# WOMEN INTELLECTUALS AND LEADERS IN THE MIDDLE AGES

# WOMEN INTELLECTUALS AND LEADERS IN THE MIDDLE AGES

EDITED BY

KATHRYN KERBY-FULTON

KATIE ANN-MARIE BUGYIS

JOHN VAN ENGEN

D. S. BREWER

First published 2020
D. S. Brewer, Cambridge

ISBN 978 1 84384 555 3

D. S. Brewer is an imprint of Boydell & Brewer Ltd
PO Box 9, Woodbridge, Suffolk IP12 3DF, UK
and of Boydell & Brewer Inc.
668 Mt Hope Avenue, Rochester, NY 14620–2731, USA
website: www.boydellandbrewer.com

A catalogue record for this book is available from the British Library



This publication is printed on acid-free paper

Typeset in Caslon and Gill Sans by www.thewordservice.com

For their gracious intellect and leadership, in memory of:

Penelope Reed Doob (1943–2017)

Mary Catherine Smith (1916–2008)

Sabine G. MacCormack (1941–2012)

# CONTENTS

## Part III. Recovering Lost Women's Authorship



## Part IV. Multidisciplinary Approaches to Gender, Patronage, and Power



## Part V. Religious Women in Leadership, Ministry, and Latin Ecclesiastical Culture

## LIST OF ILLUSTRATIONS

The editors, contributors, and publisher are grateful to all the institutions and persons listed for permission to reproduce the materials in which they hold copyright. Every effort has been made to trace the copyright holders; apologies are offered for any omission, and the publisher will be pleased to add any necessary acknowledgement in subsequent editions.

## LIST OF CONTRIBUTORS

Asma Afsaruddin is Professor of Near Eastern Languages and Cultures and Adjunct Professor of Religious Studies and Gender Studies at Indiana University, Bloomington.

Renate Blumenfeld-Kosinski is Distinguished Professor Emerita of French and Italian Languages and Literatures at University of Pittsburgh.

Amanda Bohne is Lecturer in English at University of Illinois, Chicago.

Adrienne Williams Boyarin is Associate Professor of English at University of Victoria.

Katie Ann-Marie Bugyis is Assistant Professor in the Program of Liberal Studies at University of Notre Dame.

Dyan Elliott is Peter B. Ritzma Professor of the Humanities and Professor of History at Northwestern University.

John Van Engen is Andrew V. Tackes Professor Emeritus of Medieval History at University of Notre Dame.

Thelma Fenster is Professor Emerita of French and Medieval Studies at Fordham University.

Sean L. Field is Professor of History at University of Vermont.

Sarah Foot is Regius Professor of Ecclesiastical History at University of Oxford.

Megan J. Hall is the Assistant Director of the Medieval Institute at the University of Notre Dame.

Ruth Mazo Karras is Lecky Professor of History at Trinity College Dublin.

Kathryn Kerby-Fulton, FSA, is the Notre Dame Professor of English Emerita at University of Notre Dame.

Rachel Koopmans is Associate Professor of History at York University.

F. Thomas Luongo is Associate Professor and Chair of History at Tulane University.

Leanne MacDonald is an Instructor in the English Department at Kwantlen Polytechnic University.

Gary Macy is Professor of Religious Studies at Santa Clara University.

Maureen C. Miller is Professor of History at University of California, Berkeley.

Barbara Newman is John Evans Professor of Latin and Professor of English, Religious Studies, and Classics at Northwestern University.

S.J. Pearce is Associate Professor of Near Eastern Studies at New York University.

Ian Short is Emeritus Professor of French at Birkbeck College, University of London.

Anna Siebach-Larsen is Director of the Rossell Hope Robbins Library and Koller-Collins Center for English Studies at University of Rochester.

Gemma Simmonds is Director of the Religious Life Institute at Margaret Beaufort Institute of Theology.

David Wallace is Judith Rodin Professor of English at University of Pennsylvania.

Nicholas Watson is Henry B. and Anne M. Cabot Professor of English Literature at Harvard University.

Jocelyn Wogan-Browne is Thomas F. X. and Theresa Mullarkey Chair in Literature (Emerita) at Fordham University.

# ACKNOWLEDGEMENTS

It takes a village to bring a volume like this to maturity, and among our many debts of gratitude, we would like first to offer heartfelt thanks to our patient and meticulous post-doc research assistants, Marjorie Harrington, Hannah Zdansky, Karrie Fuller, and our indexer, Richard Fahey. At the University of Notre Dame we have enjoyed the unfailing financial support of the Medieval Institute, the Institute for Studies in the Liberal Arts, the College of Arts and Letters, and the Henkels Lecture Series, which generously funded the original 2015 conference. For administrative support we thank particularly Thomas Burman and Megan J. Hall at the Medieval Institute. Finally, at Boydell and Brewer, we have benefited from the vigilance and precision of Elizabeth McDonald and Bonnie McGill, and from the steady engagement and wisdom of Caroline Palmer, through good times and bad.

Introduction

# TAKING EARLY WOMEN INTELLECTUALS AND LEADERS SERIOUSLY

KATHRYN KERBY-FULTON

Arguing for medieval women as intellectuals is a battle fraught with perils from all sides and even at times subject to friendly fire. Since women were normally denied access to public educational institutions, gateways to most leadership positions, modern scholars have naturally tended to study learned women as simply anomalies and medieval women, generally, as victims. The concept of women intellectuals, therefore, can be subject to critique as unwarranted extrapolation from the "exceptional few," or, more broadly, a gesture of disloyalty to the memory of gender victimization.[1] This volume, however, while always respectful of the historical truths and theoretical positions supporting these views, argues instead for a *via media* – not least because the evidence is not yet all in. The digital revolution is making new medieval manuscript and archival sources available daily, and scholars of medieval women are reaching further afield for more multidisciplinary methods. We suggest here that, if we look more closely, *more* medieval women attained some form of learning than scholars often assume and that women with legal, social, or ecclesiastical knowledge in turn often also wielded professional or communal leadership.[2]

This volume is intentionally trans-disciplinary, involving contributors from the fields of literature, history, and religion. It challenges several traditional views: first, the still-prevalent idea that women's intellectual accomplishments were limited to the Latin literate.[3] We take for granted the major Latin women writers because, happily, other studies of them already abound; so, too, studies of queens, the one group of medieval women whose learning and leadership have been well canvassed. With

1 On the issue of victimization, see Barbara Newman, "On the Ethics of Feminist Historiography," *Exemplaria* 2.2 (1990): 702–705; and on exceptionalism, see Newman's essay in the present volume (Chapter 21). On current theoretical trends, now broadening beyond feminism to gender studies, see Aude Mairey, "Genre et culture de l'écrit en Angleterre à la fin du Moyen Âge," *Clio* 38 (2013/2): 273–298; and Leanne MacDonald's essay in this volume (Chapter 11).

2 See, e.g., Carole Meale's lengthy Chronology Chart (twenty-seven pages), "Women and Literature in Britain, 1150–1500," listing large numbers of women authors, translators, and literary patronesses working in Latin, French, English, and Welsh, in her *Women and Literature in Britain 1150–1500* (Cambridge: Cambridge University Press, 1996), xi–xxxviii; also Julia Boffey, "Women Authors and Women's Literacy in 14th- and 15th-century England," in ibid., 159–182.

3 Alexandra Barratt, "Small Latin? The Post-Conquest Learning of English Religious Women," in *Anglo-Latin and Its Heritage: Essays in Honour of A. G. Rigg*, ed. Siân Echard and Gernot Wieland (Turnhout: Brepols, 2001), 51–65.

respect to Latin, as Megan J. Hall notes here in her essay on the Latinity of early women readers of *Ancrene Wisse* (Chapter 15), "the predominant language of literacy was shifting." So, too, our ideas of what constitutes *intellectual* accomplishment for women must shift. This collection therefore engages heavily with vernacular writings (in Anglo-Saxon, Middle English, French, Dutch, German, and Italian) and also with material culture (manuscript illumination, stained glass, fabric, and jewelry) for evidence of women's advanced capabilities. But in doing so – and here is our second challenge to traditional views – we strive to avoid a different kind of trap: the view that women's accomplishments were *limited to* the vernacular and the material, a view related in part to decades of scholarly emphasis on the "embodiment" of women's experience. While fully acknowledging the gains of scholarship on "women and the body" over several decades now, this volume proposes a newer emphasis on (so to speak) "women and the mind" as counterbalance. While of course no one imagines embodiment to be irrelevant to women's intellectual pursuits, equally, no one would wish scholarly preoccupation with the body to *obscure* such pursuits.[4] So, for instance, several of our contributors examine women at work with the sacred languages of all three Abrahamic traditions (Latin, Arabic, and Hebrew). And this brings us to the third traditional view this volume challenges: the view that women were somehow more "original" for their lack of learning and dependence on their mother tongue (arguments, of course, also made for male vernacular writers). So, for instance, the brilliant interpreter of Julian of Norwich, Felicity Riddy, wrote that "positioning Julian in the more uncontrolled oral-literate culture ... also makes possible a view of her, not as the docile heiress of monastic *lectio divina*, but as a daring thinker whose theodicy [challenges Augustinian thought]."[5] Scholars here would agree wholeheartedly that women intellectuals could be daring thinkers, and too often subject to educational limitations, but they tend to engage less judgmentally with women's learnedness in elite or sacred languages (Latin, Arabic, or Hebrew), whenever it can be found.

The present volume evolved out of a gathering of forty-two speakers in 2015 interested in discussing medieval women as serious thinkers.[6] It retains the electricity of this extraordinary event, with six thematic parts each introduced in prefaces by leading scholars on: the intellectual life of Jewish and Muslim women; authorship and the professional writer; women's authorship (both lost and found); multidisciplinary approaches to gender, patronage, and power; religious women in leadership, ministry, and Latin ecclesiastical culture; and laywomen as leaders. Recovering the voices of women thinkers requires a wide range of sources: for example, wills and

4 For prescient caveats about this problem, see Amy Hollywood, "Feminist Studies," in *The Blackwell Companion to Christian Spirituality*, ed. Arthur Holder (Oxford: Blackwell, 2005), 363–386.

5 Felicity Riddy, "Julian of Norwich and Self-Textualization," *Editing Women*, ed. Ann M. Hutchinson (Cardiff: University of Wales Press, 1998), 101–124: 108.

6 For the original 2015 conference at University of Notre Dame, on Women Leaders and Intellectuals of the Medieval World, see: https://womenleaders2015.wordpress.com/conference-program/.
We are grateful to Notre Dame's Medieval Institute for its generous support of the conference and to the College of Arts and Letters for their support via a Henckels Conference Grant.

archival records (Bohne), Exchequer court records (Boyarin), changes in liturgical texts (Bugyis), stained glass (Koopmans), phonology and metrics (Wogan-Browne), manuscript annotation (Hall), scribal interventions (MacDonald), donor portraits (Siebach-Larsen), and textiles (Miller). By inviting scholars from all three of the Abrahamic traditions that the medieval world shaped for the modern one, we have been able to trace trans-denominational continuities of the fundamental challenge for learned women: how to be taken seriously. This challenge remains ever current: in 2017, *Time* magazine chose to feature as "Person of the Year" a cover photo of the "Silence Breakers," the courageous women who had brought sexual harassment charges against once-iconic male leaders of the media, academic, and entertainment worlds.[7] Routinely the stories of these modern women share one theme: that they had asked only to be *taken seriously as professionals and colleagues*, but they instead found themselves subject to predatory abuses of workplace power. Though this volume is not a study of the "#MeToo" movement, it does examine the history of its single most urgent issue: how did historical women succeed in being taken seriously as intellectuals and professionals, navigating as they did the even more rugged terrain of earlier institutional power structures? Like their male counterparts, we argue, medieval women were capable of acting as powerful administrative, theological, and legal thinkers, innovative authors and artists, and as courageous champions of ecclesiastical and social reform.

## *Doctrix, Auctrix, Scriptrix, Magistra, Apostola*: Some Key Medieval Concepts of Medieval Women as Intellectuals and Leaders

Medieval women were officially denied most of the public forms of education (song schools, grammar schools, and universities) available to males,[8] yet paradoxically, there was a vocabulary for women performing advanced intellectual work: in Latin, for instance: *auctrix* (female author), *scriptrix* (a female scribe), *magistra* (a female teacher), and, though ideational, even *doctrix* (the female equivalent of *doctor*, the university's top rank) and *apostola* (female apostle). In fact, women were the first educators of both boys and girls in the home, a role codified even in scholastic theology by writers like Thomas Aquinas and Henry of Ghent as a woman's right to teach "sound doctrine" to the young (cf. Titus 2:1–8 or Proverbs 4:3–4).[9] For Aquinas, this private *sermo* was appropriate to women, as successive theologians agreed, including even the teaching of nuns (*secreto in claustro*).[10] Canon law granted the right of abbesses to teach, but not to teach men (*ne doceat viros; nam mulieres potest abbatissa*),[11] a position that was

7 *Time* magazine, "The Silence Breakers," http://time.com/time-person-of-the-year-2017-silence-breakers-choice/.

8 See Boffey, "Women Authors"; and Megan J. Hall, "*Ancrene Wisse* and the Education of Laywomen in Thirteenth-Century England," *Early Middle English* 2.1 (2020, forthcoming).

9 See Alcuin Blamires and William Marx, "Woman Not to Preach: A Disputation in British Library MS Harley 31," *Journal of Medieval Latin* 3 (1993): 34–63: 41, 55, and 61, n.143.

10 Blamires and Marx, 41.

11 Gloss to *Decretum*, dist. 23, c. 29, cited in Blamires and Marx, 62, n.149.

effectively challenged over the centuries by Hildegard of Bingen and others.[12] Theologians perennially debated *pro* and *contra* as to whether women could preach publicly, the *contra* arguments repeated ubiquitously by modern scholars, but the *pro* arguments more rarely, so worth mentioning here: the traditionally accepted circumstances under which women could teach theology, for instance, are summed up by Henry of Ghent in his *questio*, "*Utrum mulier possit esse doctor seu doctrix huius scientiae*." Repeating the standard biblical evidence that God called women as prophets to teach publicly (*docere publice*) or lead the Hebrew people,[13] he named four in particular: Miriam, Deborah, Huldah, and Anna – the very four, we should note, invoked in a prayer for the ordination of women in the early church (see Macy's essay in this volume).[14] Women, like anyone who has a special gift of knowledge (1 Peter 4:10), he says, are obliged to minister or lead (*debent administrare*), adding that Mary Magdalene and Martha taught just as disciples (*publice sicut Apostoli*). These women, of course, first delivered the news of the Resurrection to the disciples themselves (see Figure 1), an act that engendered the medieval term *apostola* (translated "apostolesse" in Caxton's English), applied not only to the biblical women, but to revered women figures such as Catherine of Siena (see Luongo's essay in this volume, Chapter 5). Theologians also cited in their "pro" arguments women missionaries even St. Paul had recognized,[15] building, albeit grudgingly, a case for women's teaching under defined circumstances, i.e., when there is need (a shortage of labourers in the vineyard)[16] or when there are too many corrupt or degenerate males (ironically termed "effeminati").[17]

Fortunately for medieval women, there was never a shortage of male clerical corruption. So the loophole authorizing women to teach "by a special grace" (*ex speciali gratia*) persisted,[18] and a surprising number of women took advantage of it to preach, teach, write, and minister in a variety of ways – in the present volume alone: Agnes of Harcourt, Catherine of Siena, Colette de Corbie, Mechthild of Magdeburg, and Mary Ward.[19] Especially at times of stress and crisis for the church, such women emerged: Hildegard of Bingen's preaching tours took place during the twelfth-century period of heresy and schism; the turbulent years of the late thirteenth century for the papacy and for beguines gave rise to the works of Mechthild of Magdeburg, Marguerite Porete, and the anonymous author of "Eckhart and the Lay

12 "When Women Preached: An Introduction to Female Homiletic, Sacramental, and Liturgical Roles," *Voices in Dialogue: Reading Women in the Middle Ages*, ed. Linda Olson and Kathryn Kerby-Fulton (Notre Dame: University of Notre Dame Press, 2005), 31–56.

13 See, e.g., the anonymous *Questio: Utrum liceat mulieribus docere viros publice congregatos*, hereafter cited as *Utrum liceat*, ed. Blamires and Marx, 55, echoing Aquinas especially.

14 Respectively in Exodus 15:20; Judges 4:4; 4 Kings 22:14; Luke 2:46, e.g., in Henry of Ghent, *Utrum mulier*, ibid., 50n.49.

15 Paul speaks of the mission of "Phoebe our sister," Romans 16:1–2; Blamires and Marx, 40.

16 Alluding to the shortage of *operarii* in Matthew 9:37, *Utrum liceat*, 62 and n.152, and for Henry, 54.

17 *Utrum liceat*, 62. Hildegard exploited this brilliantly by labelling her entire age "effeminate," thereby giving herself license.

18 See Henry's *Utrum mulier*, 55.

19 See essays here by Field, Luongo, Blumenfeld-Kosinski, Newman, and Simmonds (Chapters 4, 5, 17, 21, and 7).

Figure 1 Mary Magdalene preaching Christ's Resurrection to the Apostles, St. Albans Psalter. Dombibliothek Hildesheim, HS St. God. 1 (Property of the Basilica of St. Godehard, Hildesheim), p.51.

Woman" (see Newman and Van Engen in this volume, Chapters 21 and 8); the Great Schism prompted renewed arguments for women's abilities to conduct ministry, among Wycliffites, and among academics, for instance at Oxford.[20]

Outside of the church, the education of women in higher social classes involved, at minimum, rudimentary understanding of devotional Latin, and given the expectations of such women for managing estates and educating households, it is not surprising that connections between women's education and governance appear. Karen Winstead has discussed "The Problem of the Female Intellectual" and "Social Responsibility and Intellectual Debt" in John Capgrave's *Life of St. Katherine*, where Katherine outwitted learned theologians "because she knows the conventions of *disputatio*, and employs academic jargon as dexterously."[21] When Katherine is called upon to leave her studies and govern her country, Capgrave portrays in excruciating detail the plight of the woman scholar ("nowe must I leeve my stody and desire"); his character, though fictional, here parallels Christine de Pizan's autobiographical comments in her *Avision* and those of several fifteenth-century Italian humanist women.[22] Katherine is referred to with academic titles ("so gret a mayster"), and her governance is framed as the desire of the "Fyrst Mevere" that she communicate ("comoun") what God sent her.[23]

Assessing women's literacy more generally is a major scholarly issue, more complex still now that historical linguists have shown that *all* reading was taught initially via Latin, indeed itself a medieval vernacular, and that medieval readers could function at any one of four levels of literacy.[24] Also dispelled now is the more traditional notion that women were somehow illiterate if they could not (physically) write. Julia Boffey's landmark article "Women Authors and Women's Literacy in Fourteenth and Fifteenth-Century England"[25] explored how women's writings were composed "in an age when scribal skills were not concomitant with authorial ones" (true for men as well), when, in fact, using a scribe might be more a matter of convenience or social class than literacy. Boffey challenged our understanding of "writing women" – both *scriptrix* (scribe) and *auctrix* (author) – and offered caveats about over-hasty assumptions of female authorship, especially the temptation to swell the canon of women authors by sweeping up texts merely narrated in the female voice (a temptation discussed here by Sarah J. Pearce). On the other hand, as Margaret Hannay wrote about Tudor women, "the history of women's writings is often one of repeated loss and rediscovery. When a woman did write a significant work, it might be credited to a

20 See Renate Blumenfeld-Kosinski, *Poets, Saints, and Visionaries of the Great Schism, 1378–1417* (University Park: Penn State Press, 2006); Fiona Somerset, "*Eciam Mulier*: Women in Lollardy and the Problem of Sources," in *Voices in Dialogue*, 245–260; Kerby-Fulton, "Oxford," in *Regeneration: A Literary History of Europe: 1348–1418*, vol. 1, ed. David Wallace (Oxford: Oxford University Press, 2015), 208–226.

21 Karen A. Winstead, *John Capgrave's Fifteenth Century* (Philadelphia: University of Pennsylvania Press, 2007), 46.

22 Ibid., 42.

23 Ibid., 40 (discussing lines 2:1351–8) and 42.

24 Barratt, "Small Latin?" On levels of literacy, see Katherine Zieman, *Singing the New Song: Literature and Literacy in Late Medieval England* (Philadephia: University of Pennsylvania Press, 2008).

25 Boffey, "Women Authors,"159.

man."[26] In this volume, both Jocelyn Wogan-Browne and John Van Engen wrestle with these attribution issues. So much, then, militated against women's claims to authorship throughout the Middle Ages.

## Beyond the Binaries: Theories, Methodologies, and the Unexpected Triumph of the Medieval Laywoman

The scholarly paradigm known today as "women and the body" reflects the 1970s feminist movement's rejection of intellectual abstraction as complicit with a male-dominated, ivory-towered world.[27] Productive though it has been, scholars have questioned whether it runs the risk of essentializing women and whether, in its most pronounced form, it can also bracket out women's intellectual, political, and spiritual lives, or dimensions of them. Moreover, earlier women thinkers themselves often resisted this kind of construction. As Amy Hollywood notes, "women's writings before [1300] show little concern for intense bodily asceticism and paramystical phenomena. This suggests, at the very least, that women refused to describe themselves within the paradigms provided by primarily male-authored hagiography." [28]

The Middle Ages, by contrast, with extraordinarily rich concepts of cognition, memory, interiority, inner psychology, imagination, and transcendence, can offer a different set of perspectives on women's intellectual roles.[29] Women's mysticism has long been the locus of concern for scholarship on women intellectuals, but here, too, women have been too often handicapped. As Katie Bugyis has noted, more recent shifts in theoretical trends

> lead us beyond the paradigm of dichotomizing the writings of medieval mystics into distinct, gendered groups ... which associate the "feminine" with bridal eroticism, visionary experiences, and extreme corporeal asceticism and the "masculine" with apophatic theology and experiences of self-noughting and Divine *un*-intelligibility.[30]

Contributors to this volume have elegantly avoided this dichotomy by treating visionary women as *authors* (e.g. chapters by Newman and Luongo), but the larger tendency in this book is to move beyond mysticism to other genres for women's intellectual endeavor – for example to writing history (Fenster), wills (Bohne), correspondence (Boyarin), glosses (Hall), and dialogues (Van Engen).

26 Margaret Hannay, ed., *Silent but for the Word: Tudor Women as Patrons, Translators, and Writers of Religious Works* (Kent: Kent State University Press, 1985), 2.

27 Among the myriad studies, see Caroline Walker Bynum, *Holy Feast and Holy Fast: The Religious Significance of Food to Medieval Women* (Berkeley: University of California Press, 1987); Elizabeth Petroff, *Body and Soul: Essays on Medieval Women and Mysticism* (Oxford and New York: Oxford University Press, 1994); Amy Hollywood, *The Soul as Virgin Wife* (Notre Dame: University of Notre Dame, 1995).

28 Hollywood, "Feminist Studies," 372.

29 See Anna Siebach-Larsen's essay here (Chapter 12), part of a new generation of methodologies on cognition studies.

30 Katie Bugyis, paper given at St. Mary's College, 2012.

Any study of "thinking women" is likely to be beset by binaries. First, in working with medieval women who actually left or inspired written records, we recognize, of course, that we are often studying very privileged women – at times downright elite. That said, one of the great discoveries emerging from this collection is the astonishing number of *lay*women intellectuals and leaders our contributors bring forward, not all from the upper social stratum by any means. Widows (matrons, for instance, capable of authorizing a saint's miracle, as Rachel Koopmans shows), women from the wealthy merchant classes (such as the daughters of a draper discussed by Amanda Bohne), and even the daughter of an elderly carpenter (Colette of Corbie, who nonetheless became "one of the most important reformers of the Franciscan order," the focus of Blumenfeld-Kosinski's chapter) all populate our pages here. What is most surprising is to find that these laywomen were *in control*: examples here span even the lower social classes, from Colette's rise from poverty to become "a natural-born leader, inspiring some of the most powerful men and women of her time" see Chapter 17), to the two merchant-class sisters whose legal acumen in will-making negotiates an inheritance even for what appears to be a common-law relationship – or an "unmarriage," to use Ruth Karras's term (see Chapter 13 by Amanda Bohne).[31]

Secondly, we realize that no mind ever existed (at least on this planet) without a body. Among contributors who directly invoke embodiment connections are, for instance, Nicholas Watson's discussion of Bridget de Autruy's sufferings when her brother used a condemned ritual prayer to help her learn to read (see Chapter 10); or Anna Siebach-Larsen's study of a patroness's portrait that "embodies" her equality with the great theologian Robert Grosseteste when the artist breaks with convention and paints both subjects the same size (see Chapter 12). Thirdly, though we study an astonishing range of empowered women here, we also realize that women were enormously, indeed appallingly, disadvantaged in the Middle Ages. They were, moreover, subject to unthinkable kinds of physical exploitation and marital subordination. Our goal in this volume is not to play Pollyanna in the face of all the evidence for a bleak past. However, despite all this, and against all expectation, our contributors mostly brought us two consistent types of narrative: (1) narratives of women who thought or left intellectual legacies and (2) narratives addressing continuities with urgent modern social, legal, and religious injustices. A simple way of summarizing the first category might be this: my grandfather, a country doctor, used to tell the women in the family, "Whatever profession you choose, don't be the nurse, be the doctor." Metaphorically speaking, what our contributors have brought us are numerous cases in which, against all odds, medieval women "became the doctor." We embrace here, too, the "glass-half-empty" perspectives whenever they emerge and learn from them, but with so many new sources and methods of getting at the sources, twenty-first-century scholars can be forgiven for exploring the more inspirational narratives when they appear. Back in 1988, Mary Erler and Maryanne Kowaleski had examined the question of women's oppression and widespread subordination to men, suggesting that "one answer to this question has been to redefine its terms: to understand power more

31 See Ruth Karras, *Unmarriages: Women, Men and Sexual Unions in the Middle Ages* (Philadelphia: University of Pennsylvania Press, 2012).

largely and thus to draw women within its circle. This answer, however, which denies the totality of women's subordination, can be considered only a partial response to the problem of gender inequality."[32] While this is certainly true, its partial status should not be limiting, and much remains unexplored about how and where early women found the resources to wield power.

The more practical point, however, is this: when less information was available, theories and histories were built on a scarcity model and on extrapolations from scarcity. But now, a scholar of medieval women situated anywhere in the world can open up her computer to a deluge of digitized manuscripts, archives, images of material culture, and even audio recordings of unpublished music, often performed from manuscript. Suddenly, the Middle Ages are bigger, deeper, and more complex – and all the old adages about medieval women are now up for re-examination. This does not mean these adages are necessarily wrong, but it does mean that they will now have to withstand and absorb new evidence, and in spades. We believe our contributors here have made a good start on some of that.

### Eradicating the Invisibility of Medieval Women Intellectuals

Barbara Newman's essay here (Chapter 21, "Mechthild of Magdeburg at Helfta: A Study in Literary Influence") reminds us that "Medieval women writers too often confront us as lonely figures, on the margins of the usual networks of literary exchange and influence," so Newman teaches us to value all the more highly those rare cases in which "we are able to trace one female author's direct influence on another." In this case, she is discussing evidence that a laywoman (a beguine), Mechthild of Magdeburg, was an unexpected literary mentor of the better educated, Latinate nuns of Helfta (including Mechthild of Hackeborn and Gertrude the Great). Newman's essay contends, fascinatingly, that had Helfta not taken in this fleeing, vernacular-writing laywoman, these famous, elite, visionary nuns might not have set pen to parchment themselves. This startling case of a *laywoman*'s influence among the elite speaks excitingly to Dyan Elliott's crucial question in her Preface to Part VI: whether elite laywomen of the Middle Ages (such as the learned queens discussed elsewhere by Elizabeth Tyler[33] or the wealthy patronesses of Maureen Miller's essay here) ever understood themselves to have any common cause with middle-class laywomen. Elliott asks, too, whether the elite laywomen who promoted the eleventh century's ecclesiastical reforms understood that they were simultaneously *narrowing* the options for other women, for example by limiting the possibility for women to take on clerical roles (even to access the altar physically) and restricting the development of women's saints' cults. Elliott's views deal in sobering historical truths and represent classic positions from persuasive feminist readings of the Gregorian reforms. Happily, however, in this volume, they *round out* rather than cancel other more hopeful, intellective-centered

32 Erler and Kowaleski, *Women and Power in the Middle Ages* (Athens, GA: University of Georgia Press, 1988), 1–2.

33 Elizabeth Tyler's 2015 conference paper is published in her *England in Europe: English Royal Women and the Patronage of Literary Culture, c. 1000–c. 1150* (Toronto: University of Toronto Press, 2017).

methodologies often represented or cited here. So, Rachel Koopmans in Chapter 20, "Laywomen's Leadership in Medieval Miracle Cults: Evidence from Britain, c.1150–1250," offers us an astonishing window on middle-class laywomen taking it upon themselves to witness to, and thereby *authorize*, a miracle: in this episode a matron asks, "Do we not have five widows here?", a moment that captures the widows' collective decision to exercise their social right to agency (that is, free of spousal control) in a religious cause. This remarkable moment of autonomy, as Elliott astutely notes in her Preface, also seems to hark back to a time when women had the power of deaconesses. That very power is discussed here in Gary Macy's historiographical piece on the ordination of women (Chapter 16, "The Treatment of Ordination in Recent Scholarship on Religious Women in the Early Middle Ages"), building on his earlier landmark work in this manifesto excoriating modern historians (and churchmen) for their neglect of the well-established fact that women were ordained in the Early Middle Ages.[34] Macy laments, like Elliott (and with reference to Elliott's superb work elsewhere), "the dramatic change in the understanding of ordination wrought by the eleventh-century reform movement." But it is precisely in this post-reform period, traditionally scorched earth for evidence of women's clerical empowerment, that Katie Bugyis uncovers evidence for women assuming priestly roles in the liturgy of the Easter vigil. In her essay (Chapter 18, "Women Priests at Barking Abbey in the Late Middle Ages"), Bugyis studies a striking liturgical Easter drama shaped (or reshaped) by an innovative abbess, Katherine de Sutton, sometimes accounted England's first woman playwright. Bugyis shows that this liturgy was even open to the laity, the abbess insisting, most unusually, on the pastoral care of locals (an instance, I'd note, of defying the canon law rubric mentioned above that abbesses should only teach *secreto in claustro*). It was performed at an altar *in front of*, not behind, the rood screen; among its other daring features, this liturgy brought nuns in proximity to the altar, normally taboo for women. So, using a different set of sources and methods than Macy and Elliott (in this case, paleography and liturgical records), Bugyis is able to show her women breaking through a barrier (the eleventh-century reforms) long established by historians as near fatal to women's continuation in ministerial roles.

Proximity to the altar is also a theme, though explored, surprisingly, with respect to laywomen, in Maureen Miller's essay, Chapter 19, "Women Donors and Ecclesiastical Reform: Evidence from Camaldoli and Vallombrosa, c. 1000–1150." Miller looks at, among other things, the materiality of laywomen's donations of textile work for priestly robes, whether or not as a way of procuring for themselves *vicarious* proximity to the altar – just one dimension (perhaps the most "embodied" one) of the intellectual confidence of these wealthy women in fostering reformed monasticism through major donations, sometimes as founders. Miller's is one of many methodologies here showing that women's intellectual and leadership agency is a live force in the Middle Ages and that the study of it can take us beyond where more traditional methods have – that is, to a clearer sense that these women were taken seriously. The

34 See also Dyan Elliott's *The Bride of Christ Goes to Hell: Metaphor and Embodiment in the Lives of Pious Women, 200–1500* (Philadelphia: University of Pennsylvania Press, 2012) on the wide application of the title 'deaconess', as Macy notes: "one of the best summaries of the role of deaconesses in the Middle Ages to date."

kind of work is done here, of course, not in the spirit of erasing victimization, but of not allowing it to have the last word.

Turning now to the second of the twin emergent themes of this volume, after evidence of *intellectual agency*, we have *continuity* – continuities with modern traditions in which women's struggles for equal opportunity persist unevenly to this day. This comes through especially strongly in Part I ("Scholarship, Law, and Poetry: Jewish and Muslim Women") in which Asma Afsaruddin lays out stunning evidence for women's intellectual and artistic agency in early Islam, as poets, authors, and highly respected teachers (Chapter 1, "Gender, Scholarship, and the Construction of Authority in the Pre-Modern Muslim World"). These women were transmitters of sacred teachings who, strikingly for us today, gathered both *male and female* adherents in the madrasas. Asma Sayeed, whose paper (published elsewhere) was also given at the 2015 conference, in fact presented to a hushed audience a map of the medieval Middle East heavily covered in dots, each representing madrasas at which *women* taught, in some cases famously attracting adherents of both sexes from miles away.[35] The implications and resonance for the modern world of this kind of research hardly need spelling out, and among all the papers presented at the 2015 conference, these two on women's roles in early Islam easily provoked the most astonishment – and perhaps the most *hope*. Hope, a commodity often in very short supply in medieval Jewish women's history as well, also emerged unexpectedly in two essays here: first, Adrienne Williams Boyarin's "Medieval Anglo-Jewish Women at Court" (Chapter 3), which offers evidence from the Exchequer of the Jews for the polyglot legal knowledge of thirteenth-century Jewish women in England. These women were capable of working in Latin, French, and Hebrew, and in renascent written English, even as they operated under the pressures of persecution or conversion. Sarah Pearce's chapter (Chapter 2, "The Historiography of Absence: Preliminary Steps Towards a New History of Andalusi Women Poets") tackles and demolishes a long-standing assumption about the dearth of women poets, i.e., that Jewish women could not grasp the allusions to Hebrew Scripture demanded by Jewish poetics. Her essay finds evidence that in fact they *could*. Her paper also speaks eloquently to extraordinary methodological difficulties (both the dead ends and the promising leads) for recovery of women authors, another major theme addressed below.

All of these pieces speak to modern issues and are surprisingly optimistic, a factor Ruth Karras mentions in her Preface to Part I. Certainly an emphatic strand of vintage twentieth-century feminist scholarship was its understandable emphasis on the long, horrific history of women's oppression, rising against the stark backdrop of twentieth-century persecutions of Jews, magnified for medievalists by studies of heresy and other oppressed groups. By contrast, the majority of contributions here seem intent on *building* as much as remembering – building bridges from the heroic exceptions of the past to a more, we hope, humane future. Bringing to bear methodologies sometimes quite new to women's studies (a point Nicholas Watson makes in his

35 "Transmission vs. Authorship: The Spheres of Women's Intellectual Engagement in Classical Islam"; for Asma Sayeed's publications on this topic, see Asma Afsaruddin's essay here. Asma Sayeed, *Women and the Transmission of Religious Knowledge in Islam* (Cambridge: Cambridge University Press, 2015).

Preface to Part II), in part owing to newer access to sources, has helped change the narrative. Particularly impressive among the results of these newer methods is the triumph of the *learned laywoman* in this volume. As Ruth Karras notes, the lay vs. clerical distinction is less meaningful in Jewish and Islamic thought, where the power to teach is earned through learning, not through ordination (though as Pearce's essay shows, this learning was tough for Jewish women to acquire). This is another reason to include all three Abrahamic traditions. And even ordination itself, as Macy notes, also means something different before the eleventh century – another reason to keep the early medieval period in sight.

On this point, and the possibilities of twenty-first-century optimism, Sarah Foot's conclusion to her "Bede's Abbesses" (Chapter 14) is illuminating:

> I have little sympathy with readings that have depicted Bede as misogynistic and do not believe that he ever deliberately downplayed the role of women. Overall, I would argue that Bede presents us … with images of active and powerful women, women who while capitalising on their family background and influence, proved capable of using their own minds to determine their futures. Bede's abbesses appear frequently as forceful political agents; rigorous, and even transgressive thinkers; innovative authors; and courageous champions of the monastic way of life among the early English.

The biggest challenge we face, however, in recovering these transgressive thinkers and innovative authors is, once again, the *invisibility* of the medieval woman intellectual. I recently encountered this invisibility while carrying out research ostensibly unrelated to women's issues: on the literary history of medieval Oxford.[36] No one had even thought to look for women intellectuals at medieval Oxford, but from unrelated research, I knew, for instance, that Hildegard's massive *Scivias* was studied seriously at Merton (and survives from the thirteenth century as Merton College MS 160) as part of that college's specialty in astronomy and cosmology.[37] Similarly, Hildegard's prophecies were studied by Oxford friars, preserved by its Wycliffites, and quoted by the university's experts on the Great Schism when they were in dispute with Paris about solutions to the crisis. Medieval Oxford, it turned out, teemed with women book owners: both Christian and Jewish women's names appear in college book-chest pledge records (for parallels, see Boyarin's essay here); the famous *De Brailes Hours* was created for an Oxford woman in the heart of the university's scholastic book production centre (for an important parallel involving Joan Tateshal and Oxford's chancellor, Robert Grosseteste, see Siebach-Larsen's essay here); Oxford's anchoresses were prominent and numerous enough that Oxford was listed in an early redaction of *Ancrene Wisse* as among those cities whose anchoretic communities could be likened to those of the friars (for parallels, see Hall's essay here). Benefactresses of the university were vital, most notably Philippa of Hainault, wife of Edward III, a foundress of Queen's College,

36 For these examples, see Kerby-Fulton, "Oxford."

37 Kerby-Fulton, "Hildegard and the Male Reader," in *Prophets Abroad: The Reception of Continental Holy Women in Late Medieval England*, ed. Rosalynn Voaden (Cambridge: D. S. Brewer, 1996), 1–18 for these examples.

and Dervorguilla of Galloway, widow of John de Balliol, both thirteenth-century founders of Balliol College. Dervorguilla also authored the Balliol student code of conduct. And, it turns out, Godstow Abbey, on the edge of the university, was full of academic visitors (too full, as some bishop's visitation records opine). Most strikingly, in the early fifteenth century, the prioress of Godstow even drew up a Latin cartulary, acting both as its donor and compiler (*sumptibus et labore*), as a gift to the abbess, showing that convent Latin skills in writing and editing legal documents were alive and well, even as late as the reign of Henry IV.[38] But crucial for *our* purposes is that until the detailed codicological work of Emily Amt on this cartulary was published in 2014, it was wrongly assumed that the prioress – subject to our usual narratives about the decline of Latin in nunneries – had had to pay a male scribe to do this work. In fact, she performed this labour of love *herself*. This prioress, then, a *scriptrix*, *is the victim of our ignorance*, not of medieval prejudices. She provides a perfect example of how women's intellectualism is just plain *invisible* much of the time because no one is looking for it – indeed, many of our blanket narratives insist that it didn't exist.

In the present volume, there are plenty of other examples of the same phenomenon. As Megan J. Hall shows (in Chapter 15, "Women's Latinity in the Early English Anchorhold"), contrary to what scholars have assumed, there is good evidence of the Latinity of women readers in early copies of *Ancrene Wisse* and, also unnoticed, that such women had scribal abilities and are likely some of the manuscript annotators. Also showing that a medieval woman writer could wield serious historical sources, such as the first-century Jewish historian, Josephus, just as males did, is Thelma Fenster's Chapter 6, "Christine de Pizan on the Jews, in Three Texts: The *Heures de contemplation sur la Passion de Nostre Seigneur Jhesucrist*, the *Fais et bonnes meurs du sage roy Charles V*, and the *Mutacion de Fortune*".

Using the same kinds of techniques of manuscript studies, Tom Luongo shows in Chapter 5 ("Catherine of Siena, *Auctor*") how the manuscripts of her letters were designed to "cloak Catherine's Italian in the material trappings of Latin status, with a page design borrowed ... from Bolognese legal manuscripts." Luongo traces how the production team drew on various influences to give Catherine "a clear authorial identity." Similarly, Sean Field in Chapter 4, "Agnes of Harcourt as Intellectual: New Evidence for the Composition and Circulation of the *Vie d'Isabelle de France*," restores Agnes's reputation as a serious intellectual, showing her to be at the forefront of "cutting edge" hagiographical techniques, a collaborative author in her convent, and influential in "royal, monastic, and (eventually) erudite circles." What all these contributors have in common is a strong confidence – and in some ways a *new* confidence – in women's abilities to think, intervene, compose, and direct their own affairs.

So it seems that, while it is traditional and appropriately cautious to ask, as Elliott justly does, whether we can ever recover women's voices (when they are so often filtered through their clerical scribes), newer methods, pioneered by manuscript studies, editorial theory, codicology, and digitization, now offer us much more information about exactly what a woman author and/or collaborator wrote. What we were once only

38 Kerby-Fulton, "Oxford," 220–226; Emilie Amt, *The Latin Cartulary of Godstow Abbey* (Oxford: Oxford University Press, 2014).

able to know in extraordinary women's cases about women's literacy – for example, in Hildegard's complaints to her secretary, Guibert de Gembloux, that he was taking too many liberties in correcting her prose, many more than, she insisted, her previous secretary Volmar ever took[39] – we can now see in more ordinary women's cases, thanks to codicology. Katie Bugyis's work has revealed extensive manuscript corrections by women scribes and redactors, aimed at "writing their consorors into more visible roles" in their liturgy; Leanne MacDonald in Chapter 11 ("Written with her Own Hand: Perpetua's Representation of Non-Binary Gender in Old English Hagiography") also offers manuscript evidence of feminizing or other gender-related redaction; Nicholas Watson in Chapter 10 ("The Visions, Experiments, and Operations of Bridget of Autruy (fl. 1303–15)") discusses a brother–sister collaboration, a text in which the brother painstakingly records his sister's contribution in a method worthy of modern bibliographic protocol for co-authorship. While we knew from Hildegard's complaints that she must have combed through her male secretaries' drafts, checking to see that they had represented her dictation accurately, we just haven't had this kind of literacy information for rank-and-file authors. Now we are getting it, and it is changing our entire sense of what women did or could do.

Some of these methodologies are becoming very sophisticated. Part III, "Recovering Lost Women's Authorship," models a set of methodological approaches and theoretical questions by senior scholars: Jocelyn Wogan-Browne in Chapter 9 ("Recovery and Loss: Women's Writing around Marie de France") asks, for instance, what new linguistic evidence showing *multiple* "Maries de France" changes about our sense of her authorship, offering the exciting possibility that there were several unknown women writers sheltering under Marie's name. By examining the theoretical implications of the use elsewhere among medieval authors of a soubriquet, and by looking at the transmission issues that have resulted in the loss or suppression of women's signatures elsewhere, Wogan-Browne succeeds in fruitfully destabilizing our sense of Marie's identity and offers the delightful prospect of yet more women authors at work. In Chapter 8, also in Part III, John Van Engen's paper ("A Woman Author? The Middle-Dutch Dialogue between a 'Good-willed Layperson' and a 'Master Eckhart'") gives striking evidence for attributing an anonymous dialogue, supposedly conducted between a layperson and Meister Eckhart, to a *female* rather than a male author. The way he frames the discussion is applicable not only to this case, but to multiple cases in the volume. Noting that the rapid growth of vernacular writing in the later medieval period, much of it anonymous, presents us with serious methodological challenges in uncovering women writers (women, even more than men, might have reasons for anonymity or might have anonymity thrust upon them), he asks:

> At issue, perhaps now more than ever, is how we are to situate all this work: Is it friars writing for their charges…? Women writing for women, or for women and men, or in not a few cases women and men writing collaboratively?

39 See Kerby-Fulton, "Hildegard of Bingen" for the *Medieval Holy Women in the Christian Tradition, c.1100– 1500*, ed. Alastair Minnis and Rosalynn Voaden (Turnhout: Brepols, 2010), 343–370.

This is another way, a much more informed way, of asking the old question, why is "Anonymous" always assumed to be a man? This parallels Pearce's critique of the long-standing belief among Hebrew scholars that women couldn't write poetry demanding allusions to the Hebrew Scriptures, and the supposed impossibility of Hall's annotators being women because women, it was thought, did not have the requisite Latinity. The sacred language of both Judaism and Christianity respectively is at stake in these prejudices, and while earlier scholars might reach for an embodiment explanation, both Pearce and Hall, perhaps representing a younger generation, choose newer methodologies – history of literacy – instead. Sarah J. Pearce also looks at literary voice, beginning her essay (Chapter 2) with a Hebrew poem narrated by a woman that earlier scholars had (somewhat irrationally) attributed to a woman *author*. Pearce offers instead "some alternatives to the models of absence that have dominated the discourse" about whether women wrote Hebrew poetry. Wogan-Browne's chapter, too, invokes issues of female voice, narration, and performativity, while Nicholas Watson's contribution also tackles what Pearce would call "models of absence". In Pearce's definition, this is the scholarly tendency to judge a woman on whether she rises to historical prominence *with or without* connections to a famous man; for example, would Heloise have risen to fame without Abelard? (Those tempted to think this is only a medievalist's dilemma might note the challenges that faced Hillary Clinton's 2016 presidential candidacy.) In Watson's study, Bridget's collaborator, her brother John of Morigny, takes pains to record his sister's intellectual contributions and to explain how he brought her into a circle of university-educated clerks. Without John's unusually full explanations, we would never know that an Italian woman traveled in these circles and was taken seriously within them (as was, I'd note, Douceline de Digne in her brother's, Hugh de Digne's, academic circles).[40] But of course, we haven't been *trained* to expect such things – and we must now *untrain* ourselves from the older expectations of invisibility and get on with more such discoveries.

### Women's History is Not Just a Museum: Medieval Problems and Modern Continuities

One of the exciting but unusual dimensions of this volume is that several essays resonate with the recognition that certain issues medieval women faced are still faced by modern women in a surprising number of religious traditions and social settings (we have already mentioned #MeToo). Both Macy's and Bugyis's essays, which in their different ways are about the history of women in clerical roles, pick up on this strong thread by emphasizing historical continuities – that is, medieval problems that *still matter*. The chapters on both Muslim and Jewish medieval women in Part I discussed above (by Boyarin, Pearce, and Afsaruddin, and the published work of Sayeed) all address this question, as do several others. Gemma Simmonds in Chapter 7 ("Walking in Grandmothers' Footsteps: Mary Ward and the Medieval Spiritual and Intellectual Heritage"), like Macy and Bugyis, examines yet another strand of frustration with the unequal treatment of women in the Roman Catholic tradition. Simmonds discusses the author,

40 Kerby-Fulton, "When Women Preached," 45.

religious leader, and activist Mary Ward, whose passion to found her own un-cloistered religious order for women was medieval in intellectual formation. Both Mary and the order suffered persecution at the hands of church authorities (Mary's writings survive in part as "lemon juice letters", an early modern technique for secret writing), and in the seventeenth century, Pope Urban VIII officially abolished it, invoking in his pronouncement the medieval trope of heresy as weeds: "the poisonous growths in the Church of God must be torn up from the roots lest they spread themselves further". The pope's abolition provokes this spirited and amusing comment from Simmonds:

> Despite this suppression, some 400 years after their foundation in 1609, sisters of the Congregation of Jesus and the Institute of the Blessed Virgin Mary are now a worldwide group spanning over 2,000 sisters found in every continent and country from Albania to Zimbabwe. Mary Ward stands as an icon for women's struggle down the centuries to claim their legitimate voice in church and society as leaders and intellectuals....

Simmonds speaks, remarkably cheerfully, for beleaguered women, historical and modern, to be found across all three Abrahamic traditions and beyond, many passionately represented in various chapters in this volume. These women must be allowed to join others more commonly (and comfortably) discussed in the modern university. This, too, is gender inequality: just as wage inequality, reproductive control, workplace harassment, and glass-ceilinged career patterns remain social injustices,[41] the inability of women to lead services, preach, teach, or to be ordained in some denominations is a parallel injustice – even though Judaism, Christianity, and Islam *all* from their inceptions unequivocally laid to rest any notion that women's souls were unequal.

In this sense, as several contributors and I have argued in an earlier collection, the study of religious cultural history is "not just a museum."[42] And as Barbara Newman has pointed out so elegantly, no one can do history without their personal beliefs affecting their work.[43] In the 2015 conference, the closing session on women's leadership, then and now, tapped panelists from the Jewish, Muslim, Roman Catholic, Anglican and United Church of Canada traditions (the latter, a national union of Presbyterians, Methodists, and Congregationalists, began ordaining women in 1936).[44] In response to this, Ruth Karras asks (in the Preface to Part I), reasonably enough, "is the argument from history always the best one? If we were to look for women's leadership in the past and not find it, would that then justify their exclusion today?" No, but we hope it would *contextualize* it – just as scholars on other women's issues regu-

41 Sandra Fredman, "The Scandal of Gender Imbalance," *Oxford Today* 28.1 (2015): 19.

42 "'Something Fearful': Medievalist Scholars on the 'Religious Turn,'" in *"Something Fearful": Dialogues and Essays on the "Religious Turn"*, special issue of *Religion & Literature* 42.1 and 42.2 (2010): 1–18; and "The Vitality of the Past in the Present: A Response to *Acknowledged Convictions: A Forum on Religion & Literature 42.1–2*," in *Religion & Literature* 43.1 (2013): 97–112.

43 Newman, "Coming out of the (Sacristy) Closet," *Religion & Literature* 42.1 (2010): 296.

44 The *United Church Observer* wrote about the first woman ordinand: "Miss Gruchy ... comes after a probation far longer and trials far more testing than have been given the candidates for the ministry of the sterner sex, and she comes having passed the test with, to say the least, equal satisfaction to the Church." Nov. 18, 1936, reprinted in the March 1975 anniversary issue.

larly look to the past. As Macy puts it (in Chapter 16), writing of the Roman Catholic tradition: "Theologians have a particular interest and concern to determine whether the ordinations of women in the past were 'real.'" I would add that no matter what religious or political tradition one is addressing, for any institution, nation, or denomination that sees itself *as a cumulative tradition* (and this certainly describes the religious traditions studied here), then, *yes*, the argument from history is critical. And as many of the essays from this collection show, whoever controls the historical narrative wields the power. "You haven't made it till we've all made it" is the challenge laid down in a 1975 article on women in the ministry.[45]

Politicians understand this innately. The American President Jimmy Carter, for instance, severed his ties with the Baptist church in 2009 over the rights of women:

> This discrimination, unjustifiably attributed to a Higher Authority, has provided a reason or excuse for the deprivation of women's equal rights across the world for centuries. At its most repugnant, the belief that women must be subjugated to the wishes of men excuses slavery, violence, ... [and] costs many millions of girls and women control over their own bodies and lives, ... deny[ing] them fair access to education, health, employment and influence within their own communities.... The carefully selected verses found in the Holy Scriptures to justify the superiority of men owe more to time and place – and the determination of male leaders to hold onto their influence – than eternal truths. I am also familiar with vivid descriptions in the same Scriptures in which women are revered as pre-eminent leaders. During the years of the early Christian church women served as deacons, priests, bishops, apostles, teachers and prophets. It wasn't until the fourth century that dominant Christian leaders, all men, twisted and distorted Holy Scriptures to perpetuate their ascendant positions within the religious hierarchy.[46]

Even Jimmy Carter, then, knows and deploys the early history of women's ordination to which Gary Macy, Katie Bugyis, Gemma Simmonds, and Dyan Elliott all refer. Even more recently, in a letter to Pope Francis, Tim Kaine, Hillary Clinton's 2016 Vice Presidential nominee, wrote:

> If women are not accorded equal place in the leadership of the Catholic Church and the other great world religions, they will always be treated as inferiors in earthly matters as well.... There is nothing this Pope could do that would improve the world as much as putting the Church on a path to ordain women.[47]

45 Muriel Duncan, "You haven't made it ... until we've all made it," *United Church Observer*, March 1975, 12–15.

46 In 2009, Carter penned this letter: see "Losing My Religion for Equality," http://www.dailykos.com/story/2015/04/24/1379812/-Jimmy-Carter-Losing-My-Religion-For-Equality?detail=emailclassic#.

47 See: http://pilotonline.com/news/government/politics/let-women-be-priests-sen-kaine-tells-the-pope/article_55c95931–5845-52e3-9b3e-2a167040c0a6.html.

Can medievalists afford to ignore modern traditions and sub-cultures that have invested so much in medieval history? It seems to me we do so at our peril, since medieval history is our *collective history*, and medievalists, increasingly losing market share in the humanities, so often don't realize or don't bother to address the relevance to much that goes on in the modern world, often in the name of history.

The essays collected here, then, make a start at showing why women community leaders, professionals, and intellectuals of the medieval world spoke so vitally to their own day – and to ours.[48] What Gemma Simmonds wrote about Mary Ward in fact applies to every woman discussed here: they, too, "stand as an icon for women's struggle down the centuries to claim their legitimate voice in church and society as leaders and intellectuals.

48 Acknowledgments: I am especially grateful to Katie Bugyis for her unflagging assistance and advice and to John Van Engen, as always, for his perceptive and balanced judgment.

# PART I

# SCHOLARSHIP, LAW, AND POETRY: JEWISH AND MUSLIM WOMEN

Preface to Part I

# AUTHORSHIP AND INTELLECTUAL LIFE: JEWISH AND MUSLIM WOMEN

RUTH MAZO KARRAS

The intellectual and literary achievements of medieval Muslim and Jewish women are not as well known among medievalists as those of Christian women, even when we may actually have the names of more authors in a given genre. The chapters in Part I focus on people who are doubly othered in relation to medieval studies as it has traditionally been practiced in Europe and North America. But it is not just that they bring material that is well known in one scholarly community to the attention of another. Neither Jewish Studies nor Islamic Studies has been at the forefront of recognizing women's activity and leadership. These chapters therefore do important recuperative work in giving us women who have been if not totally ignored, then drastically under-interpreted by previous scholarship. None, perhaps, reaches the status of a Catherine of Siena or Christine de Pisan in terms of the amount of information available about her. Our knowledge of many women authors and scholars, across all traditions, is much more contingent, often dependent on one source or one manuscript fragment.

The Jewish and Muslim women in question, like many of the Christian women discussed in this book, were able to do what they did because of the families into which they were born or married. We do not know anything about the family background of Alice the convert of Worcester, whom Adrienne Williams Boyarin discusses, but she was wealthy, and it is unlikely that her wealth was entirely self-made. The wife of Dunash ibn Labrat, whose poetry S. J. Pearce places at the center of her analysis, is known to posterity only through her connection with her husband. Sitt al-Qudah, like other women Asma Afsaruddin discusses, was from a family of scholars. It is important to note, of course, that this was the case for most medieval men as well. Documents tended to focus on transfers of money and property, and therefore they tend to give us the names of people who controlled money and property. People who were educated were most often so because they came from families who could afford to educate them. The Middle Ages offered more opportunities for a poor but able boy than for a girl, but in either case, the opportunities were precious few. Scholars are less likely to fall into the trap of lumping all medieval men into one group and concluding that "men had opportunities" than to do so with women. Social background may trump gender: within the privileged group, women as well as men grew up in houses full of books and documents, and it makes complete sense that they shared the intellectual curiosity of their brothers and husbands, as well as in some cases their control of property.

Even within the relatively privileged segment of society where women as well as men were able to obtain an education, it is important to remember that we are not dealing here with equality. Women could and did own and manage property, write poetry, study, and teach, but even if these activities were not exceptional, they were not all found in the same times and places. Women were often restricted to certain areas of endeavor and faced greater obstacles – among them, of course, writers or copyists who recorded (or did not record) their activity or who erased or denied it in later centuries.

The women who are the focus of Part I of this book come from cultures that did not have the clear line between laypeople and the clergy that we find in Christianity. The question discussed elsewhere in this volume, of whether particular women referred to in the sources were lay or religious, simply does not arise. Of course, there was fluidity in Christianity as well between the religious and secular purposes of education, but in Muslim and Jewish cultures, the divide makes little sense at all. The lack of division between laity and clergy created different spaces for women's leadership and intellectual production. The question of women's ordination is also a non-issue. Religious leaders became such because of their knowledge and moral character, not because they participated in a specific ritual. That does not mean that they could exercise all the religious prerogatives that men could. Afsaruddin gives us women who were admired as teachers and scholars early in the Muslim tradition, in numbers that are quite surprising to someone not familiar with her sources, but they do not appear to have been among the main interpreters of religious law. Elisheva Baumgarten has used the example of Dolce of Worms to show that Jewish women could lead prayers, but she led and taught women, although she also prepared books and ritual objects for men's use.[1]

The celibacy of the Western Christian clergy, especially after the eleventh century, obviously made a difference to women's opportunities for religious leadership.[2] A Jewish or Muslim woman could participate in the scholarly activity of her father or husband; indeed, it is difficult to imagine that someone who was the daughter of one great scholar and the wife of another, like the daughters of Rashi, would not be at least literate, and Afsaruddin presents us with a Muslim judge who always consulted his more knowledgeable wife. But the great Christian scholars of the central and later Middle Ages did not have wives or daughters, although there were notable sibling pairs in the religious life, as Nicholas Watson's essay in this volume shows (see Chapter 10).[3]

1 Elisheva Baumgarten, *Practicing Piety in Medieval Ashkenaz: Men, Women, and Everyday Religious Observance* (Philadelphia: University of Pennsylvania Press, 2014), 49; Judith Baskin, "Dolce of Worms: The Lives and Deaths of an Exemplary Medieval Jewish Woman and her Daughters," in *Judaism in Practice: From the Middle Ages through the Early Modern Period*, ed. Lawrence Fine (Princeton: Princeton University Press, 2001), 429–37.

2 The enforcement of clerical celibacy varied substantially, but even before the universal invalidation of clerical marriages in the twelfth century, monks, who were the intellectual leaders of Christendom, did not have wives and children.

3 See also Fiona Griffiths, "Siblings and the Sexes within the Medieval Religious Life," *Church History* 77 (2008): 26–53.

The chapters on Jewish women raise fascinating questions about multilingualism. It is too easy to assume, with regard to both Christian and Jewish culture, that women would be literate mainly in the vernacular while the sacred or learned language was reserved for men. This is not just based on modern scholars' preconceptions; medieval Yiddish texts tell us they have been put into the vernacular so that women can read them. Pearce explodes the assumptions about the allusive nature of Hebrew poetry that have suggested women's inability to write in Hebrew and led to the exceptionalist theory of Dunash's wife. Boyarin uses the case of Alice to underscore that Jewish women as well as men in twelfth-century England operated within a documentary culture, whether or not a given woman was herself literate in the narrower sense; the fact that Alice sent letters in both French and Latin suggests the need for medieval Jews to command several languages, both vernacular and learned, minority and majority.

Because some modern versions of Islam and Judaism (and Christianity) so restrict the participation of women, Part I is particularly important in bringing to the fore a question that is addressed in varying ways throughout the volume: what is the relevance of historical experience to religious tradition? In an era when Islamophobes co-opt feminist rhetoric to critique an entire global set of cultures on the basis of their treatment of women and in which groups like the Nigerian Boko Haram and the Afghan Taliban make girls' schools their particular targets, it is especially important to show, as Afsaruddin does, that women's educational and intellectual activity has deep roots in the Qur'an and early Islam. Even if female scholars were relatively rare compared to men, the fact that it was possible for women to transmit *hadith*, and to teach and learn at madrasas, is significant. Afsaruddin makes a crucial point that the new legal history has made about medieval Christian society as well: just because we have prescriptive texts saying that something cannot happen does not mean that it did not happen. We are very fortunate that al-Sakhawi chose to depart from tradition and document the lives of contemporary and recent women.

In religions based so heavily on tradition, it is obviously of great import to contemporary believers what opportunities women were given at the founding moment and in sacred texts. The argument from history can seem to scholars or to moderate believers to refute the claims of self-identified "traditionalist" groups, but those traditionalists themselves are likely to develop their own arguments to explain away women's participation (or ignore it, as Afsaruddin shows was done in the later Middle Ages). But is the argument from history always the best one? If we were to look for women's leadership in the past and not find it, would that then justify women's exclusion today? It is crucial for a variety of reasons for both believers and non-believers to set the record straight and restore historical women to the prominence they had in their lifetimes. But it is also crucial to examine how traditions develop and change over time. The relation between past and present is always mediated in complex ways. All three chapters in Part I discuss how scholars, pre-modern and modern, have shaped the tradition of women's education and leadership by what they chose to ignore and what to emphasize. Contemporary scholars – those in this volume and others – must recognize that we are doing the same with regard to women or any other group.

I

# GENDER, SCHOLARSHIP, AND THE CONSTRUCTION OF AUTHORITY IN THE PRE-MODERN MUSLIM WORLD

ASMA AFSARUDDIN

A well-known *hadith* (statement attributed to the Prophet Muhammad) states, "The seeking of knowledge is a religious obligation for every Muslim" (*talab al-'ilm farida 'ala kull muslim*).[1] A variant version of this *hadith* explicitly makes clear that this obligation recognizes no gender difference: "The seeking of knowledge is a duty of every Muslim, *male and female*."[2] Like the practice and possession of personal piety (*taqwa*), possession of knowledge (*'ilm*) – religious and otherwise – is highly valorized in the Islamic milieu and has the potential to level gendered differences between men and women. Knowledge and piety combined sometimes conferred great status and religious authority on the individual concerned irrespective of gender and sometimes brought exceptional social and intellectual recognition in its wake. Such was the case for 'A'isha bint Abi Bakr, beloved wife of the Prophet Muhammad from the seventh century and for Rabi'a al-'Adawiyya, the famous female Basran mystic from the eighth century. To this day, the names of these distinguished women are invoked reverentially by many Muslims as paragons of moral excellence and exceptional learning whose lives are deemed to be worthy of emulation by both women and men.

There may, however, be a temptation among modern scholars to dismiss these women as exceptions to the rule, especially since many in the Western academy and beyond it often tend to portray Muslim-majority societies as peculiarly resistant to women's empowerment, particularly through education. And yet, a number of pre-modern sources document the active participation of considerable numbers of women, usually from elite backgrounds, in the production and dissemination of religious knowledge in Islamic societies, which sometimes conferred a measure of religious authority on them. Other sources list the contributions of elite and non-elite women in the more worldly realms of literary composition, which brought them distinction and renown in their own milieu and beyond.

This chapter will be concerned with selectively retrieving details of the lives of a number of such learned and accomplished Muslim women in the pre-modern period (roughly from the seventh century to the sixteenth century) whose religious and intellectual pursuits are recorded in some of the most important biographical and

1 See, for example, al-Tabarani, *al-Mu'jam al-awsat* (Riyadh: Maktabat al-Ma'arif, 1985), 1:33, 9.

2 This *hadith* is recorded by the well-known scholar Ibn Maja in his famous hadith collection known as *Sunan*; see A. J. Wensinck, *Concordance et indices de la traditions musulmane* (Leiden: E. J. Brill, 1988), 4:10.

prosopographical works of the period. We will begin with an account of an intrepid learned Muslim woman from the first century of Islam who has become a near-iconic figure in the contemporary period for reasons that will shortly become obvious. We will then proceed to provide an account of gifted women from later centuries whose contributions have left an indelible imprint in both religious and non-religious realms and whose religious and intellectual standing as a consequence was both celebrated and contested through the centuries. The larger implications of retrieving the details of their contributions to pre-modern Islamic scholarship and intellectual life for the contemporary period will be briefly explored in the conclusion.

## Reading the Lives of Pre-Modern Muslim Women: Creating Paradigms of Moral Excellence

The lives of the first generation of Muslims (Arabic *salaf*), men and women, are generally regarded as worthy of emulation by later generations of Muslims. The latter often look back to the first century of Islam (seventh century of the common era) as an ideal period during which the *Zeitgeist* of Islam was fully realized. With regard to the female Companions, that is the female associates and followers of the Prophet Muhammad (d. 632), their lives have been and are still centrally constitutive of traditionalist – and nowadays "Islamist" – views of the "proper" roles of women in Islamic societies. Traditionalists and Islamists today maintain that women's primary roles are as wives and mothers, and their access to the public sphere should thereby be limited, except in the cases of economic necessity or an emergency situation.[3] Such groups often justify these views by asserting that they are in full compliance with the norms and mores of the earliest period and that these restrictions placed on women's public roles should therefore continue to be upheld by contemporary observant Muslims. But can such assertions and claims be supported if we were to look at actual historical and biographical sources which document the lives of a considerable number of the earliest Muslim women? The answer is resoundingly in the negative; such sources, in fact, allow us to undermine such ideological, ahistorical assertions with considerable vigor.

To demonstrate this succinctly, this chapter will begin by looking at the life of one "problematic" woman Companion,[4] Umm Waraqa, as depicted by two well-known scholars, Ibn Sa'd (d. 845) and Ibn Hajar (d. 1449), of the ninth and fifteenth centuries respectively, in their important biographical works. A close scrutiny of how the details of the life of this remarkable woman are configured and reconfigured in their works will allow us to trace the attitudinal changes concerning public roles of women during the span of time separating their lives.

The rest of the chapter will then selectively discuss the intellectual contributions of a number of prominent Andalusian women poets and scholars featured in a literary work composed by the famous North African historian Ahmad ibn Muhammad

3 Muhammad Mutawalli al-Sha'rawi, *Qadaya al-mar'a al-muslima* (Cairo: Dar al-Muslim, 1982), 18 ff.

4 It will soon become clear why I refer to her as "problematic."

al-Maqqari (d. 1632), followed by a discussion of the lives of prominent women religious scholars from the Mamluk period (1250–1517), as recorded in the biographical dictionary of the well-known fifteenth- century scholar Shams al-Din al-Sakahwi (d. 1497). This will allow us to compare al-Maqqari's account of women luminaries with that of al-Sakhawi in order to derive some broad conclusions regarding the place of women's scholarship and literary activity in the larger master narrative of learning in pre-modern Muslim societies.[5]

### Umm Waraqa bint Abd Allah ibn al-Harith: A Seventh-Century Exemplar

Umm Waraqa's name is sometimes invoked by contemporary Muslims in the context of roles of religious leadership for women, particularly as prayer leader (*imam*) of mixed-gender congregations.[6] According to Ibn Sa'd, who records the details of her eventful life in his justly famous biographical work titled *al-Tabaqat al-kubra*, Umm Waraqa, on accepting Islam, personally gave her allegiance to the Prophet Muhammad and related *hadith*s from him. She is said to have memorized the Qur'an (*kanat qad jama'at al-qur'an*), and the Prophet asked her to lead her household in prayer (*qad amaraha an ta'umma ahl dariha*), which she did repeatedly. She also hired a (male) caller to prayer (*mu'adhdhin*). The Prophet would visit her frequently and conferred on her the epithet "the Martyred Woman" (*al-shahida*). At the time of the battle of Badr, Umm Waraqa implored Muhammad to let her accompany him to the battlefield and tend to the wounded so that "perhaps God may grant me martyrdom" (*anna allah yuhdi li shahada*). The Prophet assured her that God would grant her martyrdom. Umm Waraqa, Ibn Sa'd further records, continued to lead the members of her household in prayer until two servants, a male and a female, who were under her charge, murdered her during 'Umar's caliphate. 'Umar is said to have remarked that due to her violent and unjust death, she had in fact achieved martyrdom.[7]

Turning to Ibn Hajar's account of Umm Waraqa's life in his well-known biographical work *al-Isaba fi tamyiz al-sahaba*, we are struck by the fact that he does not mention that she had led "the people of her household" (Ar. *ahl dariha*; which, since we are not told to the contrary, must have consisted of male and female members) in prayer at the express request of the Prophet. He records, however, that she had asked the Prophet's permission to hire a male caller to prayer. Further doctoring on his part of the older version as contained in Ibn Sa'd's work becomes evident when he launches into an explanation of the sobriquet "the Martyred Woman" conferred

5 This next section is largely derived from my earlier essay, "Literature, Scholarship, and Piety: Negotiating Gender and Authority in the Medieval Muslim World," *Religion and Literature* 42 (2010): 111–31.

6 Invoking such early narratives, on March 18, 2005, Amina Wadud, a scholar of Islamic Studies at the University of Richmond, Virginia, led a mixed-gender Friday congregational prayer in New York which was both praised and condemned by different groups of Muslims; see this account in the article "Woman Leads Muslim Prayer Service in New York," *The New York Times*, March 19, 2005, available at: http://www.nytimes.com/2005/03/19/nyregion/woman-leads-muslim-prayer-service-in-new-york.html?_r=0; last accessed April 2, 2016.

7 Ibn Sa'd, *al-Tabaqat al-kubra*, ed. Muhammad 'Abd al-Qadir 'Ata (Beirut: Dar Sadir, 1997), 8:457.

on her by the Prophet. Ibn Hajar foregrounds the account according to which she asked Muhammad's permission to take part in the battle of Badr as a nurse. In his rendition of this event, the Prophet explicitly forbids her, using words that have Qur'anic resonance, "Remain (*qurri*)[8] in your house; for indeed God will grant you martyrdom [in another way]." In case the import of this directive is lost on the reader, Ibn Hajar supplies a variant account (not occurring in Ibn Sa'd's entry) in which the Prophet is quoted as counseling her even more bluntly, "Sit in your home, for indeed God will grant you martyrdom in your house"[9] (*uq'udi fi baytiki fa-inna allah sa-yahdi 'ilayki shahada fi baytiki*; emphasis added). The tragic dénouement to Umm Waraqa's life then teleologically falls into place: a woman can achieve the status of a martyr by remaining (and only by remaining) within her home and carrying on her usual domestic activities, like the supervision of her servants.[10]

It is worth bearing in mind that Ibn Sa'd does not record the Prophet's injunction to "remain in your house" in response to Umm Waraqa's entreaty. The only prophetic response he records is Muhammad's assurance to her that she would indeed achieve martyrdom. Ibn Sa'd's version does not rule out the possibility that Umm Waraqa did accompany the Prophet to the battlefield. Muhammad's prescient statement simply presages her tragic end but does not express disapproval of her potential presence at Badr. Given that we are now able to detect a certain editorial tendency on Ibn Hajar's part, it is not surprising that Umm Waraqa's continuing role as the prayer leader of her household, mentioned by Ibn Sa'd, goes unreported by him as well in the *Isaba*.[11]

These relatively minor deviations in detail are highly revealing of how societal conceptions of women's agency and proper conduct in the public realm came to be progressively defined and restricted in the late medieval Muslim world. Most jurists and theologians by the fifteenth century had decided that leadership of prayer of mixed congregations was not an appropriate role for women and that virtuous women best exercised their virtue within the confines of their home. These views, like others, came to be retrojected onto the lives of the earliest Muslim women.[12] Such views from the later period provide on the one hand valuable grist for ultra-conservative Muslims

8 The usage of this word here evokes Qur'an 33:33, "*wa-qarna fi buyutikunna* …;" commonly translated as 'remain in your (f. pl.) homes.' The imperative *qarna* remains problematic, however, since it is irregular and in its present conjugated form in the imperative cannot categorically be linked to the verbs *qarra* or *waqara*, which would connote 'to remain' and 'to behave with dignity' respectively. For a brief discussion of this, see Barbara Stowasser, *Women in the Qur'an, Traditions, and Interpretation* (Oxford: Oxford University Press, 1994), 172, n. 79.

9 Ibn Hajar, *al-Isaba fi tamyiz al-sahaba* (Cairo: Matba'at al-Sa'ada, 1907), 8:289.

10 This position is reflected in the *tafsir* literature in general; see for example, Ibn Kathir (d. 1373), *Tafsir al-Qur'an al-'azim* (Beirut: Dar al-Jil, 1990), 3:464, where he interprets Qur'an 33:33 as counseling the Prophet's wives "to remain in their homes."

11 See further, Asma Afsaruddin, *First Muslims: History and Memory* (Oxford: Oneworld Publications, 2008), 163–65, 190–91, for a discussion of how the details of Umm Waraqa's life are interpreted by later Muslim biographers to draw certain conclusions about gendered roles in the first century of Islam, which has important consequences for contemporary debates among Muslims regarding public religious roles for women.

12 See further, Asma Afsaruddin, "Early Women Exemplars and the Construction of Gendered Space: (Re-) Defining Feminine Moral Excellence," in M. Booth (ed.), *Harem Histories: Envisioning Spaces and Living Places* (Durham, NC: Duke University Press, 2011), 31–71.

today who wish to curtail women's legal and societal rights on the basis that such views accurately reflect the gender norms of the earliest period. On the other, earlier accounts of Umm Waraqa's life, such as Ibn Sa'd's, which celebrate the full range of her accomplishments, allow liberal and feminist Muslims today to insist that knowledge rather than gender is constitutive of leadership roles in the Islamic milieu and, therefore, women should face no barrier in their quest to gain equal access to positions of religious authority today.

### Beyond the First Generation of Muslim Women: Re-reading History

Although we are not blessed with an over-abundance of biographical notices on prominent women in Islamic societies from after the time of the Companions of the Prophet, there are a number of notable works from the post-prophetic period that preserve the names and contributions of women scholars and litterateurs who helped shape the intellectual ethos of their time. Among these works is what is popularly known as the *Kitab al-Nisa'* ('Book of Women') of the previously mentioned al-Sakhawi, which sheds valuable light on the noteworthy scholarly attainments and economic activities of a considerable number of women from the Mamluk period.[13] Another important source for the lives of particularly literary women in Muslim Spain of the eleventh and twelfth centuries is the work of al-Maqqari, mentioned above, titled *Nafh al-tib fi ghusn al-andalus al-ratib*.[14] Both of these works are exceptional for the fact that they record the lives of women in the later Middle Ages who were specifically engaged in literary and scholarly endeavors. This is in contrast to most biographical works of the late medieval period, such as the aforementioned Ibn Hajar's *al-Isaba fi tamyiz al-sahaba*, which continued to focus on women from the first generation of Islam, invoking them as role models for later generations of women.

### Poetry and Romantic High Jinks in al-Andalus (Muslim Spain)

In his introduction to the section on women in the *Nafh al-tib*, the historian and biographer Ahmad ibn Muhammad al-Maqqari al-Tilimsani al-Maqqari (d. 1632) writes:

> When I reached this point in my narrative about the people of al-Andalus, I saw it fit to mention a group of Andalusian women who were endowed with eloquence, to let it be known that the people of al-Andalus, including their women and their youth, were eminently gifted.[15]

13 For the economic activities of women mentioned in this biographical work, see Huda Lutfi, "Al-Sakhawi's *Kitab al-Nisa'* as a Source for the Social and Economic History of Muslim Women during the Fifteenth Century," *The Muslim World* 71 (1982): 104–24.

14 The edition of *Nafh al-tib* used in this article has been edited by Ihsan 'Abbas in 4 vols. (Beirut: Dar al-Sadir, 1968). Volume four contains the section on women; all page references below therefore refer to this volume. The following section on al-Maqqari's work is based on an earlier article of mine titled "Poetry and Love: The Feminine Contribution in Muslim Spain," *Islamic Studies* 30 (1991): 157–69.

15 *Nafh al-tib*, 166.

It is worthy of note that al-Maqqari is of the opinion that no intellectual history of al-Andalus would be complete without including accounts of its talented women and youth, two groups of people who were ordinarily excluded or scantily referred to in regional histories of this kind. Traditional biographical and prosopographical works focused on mature men who wielded power and influence of different kinds: political, religious, intellectual, and martial. Females of all ages and males of extreme youth tend not to figure in such accounts, except rarely and tangentially, because in most cases they were deemed incapable of exercising such types of authority in their own right. When they merited mention at all in conventional biographies, it was in connection with powerful men, a fact which underscored their mostly biologically-derivative social status in pre-modern patriarchal societies.

The aesthetic and literary domains, however, in general have been the exception to this trend. Excellence in literary and aesthetic pursuits has often been equally recognized in practitioners of both sexes. Eloquence (*al-balagha*), in particular, as we observe in al-Maqqari's introduction, continued to be a trait highly esteemed, regardless of in whom it resided, by the cultural elite in the pre-modern period, an attitude that harkened back to the pre-Islamic period. Linguistic virtuosity and poetic talent, embodied in the kind of eloquence al-Maqqari pays homage to in this introduction, often served as a leveler of culturally constructed notions of social propriety and gendered roles. Thus, al-Maqqari magnanimously acknowledges that a full appreciation of the vitality of the cultural and intellectual life in Muslim Spain in the eleventh and twelfth centuries could be achieved only through additional consideration of women's contributions in this sphere and of their considerable interaction with their male peers.[16]

In a large number of cases, our author offers us only tantalizingly brief glimpses into a woman poet's life and her contribution, while in others we are given more fulsome accounts of her literary accomplishments and relations with particularly male contemporaries, both platonic and amatory. Among these women are twenty-four poets who achieved considerable literary prominence. Details on their lives are sometimes disappointingly meager, although in a number of instances, we get more complete descriptions which allow us to draw more certain conclusions about the extent of the contributions of these women to the cultural and intellectual milieux of their time. In any case, from perusing the section on women literati in *Nafh al-tib*, one gets an overall impression of the spiritedness, prolific talent, and intellectual vibrancy evinced by these Andalusian women. Discounting the hyperbole that is sometimes typical of medieval biographical accounts, one cannot help but be impressed by the amount of personal and intellectual freedom enjoyed by these women and the high level of cultural accomplishment that distinguished them. Most of these accomplished women were from elite backgrounds. Thus the poetess Umm al-'Ala', mentioned by al-Maqqari, was the daughter of well-known poet Abu 'l-Mukhshi and received a

16 For an overall assessment of the status of Andalusian women, see the valuable articles by Maria Viguera, "Asluhu Li 'l-Ma'ali: On the Social Status of Andalusi Women," in *The Legacy of Muslim Spain*, ed. Salma Jayyusi (Leiden: E. J. Brill, 1994), vol. 2 and Nada Mourtada-Sabbah and Adrian Gully, "'I am, by God, Fit for High Positions': On the Political Role of Women in Al-Andalus," *British Journal of Middle Eastern Studies* 30 (2003): 183–209.

thorough education in poetics, among other subjects.[17] Buthayna bint al-Mu'tamid ibn 'Abbad was from a caliphal family and became a well-known poetess like her mother al-I'timad, as did Hafsa bint Hamdun, who was from one of the most prominent families in Wadi al-Hijara.[18]

A towering and formidable literary and historical personality of the time was Wallada bint al-Mustakfi billah. When one compiles a list of the most accomplished Andalusian women poets, Wallada, daughter of the Umayyad caliph al-Mustakfi, easily heads the list. Wallada was a headstrong, willful, beautiful, and gifted woman who often defied the conventions of her time. She was, as al-Maqqari puts it, "unique in her time, endowed with gracious speech, lavishly praised and the cynosure of attention."[19] Wallada never married, although she had her share of powerful suitors. When her father died, she opened up her home in Córdoba to the famous poets, belle-lettrists and savants of her time. She is said to have presided with dazzling charm and wit over this literary salon, which gained wide repute. Ibn Bashkuwal in his *al-Sila* remarks that she was a cultured poetess of eloquent diction who wrote refined poetry and was inclined to engage in contests of superiority with her fellow poets.[20] Wallada died at an advanced age in 1087.

A less famous poetess, Hamda, also known as Hamduna bint Ziyad al-Mu'addib, became renowned as the "Khansa' of the West." This sobriquet confers singular distinction on her, for the original Khansa' from seventh-century Arabia was celebrated for her poetry, particularly for the elegies (*marthiyyat*) she had composed to commemorate the deaths of her brothers, Mu'awiya and Sakhr. When Khansa' converted to Islam and met the Prophet Muhammad in Medina, he praised her poetry, thus winning for herself and her poetry a special position in Arabic literature.[21]

Favorable comparison with the original Khansa' highlighted the distinctive nature of Hamda's poetic talent and also her exceptional linguistic ability. Al-Maqqari mentions that there was a group of women in Granada collectively known as *al-'Arabiyyat* ('the Arab women') on account of their mastery of the Arabic language. In this group were included Hamda and her sister Zaynab bint Ziyad, another accomplished litterateur.[22]

In her own time, 'A'isha bint Ahmad al-Qurtubiyya was among the most celebrated Andalusian on account of her learning, quick mind, eloquent speech, and excellent poetic skills. Al-Maqqari includes only a brief entry on her, according to which she sang the praises of the Andalusian kings in her poetry and had close connections with a number of them, such that she could write to them any time she required something of them. 'A'isha's penmanship is said to have been beautiful, and

17 See my earlier "Poetry and Love," 157–58.

18 Ibid., 163–64.

19 *Nafh al-tib*, 205.

20 Ibid., 207.

21 The original Khansa''s proper name is Tumadir, daughter of 'Amr b. al-Sharid of the Banu Sulaym, and is one of the *mukhadramun* poets, that is, those poets whose lives spanned the pre-Islamic and Islamic periods. See further "Khansa'" in the *Encyclopaedia of Islam*, New Edition, ed. H. A. R. Gibb et al. (Leiden: Brill, 1960–2003).

22 *Nafh al-tib*, 287–90.

she copied manuscripts, which was by no means a common accomplishment, especially for women.[23] She never married and died in the year 1010.[24]

A Castilian woman known simply as al-Shilbiyya, from the town of Lucena, merits an entry in al-Maqqari's biography. According to al-Maqqari, her talents extended far beyond her skills at versification, for she had also gained renown for her remarkable knowledge of Islamic law and jurisprudence, so much so that it became widely circulated that there was a *qadi* in Lucena (al-Shilbiyya's husband) whose wife surpassed him in knowledge of the law and of judicial proceedings. In fact, it was said that her husband had married her on that account. Al-Maqqari reports that at judicial assemblies, al-Shilbiyya's husband, before uttering any legal pronouncement, would consult with her, and she would indicate to him the correct legal decision. In recognition of this fact, some of his colleagues jestingly composed the following poem:

In Lucena there is a *qadi* who has a wife
Her decisions hold sway over the people
If only he were not the judge (*qadi)*
And she was the judge (*qadiya*) instead![25]

The last verse is actually a verbatim and clever deployment of Qur'an 69:27, which states in Arabic, "*Ya laytaha kanat al-qadiya*!" In the Qur'anic context, the verse means, "If only it (sc. death) had made an end of me!" – referring to wrong-doers on the last day who realize that their sins have caught up with them and who, therefore, wish for extinction. The clever and sarcastic pun generated by the contrast between *qadi* and *qadiya* can only be appreciated in the original. It is not hard to infer that the punster regarded this situation – a male *qadi* conferring with a more knowledgeable female scholar for legal advice – as rather calamitous.

### The World of Religious Scholarship as Described in al-Sakhawi's Kitab al-Nisa'

Shams al-Din Muhammad ibn 'Abd al-Rahman al-Sakhawi's[26] comprehensive biographical dictionary of the most notable personalities of the fifteenth century – titled *al-Daw' al-lami' li-ahl al-qarn al-tasi'a* – remains until today an invaluable primary source on the scholarly and religious elite of his time and, more broadly, of the Mamluk period.[27] In the last volume of this work, popularly known as the *Kitab al-Nisa'* ('Book of Women'), the author records entries on 1,075 women, an overwhelming number

23 There was of course a well-established class of secretaries and scribes who more commonly copied manuscripts, especially for formal occasions, since the early 'Abbasid period (ninth century); see "Katib" in the *Encyclopaedia of Islam* (online version available at: http://referenceworks.brillonline.com.proxyiub.uits.iu.edu/entries/encyclopaedia-of-islam-2/katib-COM_0466?s.num=6&s.f.s2_parent=s.f.book.encyclopaedia-of-islam-2&s.q=insha.

24 *Nafh al-tib*, 290.

25 Ibid., 294–95.

26 For more details on the author, see the entry "al-Sakhawi," *Encyclopaedia of Islam*, 8:881–82.

27 For most of these details regarding al-Sakhawi and his *Kitab al-Nisa'*, I am drawing on my study titled "Knowledge, Piety, and Religious Leadership in the Late Middle Ages: Reinstating Women in the Master Narrative," forthcoming in Sebastian Guenther, ed., *Knowledge and Education in Classical Islam: Historical Foundations and Contemporary Impact* (Leiden: Brill, 2020).

of whom are distinguished for their exemplary religious piety and excellence in and dedication to religious scholarship. Al-Sakhawi's interest in contemporary women was by no means commonplace among male biographers who preceded him or came after him. Although traditionally most biographical dictionaries have a section on women, these women are mostly from the first two generations of Muslims who were still close to the time of the Prophet and therefore served as moral exemplars for succeeding generations of women, as we saw in the case of Umm Waraqa, for example. There was far less interest in documenting the lives of women contemporary to the biographer's time or from the generations following the second generation of Muslims. By departing from convention, al-Sakhawi has provided us with a precious source for reconstructing women's contributions to religious scholarship in the Mamluk period.

In the *Kitab al-Nisa'*, the general picture that emerges is of women who were active in both receiving and imparting religious knowledge, particularly in the transmission of *hadith*. The notion of sexually segregated space that we take for granted as a defining feature of medieval Muslim society is challenged by what these biographical accounts have to tell us about the formal and informal settings in which women scholars conducted their activity. Women are depicted as freely studying with men and other women; after becoming credentialed as teachers, they would go on to teach both men and women. The settings include the *madrasa*, the institution of higher learning, informal study circles (*halaqas*), and private homes. One of the most important *madrasas* mentioned by name in which one of these women scholars taught is the famed *madrasa* al-Zahiriyya in Damascus, Syria.

Al-Sakhawi's protagonists are mostly women from elite backgrounds; almost without exception, they are described as being of noble birth, and/or from families which were already distinguished for a tradition of learning, and for producing religious and legal scholars. The male relatives of these women appear to have been quite encouraging of the desire of these women to acquire advanced religious instruction. Like their male counterparts, female children from wealthy and learned families often began their education at a very early age. Al-Sakhawi refers, for example, to Zaynab bint 'Abd al-Rahim who started going to classes taught by her father and by other scholars with her brother when she was barely five years old.[28] She went on to receive teaching certificates from the prominent scholars of her time, such as Abu 'l-Khayr al-'Ala'i, Abu Bakr ibn Muhammad ibn 'Abd al-Rahman al-Mizzi, and Abu Hurayra ibn al-Dhahabi.[29]

These women scholars, like their male counterparts, spent years in scholarly apprenticeship, making the usual rounds of academic circles, choosing to study closely with specific well-known teachers, and finally earning the coveted *ijaza* ('license'), or the teaching certificate which permitted them to instruct others. Like their male colleagues, they clearly worked hard to make their entrance into the world of formal religious training. Obviously, their familial prominence and their well-to-do circumstances, which are often implied and sometimes explicitly stated, facilitated their access

28 For comparative purposes, one may refer to a recent study of schooling for women in medieval England by Megan J. Hall, "Learning and Literacy Outside the Convent: Early Middle English Women Readers and the *Ancrene Wisse*," Ph.D. Dissertation, University of Notre Dame, 2016.

29 Al-Sakhawi, *al-Daw al-Lami'a li-ahl al-qarn al-tasia* (Beirut: Dar Maktabat al-Hayat, n.d.), 12:41–42.

to the refined world of scholarship and their formal induction into academia. There is no doubt that these elite women were empowered by their privileged social and familial circumstances which appear not to have recognized a gender barrier, at least in the acquisition and dissemination of religious scholarship. Based on al-Sakhawi's depiction, the actual academic training of the best of these women scholars often appears to match that of the best male scholars in rigor and thoroughness, a fact that was acknowledged in their own time, given the amount of academic recognition that came their way as a result. This is reflected primarily in the number and quality of the students they supervised, which included al-Sakhawi himself, and prior to him, his own teacher, the famous Mamluk scholar Ibn Hajar, for example.[30]

A key descriptive term used for a number of the women scholars in al-Sakhawi's biographical work is *ra'isa* (lit. 'a female leader'); the more elevated form *kathirat al-ri'asa* ('having plenitude of leadership') is occasionally used. These terms are particularly significant since they connote some form of religious leadership and prominence in learning. One woman, Halima bint Ahmad ibn Muhammad, who is described as possessing "plenitude of leadership," is clearly deserving of this accolade. She is described as having been subjected to a rigorous examination before being granted her certificate to teach, a fact that is not cited too frequently in these biographical notices. Her board of examiners was constituted by a number of the most distinguished scholars of the day, including Ibn al-Hayyil, Ibn Mayla, al-Salah ibn Abi 'Umar, Abu Bakr ibn Muhammad ibn al-Hibal, and others. The entry on Halima continues by recording the fact that prominent scholars audited her transmission of *hadith*. She lived to an advanced age and achieved singular excellence in her profession (*tafarradat*). No doubt her aristocratic background was a help, not a hindrance, to her outstanding academic career. Her father was the head of the notables of the Syrian town of Aleppo, which would have facilitated her access to the best social and intellectual circles of her time and stimulated in her at a young age the desire to emulate the learning displayed in these circles.[31]

Al-Sakhawi also refers to a number of women who had studied works of jurisprudence, like 'A'isha bint 'Ali ibn Muhammad ibn 'Ali ibn 'Abd Allah, who is described as being thoroughly familiar with *fiqh* in addition to the usual sciences.[32] Another scholar, Ruqayya bint al-Sharaf Muhammad, who achieved enviable fame during her lifetime for her prolific transmission of *hadith*, attended court proceedings when al-Sakhawi was presiding.[33] No further details are forthcoming in this entry about her particular role in court, but it is very clear that she had a right to be there.[34]

Al-Sakhawi often highlights the personal piety and moral uprightness of many of the Mamluk women scholars. Thus, Halima bint Ahmad, mentioned above, is also

30 For further details, see my "Knowledge, Piety, and Religious Leadership," forthcoming.

31 *Al-Daw al-Lami'a*, 6:22.

32 Ibid., 12:78.

33 Ibid., 12:35.

34 For recent comprehensive studies of Muslim women scholars and their seminal role in particularly the transmission of *hadith*, see Mohammad Akram Nadwi, *Al-Muhaddithat: The Women Scholars in Islam* (Oxford: Interface, 2007) and Asma Sayeed, *Women and the Transmission of Religious Knowledge in Islam* (Cambridge: Cambridge University Press, 2015).

praised for her personal virtue and moral excellence (*kanat saliha khayra*) and described as modest (*al-hashima*).[35] Besides *khayra* and *saliha*, other commonly occurring epithets for our women scholars include *fadila* and *asila*. Like *khayra* and *ṣaliha*, *fadila* testifies to the women's moral excellence and personal piety. A less frequently used related term is *muta'abbida*, which refers to the individual's devoutness and godliness. The epithet *asila*, however, refers specifically to the individual's noble birth and, secondarily, to her strength of character. A related adjective used for a few women is *jalila*, which indicates her high-born social status in most cases, but also her distinguished academic status.

It is worthy of note that, with one exception, al-Sakhawi does not refer to the physical attractiveness of these women, even though such comments were practically *de rigueur* in biographical entries on women, as for example, in the *Tabaqat al-kubra* of Ibn Sa'd. Appropriately, al-Sakhawi focuses rather on the scholarly training and accomplishments of the women he includes in his biographical entries. There is also relatively less attention paid to the male relatives of these women, particularly husbands and fathers, as, for example, when compared with Ibn Sa'd's biographical dictionary. Rather, the women scholars are protagonists in their own right, and it is their individual scholarly efforts and achievements which receive the bulk of al-Sakhawi's attention.[36]

## Comparison between the Biographical Dictionaries of al-Maqqari and al-Sakhawi

Like al-Sakhawi's work, al-Maqqari's *Nafh al-tib* primarily focuses on highly cultured elite women whose socio-economic background granted them privileged access to learning circles and scholarly training in the literature and arts. Classical Arabic poetry, with its complex system of prosody and rhyme, required rigorous training and apprenticeship along with natural talent. Such elevated learning was typically available to families of great privilege and with a tradition of learning. Thus, as we noted, the poetess Umm al-'Ala' followed in the footsteps of her well-known poet father Abu 'l-Mukhshi, while Buthayna bint al-Mu'tamid ibn 'Abbad, member of a caliphal family, became a well-known poetess like her mother al-I'timad.

Men are sometimes depicted as having unabashedly learnt from accomplished women and publicly acknowledged this fact. This is a prominent fact in al-Sakhawi's work, as we already noted, and it is also intermittently documented in al-Maqqari's work. Besides literary skills, a few Andalusian women also seem to have excelled in the traditionally highly esteemed, male-dominated disciplines of law and jurisprudence. Thus, we have reference to al-Shilbiyya who, besides being a gifted poetess, was also well-versed in law. Her husband, who was a *qadi*, openly consulted with her before rendering a judicial decision, a situation that seems to have been greeted with part admiration and part derision, as we saw. In his biographical work, al-Sakhawi also refers to a number of women who had studied works of jurisprudence, like 'A'isha bint 'Ali and Ruqayya bint al-Sharaf Muhammad. This establishes that women's religious scholarship often extended beyond the realm of *hadith* transmission, a phenomenon that needs to be more comprehensively studied.

35 Ibid.

36 Cf. "Knowledge, Piety, and Religious Leadership," *passim*.

## Conclusion

The sources consulted above remind us that whether as religious scholars, poets, jurists, military heroes, and/or learned citizens of their communities, Muslim women helped shape Islam's storied past to a considerable degree. This is a fact often acknowledged by their contemporaries and sometimes given due recognition in the writings of their male students, colleagues, and consorts, as we saw. However, later scholars (after the seventeenth century) have consigned these remarkable women to relative oblivion and elided their contributions with the shaping of the Islamic intellectual tradition. Reading and re-reading biographical works, historical sources, and other literary artifacts from the medieval period, especially in its nooks and crannies into which women (and other marginalized people) typically tend to fall, can yield rich dividends, as this chapter demonstrates. Forensic scholarship of this kind has, in fact, led to the excavation of a past peopled by learned and gifted women who distinctively shaped the trajectory of early and medieval Islamic society but whose contributions were, over time, subjected to benign and not-so-benign neglect. Given the fractious present of many Muslim-majority societies today and the contestation of the roles of women in the public domain that have ensued as a consequence, it has never been more important to help revive the memory of these distinguished women scholars, religious leaders, and litterateurs who bear testimony to Islam's valorization of learning – irrespective of gender – that empowered them. The implications of such a project of revival for contemporary Muslim-majority societies cannot be underestimated.

2

# THE HISTORIOGRAPHY OF ABSENCE: PRELIMINARY STEPS TOWARDS A NEW HISTORY OF ANDALUSI WOMEN POETS

S. J. PEARCE

> "If I am woman by nature, I am man by poetry."[1]
> – Nazhūn al-Mājinah (twelfth century, Granada)

In a widely reported 2011 interview at the Royal Geographic Society, the British–Caribbean novelist and essayist V. S. Naipaul shocked his interlocutors and many members of the reading public when he said: "I read a piece of writing and within a paragraph or two I know whether it is by a woman or not. I think it is unequal to me." He continued: "A woman is not a complete master of a house, so that comes over in her writing, too. My publisher, who was so good as a taste-maker and editor, when she became a writer, lo and behold, it was all this feminine tosh." Naipaul's valedictory flourish was the clarification: "I don't mean this in any unkind way."[2]

The notion that a reader may discern the gender of a text's author through close reading is, paradoxically, antithetical to the notion of close reading itself; nevertheless, it still finds roots deep in various literary historiographies and methodologies. In the early years of his career, before becoming the doyen of the social history of the medieval Mediterranean, S. D. Goitein claimed that while listening to the performance of Arabic poetry in Yemen, he could always tell whether a poem had been written by a man or a woman regardless of the gender of the performer.[3] Such a belief, in no way limited to Naipaul and Goitein, bears serious interpretive consequences that have limited scholarly ability to comprehend the boundaries of women's writing. In this chapter, I propose to examine those consequences as they bear upon the construction of a literary history of Andalusi women poets and argue that only by overcoming both gender-essentialist and female-exceptionalist interpretation, two faces of the same critical coin, can we arrive at sound explanations for women's

1 Nazhun al-Mājinah, cited in Aḥmad al-Maqqarī, *Nafḥ al-Ṭīb min ghusn al-Andalus al-raṭīb*, vol. 4, ed. Iḥsān 'Abbās (Cairo: 1968), 205.

2 Naipaul's comments were reported in the British newspaper *The Guardian*, among other news outlets. Amy Fallon, "V. S. Naipaul Finds No Woman Writer His Equal," *The Guardian*, 6/1/2011. http://www.theguardian.com/books/2011/jun/02/vs-naipaul-jane-austen-women-writers (accessed 10/2015).

3 S. D. Goitein, "Women as Creators of Biblical Genres," in *Studies in Scripture* (Tel Aviv: Yavneh Press, 1957), 248–82. An English-language version of this article appears in *Prooftexts* 8 (1988): 1–33.

participation in the world of Andalusi courtly literature and the nature and extent of the limits placed upon that participation during the medieval period. The example of the single medieval Hebrew poem attributed to an Andalusi woman, both within its medieval context and in the light of the literary historiography that has tried to interpret and contextualize it, will be the test case for such a reassessment of that literary historiography. And through a consideration of the primary materials that offer evidence of women's literacy in Hebrew and a review of the methodologies that have allowed for the development of women's history in the last decades, this present chapter will offer some alternatives to the models of absence that have dominated the discourse about the possibility of women writing Hebrew poetry in al-Andalus and suggest ways forwards to better account for the dearth of women poets writing in Hebrew in western Islamic lands.[4]

## History, Historiography, and the State of the Question

With the arrival of Islam in the Iberian Peninsula in the eighth century, the social, economic, and cultural lives of the local Jewish populations improved dramatically over what they had been under Visigothic rule, since they were suddenly afforded much greater religious freedoms and protections and were integrated much more completely into politics, into economic spheres, and into society at large.[5] As Iberia's Jews began to participate more actively in public society, they adopted and adapted the prevailing and prestigious forms of cultural production, including Arabic poetry and poetics, a literary tradition whose prestige dates back to the pre-Islamic period.[6] In the early decades of the tenth century, the Córdoba-based poet Dunash ben Labrat began to adapt the system of quantitative meter that is an integral part of Arabic poetics to be used for Hebrew poetry, which had, up until that point, never had a system of quantitative meter. This was a controversial innovation, with Dunash's

4 When I write about an absence model for women's history, it may evoke, for some readers, María Rubiera Mata's model of women's history that she established in her essay, "La voz de las poetisas en al-Andalus y la problemática de la voz feminine literaria medieval," in *La Voz del silencio* (Madrid: Asociación Cultural, 1992), in which she distinguished between women who are well-known in the sources because of their famous fathers, brothers, or husbands and women who rose to prominence on their own, in the "*ausencia de varón*" (absence of a man). However, it is important to assert that I am not writing here about the absence of men in women's history, but rather about how we work with the absence of sources.

5 For an overview of the status of Jews in the Umayyad emirate and caliphate, see Raymond Scheindlin, "Merchants and Intellectuals, Rabbis and Poets: Judeo-Arabic Culture in the Golden Age of Islam," in *Cultures of the Jews*, ed. David Biale (New York: Shocken Books, 2002), 313–88; David Wasserstein, "Jewish Elites in al-Andalus," in *The Jews of Medieval Islam*, ed. Daniel Frank (Leiden: Brill, 1995). A foundational, if somewhat outdated, study is Norman Roth, *Jews Visigoths, and Muslims in Medieval Spain* (Leiden: Brill, 1994); also canonical and comprehensive, if outdated, is Eliahu Ashtor's *The Jews of Moslem Spain* (Jewish Publication Society, 1993; originally 1973). On the subsequent historical period, see the third section of David Wasserstein, *The Rise and Fall of the Party Kings* (Princeton: Princeton University Press, 1985).

6 For an overview of the literary history of the Arabized Jews of Islamic Spain, see Ross Brann, "The Arabized Jews," in *The Cambridge History of Arabic Literature: The Literature of al-Andalus*, ed. María Rosa Menocal et al. (Cambridge: Cambridge University Press, 2000).

detractors arguing that they were debasing the holy tongue by conflating it with Arabic; this was a period in which delving too far into analysis based on comparisons between Semitic languages could be cause for internecine strife. Yet Dunash won the day, and within a generation, the Jewish poets of al-Andalus were writing Arabizing Hebrew poetry that rivaled the best Arabic-language examples in technical skill and aesthetics.[7]

Much of what we now know about the literary trajectory of the Arabizing Hebrew poetry of al-Andalus comes from the cache of documents found in the Cairo Genizah, a store-room in which despoiled religious texts, as well as a whole host of other literary and day-to-day texts, were stored, awaiting a proper disposal by burial in Fustat's Basaat' cemetery that would never come to pass; the fragments, which number in the hundred-thousands, came to light as an important scholarly source in the last years of the nineteenth century when they were rediscovered by the sisters Agnes Lewis and Margaret Gibson, in concert with the Cambridge academic Solomon Schechter.[8] In the late 1930s, while sorting through photographs of Genizah fragments, one in particular caught the eye of Nehemiah Allony, a scholar of medieval poetry and the first director of the Institute for Microfilmed Hebrew Manuscripts. He read the heading, a common paratextual device in Arabic and Arabizing Hebrew poetry that introduces the poem within a cycle or explains the circumstances under which it was written, as an Arabic phrase reading: "ben Labrac, ileyhi" (Ben Labrat, to him).[9] On that basis, Allony attributed the poem to Dunash. He attempted to reconstruct the first half of the poem, something that would never be done today, publishing it in the *Jewish Quarterly Review* in 1944 along with three other Andalusi and Andalusi-style poems. About its contents, he speculated: "Dunash wrote this poem, I suppose, in honor of the wedding of a friend of his."[10] Forty years thence in the history of scholarship, Ezra Fleischer, the veritable dean of medieval Hebrew poetry, found a complete

7 Most of the canonical historical overviews of the Arabizing Hebrew poetry of al-Andalus are written in Hebrew. This includes Ḥwrit Schirmann's *Studies in the History of Hebrew Poetry and Drama* (Jerusalem: Mosad Biyalik, 1979), and his edition with commentary, *Hebrew Poetry in Spain and Provence* (Jerusalem: Mosad Biyalik, 1964), as well as Schirmann's two-volume history, completed by Ezra Fleischer, *The History of Hebrew Poetry in Muslim Spain* and *The History of Hebrew Poetry in Christian Spain and the South of France* (Jerusalem: The Magnes Press, 1995 and 1997). Additionally, see Ezra Fleischer, *The Hebrew Poetry of Spain and Its Sphere of Influence* (Jerusalem: Ben Zvi Institute, 2010) and Dan Pagis, *Change and Tradition in Secular Poetry* (Jerusalem: Keter, 1976). Anglophone readers should consult Pagis' *Hebrew Poetry of the Middle Ages and the Renaissance* (Berkeley: University of California Press, 1991), and the translator's introduction to Peter Cole, *The Dream of the Poem* (Princeton: Princeton University Press, 2007), which synthesizes the non-English-language scholarship, as well as monographs such as Ross Brann, *The Compunctious Poet* (Baltimore: Johns Hopkins University Press, 1992).

8 A good overview of the Genizah and the history of its scholarship is Peter Cole and Adina Hoffman, *Sacred Trash* (New York: Random House, 2011). The canonical study of the social history reflected in the Genizah is S. D. Goitein's *A Mediterranean Society* (Berkeley: University of California Press). A proliferation of recent monographs treats specific subjects within the social history of the Genizah world. Scholarship on the literary Genizah materials may be found in the work of Fleischer and Schirmann.

9 Cambridge University Library, MS Mosseri VIII.202.

10 Nehemiah Allony, "Four Poems," *Jewish Quarterly Review* 35, no. 1 (1944): 79–83.

copy of that same poem[11] and, shortly thereafter, the right-hand side of the fragment Allony had published.[12] Fleischer now not only had two complete copies of the poem; he also had two complete copies of the heading, which he could now read not as "ben Labrat, ileyhi," marking the discourse of Dunash speaking to an unidentified male friend, but rather, "li-zawjat Dunash ben Labrat, ileyhi," that is, "by Dunash ben Labrat's wife, to him." Fleischer understood this heading to mean that the wife of Dunash was not just the poetic voice, but the poet herself, making the text the only example of Arabized Hebrew poetry written by a woman. The historic text could finally be read in full:

*Ha-yizkor ya'alat ha-ḥen yedidah*
*be-yom perud u-vi-zero'ah yeḥidah*
*Ve-sam ḥotam yemino 'al-semolah*
*u-vi-zero'o ha-lo' samah ẓemidah*
*Be-yom laqḥah le-zikaron redido*
*ve-hu' laqaḥ le-zikaron redidah*
*Ha-yishsha'er beḫol erez sefarad*
*ve-lu laqaḥ ḥaẓi malḫut negidah?*[13]

(Will her beloved remember the elegant doe, her only son in her arms at the moment of his departure? On the day he placed the signet ring from his right hand on her left and she placed her bracelet on his arm, she took his cloak as a memento and he took her cloak as a memento. If he could hold half the prince's kingdom, is there anywhere in Sefarad he would remain?)[14]

Almost immediately, Goitein signed on to Fleischer's identification of the poet, not as Dunash, but as his wife, writing: "I personally believe that she was the author, although the poem gives the impression of a perfection in composition and style not expected at that early period (especially as compared with the stiff and unimaginative

11 Cambridge University Library, MS Taylor-Schechter New Series 143.46.

12 Cambridge University Library, MS Mosseri IV 387.2. Many Genizah fragments are torn and with the pieces separated within the mass of documents. One of the major prongs of current scholarship is to identify "joins" between separated pieces, aided by new techniques in the digital humanities. On joining fragments, see Lior Wolf et al., "Identifying Join Candidates in the Cairo Genizah," *International Journal of Computer Vision*. Published online, September 2010: http://www.cs.tau.ac.il/~wolf/papers/genizahijcv.pdf. In the case of the two Mosseri fragments that contain the Wife of Dunash poem, the sheet on which they were written was created by pasting two smaller sheets together, and these came apart almost neatly at the seam when the adhesive dissolved over time.

13 Attributed to the wife of Dūnash ben Labrāt, published in Ezra Fleischer, "On Dūnash ben Labrāt and His Wife and Son," *Jerusalem Studies in Hebrew Literature* 5 (1984): 196.

14 I have translated the poem here into prose; for a good verse translation, see: "Will His Love Remember?" trans. Peter Cole, *The Dream of the Poem* (Princeton: Princeton University Press, 2007), 27.

creations of her husband)."[15] Despite Goitein's aforementioned early-career assertion that it was always possible to identify the gender of a poet from the composition itself, he agreed with Fleischer that the personal identity and, consequently, the gender of this poet should be reassessed. Fleischer asserted that the poem must have been written after one of the court conflicts over poetic and scriptural languages had not gone his way, forcing his departure from Spain and from his wife and son.[16] There is no evidence external to this poem to support such an interpretation, no evidence to suggest that Dunash's wife was a poet, and none to suggest that the poem was written by a woman rather than simply in a woman's voice; nevertheless, the attribution of the poem to a poet known only as the wife of her husband has come to be authoritative. In other words: very suddenly and in 1984, the only woman to have written poetry in Hebrew in the Middle Ages was born. And she created a whole host of historiographic problems.

These historiographic and interpretive problems ultimately boil down to criticism that accepts the idea that a female poetic voice reflects the work of a female poet and, furthermore, that the exceptional presence of a female poet writing in Hebrew is, in and of itself, a sufficient critical conclusion. To be sure, the poem is short; this does not give critics much room to maneuver, and so, frequently, the ostensible fact of the poet as a woman is taken as the end point of any interpretation. In the case of the Wife of Dunash poem, this kind of critical non-intervention manifests itself in comparisons between the poet and the biblical poet–prophet Deborah. An interpretation that takes the gender of the poet as the only conclusion can make that comparison between the two female poets or poetic voices regardless of the material differences between the two texts.[17] Yet those differences do exist: the poetic voice of the Wife of Dunash poem is that of the biblical Shulamite, who appears in the Song of Songs, rather than that of the warrior Deborah. The poem refers extensively to the Song of

15 Goitein, *Mediterranean Society*, vol. 5.

16 There is no indication of this in his published work, but one must wonder whether Fleischer did not have the model of Christine de Pizan in mind, as the abandoned wife turned poet making her way in the world, as a trope or model for constructing a context for this text and his identification of its poet as Dunash's wife.

17 I have written previously about this poem and will cite my own interpretation a little bit further on in this chapter, but at this particular juncture, I would like to reference some of the feedback I received on drafts of that article because it reflects the extent to which these attitudes are entrenched within the academy. Despite the juxtaposition of Deborah and the wife of Dunash in every single discussion of the poem, an anonymous reviewer of that article insisted that "nobody is seriously making a comparison between Mrs. Dunash and Deborah." He went on to describe the proposition that we decouple the two literary figures as "so much hot air about a non-issue" and reflective of my "inability to distinguish between what is important and what is not" (anonymous reviewer, personal communication, 7/2013). Although I know of no literary critic who would dismiss such a consistent juxtaposition as *not* drawing some kind of analogy between the juxtaposed terms, even if we were to accept such a contention, then a non-serious comparison or a non-comparison invoking the figure of Deborah still does an interpretive disservice, again simultaneously gender-essentializing and female-exceptionalizing by casting the voice of the Wife of Dunash poet in a biblical mode that does not apply. If we are to speak seriously about women poets in some kind of thickly described medieval context, then biblical analogies must not be the starting point or the end point. In fact, it is this kind of response to a revision of the standard literary history and interpretation that demonstrates precisely the need for a wider study that reassesses women's literary history in medieval Spain.

Songs through a literary technique common in Arabizing Hebrew poetry known as the *shibbui*, or reference to elements of the biblical text in verse so as to elicit recognition from the reader; in this case, the poem makes use of the Song of Songs' imagery of the lovers' possessions and, in more general terms, builds upon the motif from the biblical text of the departure and absence of the beloved.[18] And although medieval Hebrew poetry does not always use biblical citation to allude directly to the Bible,[19] the concentration of quotations from the Song of Songs demands an allusive and intertextual reading in this case. This is not a poem written in a voice that co-identifies with Deborah, nor does it speak to the same poetic tradition; a biblicizing interpretation must begin with the biblical text that appears within the medieval text rather than with comparisons that might be drawn externally by modern observers who see two women poets or poetic voices and are eager to file them under the same heading.

## Reassessing the Wife of Dunash Poem in Light of Genizah Documents[20]

The poem instead requires a different approach, one that does not simultaneously and paradoxically identify the poet with the author of a biblical rally to war and the sentimental victim of circumstance in a man's grammar game. Rather than being the sentimental, tender farewell between a woman about to be abandoned by her husband, if we read the poem in conjunction with economic documents and personal correspondence found along with it in the Cairo Genizah, we begin to see the woman portrayed in the poem as a savvy, independent actor who both sets herself up well in anticipation of a long separation from her husband, and also plays a crucial role in ensuring his economic solvency during his time away. What follows is a reading of the poem that neither begins and ends with the gender of the poet nor is contingent upon it. Rather, this reading situates the poem in the context of the mercantile economy of tenth-century Córdoba.

The first exchange of gifts between husband and wife consists of her bracelet for his signet ring as mementos, the poem tells us; however, this is more than mere tokenism and a far cry from the exchange of two pieces of jewelry that could be monetized equally if either spouse were in financial need during their separation. Both dowry lists and personal correspondence found in the Cairo Genizah cache show that bracelets were uniquely and securely the property of women and could be used as a metallic store for her own funds.[21] The best example of a woman taking her fortune, in the form of silver bracelets, and using it to move her own personal wealth and ensure her solvency and personal leverage while separated from her husband

18 Specifically, see Song of Songs 8:6–8.

19 Pagis, *Change and Tradition*, 34–5.

20 This section is a distillation of the article mentioned in the above footnote: S. J. Pearce, "Bracelets Are for Hard Times: Economic Hardship, Sentimentality, and the Andalusi Hebrew Poetess," *Cultural History* 3, no. 2 (2014): 147–69.

21 Goitein, *Mediterranean Society*, 4.190–201 and idem, "Three Trousseaux of Jewish Brides from the Fatimid Period," *AJS Review* 2 (1977): 77–110. See also Maya Shatzmiller, "Women and Property Rights in al-Andalus and the Maghrib," *Islamic Law and Society* 2, no. 3 (1995): 219–57. For a material example of this type of bracelet from al-Andalus, see the silver bracelets that form a part of the Mondújar hoard, now housed in the Museo Arqueológico Nacional in Madrid (MAN 50864–66 and MAN 50893–5).

comes in a letter written by a man to his niece. At the time of writing, she was living apart from her husband, who had moved from Cairo into the outer provinces. He advises her that she must join her husband before he takes a second wife and then instructs her in how to handle her financial affairs in preparation for the move:

> Take the articles that you wish to, and whatever is heavy, and put it in the custody of the judge and get a receipt for them. The wine should be sold and a silver bracelet purchased for your wrist. Get in touch with Abu l- Ḥajjāj ibn al-Ṭabīb, may God the exalted have mercy upon him. He will undertake its sale and will purchase the bracelet for you.[22]

Here we see a woman being instructed to convert her property into silver, in the form of a bracelet that she could carry with her as she traveled; other documents show that silver bracelets were very definitively the property of women, not only their personal adornments, but also stores, in the form of precious metal, of funds that were uniquely theirs. Bracelets were typically worn in pairs[23] – a detail to which I will return momentarily – and price lists and dowries indicate that the value of such a pair of silver bracelets was sufficient to hire household help for a considerable length of time; this was not a small sum. The husband in the poem offers his signet ring in return. In this case, it was more like a memento. Goitein has shown that property lists that include prices typically exclude, by scribal convention, signet rings; this is because the stones that made up the face of the signet were too difficult to authenticate accurately and could easily be substituted with glass undetected.[24] Unlike bracelets, a signet ring was a symbol and instrument of power for its owner but worthless as an economic instrument. And so, in the second line of the poem, we see the wife using perhaps the only property that belonged fully to her to fund her husband's travel, while she receives a simple memory token in exchange: a mere symbol of his erstwhile status at court.

The exchange of cloaks is almost the diametric opposite. While a modern reader might find it puzzling that a man might go off on a long voyage with his wife's coat, the documentary sources tell us that in this society, in which social norms and sumptuary laws strictly forbade cross-dressing, coats were uniquely and almost always unisex in design and size and often shared between husband and wife;[25] in this case, each spouse prepares for their impending separation with a

22 TS 13 J 28.19, published in Goitein, *Mediterranean Society*, 3.167–8, 77–9. This text is also cited in Joel Kraemer, "The Women Speak for Themselves," in *The Cambridge Genizah Collections: Their Contents and Significance*, ed. Stefan Reif (Cambridge: Cambridge University Press, 2002), 197–8.

23 In addition to textual sources, such as dowry lists, that document pairs of bracelets, archaeological evidence tends to yield bracelets in pairs, and contemporaneous depictions of women also show them wearing two bracelets (such as, for example, the eleventh-century ivory plaque (Meyer-Riefstahl 1914 OA 6701) depicting a woman wearing a pair of bracelets that forms part of the collection at the Musée du Louvre).

24 Goitein, *Mediterranean Society*, 4.206–7.

25 Yedida Stillman, "Female Attire of Medieval Egypt: According to the Trousseau Lists and Cognate Material from the Cairo Geniza" (Ph.D. Dissertation, University of Pennsylvania, 1972). See, in particular, glossary entries for the following types of cloaks, which were worn by both men and women: *kisā'* (51), *milḥafa* (52–3), *mulā'a* (55), and crucially for our purposes, *ridā'* (59–61), cognate with the *radid* mentioned by the poet. References to husbands and wives

garment that will serve both as a memory token and a practical garment. He can remember her by her coat, but he can also stay warm in it. As we reach the last line of the poem, I would like to return for a moment to the image of the women handing a bracelet to her husband. Another thing that we know from the Genizah documents is that women tended to wear their silver bracelets in pairs, a detail so ubiquitous in the Genizah documents that we must assume that any reader or hearer of the poem would recognize her handing over a single bracelet as handing off one half of a pair. The last line of the poem inquires if anything could be done to keep the husband from leaving, asking: "Would he settle now in the land of Spain if its prince gave him half his kingdom?" And so, we see a woman handing over half her personal fortune to her husband to fund his leaving because he could not be offered half a kingdom to stay. Actually, reading and interpreting the text does not detract from the feminist reading of the entire *mise-en-scène* that a female-exceptionalist reading of the context seems to desire; instead, it strengthens it through the literary representation of a woman as the principal financial support of her family and as a stand-in to compensate for the failures even of high-ranking political leaders.

## Towards a Literary History of Missing Women Poets

I have made the argument that gender-exceptionalism is not a sufficient critical approach to the Wife of Dunash poem, offered an alternative reading that engages with the text of the poem in its cultural context rather than focusing on the gender of the poet, and have noted that the available evidence does not allow us to conclude firmly that the poet was, in fact, a woman and not a man composing poetry featuring the voice of a woman.[26] This leaves one final point of discussion: if we return to the scholarship that holds that the Wife of Dunash poet is, in fact, the wife of Dunash and that then tries to explain why she might have been the only woman writing Hebrew poetry in the Middle Ages, we find ourselves confronting a much broader and potentially more productive question that lies in how the historiography explains the dearth of women poets writing in Hebrew even when there is better evidence that both Jewish and Muslim Andalusi women were writing poetry in Arabic. This is a question that holds up regardless of whether we believe that Dunash's wife was a poet and regardless of whether we believe that she was the author of this poem. It is a question that holds up regardless of whether we believe that there was only one woman writing poetry in Hebrew in the whole of the Middle Ages or whether we believe that there were zero. The question is this: why not?

sharing cloaks may be found in Goitein, *Mediterranean Society*, 4.153–4 and 186.

26 Other examples of male poets writing in a female voice include Ibn Khalfun's poem "*Bi-'et ḥesheq ye'ireni*," which Tova Rosen explicates in view of the female poetic voice in her "Gender and Genre in a Love Poem by Isaac ibn Khalfun," *Prooftexts* 16 (1996): 5–13. Also rather well-known is the poet Qalonymos ben Qalonymos who explores the boundaries of gender roles in verse; it may be worth noting that although his poem is frequently read with a feminist bent that understands it to be subverting social and religious limitations on women, I read it in a much more sarcastic and patronizing tone as a reinforcement of those roles.

Scholarship has typically explained this absence in one of two ways. Goitein argues that a wider range of women could not have written Arabizing poetry in Hebrew because the form requires citation from the Hebrew Bible, and women did not have sufficient education in or experience with the biblical text in order to be able to cite it.[27] Ezra Fleischer, on the other hand, argues that women did not write Hebrew poetry because they would not have had access to works of Hebrew poetics, such as Moses ibn 'Ezra's *Book of Conversation and Discussion*, a somewhat misleadingly titled literary history of al-Andalus and practical manual of poetics.[28] Each explanation is strangely circular, presuming not that too many women were totally illiterate or excluded completely from intellectual life, but rather that certain, very narrow elements of intellectual endeavor were so far off-limits to women that they could not overcome the barriers even as they were participating in the intellectual and literary lives of their communities in other ways. Goitein's explanation presumes that even though women heard the Torah read out in their synagogues, and even though we have documentary evidence of women as teachers (of students up to a certain age) of a curriculum that included the Hebrew Bible, this familiarity with the text would have still been insufficient to be able to incorporate it in verse compositions.[29] Fleischer presumes that women would have had access to their fathers' and brothers' and husbands' libraries – I have not yet found evidence of a woman's own proprietary library in this setting, but my work with library lists is still in its beginning stages – without ever wishing to pick up one of the works of practical or descriptive poetics that very many of these libraries contained. We have some evidence of women participating in many other types of literary pursuits, including writing poetry in Arabic. Some evidence, like the manuscript paintings in the thirteenth-century manuscript now housed in the Vatican that contains a version of the legend of Bayad and Riyad, also shows that women participated in the kinds of social gatherings in which poetry was read out.[30] Women were not excluded from the world of poetry in al-Andalus. In fact, as Asma Afsaruddin observes: "Excellence in literary and aesthetic pursuits have been equally recognized in practitioners of both sexes.... Linguistic virtuosity and poetic talent often served as a leveler of culturally constructed notions of social propriety and gendered roles."[31] Yet despite the conditions of literacy and access that should have produced women poets, we have none; instead, we have an entire generation of twentieth-century scholars re-imposing those gendered notions and roles in ways that defy logic and contemporaneous practice in the medieval period in order to try to explain the discrepancy. Afsaruddin notes that this kind of documentary silence allows modern readers, both scholars and religious practitioners, to claim textual authority and precedent for writing women out of literary and other kinds of history;[32] however, as she has also

27 Goitein, *Mediterranean Society*, 5.469.

28 Fleischer, "On Dūnash."

29 Goitein, *Mediterranean Society*.

30 Vatican MS Ar. 368. On the illustrations of this manuscript, see Cynthia Robinson, "Preliminary Considerations on the Qiṣṣat Bayād wa-Riyāḍ," in *Al-Andalus und Europa: zwischen Orient und Okzident*, ed. Martina Müller-Wiener (Petersberg: Imhof, 2004), 284–96.

31 Asma Afsaruddin, "Literature, Scholarship, and Piety: Negotiating Gender and Authorship in the Medieval Muslim World," *Religion and Literature* 42, no. 1 (2010): 119.

32 Afsaruddin, "Literature, Scholarship, and Piety," 113.

demonstrated, the types of sources consulted can, like a kaleidoscope, shift and reveal the always-already presence of women in the history. I am not yet prepared to argue that women were, in fact, writing poetry in Hebrew; there may never be evidence of this, and it may never have happened. However, the goal of the remaining short sections of this chapter is to lay out the panorama of sources for women's writing that may help us come to a better answer to the "why not?" question posed above and to propose an investigative way forward to that answer.[33]

## Tropes of Authorship in Narrative Sources

One of the greatest challenges in reassessing the evidence for women poets writing in Hebrew is the delicate puzzle of detangling tropes and models of authorship from authorship itself. This is a question that will recur in all of the following sections, with the question of literary modeling playing a slightly different role with respect to each type of source and in answer to each way of framing the central question of why women seem not to have written poetry in Hebrew. It is ultimately a question that finds its theoretical grounding in the New Medievalism, an approach to pre-modern text that draws upon the disruptive reliance upon literary criticism brought to bear on ostensibly historical texts by the scholars of the New Historicist school of thought; and although this approach finds its origins in literary criticism, it walks the fine, modern line between history and literature that can become blurred in the context of cultural, intellectual, and literary history but that even documentary and social historians are beginning to recognize as not a completely inviolate one.[34]

Tova Rosen and other scholars have productively utilized tropes of women found within literature to attempt to reconstruct realities of and expectations for women through a careful analysis of the tropes used to represent women in literary texts. Rosen describes the need for such a methodology given the landscape of sources available:

> The prospects of recovering more women-authored literary materials in this no-woman's-land of Hebrew literature are scant. This makes the feminist project termed by Elaine Showalter as "gynocentrics" impracticable. The path left for the Hebrew medievalist feminist is thus approaching the issues of women and gender via male-authored texts.[35]

33 María Ángeles Gallego wrote a similar methodological proposal for studying Jewish women poets writing in Arabic in her article "Approaches to the Study of Muslim and Jewish Women in the Medieval Iberian Peninsula: The Poetess Qasmuna bat Isma'il," *Miscelanea de Estudios Arabes y Hebraicos* 48 (1999): 63–75. This present study is particularly interested in women poets writing in Hebrew. We will return to Gallego's approaches in the discussion of literary models for the Wife of Dunash poet in the following section of this chapter.

34 Some of the foundational texts of the New Medievalism may be found in *Speculum* 65, no. 1 (1990); most recently, for an application of the historicizing literary approach to documentary materials, see Miriam Frenkel, "Genizah Documents and Literary Products," in *From a Sacred Source: Genizah Studies in Honour of Professor Stefan C. Reif*, ed. Ben Outhwaite (Leiden: Brill, 2010), 139–56.

35 Tova Rosen, *Unveiling Eve* (Philadelphia: University of Pennsylvania Press, 2003), 3.

Yet this approach still does not get to authorship even through representation, whereas a different approach to literary tropes in different kinds of sources may prove more productive in attempting to answer the kind of question posed here in the present study.[36] Tropes of authorship that occur in chronicles, biographical dictionaries, and other sources that make certain claims to historicity but that must still be read and understood with a literary sensibility may be what give us the best information for the Andalusi women poets, both Muslim and Jewish, who composed their poetry in Arabic.

Both building upon and departing somewhat from Rosen's approach, historical sources are an important way of seeking and interpreting representations of women and, in this case in particular, of women's authorship; however, they must be treated as carefully as literary sources and read with the idea that they, too, deal in tropes of authorship as much as in a more mimetic narrative. In an article on the social roles of women in al-Andalus, María Jesús Viguera Molins seems to go so far as to question whether we may accept the identification as women of any of the female poets mentioned in these sources or must treat them as tropes, describing the output attributed to them as "verses composed by women poets in al-Andalus, or put into their mouths."[37] I do not find cause to take the question that far; even if some of these women come into the source material as tropes, the regular occurrence of the trope of the female poet would seem to suggest some verisimilitude and intelligibility to readers; in other words, the trope of a woman poet is hardly likely to occur in the literature of a society that knows no women poets. In fact, in the course of writing about women poets in the Bedouin community of Awlad 'Ali, Lila Abu-Lughod cites the question of women's poetry as one in which text and ethnography are particularly closely intertwined.[38] And despite her skepticism, Viguera Molins acknowledges that the biographical dictionaries as supplements to poetry offer a path by which "the true facts concerning women's poetry in al-Andalus can now be inferred."[39] Viguera Molins' study of these sources concludes that significant limitations were placed on the Arabic-language women poets, and her sources and methods may, therefore, be particularly instructive in looking at the restrictions that led to the absence of Hebrew poetry written by women.

The biographical dictionaries, while extremely well-known and well-trodden sources within the field of Islamic Studies, continue to yield up new discoveries[40] that are particularly relevant to Jewish Studies, in part because those texts have been seen in the past solely as the provenance of the former discipline. Women faced severe social restrictions, and poetry was one of the ways in which they could reject those

36 David Wasserstein's study, "Samuel ibn Naghrīla ha-Nagid and Islamic Historiography in al-Andalus," *Al-Qantara* 14, no. 1 (1993): 109–25 and Ross Brann's monograph *Power in the Portrayal* (Princeton: Princeton University Press, 2002) both offer models for scholarly negotiation between poetry and prose in the service of historiography.

37 María Jesús Viguera Molins, "On the Social Status of Andalusi Women," *The Legacy of Muslim Spain*, ed. Salma Khadra Jayyusi (Leiden: Brill, 2000), 709.

38 Lila Abu-Lughod, *Veiled Sentiments* (Berkeley: University of California Press, 1986), 234–8.

39 Viguera Molins, "On the Social Status," 713.

40 The most significant example of these relatively new discoveries is Joseph Sadan's discovery of a biographical note on the literary polymath Judah al- Ḥarīzī, published in "Judah al- Ḥarīzī as a Cultural Junction," *Pe'amim* 68 (1996): 16–67.

restrictions while simultaneously appearing to uphold them; and so, the biographical dictionaries might well be a place in which their forms of resistance are noted in prose form. The dictionaries, which do include verse, might or might not give direct evidence of women's poetry but might do so for women poets; it is certainly worth a comprehensive return to those books with the possibility of women poets in mind. In the following sections, we will look at some of the particular restrictions as they applied to Andalusi Jewish women and to Jewish women in the wider Mediterranean basin.

The closest medieval model for or comparison to the Wife of Dunash poet as she is represented in the scholarship is another Andalusi Jewish poet also known most principally as the relative of a recognizable male poet. This poet, who wrote in Arabic rather than in Hebrew, is known as Qasmūna bint Isma'īl. Scholarship suggests that she was the daughter of the poet-vizier Samuel ibn Naghrīla[41] and so resembles (at least as Fleischer interprets the evidence) the Wife of Dunash poet in being known principally as a poet who was the female relative of a more famous male poet. Both Qasmūna's biography and her surviving poetry are recorded in Jalāl al-Dīn al-Ṣuyūṭī's *Nuzḥat al-julasā' fī ash'ar al-nisā'* (*Entertainment for Boon Companions through Women's Poetry*) and Ahmad al-Maqqarī's *Nafq al-Ṭīb*, which is dependent upon Ṣuyūṭī's work. Surviving amongst those works are two of Qasmūna's poems as well as a few details about her education that suggest she learned to compose poetry orally. We have many records of Arabic-language poets composing extempore and orally in addition to in writing, and this practice, and the evidence that it was practiced by women, also raises certain questions about the fallibility of literacy versus orality as potential limitations to women poets. It is also worth noting, as Wasserstein points out, that our only knowledge of Qasmūna comes from Islamic sources while she is unacknowledged in Jewish ones.[42] Just as tropes of authorship will be a recurring theme and problem throughout this chapter, so, too, will questions of oral and written composition; these are very much in flux and must be accounted for in any future study of women poets.

Just as is the case with the biographical dictionaries discussed above, chronicles of literary history such as Ṣuyūṭī's, and even chronicles with a wider scope, such as al-Maqqarī's, must be read with a literary sensibility rather than as a clear-eyed reporting of history. With that in mind, Qasmūna is sometimes looked to as a model for writing about women's poetry and biography in al-Andalus and might continue to be workable in that capacity. Yet a historiography of absence demands not only a comparative approach between the Wife of Dunash poet and the abstract potentiality of women poets working in Hebrew, but also a departure from comparison through differentiation from the literary tropes that govern the information that has survived; in other words, we cannot only set up the conditions under which poetry might or might not have been written by women in Hebrew, but must also use these tropes and models as far as they will go but perhaps not to create so idealized a paradigm that it keeps us away from the historical task at hand.

41 J. M. Nichols, "The Arabic Verses of Qasmuna bint Ismā'il ibn Baghdalah," *International Journal of Middle East Studies* 13, no. 2 (1981): 155–28 and James A. Bellamy, "Qasmūna the Poetess: Who Was She?," *Journal of the American Oriental Society* 103, no. 2 (1983): 423–4.

42 Wasserstein, "Samuel ibn Naghrīla," 123.

## Women's Literacy and Reading Habits in Hebrew and in Arabic

One of the foundational questions that would help to inform an explanation of the dearth of women's poetry written in Hebrew, not only in al-Andalus, but during the whole of the Middle Ages, is women's level of literacy and the kinds of books that they read. Even more fundamental than questions of the models, tropes, and social possibilities for women as poets is the foundational question of whether women could read at a level that would allow them to write poetry, whether they were familiar enough with the text of the Hebrew Bible to participate in a poetic culture that demanded reliance upon that text, and whether they had access to the kinds of books and social settings that would allow them to read and hear poetry and familiarize themselves with the detailed literary principles required for the composition of Arabizing Hebrew poetry.

Some of the best specific evidence comes in an incredibly detailed autobiography written by a North African Jewish convert to Islam, who wrote his autobiography to demonstrate that he had made his decision to convert through rationally guided choices, and he wrote it late in life out of deference to his family, waiting until after his father's death to disseminate the work. That convert, Samawal al-Maghrebi, wrote extensively about his own education and about the education of those around him; although the comments about his own education are framed teleologically to justify his conversion in intellectual terms, his observations about women's education serve lower stakes and so may not be subject to quite the same level of reframing and refinement. Samawal first introduces his mother and his aunts into the narrative of his autobiography in terms of their intelligence and education: "She came from Basra and was one of three distinguished sisters well-versed in Torah studies and Hebrew writing."[43] This kind of evidence, read in concert with scholarship on literacy in pre-modern societies, should offer a more complete panorama of the extent and limits of women's literacy and how that might have restrained poetic production or, perhaps, whether it should have encouraged it.

Documentary evidence also helps to shed light on the conditions of women's literacy, such as the corpus of women's letters that Joel Kraemer assembled from within the Cairo Genizah cache. One of the letters he discusses in detail is written to a woman named Ballūta, resident in Toledo. Kraemer notes that "the letter's tone implies that Ballūid was educated." In addition, the basmallah, or opening invocation of the divine name – *bi-shem ram ve-nisa* (in the lofty and elevated Name) – seems to be a bilingual pun that acknowledges that the recipient is a woman and one with sufficient facility in both languages to appreciate the pun: the Hebrew word for elevated, *nisa*, is homophonous with one of the Arabic words for women, that is, *nisā'*.[44] Women were clearly reading works of *adab* (Arabic courtly literature, examples of which will be discussed in the following section in conjunction with biblical poetry), and despite

43 Samaw'al al-Maghribī, "The Conversion to Islam and the Narrative of his Vision of the Prophet," in *Ifḥām al-Yahūd: Silencing the Jews*, ed. and trans. Moshe Perlmann (New York: American Academy for Jewish Research, 1964), 75.

44 Cambridge University Library, MS T-S 13 J 9.4, recto, line 1.

Fleischer's claim, noted earlier, that women did not read works of poetics, documentary texts from the Genizah directly contradict his evidence, as Viguera Molins is able to demonstrate quite clearly that women were reading not only *adab*, but works of poetics as well.[45] Additionally, there is some evidence in manuscript colophons suggestive that there were women well enough educated to have worked as scribes copying Hebrew books.[46]

Nevertheless, praise of women for their intelligence is rare and the cases when it occurs, notable and enumerable. The Granada-born translator Judah ibn Tibbon composed an autobiographical ethical will which goes into great detail about how he chose to educate his son, Samuel, but which does not mention the education of his daughters, instead focusing on the lengths to which he went to arrange their marriages.[47] At the same time, though, he uses the Hebrew term *maskelet* (clever, educated)[48] to describe his daughter-in-law, Samuel's wife; this is the same term that the poetic voice uses to describe his wife in a poem attributed to Dunash himself and that has been used to argue for the literacy of the historical wife of Dunash and her role as the Wife of Dunash Poet.[49]

If we return to the case of Qasmūna bint Ismā'il, the central question that she poses as a counterpart to the Wife of Dunash poet and any other possible women poets writing in Hebrew is that of language and language choice for women poets. Wasserstein sets that question out quite clearly in his study of the historiography of Qasmūna's father's biography, explaining jointly that the study of women poets demands a better understanding both of women's education and literacy as well as the linguistic, literary, and cultural choices they might have been able or willing to make in their writing:

> Jewish poets writing in Arabic are not unknown... but they are decidedly uncommon; and poetesses, writing in Hebrew or in Arabic, are very rare indeed. To find the daughter of such a man as the Nagid among those writing in Arabic is particularly striking, for it implies a crossing of linguistic, cultural, and social boundaries which, while far from impossible for a man, was not easy, and will have been of vastly greater difficulty for a woman. We are bound to wonder about the means by which Qasmūna acquired her skills in Arabic poetic compo-

45 Viguera Molins, "On the Social Status," 714.

46 Judith Baskin and Michael Reigler, "May the Writer Be Strong: Medieval Hebrew Manuscripts Copied By and For Women," *Nashim* 16 (2008): 9–28.

47 Judah ibn Tibbon, "A Father's Admonition," in *Hebrew Ethical Wills*, ed. Israel Abrahams (Philadelphia: Jewish Publication Society, 1926), 66. In writing about Qasmūna bint Isma'il, James Bellamy argues that her penchant for poesy must have come about because "it is not likely that a liberal-minded man of such poetic talents as Ibn Naghrilla would instruct only his sons in the art and neglect the education of his daughter" (424), yet this omission in the Ibn Tibbon ethical will reminds us that we must not take for granted that poets and other intellectuals would have necessarily educated their daughters, as well as their sons, in their craft.

48 Judah ibn Tibbon, "A Father's Admonition," 66.

49 In the fragment TS 143.46, the Wife of Dunash poem is followed by one attributed more securely to Dunash himself and which contains the line "*ve-eich evgod be-maskelet kemotach*?" ('How could I betray a woman as clever [*maskelet*] as you?')

> sition, and to enquire what were the mechanics which might have made such a development possible. Whatever the answers to such questions (and it is unlikely in the extreme that any exact or direct answers to them can be provided), it seems likely that Qasmūna represents something very different from what the traditional image of her father might suggest to us.[50]

Although Wasserstein then takes this discussion in a direction that suggests more separation between Arabic literary culture and Jewish faith than I believe is warranted (as will be elaborated upon in the subsequent section of this chapter on writing in a polysystem), he concisely delineates the parameters of the problem. The possibility of women poets writing in Hebrew is not a question of their ability to cross boundaries, but rather to negotiate their language choices and the cultural backgrounds and freightedness of each of the two languages within their respective religious and combined cultural traditions that inform and facilitate those choices.

Returning to the question of what kind of works literate women might have read, and specifically whether they would have read poetics and had familiarity with the Hebrew Bible, it is worth considering women's ownership of books as a metric for what they might have read. A preliminary review of the library lists published in *The Jewish Library in the Middle Ages* does not suggest any particular library collection as the personal property of a woman; however, many of the lists contain borrowing and lending information, and so a more detailed study of those documents could potentially yield information about women who were lending out their own books or borrowing them from collection owners or community institutions that owned libraries.

## The Hebrew Bible in Women's Reading and Writing

Tropes and models for literacy aside, evidence for women's education and the writing that resulted from that education (and the kinds of mediated writing that were necessitated by a lack of education or by social convention) provides the best evidence for the kinds of literacy that might or might not yield the possibility of poetic composition. In fact, study was not considered a legal, but rather, a religio-cultural obligation: "Piety required some kind of literacy."[51] In fact, Kraemer interprets one letter-writer's decision to write in Hebrew to the possibility that his wife was educated and, therefore, might have been able to read it herself.[52] While biblical quotation in poetry and documentary sources are qualitatively different matters, looking at biblical citations in women's letters may also go a way to addressing the contention that women did not know the text of the Hebrew Bible well enough to cite it. While a considerable amount has been written on the linguistic aspects of a female sociolect of the Judeo-Arabic of women's letters, an assessment of those letters' contents with an eye towards biblical citation remains a desideratum. Such an analysis, were it able to disentangle citations included in compositions by women themselves

50 Wasserstein, "Islamic Historiography in al-Andalus," 120–1.

51 Kraemer, "Women Speak for Themselves," 186.

52 Kraemer, "Women Speak for Themselves," 201.

and those added by scribal convention, might serve as a metric for women's ability to quote from the Hebrew Bible in textual situations.

Exceptionally well-educated women read biblical poetry alongside other works of Arabic literature. For example, Kraemer has identified the case of a woman named Ra'isa,[53] whose brother advised her to read the biblical book of Proverbs, the biblical–poetic book of Ecclesiastes,[54] and the classic of Arabic prose literature, *Kitāb al-Faraj ba'd al-shidda* (*The Book of Consolation After Distress*) by the tenth-century Baṣran writer Muḥassin ibn 'Alī al-Tanuḫī. The letter advises her to take stock of the juxtaposition of themes of consolation across the three works – two biblical and one of *adab*. This is suggestive of a reading practice that draws lines of congruence across biblical and secular Arabic and Arabizing literature that would not seem to suggest the exclusion of women from Hebrew poetry. Further pursuit of this avenue may yield additional light on the conditions that might have fostered or inhibited poetic composition amongst women.

## Writing in a Linguistic Polysystem

Approaches most firmly grounded in the field of comparative literature may also prove productive, looking at models for women poets in other national–linguistic traditions and points of contact that might have yielded the literary cross-pollination that allows for the transgression of those nationally defined modern boundaries between textual corpora. The terms that I have used to set out the first premise of this section, textual models and their points of contact, are drawn very directly from the Tel Aviv post-structuralist school of thought, which espouses the notion of the literary polysystem that was specifically adapted for the Andalusi context by Rina Drory in her field-changing monograph, *Models and Contacts: Arabic Literature and Its Impact on Medieval Jewish Culture*.[55] The notion of a literary polysystem holds that certain types of literature are best understood as a complex but unified system comprising overlapping component parts that allows its readers and writers multiple cultural and linguistic options and possibilities that they negotiate according to their literary needs and preferences.[56] In implicit ways, some of the approaches I have suggested up to this point treat the possibility of women Hebrew poets as a component in a polysystem. One final approach towards a new literary history of Andalusi women poets is by a comparative consideration of other women poets or female poetic voices that negotiate such systems. Possibilities for comparison along this axis include the corpus of *kharjas*, the vernacular couplets written in a female voice that conclude certain poems written in classical Arabic and Hebrew, and female poets writing in the Romance languages, where there is also a relationship with Latin as a sacred language in play.

53 Cambridge University Library, MS T-S 10 J 9.1.

54 Although biblical poetry does not conform to the poetics of the Arabizing Hebrew poetry of the Middle Ages, medieval commentators such as Abraham ibn Ezra and Samuel ibn Tibbon did recognize biblical–poetical works such as the book of Ecclesiastes as poetry.

55 Rina Drory, *Models and Contacts* (Leiden: Brill, 2000).

56 Itamar Even-Zohar, "Polysystem Theory," *Poetics Today* 1 (1990): 1–6.

## Conclusions: Accounting for Absence in the Evidence

It remains a possibility that new evidence will be uncovered that offers us a whole host of women poets writing in Hebrew, just as new evidence gave us the possibility of the wife of Dunash. The Cairo Genizah is still giving up mysteries here and there; the idea that there is another similar Genizah out there, perhaps in one of the larger towns in the foothills of the Atlas Mountains or at the northern edge of the Sahara, such as the historic site of Sijilmasa (modern-day Rimode), is a persistent hope of scholars in the field; and the Kati Trust cache of manuscripts from Timbuktu seems to contain much Andalusi material and will yield all kinds of treasures and perhaps some in this area of women's literacy and poesy. Much of the evidence currently available suggests that there should be women's poetry in Hebrew, and this raises questions about the survival of sources.

Nevertheless, although their caveats were made before the more recent interest in and availability of the Timbuktu cache, both Wasserstein and Rosen are correct in noting that it is unlikely that new sources will emerge that radically change the picture of women as Hebrew-language poets. And so, barring new discoveries, what do we do to better explain the literary landscape as it now exists? Like the text of the poem attributed to the wife of Dunash, the literary history might also benefit from a reassessment that situates it within its economic context. In a setting in which poets either served patrons, sold their work as freelancers, or worked for a congregation, it is necessary to examine the system of patronage and payment and whether the participation of women in certain aspects of the professional, paid life of poets might have limited the literary possibilities. All of these different types of evidence suggest, in a very limited way, conditions under which women should have been writing poetry in Hebrew just as their counterparts in other language traditions; this is ultimately not just a question of why women did not write poetry, but also of whether we must conclude that they did, either anonymously or in forms that have not survived.

In an interview given to the journal *Itinerario*, Natalie Zemon Davis asserts that the silence of sources need not dictate the silence of scholars:

> Just because he [Ḥassan al-Wazan, in his autobiography] was silent, am I not going to broach the subject of marriage? How could I do that? I write about the history of women and gender – it's against my principles not to pose such a question. So you take what clues you have from his writing and collateral evidence from others around him and you make a "thought experiment." You speculate and you make it clear you're speculating. But even if you can't resolve the matter, it's important to venture it. Resorting to speculation is better than not asking the question at all.[57]

57 Jessica Roitman and Karwan Fatah-Black, "An Interview with Natalie Zemon Davis," *Itinerario* 39:1 (2015): 6.

It may very well be that we never find any women writing Hebrew poetry in medieval Islamic Spain; it may well be that this practice was unknown. But our understanding of the role of women as authors and intellectuals in that time and place will benefit greatly if we can, at a minimum, ascertain a more productive way to read the source materials – and yes, perhaps, to speculate – and, therefore, arrive at a better answer to the deceptively simple question that we must insist upon asking: why not?

3

# MEDIEVAL ANGLO-JEWISH WOMEN AT COURT

ADRIENNE WILLIAMS BOYARIN

## Anglo-Jewish Women and Modern Scholarship

Medieval Anglo-Jewish women were a constant presence in law courts. There are whole generations of women who survive in the records of the extraordinary bureaucracy of thirteenth-century England, most notably in the seventy-two extant rolls of the Exchequer of the Jews for the dates 1219–1290,[1] but also in marriage contracts, close rolls, letters, tallages, and *shetarot* (i.e., starrs, bonds of debt or acquittance written in Hebrew and according to Jewish custom), among other miscellaneous documents. Michael Adler in 1934 proclaimed the Anglo-Jewess, for the vital role she played in the English economy and courts, "unequalled in those days in any country."[2] Barrie Dobson maintained that the Anglo-Jewish woman was "a more influential and even formidable figure than her Christian counterpart."[3] Victoria Hoyle's work on moneylending between Anglo-Jewish and Christian women documents "641 references to 310 distinct and individual Jewish women…in the published plea rolls" of the Jewish Exchequer, not counting cases of ambiguity.[4] Hannah Meyer, in her impressive 2009 Cambridge dissertation, concluded that "using gender as a

1 On the institutional history of the Exchequer of the Jews, see Paul Brand's introduction to *Plea Rolls of the Exchequer of the Jews Preserved in the National Archives (formerly the Public Record Office)*, vol. 6 (London: The Jewish Historical Society of England, 2005); J. M. Rigg's introduction to *Select Pleas, Starrs, and Other Records from the Rolls of the Exchequer of the Jews, 1220–1284*, Publications of the Selden Society 15 (London: Bernard Quaritch, 1902); and Hilary Jenkinson's introduction to *Calendar of the Plea Rolls of the Exchequer of the Jews*, vol. 3 (Colchester, London, and Eton: Spottiswoode, Ballantyne & Co. for the Jewish Historical Society of England, 1929).

2 The presidential address to the Jewish Historical Society, 19 November 1934, printed as "The Jewish Woman in Medieval England," in *The Jews of Medieval England* (London: Edward Goldston for the Jewish Historical Society of England, 1939), 17–45.

3 "The Medieval York Jewry Reconsidered," in *The Jews in Medieval Britain: Historical, Literary and Archaeological Perspectives*, ed. Patricia Skinner (Woodbridge: Boydell Press, 2003), 145–156, at 153.

4 "The Bonds that Bind: Money Lending Between Anglo-Jewish and Christian Women in the Plea Rolls of the Exchequer of the Jews, 1218–1280," *Journal of Medieval History* 34, no. 2 (2008): 119–129, at 122. In my own ongoing survey of the unpublished rolls, I have found an additional 54 cases featuring Jewish women. For information on what is and is not published, see Brand, *Plea Rolls*, vol. 6, 57–68 ("Appendix III: List of Surviving Plea Rolls, 1219–1290").

primary tool of analysis" for the available records means "the inescapable visibility of Jewish [female] uniqueness."[5]

In the thirteenth century, several major Anglo-Jewish financiers were women. Licoricia of Winchester, about whom Suzanne Bartlet wrote a posthumously published book,[6] is only the wealthiest and most famous among them. Others include Henna of York, Mirabelle of Gloucester, Belia of Bedford, Chera of Winchester, and Abigail of London. These are women for whom we can track full careers, who travelled and appeared in court independently, owned properties, and lent mostly to men of various social and ecclesiastical stations. They and lesser figures appear startlingly frequently in national records, and it appears that they were literate and leading figures in Jewish–Christian business relations. In attempts to understand and reconstruct their lives, literacies, and agency, there is a glut of archival material to explore – "a gigantic lucky dip," as Dobson called it.[7]

And yet these women receive relatively little scholarly attention. They are caught between academic disciplines and between deep scholarly histories that say there is little Jewish material to study from medieval England or that Jewish women are simply not much depicted in the medieval sources of the dominant Christian culture. Those who work on English illustration, poetry, or liturgy find little evidence of post-biblical Jewish women's importance there. Jewish Studies scholars have little Hebrew to work with from England, much of it financial in nature. Elisheva Baumgarten, in her authoritative studies of Ashkenazi women's ritual and family life, twice notes that English Jews are "not included" in her books because the evidence they leave behind is "not the same" and "not plentiful enough."[8] Sara Lipton, in her book *Dark Mirror* and in an earlier essay, asks "Where are the Jewish women?" but finds little evidence of stereotypes or remarkable attitudes toward Jewesses until the end of the Middle Ages. Jewish and Christian women, she argues, are frequently indistinguishable because "in the Christian imagination, for better or worse, the Jewess's femaleness trumped her Jewishness."[9] Her gender already othered her and left little room for further distinction, positive or negative. Jewish Studies cannot easily approach Anglo-Jewish women through traditional disciplinary methods, languages, or commitments; art historical and literary analyses of English materials usually approach Jewish women from the perspective of anti-Jewish discourse, representation, and post-Expulsion

5 "Female Moneylending and Wet-Nursing in Jewish–Christian Relations in Thirteenth-Century England" (Ph.D. Dissertation, University of Cambridge, 2009), 293.

6 *Licoricia of Winchester: Marriage, Motherhood and Murder in the Medieval Anglo-Jewish Community*, ed. Patricia Skinner (London and Portland, OR: Vallentine-Mitchell, 2009), edited for publication by Skinner after Bartlet's death in June 2008.

7 "A Minority within a Minority: The Jewesses of Thirteenth-Century England," in *The Jewish Communities of Medieval England: The Collected Essays of R. B. Dobson*, ed. Helen Birkett, Borthwick Texts and Studies 39 (York: The Borthwick Institute, University of York, 2010), 149–166, at 151.

8 *Mothers and Children: Jewish Family Life in Medieval Europe* (Princeton: Princeton University Press, 2004), 6; *Practicing Piety in Medieval Ashkenaz: Men, Women, and Everyday Religious Observance*, Jewish Culture and Contexts (Philadelphia: University of Pennsylvania Press, 2014), 4.

9 *Dark Mirror: The Medieval Origins of Anti-Jewish Iconography* (New York: Metropolitan, 2014), 219; "Where are the Gothic Jewish Women? On the Non-Iconography of the Jewess in the *Cantigas de Santa Maria*," *Jewish History* 22, no. 1/2 (2008): 139–177, at 158.

absence. Not many who study literature, art, or religion are trained to search through legal and governmental bureaucratic records. Much is unedited. Much depends on knowledge of Latin, French, and Hebrew – or collaboration with those who can provide the combined knowledge.

Barrie Dobson hit the nail on the head, however, when he lamented that "the Jewish woman is nearly always revealed at the most personal, painful, and significant interface between" Christianity and Judaism in medieval England.[10] She is so unavoidably present for those who work on medieval Anglo-Jewish history, so clearly significant, yet she survives mostly in texts recorded by Christian scribes and at some of the most difficult times of her life: deaths of husbands or children, disputes over conversions, disputes over property seizure, fines, imprisonment – always at an interface, a juncture point where two or more separate systems interact. There are more surviving medieval records of the daily life and interactions of Jewish communities in England than anywhere on the continent – as Cecil Roth quipped, never has it been "possible to assemble so much about so few"[11] – but these records, because of their nature, yield painfully little about things like authorship, ritual, and intellectual activity.

I approach Jewish women in England from the perspective of a literary scholar, and, notwithstanding the difficulties, I find not only that it is hard to see how Jewish women matter in medieval English literature without knowing the historical and legal records, but also that a focus on the interfaces, the juncture points, illuminates Anglo-Jewish women across disciplinary and perspectival lines. These women rightly cease to look marginal when a creative mix of source material is employed, and in this chapter, I seek, provocatively, to model the potential of working at the points of interface. I focus on the question of Anglo-Jewish women's literacy and on the kinds of agency and authorship we might theorize for them from available evidence. Finally, by way of an argument for the value of the interfaces to both Jewish Studies and English literary history, I offer a nascent case study of one Anglo-Jewish woman who converted to Christianity in the thirteenth century.

## Anglo-Jewish Women in Documentary Culture

We can be certain that Anglo-Jewish women were immersed in documentary and book culture. Both Jewish and Christian chroniclers mention the plentiful books of the Anglo-Jewish community. Ephraim of Bonn writes that, in the 1190 massacre at York, not only were Jewish people killed, but also that "the choicest of books – which they had written many of, more desirable than gold, of which there are [now] none as worthy" – were pillaged and sold on the continent,[12] and Bartholomew Cotton in his *Historia*

10 "The Role of Jewish Women in Medieval England (Presidential Address)," in *Christianity and Judaism: Papers Read at the 1991 Summer Meeting and the 1992 Winter Meeting of the Ecclesiastical History Society*, ed. Diana Wood, Studies in Church History 29 (Oxford and Cambridge, MA: Blackwell, 1992), 145–168, at 146.

11 Quoted in Dobson, "Minority within a Minority," 150.

12 I use Shamma Boyarin's translation of Ephraim of Bonn's Hebrew account in his *Book of Historical Records*, in "Appendix D. Other Medieval Anti-Semitisms and the Crusade Context," *The Siege of Jerusalem*, ed. and trans. Adrienne Williams Boyarin (Toronto: Broadview, 2014),

*Anglicana* writes of the 1290 Expulsion that many Jews drowned crossing the channel, "each one with books" [una cum libris suis].[13] Judith Olszowy-Schlanger has described medieval English Jews in general as "highly literate, by which [we] mean not that all knew how to read and write, but that their very existence was based on bureaucracy, reading and writing, documents. Everybody, not just scholars, grammarians and sages, needed to be literate." Olszowy-Schlanger, who has spent much of the last decades radically reorganizing our sense of medieval Anglo-Hebrew literature and records, also summarizes the linguistic case thus: "People who dealt with documents had to know other languages. The Jews had to know Latin, and some Christians knew Hebrew."[14] In England, this naturally extended to Jewish women and surely included French and English vernaculars as well, as Michael Clanchy intuited some time ago.[15]

While there is little surviving evidence of writing done by Anglo-Jewish women, there is some. A list of acknowledgements of *shetarot* for Easter Term 1270 in the Jewish Exchequer rolls records that a starr of Henna of York, a significant financier after her husband Aaron's death in 1268, was "signed in her Hebrew character" [scrip-

156–158. The Hebrew can be found in A. M. Habermann, ed., *Sefer Gezerot Ashkenaz ve-Zorfat* (Jerusalem: Tarshish, 1945), 127.

13 *Bartholomaei de Cotton Monachi Norwicensis Historia Anglicana*, ed. Henry Richards Luard, Rerum Britannicarum medii aevi scriptores 16 (London: Longman, Green, Longman, and Roberts, 1859), 178. Bartholomew is an independent authority for the years 1285–1291, writing nearly contemporaneously with the 1290 Expulsion. The same passage was also mentioned by Judith Olszowy-Schlanger in her Oxford 2014 lecture (see n. 14 below), where she translated the phrase "una cum libris suis" as "each one with his book"; however, since Latin *suis* is grammatically masculine here only because it modifies *libris*, I translate the phrase to remove the gendered pronoun.

14 I am quoting from Olszowy-Schlanger's lecture, "Hebrew Documents in Medieval England," delivered 8 December 2014 and now posted in a slightly garbled form on the *Oxford Jewish Heritage* website (http://oxfordjewishheritage.co.uk, under the "News and Events" tab). For her most important published works on the larger topic of Anglo-Hebrew materials, see *Les manuscrits hébreux dans l'Angleterre médiévale: étude historique et paléographique*, Collection de la Revue des Études Juives 29 (Paris: Peeters, 2003); with Patricia Stirnemann, "The Twelfth-Century Trilingual Psalter in Leiden," *Scripta* 1 (2008): 103–112; "A School of Christian Hebraists in Thirteenth-Century England: A Unique Hebrew–Latin–French and English Dictionary and its Sources," *European Journal of Jewish Studies* 1, no. 2 (2007): 249–277; "Robert Wakefield and his Hebrew Manuscripts" *Zutot* 6, no. 1 (2009): 25–33; "Christian Hebraism in Thirteenth-Century England: The Evidence of Hebrew–Latin Manuscripts," in *Crossing Borders: Hebrew Manuscripts as a Meeting-place of Cultures*, ed. Piet van Boxel and Sabine Arndt (Oxford: Bodleian Library, University of Oxford, 2009), 115–122; and her groundbreaking two-volume *Hebrew and Hebrew–Latin Charters and Tallies from Medieval England: A Diplomatic and Palaeographical Study*, Brepols Monumenta Palaeographica Medii Aevi: Series Hebraica (Turnhout: Brepols, 2016). Pinchas Roth is also currently working on medieval Anglo-Jewish rabbinic culture: see, for example, his "New Responsa by Isaac ben Peretz of Northampton," *Jewish Historical Studies* 46 (2014): 1–17.

15 See *From Memory to Written Record: England 1066–1307*, 2nd ed. (Oxford and Cambridge, MA: Blackwell, 1993), 201–203, discussed in further detail below. An interesting comparative case for the participation of Christian women in legal-documentary and epistolary culture in the later middle ages is Malcolm Richardson, *Middle-Class Writing in Late Medieval London*, The History of the Book 7 (London: Pickering and Chatto, 2011), especially Chapter 4.

tum littera sua ebraica consignauit].[16] In Trinity Term 1267, Belia of Bedford appeared to quitclaim one Alexander of Stokes of all debts to her, in acknowledgement of which "Belia was to make for him her starr of acquittance" (*CPREJ* 1.149) [dicta Belya... faciet ei starrum de acquietancia]. Henna of London in Trinity Term 1277 similarly promised to make her starr and "swore on the Law of Moses that no starr of acquittance was previously made, neither by herself nor by her command" (*CPREJ* 3.305) [iurauit predicta Henna super legam moysi quod nec per ipsam nec per preceptum suum factum starrum de acquietancia], suggesting a distinction between a recognized ability to write her own documents and her (probably more typical) practice of commissioning them to be made. Henna was, in court, swearing on a Hebrew Torah, as seems to have been standard practice for Jews appearing before the Justices.[17]

One of the most well-known documents in Hebrew that survives from thirteenth-century England is the 1271 pre-marital agreement (*shidduch*) between Belaset bat Barakhyah of Lincoln and Benjamin ben Joseph, parents of their betrothed children. In it, Belaset makes arrangements for the marriage of her daughter Judith to the young man Aaron and promises a dowry that includes twenty marks and a Bible. Four years in advance of the planned wedding, Belaset transfers her Bible to Benjamin (Aaron's father): "twenty-four books in one volume, properly corrected, with vocalization and Masora, on calf parchment with six columns on each sheet and, separately, the Targum for the Pentateuch and Haphtarot, with all written in it." This volume is presented as the property of the mother, passes from her hands and by her arrangement alone, and is designated by her for the "use of the young couple," both of them. The contract further stipulates that, should the marriage not happen, the Bible must be returned to Belaset.[18] In another agreement between Jews, enrolled in Latin in Hilary Term 1276,

16 J. M. Rigg, ed. and trans., *Calendar of the Plea Rolls of the Exchequer of the Jews*, vol. 1 (London: Macmillan for the Jewish Historical Society of England, 1905), 270. Other volumes in this series include J. M. Rigg, ed. and trans., *Calendar of the Plea Rolls of the Exchequer of the Jews*, vol. 2 (Edinburgh: Ballantyne for the Jewish Historical Society of England, 1910); Jenkinson, ed. and trans., *Calendar of the Plea Rolls of the Exchequer of the Jews*, vol. 3; H. G. Richardson, ed. and trans., *Calendar of the Plea Rolls of the Jews Preserved in the Public Record Office*, vol. 4 (Colchester: Spottiswoode for the Jewish Historical Society of England, 1972); Sarah Cohen and Paul Brand, eds., *Plea Rolls of the Exchequer of the Jews Preserved in the Public Record Office*, vol. 5 (London: Jewish Historical Society of England, 1992); and Brand, ed., *Plea Rolls of the Exchequer of the Jews*, vol. 6. I cite these hereafter as *CPREJ*, followed by volume and page number. Though I lean on previous translations where possible (inconsistently available in vols. 1–4), all translations are modified by me. Latin text, unless otherwise noted, is from my own transcriptions; the Latin is not included at all in *CPREJ* vols. 1–3, and only intermittently in vol. 4.

17 Justice of the Jews Hamo Hauteyn amerced the York Sergeant of the *Judaismo* Meyrot of Stamford for contempt in Hilary Term 1278 when "he did not have the book of Judaic Law on which Jews could make an oath" [non habuit librum legis judaice super quem judei potuerunt sacramentum facere], which evidently made continuing proceedings difficult. See *CPREJ* 5.46. Cf. Dobson's confused assessment of the same entry in "The Medieval York Jewry Reconsidered," 151–152.

18 I use the translation (from Hebrew) of Olszowy-Schlanger, *Hebrew and Hebrew–Latin Charters and Tallies*, 1.300–301 (item no. 66, Westminster Abbey Muniments 6797). This *shidduch* is also translated by Adler in *Jews of Medieval England*, 42–43, after the Hebrew available in M. D. Davis, ed., *Hebrew Deeds of English Jews before 1290*, Publications of the Anglo-Jewish Historical Exhibition 2 (London: Jewish Chronicle, 1888), 299–302.

a Belaset of London arranges free control over her inheritance after her husband's death, including her household books, explicitly those "which ever belonged to…her uncle" [que vnquam fuerit…auunculi sui] but excluding "books that fell to her in the presence" of a certain Aron and Josce (*CPREJ* 3.112) [excepta libri qui ei acciderint coram Aron…et Josc]. The record is specific enough to indicate that certain books are especially dear to this Belaset, or perhaps that she had hoped to keep them all.

Anglo-Jewish women were also dealing in the trade and sale of Christian and Latin books, no doubt those acquired as surety for debts. In Easter Term 1278, a Jewess called Margarina was sued by Oxford Carmelites for unlawful detinue of three books, "to wit, Paul's epistles, glossed, worth 40 shillings, Matthew glossed, worth 7 shillings, and a *Sentences*, glossed, worth 10 shillings [videlicit, epistolas pauli glosatas pretium xl s. matheum glosatum pretium vii s. et sententias pretium x s]; after an inquest by a mixed jury of Christian and Jews, Margarina "acknowledged before them that she had received the said books from the said brothers in pledge, and afterwards, because of the time elapsed, had sold them" [coram eis recognouit quod predictos libros a dictis fratribus in vadium recepit et postea per lapsum temporis eos vendidit].[19] In 1281, two female converts from Judaism, Belaset and Hittecote of Oxford, and their books, were the subject of a writ sent to the Justices of the Jews by Edward I: he ordered their belongings sent to the Domus Conversorum in London "for the maintenance of the converts … [and] to be assigned to the same Belaset and Hittecote" [ad sustentacionem Conversorum … [et] eisdem Belassez et Hittecote faciat assignari]. The Exchequer scribe listed their only movable belongings as delivered: nine Latin books, all concerning grammar, logic, and natural science.[20] This kind of interaction suggests a trade in books between Jewish women and religious and scholarly institutions – notably around Oxford – as well as the willingness of Jewish women to appeal directly to royal authority.

Whatever we determine from this admittedly sparse evidence about the likelihood of Anglo-Jewish women's literacy in, or use of, Hebrew or Latin, there is important emphasis to be placed on the idea that Anglo-Jewish women were associated with "the

19 Kew, TNA E 9/27 membrane 7; Rigg, *Select Pleas*, 103–104. The fact that Margarina's case was heard by a mixed jury is not unusual. The Exchequer of the Jews was in many ways a joint Christian and Jewish institution, with chirographers and officials of both religions, and recourse to all-Jewish or mixed juries was dependent on claimants, defendants, and cases. See Brand's Introduction to *CPREJ*, vol. 6, especially 6–16 and 44–45, and Marianne Constable, *The Law of the Other: The Mixed Jury and Changing Conceptions of Citizenship, Law, and Knowledge* (Chicago and London: University of Chicago Press, 1994), 18–21.

20 Rigg, *Select Pleas*, 114. The books listed are: "unus liber Prisciani Constr'… unus Grecismus … una Logica vetus … unum Doctrinale magnum … quidam liber Institutionum … quidam Codex … quoddam Inforciatum … liber Nature … [et] quidam Grecismus." This supports evidence noted by Malcolm Parkes of the role of Oxford Jewry in the medieval Oxford University book trade. See his "The Provision of Books," in *The History of the University of Oxford*, vol. 2, *Late Medieval Oxford*, ed. J. I. Catto and Ralph Evans (Oxford: Clarendon Press, 1992), 407–483, at 410. Kathryn Kerby-Fulton's "Afterword: Social History of the Book and Beyond: *Originalia*, Medieval Literary Theory, and the Aesthetics of Paleography," in *The Medieval Manuscript Book: Cultural Approaches*, ed. Michael Johnston and Michael Van Dussen (Cambridge: Cambridge University Press, 2015), 243–254, at 247, emphasizes that Parkes demonstrated that some books "were even owned by Jewish women."

letter of the law" just as much as Jewish men and that they must have *seemed* to be literate by virtue of their participation in documentary and book culture. Clanchy, who posits Hebrew as such an important language of record in England that "indebted magnates of the thirteenth century would probably have come across more writing in Hebrew than in English," concludes that "it was evidently normal for both male and female English Jews to be literate. The men, and a notable number of women, who had business dealings with Christians, had to understand Latin, French, and English as well."[21] The people who produced and carried the bonds to those indebted magnates, that is, were male *and* female, whether they wrote the documents themselves or not.

Standard proclamations in synagogues concerning summary settlement of debts of Christian individuals (because they had died or were, for instance, going on crusade) suggest that Clanchy's inference is true: the formula, frequently copied into the Exchequer rolls, reads, "if any Jew *or Jewess* [Jud' vel Judeam] have claim against X, he or she must be before the Justices by X day with chirographs, tallies, and all other instruments."[22] Licoricia of Winchester was summoned to appear before the court and "have her chirographs" [haberet chirographa] with her, that is, she was to appear with the indented duplicates of all debt bonds held in her name.[23] The earliest mention of a Jewess that appears in the Fine Rolls of Henry III in 1218 states simply, "she has the writ" [habet brevem].[24] This evidence is made more remarkable by comparison with French Jewish women financiers of the same period, who were involved primarily if not exclusively in small-scale, woman-to-woman lending.[25]

All of this must impact how we read representations of Jewish women in the dominant Christian contexts as well as how and where we might look for stereotypes or cross-cultural resonances around women in court, women with text, or women in business. As I have argued elsewhere, the frequent depiction of the Virgin Mary in England displaying charters or contracts, alongside literary emphasis on the fact of her Jewishness, is fruitfully connected to the role of Jewish women financiers and book traders in twelfth- and thirteenth-century England.[26] The idea that people asked

21 *From Memory to Written Record*, 202.

22 Such proclamations can be found in *CPREJ* 1.89, 1.91, 1.115, 1.193, 1.194, 1.197, 1.200, *et passim* through all six of the *CPREJ* volumes.

23 Rigg, *Select Pleas*, 19. This is just one convenient example, however. Licoricia was frequently in court with her documents. For more on her long career and business dealings, see Bartlet, *Licoricia of Winchester*, especially chapters 1 and 4.

24 Kew, TNA C 60/9 membrane 6 (11 April 1218). Image and text available online through the *Henry III Fine Rolls Project* (http://www.finerollshenry3.org.uk/).

25 On the French situation and comparison with England, see William C. Jordan, "Jews on Top: Women and the Availability of Consumption Loans in Northern France in the Mid-Thirteenth Century," *Journal of Jewish Studies* 29, no.1 (1978): 39–56; Joe Hillaby and Caroline Hillaby, *The Palgrave Dictionary of Medieval Anglo-Jewish History* (New York and Houndmills: Palgrave Macmillan, 2013), s.v. "Women of the Medieval Anglo-Jewry"; and Meyer, "Female Moneylending and Wet-Nursing," especially Chapter 5 and her conclusion.

26 I refer to my *Miracles of the Virgin in Medieval England: Law and Jewishness in Marian Legends* (Woodbridge: D. S. Brewer, 2010) and my "Inscribed Bodies: The Virgin Mary, Jewish Women, and Medieval Feminine Legal Authority," in *Law and Sovereignty in the Middle Ages and the Renaissance*, ed. Robert S. Sturges, Arizona Studies in the Middle Ages and Renaissance 28 (Turnhout: Brepols, 2011), 237–259.

Margery Kempe "whyder sche wer a Cristen woman er a Jewe" might be taken seriously as a historically savvy barb in late-medieval England,[27] a place that certainly could have had long-standing stereotypes of the female Jewish businesswoman, travelling without a husband, handling her own money, appearing before courts, laden with documents. This evidence may speak to why the unique early Middle English "Judas Ballad," unlike any other known Judas literature, posits for the betrayer a Jewish sister who manipulates Judas and takes his thirty coins.[28] It makes some sense of why the late thirteenth-century ritual murder story of Adam of Bristol features a widowed Jewish sister who speaks Hebrew and French, understands English, is familiar with Latin liturgical formulations, and is able to negotiate body-disposal fees with a visiting Irish priest whose English is shaky.[29] Bureaucratic and literary records *together* reinforce that Anglo-Jewish women were seen to be literate, multilingual, involved in finance and negotiation, willing to appeal to the law, and remarkably independent.

## Case Study: Alice the Convert of Worcester

One of the best cases for authorship and literacy on the part of an Anglo-Jewish woman, especially if we leave aside the question of Hebrew literacy, comes from a woman who rejected her Judaism. Alice of Worcester converted to Christianity before 1272, and she wrote two letters that survive – one in Latin and one in French – requesting support for herself and her son John, who apparently converted with her.[30] It is difficult to say who Alice was before her conversion, as converts took a Christian name upon baptism, but she was, indeed, likely a Jewess from Worcester and was also likely a prominent figure before her conversion.[31] The Worcester and Gloucester Jewish communities were small and intermarried but boasted leading national financiers, of both genders, throughout the thirteenth century.[32] Alice feels

27 Lynn Staley, ed., *The Book of Margery Kempe*, TEAMS Middle English Texts Series (Kalamazoo: Medieval Institute, 1996), 29–33.

28 Cambridge, Trinity College, MS. B.14.39, fol. 34r. The ballad is edited and translated as an appendix in Irina A. Dumitrescu, "Debt and Sin in the Middle English 'Judas,'" *Anglia* 131, no. 4 (2013): 509–537.

29 See Cristoph Cluse, "'Fabula ineptissima': Die Ritualmordlegende um Adam von Bristol nach der Handschrift London, British Library, Harley 957," *Aschkenas* 5, no. 2 (1995): 293–330. The Jewess's interactions with the oblivious priest in this text also implicates the Irish, another much-maligned group in English and Welsh literature of the period. The related linguistic complexities – and associated political, legal, and literary echoes and negotiations – in Irish and Welsh border regions and archives is recently discussed by Kathryn Kerby-Fulton in her "Competing Archives, Competing Languages: Office Vernaculars, Civil Servant Raconteurs, and the Porous Nature of French during Ireland's Rise of English," *Speculum* 90, no. 3 (2015): 674–700.

30 These are Kew, TNA SC 1/16/63 and SC 1/24/201, respectively.

31 On Jewish converts in thirteenth-century England generally, see Adler, *Jews of Medieval England*, 277–379; and Robert Stacey, "The Conversion of Jews to Christianity in Thirteenth-Century England," *Speculum* 67, no. 2 (1992): 263–283.

32 On the Worcester and Gloucester communities, see Hillaby and Hillaby, *Palgrave Dictionary of Medieval Anglo-Jewish History*, s.v. "Worcester" and "Gloucester"; and Joe Hillaby, "The Worcester Jewry 1158–1290: Portrait of a Lost Community," *Transactions of the Worcestershire Archaeological Society* 3rd series, no. 12 (1990): 73–122.

empowered to write directly to Edward I, cites her son's presence at the king's court in Gascony, and she appeals emotionally to Robert Burnell, Bishop of Bath and Wells, Chancellor of England, and regent during Edward I's absence on crusade and in Gascony early in his reign. A fifteenth-century copy of a third letter, from Edward I to Worcester Cathedral Priory, takes up Alice's case and shows that the king did indeed advocate on her and her son's behalf.[33] All three letters are transcribed and translated in an appendix below, now printed and translated together for the first time.

The surviving letters by and about Alice fall into a period of eight years at most, between August 1274 and March 1282. The chronology is implicit in the events mentioned: in her French letter, Henry III is dead, and Edward has recently returned from Gascony, probably for his August 1274 coronation. Robert Burnell was consecrated Bishop of Bath and Wells in April 1275, and Alice uses that title for him. The regnal year on Edward's letter is partially obscured by damage, but 1282 (the tenth year of his reign) is most likely. Alice's situation changed dramatically between the time of Edward's return from Gascony – when she asks for renewed confirmation of royal support through Worcester Priory because "the Prior and the good people of the house truly desire it" – and Edward's later letter admonishing Worcester Priory for disobeying his direct order regarding Alice and her son by withholding support. In between, Burnell had for some reason sent Alice to Coventry (probably St. Mary's Priory); but Coventry refused her, and she reports that she is destitute at Chester. Before her wanderings ended, she was for some time at the Domus Conversorum in London: post-Expulsion records list her among residents in 1280 (apparently without her son), but her whereabouts were unknown by 1308, when Edward II ordered officials to assess the Domus and its residents.[34]

Alice's personal and impassioned appeal to Robert Burnell and the dates of her letters suggest that she may have found sponsorship in the Giffard family, an influential family in Worcester and nearby Hereford, who were significantly involved with the Jewish communities of both towns in the same period. Godfrey Giffard was Bishop of Worcester, 1268–1302, and Walter may have been Bishop of Bath and Wells at the time of Alice's conversion: he was elected May 1264 and held the office until October 1266, when he was transferred to York, and we know from Alice's letter to Edward I that she converted and received royal orders for monastic support sometime during the reign of Henry III, certainly after 1255.[35] Both Giffard brothers were "notorious traffickers in

33 Oxford, Bodleian Library, MS Bodley 692, fol. 89v.

34 Adler prints the surviving 1308 Domus inventory in *Jews of Medieval England*, 350–352; he discusses the situation of extant warden's and inquiry records at 307–310.

35 In 1255, Henry III made provision for about 150 converts to be maintained at monasteries across England, as recorded in TNA C 60/52, on the dorse sides of membranes 2 and 12–14 (images are available online through the *Henry III Fine Rolls Project*). On these provisions, see Adler, *Jews of Medieval England*, 341–347 and Joan Greatrex, "Monastic Charity for Jewish Converts: The Requisition of Corrodies by Henry III," in *Christianity and Judaism: Papers Read at the 1991 Summer Meeting and the 1992 Winter Meeting of the Ecclesiastical History Society*, ed. Diana Wood, Studies in Church History 29 (Oxford and Cambridge, MA: Blackwell, 1992), 133–143. Greatrex calls 1255 "a turning point in the billeting of *conversi* in monastic establishments" (137) but notes that "there is sufficient evidence [Alice's letters among them] to show that the allocation of places for both *conversi* and other royal nominees continued through the remaining years of Henry's reign and beyond" (140).

Jewish debts,"[36] specifically those of the Worcester community, and both would have had to work with Burnell in local and national business. Both, like Burnell, served as Lord Chancellor (briefly but in quick succession, 1265–1268). Property that came to them from purchased Jewish bonds was gifted to their sister Alice Giffard after 1264, and Walter's son and heir to the Worcester bishopric was called John.[37] If our convert Alice was a Worcester financier, she would certainly have known and had dealings with this family, with Burnell, and with their associated institutions.

One might also conjecture that Alice's change of circumstances had something to do with the 1275 expulsion of Jews from Worcester. Jews were expelled from the dower towns of Edward's mother Queen Eleanor in that year – Worcester among them – and those expulsions were complete by the end of 1275.[38] It is possible that Worcester Priory viewed their resident Jewish converts as Jews despite their conversion. Converts had little luck shedding their Jewish identity; apostasy was possible and sometimes just suspected, and conversions were occasionally disputed.[39] The religious houses to which Henry III had assigned converts certainly resented the burden,[40] and it is also possible that Alice had lingering ties to her former community that caused tension or compelled her to want to move when they were forced out by expulsion.

Under these circumstances, the survival of Alice's letters is extraordinary. Very little has been written about them. Michael Adler knew of one in the 1930s, and Joan Greatrex briefly mentioned all three in her 1992 essay on monastic care of Jewish converts. Until now, only one of the three has been published, and Greatrex incorrectly summarized the content of the Latin letter to Burnell in her essay, taking the passive verb form "agar" (I shall be driven, compelled) as a reference to the biblical Hagar – an allusion that is not, in fact, anywhere in the letter.[41] The two letters from

36 Hillaby and Hillaby, *Palgrave Dictionary of Anglo-Jewish History*, s.v. "London, Abigail and Family of," where the Giffard siblings' profits from debt trafficking are incidentally discussed.

37 Ibid. See also *The Oxford Dictionary of National Biography* (Oxford: Oxford University Press, 2004–2016), s.v. "Giffard, Walter (c.1225–1279)" and "Giffard, Godfrey (c.1235–1302)"; and material related to John Giffard's inheritance in Francis Joseph Baigent, ed., *A Collection of Records and Documents relating to the Hundred and Manor of Crondal in Southampton*, vol. 1 (London: Simpkin, 1891), xxv and 416–420.

38 See nn. 31–32 above. Barrie Dobson also discusses the dower-town expulsions in "The Jews of Medieval Cambridge," in *The Jewish Communities of Medieval England: The Collected Essays of R. B. Dobson*, ed. Helen Birkett, Borthwick Texts and Studies 39 (York: The Borthwick Institute, University of York, 2010), 101–126, especially at 115–118.

39 See Adler, *Jews of Medieval England*, 277–379 ("History of the Domus"); Stacey, "Conversion of the Jews"; and F. D. Logan, "Thirteen London Jews and Conversion to Christianity: Problems of Apostasy in the 1280s," *Bulletin of the Institute of Historical Research* 45 (1972): 214–229. There is lengthy back-and-forth and confusion (on both Jewish and Christian sides), for example, evident in the Jewish Exchequer rolls and royal documents (cited by Logan) concerning a certain Melkana, a Jewess who apparently converted but later claimed she had always been a Jewess. See Rigg, *Select Pleas*, 100 and *CPREJ* 3.22, 3.34–35, and 3.177.

40 On resistance to Henry III's placements, see Greatrex, "Monastic Charity for Jewish Converts."

41 Adler published the French letter to Edward I (with a translation) in *Jews of Medieval England*, 347–348. It had previously been printed in F. J. Tanquerey, ed., *Recueil de lettres Anglo-Françaises 1265–1399* (Paris: Édouard Champion, 1916), no. 61. An English translation can also be found in Anne Crawford, ed., *Letters of the Queens of England 1100–1547* (Thrupp: Sutton,

Alice are not written in the same hand, and both mention that her son is carrying letters for her. It is likely that she employed scribes, though this fact does not, of course, exclude her authorship. Alice's determination to advocate for herself in writing with appeal to the highest levels of authority is related to the kind of literacy we might expect for Anglo-Jewish women of her time and, especially, for those involved in the business workings of the wealthiest Jewish families. Furthermore, Alice's letters place her in an environment of religious learning, and they suggest a facility with both Latin and French as well as an ability to use biblical stories persuasively.

This last skill is most evident in the final sentence of her letter to Burnell: "Have mercy on me, a captive, according to the great mercy with which Lord Jesus Christ showed mercy to the blessed Mary Magdalene." She is, she says elsewhere, "praying tearfully" to Burnell, and she worries that "in [her] weakness" [in infirmitate mea] she will be forced to beg and crawl. Her evocation seems to make full use of the medieval figure of the Magdalene, a composite of several women, including the woman in Luke 7:37–38, who washes Christ's feet with her tears, and St. Mary of Egypt, who while alone in the desert was fed by manna from heaven when she prayed. But Alice's phrase "in infirmitate mea" most explicitly echoes the Magdalene as she is described by name in Luke 8:2, among "certain women who had been healed of evil spirits and infirmities" ("et infirmatibus" in the Vulgate). The fact that Alice has experienced a conversion and wanders in need of support connect her to the Mary of Egypt–Mary Magdalene conflation that is evident, for instance, in the *Legenda aurea*, but Alice's self-fashioning as an anxious and wandering "captiva" is more likely a biting allusion to Isaiah 49 and 52, where Zion worries that she is "led away, and captive" (Isaiah 49:21) [transmigrata et captiva] and where the "captive daughter of Sion" [captiva filia Sion] is urged to "loose the bonds from off [her] neck" [solve vincula colli tui] and rejoice (Isaiah 52:1–2).[42]

Alice calls herself "captiv[a]" in the valediction of this letter to Burnell, but she also opens the letter by calling herself "his [Burnell's] captive" [sua captiua]. The repetition is striking as much for its pathos as for its evoking of biblical vocabulary specific to Jewish femininity. If this is an allusion to Isaiah, as I think it is, Alice uses "captiva" here to marshal – powerfully so because from a female author – commonplace gendered metonyms for Jerusalem (Zion) and for the Jewish people (the daughter of Zion). These may seem stark allusions for Alice the Anglo-Jewish convert to make: they suggest that she casts herself, in her post-conversion destitution and wandering, as a figure of Jerusalem before its salvation, a Jewish captive in foreign (Christian) bonds. But there are only six instances of the word *captiva* in the Vulgate, and only in Isaiah is the *captiva* a woman worried about her children (as Alice is worried about

1994), 246–47. For the incorrect summary of the Latin letter to Burnell, see Greatrex, "Monastic Charity for Jewish Converts": "She [Alice] likened herself first to Hagar, the bondwoman in the Old Testament, who was persecuted and driven into exile" (141). Ruth Nisse, *Jacob's Shipwreck: Diaspora, Translation, and Jewish-Christian Relations in Medieval England* (Ithaca: Cornell University Press, 2017), 116, repeats Greatrex's misreading to interpret Alice's words as a "typological identification of Hagar with Mary Magdalene."

42 *Biblia sacra iuxta Vulgatam versionem* (Stuttgart: Deutsche Bibelgesellschaft, 1994); translations from the *Douay-Rheims Holy Bible* (Fitzwilliam, NH: Loreto, 2000).

her son in her letters), "transmigrata et captiva … destituta et sola" (Isaiah 49:21). Alice's framing choice of the word "captiva" is clearly figurative, and its opening and closing use suggests that it is as essential to her identity as Burnell's official titles are to his. She both takes on the character of a Christian feminine ideal (and convert from Judaism) through Mary Magdalene *and* straddles Jewish and Christian ideas of the redemption of Jerusalem and the Jewish people by insisting nonetheless on her continued captivity. This suggests a familiarity with the Vulgate, an awareness of her own liminality, and a persuasive facility with a Christian rhetoric of urgency and spiritual need. As Edward I's annoyed letter to Worcester Priory later makes clear, Alice is nothing if not persistent in her appeals: Edward does not want to have to hear her complaints again.

What can we take away from the French and Latin letters of one Anglo-Jewish woman convert writing in the 1270s? It is clear to me that the literate, bilingual, and commanding modes of Alice's experience communicate the usefulness of looking to such in-between spaces to glean information about women's lives and agency in the Middle Ages and, especially, about Jewish women in England. Alice, because of her conversion, might not be considered a Jew. Clearly, she understood herself as separate from her former people, but plausibly her Jewishness was part of her literacy, documentary agency, and confidence; *certainly*, it was part of her forced wanderings and destitution. Her willingness and ability to go directly to the highest authority in her own voice, to send her son as a courier to the king's court, and to write in the king's own vernacular, all correspond with what we know of Anglo-Jewish women's positions in business, legal, and family life. Her place at the interface of religions, languages, and scholarly disciplines, furthermore, activates the historic and interpretive potential of her story. Alice can inform us about Jewish women's place within the dominant Christian culture of thirteenth-century England as much as the women recorded in the Jewish Exchequer rolls (and she may, in fact, be one of those women). Though she had been a Christian for some time when she authored her letters, Alice provides further and specific evidence for Jewish women's literacy, multilingualism, and agency in thirteenth-century England.[43]

43 For more on Alice of Worcester and many of the topics and texts discussed in this chapter, see Adrienne Williams Boyarin, '*Polemics of Sameness: Jews and the Jewess in Medieval England*, The Middle Ages Series (Philadelphia: University of Pennsylvania Press, forthcoming 2020).

## Appendix: Alice the Convert of Worcester's Letters[44]

### 1. TNA SC 1/16/63, Alice the Convert of Worcester to King Edward I, c. 1274–1275

A nostre seygnur le Rey si li pleyt Alice la conu*er*se de Wyrecestr' monstre cu*m* el aueyt p*ar* le graunt le Rey Henri ke fu vost*re* pere ke deu de sa alme eyt merci charite en la Priorie de Wyrcestr' e pus par vostre graunt ke vos ly grauntates en Gascoyne la ele vaya sun fiz kaunt vos fuces en ses p*ar*ties e la vos ly grauntates vne Lecter ke ele dute ressayuer la charite ieskes a uost*re* venue en Engletere cu*m* ele aueyt ressu deuaunt ses oures / dunt pus ke vos estes venu en Engletere mercie seyt nost*re* seygn*ur* ele vos pri pur deu e par seynte charite si vos pleyt ke vos ly grauntes vost*re* lecter au Priour e au Couent de Wyrecstr' deauer e resseyure la charite cu*m* ele a ressu deuaunt ses oures kar le Priour e les bone gent de la mesun le volunt ben.

To our Lord the King, if it please him, Alice the Convert of Worcester shows how she had charity in the Priory of Worcester by the grant of King Henry who was your father (may God have mercy on his soul) and then by your grant that you gave her in Gascony, where she sent her son when you were in those regions and where you granted him a letter that she ought to receive the charity until your coming into England, as she had received it formerly. Wherefore, since you have arrived in England (thanks be to our Lord), she begs you for the sake of God and holy charity, if it please you, that you grant her your letter to the Prior and Convent of Worcester that she might have and receive the charity as she received it formerly, for the Prior and the good people of the house truly desire it.

### 2. TNA SC 1/24/201,[45] Alice the Convert of Worcester to Robert Burnell, Bishop of Bath and Wells and Chancellor of England, c. 1275–1280

Viro ven*er*abili *et* discr*et*o R*oberto* dei gr*ati*a Ep*iscop*o de Baa . nec*non* *et* d*omi*ni E*dwardi* reg*is* n*os*tri Cancellario . sua captiua Alic*ia* de Wyrcestr' conu*er*sa si plac*et* sal*ut*em . pontificali Excellencie v*est*re notifico . q*uod* dom*us* Couentrenc' que me cu*m* filio meo latore p*re*sentiu*m* mandasti ? lit*er*atorie vt m*ihi* victus meos don*ec* m*ihi* melius p*r*ouideretis t*ri*bueret . l*ite*ras v*est*ras m*ihi* sub sigillo v*est*ro t*ri*butas n*u*llo m*odo* suscip*er*e dignant*ur* . Quap*ro*p*ter* vob*is* *con*uolo ta*m*q*uam* ad re-

44 Medieval punctuation is maintained in these transcriptions and expanded abbreviations are marked by italics. My thanks to my colleagues at the University of Victoria – Margaret Cameron, Cedric A. J. Littlewood, and Iain Higgins – who generously assisted with translations. These texts are also printed in Williams Boyarin, *Polemics of Sameness*, appendix 3.

45 Note that the page of the archival binder in which this letter is now bound (that is, in SC 1/24) reads 202, but the PRO stamp on the dorse side of the letter reads 201.

fugium meum lac*ri*mabil*ite*r exorando . q*ua*tin*us* sup*er* hiis m*ihi* aliq*uid* remediu*m* volitis t*ri*buere . Sciat*is* me *com*morante*m* ap*u*d Cestr' don*ec* no*n* valente*m* itin*er*ando laborare . su*m*ptib*us* carendo . don*ec* m*ihi* aliq*uid* ben*eficiu*m si vob*is* placuerit p*er* latore*m* p*re*sentiu*m* m*it*tere dignenu*m* . T*amen* s*upe*r hiis faciat*is* ne in inf*ir*mitate mea vos pet*ere* agar *et* si pedib*us* ac ma*n*ib*us* op*or*tet incedere . valet*e* . Miserere mei captiue p*ro* max*ima* mis*er*icordia q*uam* d*omi*n*us* i*esus christus* misert*us* fuit s*upe*r b*eat*am maria*m* magdalen'. valet*e* .

To the venerable and prudent man Robert, by God's grace Bishop of Bath and likewise Chancellor of our lord king Edward, from his captive Alice of Worcester, a convert, if it please, greetings. I notify your pontifical excellency that the Coventry house to which you assigned me with my son, the bearer of the present document, in writing, to contribute to my sustenance until you provide better for me, in no way deigns to receive your letters, which were granted to me under your seal. Therefore, I fly to you as to my refuge, praying tearfully, that you might give me relief in the matter of these desired things. Know that I am staying at Chester for as long as I cannot manage travelling, lacking means, until it pleases you to send some worthy benefit to me through the bearer of the present document. Would that you act on these things, lest in my weakness I am driven to beg and, if necessary, go on feet and hands. Farewell. Have mercy on me, a captive, according to the great mercy with which Lord Jesus Christ showed mercy to the blessed Mary Magdalene. Farewell.

3. Bodleian Library, MS Bodley 692 (fol. 89v),[46] King Edward I to the Prior and Convent of Worcester, 18 March 1282(?), as copied in 1446 by John Lawerne, Worcester monk and D.Theol. (Gloucester College, Oxford)

[In margin:] L*ite*ra d*omi*ni rege p*ro* Alicia*m* la co*n*uerse ad p*r*iore*m et con*uen*tum* Wygorn*ensis*

Edward dei gra*tia* Rex Angl*ie* . D*omin*us Hib*ernie et* Dux Aquit*ania* . dilect*is* sibi i*n Christ*o P*r*iori *et* Co*n*uentui Wyg*ornensis* sal*u*tem . Ex graui querela Alicie la co*n*uerse de Wyg*ornia et* Ioh*annis* filii eius nobis e*st* ostensu*m* . q*uod* cu*m* ip*s*i habere debea*n*t quanda*m* certa*m* sustentac*io*nem de domo *vest*ra que eis ad ma*n*dat*us* d*omi*ni *et* quo*n*dam regis Angl*ie* pa*t*ris n*ost*ri . Ad tota*m* vita*m* eor*um*dem Alicie *et* Ioh*annis* p*e*rcipienda*m* p*er* vos extiti*t* assignata ; qua*m* quid*e*m sustentac*io*nem . iid*e*m Alicia *et* Ioh*an*nes ta*m* d*ic*ti pa*t*ris n*ost*ri temp*ore* q*uam* n*ost*ro iux*ta* forma*m* assignac*io*nis p*re*d*ict*e diutius p*er*ceperu*n*t *et* h*ab*ueru*n*t ; Vos nich*il*omi*nus* d*ict*am sustentac*io*nem eisd*e*m Alicie *et* Ioh*ann*i

46 The lower portion of this leaf is significantly damaged by water as well as by minor tearing or trimming. Ultra-violet light was used to read smudged and faded portions. Only the top portion of the letter indicating the regnal year is visible; an earlier date is not out of the question.

subtrahit*is* ia*m* de nouo . *et* ea*m* eis sic*ut* asseru*n*t renuitis amplius exhibere . in ip*s*oru*m* Alic*ie et* Ioh*ann*is dampnu*m et* depaup*eracion*em ma*n*ifesta*m* . Et q*uia* nolum*us* q*uo*d eisd*e*m Alicie *et* Ioh*ann*i iniuri[*ari*] aliqua*liter* in hac p*ar*te vobis mandam*us* sic*ut* alias ma*n*dauim*us* . q*uod* si ita e*st* eisd*e*m Alicie *et* Ioh*ann*i ta*l*em sustentac*ion*em de domo v*est*ra p*redic*ta exhiberi faciat*is* . quale*m* eis in te*m*po*r*e d*ic*ti p*at*ris n*ost*ri exhibuist*is* . Et talli*ter* vos habeat*is* in hac p*ar*te q*uo*d n*on* op*or*teat ip*s*os in v*est*ri def*e*ctus ad nos it*er*ato req*ui*rere ex hac c*aus*a . v*e*l ca*us*am nobis sig*n*ificat*is* . quare ma*n*dato n*ost*ro alias vobis inde directo minime paruistis . T*este* me ip*s*o ap*u*d Westm*onisterium* xviii[mo] die Martii anno regni n*ost*ri [x][o]

Letter from the Lord King for Alice the Convert to the Prior and Convent of Worcester:

Edward, by God's grace King of England, Lord of Ireland, and Duke of Aquitaine, to his beloved in Christ, the Prior and Convent of Worcester, greetings. On the grievous complaint of Alice the Convert of Worcester and her son John, it was shown to us that they should have had certain guaranteed support from your house that was set for them by order of the Lord and once-King of England our father. It was assigned to you in order to secure the whole life of the said Alice and John; indeed, the same Alice and John secured and held this support both in the time of our father and in our own time, according to the form of the aforesaid assignment, for a long time. You nevertheless withhold the said support from this Alice and John even now, and, as they assert, refuse to pay it to them further, to the manifest damage and impoverishment of this Alice and John. And because we do not wish to do injustice to the same Alice and John, so we command you in this matter, as we have commanded before, that you are to effect such support of the same Alice and John from your aforesaid house as you did for them in the time of our said father, and so deal in this matter that they need not inquire at us for this reason again because of your failure, or show us cause why you have not previously performed our direct order to you. Witness myself at Westminster on the 18[th] day of March in the [tenth?] year of our reign.

# PART II

# AUTHORSHIP, INTELLECTUAL LIFE, AND THE PROFESSIONAL WRITER

# Preface to Part II

## INTELLECTUALS, LEADERS, *DOCTORES*

DAVID WALLACE

In the first of the four chapters gathered together as Part II, Sean Field maintains that Agnes of Harcourt was "a leader in her world," but then wonders: "was she an intellectual?" Towards the end of the chapter, having unearthed a wider range of sources and textual witnesses than hitherto associated with Agnes, he affirms that she was "an important intellectual." Agnes flourished at or near Paris, and Parisian academics of our own time would have fewer hesitations in recognizing her status *as* an intellectual than their Anglo-American counterparts, since "the terms 'intellectual/ intellectuals'," Rita Copeland has argued,

> ... are still not accepted or used comfortably in all quarters. The terms have found a more secure usage among French and other continental historians of the Middle Ages than among Anglo-American historians of medieval English universities.[1]

Mention of "universities" here invites us to consider a peculiarity of Paris: that university, royal court, and commercial city were all gathered at one site, whereas in England (particularly) and elsewhere this was not often the case.[2] Jacques Le Goff has associated "the appearance of the intellectual as a distinct social type in the twelfth century"[3] with the appearance of towns, and in a city such as Paris there is scope for university learning to bleed into urban institutions (as it bleeds into Jean de Meun's unmistakably Parisian, secular continuation of the *Roman de la Rose*). But for the two Paris-identified women in Part II, Agnes de Harcourt and Christine de Pizan, it is sponsorship of the royal court that decisively enables their authorly work. Again, such an option was hardly on offer in England for literary authors, male or female. Chaucer and Gower tried to float the *idea* that royal personages might protect and encourage literati, with Chaucer placing his faith in queenly rather than kingly fictional surrogates. But there is scant support for royal-sponsored, institutional provision of literary learning in England before the monks of Sheen begin supplying the Bridgettine nuns of Syon with texts for perusal within private, enclosed spaces.[4] The great, royally

1 *Pedagogy, Intellectuals, and Dissent in the Later Middle Ages: Lollardy and Ideas of Learning* (Cambridge: Cambridge University Press, 2001), 34.

2 On Paris see Stephen G. Nichols, "Paris," in *Europe: A Literary History, 1348–1418*, ed. David Wallace, 2 vols (Oxford: Oxford University Press), I, 11–42.

3 Cited in Copeland, *Pedagogy, Intellectuals*, 35.

4 Vincent Gillespie (ed.), *Syon Abbey*, Corpus of British Medieval Library Catalogues, 9 (London:

approved program of vernacularization instituted by Charles V of France finds no counterpart in England; the literary and lordly productions of Berkeley castle, Gloucestershire,[5] are more impressive than anything essayed at Westminster.

Medieval women authors are routinely dogged by readers' doubts about whether they *really* wrote a given text, and in ways that rarely attend writings ascribed to men: as someone once said, wittily, there has never been a *female* anonymous.[6] Of the four women in this section, it is Catherine of Siena whose claims to "authorship" have been most subjected to scrutiny; Tom Luongo in Chapter 5 here carries forward work valiantly pioneered by Jane Tylus.[7] But the importance of *writing* has been greatly exaggerated. That is to say, the physical act of pulling pen across parchment – often likened to ploughing a furrow – forms but a minor, ancillary part of textual composition. Few would claim that the true *authors* of documents from the mid-twentieth century, taken down in shorthand or bashed out by typewriter, are those *taking dictation* – especially since that underpaid labor pool was overwhelmingly female. So there is no need to get excessively hung up on what, exactly, Catherine of Siena did in producing texts that are, undoubtedly, hers. Her own description of her God-given gift of textual composing is wonderfully eloquent in being just a little opaque: she has been granted, she says, and as Luongo notes, *l'attitudine dello scrivere.* Implicit here is the recognition that *all* textual composition and conservation is collective, takes a village, is *institutional.* The notion that every aspect of a given text must represent the will of a single, sovereign author is, under current scrutiny, falling apart. Shakespeare, it (only now) seems, employed many hands in the writing of his plays: but then he was, after all, a commercial playwright. The text of Dante's *Commedia*, for centuries tapped as the gold standard of the Tuscan that would become normative for Italy, may actually find its earliest witnesses in manuscripts form the north – where Dante was exiled, and where northern scribes first copied his work.[8] Will the *sacro poema* now admit northern inflections, undoing the data scrubbing carried out by Pietro Bembo in his quest for a pure Tuscan fit for marketing through Venetian printing presses? But what if Dante had been living in exile so long that his Florentine became tainted with northernisms? Ovid, after all, when exiled to the Crimea, feared, or pretended to fear, that his pure Roman diction would be compromised by local usages; should he now, at the edge of the world, become a Getic poet?[9] All this is to say that the kinds of *worrying* over the authenticity of women's texts can just as easily be turned back onto the heads of male

The British Library, 2001); *Syon Abbey and its Books: Reading, Writing and Religion c.1400–1700*, ed. E. A. Jones and Alexandra Walsham (Woodbridge: Boydell Press, 2010).

5 See Emily Steiner, "Berkeley Castle," in *Europe*, ed. Wallace, I, 227–39.

6 For reflection on such matters see Marcy L. North, "Women's Literary and Intellectual Endeavors: A Case for the Anonymous Riposte," in *A Companion to British Literature*, ed. Robert DeMaria Jr., Heesok Chang, and Samantha Zacher, vol. II, *Early Modern Literature 1450–1650* (Oxford: Wiley Blackwell, 2014), 143–63.

7 *Reclaiming Catherine of Siena: Literacy, Literature, and the Signs of Others* (Chicago: University of Chicago Press, 2009).

8 See Paolo Trovato, "Primi appunti sulla veste linguistica della Commedia." *Medioevo Romanzo*, 33/1 (2009), 29–48.

9 See Luigi Galasso, "*Epistulae ex Ponto*," in *A Companion to Ovid*, ed. Peter E. Knox (Oxford: Wiley-Blackwell, 2009), 194–206 (205).

authors. Each of the four women here produced texts through collective effort, and an *institutional* model, I am suggesting, may help us read them aright.

Our Parisian pair, while active more than a century apart, shares associations not just through royal circles, but specifically beneath the penumbra of the saintly Louis IX. Agnes's father had crusaded with Charles IX, Sean Field tells us, and Agnes herself formed part of the entourage of Isabelle of France, Charles's sister; Isabelle became the first abbess of Longchamp, and Agnes the third. Christine de Pizan wrote a *Dit de Poissy* c. 1400, describing a visit to her daughter who lived in the abbey there as part of the entourage of Princess Marie, daughter of Charles IV.[10] Poissy, a favorite haunt of the French royal family since the twelfth century, had been the birth and baptismal place of the future saint and king, Louis IX, later becoming the center of his cult. In her *Vie d'Isabelle*, Agnes made use of the earliest French prose life of Elizabeth of Hungary, the thirteenth century's chief model of papally approved queenly sanctity; her writings on Isabelle then formed part of the documentary grounding of Longchamps for some 500 years, right up to the French Revolution. The specific form of her intellectualism, that is, may be seen as *institutional*, supportive of religio-monarchist fabric right up to the moment of its abolition. The same can be said of Christine de Pizan, more broadly in her writings but specifically in her *Mutacion de Fortune*. Thelma Fenster begins by speaking of Charles VI reversing the policy of his father, Charles V, by expelling the Jewish community from France in 1394. This formed part, one should note, of a western European pattern of violent persecution in this decade, initiated in Castile in 1391.[11] During the summer of 1392, Charles VI went mad *pro tempore* while travelling in Brittany, killing a number of knights (and almost his own brother, Louis of Orléans); such bouts of insanity, leading the monarch to believe he was made of glass, and had no wife or children, grew more frequent through his reign.[12] Thus it seems better to imagine Christine de Pizan, in her lengthy *Mutacion*, not to be following the inclinations of a single individual, King Charles VI, unhappily unstable, but rather serving the institution of which he formed part: the Crown. And as Fenster astutely observes, in her final sentence, the *Mutacion*'s irreconcilable contradictions simply track those of the French royal state, embodied by a monarch who was pledged to at once protect and persecute Jews.

10 "The documentary style of the opening of the *Dit de Poissy*," observes Barbara K. Altmann, "is unique in the way it anchors its debate in an historical construct so elaborate and accurate that it ceases to function as background material and constitutes a major focus – if not *the* major focus – of the poem" (*The Love Debate Poems of Christine de Pizan* (Gainesville: University Press of Florida, 1998), 18).

11 "The succession of violent pogroms and forced conversions that begin in Seville in early June [1391] and spread throughout the peninsula," writes John Dagenais, "mark the beginning of the end of openly practised Jewish culture and identity in the Iberian peninsula" ("The Crown of Aragon," in *Europe*, ed. Wallace, II, 41–65 (59).

12 For a study of the precise vocabulary of mental disturbance applied to Charles VI by a contemporary chronicler, Michel Pantin, a monk of St-Denis, see Bernard Guenée, "La folie de Charles VI. Études de mots," in Guenée, *Un roi et son historien: Vingt études sur le règne de Charles VI* (Paris: Boccard, 1999), 277–83. "En 1392," writes Guenée, "la prèmiere crise frappe Michel Pintoin de stupeur"; following the crisis of 1395, however, the king's malady comes to be considered "habituelle, *solitus, consuetus*" (281).

Catherine of Siena (1347–1380) and Mary Ward (1585–1645) also lie rather far apart in time but invite comparison as *charismatic* individuals. Whereas Agnes and Christine dedicate themselves to chronicling the lives of great women, in spirited but ancillary ways, Catherine and Mary are, for their contemporary followers, the main event. Charismatic individuals by definition, as brilliantly discussed by Max Weber,[13] live in the present, moment by moment; it is for their entourage or followers to formalize their utterances, publish their works, preserve their memory, routinize their charisma, become Bonaventure to Francis. Such figures court danger and surprise: taming a wild wolf (Francis), laying her head on an executioner's block (Catherine), scratching a greeting on a window for her chief persecutor (Mary Ward, to the Archbishop of Canterbury). Catherine makes herself brilliantly present through her letters that begin, famously, "I, Catherine."[14] Even these, however, rely upon collaborating amanuenses and scribes, and that "I" is a complexly rhetorical construct. Catherine's ambition to achieve a more systematic theological statement, spurred by encounters with Bridget of Sweden's textual team, requires the collaboration of a compositional and publishing team of her own. Mary Ward's followers were keen for their leader to provide the makings of a *vita*. Her times of autobiographical reflection, however, seem largely confined to moments of illness or incapacitation: for she was, as Gemma Simmonds emphasizes, perennially a woman *in motion*. It was again the task of her chief followers to parlay such fragments as she had left into more formal, biographical accounts; to transform life to *life*.[15] This work was carried on in both word and image, since we have both literary biographies (in English, Italian, and French) and *The Painted Life*. Simmonds makes a welcome beginning to the business and pleasure of *reading* these fifty paintings, hitherto under-studied, uncovering secrets that (given the persecution of Mary Ward's movement by Rome) could be *gestured to* in paint, but not laid bare in words. The German texts later imposed upon the paintings were, it seems, commissioned by a Jesuit confessor; the paintings themselves were likely guided by the women who knew Mary Ward best.

Mary Ward championed the teaching of Latin to young women and was dedicated to the schools that, for centuries after her birth, were the chief vestige of her banished movement. But can she be considered an intellectual? Certainly, the central drama of her life and *life* is a protractedly long process of thinking: what form of life should she, and her followers, embrace? This process began early on, in childhood, through a process of retreat *within* a series of Recusant houses; it continued into exile in the Spanish Netherlands as Mary lived first with Poor Clares and then in a house

13 *Economy and Society: An Outline of Interpretive Sociology*, ed. Guenther Roth and Claus Wittich, tr. Ephraim Fischoff *et al.*, 2 vols (Berkeley, CA: University of California Press, 1978), 241 ff.

14 See *I, Catherine: Selected Letters of St Catherine of Siena*, ed. and tr. Kenelm Foster OP and Mary John Ronayne OP (London: Collins, 1980). For the letter in which Catherine tells of "placing my own head on the [executioner's] block," by way of encouraging a condemned man, see 71–5 (73).

15 On this (unreliable) "life/ *life* binome, marking a distinction between biological being and textual accounting," see David Wallace, *Strong Women: Life, Text, and Territory, 1347–1645* (Oxford: Oxford University Press, 2011), xxvii.

of English-speaking female religious of her own devising. This last step of the journey made her very popular with Catholic authorities; the next, in which she left the security of said house for an apostolate of the streets, brought opprobrium. Mary's struggle, I would suggest, is largely driven by the nagging question *how might the poor Catholics of England, deprived of the services of priests and hence sacraments, best be served?*[16] Her answer, finally, takes the form of an Institute for female religious – resisting enclosure, embracing the open road, and based upon the Jesuit constitutions. Her vision is thus above all, as this name suggests, institutional; the great body of writings associated with her, now finally and brilliantly edited in four volumes, speaks above all of the efforts of Mary and her compeers to realize it. In the beginning, the Institute comes to Mary as an ideal in a mental vision. Decades later, the Institute is realized like a multi-national corporation, with correspondence between sisters extending from Bratislava to Naples. Later still, after Mary Ward's death, the Institute lives on as a scattered teaching mission, but also as an ideal of female religious activism, collective and yet singular, yet to be realized.

Mary Ward travelled as a pilgrim from Liège to Rome late in 1621, keen that her Institute should receive official papal backing. She cooled her heels there for five years as her proposal was picked apart by curial committees. Later, her Institute having been abolished in 1629, she was detained in Rome under a regime corresponding, loosely, to modern electronic tagging; eventually she headed back north to regions where the sight of women on the streets was less shocking, to masculine sensibilities, than in Rome. Bridget of Sweden, sometimes a spectacular traveller, was content to lead much of her last, long phase of life in Rome. The curia was keen for Catherine to succeed Bridget at Rome as in-house mystic, but Catherine had other ideas, travelling on a wide circuit among the rural poor. Even so, Catherine's decision to write "my book" ("il mio libro") and to address issues of Latin-related authoritativeness, as Tom Luongo details, suggest a form of intellectuality seeking institutional expression: she could not produce a book alone.

In struggling to situate these women between the terms *leader* and *intellectual* we might, by way of conclusion, settle for a middle term actually applied to Catherine of Siena herself by her Church, namely *doctor*. This title was bestowed on 4 October 1970 by Pope Paul VI, just one week after he similarly recognized Theresa of Ávila. This came belatedly, since the first three Roman *doctores* (Ambrose, Augustine, Jerome) had been announced by Boniface VIII on 20 September 1295. There are now thirty-six Doctors of the Church, with just Thérèse of Lisieux (19 October 1997) and Hildegard of Bingen (7 October 2012) joining the class of 1970. But the term *doctor* has some merit, I would suggest, in looking both to *teacher* and *intellectual*, our twin organizational terms. A *doctor* should possess some dossier of speculative and original writings, comparable in part to those of *doctores* who inhabit universities (although Thérèse of Lisieux's page count is rather low). But she should also be a *doctor* in the original, Latinate sense as *one who leads*. Catherine of Siena was canonized in 1461, but Mary Ward's name remained Tiberian mud until 1909. One hundred years after this, however, she was pronounced "Venerable" by Benedict

16 See further Wallace, *Strong Women*, 156–70.

XVI.[17] She may have to wait a while longer to achieve official *doctor* status, but there is no doubt that she, like the three other women considered in Part II, was indeed a leader and also, in her own fashion, both mystical and practical, an intellectual.

17 Young seminarian–schoolboy Ratzinger was for a while taken care of, following the requisitioning of his seminary at Trauenstein as a military hospital in 1939, by the Mary Ward sisters at Sparz, in the hills above Trauenstein.

4

# AGNES OF HARCOURT AS INTELLECTUAL: NEW EVIDENCE FOR THE COMPOSITION AND CIRCULATION OF THE *VIE D'ISABELLE DE FRANCE*

SEAN L. FIELD

Agnes of Harcourt (c. 1240–c. 1291) served for some seventeen years as the abbess of Longchamp, the female Franciscan community founded just west of Paris in 1260. Although a thorough study of her activities as abbess remains to be undertaken, the general outlines of her career seem fairly clear.[1] Her parents, Jean I of Harcourt (d. 1288) and Alix of Beaumont (d. 1275), probably married around 1240. Agnes was likely one of their first children, if not their very first. By the 1250s, Agnes seems to have been part of the entourage of Isabelle of France (1225–1270), the sister of King Louis IX. Isabelle, for her part, was living a startlingly unusual life as a celibate princess at the Capetian court, but by 1254 she was working to found the first female Franciscan community in the Île-de-France.[2] A first version of the community's rule was approved by Alexander IV in 1259, and the initial group of nuns, including Agnes of Harcourt, took the veil in June 1260.[3] In 1263 Urban IV approved a revised version

1 The biographical sketch here is largely drawn from Sean L. Field, "The Princess, the Abbess, and the Friars: Isabelle of France and the Course of Thirteenth-Century Religious History" (Ph.D. diss., Northwestern University, 2002), ch. 7. Generally on Agnes's family background see Gilles-André de la Roque, *Histoire généalogique de la maison de Harcourt*, 4 vols. (Paris: Carmois, 1662); Anselm, *Histoire généalogique et chronologique de la maison royale de France*, 3rd ed., vol. 5 (Paris: Libraires associez, 1730), 114–61, esp. 127–30; Georges Martin, *Histoire et généalogie de la maison de Harcourt* (La Ricamarie: Private Printing, 1974), and (more reliably) Léopold Delisle, *Histoire du château et des sires Saint-Sauveur-le-Vicomte* (Paris and Caen: Valognes, 1867). There is some doubt about how many times Jean I of Harcourt married, and thus whether all the siblings of Agnes's generation had the same mother.

2 For the sources on Isabelle's life, see Jacques Dalarun, Sean L. Field, Jean-Baptiste Lebigue, and Anne-Françoise Leurquin-Labie, *Isabelle de France, sœur de saint Louis: Une princesse mineure* (Paris: Éditions franciscaines, 2014), hereafter cited as *Princesse mineure*. The most useful studies of her career include William Chester Jordan, "Isabelle of France and Religious Devotion at the Court of Louis IX," in *Capetian Women*, ed. Kathleen Nolan (New York: Palgrave, 2003), 209–23; Field, *Isabelle of France: Capetian Sanctity and Franciscan Identity in the Thirteenth Century* (Notre Dame, IN: University of Notre Dame Press, 2006); and Anne-Hélène Allirot, *Filles de roy de France: Princesses royales, mémoire de saint Louis et conscience dynastique (de 1270 à la fin du XIVe siècle)* (Turnhout: Brepols, 2010), ch. 8.

3 On Longchamp see Gaston Duchesne, *Histoire de l'abbaye royale de Longchamp (1255–1789)*, 2nd ed. (Paris: Champion, 1906); Gertrud Młynarczyk, *Ein Franziskanerinnenkloster im 15. Jahrhundert: Edition und Analyse von Besitzinventaren aus der Abtei Longchamp* (Bonn: Ludwig

of Longchamp's rule, which created the Order of *Sorores minores inclusae*, a distinct branch of the Franciscan family.[4] Soon after, Agnes of Harcourt became the community's abbess for a first term that spanned approximately the years 1264 to 1275, and then a second from 1281 to 1287.

Agnes's status as daughter of an important noble family evidently bolstered her position at Longchamp. At least two other women from the Harcourt family in fact became nuns there as well: Agnes's aunt Jeanne (sister of Jean I of Harcourt) entered along with Agnes in 1260 and made over lands and goods to the community upon her profession,[5] while Agnes's younger sister, also named Jeanne (d. 1315), joined the community around 1277 and eventually served as abbess herself from 1294 to 1299. Jean I of Harcourt gave lands and rents to the abbey, including in 1281 a donation for the younger Jeanne.[6] The *famille d'Harcourt* was a pillar of support for Longchamp in its formative years.

Moreover, these family networks tied Agnes of Harcourt to the very heart of power in Capetian France. In these decades Agnes's father and her oldest brother, Jean II (d. 1302) of Harcourt, Marshal of France, went on crusades with Louis IX and with Philip III. Jean II also accompanied Charles of Valois on his Italian adventure of 1301–1303, while his brother Guillaume (d. c. 1327) was likewise a leading military figure under the later Capetians. Moreover, three younger brothers were eminent churchmen: Raoul (d. 1307) held offices including archdeacon of Coutances and Rouen, and founded the College d'Harcourt; Robert (d. 1315) was bishop of Coutances (d. 1315); Guy (d. 1336) was bishop of Lisieux and founder of the College of Lisieux. These men often played important parts in the political and ecclesiastical affairs of the realm under Philip IV.[7]

---

Röhrscheid Verlag, 1987); Field, "The Abbesses of Longchamp up to the Black Death," *Archivum franciscanum historicum* 96 (2003): 237–44; Gabrielle Joudiou, *Isabelle de France et l'abbaye de Longchamp* (Paris: Éditions franciscaines, 2006); Field, "The Abbesses of Longchamp in the Sixteenth Century," *Archivum franciscanum historicum* 100 (2007): 553–59; Anne-Hélène Allirot, "Longchamp and Lourcine: The Role of Female Abbeys in the Construction of Capetian Memory (Late Thirteenth Century to Mid-Fourteenth Century)," in *Memory and Commemoration in Medieval Culture*, ed. Elma Brenner, Meredith Cohen, and Mary Franklin-Brown (Farnham, UK: Ashgate, 2013), 243–60; Fabien Guilloux, "*La Regle et la Vie des Sereurs meneurs enclose*: Un traduction en langue romane de la règle d'Isabelle de France (ca. 1315–1325)," *Archivum franciscanum historicum* 106 (2013): 5–39; and Linda Barney Burke, "'She is the Second St. Clare': The Exemplum of Jehanne de Neuville, Abbess of Longchamp, in a Fourteenth-Century Defense of Women by Jehan Le Fèvre," *Franciscan Studies* 71 (2013): 325–60.

4 Sean L. Field, *The Rules of Isabelle of France: An English Translation with Introductory Study* (additional documents trans. Larry F. Field) (St. Bonaventure, NY: Franciscan Institute Publications, 2014). Aleksander Horowski, "Una raccolta giuridica dei Frati minori nel codice ottoboniano latino 15," *Collectanea Franciscana* 85 (2015): 427–86, identifies a "new" manuscript copy of the Rule of 1263, as well as copies of two other papal bulls destined for Longchamp.

5 Paris, Archives nationales (hereafter "AN") L 1020, no. 5C.

6 AN K 35, no. 4².

7 For example, Robert of Harcourt is mentioned repeatedly in Joseph R. Strayer, *The Reign of Philip the Fair* (Princeton: Princeton University Press, 1980), 86–88, 94–97, in his discussion of "The King and his Councilors"; more broadly, see H. L. Bouquet, *L'Ancien Collège d'Harcourt et le Lycée Saint Louis* (Paris: Delalain, 1891).

The Harcourt were thus literally a "leading" family of France, and Agnes was very much a part of that leading status. The rich and still under-used archives of Longchamp demonstrate Agnes's active leadership of her community: she bought land, negotiated with other monastic houses, secured royal privileges, filed legal claims, left numerous documents (some still bearing her seal), and kept meticulous records.[8] After the founder Isabelle of France, Agnes of Harcourt was clearly the most important figure in the community's early history, providing stability as abbess for seventeen of Longchamp's first twenty-seven years and enjoying the honor of being the first woman to be re-elected to that office.

In terms both of monastic standing and family status, Agnes of Harcourt can certainly be considered a leader in her world. But was she an "intellectual"? Obviously this judgement must be subjective. Certainly Agnes was an author. She composed a *Letter on Louis IX and Longchamp* as a contribution to Louis IX's canonization process in 1282, and she wrote her much more substantial *Vie d'Isabelle de France* around 1283.[9] But of course not all authors merit the title "intellectual." One might suggest that to be reasonably considered an intellectual, an author should show evidence of self-conscious engagement in a sustained creative process reflecting critical thought.

Scholars and commentators before the twenty-first century did not place Agnes of Harcourt in this kind of intellectual framework. Instead they generally saw her (to the extent she was seen at all) as a simple woman whose vernacular style was refreshingly free of artifice or scholastic pretension. For example, Paulin Paris in the mid-nineteenth century wrote glowingly that the *Vie d'Isabelle* was written "avec naturel et simplicité" (with a natural quality and with simplicity), causing him to gush that "nous croyons y respirer un parfum de candeur et de sincérité" (we feel as though here we are breathing in a scent of candor and sincerity).[10] Although the assessment was meant to be complimentary, it obviously assumed a lack of intellectual sophistication. Scholars today would be less likely to offer such a mix of praise and condescension in assessing the writings of a medieval woman. And yet because few scholars have devoted to Agnes's works the kind of close study accorded those of better-known writers such as Marie

8 The core of the Longchamp archives is held as AN L 1020–29, with carton L 1020 containing the largest number of documents stemming from Agnes's terms as abbess. Many other early documents and privileges, however, are scattered elsewhere in the Archives nationales.

9 Sean L. Field, *The Writings of Agnes of Harcourt: The Life of Isabelle of France and the Letter on Louis IX and Longchamp* (Notre Dame, IN: University of Notre Dame Press, 2003) (hereafter cited as *Writings of AH*); Anne-Hélène Allirot, "Isabelle de France, sœur de saint Louis: La vierge savante. Étude de la *Vie d'Isabelle de France* écrite par Agnès d'Harcourt," *Médiévales* 48 (2005): 55–98; Anne-Françoise Leurquin-Labie's translation in *Princesse mineure* offers the most up-to-date notes and interpretations. Jean-François Kosta-Théfaine's 2012 translation into modern French for Éditions du Cerf is less useful for scholarly purposes.

10 Paulin Paris, "Agnès d'Harcourt, abbesse de Longchamp," *Histoire littéraire de la France* 20 (1842): 98–103. A similar judgement was rendered by Henri Carton, *Histoire des femmes écrivains de la France. Illustré de six portraits* (Paris: A. Dupret, 1886), 31, who praised Agnes's control of French while describing the *Vie d'Isabelle* as "écrit avec un charme et une naïveté." A brief but quite credible history of "Longchamps" printed in *The Ladies' Cabinet of Music, Fashion, and Romance*, vol. 3 (London: G. Henderson, 1840), 328–34, at 330, praised Agnes for the "naïveté of the style and the honest simplicity of the feelings expressed."

de France or Christine de Pizan, we are still left without a detailed understanding of Agnes's critical and creative process as an author.

This chapter contends that Agnes of Harcourt can well be considered an early Parisian intellectual. Five new findings shed fresh light on her engagement with other texts, on aspects of her writing process, and on her long-term legacy. The credit for these recent advances belongs to a number of different scholars working across several fields. The goal of the present essay is to bring them together in order to point out their larger implications for the composition and circulation of the *Vie d'Isabelle de France,* and in turn for our understanding of Agnes of Harcourt as an intellectual.

The first of these five findings is Martine Pagan's demonstration that the earliest French translation of Thomas of Celano's Latin *Legenda* of Clare of Assisi was made at Longchamp between approximately 1275 and 1280.[11] Clare had died in 1253 and was quickly canonized in 1255. Celano wrote his *Legenda* in several stages over the next few years, completing it around the time Longchamp was founded and not long before the Order of St. Clare and the Order of *Sorores minores* were created in 1263.[12] The first translation of his *Legenda* into French (preserved in Paris, Bibliothèque nationale de France [hereafter BnF] ms. fr. 2096 and Archives nationales [hereafter AN] LL 1601) could have been done by a friar associated with Longchamp, but Pagan also suggests the intriguing possibility that Agnes herself could have been directly involved as translator, as part of a team of translators, or as commissioner of the translation. More concretely, and more importantly for the present article, Pagan (collaborating with Jacques Dalarun and myself) was able to show that Agnes of Harcourt definitely drew on this newly translated French *Vie de Claire* when composing her *Vie d'Isabelle* just a few years later.[13] Only in a few small places did Agnes literally reuse passages from the *Vie de Claire*, yet, as Pagan noticed (and I concur), "an inflexion, a phrasing, a tonality" seem to link the two texts.[14]

11 Martine Pagan, "Les légendes françaises de Claire d'Assise (XIII^e^–XVI^e^ siècle): I. Inventaire et classement des manuscrits," *Études franciscaines*, n.s. 7, no. 1 (2014): 5–35; Pagan, "Les légendes françaises de Claire d'Assise (XIII^e^–XVI^e^ siècle): II. Édition du plus ancien manuscrit de la version longue (BnF, fr. 2096)," *Études franciscaines*, n.s. 7, no. 2 (2014): 221–72. A third installment of Pagan's study should be noted, although it does not bear directly on Agnes or Longchamp: "Les légendes françaises de Claire d'Assise (XIII^e^–XVI^e^ siècle): III. Édition et commentaire du manuscrit 663 de la Bibliothèque de l'Institut de France," *Études franciscaines*, n.s. 8, no. 1 (2015): 5–25. Pagan's forthcoming book, provisionally titled *Laisser parler les manuscrits: Variations sur la Vie française de Claire d'Assise*, promises to add substantially to what we know about both the *Vie de Claire* and the *Vie d'Isabelle.*

12 For a convincing demonstration of Celano's authorship (which had not always been previously accepted), see Marco Guida, *Una leggenda in cerca d'autore: la Vita di santa Chiara d'Assisi. Studio delle fonti e sinossi intertestuale,* preface by Jacques Dalarun (Brussels: Société des Bollandistes, 2010).

13 I consider implications of Martine Pagan's findings more closely in "Revisiting the Links between the Women's Religious Movement and the Origins of a Female-Authored Vernacular Religious Literature in France," in *Between Orders and Heresy: Religious Movements in the Middle Ages Revisited, Revised, and Reimagined,* ed. Jennifer K. Deane and Anne E. Lester (Toronto: University of Toronto Press, forthcoming). Appendix A to that essay prints some of the textual parallels between Celano, the French *Vie de sainte Claire*, and the *Vie d'Isabelle de France.*

14 Pagan, "Les légendes françaises II," 222.

Suddenly Agnes's authorial process appears in an entirely new light. Rather than an author working from a position of naive "simplicity" and "naturalness," Agnes was spurred on by intellectual engagement with a fresh text at the cutting edge of her creative project. As Agnes of Harcourt began to construct the life of her monastery's royal founder, she could draw ideas and concepts from the newly available *Vie* of the recently canonized Clare, and redeploy them for her own purposes.[15] Indeed, it is not impossible to imagine (as Pagan has again suggested) that the translation of the *Vie de Claire* could have been undertaken at Longchamp at least in part as a preparatory step toward an envisioned life of Isabelle.

This initial re-evaluation of Agnes's writing process leads to our second point, which stems from an exchange of ideas with Jacques Dalarun and Anne-Françoise Leurquin-Labie during the preparation of new modern French translations of the *Letter on Louis IX and Longchamp* and the *Vie d'Isabelle*:[16] While Agnes of Harcourt absolutely deserves the title of "author" of the texts associated with her name, they were evidently produced in collaboration with other nuns at Longchamp. Taking the collaborative nature of Agnes's authorship seriously helps to bring into focus the intellectual engagement involved in her creative process.[17]

The clearest example of this collaboration is found in the *Letter on Louis IX and Longchamp*, composed in December 1282 and detailing Louis's support for the abbey.[18] This *Letter* is in fact issued in the name of "Agnes of Harcourt, humble abbess of the Enclosed Sisters Minor of the Abbey of the Humility of our Lady, and the whole convent of this same place." Following this greeting, with its explicit statement of group responsibility, the first anecdote begins with a "We" (*nous*) and uses the first-person plural to relate the nuns' recollection of how the royal family laid the first stones

15 Thus Allirot, "La vierge savante," 59, was quite right (more than anyone could have known at the time) to suggest in 2005 that for Agnes "les textes concernant sainte Claire d'Assise et sainte Élisabeth de Hongrie ont pu lui fournir un modèle." Until recently I was reluctant to see Clare's *Legenda* as a model for the *Vie d'Isabelle*. It is still important to note that Isabelle's own goals during her lifetime were not identical to Clare's, and to remember that Longchamp belonged to the Order of *Sorores minores*, not the Order of St. Clare (it was thus not a house of "Clarisses" or "Poor Clares.") But it now seems clear that Allirot was quite correct to look for parallels between Clare's *Legenda* and Isabelle's *Vie*.

16 *Princesse mineure*, 267–313.

17 Such creative and authorial collaborations between nuns were not unusual, and could take numerous forms. For instance, one sister might act as scribe for another, or multiple sisters might help compile an ongoing chronicle or visionary text, or sisters could revise a work commenced by another sister. The (largely German and Dominican) Sister-books might be the best example of several of these modes of authorial cooperation. For an overview see John Van Engen, "Communal Life: The Sister-books," in *Medieval Holy Women in the Christian Tradition, c. 1100–c. 1500*, ed. A. J. Minnis and Rosalynn Voaden (Turnhout: Brepols, 2010), 105–31. See also Alison I. Beach, *Women as Scribes: Book Production and Monastic Reform in Twelfth-Century Bavaria* (Cambridge: Cambridge University Press, 2004); the rich collections of essays in *Nuns' Literacies in Medieval Europe: The Hull Dialogue*, ed. V. Blanton, V. O'Mara, and P. Stoop (Turnhout: Brepols, 2013), *The Kansas City Dialogue* (2015), *The Antwerp Dialogue* (2017); and, for a recent discussion of the excellent example of the nuns of Helfta, see Barbara Newman, "Annihilation and Authorship: Three Women Mystics of the 1290s," *Speculum* 91 (2016): 591–630, esp. 595.

18 *Writings of AH*, 46–49; *Princesse mineure*, 267–71.

of Longchamp. Then, as though giving a witness list, the "we" is expanded, to "I (*je*) sister Agnes of Harcourt, I sister Isabelle of Reims, I Sister Angre, I sister Julienne, I sister Mahaut of Gondarville, and many other sisters," who heard these things from Queen Marguerite of Provence, wife of the late King Louis IX. Although this is the only place in the *Letter* where such witnesses appear in the first person, the authorial voice continues to be expressed as *nous* throughout the text, concluding that "we" have affixed our seals to the present letter. The original document in fact carried both the abbey's corporate seal and also (almost certainly) Agnes of Harcourt's seal as abbess.[19] When I first published this text in 2003 I wanted to emphasize Agnes's legitimate status as author, and so I simply treated the *Letter* as her work. That treatment was not entirely misleading; Agnes of Harcourt does indeed stand out in the salutation of the letter, as first in the list of witnesses, and again with the affixing of her personal seal. Yet it now seems more useful to envision Agnes as the "lead author" in the team of senior sisters that put together the *Letter*.

The *Vie d'Isabelle* presents a variation on this theme. Throughout most of this longer work one encounters a very firm and singular first person (I/*je*) authorial presence. Although other nuns are sometimes referred to as witnesses, and various other figures are credited as the source of stories, in the body of the *Vie*, the "*je*" is always, without exception, reserved for Agnes of Harcourt. The first instances (in pars. 8 and 10) again put Agnes forward as a witness: "And I, Sister Agnes of Harcourt, heard these things [...]."[20] Similarly, when Agnes stands as the first in a longer list of witnesses, in this text (unlike in the *Letter*) the others are all referred to in the third person. For instance, in authenticating events recorded in par. 11, the text reads "And I, Sister Agnes of Harcourt, heard this from the mouth of Monseigneur the holy king Louis, who recounted it to us, and Mahaut of Gondarville, who was in [Isabelle's] service, heard the same thing from the mouth of Madame Helen of Buisemont, who was with Madame from her childhood."[21] Although there is a collective "*nous*" embedded in the middle of the clause, Agnes accords only herself the singular first-person authorial voice. Eventually (for example, in par. 27) Agnes's role expands beyond witnessing to recalling: "And sometimes I saw that for some things that displeased her she would strongly reprimand some people before me, Sister Agnes of Harcourt."[22] On this level, Agnes indeed presents a very strong and distinct authorial voice.

After recounting Isabelle's life, the text then appends forty miracles, and the reservation of the first-person "*je*" for Agnes of Harcourt carries through to the miracles that occurred during Isabelle's life and shortly after her death. In addition to Agnes, many sisters and Franciscans are again listed as witnesses to these early miracles, but always in the third person. And yet, the last time Agnes of Harcourt is accorded first-person status is in miracle 12. In fact, at miracle 20, Agnes appears at the head of a list of three sisters who are said to remember a miracle, but now suddenly she is referred to in the third person: "Sister Agnes of Harcourt, Sister Agnes

19 For a description of the now-lost original document and its seals, see *Writings of AH*, 34 n. 65.

20 *Writings of AH*, 56–57; *Princesse mineure*, 278–80.

21 *Writings of AH*, 58–59; *Princesse mineure*, 281.

22 *Writings of AH*, 68–69; *Princesse mineure*, 292.

of Anery, Sister Marguerite of Guise, and several other sisters remember this miracle well."[23] After this point, no further first person singular references occur, and increasingly the voice is a plural "*nous*/we."

Thus, it seems likely that there was a first phase of composition in which miracles attributed to Isabelle during her life and around her death were recorded. Agnes of Harcourt retained her strong first-person presence throughout that phase. But there was apparently a process of adding on to the original list of miracles (perhaps as they occurred, but more likely as they were remembered or solicited), and the later phases of this process may have been carried out more as a project of group remembrance and less as Agnes's individual creation. In light of this reconstruction, we can picture Agnes not only as an intellectual herself, but also as the leader of a sustained process by which her community gathered and shaped its collective memories.

The third exciting discovery bearing on Agnes of Harcourt's intellectual engagement is the Hungarian scholar Levente Seláf's 2009 demonstration that the Prologue to the *Vie d'Isabelle* was drawn directly from the earliest French prose life of Elizabeth of Hungary.[24] Elizabeth died in 1231 and was canonized in 1235, making her one of the two main models of papally approved thirteenth-century female sanctity, along with Clare of Assisi. One of the earliest hagiographic writings stemming from Elizabeth's canonization process recorded four of her companions' memories; those recollections were given an introduction and conclusion and compiled into a text known as the *Libellus de dictis quatuor ancillarum*.[25] Of the numerous lives of Elizabeth subsequently written in France, generally based directly or indirectly on the *Libellus*, the earliest French *Vie* was composed between 1243 and 1264. Quite surprisingly, it has not yet appeared in print, though Seláf's edition is nearing completion. The incipit for the main body of this French prose text (after a separate prefatory section) reads: *Madame sainte Elizabeth fut estraite de reaul lignie quar ele fut fille au roi Andrieu de Honrie* (Madame St. Elizabeth came from a royal lineage, because she was the daughter of King Andrew

23 *Writings of AH*, 80–81; *Princesse mineure*, 304.

24 Levente Seláf, "Párhuzamos Életrajzok: Szent Erzsébet és Isabelle de France Legendái," in *Árpád-házi Szent Erzsébet kultusza a 13–16. Században* (Budapest: Magyarok Nagyasszonya Ferences Rendtartomány, 2009), 141–50 (with a French résumé). I thank the author for kindly corresponding with me in 2009, for further updating me in 2015 on the status of his forthcoming critical edition, and for sending me a pre-publication copy of his article "Le Modèle absolu de la princesse charitable: La première légende vernaculaire de sainte Élisabeth de Hongrie et sa réception," *Le Moyen Âge* 124 (2018): 371–96. I develop the implications of his findings further in "Revisiting the Links between the Women's Religious Movement and the Origins of a Female-Authored Vernacular Religious Literature in France," where Appendix B offers textual examples of Agnes's dependence, building on the already convincing demonstration by Seláf.

25 Albert Huyskens, *Der sog. Libellus de dictis quatuor ancillarum s. Elisabeth confectus* (Kempten und München: Verlag der Jos. Kösel'schen Buchhandlung, 1911). For a useful survey of writings on Elizabeth, see Ottó Gecser, "Lives of St. Elizabeth: Their Rewriting and Diffusion in the Thirteenth Century," *Analecta Bollandiana* 129 (2009): 49–107, at 52–55. On Elizabeth's cult see Kenneth Baxter Wolf, *The Life and Afterlife of St. Elizabeth of Hungary: Testimony from Her Canonization Hearings* (Oxford: Oxford University Press, 2011), and Gecser, *The Feast and the Pulpit: Preachers, Sermons, and the Cult of St. Elizabeth of Hungary, 1235–ca. 1500* (Spoleto: Fondazione Centro Italiano di Studi sull'alto medioevo, 2012).

of Hungary).[26] A comparison with the corresponding opening of Agnes of Harcourt's *Vie d'Isabelle* is enough to reveal its dependence: *Nostre saincte mere et dame madame Ysabeau fut estraicte de royal ligniee et fu fille du tres noble roy Loys de France*. This direct textual dependence continues through paragraph four of Agnes's *Vie*. Perhaps because Seláf announced this discovery in a Hungarian-language publication, it has not yet garnered a great deal of attention. But, much as with Agnes's use of the first French version of Thomas of Celano's *Legenda* of Clare of Assisi, this new information demonstrates that the *Vie d'Isabelle* was constructed with models at hand that included the most recent French hagiographic texts, focused on the most famous female saints of the century. Agnes, like any intellectual, engaged with exciting new material as she went about her own creative process.

Moreover, a seventeenth-century description of Agnes of Harcourt's original manuscript adds useful information here.[27] The original copy was a roll, treasured at Longchamp until the eighteenth century. When a would-be biographer of Isabelle of France, Pierre Perrier, examined this roll in 1699, he described it as made up of eight sheets of parchment sewn together. The first sheet, which contained the prefatory material that had been adapted from the *Vie d'Elisabeth*, was written in a different hand. Although one could imagine a number of possible hypotheses that might accord with Perrier's description, Jacques Dalarun, Anne-Françoise Leurquin-Labie, and I have argued that the prefatory material was actually written last, and added on to the roll by Agnes and/or her collaborators, after the bulk of the life and miracles had already been recorded.[28] If this argument is correct, then it would seem that once the *Vie d'Isabelle* was written, Agnes and/or her sisters at Longchamp decided that a polished, accepted introduction would help to lend literary legitimacy to their new life. This finding in turn demonstrates that the *Vie d'Isabelle* resulted from a sustained process not only of creation and collaboration but rethinking and revision.

Just as Agnes of Harcourt collaborated with those around her at Longchamp, but also engaged with texts created by authors she had never actually met herself (Thomas of Celano, the anonymous author of the French prose *Vie d'Elisabeth*), so too her own writings went on to impact other intellectual milieus remote in time and space. Certainly at Longchamp itself Agnes's writings continued to underpin virtually every new presentation of the abbey's founder for the next 500 years. New textual representations of Isabelle of France's career and cult began to emerge in the later fifteenth century, with a new epitaph hung over her tomb, a new *Vie* composed at Longchamp around 1519, texts attached to the successful petition for papal recogni-

26 See Anne-Françoise Leurquin and Marie-Laure Savoye, notice for "Vie de sainte Elisabeth de Hongrie, anonyme," in the database Jonas-IRHT/CNRS, at http://jonas.irht.cnrs.fr/oeuvre/2150. While awaiting Seláf's critical edition of the text, interested scholars can access one of the earliest (though incomplete) manuscripts of the text, BnF ms. fr. 13496, fols. 155rb–172vb, through the BnF's Gallica portal. Excerpts translated into modern French can also be found in André Vauchez and Armelle Le Huërou, eds., *Élisabeth de Hongrie: Princesse, servant, sainte. Vies et documents* (Paris: Éditions franciscaines, 2017), 391–96.

27 The description is from AN L 1029, no. 37. See Sean L. Field, "Pierre Perrier's 1699 *Vie de sainte Isabelle de France*: Precious Evidence from an Unpublished Preface," *Franciscan Studies* 73 (2015): 215–47.

28 *Princesse mineure*, 276 n. 1.

tion of her cult in 1521,[29] a still unpublished life copied in 1569,[30] and into the first printed biographies produced in the seventeenth century.[31] Even as multiple layers of new interpretations (and records of new miracles) made their appearance, recent studies have demonstrated that all of these texts can accurately be described as developments of and commentaries on Agnes's original *Letter* and *Vie*.

At Longchamp, the original copy of the *Letter on Louis IX and Longchamp* was preserved into the eighteenth century, and the text was also copied into one of the community's most important manuscripts (BnF ms. fr. 11662) in the fifteenth century.[32] Likewise, the original of the *Vie d'Isabelle* (the roll discussed above) could be consulted at Longchamp up to the Revolutionary era,[33] and at least one other copy was held at the abbey, mentioned in inventories from 1325 through the fifteenth century.[34]

But the impact of Agnes's writings was felt outside Longchamp as well. It has long been known (though often forgotten), that a copy was recorded in the first inventory of the royal library in 1373.[35] Since this copy is no longer thought to be extant,

29 For editions of these texts, see Sean L. Field, "Imagining Isabelle: Isabelle of France's Fifteenth-Century Epitaph at Longchamp," *Franciscan Studies* 66 (2007): 371–403; Field, "A New Life of Isabelle of France from the Early Sixteenth Century," *Studies in Medieval and Renaissance History*, 3rd series, 8 (2011): 27–80; Field, "Paris to Rome and Back Again: The Nuns of Longchamp and Leo X's 1521 Bull *Piis omnium*," *Studies in Medieval and Renaissance History*, 3rd series, 11 (2014): 155–223.

30 BnF ms. nouv. acq. fr. 10871.

31 Sebastian Roulliard [sic], *La saincte mère, ou vie de M. saincte Isabel de France, sœur unique du roy s. Louys, fondatrice de l'abbaye de Long-champ* (Paris: Taupinart, 1619); Aubertus Mireaus, *Isabellae sanctae: Elisabetha Ioannis Bapt. mater, Elisabetha Andr. Regis Hung. filia, Isabella regina Portugallix, Isabella, S. Lud. Galliae regis soror* (Brussels: Ioannem Pepermanum, 1622); *L'abrégé de la vie et miracle fait à l'abbaye de Long-champ sur le tombeau de la bienheureuse Isabel de France, fille du roy Louys VIII & soeur du bon roy S. Louys* (Longchamp, 1637); Nicolas Caussin, *La vie de Ste Isabelle, sœur du roy saint Louis et fondatrice du monastère royal de Long-champ, Qui a donné un parfait example de la vie neutre des personnes non mariées ny religieuses* (Paris: Sonnius, Bechet, Bray, 1644). On this era see Thomas Worcester, "Neither Married nor Cloistered: Blessed Isabelle in Catholic Reformation France," *Sixteenth Century Journal* 30 (1999): 457–72. The history of Longchamp written by the nuns in this period, preserved as AN LL 1604, remains unedited, but Fabien Guilloux and I have begun work on an edition.

32 *Writings of AH*, 35. This manuscript can currently be consulted through Gallica.

33 Described as late as 1741 in the *Acta sanctorum* by the Jesuit Étienne Souciet. See *Writings of AH*, 25 n. 42.

34 The first inventory in which it is mentioned (1325) is AN L 1027, no. 5: "Item .i. autre livre ou est la rieule, est en francois et en Latin, et la vie madame." This manuscript is now lost, but it contained Latin and French copies of the abbey's rule and a "Vie d'Isabelle." It was evidently a pair with AN LL 1601, which is still extant and contains French and Latin copies of Longchamp's rule and one of the two early copies of the *Vie de Claire* made at Longchamp. On this manuscript, see François Berriot, "Les manuscrits de l'abbaye de Longchamp aux Archives de France et la Vie de sainte Claire inédite (début XIVe s.)," *Archivum franciscanum historicum* 79 (1986): 329–58; and now the important advances in Fabien Guilloux, "*La Regle et la Vie des Sereurs meneurs enclose*." Guilloux dated the original parts of the manuscript to 1305–25, but Martine Pagan's re-dating of AN LL 1601 to the 1280s implies a re-dating of this lost "twin" to the same period as well.

35 Léopold Delisle, *Le cabinet des manuscrits de la bibliothèque nationale*, vol. 3 (reprint, New York, 1973), 158. It is of course possible that the "Vie suer Ysabeau de Longchamp, qui fu suer S.

it is impossible to say whether it was presented to the royal court on the nuns' initiative, commissioned by someone at court, or simply left to the king as a bequest by some noble book-owner. But in any case, Agnes's work was known, or at least could be found, at the very center of political power in France by the reign of Charles V.

And now new evidence (our fourth point) reveals that the *Vie d'Isabelle* was circulating even more widely in the later Middle Ages. The relevant discovery here is Marie-Françoise Damongeot-Bourdat's demonstration that Marie of Brittany (1424–77), abbess of Fontevraud, left a copy of "La *Vie de madame Ysabeau de France*" at the time of her death.[36] Marie of Brittany was the oldest daughter of Richard of Brittany, Count of Étampes, and his wife Marguerite of Orléans, and thus came from the highest French nobility (the poet Charles of Orléans was her uncle; Duke François II of Brittany was her brother). This family in fact developed deep ties to Longchamp in the fifteenth century. Marguerite of Orléans may have spent time there after her husband's death in 1438, and she is securely recorded as visiting the abbey as early as 1445.[37] In fact, a surviving act of 1450 demonstrates that Marguerite of Orléans envisioned her daughter Marie joining the community at Longchamp;[38] Longchamp's seventeenth-century chronicle even claimed that Marie had lived there for six years, while being groomed to become abbess of Fontevraud.[39] But after Marie entered Fontevraud in 1457, it was her younger sister Madeleine who took the veil at Longchamp in November 1461. Marguerite of Orléans was present for Madeleine's profession, and insisted on opening Isabelle of France's tomb, an event which led to the recording of several dramatic miracles.[40] Thus Marie of Brittany's family was in close and sustained contact with Longchamp during these years, and exhibited a notable veneration for Isabelle of France. These factors explain how a copy of Agnes of Harcourt's *Vie d'Isabelle* would have come into Marie of Brittany's possession, as a gift from her mother or sister, as a volume she herself commissioned, or as a presentation from Longchamp to Fontevraud.[41]

---

Loys, et ses miracles" recorded there was an otherwise unknown early reworking of Agnes's original text. But in the absence of any evidence to support that interpretation, it seems most likely that this "Vie" was simply a copy of Agnes of Harcourt's work.

36 Marie-Françoise Damongeot-Bourdat, "Le Coffre aux livres de Marie de Bretagne (1424–1477), abbesse de Fontevraud," in *Livres et lectures de femmes en Europe entre Moyen Âge et Renaissance*, ed. Anne-Marie Legaré (Turnhout: Brepols, 2007), 81–99, at 94, citing Archives départementales de Maine-et-Loire, 101 H 5 15 no. 7, fol. 17r : "Item la Vie de madame Ysabeau de France, en papier, couvert d'ung parchemin dur."

37 Młynarczyk, *Ein Franziskanerinnenkloster im 15. Jahrhundert*, 257, n. 22, citing AN LL 1602, fol. 71. For papal permission allowing Marguerite of Orléans to visit Longchamp in 1448, a donation of relics, and other associations with the abbey, see ibid., 49 n. 62, 98, and 195. Marguerite of Orléans in fact died at La Guiche, a sister house following the Rule of the *Sorores minores*, in 1466.

38 Damongeot-Bourdat, "Le Coffre aux livres de Marie de Bretagne," 88, citing AD Maine-et-Loire, 11 H 15 n° 5.

39 AN LL 1604, fols. 18v–19r.

40 Field, "A New Life," 72–73. Madeleine of Brittany's career at Longchamp was unfortunately cut short by her death in March 1462.

41 There is no evidence for this volume's fate after Marie of Brittany's death. As Damongeot-Bourdat remarks ("Le Coffre aux livres de Marie de Bretagne," 89) for Marie's books generally, it would be nice to imagine it coming into the hands of Anne of Brittany (daughter of François

Damongeot-Bourdat's identification has great importance, because it suggests the kind of channels by which the *Vie d'Isabelle* could become more widely known outside Paris. As long as scholarship had given the impression that Agnes's work never left Longchamp, it was easy to assume that the *Vie d'Isabelle* simply had no circulation outside that abbey's walls. But once it is realized that copies were entering other collections in the fourteenth and fifteenth centuries, there is no particular reason to think that some additional circulation did not occur. Indeed, it seems reasonable to speculate that the *Vie d'Isabelle* might have been known at other houses of *Sorores minores* in France and England, particularly those founded by women from or close to the French royal family. For instance, Saint-Marcel (or Lourcines) was founded in the Parisian *faubourgs* with the help of Isabelle of France's sister-in-law Marguerite of Provence, who was herself one of Agnes of Harcourt's main sources of information in writing Isabelle's *Vie*.[42] Would not a copy of the work have been likely to have made its way to Saint-Marcel, where Marguerite retired before her death in 1295? Moreover, nuns and former abbesses from Longchamp are known to have traveled to help found a number of new sister houses of *Sorores minores* on both sides of the English Channel,[43] and books are known to have passed back and forth through these networks.[44] One might go so far as to say that it would be surprising if copies of Agnes's *Vie d'Isabelle* had *not* circulated through these channels.

Our fifth and final point concerns new evidence for a veritable scholarly scramble to gain access to Agnes's writings in the seventeenth century. Until the twenty-first century no manuscripts of the *Vie d'Isabelle* were known to be extant, and the French text could only be consulted in the 1668 edition by Charles Du Cange.[45] Du Cange

II of Brittany and hence niece of Marie and Madeleine of Brittany), but no surviving evidence supports this pleasant speculation. See Cynthia J. Brown, *The Queen's Library: Image-Making at the Court of Anne of Brittany, 1477–1514* (Philadelphia: University of Pennsylvania Press, 2011). More likely the book remained at Fontevraud.

42 On this context see Anne-Hélène Allirot, "Longchamp and Lourcine." Isabelle, the daughter of Louis IX and Marguerite of Provence, and her husband Thibaut of Navarre were also important early patrons of Saint-Marcel; another of Marguerite and Louis's daughters, Blanche de la Cerda, retired there as well.

43 For instance, Julianne of Troyes, fourth abbess of Longchamp, went to help found La Guiche around 1285 (founded by Jean of Châtillon, his wife Alix, and their daughter Jeanne, wife of Isabelle of France's nephew Pierre of Alençon); Jeanne of Nevers, fifth abbess of Longchamp, was first abbess of Waterbeach in England, founded around 1293; and Marie of Lyon, tenth abbess of Longchamp, went to Moncel (founded by Philip IV) to help with its foundation, though the date of her stay there is not clear. See Field, "The Abbesses of Longchamp up to the Black Death."

44 For examples of books moving back and forth across the English Channel through these networks see Sean L. Field, "Marie of Saint-Pol and Her Books," *English Historical Review* 125 (2010): 255–78.

45 Charles du Fresne, sieur du Cange, *Histoire de S. Lovys IX. dv nom, roy de France, ecrite par Iean sire de Ioinville, senéchal de Champagne : Enrichie de nouvelles Obseruations & Dissertations Historiques Avec les Établissements de S. Lovys, le Conseil de Pierre de Fontaines, & plusieurs autres Pieces concernant ce regne, tirées des Manuscrits* (Paris: Marbre-Cramoisy, 1668), 169–81. The French text was translated into Latin by J. Stilting for the *Acta sanctorum*, Aug., vol. 6 (Antwerp, 1743), 787–809. Allirot's edition in "Isabelle de France, soeur de saint Louis: La vierge savante. Étude de la *Vie d'Isabelle de France* écrite par Agnès d'Harcourt," is in fact an annotated reprinting of Du Cange.

thanked the well-known *érudit* Vyon d'Herouval for providing him with the manuscript from which he worked,[46] but that manuscript was not thought to survive. In 1999–2000 I discovered a manuscript copy which Antoine Le Maistre had made in 1653 directly from the original roll at Longchamp. It had then passed to Le Maistre's former pupil, Sébastien Le Nain de Tillemont, and is now found in his notebook "B" (BnF ms. fr. 13747).[47] This copy (compared with Du Cange's edition) thus formed the basis for my 2003 edition of the *Vie d'Isabelle*.[48] Already, then, it should have been clear that some of the seventeenth century's most famous scholars and historians had concerned themselves with the text. But two recent discoveries, neither one of which has yet received more than a few sentences in print, significantly expand this picture of Agnes of Harcourt's intellectual legacy and thus warrant more detailed description.

First, in 2007 (in the same article that studied Marie of Brittany's books), Marie-Françoise Damongeot-Bourdat indicated that another seventeenth-century copy of the *Vie d'Isabelle* could be found in BnF ms. Duchesne 38.[49] This copy is a vital new witness to the text, but thus far it has not received significant attention beyond Damongeot-Bourdat's footnote. Most manuscripts in the Duchesne collection are compilations of copies and extracts made by many scholars, from many different original documents, for the great *érudit* André Duchesne (1584–1640) or his son François (1616–93). This manuscript of iiii + 394 folios is no exception, gathering together copies of numerous saints' lives and related ecclesiastical texts.[50] Some copies were probably made by André himself, but doubtless most were procured on his behalf by others. Consequently, they are in many different hands, on many different kinds and sizes of paper, only at a later date all pasted into the manuscript as it now stands. The folios which contain the *Vie d'Isabelle* are large, un-ruled paper, originally three six-folio quires. The text of the *Vie* runs from 72r–89r, with 89v blank. Although elsewhere André Duchesne sometimes added a note to indicate the original source of his copy, in this case there is no such indication. The copyist's hand does not seem to appear anywhere else in the manuscript; it is thus unlikely that the copy was made by André himself, or by his son. At this point the exact date of the copy remains unclear, but it seems virtually certain that it was made before 1668, since Du Cange's

46 Repeated credit given in the notes of Gilles-André de la Roque's 1662 *Histoire généalogique de la maison de Harcourt* demonstrates that Hérouval was on the lookout for material related to the Harcourt family, which may explain why this manuscript passed through his hands.

47 On Tillemont's own life of Isabelle, see Sean L. Field, "The Missing Sister: Sébastien Le Nain de Tillemont's Life of Isabelle of France," *Revue Mabillon* n.s. 19 (2008): 243–70.

48 *Writings of AH*. I was also able to use two copies of part of the opening of the text, made directly from the original roll by Pierre Perrier and preserved in AN L 1029 no. 37. See now Field, "Precious Evidence."

49 René Poupardin, *Catalogue des manuscrits des Collections Duchesne et Bréquigny* (Paris: Leroux, 1905), 44, listed this text only as "Vie française de sainte Isabelle, fille de Louis VIII.» The table found on unnumbered folio iii of this manuscript, written in an early modern hand, gives only the Latin heading as found on fol. 72r.

50 The manuscript also includes one original letter to André Duchesne and one to François. Except for these letters and a brief *Mémoire sur saint Alpin de Châlons* (fols. 261r–v), the copy of Agnes of Harcourt's *Vie* is the only French text in this learned collection of Latin *vitae*.

edition would have been readily available to François Duchesne and his circle after that date (and this copy was definitely not made from the printed text).

In fact, the Duchesne copy was almost certainly made directly from the original roll held at Longchamp, since it is a near perfect match with Le Maistre's copy, which was without any doubt made directly from that roll. The following comparison shows that after completely different descriptive titles, the opening text is virtually identical (this fact is highlighted by comparison with the two other copies of the same passage given below):

| Le Maistre: | Duchesne: |
|---|---|
| La vie de la bienheureuse Isabelle de France soeur du roy S. Loys fondatrice de Longchamp. Copiée tres fidellement sur le manuscrit composé par sœur Agnes de Harcourt, 3e abbesse de cette maison. C'est un long rouleau de parchemin. | De egregia vita et conversatione nobilissimae dominae Isabellis regiae fundatricis nostrae, et de signis a deo factis suis meritis invocatis. |
| Nous avons proposé d'escrire la vie de nostre saincte et benoite dame et mere madame Yzabeau de France a la requeste de monseigneur le roy de Cecile son frere germain selonc ce que Diex nous donrra sa grace a l'onneur de Nostre Seigneur Jesu Crist et de ceste benoite saincte et a l'edification de sainte eglise. | Nous avons proposé d'escrire la vie de nostre saincte et benoite dame et mere Madame Yzabeau de France a la requeste de Monsieur le roy de Cecile son frere germain selonc ce que Diex nous donrra sa grace a l'onneur de Nostre Seigneur Jesu Crist et de ceste benoite sainte et a l'edification de saincte eglise. |
| Et premierement nous dirons qui elle fut et de quex gens estraite et apres dirons de s'enfance et de sa conversation quelle vie elle mena. | Premierement nous dirons qui elle fut et de quex gens estraite et apres dirons de s'enfance de sa conversation quelle vie elle mena. |

Yet the Duchesne manuscript cannot be a copy of Le Maistre's transcription, because Le Maistre left out two miracles (numbers 26 and 27, which Perrier described as crossed out in the original roll), whereas the Duchesne copy includes them. This newly discovered copy thus represents a second independent witness to the now-lost original, and so offers the possibility of substantial advances in textual certainty.

More recently, I have pointed out an additional seventeenth-century copy preserved in Paris, Bibliothèque de l'Institut, ms. Godefroy 531, fols. 339r–363r.[51] As with many manuscripts in the Godefroy collection, 531 is a *mélange* of copies (in many hands) and printed originals of many documents, made for or by the great royal historian Théodore Godefroy (1580–1649) and his son Denys II Godefroy (1615–1681).[52] Within

51 When I first examined this copy in 2009, it had not yet, to my knowledge, been referred to by any scholar writing about Agnes of Harcourt or Isabelle of France. But the text is clearly labeled "Vie d'Isabelle de France, fille de Louis VIII, fondatrice du monastère de Longchamp, par Agnès d'Harcourt," in François Gébelin, *Catalogue général des manuscrits des bibliothèques publiques de France. Paris, Bibliothèque de l'Institut, Collection Godefroy* (Paris: Plon, 1914), 693, so I can hardly claim to have made a true "discovery" here. I first referred in print to this copy's existence in my 2014 article "Paris to Rome and Back Again."

52 The Godefroy Collection passed through the hands of several further relatives before being purchased by Antoine Moriau (1699–1760) in 1746 (his *ex libris* stamp is found on fol. ii$^{r}$ of ms. 531) who then left his books and manuscripts to help found the municipal library of Paris which

this large manuscript of ii + 537 folios, fols. 339r–363r (363v–364r are blank) contain the *Vie d'Isabelle*, copied on 13 bi-folios of unlined paper. The text is written in an extremely neat, clear, printed hand, with wide margins and virtually no corrections or additions. This was not a scholar's quick working copy, but a finished and polished text for presentation or formal reference.

Unfortunately, the copy itself is not dated and records no explicit information about its exemplar. But many documents in this *mélange* are either manuscript copies of dated decrees, or printed texts bearing dates of publication.[53] Although one of these printed texts dates from as early as 1613,[54] most of the dated material (printed and manuscript) is from the 1640s. Moreover, some of the documents from that decade then bear slightly later additions or corrections. For instance, fols. 13r–18r contain a carefully copied list of the archbishops and bishops of France for 1640, which must have been made for or by Théodore Godefroy. The list was then updated by Denys II in 1654.[55] Similarly, fols. 19r–20v, also copied in a formal printed hand (on smaller paper), give a list of ambassadors accredited to France for February 1648, and then fols. 20bis–20ter (on even smaller paper, in a script hand) updated this list to 1662. The latter in fact seems to be the latest date explicitly given in the entire manuscript (for the printed material, no date of printing seems to be later than 1648). The manuscript therefore evidently represents a group of texts compiled in the 1640s by (or for) Théodore Godefroy, with some later updates and additions by Deny II Godefroy from the 1650s and early 1660s.[56]

opened in 1763. See Evelyn M Acomb, "The Library of the Institute de France," *French Historical Studies* 2 (1961): 247–53. According to Gébelin's introduction to his 1914 catalogue (xv–xvi) most of the copies were made by Théodore or for him, while Denys II added most of the originals, some of which were acquired through friends, including Vyon d'Herouval. On Théodore Godefroy, see Erik Thompson, "Commerce, Law, and Erudite Culture: The Mechanics of Théodore Godefroy's Service to Cardinal Richelieu," *Journal of the History of Ideas* 68 (2007): 407–427; more generally see D.-C. Godefroy-Ménilglaise, *Les savants Godefroy. Mémoires d'une famille pendant les XVIe, XVIIe et XVIIIe siècles* (Paris, 1873; reprint Gevena: Slatkine, 1971).

53 The 1914 catalogue in fact omits mention of many texts. For instance, it indicates that the next document after the *Vie* begins on fol. 389, whereas in fact at least six printed documents appear (dated in the 1640s) between fols. 364 and 389.

54 A few copies are of much older documents. For instance, on fols. 336r–337v (one of many texts not mentioned in the catalogue) is found a copy of a document (given in seventeenth-century French) issued by the Provost of Paris, Jean Ploiebauch, concerning a land transaction between one Huguenin and his brother Oudin de Guinegaut in 1313.

55 The catalogue entry credits the updates to Deny II. The first, printed, hand is similar to the one that copied the *Vie*, but I cannot say with certainty that it is identical.

56 Scholars interested in the Godefroys might wish to know that Silver Special Collections at the University of Vermont holds a copy of [Jean Tixier, Seigneur de Ravisy], *De memorabilibus et claris mulieribus aliquot diversorum scriptorum opera* (Paris: Ex aedibus Simonis Colinaei, 1521), which bears the signature "Dionisius Godeffroy" on the verso of the final folio, and a related inscription on the recto of the first folio. Women treated in the book include Clare of Assisi, Elizabeth of Hungary, Joan of Arc, Blanche of Castile, Jeanne de Navarre, and even Pope Joan (among many others), possibly indicating a particular interest in medieval women by this Denys Godefroy, though a specialist would have to examine the signature to be certain it is that of Denys II and not one of the other men by that name in the family.

To return to the relevant fols. 339–63, the most striking thing about the text found there is that it is virtually identical to the version of the *Vie* printed by Du Cange. Word for word, letter for letter, and even in terms of punctuation and accents, the two are near perfect matches (a point which is again greatly strengthened when compared with the text already given above for the Le Maistre and Duchesne copies). Consider again the opening text, given here in a version that respects orthography and punctuation:

| Godefroy: | Du Cange : |
|---|---|
| De Egregia uita, et Conuersatione Nobilissimae Dominae Isabellis Regiae Fundatricis nostrae,[57] et de signis à Deo factis suis meritis invocatis. Par madame Agnes de Harecourt sa Damoiselle suiuante, et depuis Religieuse au dict Conuent et 3. Abbesse. | LA VIE D'ISABELLE SOEVR DE S. LOVYS, FONDATRICE DE L'ABBAYE DE LONCHAMP. ÉCRITE PAR AGNES DE HARCOVRT sa Damoiselle suiuante, & depuis troisiéme Abbesse de ce Monastere. |
| | Sur le Manuscrit communiqué par Monsieur D'HEROVVAL. |
| Nous auons proposé d'escrire la Vie de nostre Saincte, et benoiste Dame, et Mere Madame Isabeau de France à la Requeste de Monsieur le Roy de Sicile son frere germain selon ce que Dieu nous donnera sa grace à l'honneur de nostre Seigneur Iesus Christ, et de ceste benoiste Saincte, Et à l'Edification de la Saincte Eglise. | Novs auons proposé d'écrire la vie de nostre Saincte, & benoiste Dame, & Mere Madame Isabeav de France, à la requeste de Monsieur le Roy de Sicile son frere germain, selon ce que Dieu nous donnera sa grace à l'honneur de nostre Seigneur Iesus-Christ, & de cette benoiste Sainte, & à l'edification de la saincte Eglise. |
| Premierement nous dirons qui elle fust, et de qu'elles Iens extraicte, et apres dirons de son enfance, de sa Conuersation, qu'elle [sic] uie elle mena. | Premierement nous dirons qui elle fut, & de quelles jens extraicte, & aprés dirons de son enfance, de sa conuersation, quelle vie elle mena. |

Although a full textual demonstration is beyond the scope of this essay, the two texts do in fact remain virtually identical throughout, with orthography and syntax that has clearly been modernized from the thirteenth-century original. It would seem very likely that either Godefroy's copy was made from the 1668 printed edition, or his copy served as Du Cange's exemplar. Several factors indicate that the latter possibility is far more probable. The dating established above has already pointed strongly in this direction. By and large the *mélange* in Godefroy 531 dates from the 1640s, and no date later than 1662 seems to appear in the manuscript. Everything suggests that the copy thus pre-dates the 1668 printing. Moreover, Deny II Godefroy would certainly have had easy access to that printing once it was available, and so meticulously copying it out would have made little sense (especially since this *mélange* routinely included printed texts). Furthermore, the Godefroy copy gives the text the Latin title that is found in the Duchesne manuscript, but not in the Du Cange edition. Since it cannot be a coincidence that the Godefroy and Duchesne copies provide

57 Above the line a later script hand has added: *de l'Abbaye de Longchamp proche [?] le bois de Madrid ou de Bolongne.*

identical Latin titles, and since the Godefroy copy is clearly independent from the Duchesne, this Latin title must have been written on the original roll (whether at the original time of composition or by a later hand). Du Cange replaced the Latin with a French equivalent (similar but not identical to the French title employed by Le Maistre). But Du Cange's French wording attributing the work to Agnes then clearly drew from the heading of the Godefroy manuscript.

Very close comparison of the two texts offers further confirmation for this hypothesis. Consider a telling passage where a phrase in Godefroy's copy does *not* in fact appear in Du Cange. On one hand, this omission confirms again that the Godefroy manuscript could not have been copied from Du Cange. But a close examination is even more suggestive:

| **Godefroy, fol. 343v (respecting line endings and beginnings):** | **Du Cange, p. 171 (this text appears all on one printed line):** |
|---|---|
| ... elle faisoit dire le diuin office<br>moult diligement, et l'escoutoit tout<br>moult deuotement, et moult ententivement ... | ... elle faisoit dire le diuin office moult deuotement & moult ententiuement ... |

The fact that two successive lines in the Godefroy copy began with "moult" makes it likely that this exact *mise-en-page* was what caused Du Cange or his printer to skip from the first "moult" directly to "deuotement" and thus omit "diligement, et l'escoutoit tout."

There are other small indications, such where Godefroy left an unexplained space before a word, and the space reappears in Du Cange. For example:

> Godefroy, 347v: "... estoient touiours illec [space] Freres Mineurs Maistre de diuinité..."
>
> Du Cange, p. 173: "... estoient toûjours illec [space] freres Mineurs, Maistres de Diuinité... "

Thus, although further questions remain,[58] it seems very likely that the folios now in Godefroy MS 531 were indeed the manuscript provided by d'Herouval to Du Cange.

The identification of these two new manuscript copies has helped clarify a picture of Agnes of Harcourt's wide seventeenth-century circulation among elite scholars. At least six *érudits* (Le Maitre, Tillemont, Duchesne, Godefroy, d'Herouval, and Du Cange) can now be tied to the three known copies, as two (closely related but distinct) versions of the text were being copied and circulated among some of the most illustrious French scholars of the age of Louis XIV. The greatest French intellectuals of the day were, in a certain sense, engaged in a continuing conversation with their predecessor, Agnes of Harcourt.[59]

As this essay hopes to have shown, Agnes of Harcourt was an influential noblewoman, a leader of her Franciscan community, and an impressive intellectual. As an

58 It can be noted that these folios did enter the manuscript at the time of its original binding, since the titles scrawled on the original spine include "Vie d'Issabelle soeur du St. Louys."

59 On a textual level these two seventeenth-century copies complete each other and suggest the

author, she sought and drew inspiration from the most recently available hagiographic models, collaborated with those around her, revised and rethought her work, and found a ready audience for her writings not only at Longchamp but in royal, monastic, and (eventually) erudite circles.

But after the intense seventeenth-century interest in her work, she receded from scholarly consciousness, languishing in relative obscurity into the 1990s.[60] In fact, one of the few places in which Agnes was accorded notable intellectual respect was Judy Chicago's iconic installation *The Dinner Party*, begun in 1974 and now housed at the Elizabeth A. Sackler Center for Feminist Art at the Brooklyn Museum.[61] The work pays tribute to 1,038 women in history, with 39 women represented by place settings around a table in the shape of an equilateral triangle and another 999 names inscribed in the floor on which the table rests. The featured 39 include such towering figures from the European Middle Ages as Hildegard of Bingen and Christine de Pizan. Much more surprising is the inclusion of Agnes of Harcourt among the 999 "women of achievement." My hat is off to Judy Chicago for extending this well-deserved dinner invitation to Agnes, at a time when she remained practically unknown to scholars. My only suggestion is that it might be time to make a place at the table itself, perhaps between an erudite abbess such as Hildegard and a formative female author of French prose such as Christine, for the important intellectual Agnes of Harcourt.[62]

---

necessity of a new critical edition. Without the Le Maistre copy, we could not be sure that the Duchesne copy was made directly at Longchamp from the original (since the scribe gave no indication to this effect); without the Duchesne copy we would have much less confidence in some of the unusual readings attested by Le Maistre, and we would have to continue to rely on Du Cange for the missing two miracles.

60 Biographers of Isabelle of France did of course consult Agnes's work in the intervening period, most notably Albert Garreau's *Bienheureuse Isabelle de France, sœur de Saint Louis* (Paris: Éditions franciscaines, 1943; expanded edition 1955) and then the pioneering observations by William C. Jordan in *Louis IX and the Challenge of the Crusade: A Study in Rulership* (Princeton: Princeton University Press, 1979), 9–12 (Jordan, however, worked from the Latin translation in the *Acta sanctorum*).

61 For information and bibliography on Judy Chicago (b. 1939), see her website at http://www.judychicago.com/

62 I would like to thank the organizers and participants of the conference "Women Leaders and Intellectuals of the Medieval World" for thoughtful comments on the first version of this paper, and Jacques Dalarun, Anne-Françoise Leurquin-Labie, Martine Pagan, and Levente Seláf for helpful discussions and access to pre-publication work. Although I never had the pleasure of meeting the late Marie-Françoise Damongeot-Bourdat, the reader will see that this essay benefits greatly from one of her articles. I also am grateful to the College of Arts and Sciences at the University of Vermont for a Lattie F. Coor Faculty Development Award that helped make manuscript research possible in Paris at the Bibliothèque de l'Institut de France, Bibliothèque nationale de France, and Archives nationales de France, and to the directions and staffs of those three institutions.

5

# CATHERINE OF SIENA, *AUCTOR*

F. THOMAS LUONGO

> Who while reading her letters ... is not amazed by their high style, and their deep thoughts, so useful above all for the saving of souls? Although in them she speaks in her own vernacular, since she did not know letters, nevertheless she entered into the power of God using the key to his depths, so that to anyone who looks into them carefully they will seem to be by Paul rather than Catherine – by an apostle rather than some girl [*cuiuscumque puelle*]. She dictated these letters quickly, without the slightest delay, as if she was reading what she spoke from a book placed before her. I myself often saw her dictating at the same time to two different secretaries two different letters, addressed to different persons and on different subjects, and neither secretary ever had to wait even a moment for the dictation he was taking, nor did either of them hear anything except what was intended for him. If we then turn to the book that she composed in her own language, manifestly at the dictation of the Holy Spirit, who could imagine or believe that it was done by a woman? Its style is so lofty that one can scarcely find Latin expressions equal to the loftiness of its style, as indeed I myself have found in the Latin translation in which I am engaged at present. Her thoughts [*sententiae*] are at the same time so lofty and so profound that if you heard them read out in Latin you would think that they were the work of none other than Aurelius Augustinus.
>
> – Raimondo da Capua,
> *Legenda maior sive Legenda admirabilis virginis Catherine de Senis*.[1]

This assessment of Catherine of Siena's writings by Raymond of Capua, her confessor and (when he wrote his authoritative *Legenda* of Catherine) Master General of the Dominican Order, addresses directly the theme of this volume and the conference on which it is based. Raymond presents Catherine as an *auctor* on the level of the highest scriptural and Patristic authorities – in other words, as an intellectual leader. Raymond himself contributed to the translation of Catherine into an *auctor*, as he notes, by

1 Edited by Silvia Nocentini, Edizione Nazionale dei Testi Mediolatini d'Italia 31, Serie 1, 19 (Florence: SISMEL Edizioni Galluzzo, 2014), 120–21.

producing a (partial) Latin version of the *Libro*. Complete translations of the *Libro* were produced by two others of Catherine's close followers and sometime scribes: the Sienese noble Stefano di Corrado Maconi (who joined the Carthusians after Catherine's death and became that order's Master General) and the Sienese notary Cristofano di Gano Guidini. The Latin versions of Catherine's book, alongside the version in Italian, played an important role in the reception of her texts and authorship in the fifteenth century.[2]

In material terms, Catherine's translation into an *auctor* was the responsibility of her other significant hagiographer and the main promoter of Catherine's sanctity in the decades after her death, the Sienese Dominican friar Tommaso da Siena, better known as "Caffarini," who established a scriptorium in Venice largely for the production of works by and about Catherine. Caffarini saw to it that Catherine's texts circulated in the prestigious form – both in the parchment materials and in choice of scripts and page design – of Latinate desk books, as we can see from his scriptorium's manuscript of the Latin version of the *Libro* by Stefano di Corrado Maconi, which includes Raymond of Capua's prologue to the *Legenda maior*, including the passage cited above. While Caffarini in his own writings on Catherine attributed to her a miraculously acquired ability to write not acknowledged by Raymond – more on this below – the illustrations here and elsewhere do not show her with pen in hand. Instead, the portrait of Catherine as author at the incipit of the *Libro/Liber* shows her in one of the moments of inspired dictation described by Raymond. Catherine is shown in a pose of humility, receiving dictation from God and dictating in turn to the scribes who do the actual writing (see Figure 2). The scribe with the *capello* on his head is presumably meant to be the Florentine notary Barduccio Canigiani, Catherine's most important scribe in the last two years of her life and one who we know worked most assiduously with her on the *Libro*, and whose presence here as a notary perhaps adds to the authorization of the text contained in the manuscript.

And yet Raymond's hagiographic case for Catherine's *auctoritas* might seem to undermine her as a writer. Raymond appeals to a standard trope of medieval female sanctity, and the author portrait in Caffarini's manuscript echoes this trope, by drawing attention to Catherine's inadequacies – her femininity and lack of learning – to emphasize her dependence on God and her male scribes. Catherine is presented in terms that augment her authority as a saint, but that would also seem to deprive her of the agency, craft, and self-awareness expected of authors. Not only does Catherine becomes an *auctor* through God's wonder-working hand and not through her own efforts or agency, but her status as an intellectual leader requires that her writings undergo a process of gender and cultural translation, into Latin and as if they were authored by a man, rather than in the vernacular of "some girl."

We are faced here with a number of issues that should be familiar from the last several decades' scholarship on medieval women saints and female spiritual authors, for instance the question of how to locate the agency and identity of a female author in light of her dependence on confessors and (male) scribes for the production of her texts.

2 Silvia Nocentini, "'Fare per lettera': Le traduzioni latine del 'Libro di divina dottrina' di Caterina da Siena," *Studi medievali* 56, no. 2 (2015): 639–80.

Figure 2 Catherine of Siena, *Liber divine doctrine* – Latin translation of the *Libro di divina dottrina*. (Siena, Biblioteca Comunale, T.II.4, 6v.; reproduced by permission of the Biblioteca Comunale degli Intronati, Siena.)

And Raymond seems to confirm what the last several decades of scholarship have identified as a tendency of male hagiographers to rewrite the lives of their subjects into clerically sanctioned hagiographic categories, in effect controlling or even repressing their saintly subjects' agency and identity. The tendency in Catherinian scholarship (my own included) has been to emphasize the distance between Raymond's version of Catherine's life and her actual career and self-identity, in particular as a woman writer. This distance is emphasized dramatically, for example, in Jane Tylus' recent case for Catherine as a writer committed to writing as an expression of her body and to using her own Sienese vernacular.[3] Indeed, there is a gap between Raymond's portrait of Catherine as *auctor* and Catherine's own sense of herself as a writer, one that opens up most clearly in his omission from the *Legenda maior* of a letter Catherine addressed to him in October 1377; in the postscript to that letter, Catherine announces that she has learned to write and has written the letter in her own hand. For Tylus, therefore, Raymond makes Catherine a figure of orality – not literacy, or literature.

In response to these questions of female agency and literacy there are two points that need to be made at the outset. First, the more obvious point that in the Middle Ages dictation to scribes was a form of writing – indeed often a more authoritative form of writing than penning a text oneself – not a marker of orality or illiteracy.[4] We have to think about writing for Catherine, as with other writers, as including processes more complicated than an alternative between doing the writing herself or working with her scribes. If Catherine was able to write (which seems on the whole likely), she might have alternated between dictation and solo writing, and she might also have transmitted texts to scribes through rough notes on paper or wax tablets. In any case, the evidence is that she was always to some extent dependent on her scribes for the composition of her letters and *Libro*.[5] As we will see, writing in her own hand did

3 *Reclaiming Catherine of Siena: Literacy, Literature, and the Signs of Others* (Chicago: University of Chicago Press, 2008).

4 On the authorizing effect of scribes, see Lynn Staley, "The Trope of the Scribe and the Question of Literary Authority in the Works of Julian of Norwich and Margery Kempe," *Speculum* 66 (1991): 820–38. See also Jennifer Summit's comments on Margery Kempe's use of scribes: "by collating Margery Kempe within an existing canon, the scribe established Margery's authority by showing precisely that she is not an original creator, but rather one that upholds pre-existing models of *traditio* and *auctoritas*." Jennifer Summit, "Women and Authorship," in Dinshaw and Wallace, eds., *The Cambridge Companion to Medieval Women's Writing*, ed. Carolyn Dinshaw and David Wallace (Cambridge: Cambridge University Press, 2003), 71.

5 It is not the case that Catherine depended on scribes early in her career and then ceased to depend on them later. Catherine's scribes developed an increasingly formal kind of chancery, one that became more organized and professional in the last two years of her life, perhaps under the influence of the Florentine notary Barduccio Canigiani, who joined her circle in 1378. For example, from the last years of her life we have a number of letters sent to different recipients that are almost identical in content, save for the opening and closing protocols, a sign that Catherine and her scribes were working with and from base texts that existed in registers of some kind. As for the *Libro,* Catherine's followers, including those who served as her scribes, in their writings about her almost never mention that work without stating that it was dictated in a state of ecstasy. Apart from these comments, for practical reasons it is very unlikely that Catherine herself wrote out a lengthy work like the *Libro*. On the other hand, as Silvia Nocentini has pointed out ("Il problema testuale," 260), it is not impossible that Catherine dictated the entire book over the course of several days, as Raymond of Capua recounts. On the

mean something special to Catherine. But Catherine's being a writer does not depend on her independence from her scribes. After all, Catherine begins all of her letters, which we know she dictated to scribes, with some variation of "Io Caterina scrivo a voi" (I, Catherine, write to you).

And second, as others before me have pointed out, there are plenty of reasons to question the understanding of agency and the power relations between male clerics and female saints that might lead us to read Raymond's hagiographic treatment of Catherine as oppressive.[6] As John Coakley, among others, has shown, relationships between male confessors/hagiographers and their female subjects could involve mutual influence instead of, or in addition to, coercion.[7] As several studies of the *Legenda maior* have noted, while Raymond's account of Catherine's life and Catherine's own account are not the same, they overlap in complicated ways; the *Legenda maior* is an interpretation of Catherine's sanctity and not simply a rewriting of Catherine's life into a series of hagiographic tropes.[8] Sometimes even the tropes may not be what we would expect. For example, as Maria H. Oen has recently pointed out, Raymond's emphasis on Catherine's marvelous dictation to several scribes and the reference to that dictation in the manuscript iconography appeal to similar episodes in the hagiography of Thomas Aquinas – in other words, as claiming for Catherine a kind of intellectual authority rather than imposing on her the trope of female saintly passivity.[9] And while Catherine in her letters mostly avoids accounts of visions and the kind of auto-hagiography familiar from the writings of many other medieval female visionaries or mystics (the *Revelations* of Birgitta of Sweden, for example), the exceptions are her letters to Raymond. Catherine wrote several letters to Raymond that narrate key episodes in her career, including a number of mission-defining visions, along with her

mechanics of Catherine's writing and discussion of what it might have meant for her to participate by writing herself, alongside her scribes, see my "Birgitta and Catherine and their Textual Communities," in Maria H. Oen and Unn Falkeid, eds., *Sanctity and Female Authorship: Birgitta of Sweden and Catherine of Siena*, Routledge Studies in Medieval Religion and Culture (London and New York: Routledge, 2019), 14–34.

6 On the question of agency, see Amy Hollywood, "Gender, Agency, and the Divine in Religious Hagiography," in *Acute Melancholia and Other Essays* (New York: Columbia University Press, 2016), 117–28; and my "Inspiration and Imagination: Inspired Authorship in the Early Manuscripts of the *Revelations* of Birgitta of Sweden," *Speculum* 93 (2018): 1102–50, esp. 1111–19.

7 John Coakley, *Men, Women, and Spiritual Power: Female Saints and their Male Collaborators* (New York: Columbia University Press, 2006). See also the discussion of the different forms taken by spiritual relationships of men and women in Amy Hollywood, "Feminist Studies in Christian Spirituality," in *Acute Melancholia*, 93–116, esp. 96.

8 See for instance the essential essay by Sophia Boesch-Gajano and Odile Redon, "La *Legenda maior* di Raimondo da Capua, costruzione di una santa," in *Atti del simposio internazionale Cateriniano-Bernardiniano* (Siena 17–20 aprile 1980), ed. Domenico Maffei and Paolo Nardi (Siena: Accademia Senese degli Intronati,1982), 15–36. See also Silvia Nocentini, "The *Legenda maior* of Catherine of Siena," in *A Companion to Catherine of Siena*, ed. Carolyn Muessig, George Ferzoco, and Beverly Mayne Kienzle (Leiden: Brill, 2012), 339–61.

9 Maria H. Oen, "Ambivalent Images of Authorship," in Oen and Falkeid, eds., *Sanctity and Female Authorship*, 113–37; Constant Mews, "Thomas Aquinas and Catherine of Siena: Emotion, Devotion and Mendicant Spiritualities in the Late Fourteenth Century," *Digital Philology: A Journal of Medieval Cultures* 1, no. 2 (2012): 235–52. Note that Mews' very suggestive essay contains several errors, particularly in his reading of Catherine's postscript to letter 272.

letter in October 1377 referred to already.[10] While Raymond did not incorporate all the details of Catherine's letters into his *Legenda*, these letters can nevertheless be taken as some evidence of a collaborative relationship between Catherine and her confessor. For example, in her final, valedictory letter to Raymond, Catherine asks that Raymond and others of her clerical followers "take in hand [*ve le rechiate per le mani*] the book and any writings of mine, and do with them what seems to you best for the honor of God."[11] This request testifies to Catherine's identification with her writings – especially her *Libro* – and her determination that they would be preserved and published after her death. But there is no sense here that Catherine was determined that her writings remain in the vernacular. Instead, her request shows that she trusted Raymond and other clerics in her circle to shape the forms in which her texts would circulate – including (implicitly) translation into Latin.[12]

In what remains of this essay I would like to reconsider the idea of Catherine as an intellectual leader by taking Raymond of Capua's statement at face value, and asking what it meant for Catherine to enter the world of books – to be or become an *auctor* like Augustine. I will begin with Catherine's use of manuscript books as metaphors in her writings as a glimpse of a world of books and a bookish culture she viewed from a certain distance. But I will argue that Catherine entered into that world decisively and intentionally and became an *auctor* in writing of her *Libro*. What her authorship meant for her can be seen in the extraordinary letter she wrote to Raymond in October 1377, in which she reveals to him the revelation that became the basis for the *Libro*, and in a postscript announces that she has learned to write and has written this letter herself.

### The Book as Metaphor in Catherine's Writings

Catherine uses the book as a metaphor a number of times in her letters and *Libro*. For instance, in a couple of early letters, Catherine adapts Colossians 2:14, in which the act of Christ's redemption is described as the canceling of the contract or decree (*chirographum*) written out against us on account of our sin. Catherine plays on the analogy between the lambskin of the *carta* (document, and by implication contract or bond) and the Lamb of God, to describe the contract cancelled by being torn up on the cross:

10 In addition to letters 272 and 273, discussed below, these include letter 219, which describes a vision confirming Catherine's mission; and 295, which describes her near martyrdom in the Ciompi revolt.

11 Letter 373. All quotations in this essay from Catherine's letters are taken from Antonio Volpato's edition, in *Santa Caterina da Siena: Opera Omnia. Testi e concordanze*, ed. Fausto Sbaffoni (Pistoia, 2002) (CD-ROM Edition). The translations are my own.

12 Giovanna Frosini has pointed out that the phrase Catherine uses here to instruct Raymond to collect her writings, "ve le rechiate per le mani," when used in other contemporary sources suggests that she intended to give Raymond agency to circulate, adapt and even change Catherine's texts. See Frosini, "Lingua e testo nel manuscritto Viennese delle lettere di Caterina," in *Dire l'ineffabile: Caterina da Sienae il linguaggio della mistica*, ed. Lino Leonardi and Pietro Trifone (Florence: SISMEL–Edizioni del Galluzzo, 2006), 94–5. There is in fact no evidence that, as Jane Tylus claims, Catherine "insisted to her scribes" (*Reclaiming Catherine of Siena*, 123) that her words circulate in *volgare* rather than in Latin.

> Oh inestimable and most sweet charity, you have destroyed the *carta* that existed between man and the devil, by tearing it up on the wood of the most holy cross. The *carta* was made of none other than lamb, that immaculate Lamb who has inscribed us on himself, but then has torn up the *carta*. Let our souls therefore be comforted, since we were bound by contract [literally, "written," *scritti*], but that *carta* has been torn up, and our opponent and adversary can never demand to have us back.[13]

In several letters to clerics and members of religious orders, Christ becomes "our rule and instruction [*dottrina*]" and the "book of life," which we are called to study.[14] The idea of Christ as a book, juxtaposed against other, more worldly books occurs elsewhere in her letters and even more vividly in her *Libro*, where God the Father complains to her about unfit priests, who "instead of making wives of their breviaries," betray their breviaries like adulterers so that "their books are their troops of (illegitimate) children [*i libri suoi sono la brigata dei figliuoli*]."[15]

In several letters to lay followers, Catherine expands on the image of Christ as parchment page in a more elaborate, and more specifically codicological, image she borrowed from the fourteenth-century Florentine Dominican Domenico Cavalca's *Speccio di croce*, a very popular work of theological *volgarizzamento*.[16] In these letters, Catherine offers her correspondents the image of Christ on the cross as a book, sometimes "il libro della vita" – whose letters are large or clear enough that "even slow and blind people are able to read it." She elaborates at length on this image in a couple of letters written to laymen, for instance in one written from Rome in 1379 to her close follower, the Sienese wool master Sano di Maco, through whom during her travels she often addressed her spiritual famiglia in Siena, as indeed she does in this letter. Here Catherine describes Christ as a teacher who teaches from a book written on his own body, whose wounds can be "read" like rubricated capitals on a manuscript page:

> Whom we see with the light of faith, raised onto the cathedra of the cross, from which he teaches us his doctrine, which he has written on his body. He makes of himself a book, with capitals so large [*con capoversi sì grossi*] that no man is so unlearned [*tanto idiotto*] nor has so little sight that he cannot slowly and perfectly read them.

She invites Sano to meditate on Christ's body – as if before a painted crucifix – by "reading" it as if it were a manuscript. For instance, from what we "read" in the wound in Christ's side we learn of Christ's love, and from there we learn to have patience with others. Catherine extends the metaphor here at length: Christ's body is the source from which we acquire virtue if we read it correctly. Reading well, and from the right book, becomes here a metaphor for an education in the Christian

13 Letter 69, to her Sienese follower Sano di Maco di Mazzacorno.

14 Letter 11, to Cardinal Pierre d'Estaing, in October 1377.

15 *Dialogo,* chapter 130, 401–2.

16 Suzanne Noffke, *The Letters of Catherine of Siena* (Binghamton, NY: ACMRS Publications, 1988), 1:93n.

life, whereas becoming a sinner is a result of reading badly, or of reading from the wrong book.[17]

What, if anything, can we take from this metaphor about Catherine's sense of herself as a writer? The way in which the metaphor of the book links reading both to Christ's body and to Christian virtue might suggest, as Jane Tylus and Catherine Mooney have stressed, a link between Catherine's writing – as someone who avowedly wrote her letters in Christ's blood – and Catherine's suffering and bodily *imitatio Christi.*[18] On the other hand, the metaphor here is about reading, not writing. And the book in this metaphor is not only a figure for Christ and the Christian life, but also a cultural point of reference and an object with a particular appearance. The image of the book as the crucified Christ evokes an immediately recognizable type of medieval manuscript book: a codex with pages made of parchment, with decorated capitals, rubrication and the other trappings of prestige, Latinate medieval manuscript books. Catherine's use of the image of Christ as manuscript book shows her recognition of the different cultural registers denoted by different material forms of writing, including elite forms of writing that we might not associate with Catherine's experience as a reader or writer. The image from Cavalca that Catherine adapts was, after all, written for laypeople, for the culture of the *volgare*, and assumes a very *haut en bas* attitude towards lay literacy, as if for laypeople such books were icons, to be looked at rather than read. Indeed, Catherine uses the metaphor in just this way, and with particular emphasis in letters to lay followers: the metaphor depends on viewing the book as icon, as image, gazing at and into the wounds of Christ the way one would meditate visually on a painted crucifix – not perhaps the way an educated reader reads a text, but as an object of fascination and power. In this connection it is interesting to consider that for Caffarini, the manuscripts of Catherine's writings that he produced could serve a similarly iconic purpose, as objects that testified to Catherine's sanctity rather than (or in addition to) books to be read: in one of his hagiographical works on Catherine he cites as evidence of her sanctity the material quality of these manuscripts, "well bound and covered, and of goatskin parchment, and all similarly written in an expert hand." He mentions that once, preaching in Venice on Catherine's feast day, he stopped his homily to show the people these volumes, as testimony to various things Catherine had said.

Catherine's recognition of the power of the book, and her identification of it with the crucified body of Christ, speaks to the way in which, as Tylus has suggested, Catherine was "intrigued by the technology of writing."[19] As we will see, Catherine's letter to Raymond in October 1377 expresses a desire to enter directly and intimately into the physical act of writing and the world of the decorated, Latinate manuscripts she evokes as metaphors.

17 Letter 318.

18 Catherine M. Mooney, "Wondrous Words: Catherine of Siena's Miraculous Reading and Writing According to the Early Sources," in *Catherine of Siena: The Creation of a Cult*, ed. Jeffrey Hamburger and Gabriella Signori (Turnhout: Brepols, 2013), 287.

19 Tylus, *Reclaiming Catherine of Siena*, 18.

## Catherine's Letter and Writing "Miracle"

Letter 272 is one of the most important, and perhaps the most complex, of the series of self-disclosing and mission-defining letters Catherine addressed to Raymond. Catherine begins by calling on Raymond to be "manly [*virile*] and without fear" in response to the "thorns of persecution, because only a crazy person would give up the rose for fear of the thorns." She refers to the sense of bitterness she and Raymond felt in response to the harm done to the Church, "the sweet Bride of Christ," and promises that the "more numerous [*più abonda*] is her tribulation and bitterness, even more does divine Truth promise to make her overflow [*farla abondare*] in sweetness [*dolcezza*] and consolation." It is clear from the context that Catherine means the harm caused by poor pastoral leadership, as well as (perhaps) harm caused by Florence and the Church's enemies in the War of the Eight Saints; she notes that the promised *dolcezza* is the "reform of holy and good pastors," and calls on Raymond to "rejoice therefore in the bitterness, since Truth has promised to give us refreshment [*refrigerio*]." She then describes how she responded to the latest news contained in letters from Raymond and from the Pope – to whom she refers in her usual way, as *babbo* (daddy) – by turning to God in intense prayer. In the course of her account of her experience, Catherine begins to refer to herself in the third person, as a "servant of God":

> After the bitterness and consolation [*amaritudine e consolazione*] that I had by receiving the letter of sweet *babbo* and your letter, since I had great bitterness [*amaritudine*] for the harm to the Church, and for your bitterness, which I had felt internally on the feast of St. Francis, and happiness [*allegrezza*] too, because it took me a great deal of thought reading the letter and understanding everything, I begged a servant of God to offer tears and sweat before God for the Bride and the infirmity of *babbo*. Whence suddenly by divine grace there grew a desire and happiness beyond all measure. And waiting until the morning to have Mass – it was Mary's day [i.e., Saturday] – and the hour of Mass having arrived, she took her place with true knowledge of self [*con vero cognoscimento di sé*], ashamed before God in her imperfection. And raising herself above herself with anxious desire [*levando sé sopra di sé con ansietato desiderio*], and gazing with the eye of the intellect on Truth Eternal, she requested four petitions, holding herself and her father [i.e., Raymond] in the presence of the Bride of the Truth.

Catherine then describes the four petitions – for reform of the Church, for the whole world, for Raymond's salvation, and for the particular situation of someone she does not name – and Christ's responses to them. The petitions and responses form the basis for her book, her *Libro*, which is an expanded version of the material in the letter, and which she evidently began to write at this time.

As remarkable as the letter is, Catherine's postscript is perhaps even more so. After closing the letter in her usual way, Catherine announces to Raymond in ecstatic terms – the translation here maintains the somewhat scattered syntax of the original – that God has given her the ability to write, and that she has written this letter, and another she sent him, in her own hand:

> This letter, and another I have sent you, I wrote in my own hand in the Isola della Rocca, with many sighs and an abundance of tears, so much so that the eye, seeing, could not see. But I was full of amazement at myself, and in the goodness of God, considering his mercy towards his creatures who possess reason, and his Providence, which overflowed [*abondava*] over me, in that for refreshment – having been deprived of this consolation, which on account of my ignorance I did not know – he had given me, and provided for me by giving me the ability of writing [*l'attitudine dello scrivere*], so that having descended from the heights, I might have some small way in which to vent the heart [*sfogare 'l cuore*], so that it not burst. Not wishing to take me yet from this shadowy life, in a marvelous way he fixed it in my mind, just as a master does to a boy when he gives him an exemplar. Whence, immediately he parted from me, with the glorious Evangelist and Thomas Aquinas, thus sleeping I began to learn. Pardon me for writing too much, for the hands and the tongue agree with the heart [*le mani e la lingua s'accordano col cuore*].

Not only does Raymond of Capua not include the details of this letter in the *Legenda maior*, none of Catherine's closest followers – the ones who served as her scribes – ever mention that Catherine could write. They all emphasize instead her practice of dictating her letters, and eventually her *Libro*, to scribes – as we saw illustrated in the manuscript of the Latin version of the *Libro* produced by Caffarini's scriptorium. This silence, and probably also the audaciously self-authorizing nature of Catherine's announcement, caused difficulties for twentieth-century Catherinian scholars; some doubted its authenticity (for reasons that now appear unsound) and others chose simply to ignore the letter.[20]

But the question of whether Catherine could or could not write, miraculously or otherwise, does not address the more important question of what Catherine is saying about herself here. On this issue, this letter has been a focus of discussion in analysis of Catherine's status and self-awareness as a writer by Tylus and Marina Zancan, among others.[21] That Catherine's announcement of the ability to write is connected to her embarking on the *Libro* seems obvious, but beyond that it is not clear what Catherine means by this announcement. When Catherine writes that she acquired "l'attitudine

20 See Luongo, *The Saintly Politics of Catherine of Siena* (London: Cornell University Press, 2006), 193. See also Catherine Mooney's astute analysis of this letter and the hagiographical treatments of it in "Wondrous Words." On the mechanics of Catherine's writing and discussion of what this letter might have meant in more practical terms, see my "Birgitta and Catherine and Their Textual Communities," in Oen and Falkeid, eds., *Sanctity and Female Authorship*

21 Tylus, *Reclaiming Catherine of Siena*; Marina Zancan, "Lettere di Caterina da Siena," in *Letteratura italiana. Le opere*, vol. 1, *Dalle origini al cinquento*, ed. Alberto Asor Rosa (Turin: Einaudi, 1992), 593–633; Marina Zancam, "Lettere di Caterina da Siena. Il testo, la tradizione, l'interpretazione," *Annali d'italianistica* 13 (1995): 151–61.

dello scrivere," she seems to have meant more than the "ability" to write; as other scholars have noted, "attitudine" here seems to mean something more like "disposition" or even "vocation." In other words, as Marina Zancan argued long ago, Catherine's announcement is symbolic, intended to signal a departure from the kind of writing she had done before and a new kind of authorial identity connected to her embarking on the project of her book.[22] But how or why does taking the pen into her hand signal this new authority and direction? Jane Tylus is surely right that Catherine in her announcement intended, in her new identity as a writer, to liberate herself in some sense from her scribes.[23] But it seems that the point of this liberation had more to do with the kind of writing she was beginning in her book than any actual independence from her scribes, on whom she depended for the composition of her *Libro.*

Perhaps what Catherine was really liberating herself from by shifting from letter writing to the writing of a book is the kind of engagement with worldly politics that was increasingly a source of the *amaritudine* that she mentions at the start of her letter to Raymond. Letter writing was for Catherine the business of the religious life – the equivalent of the preaching and teaching with which her male, clerical associates were burdened.[24] This business was at this point in her career closely associated with her scribes and the formal and efficient semi-chancery that had developed to produce her letters. Here she is responding to the bitterness by uniting with God and, in Christ's responses to her petitions, receiving the consolation of a divine perspective on her and Raymond's frustrations and disappointments. In the vision Catherine is alone with God, and this form of writing is, as she makes clear, a gift – a source of refreshment and spiritual consolation that "overflows" (*abondare*) in exactly the way she had promised Raymond divine goodness would do, in proportion to his and her experience of bitterness. Indeed, Catherine's language in her letter to Raymond as well as in the opening pages of the *Libro* resonate with the traditional language of spiritual consolation or spiritual pleasure, in particular the idea that the soul's experience alternates between the bitterness of God's absence and the sweetness and pleasure of God's presence – a truth with which Catherine reassures Raymond at the beginning of her letter.[25] In her postscript Catherine makes it clear that this new kind of writing is connected to the *consolazione* and *refrigerio* she received from God's presence in the experience she describes to Raymond. Writing is a way for her to vent her heart, which has expanded in the pleasure of God's presence, an image that echoes Thomas Aquinas' description of spiritual pleasure as a kind of enlargement (*dilatatio*).[26]

22 Zancan, "Lettere di Caterina da Siena" (1992). On the transition from letters to book, and on the implications of the origins of Catherine's book as a letter, see Luongo, *Saintly Politics*, chapter 5, "Prophetic Politics."

23 Tylus, *Reclaiming Catherine of Siena*, 213–14.

24 I am indebted to John Van Engen for this observation, and for the suggestion that I look deeper into the traditional idea of spiritual consolation or refreshment in connection with Catherine's sense of vocation as she turned to writing her book.

25 See Louis Poullier, "Consolation spirituelle," in *Dictionnaire de Spiritualité* (Paris: G. Beauchesne, 1937), vol. 2, 1618–34.

26 *Summa theologiae*, I–II, a.33. Thomas appeals to Isaiah 60:5: "videbis, et affluens, et mirabitur et dilatabitur cor tuum [Thou shall see and abound, thy heart shall wonder and be enlarged]."

But why does it matter to Catherine that she write in her own hand? As already noted, dictation as a form of writing was in some ways more authoritative than writing by hand, and Catherine had "written" letters through dictation for years. What is it about becoming her own scribe that makes this new kind of writing a form of such special consolation, and one expressed in such intensely physical terms, so that *le mani e la lingua s'accordano col cuore* – so that her hands and heart agree with, or express, what is in her heart? A hint might be provided in the very specific way this enigmatic final line of Catherine's postscript, as well as her description of writing as a way to "vent the heart," connect the idea of spiritual consolation/refreshment/pleasure to the vocation of the writer as scribe. Catherine's language here seems obviously to evoke Psalm 44: 2–3: "eructavit cor meum verbum bonum, dico ego opera mea regi, lingua mea calamus scribae velociter scribentis; speciosus forma prae filiis hominum diffusa est gratia in labiis tuis propterea benedixit te Deus in aeternum" (My heart hath uttered a good word. I speak my works to the king; My tongue is the pen of a scrivener that writeth swiftly. Thou art beautiful above the sons of men: grace is poured abroad in thy lips; therefore hath God blessed thee forever). These verses, like the closing passage in Catherine's letter, make writing an expression of a heart overflowing with divine goodness, and make writing a very physical form of union with God, by which the author's tongue is transformed into the pen of the Holy Spirit, to write what the Holy Spirit has inscribed on his heart.[27]

Indeed, this passage from the Psalms was very frequently used in the Middle Ages as a model for writing produced by inspiration rather than the writer's own erudition or education.[28] It was also especially prominent in the liturgy: combinations of these two verses were used frequently as introits and prefaces in the Mass, particularly on the feasts of virgin saints and of the Virgin Mary.[29] Indeed, while it is not certain that the verse was used for the particular Saturday in October (after the feast of Francis of Assisi on October 4) on which Catherine experienced the vision she describes, it was closely associated with the Saturday commemoration of the Virgin Mary. And it seems to have been a verse already associated with Catherine among her followers, as is suggested by a letter from 1376 in which the Florentine Vallambrosian Giovanni dalle Celle defends Catherine's sanctity by arguing for her authority in terms borrowed from Psalm 44 and the Song of Songs.[30] It seems very likely that Catherine is justifying her loquacity – and authorizing her writing – by comparing herself to the Psalmist, the very model of an inspired author.[31]

27 For emphasis on the physicality of the imagery in the Psalm, see for instance Thomas Aquinas' commentary: *Sancti Thomae de Aquino in psalmos Davidis expositio* (Parma, 1863); http://www.corpusthomisticum.org/cps41.html.

28 It is used precisely this way in Thomas' commentary. For example, this verse is probably a source for Dante's famous identification of his persona as an inspired poet in Purgatorio 24, 52–4: "E io a lui: 'I' mi son un che, quando/ Amor mi spira, noto, e a quel modo/ ch'e' ditta dentro vo significando.'"

29 Susan Boynton, "The Bible and the Liturgy," in *The Practice of the Bible in the Middle Ages: Production, Reception, and Performance in Western Christianity*, ed. Boynton and Diana J. Reilly (New York: Columbia University Press, 2011), 20–1.

30 Giovanni dalle Celle and Luigi Marsili, *Lettere*, ed. Francesco Giambonini, Istituto Nazionale di Studi sul Rinascimento, Studi e Testi 22, 2 vols. (Florence: Olschki, 1991), 2: 370–1.

31 I am correcting to some extent my argument in *Saintly Politics of Catherine of Siena*, 194–5. It

It is worth pausing to recall that one model available to Catherine when she set out to write her *Libro* was the *Liber celestis revelacionum* of Birgitta of Sweden, manuscript copies of which had begun to circulate before Catherine's vision and letter to Raymond in October 1377. And it is intriguing to think that Catherine might have known of Birgitta's book when she began her own, and perhaps even knew Birgitta's standard iconography, which showed her receiving her revelations pen in hand.[32] But Catherine as a writer did not imitate Birgitta's *Revelations*, and Birgitta is not a model she invokes here.

The models Catherine does invoke in her postscript are "the Evangelist" – by which she certainly means John – and Thomas Aquinas, who are present with her but do not act. What are they doing here? John is of course the paradigm of the inspired, indeed visionary author and authority. But it is important to note that for Catherine, Thomas Aquinas was a similar kind of figure. In several places in her letters and in her book, Catherine appeals to John and to Thomas Aquinas, as well as to Augustine, as visionary authors, indeed in terms like those used by Raymond to describe Catherine.[33] That Catherine saw herself as entering, as least in one sense, into the world of the Fathers of the Church is suggested in the way she describes God teaching her to write by way of an *exemplar*. The image of schooling that Catherine evokes here is explicitly male – God teaches her the way a master teaches a boy – and distinctly Latinate: there was no formal schooling in the vernacular in fourteenth-century Tuscany – no teachers teaching the vernacular by way of exemplars.[34] By comparing her inspired instruction to a classroom exercise, Catherine gestures to Latinity – if not perhaps to the Latin language itself, then certainly to the cultural place occupied by Latin letters and Latinate books. We have seen that Catherine was aware of the cultural resonance of different book cultures. Here we have Catherine showing that she was conscious of the way in which by embarking on her book, she was venturing into Latin literary culture. The experience Catherine describes to Raymond is clearly a pivotal one in her vocation as a writer. The consolation and refreshment she receives from God's presence is also a call to join her masters, John and Thomas Aquinas, as an author of an inspired book of divine teaching.

is also worth noting that Jane Tylus gives Romans 10:8 as Catherine's scriptural source, which is plausible – in the sense that Paul was a frequent source for Catherine – but Psalm 44 seems much more apt. Psalm 44 is about writing, whereas Romans 10:8 is about preaching.

32 For example, in the famous frontispiece full-page miniature in the Morgan Library manuscript of the *Revelations*, produced in Naples probably under the direction of Alfonso Pecha in 1377 or 1378: https://www.themorgan.org/manuscript/85653.

33 In her *Libro*, Catherine describes these doctors in terms that suggest intellectual vision. See for instance *Dialogo*, ch. 85, 222.

34 Alison Cornish has drawn attention to this incongruity in Catherine's reference to pedagogical practice: *Vernacular Translation in Dante's Italy: Illiterate Literature* (Cambridge and New York: Cambridge University Press, 2011), 120–1. For a fuller discussion of the relevant pedagogical practices and the distinctions between Latin and the vernacular, see Robert Black, *Humanism and Education in Medieval and Renaissance Italy: Tradition and Innovation in Latin Schools From the Twelfth to the Fifteenth Century* (Cambridge and New York: Cambridge University Press, 2001), 41–4.

## Conclusion

There are of course differences in the way Raymond represents Catherine's authorship and the way Catherine herself does. Catherine in this letter gestures dramatically to the pen in her hand in a way that did not serve Raymond's plan for how to present her, and in a way that perhaps might be seen as violating the conventional image of an inspired female spiritual author – although on this point it is worth remembering that Birgitta of Sweden's iconography, standardized in roughly the same year as Catherine's letter, shows Birgitta with pen in hand. In his discussion of Catherine's persona as author, Raymond does not mention the role of spiritual consolation, which as we have seen dominates Catherine's discussion of her authorship as well as her description of her crucial vision, both in letter 272 and in the *Libro* itself, although it could be argued that this theme surfaces elsewhere in the *Legenda maior*. Raymond's omission of letter 272 also perhaps served his purposes by casting Catherine more strictly in the role of an author of transcendent and eternal spiritual teaching. Catherine's letter and the spiritual consolation described in the postscript, on the contrary, are grounded in the particularities of her activities in the world and related ecclesiastical and Italian politics; indeed, it is worth thinking more about the fact that the gift Catherine received in writing was consolation specifically for the bitterness she had experienced in politics and especially as a result of the failures of the Pope and other prelates to lead the church properly. Indeed, in his account in the *Legenda maior*, Raymond locates the major part of Catherine's dictation of the *Libro* to a short period of time following the election of Pope Urban VI on 8 April 1378 and the peace settlement between the new pope and Florence in August 1378, further distancing the book from the letter and the contingent circumstances of her vision and the book's origin.[35] Raymond's account misses, therefore, some of the interesting oscillation in Catherine's account of her vision between the public/political and private/personal meanings of her experience of God's presence.

On the other hand, it should be clear now that the aspects of Raymond's presentation of Catherine that might seem to deny her agency and identity are in fact very close to the self-understanding she expresses in letter 272 and its postscript. Raymond's account of Catherine's marvelous dictation "without the slightest delay, as if she was reading what she spoke from a book placed before her" depends on the trope of the inspired author of Scripture as God's pen – the key idea in the verses of Psalm 44 to which Catherine seems to appeal in her postscript in order to define her new authorial identity. Just as Raymond makes Catherine's literary achievement an effect of "the power of God," for Catherine it is God's presence that gives her the consolation of writing in a new mode, in closer communion with God. And the way in which Raymond and others "translated" Catherine into a male Latin author is anticipated in Catherine's own determination, in her new mode of writing, to join John the Evangelist and Thomas Aquinas. When Catherine set out to write her book, she did

35 There are references in Catherine's letters that suggest strongly that she had completed at least part of the dictation while still staying with the Salimbeni family in late 1377. See for instance letter 365.

so by appealing to the same kinds of cultural transformations at the basis of Raymond of Capua's account of the virtual Latinity of her texts and Caffarini's packaging of Catherine's texts in Latinate manuscripts. Indeed, when Catherine invoked Thomas as a model she may have come very close indeed to Raymond's vision of the role he wanted her to play as an *auctor* and *auctoritas* for the Dominican Order.

Raymond and Catherine's other followers did translate Catherine's *Libro* into Latin, and the manuscripts (both the Italian and Latin ones, as Silvia Nocentini has emphasized) witness the development of a chapter structure and other divisions of the work.[36] Translation into Latin was not a way of suppressing Catherine's voice or an expression of contempt for her lack of learning, but merely a way of transmitting her writings to a larger audience; indeed, in the passage quoted at the start of this essay, Raymond suggests that the Latin translation is not the equal of the original. It is clear that Catherine's followers did not do much to change what she wrote – even where in her letters her syntax is confusing or in the *Libro* where some trimming and organizing might have been useful.[37] The production of Catherine's writings was a cooperative effort, one in which both Catherine and her scribes participated, but one from which Catherine nevertheless emerges with a clear authorial voice. Neither Catherine nor her followers, by emphasizing the divine source of her texts, intended to undermine her claim to the status of an author, any more than they did John, or Aquinas, or Augustine.

If we can read Catherine's announcement to Raymond of Capua as a statement of her aspiration not merely to write, but to compose a book that could take its place on the shelf alongside Latinate classics, perhaps we should take Raymond of Capua's hagiographic comments about her writings more seriously as an argument for the intellectual and cultural stature of her writings, rather than to draw hasty and overly simple conclusions from his emphasis on Catherine's passivity before God. Raymond's comments on Catherine's writing, like his *Legenda* as a whole, should be taken as an expression of his fascination with Catherine, her sanctity and her genius as a spiritual writer – part of a larger fascination with visionary or inspired authors in the later Middle Ages – and not necessarily as a form of repression.[38] To be sure, Raymond and Catherine's other hagiographers transformed her identity to some degree in the process of making her an author, but that is what we do when we write hagiography, whether we write it for a saint's *Legenda* or for book jacket copy. Like Catherine in her account of learning to write, they did this not to suppress some essential aspect of her experience or identity, but rather to usher her into the canon of Christian literature and the world of books.

36 Nocentini, "Il problema testuale."

37 It has long been the consensus among scholars of Catherine's life and writings that her followers in their copies of her texts were faithful to Catherine's original. See for instance Eugenio Dupré Theseider, "Caterina da Siena," *Dizionario biografico degli italiani* (Rome: Istituto della Enciclopedia Italiana, 1960), 22: 361–79.

38 On the increased "visibility" of inspired authors in the later Middle Ages, see my "Inspiration and Imagination," esp. 1149.

6

# CHRISTINE DE PIZAN ON THE JEWS, IN THREE TEXTS: THE *HEURES DE CONTEMPLATION SUR LA PASSION DE NOSTRE SEIGNEUR JHESUCRIST*, THE *FAIS ET BONNES MEURS DU SAGE ROY CHARLES V*, AND THE *MUTACION DE FORTUNE*

THELMA FENSTER

Christine de Pizan (c. 1364–c. 1430) led a life of learning and engagement, stimulated by her reading and intellectual gifts. She produced an astonishingly large and varied body of work, covering politics, philosophy, government, ethics, the conduct of war, autobiography and biography, and religious, homiletic, and consolatory subjects. The times she lived in were calamitous, especially after the death of the French king Charles V in 1380: power struggles between King Charles VI's uncles, shifting loyalties, betrayal, murder, bouts of plague, war with England – all would have tested the hardiest among the French. Widowed in 1390 at the age of twenty-five, Christine spent fourteen years in court protecting her property from the predations of those who sought to cheat her, all the while lamenting the death of her beloved husband, the royal secretary Étienne de Castel. In spite of this, she was uniquely fortunate to have had an educated father, Tommaso da Pizzano, who, in being invited to France to be Charles V's astrologer, brought her to the court of that enlightened medieval French monarch when she was a small child. The happy coincidence of her father's openness to his daughter's scholarly interests (as she tells us in the *Cité des dames*[1]) and the intellectual fertility of the royal court created the ground for her to follow what she saw, in the philosophical language of the time, as her God-given "inclination" to study. Proximity to the French humanists of the king's chancellery and her marriage to Étienne furthered her opportunities to acquire both knowledge and literary skill, and she felt she had become a man by profession, a writer supporting herself and her family.

Christine did most of her writing in the space of a little over a decade, starting in 1399. By any standards, she was extremely energetic, prolific, and quick. A selected list of her most important works from that period, in addition to those to be discussed here, would include the *Epistre Othea* (*Othea's Epistle*, 1400–1), a work of advice to her son in which she makes accomplished use of allegory; the Debate on

1 In the *Cité*, the figure of Droiture, one of three allegorical figures who come to help Christine build the city, reminds Christine that her father was pleased with her inclination to learn and did not think women were worth less by learning. *La città delle dame*, ed. E. J. Richards; trans. (into Italian) Patrizia Caraffi (Milan: Luni Editrice, 1997), 316. Whether he would have approved of the writing she undertook after his death may be another matter.

the *Romance of the Rose* (1401–4), in which her letters show her unafraid to confront influential French humanists; the *Chemin de lonc estude* (*Path of Long Learning*, 1402–3), a dream vision, which includes her first significant consideration of the qualities of an ideal ruler; the *Livre de la mutacion de Fortune* (*Book of Fortune's Mutability*, 1403); the *Livre des fais et bonnes meurs du sage roy Charles V* (*Deeds and Good Practices of the Wise King Charles V*, 1404), a flattering prose biography of the king commissioned by Philip, duke of Burgundy, who admired the *Mutacion*; the *Livre de la cité des dames* (*City of Ladies*, 1404–5), a prose history of women, the first composed by a woman; the *Livre des trois vertus* (*Book of Three Virtues*, 1405–6), also known as the *Tresor de la Cité des dames* (*Treasury of the City of Ladies*), innovative in its advice to women of all classes and again a first by a woman; the *Advision Cristine* (*Christine's Vision*, 1405), a partly autobiographical, philosophical reflection; the *Corps de policie* (*Body Politic*, 1406–7); the *Fais d'armes et de chevalerie* (*Deeds of Arms and of Chivalry*, 1410); the *Lamentation sur les maulx de France* (*Lamentation on the Ills of France*, 1410); and the *Livre de paix* (*Book of Peace*, 1412–14). In spite of this copious output, Christine's writing fell into obscurity after the early modern period, rescued from time to time by interest in one or another of her books, frequently her biography of King Charles V. In the wake of the twentieth-century women's movement, it was at first her defense of women that attracted scholars; over time, and in keeping with the modern feminist desire to uncover neglected work by women, that initial focus broadened into study and evaluation of as much of her work as could be made available.[2]

When Christine wrote on political subjects, civil harmony under a good king was her principal concern.[3] Urging the noble classes to set a standard of public behavior, thereby to ensure the health of the kingdom of France, was never far from her mind, nor was it always a discrete category: as early as the opening verses of her *Epistre au dieu d'Amours* (1399), otherwise thought to be a "courtly" composition, she says that good behavior is especially the purview of French nobles, who should make France an example to the world.[4] It goes without saying, but may be worth emphasizing, that the exemplary king would be a good *Christian* king. How then should that king act toward Jews, regarded as Christianity's enemies? History shows that this was not an

2 All the compositions mentioned above have now appeared in modern editions, with most translated into modern French or English. The list does not include Christine's lyric or courtly poetry, written in the same decade. Courtly narrative includes the *Epistre au dieu d'Amours* (*Letter from the God of Love*, 1399) *Dit de la Rose* (*Tale of the Rose*, 1402), *Debat de deux amants* (*Debate of Two Lovers*, 1400), *Trois jugemens* (*Three Judgments*, 1400), *Dit de Poissy* (*Tale of Poissy*, 1400), *Dit de la pastoure* (*Tale of the Shepherdess*, 1403), and *Duc des vrais amans* (*Duke of True Lovers*, 1403–5); her important later poem, the *Ditié de Jeanne d'Arc* (*Poem of Joan of Arc*) was written shortly before she died. A commented list of Christine's individual works, with their modern editions and translations, where available, is given in Nadia Margolis, *An Introduction to Christine de Pizan* (Gainesville, FL: University Press of Florida, 2011), 202–11.

3 Claire Le Ninan, "la concorde civile autour d'un bon roi est le sujet principal de ses textes politiques"; *Le Sage Roi et la clergesse: L'écriture du politique dans l'oeuvre de Christine de Pizan* (Paris: Honoré Champion, 2013), 10–11.

4 *Poems of Cupid, God of Love: Christine de Pizan's* Epistre au dieu d'Amours *and* Dit de la Rose, *Thomas Hoccleve's* The Letter of Cupid, *with George Sewell's* The Proclamation of Cupid, ed. and trans. Thelma Fenster and Mary Carpenter Erler (Leiden: E. J. Brill, 1990), 34–5.

idle question: under the Capetian kings, and then the Capetian branch of the Valois, the Jews of France were subject to alternating attempts to tolerate, convert, kill, or expel them. In 1182, Philip Augustus banished the Jews, but in 1198, he recalled them. In 1306, Philip the Fair again expelled the Jews,[5] but in 1315, Louis X invited them back. King John the Good, Charles V's father, captured in 1356 at the Battle of Poitiers, needed Jewish financial skill to help pay the enormous ransom to the English stipulated in the Treaty of Brétigny (1360), and his son, always in need of funds, allowed the Jews to remain in France throughout his own reign. In 1394, Charles VI became the last medieval king to expel the Jews from France, and this time, they were gone for good, or at least until the seventeenth century. What William Chester Jordan, studying an earlier period in French medieval history, has called the French royal court's "obsession with the place of the Jews in society"[6] could easily be extended to the French Middle Ages up to 1394.

In view of that "obsession," and considering Christine's abiding interest in the ways of government, her silence about royal policy toward the Jews is surprising. What the king should do about the Jews seems not to enter openly into Christine's deliberations on royal exemplarity: in every instance where she mentions the Jews, the terms of their residency have already been settled extratextually. Was the king's attitude toward and treatment of the Jews an element in the conduct of a good king? Would a good medieval king be tolerant, or would he punish the confirmed enemies of Christianity? We know that important shapers of doctrine, from Augustine to Aquinas, had each proposed somewhat different solutions. Which position did Christine take? Should the Jews have remained as witnesses, as Augustine held, or was their expulsion the better course?

Christine mentions Jews in three works, each an illustration of a distinct orientation. Her most straightforward commentary is found in a late work, the *Heures de contemplation sur la Passion de Nostre Seigneur Jhesucrist* (*Hours of Contemplation on Our Lord's Passion*, 1418–28, hereinafter *Heures*), a devotional treatise notable for having been written by a layperson and a woman, which condemns the Jews for Jesus's death. In the *Livre des fais et bonnes meurs du sage roy Charles V*, written at least fourteen years earlier, she praises Charles V's legal judgment in favor of a Jew; but her account of Jewish history in the *Livre de la mutacion de Fortune*, and especially its framing, offers puzzles as yet to be seriously considered.[7] Of the three, the *Heures* events are played out against

5 See Danièle Iancu-Agou and Elie Nicolas, *Philippe le Bel et les Juifs du royaume de France (1306)*, Nouvelle Gallia Judaica 7 (Paris: Éditions du Cerf, 2012). The 1306 expulsion in particular left a literary record of Jewish grief; see Susan L. Einbinder, *No Place of Rest: Jewish Literature, Expulsion, and the Memory of Medieval France* (Philadelphia: University of Pennsylvania Press, 2009).

6 William Chester Jordan, "Anti-Judaism in the Christina Psalter," in *Christianity and Culture in the Middle Ages: Essays to Honor John Van Engen*, ed. David C. Mengel and Lisa Wolverton (Notre Dame, IN: University of Notre Dame Press, 2014), 288. See also Jordan, *The French Monarchy and the Jews from Philip Augustus to the Last Capetians* (Philadelphia: University of Pennsylvania Press, 1989).

7 Editions are *Les heures de contemplacion sur la Passion de Nostre Seigneur Jhesucrist*, ed. Liliane Dulac and René Stuip, with E. J. Richards (Paris: Honoré Champion, 2017); *Le livre des fais et bonnes meurs du sage roy Charles V*, ed. Suzanne Solente, 2 vols. (Paris: Honoré Champion, 1936); *Le livre de la mutacion de Fortune*, ed. Suzanne Solente, 4 vols.; Jewish history appears in volume 2. Société des

an ancient history whose interpretation was, to medieval Christians, a settled matter. The *Fais et bonnes meurs* and the *Mutacion* passages, however, achieve greatest meaning only in the context of medieval French history, to which both bear witness.

### On the Death of Jesus

Medieval writers talking of Jesus' death inevitably invoked the Jews as the responsible party, and Christine was not an exception. Blame of the Jews appears early in her career in the *Oroyson de Nostre Seignur* (1402–3), where the Jews are called false, a people of unparalleled cruelty,[8] but for a statement justifying their censure, we must turn to the *Heures*. Now conceivably retired to the convent at Poissy where her daughter resided, Christine may have composed the *Heures* there, possibly for the convent's residents, mostly noble women who lived within its walls.[9] Many would also have suffered the loss of family members at Agincourt and the ensuing English depredations (including no doubt the Duke of Bedford's removal of Charles V's library, presumably an erstwhile important resource for Christine). Using a popular version of crucifixion history, she condemns the Jews, perceived as Jesus's murderers, but she exonerates Pilate. Addressing Jesus directly, she says:

> Mais, mon doulx Sauveur, quant Pilate te ot par pluseurs fois sur ces choses bien interrogué et mis a question, apperceut et vist ton innocence et purté, et clerement congneust la fraude, mauvaistié et envye de ceulx qui t'accusoient, dont briefment leur dist qu'il ne trouvoit en toy nulle cause de mort. O Pilate, se bon juge feusses et droit justicier, ceulx eusses condempnez et Jhesucrist delivré.
>
> (But my sweet Savior, when Pilate had interrogated and questioned you many times about these things, and perceived and saw your innocence and purity, and clearly saw the deception, evil and envy of those who accused you – about this he shortly told them that he found no reason to put you to death. Oh, Pilate, if you had been a good judge and a good administrator, you would have condemned them and set Jesus Christ free.)

She concludes by saying to the Jews that "Certes a bon droit l'avez puis chierement compaiez" (You have certainly paid rightly and dearly for that.)[10] Here, then, is a stated position, and a long-held one, because Christine had first uttered it at least fifteen

Anciens Textes Français (Paris: A. & J. Picard, 1959–66); English: Geri L. Smith, trans., *Book of the Mutability of Fortune* (Toronto: Iter; Tempe, AZ: Arizona Center for Medieval and Renaissance Studies, 2017). In this essay English translations from the *Mutacion* are my own; see my n. 35.

8 "Une Oroyson de Nostre Seigneur," in *Oeuvres poétiques de Christine de Pisan*, ed. Maurice Roy, 3 vols. (Paris: Firmin Didot, 1888–96), 3 : 15–26, at 18, 21.

9 *Heures*, xxi–xxii.

10 Christine de Pizan, *Les Heures de contemplacion sur la Passion de Nostre Seigneur Jhesucrist*, ed. Liliane Dulac and René Stuip, with E. J. Richards (Paris: Honoré Champion, 2017). For a description of the *Heures*, see Maureen Barry McCann Boulton, *Sacred Fictions of Medieval France: Narrative Theologies in the Lives of Christ and the Virgin, 1150–1500*, Gallica 38 (Cambridge: D. S. Brewer, 2015), 249–53.

years earlier, in the *Mutacion*. Before discussing the *Mutacion*, however, I turn first to the *Fais et bonnes meurs*, treating the two works in the order of their internal chronology, Charles V to Charles VI, thereby following the trajectory in late medieval France from toleration of the Jews to their expulsion.

## A Jew in Court

The anecdote of the *Fais et bonnes meurs*, "a moral and philosophical treatise on the nature and effects of kingly virtue," suggests more than it says.[11] In it Charles V adjudicates a case brought by a Jew against a Christian who had given the Jew a false pledge, and he finds in favor of the Jew. The episode provides a rare glimpse into the king's Jewish policy at work. It is not likely that Charles himself would have acted as *justicier* in the case had there not been a political and financial infrastructure in place which called for the Jews to supply funds to the crown in return for residence in France under the king's protection; these were the "king's Jews."[12] Charles is exemplary because he honored the terms of his compact with the Jews, that is, he "feist droit aux Juifs": he did what was right toward the Jews, dispensing justice toward them.[13] Christine may have applauded Charles' policy, but she was writing the *Fais et bonnes meurs* under his son's reign, and by then the Jews were gone from France.

The king's agreement with the Jews depended upon arrangements most immediately traceable to Jean II le Bon, Charles V's father. In 1361, burdened by the enormous ransom owed to the English after his capture at Poitiers and the expenses of war with England, not to mention costly internal strife, Jean issued an ordinance allowing financially skilled Jews to return to France under very favorable circumstances.[14] Jean's edict specified a limited term of twenty years, but it was renewed several times under Charles V (in 1370, 1372, and 1380) and even once under Charles VI (1392). Jean, and Charles after him, granted the Jews the right to own or rent houses and to retain plots of land for cemeteries; they could own whatever books they desired (the Talmud, burned in Paris in 1242 and confiscated in 1284, 1290, and 1299, and in Toulouse in 1319, was not forbidden). They were permitted to charge their Christian clients at high interest: the higher the interest, the greater the sums flowing into the royal coffers in the form of loans, taxes and *captiones*, or "takings" from Jews (which in turn amounted to an indirect taxation by the king on his Christian subjects). The Jews could not be prosecuted if goods given them as pledges had been stolen. In turn, they paid a fixed sum of money annually to the crown, in addition to initial fees for the right of entry.[15]

11 Daisy Delogu, *Theorizing the Ideal Sovereign: The Rise of the French Vernacular Royal Biography* (Toronto: University of Toronto Press, 2008), 180.

12 Jordan, *French Monarchy and the Jews*, 249.

13 *Fais et bonnes meurs* I:XXIII, 61.

14 This implies that the Jews already in France did not have any legal authorization (Roger S. Kohn, "Les Juifs de la France du nord à travers les archives du Parlement de Paris (1359?–1394)," *Revue des Etudes Juives* 141 (1982): 13–29, at 20.

15 Kohn, "Les Juifs de la France du nord," 18–21, and Kohn, "Les Juifs en France du Nord dans la seconde moitié du XIVe siècle: un état de la question," in *L'Expulsion des Juifs de France, 1394*, ed. Gilbert and Elias Nicolas (Paris: Éditions du Cerf, 2004), 13–30, at 22.

To function, that system needed the king's protection of the Jews: "across Europe, those who claimed power came to claim a special power over Jews."[16] But the king's protection of the Jews affected his officers, for if he discovered that any of them had violated his example, he ordered their immediate dismissal and punishment.[17] Such decisions would have reminded the king's Christian subjects that cheating a Jew amounted to cheating the king himself. In the middle were the Jews, potentially objects of (sometimes violent) resentment.

The Jews residing in Christian France and speaking French were never strictly French. Although we may hope that individual Jews enjoyed reasonable relations with individual Christians, given their commercial contacts, the Jews as a group had never been assimilated into French medieval culture with the same rights as Christians. The circumstances of their residency – their place – in France for a good part of the fourteenth century can be glimpsed in this *lettre de sauvegarde* issued by Charles V, outlining the conditional welcome he extended to those Jews with financial skill:

> il n'ont pas ne bien propre aucun en toute chretianté, ou ils puissent demourer, frequanter ne y habiter, si ce n'est de la propre et pure licence et volonté du Seigneur ou Seigneurs soubz qui il se vouldroient asseoir pour demourer soubz eulz comme leurs subgiez, et qui à ce les recueillir et recevoir
>
> (they own not a single property in all of Christianity, wherever they may reside, visit, or live, unless by the personal, unconditional authorization and will of the lord or lords who agree to receive and welcome them and under [whose jurisdiction] they wish to install themselves, to reside under them as their subjects.)[18]

Charles V's need for money encouraged a pragmatic tolerance toward the Jews, with the granting of favorable terms. But his view of the Jews was not necessarily shared by the French people or clergy, and upon his death in 1380 rioters pillaged all forty houses of the Jewish quarter in Paris, killing people and snatching away and baptizing Jewish babies. The Religieux de Saint-Denis railed against the subsequent return of the babies to their parents, slandering the Jews as enemies of Christ and a disgrace to the French people. It is the Religieux who tells us that Charles VI, having been informed of the civil disorder, and in spite of the enormous sums extracted from the Jews to fill the royal coffers, listened to "wise counsel and to the pleas of the queen," and the 17th of September 1394 the Jews were required by ordonnance to leave France before Christmas.[19]

16 David Nirenberg, *Anti-Judaism: The Western Tradition* (New York: W. W. Norton, 2013), 189–90.

17 *Fais et bonnes meurs*, I.XXIII:61.

18 Roger S. Kohn, "Les Juifs de la France du nord à travers les archives du Parlement de Paris (1359?–1394)," *Revue des Etudes Juives* 141 (1982): 13–29, at 21.

19 Bernard Guenée, *La Folie de Charles VI, roi bien-aimé* (Paris: Perrin, 2004), 183–4.

## How Odd the Jews: The *Mutacion*

Questions still surround the decision by Charles VI to expel the Jews.[20] As mentioned, in 1392 the king renewed his father's contract with the Jews, but a mere two years later he broke the contract and banished them. It was during that two-year period that the "mad king" had begun to suffer from the mental illness that would soon incapacitate him. The first episode occurred in mid-summer 1392 and lasted until October. The second episode took place from June 1393 to January 1394, and the third in mid-1395; it was not until 1397, however, that Charles's "absences" became more frequent. Contemporary opinion was divided as to whether the king ever regained the ability to make complex decisions, but it matters that at times many considered him sane.[21]

In 1400 Christine began to write the *Mutacion*, a universal history in nearly 24,000 octosyllables in rhyming couplets on the theme of Fortune's unaccountable capriciousness.[22] Fortune was known to determine – or interrupt – the course of individual lives, including Christine's own, without regard to what was deserved. As Christine readily (and pointedly) admits, the Jews do not belong in the *Mutacion*, for it was God directing Fortune, not Fortune acting alone, who determined what happened to the Jews, both their rewards and their punishments. But it is *how* Christine tells Jewish history in the *Mutacion* that has challenged modern understanding more than many other aspects of Christine's writing, and so the remaining space of this essay will be devoted to a discussion of the *Mutacion*'s Jewish history.

About 300 verses before commencing Jewish history, Christine prepares her readers to expect that it will be told "differently," emphasizing that the Jews stand squarely outside her theme and she will have to expand what she is writing in order to accommodate their story:

> Affin que mon oeuvre accomplie
> Soit, et que riens je n'y oublie,
> Ancore un peu dilateray[23]
> Mon propos, car je me tairay
> Des choses que Fortune meine
> Puis hault, puis bas, en maint demaine,

20 Elie Nicolas, questioning the motives for Charles VI's decision to banish the Jews, points out that usury continued in any case after 1394, as did the royal need for money ("Typologie des sources chrétiennes," in *L'Expulsion des Juifs de France, 1394*, ed. Dahan and Nicolas, 95–122, at 110.

21 See R. C. Famiglietti, *Royal Intrigue: Crisis at the Court of Charles VI 1392–1420* (New York: AMS, 1986), 19.

22 Christine wrote the *Mutacion* over a period starting in summer 1400 and ending in November 1403. She presented a first copy to the Duke of Burgundy on January 1, 1404, and a second to the Duke of Berry in March of the same year (Margolis, *Introduction to Christine de Pizan*, 88).

23 The *DMF* gives this very passage to illustrate *dilater* in the meaning *développer*, "develop" (*DMF* s.v. *dilater*).

En touchant les vrayes histoires
Des Juïfs anciennes et voires,
Car leurs fais et prosperitez,
Ou leurs grandes adversitez,
A Fortune je n'enjoing mie,
Car Dieux, cuy la loy ert amie,
Les punissoit et meritoit,
Selon leur dessarte, et metoit
Puis hault ou bas, selon leur vice
Ou merite, par sa justice.
Combien que je pourroie dire,
Ce me semble que Nostre Sire
Consentoit, selon leur desertes,
Que Fortune gaignes et pertes
Leur envoyast,...

> (In order that my work may be complete, and so that I don't forget anything, I'll expand my story a bit, for I'll be silent about the things that Fortune brings, high and low, in many a place, by treating the true history, ancient and true, of the Jews, for I do not attribute their deeds and successes or their great adversities to Fortune. For God, religion's friend, punished and rewarded them according to what they deserved, [and brought them] high or low, according to their bad or good deeds, through his justice. Whatever I might say, it seems to me that Our Lord allowed Fortune to send them gains and losses, as they merited; vv. 8415–33).

In fact, it was more immediately the kings of France who determined the fate of the Jews of France.

Christine is reluctant to include the Jewish past, and she does so, she says, only in the interests of completeness, so as not to be accused of having forgotten something. When later she arrives at the story of the Jews, then, we should not be surprised that she does something quite unusual: departing from the octosyllables of the rest of the poem, she recounts Jewish history not in poetry but in prose. Considering the cost to the integrity of her poem and to the aesthetics of a major work by a cautious woman always eager to demonstrate her skill, the alteration surprises. Is this a flaw, or a demonstration of skill?

As for her source for Jewish history, Christine claims to find it in the topmost room of Fortune's abode, a many-chambered castle set on an icy, perpetually revolving rock in the sea. The walls of the room feature depictions of the branches of medieval knowledge; also affixed to the walls are paintings of stories of the Hebrews. On a table, she discovers a bible, an authoritative source for Jewish history (v. 8740). But now, seeming to prepare her readers anew, she makes a second announcement about the Jewish history she proposes to relate: she has been stricken by a fever and lacks the strength to write poetry. Instead, she will tell the history of the Jews in prose:

> Or me couvient cy excuser
> Un petit, car ne puis muser
> A rimer, pour fievre soubdaine
> Qui m'a seurpris, dont suis en peine.
> Sus ce pas faut laisser ester;
> Mais, pour mon ouvrage haster,
> Mettray la prose en la maniere
> Que mot a mot l'escri plainiere,
> En la sale cy devant dicte,
> Ou la Bible trouvay escripte;
> Si ne soit pas tenu a faute,
> Pour ce qu'ay de santé deffaute,
> Dont troublé mon entendement
> Est a present aucunement;
> Et qui de bien rimer se charge,
> Ce n'est mie petite charge,
> Et par especial histoires
> Abriger en parolles voires!

(At this point I must excuse myself a bit, for I can't think of rhyming [or writing in meter] because a sudden fever has overwhelmed me and put me in discomfort; in the circumstances, I must leave things as they are. But to speed my work along, I shall write in prose in such a way that I do it plainly in the room I mentioned before, where I found the bible written. May I not be judged at fault because my health has failed me and [because] my thinking is somewhat confused at the moment. And whoever takes the responsibility of writing poetry, that is not a small task, and especially [when] abbreviating stories in truthful words; vv. 8731–48)

When Christine finishes her account of Jewish history, she moves on to Assyrian and Babylonian history, reverting to poetry and remarking that she has now recovered her health:

> Or est (Dieu merci!) respassee
> La grevance, qui ma pensee
> A troublee et foibli mon corps.
> Si remeray, com j'ay amors,
> Suivant mon stile premerain.

(Now, God be thanked, the malady that confused my thinking and weakened my body is past. So I will rhyme, as is my custom, following my first style, vv. 8749–53)

This curious passage has not been much discussed in modern criticism. Many present-day readers have silently accepted the comments of Suzanne Solente, editor of the *Mutacion*, who found this explanation curious, enough to try to corroborate

Christine's illness by consulting her other works. She notes that Christine talks of an illness that befell her in the partly autobiographical *Advision*, written in prose and completed in 1405. Christine describes a debilitating illness that struck her in the past, but not at the moment of writing; there seems no cause to doubt her.[24] Solente adduces a second example, however, which is less persuasive: in ballad 43 of her *Cent balades* Christine laments a severe illness which she says is afflicting her at the very moment of composing her poem.[25] Made up of three eight-line stanzas of rhyming heptasyllables plus *envoi*, ballad 43 must be considered a *tour de force*, if only because the poet, who says she is so weak she cannot stand, has in fact composed poetry. Illness here could of course have been an after-the-fact literary construction, and there could have been no illness at all, but the ballad, a pretext for writing, nonetheless puts the illness explanation of the *Mutacion* in question.

Current discussion, such as it is, has crystallized around only two possible readings: either Christine was "really" ill, or, if she wasn't, she was an antisemite. Those limits, I suggest, put an end to any effort to understand another reading – indeed, even *that* there may be another reading, although it is clear that illness alone cannot begin to address the range of questions this passage raises. Even those who accept it have nonetheless noticed one irreducible piece of the enigma: timing, as the malady begins and ends precisely around Jewish history. In fact, Christine's explanations are noticeably overdetermined: first, there is the announcement of an intended digression 300 lines before the beginning of the account, as if anticipating her reader's curiosity; then, there is the onset of illness occurring precisely at the beginning of the history (had it happened in the midst of the history it might have been more believable); finally, a celebration of returned good health just as that history finishes (that too could have occurred at a different, perhaps more persuasive point) – this is a passage that begs to be read otherwise.

In the early, most prolific part of her career, it was Christine's habit to work on several pieces simultaneously, which lends itself to the modern technique of dating the events of one text according to the events of other textual witnesses. I suggest, however, that it is unlikely that Christine's medieval readers would have needed to corroborate the truth of this illness with other such instances in order to make sense of the passage. Perhaps we modern readers bring to the text an urgency of exculpatory interpretation that medieval readers, persuaded that Jews were the enemies of Christianity, and unchallenged in their right to think so, did not and could not feel. There is in fact no evidence to show that she did not share her contemporaries' negative views of the Jews. Even for medieval Christians who may have enjoyed reasonable relations with individual Jews, the Jews as a group were deeply anomalous, a perspective embedded in the anti-Judaism David Nirenberg has written about so

24 *Le livre de l'advision Cristine*, ed. Christine Reno and Liliane Dulac (Paris: Honoré Champion, 2001), 101, ll. 65–7.

25 *Oeuvres poétiques de Christine de Pisan*, ed. Maurice Roy, 3 vols., Société des Anciens Textes Français (Paris: Firmin Didot, 188696), 1:44. The illness adduced in this poem is is debatable on other grounds, since some have read it instead as a love poem; see James Laidlaw, "L'unité des 'Cent balades'", in *The City of Scholars: New Approaches to Christine de Pizan*, ed. Margarete Zimmerman and Dina Di Rentiis (Berlin: Walter de Gruyter, 1994), 96–106, at 104.

well and which he characterizes as not simply "an attitude toward Jews and their religion, but a way of critically engaging the world." Meditating upon the place of the Jews allowed Christians to construct their own place in the world and in history, defining themselves as a people in "fundamental opposition to Jews and Judaism."[26]

Further, the prose passage has struck some modern scholars as so jarringly detrimental to the integrity of the *Mutacion* (Jeanette Beer has dubbed it *décousue*, implying that it had come unraveled[27]) that they have wondered why Christine never took the trouble to revise it.[28] This aesthetic question, combined with the challenge of being a woman writing, in my view presents a strong argument against considering the prose Jewish history to be a result of simple happenstance: Christine, deeply conscious of her situation as a woman in a masculine sphere, was always careful, even eager, to prove her skills (sometimes she herself points out her talent). It is extraordinarily unlikely that she would have willingly compromised her reputation as a poet, a point that has been made over and over in modern scholarship. Further, the departure from stylistic protocol in the *Mutacion* is an isolated action, not a technique duplicated any place else in Christine's work. We can only wonder whether writing about the popularly perceived shortcomings of the Jews did not in fact suit the ethics of a book written after the Jews were expelled from France and while memory of the event was still relatively fresh.

Christine's *oeuvre* does not provide a strict demarcation of uses as between poetry and prose. There is a *tendency* for prose or verse to be used for separate types of writing: her early courtly narratives are done in verse, for instance, while some texts, such as the *Livre du duc des vrais amans* and the learned *Epistre Othea* systematically mix poetry and prose. Notable prose compositions include the letters in the Debate of the Rose, the *Cité des dames*, the biography of King Charles V, and the *Advision Cristine*, at once a mirror for princes and an autobiography. It would be wrong, however, to leave the impression that all Christine's "serious" work was written in prose, for her *Chemin de lonc estude* was also composed in octosyllables.[29] The pointed separation between prose and poetry in the *Mutacion* not only asks about the use of prose, it also leads to questioning how Christine saw poetry. Her most extended commentary on

26 Nirenberg, *Anti-Judaism*, 3.

27 Jeanette Beer, "Christine et les conventions dans *Le livre de la Mutacion de Fortune*: 'abriger en parolles voires'", in *Une femme de lettres au Moyen Age: Études autour de Christine de Pizan*, ed. Liliane Dulac and Bernard Ribémont (Orleans: Paradigme, 1995), 355 n. 7. See also Margolis, *Introduction to Christine de Pizan*, 92.

28 Four manuscripts containing the *Mutacion* show Christine's personal intervention in various ways, and all were prepared simultaneously: MS Brussels, KBR, 9508, end 1403–beginning 1404 (presented to Philip the Bold end 1404); MS The Hague, KB, 78 D 42, 1403–4 (presented to the Duke of Berry in March 1404); MS Chantilly, Bibliothèque du Château, 494, toward 1404; MS ex-Phillips 207, private collection, toward 1404; MS Munich, BSB, Cod. Gall. 11, toward 1410–11. Solente chose the Brussels manuscript, which contains only the *Mutacion*, as the base of her edition. The *Mutacion* appears in whole or in part in additional manuscripts; see Solente's discussion, *Mutacion*, vol. 1, xcix–cxxxviii.

29 Earlier scholarly claims that prose arose with historiography (specifically, with the *Pseudo-Turpin*) have not gained consensus: Gabrielle Spiegel, *Romancing the Past: The Rise of Vernacular Prose Historiography in Thirteenth-Century France* (Berkeley: University of California Press, 1993), 63.

poetry, in the *Fais et bonnes meurs*, may shed light.[30] As she presents it, poetry is composed of an *introduction*, a superficial level which has its own meaning but which also signifies other meanings *occultement* (in hidden fashion), and the aim of this is truth. Doctrine is re-dressed (*revestue*) in unfamiliar ways, the manner of it done according to appropriate signs or signals (*figures*). This was the way of the Hebrew bible, and even Jesus Christ spoke in *figures*, because that way is more accessible (*comprehendieuse*), better welcomed, and gives greater pleasure. Although writing in prose is credibly less demanding than writing in verse, in the *Mutacion* Christine also points to another important advantage: prose allows her to write *mot àmot* (word for word, v. 8738). Medieval translation theory had distinguished between rendering word for word and sense for sense, a tradition handed down by Jerome, who normally advocated rendering sense for sense, except in the case of the Bible.[31] But medieval hermeneutics of Scripture made a further distinction, between a literal reading and a spiritual one. To reach the spiritual meaning hidden behind the literal meaning of Scripture, one had to read not literally, the way the Jews were alleged to do, but spiritually, as advocated by Paul and the church fathers, on the grounds that the mystery of holy writing could be uncovered only in that way. To explain why Jews refused to see the superior message of Christianity, the church fathers, including Origen, Ambrose, Jerome and Augustine, using *ad hominem* exegesis, argued that the Jews, unable to read the spiritual sense of scripture, were blind to its mysteries – they could read only its surface, only its letters and its words.[32] Christine has combined these two traditions, translation theory and scriptural hermeneutics: she invokes the notion of "sense for sense" from translation theory, and combines it with the notion from hermeneutics that the spiritual sense gives access to deeper meaning, and with this move attempts to explain the mysterious character of poetic figuration in general. Her move away from the intricacies of poetry to relate Jewish history in prose signifies that certain kinds of prose invite no spiritual interpretation. Prose speaks to the limit of the Jewish hermeneutic.

Closely related to the prose presentation of Jewish history is the rather flat, decidedly unlyrical rhythm of its chronicle listing of names and dates, which diverges markedly from the rounded stories in the *Mutacion*. Christine borrows this Jewish history from the *Fleurs des chroniques,* a French translation of Bernard Gui's (1260–1331) *Flores chronicorum*,[33] a collection of works translated from Latin into French in 1368

30 See "Cy dit de poesie," *Fais et bonnes meurs*, II :176–8.

31 See Rita Copeland, *Rhetoric, Hermeneutics, and Translation in the Middle Ages: Academic Traditions and Vernacular Texts* (Cambridge: Cambridge University Press, 1991), ch. 2, 37–62.

32 See Nirenberg's chapter "Early Christianity: The Road to Emmaus, the Road to Damascus," in *Anti-Judaism*, 48–134. See also Jeremy Cohen, *Living Letters of the Law: Ideas of the Jew in Medieval Christianity* (Berkeley: University of California Press, 1999), and idem, *The Friars and the Jews: The Evolution of Medieval Anti-Judaism* (Ithaca: Cornell University Press, 1982).

33 More than forty Latin manuscripts contain the *Flores*, but only one corresponds to the text in the French translation: Bibliothèque Nationale de France MS lat. 4975. See Thomas F. Coffey, ed., "Bernard Gui, *Les Fleurs des Chroniques*: An Introduction and Commentary" (Ph.D. diss., Catholic University of America, 1974), vii. For discussion, see Léopold Delisle, *Notice sur les manuscrits de Bernard Gui* (Paris: Imprimerie Nationale, 1879). Gui executed five [?]"editions" of his universal chronicle: 1315–16, 1319, 1320, 1321, 1327, and 1330 or 1331.

at the command of King Charles V.[34] In the *Flores* Gui calls himself a chronographer (*chronographe*), a recorder of events and dates. He distinguishes this from the work of an historiographer (*hystoriographe*), someone who relates or expatiates on the character of an individual or an event, elaborating on its exceptionality. These descriptive terms could well characterize the difference between Christine's "chronographic" Jewish history and her fuller "historiographic" approach throughout the rest of the *Mutacion*. She concludes each list, as does Gui, with the assertion that the Jews were undone because they worshipped idols, as in the following:

> Aprés vint Gedeon qui gouverna .XL. ans, lors vivoit Herculés. En ce temps furent derechief desconfis de Madian et de Amalech, pour la cause dessus dicte, et furent serfs l'espace de .VII. ans, dont Gedeon les delivra, et furent en paix .XL. ans, tant comme Gedeon les gouverna. Aprés vint Abimelech, son filz, qui gouverna .III. ans. Aprés vint Thola, qui gouverna .XXIII. ans, et, en ce temps, flourissoit la tierce Sebile Seurnommee delphique et Priamus regnoit en Troye. Aprés gouverna Jaïr .XXII. ans. Aprés gouverna Jepté .VI. ans, et, en son temps, delivra les Juifs de la servitude, ou ilz avoient esté .XVIII. ans des Philistines et Amon, qui les avoient desconfis, et la cause avoit esté ydolatrie a Baalim
>
> (Gideon came after, who governed for forty years; Hercules lived then. At that time they were once again ruined by the Midianites and the Amalekites [...], and were slaves for seven years, from which Gideon delivered them; and they were at peace for forty years, for as long as Gideon governed them. Afterward came Abimelech, Gideon's son, who ruled for three years. After him came Thola, who ruled for twenty-three years, and at this time the Sibyl named Delphic flourished, and Priam reigned in Troy. Afterward Jephthah ruled for six years, and during his time he delivered the Jews from the servitude in which they had been [placed] by the Philistines and Amon, who had defeated them, and the cause of that was their idolatrous worship of Baal).[35]

34 The copy Christine consulted remained in the royal library at the Louvre until 1425, when it was sold. It is now Bibliothèque Nationale de France MS Nouv. acq. fr. 1409. Two other extant manuscripts contain the same chronicle: Bibliothèque Nationale de France MS fr. 17180 (dated 1468) and the fourteenth-century Biblioteca Apostolica Vaticana Regina MS 700. Both, with MS 1409, appear to be copies of a lost French prototype.

35 *Mutacion*, 2: 159; this is omitted in Smith's abridgment of Christine's Jewish history.

Gui was appointed inquisitor of Toulouse for the Dominicans on January 16, 1307, a post he occupied until 1323, along the way writing an inquisitor's guide, the *Practica inquisitionis heretice pravitatis*, in which he listed Jews among heretics.[36] The ultimate source for his Jewish history, the Hebrew "historical" books of Joshua, Judges, Samuel, and Kings, gave material for the theme Gui wished to develop, Jewish idolatry and sinning toward God. The books, which are not part of the Torah (the Pentateuch, or Five Books of Moses), constitute a continuous history from Moses' death through the Babylonian exile, and they share one ideology: exclusive worship of God and belief in an eternal and supreme Davidic dynasty. They warn against idolatry and stress its terrible consequences, attributing Jewish defeats to the Jews' failure to obey God. Although Christine's choice of Gui's history to represent a generic Jewish history may have been a matter of what she found translated into French in King Charles's library – the Duke of Berry owned a French translation of Josephus's *Antiquities of the Jews*, but it did not enter the royal library before 1410[37] – there is no reason to suppose that she was a slavish imitator, either in content or in style, or that the blame for what she says about the Jews can be laid at Gui's feet. Gui's chronicle offers little in the way of the drama that accompanies so many of Christine's historiographic stories, and its shape as a list may have presented special challenges, but to question Christine's virtuosity as a storyteller and metricist in this one instance – to imagine, that is, that she was unable to convert the material into more pleasing form at any point, as some have briefly thought – does her a serious injustice. If one had to talk about the Jews, as Christine clearly thought she did, it would have been absurdly out of place to have claimed publicly that the "enemies" of Christianity did not deserve their fate. At the end of her passage on the Jews, Christine says by way of summation, that the Jews are:

> vagues et inestables, *sanz pays at sanz seigneur*, en punicion du pechié, qu'ils commirent, en crucifiant Nostre Seigneur
>
> (errant and unstable, *without a country and without a ruler*, in punishment for the sin they committed in crucifying Our Lord; my emphasis)[38]

In other words, the Jews were deeply unlike the French, who had a land and someone to rule it, a well-placed reminder to Christine's readers of what was most important for France.

The medieval idea that the Jews were fated to wander is said to go back to Vespasian's conquest of Jerusalem and his claim to all its captured Jews, although it no doubt had other sources as well. As the story goes, Vespasian sold all but 180 Jews to his soldiers, sending the 180 into exile and dooming them to wander, but under his

36 For Gui's life and writing, see Delisle, *Bernard Gui*, 179. According to Jeremy Cohen, Gui's *Practica* made "concern with the Jews a permanent aspect of the operations of the Papal inquisition" (*The Friars and the Jews*, 96).

37 The library did contain a copy of Josephus in Latin; see Léopold Deslisle, *Recherches sur la bibliothèque de Charles V* (Paris: Honoré Champion, 1907), 119. Christine did not have access to copies of Josephus in French in the Louvre library, as I misstated in Fenster, "Fortune of the Jews," 84.

38 *Mutacion*, 2: 170.

protection. Vespasian was of course not a Christian, but his actions were later interpreted by Christians as retribution for the death of Christ. As Nirenberg observes, he "represented medieval ideals about the proper behavior of rulers toward Jews."[39]

We do not know whether Vespasian provided an ideal policy for Charles VI and, therefore, for Christine, but actions like Vespasian's could have figured among the legends adduced to authorize expulsion of the Jews. Christine's *Mutacion* passage banishes the Jews not only from France and its history but also from world history as Christine knew it: a history preceded by cultures that made important contributions to Christianity. The "Hebrews" of the bible, who lived before Christ, gave their culture to the Christian bible; the "Jews" wanted to take it away. Christine's *Mutacion* history acknowledges the persistent presence of Jews in the world, but it captures the blemish they constituted for her in post-Crucifixion history. Expelled from poetry, they are marked as the *Mutacion*'s single deviant category of people.[40]

Could Christine's illness have been a metaphor for the Jews and for Jewish history? Irven Resnick has shown that where there was interest in the natural world and its systemization of ideas about physiognomy, Jews came to be depicted "with physical deformities and associated with disease and illnesses that somehow reflect a persistent sinful state, seeing that they remain throughout their lives subject to original sin and its consequences, which Christians overcome through the sacrament of baptism. Jewish bodies will reveal the corruption of their souls, souls whose very rationality will become subject to doubt in light of their general unwillingness, over many centuries, to acknowledge the truths of Christian faith."[41] Christine's is a powerful literary move: mimicking the situation of Jews who cannot see the truth of Christ, she has developed an illness that leaves her unable to think clearly, as she says: "Dont troublé mon entendement / Est a present aucunement" (From which my understanding/ ability to think is at present somewhat troubled).

The history of European literature includes any number of famous, gifted male authors, professed Christians who expressed distasteful attitudes toward the Jews. Piety offered no corrective, given that condemnation of the Jews could be intrinsic to Christian religiosity, the example of erroneous belief against which Christianity measured itself. In no way could the Jews have been presented as the innocent victims of capricious Fortune; that would have been reprehensible, perhaps even punishable. Christine accepted the royal policies of both Charles V and Charles VI, even though they contradicted one another. In her biography of Charles V she notes without substantive comment that the king had tolerated a Jewish presence in France. As I argue here, in the indirection of the *Mutacion* record of Jewish history, her doubly determined placement of the Jews *outside* her narrative supports Charles VI's expulsion of the Jews. These are not evidence of a changed opinion: instead, they speak to

39 Nirenberg, *Anti-Judaism*, 187.

40 Margolis muses that this could be "historiographical mimesis at its finest, since the Jews have so often been outcasts and marginalized undesirables"; she does not situate the passage against historical events in France ("The Rhetoric of Detachment in Christine de Pizan's *Mutacion de Fortune*," *Nottingham French Studies*, 38 (1999), 170–81, at 176).

41 Irven M. Resnick, *Marks of Distinction: Christian Perceptions of Jews in the High Middle Ages* (Washington, D.C.: Catholic University of America Press, 2012), 33–4.

Christine's steady support for French royalty. The *concorde civile* that she sought was certainly best realized when the kings of France did God's will and the people of France concurred; this was political philosophy aligning with divine intent: "For God, religion's friend, punished and rewarded [the Jews] according to what they deserved." Charles V rewarded the Jews, Charles VI punished them.[42]

42 Parts of this essay appeared earlier in my "The Fortune of the Jews in the *Mutacion de Fortune*," *Christine de Pizan et son époque: Acts du Colloque international des 9, 10, et 11* décembre 2011 à Amiens, ed. Danielle Buschinger, Liliane Dulac, Claire Le Ninan, and Christine Reno, *Médiévales* 53 (Amiens: Presses du Centre d'Etudes Médiévales, 2012), 80–7. Various stages in its development have been presented as talks at conferences in Amiens, Kalamazoo, Liège, and Fordham University. For valuable comments and questions, I am grateful to Deborah Fraioli, Angus Kennedy, Thomas O'Donnell, John Van Engen, David Wallace, and two anonymous readers for the press. My heartfelt gratitude goes to Jocelyn Wogan-Browne.

7

# WALKING IN GRANDMOTHERS' FOOTSTEPS: MARY WARD AND THE MEDIEVAL SPIRITUAL AND INTELLECTUAL HERITAGE

GEMMA SIMMONDS

Mary Ward was born in Yorkshire in 1585 and died during the English Civil War in 1645, but her life's trajectory so clearly bridges the world of medieval and early modern women that she needs no apology for appearing in this collection of essays. Connecting Mary Ward and the medieval spiritual and intellectual heritage is a matter of circumstantial evidence, since she makes little or no reference to books or writers other than the Scriptures, the Ignatian *Spiritual Exercises* and Lorenzo Scupoli's *Spiritual Combat.* Nevertheless Thomas à Kempis and the *Devotio Moderna* underlie Mary's spiritual perspective as they do that of Ignatius of Loyola.[1] James Walsh, one of Julian of Norwich's foremost twentieth-century editors, also edited Mary Ward and detects within her writing, as in Julian's, the language and rhythms of the Latin Vulgate as well as a rhetoric expressive of the theology and spirituality of the monasticism of the Late Middle Ages.[2] He underlines Mary's conviction that a love of learning is as indispensable as holiness for candidates to the new religious congregation she founded, but maintains that her own "Third Instruction" to her sisters is more reminiscent of Thomas à Kempis' views on learning.[3] Like Thomas she claims that women can achieve a "true knowledge and right understanding," without the learning that is the privilege of men, through the infused gift of a love of truth for the sake of God, who is Truth itself.[4] Here and elsewhere she acknowledges the intellectual capacity of women while pointing to an aptitude for spiritual leadership greater than the learning of those men who "practis not what they know nor perform what they preach".[5]

1 See John Van Engen, *Sisters and Brothers of the Common Life: The* Devotio Moderna *and the World of the Later Middle Ages* (Philadelphia: University of Pennsylvania Press, 2008) for the context of Thomas à Kempis and his spiritual heritage.

2 See James Walsh's introduction to *Till God Will: Mary Ward through her Writings*, ed. Gillian Orchard (London, Darton, Longman and Todd, 1985), xi–xxx.

3 See Robert Jeffery, ed., *Thomas à Kempis: The Imitation of Christ* (London: Penguin, 2013), 1, 3.

4 Orchard, *Till God Will*, 58–59.

5 Ursula Dirmeier ed., *Mary Ward und ihre Gründung: Die Quellentexte bis 1645* (Münster: Aschendorf, 2007), 1, 363. Cf. Alcuin Blamires and C. W. Marx, "Woman Not to Preach: A Disputation in British Library MS Harley 31" in *The Journal of Medieval Latin*, 3 (1993), 34–63.

Additionally, we know that Julian's *Revelations* were printed and propagated in seventeenth-century England within a recusant network with which Mary was closely connected. Her access to a copied manuscript must remain a matter of conjecture, but the *dramatis personae* behind Serenus Cressy's 1670 edition of Julian reads like a roll call of Mary's family and close collaborators. Cressy's edition was supported financially and intellectually by members of the Gascoigne, Ingleby and Constable families, all strongly connected with Mary Ward's circle of educated female educators.[6] A recent essay by Jonathan Juilfs points to recusant nuns from Yorkshire living on the Continent as the main instigators for getting Julian and other medieval texts into print.[7] This draws a suggestive line of succession from earlier medieval monastic spiritual and intellectual influences on the Catholics of Yorkshire through to their descendants, living after the suppression of the monasteries but recreating monastic ways of living and praying within their homes, as described by a priest who lived in the Babthorpe household of Mary's childhood alongside her.[8] The Yorkshire Charterhouse of Mount Grace, to which she and her sisters had a considerable devotion, witnessed the translation of the *Cloud of Unknowing* into Latin in 1491. John and Eleanor Ingleby (ancestors of the Ingleby family mentioned above) were numbered among the founders of Mount Grace, and its prior Nicholas Love translated the highly influential *Meditationes vitae Christi* into English there.[9] This translation was in turn highly influential, leaving its mark upon *The Book of Margery Kempe*, a text long conserved by the monks of Mount Grace. Books from monastic libraries were often acquired by pious gentry after the suppression, becoming the nourishment of these quasi-monastic recusant households.

The passage of time admittedly separates the spiritual and intellectual leadership of medieval monastic women from the claims implicit in Mary's foundation of her religious congregation of "Jesuitesses".[10] Yet the Council of Trent's suppression of women's potential through its reform of alleged monastic disorders was in itself a continuation of centuries of anxiety about women's aspirations to a life of holiness outside the cloister. An attempt in 1298 by Boniface VIII to enforce enclosure more strictly met with limited success, especially in Yorkshire, although the later bull *Circa pastoralis*, issued by Pius V in 1566, exerted greater force across Europe, riding a wave of Counter-Reformation anxiety.[11] On May 31, 1631, the papal bull *Pastoralis Romani*

6 See *A Book of Showings to the Anchoress Julian of Norwich*, ed. Edmund Colledge and James Walsh (Toronto: Pontifical Institute of Medieval Studies, 1978), 12ff. and Jonathan Juilfs, "'*This boke is begonne… but is not yet preformyd*': Compilations of Julian of Norwich's *A Revelation of Love*, 1413–1670" in *Women and the Divine in Literature before 1700*, ed. Kathryn Kerby-Fulton (Victoria BC: ELS Editions,), 171–184.

7 Juilfs, "'*This boke is begonne*," 159 ff.

8 Catherine Chambers, *The Life of Mary Ward: 1585–1645*, vol. 1 (London: Burns and Oates, 1882–1885), 40–41.

9 See *Nicholas Love: The Mirror of the Blessed Life of Jesus Christ*, ed. Michael G. Sargent (Exeter: University of Exeter Press, 2005).

10 A pejorative name never claimed by Mary Ward herself.

11 See David Wallace, "Nuns" in *Cultural Reformations: Medieval and Renaissance in Literary History*, ed. Brian Cummings and James Simpson (Oxford: Oxford University Press, 2010), 502–523, esp. 508–509, 519; John Tillotson, "Visitation and Reform of the Yorkshire Nunneries in the Fourteenth Century," *Northern History*, 30 (1994), 1–21.

*Pontificis* suppressed Mary Ward's "English Ladies" in violent terms reminiscent of the Council of Vienne's condemnation of the Beguines in *Cum de quibusdam mulieribus*.[12] The 1631 Bull spoke of the offence done to the church and Christian civilization by women who "have been accustomed to attempt and to employ themselves at [...] works which are most unsuited to maidenly reserve – works which men of eminence [...] undertake with much difficulty and only with great caution."[13] This sense of outrage raises strong echoes of reactions to Margery Kempe's attempts at uncloistered holiness.[14] Among offences the Bull lists are the "Jesuitesses'" claim to an educated female public voice and to mobility for women with a call to ministry outside the monastic enclosure. So toxic and dangerous was this considered to be to church and society that the Bull decreed "the poisonous growths in the Church of God must be torn up from the roots lest they spread themselves further [...] we wish and command all the Christian faithful to regard and repute them as suppressed, extinct, rooted out, destroyed and abolished."

Despite this suppression, some 400 years after their foundation in 1609, sisters of the Congregation of Jesus and the Institute of the Blessed Virgin Mary are now a worldwide group spanning over 2,000 sisters found in every continent and country from Albania to Zimbabwe.[15] Mary Ward stands as an icon for women's struggle down the centuries to claim their legitimate voice in church and society as leaders and intellectuals, and to do the great things of which God has made them capable. Her early life as a persecuted recusant Catholic was characterized by immobility, silence and conformity to the ideals of the social and religious enclosure of women prevalent in her day. A process of personal conversion transformed the hidden recusant into a trailblazing pioneer whose attempt to found the first entirely unenclosed religious order of women on the Jesuit model earned her a death sentence at the hands of the Protestant English state and imprisonment as a heretic by the Catholic Inquisition.

The Pope's insistence in 1631 on suppression and extinction took many concrete forms. There was the canonical suppression of the nascent order itself. More insidiously and more effectively this brought about the suppression of Mary Ward's voice as an original writer. Her authentic voice comes to us principally through her letters, some of which were written from an Inquisition prison, coded and in lemon juice, in the tradition of English recusants, who would hold the invisible ink close to fire, thus revealing the written words when it was safe to do so.[16] A great many of Mary's letters and papers were destroyed by her own sisters in obedience to subsequent papal sanctions, leaving only remnants of her letters and the written *Lives* produced after her death by her

12 Walter Simons, "In Praise of Faithful Women: Count Robert of Flanders's Defense of Beguines against the Clementine Decree *Cum de quibusdam mulieribus* (ca. 1318–1320)" in *Christianity and Culture in the Middle Ages*, ed. David C. Mengel and Lisa Wolverton (Notre Dame, IN: University of Notre Dame Press, 2015), 331–357.

13 Margaret Mary Littlehales, *Mary Ward: Pilgrim and Mystic* (London: Burns & Oates, 1988), 253–257.

14 Van Engen, *Sisters and Brothers of the Common Life*, 18.

15 Mary Wright, *Mary Ward's Institute: The Struggle for Identity* (Sydney: Crossing Press, 1997).

16 See Dirmeier, *Mary Ward und ihre Gründung*, 3, 213–217.

contemporaries.[17] Her earliest biography, the *Briefe Relation*, reads as her companions' *apologia* for Mary's life and inspiration, underlining her obedience to Church authorities while also making clear her fidelity to a God-given call, confirming future sisters in the validity of their vocation while refuting the accusations of rebellion and error made by the foundress's legion of enemies.[18]

Mary Poyntz and Winefrid Wigmore, two of Mary Ward's earliest companions, were responsible for the first written *Lives*. Their anxiety both to vindicate Mary Ward personally and to justify the way of life she initiated claims divine inspiration for this apostolic and Jesuit-inspired life for women, unacceptable though it remained for subsequent generations. In archpriest William Harrison's *Informatio* of 1621 we find a litany of complaints against women who undertake apostolic work despite their gendered incapacity for it. They dare to speak in public on religious matters in defiance of biblical, patristic and canonical prohibitions, risking damage to their own and the church's reputation through their scandalously free behavior. These are the same complaints made against women identified as Beguines over a long period of medieval history.[19] Women are by nature weak, inconstant, deceitful novelty-seekers, so the story runs, prone to error and thousands of dangers.

Words from or about Mary Ward were dangerous both in her own lifetime and in centuries to follow as was a non-verbal resource which operates in a similar way to the coded letters, namely the *Painted Life of Mary Ward,* a series of seventeenth-century devotional paintings now hanging in the Congregatio Jesu house in Augsburg, Germany.[20] Dating from the second half of the seventeenth century, *The Painted Life* offers a commentary on Mary's life and work and was revered as a spiritual treasure by those who followed her, as stated in 1718 in a letter from the then general superior, Mary Agnes Babthorpe, to the Bishop of Munich-Freysing:

> We will always more and more apply ourselves to following [Mary Ward's] saintly life by exercising [ourselves] in virtues and we will perform with all possible diligence what our least Institute requires, which puts before us the most excellent virtues: this was done by our ancestors who, many years ago, had pictures painted of the saintly life of our foundress.[21]

Votive pictures along the lines of similar frescoes and engravings of the lives of medieval and early modern saints Ursula, Catherine of Siena, and Ignatius Loyola,

17 A great deal is owed in this respect to Sister Christina Kenworthy-Browne CJ for her edition of the earliest biography, known as the *Briefe Relation*. Kenworthy-Browne, ed., *Mary Ward (1585–1645): A Briefe Relation… with Autobiographical Fragments and a Selection of Letters* (Woodbridge: Catholic Record Society, 2008).

18 See, as an example, the "Information" of Archpriest William Harrison of 1621 in Dirmeier, *Mary Ward und ihre Gründung*, 1, 521–528, translated and summarised in Henriette Peters, *Mary Ward: A World in Contemplation*, trans. Helen Butterworth (Leominster: Gracewing, 1994), 338–346.

19 Van Engen, *Sisters and Brothers of the Common Life*, 37–44.

20 Fifty of the original fifty-four paintings survive. All paintings are referred to by the number assigned to them on this website, where they are reproduced. Congregatio Jesu, *Painted Life of Mary Ward*, http://www.congregatiojesu.org/en/maryward_painted_life.asp.

21 Letter in Congregatio Jesu archives, Rome, quoted in Immolata Wetter CJ, *Letters of Instruction* (unpublished, c. 1982).

the paintings bear inscriptions, probably added years after the paintings were commissioned, by Tobias Lohner, Jesuit confessor to the "English Ladies" of Munich, and Mary's first German biographer. Mary's letters are full of coded names and clandestine references. Since words proved dangerous, I argue that the *Painted Life* contains similarly encrypted themes and motifs supplementing and fortifying the written word, pointing to the uniqueness of Mary's life and vision, and linking it with the Ignatian *Spiritual Exercises* and Jesuit Constitutions as well as with medieval pictorial tropes.

Persecuted English Catholicism at the time of Mary's birth was marked by the absence of structure, hierarchy and regular priestly ministry. This provided an unexpected opening for the collaboration of women with itinerant missionary priests, since they could move around undetected more easily than men.[22] Her insistence on mobility, across Europe and "even to those who live in the region called the Indies," was to prove Mary Ward's downfall.[23]

She records her childhood self as being so painfully averse to public social interaction that the silent life of the monastic cloister, though long disappeared from Protestant England, became a strong attraction.[24] Pope Boniface VIII's papal decree *Periculoso* of 1298, noted above, had attempted to clamp down on early medieval freedoms and impose strict enclosure on all nuns in the Western church, making it impossible for female religious to undertake works of charity outside the monastic enclosure, save for the education of girls. Women's options in society were reduced to *aut maritus aut murus* (either a husband or a cloister); domestic or monastic enclosure providing the necessary protection for women's weaker minds and bodies. The Council of Trent reinforced *Periculoso*'s restrictions, obliging tertiaries like Angela Merici's Ursulines to take solemn vows and observe pontifical enclosure.[25]

A pious maidservant, Margaret Garrett, told young Mary Ward and her cousin Barbara Babthorpe stories of a religious life now lost to England; it was this echo of a disappeared medieval world that inspired her to seek monastic life overseas.[26] Mary's autobiography tells of her strongly internalizing the notions prevalent at the time of women's place within society and church:

> I had no inclination to any Order in particular, only I was resolved within myself to take the most strict and secluded, thinking and often saying that as women did not know how to do good except to themselves (a penuriousness which I resented enough even then) I would do in earnest what I did.[27]

22 See Blamires and Marx, "Woman Not to Preach," 40.

23 See David Wallace, *Strong Women: Life, Text and Territory, 1347–1645* (Oxford: Oxford University Press, 2011), 133–134 and Orchard, *Till God Will*, 65.

24 Dirmeier, *Mary Ward und ihre Gründung*, 1, 21–22.

25 See Francesca Medioli, "An Unequal Law: The Enforcement of *Clausura* Before and After the Council of Trent" in *Women in Renaissance and Early Modern Europe*, ed. Christine Meek (Dublin: Four Courts Press, 2000), 136–152.

26 Ibid., 22 and one of the more charming pictures of the *Painted Life*, painting 9.

27 Kenworthy-Browne, *A Briefe Relation*, 122.

Mary's flight to Flanders to enter the cloistered Poor Clares ended when she understood God to be calling her to "some other thing," as yet unimagined. In 1606 she returned to London, undertaking apostolic work within Catholic underground networks, at great personal danger.[28] This experience of apostolic mobility pointed the way forward. A powerful mystical insight, known as the "Glory Vision," convinced her that the "assured good thing" to which God was drawing her would be greatly to God's glory.[29] Echoing the Jesuit motto *ad maiorem Dei gloriam* (to the greater glory of God), that Ignatian verbal framing already foretold her future course. The painting of this event shows Mary looking at her own image in a mirror, so overwhelmed by God's assurance that she "remained for a good space without feeling or hearing anything but the sound, 'Glory, glory, glory'" (see Figure 3).[30]

Figure 3 *Mary Ward's "Glory Vision," Painted Life*, painting 21. (Photograph: Studio Tanner, Nesselwang; © Center Maria Ward, MEP Munich.)

Irenaeus of Lyon speaks of the glory of God as a human being fully alive.[31] Mary sees her own image as a woman, considered by many contemporary thinkers as of a lower order of humanity than men, yet within that image she beholds God's glory. This vision became the background to all her subsequent efforts for

28 Ibid., 15 and *Painted Life*, painting 17; on the London Catholic milieu see Wallace, *Strong Women*, 160–168.

29 See *Painted Life*, painting 21.

30 Kenworthy-Browne, *A Briefe Relation*, 139.

31 Irenaeus, *Adversus Haereses*, 4.34.5–7.

herself and "women in time to come," struggling to create a space in which women could fulfil their God-given potential. An unpublished commentary on the *Painted Life* by historian Immolata Wetter expresses little enthusiasm for the paintings' visionary content, reminding us of Mary Ward's own reticence towards supernatural insights or occurrences in her life. In an echo of objections to the medieval Beguines of the Low Countries and their mystical claims, successive German bishops declared the paintings guilty of portraying unfounded revelations and order them "completely banished."[32] Reinstated on the walls of Augsburg convent in 1773, they were once again banned in the mid-nineteenth century but rehung in 1891.[33]

Suppressed as were Mary Ward's writings, the *Painted Life* offers a telling companion narrative to what has been saved of the written word. Mary had lost three uncles in the Gunpowder Plot, and gathered a group of companions, many related by blood or marriage to the Plotters. While the men of these families planned an act of religiously inspired terrorism, their female relatives planned an undertaking for women that was to prove even more explosive. The famous "Plotters' Portrait," hanging in London's National Gallery, depicts Guy Fawkes and his confederates in animated conversation, planning the deaths of king and parliament. Painting 22 of the *Painted Life* shows Mary Ward and her first companions in similarly animated conversation (see Figure 4). In the other half of this two-part picture, we see the women escaping by boat to Flanders in 1609 to begin their adventure, claiming the voice and mobility for women of the future which originally prevailed in medieval Flanders among the Sisters of the Common Life.

Mary and her companions were unable to clarify what sort of religious life they felt called to embark upon, but clarity came in 1611 when she received an intellectual understanding that they were to "Take the same of the Society, soe understood, as that we were to take the same both in matter and in manner, that onely excepted which God by diversity of Sex hath prohibited."[34]

In this call she saw not a divine veto but an invitation for women to form an autonomous female branch of the Society of Jesus, taking the Jesuit Constitutions and living a religious life as closely resembling that of the Jesuits as was possible for women and non-clerics. In direct contradiction to the Council of Trent, this also contravened the ban, stemming from two unhappy episodes in his own lifetime, which Ignatius of Loyola himself had placed on there ever being a female branch of his order.[35] Mary Ward's Jesuit contemporaries reacted with predictable horror.[36] Her decision to use the name Society of Jesus gave rise to further objections, the panic of the Jesuits striking a faintly comical note:

32 See reactions to Marguerite Porete in Van Engen, *Sisters and Brothers of the Common Life*, 25–26.

33 Wetter, *Letters of Instruction*, I.iv-v and Bibl. Casan., MS 2426, fol.252v.

34 Kenworthy-Browne, *A Briefe Relation*, 146.

35 Gemma Simmonds, "Women Jesuits?" in *The Cambridge Companion to the Jesuits*, ed. Thomas Worcester (Cambridge: Cambridge University Press, 2008), 122.

36 Immolata Wetter, *Mary Ward: Under the Shadow of the Inquisition* (Oxford: Way Books, 2006), 20–22.

Figure 4a *Mary Ward and Companions, Painted Life*, painting 22, left-hand side, cropped. (Photograph: Studio Tanner, Nesselwang; © Center Maria Ward, MEP Munich.)

> My confessor resisted, all the Society opposed [...they] would needs that at least we should take the name of some order confirmed, or some new one, or any we could think of, soe not that of Jesus: This the Fathers of the Society urged exceedingly and doe still so every day [...], telling us that to any such name we may take what Constitutions we will, even theres in substance, if otherwise we will not be satisfied, but by noe means will they that we observe that forme which there Constitutions and rules are writ in.[37]

In 1615 Mary received further spiritual confirmation in a vision of a soul returned to its original state of innocence and freedom, fully oriented towards its original purpose (rather than disposed as prevailing religious or social culture said she should be). This emphasis on the restoration of a lost original freedom and purity carries resonances of Beatrice of

37 Kenworthy-Browne, *A Briefe Relation*, 146–147.

Figure 4b *Mary Ward and Companions, Painted Life*, painting 22, right-hand side, cropped. (Photograph: Studio Tanner, Nesselwang; © Center Maria Ward, MEP Munich.)

Nazareth's *Seven Manners of Loving.*[38] Mary understood from this vision that women as well as men were called to the apostolic life, capable of responding to God in a "singuler freedome [...] intyre application, and apte disposition to all good works."[39]

By 1616 her companions had multiplied across Europe, drawn by a call to the apostolic life, free from enclosure and from monastic practices and dress. The apostolic aims had spread from the education of girls to "the salvation of our neighbour [...] by any other means that are congruous to the times."[40] Some of her patrons were powerful prelates who tried every conceivable manoeuver to help her minimize enclosure and thus bypass the ban on uncloistered sisters. Mary Poyntz records Mary Ward's independence of mind and judgement in this matter. Cardinal Bandino, eager

38 See Bernard McGinn, *The Flowering of Mysticism: Men and Women in the New Mysticism – 1200–1350* (New York: Crossroad, 1998), 171.

39 Dirmeier, *Mary Ward und ihre Gründung*, 1, 290.

40 Orchard, *Till God Will*, 44.

to open new houses across Europe, had tried to persuade her to accept the very mitigated enclosure of the nuns of the Torre di Specchi in Rome which was effectively less than that actually observed by the Jesuitesses. "But to this faire offer our dearest Mother gave for answer, that to obtayne the foresaid grace of propagating etc. she wou'd not admitt of two stakes putt in crosse in forme of enclosure."[41] Instead she presented her plan to the Pope, stressing the Ignatian characteristics of freedom from enclosure and episcopal authority, and the role of the general superior. Some Jesuits with experience of women's apostolic potential from the English mission supported them. Others were immovably opposed.[42] Margaret Garrett's story of religious life which had so profoundly influenced the young Mary told of a pregnant nun doing severe penance for having broken enclosure and her vow of chastity. Fear of violations of discipline among sisters fueled a more generalized social and ecclesial antipathy to women claiming a voice, mobility and a public space, themes which appear both directly and by implication in Mary's letters and more strongly as an underlying source of contention in the *Painted Life*.[43] The fear of lost virginity, ruined chastity and secret pregnancies runs through the Inquisition spies' reports and attacks on the "Jesuitesses" with tedious regularity. Clergy accused the sisters of immorality, financial irregularity and usurping priestly functions in reports based on lurid imagination and baseless rumor.[44]

Images of enclosure and mobility, themes of withdrawal from the world and engagement with life in the public space emerge repeatedly in the *Painted Life*. Mary is frequently depicted praying in her room or lying in the enclosed space of a four-poster bed while being called to a life outside.[45] One painting shows her receiving a false message, allegedly from her father, telling her to refrain from making her First Communion. A beloved fatherly authority sends a message which Mary has read to her, but is not permitted to see, which would prevent her from receiving the sacraments. The *Briefe Relation* tells of her suffering "pangs as of Death to disobey him [while,] on the other side, not to communicate caused her such remorse and griefe, as betweene both her Life was unconsolable."

41 Kenworthy-Browne, *A Briefe Relation*, 88.

42 Jesuit John Gerard was a major supporter, allegedly lending Mary his copy of the Jesuit *Constitutions* from which she drew the third, final and most Ignatian plan for her Institute, while providing for independent governance in respect for Ignatius's wishes. His lack of prudence was to cause Mary Ward's sisters considerable trouble and his support did not survive the suppression of the Institute. See Philip Caraman, ed., *John Gerard: The Autobiography of an Elizabethan* (London: Longmans, Green and Co.,1951); Dirmeier, *Mary Ward und ihre Gründung*, 1, 542–548; Peters, *A World in Contemplation*, 218–221; and Wetter, *Under the Shadow*, 23–25, 35–36.

43 See Kenworthy-Browne, *A Briefe Relation*, 114 and Elizabeth M. Makowski, *Canon Law and Cloistered Women:* Periculoso *and its Commentators 1298– 1545* (Washington: Catholic University of America Press, 1997), 40, 46.

44 Orchard, *Till God Will*, 48–50, 69; Dirmeier, *Mary Ward und ihre Gründung*, 2, 326, 1.664–666; Peters, *A World in Contemplation*, 468–469.

45 See *Painted Life*, paintings 21, 24 and 25. I am grateful for this insight to a student of the *Painted Life* and Anglican priest, Stuart Owen.

Figure 5 *The False Messenger*, *Painted Life*, painting 6. (Photograph: Studio Tanner, Nesselwang; © Center Maria Ward, MEP Munich.)

A similar scenario would take place in 1631 during her incarceration in a cloistered monastery by the Inquisition in Munich after the suppression of her Institute, where she was denied the sacraments. The *Painted Life* remains resolutely silent on this period in her life, but the play on medieval iconography in painting 6 is telling (see Figure 5). A typical scene of religious women enclosed within a garden is interrupted by a messenger mounted on a horse, symbolizing male power and mobility, standing outside the enclosure, with a church dominating a hill in the background. The messenger holds out a letter to the young Mary which determines her access to the sacraments. Despite her agony of anxiety and love for her father, Mary decides to follow her conscience. During her imprisonment by the Inquisition, the dangerously ill adult Mary was offered the last rites on condition that she sign a paper repenting of any possible errors. In order to save her followers from accusations of having been deceived by a leader who subsequently recanted, she refused to sign, saying, "I will cast my selfe on the mercyes of Christ, and rather dy without Sacraments." The *Briefe Relation* comments, "Her adversaryes thought heare had beene a notable proofe of her obstinacy and perverseness [...] but wise and prudent People knew the obligation there is for each to stand upon their owne right, especially in that abominablest of crimes." She delivered instead a paper of her own, passionately professing her service and obedience to the Church, and telling the Dean of Munich Cathedral that if she died without the Sacraments it would be on his own conscience. She was given the last rites shortly afterwards.[46]

46 *Painted Life*, paintings 4 and 6; Kenworthy-Browne, *A Briefe Relation*, 5–6, 50–51.

Mary's clandestine work in London, using disguises to escape detection, drew from George Abbot, Archbishop of Canterbury, the criticism that she "did more hurt than six Jesuits."[47] The comment provoked her into visiting Lambeth Palace and leaving her signature carved with a diamond on a window pane.[48] In a sign of different times, a present-day sister of Mary Ward's congregation is working in happy collaboration with the current Archbishop of Canterbury in his founding of the ecumenical Community of St. Anselm, based in Lambeth Palace.[49]

Mary's conviction of the aptness of women for the Jesuit way of life was based on her years of apostolic experience and her understanding of the life of Jesus' women disciples and of the fundamental equality of women and men before God. Hearing of a Jesuit's conviction that women were not able to comprehend God as men are, Mary refuted his assumption in a speech recorded in 1617.[50]

> Ther was a father that lately came into England whom I hard say, that he would not for a 10,000 of worlds be a woaman, because he thought a woaman could not apprehend god: I answered nothing but only smyled, allthough I could have answered him by the experience I have of the contrarie: I could have been sorry for his want of iudgement, I mene not want of iudgment, nor to condem his iudgment, for he is a man of a verie good iudgment; his want is in experience.[51]

This marginalization of women's experience within the church, based on the conviction that their access to God was of an inferior order from that of men, led to a high degree of invisibility and inaudibility in spiritual and ecclesial spheres. Women seeking to find a voice and a place in the public forum were not welcome. Without papal approval, the women of differing nationalities who joined Mary Ward's congregation in increasing numbers could not access dowry funds, leaving them little or nothing to live on.[52] Deciding to plead her cause to the Pope in person, Mary set out in 1621 with a few companions on foot across the Alps, braving war, plague and treacherous conditions. There were initial signs of approval for their work among girls and women. The *English Life* reports that so successful was their ministry educating the poor girls of Rome that "the wicked sayd if this went on the Stewes of Rome wou'd fayle".[53] Despite this it became clear that canonical approval for an order of female Jesuits would not easily be forthcoming.[54]

47 *Painted Life*, painting 18.

48 Kenworthy-Browne, *A Briefe Relation*, 21–22. Peters disputes the tale; see *A World in Contemplation*, 162.

49 "The Community of St Anselm," http://stanselm.org.uk.

50 Cf. Blamires and Marx on Henry of Ghent's discussion of the "inadequacy of the female intellect" for teaching and evangelizing, "Woman Not to Preach," 40.

51 Dirmeier, *Mary Ward und ihre Gründung*, 1, 359.

52 Jennifer Cameron, *A Dangerous Innovator: Mary Ward (1585–1645)* (Strathfield NSW: St. Paul's, 2000), 101–110, 125–136.

53 Immolata Wetter, *Mary Ward in Her Own Words* (Rome: Istituto Beata Vergine Maria, 1999), 95; Kenworthy-Browne, *A Briefe Relation*, 26. "Stewes" here refer to brothels.

54 Orchard, *Till God Will*, 71–77.

In a two-page memorandum of 1622 entitled "Reasons Why We May Not Alter," Mary outlines her conviction that the Jesuit way of life, approved by the church, was suitable for women and had been successfully tested over time by the virtuous lives and effective apostolates of her sisters. Appealing to social changes and their own experience she argued the need for a new form of religious life for women, claiming the God-given freedom each person has to choose their own vocation, arguing that if God gives someone a vocation, no other authority should seek to countermand it.

> And yf yt wear wronge to force anie privet man to marrie a wife whom he can not affect: much more must the election of every ones vocation in this kind be free [...] This ys the reason [...] that the Kinge of Kings should chuse his owne spowses, and that God, and not man should give vocations. And yf so to every privet soule, how much more to a beginning order and so much importing the service of his Church, and good of souls.[55]

Rome interpreted this insistence as disloyalty to the church and placing her authority as general superior above that of the Pope and his representatives. She was arrested and imprisoned on a charge of heresy, schism and rebellion against the church, the houses of the order suppressed and the penniless sisters dispensed from their vows, dispersed and left to fend for themselves.[56]

The *Painted Life* contains a recurrent theme of Mary Ward exercising speech, the right to which is denied women in scripture.[57] Her claim to public speech is the basis for many of the denunciations of her sent to the Inquisition.[58] The first image in the *Painted Life* illustrates Mary's own story of how her first spoken word was a repetition of her mother calling on the name of Jesus (see Figure 6). Mary Poyntz recounts a further childhood incident in which Mary fell on her head and was taken up stunned and speechless. 'She had her understanding good, and thought with her selfe, could she but once say JESUS she would willingly dy; which sacred name she at last pronounced, and it brought her so much sweetnes and Love, as all her Life after she was most sensible of, and in that instant restored to her former health.'[59]

55 Dirmeier, *Mary Ward und ihre Gründung*, 1, 604–605 and Peters, *A World in Contemplation*, 332.

56 Wetter, *In Her Own Words*, 68–72. Peters remarks that it was Mary's subsequent submission to the Pope that proved her a true Jesuitess; see Peters, *A World in Contemplation*, 565.

57 For an overall summary with multiple essays on the subject, see *Voices in Dialogue: Reading Women in the Middle Ages*, ed. Linda Olson and K. Kerby-Fulton (Notre Dame: University of Notre Dame Press, 2005), especially K. Kerby-Fulton, "When Women Preached: An Introduction to Women's Homiletic, Liturgical and Sacramental Roles in the Middle Ages," 31–56 and David Wallace, "Response to Genelle Gertz-Robinson: Stepping into the Pulpit?" 483–592.

58 See the report from archpriest William Harrison to the Holy See, published in Dirmeier, *Mary Ward und ihre Gründung*, 1, 521–528 and Littlehales, *Pilgrim and Mystic*, 253–257.

59 Kenworthy-Browne, *A Briefe Relation*, 28.

It is the name of Jesus, in both instances, that gives her speech, and this significance was not lost on the adult Mary and her companions, struggling to remain women of speech and mobility. One of the many causes of contention between Mary Ward and her Jesuit opponents was the setting up of the IHS monogram above their chapel door, marking them as members of a society that bore the name of Jesus.[60] Mary was adamant, not countenancing that a name should be silenced that had been given her by God, "Concerning the name, I have twice in severall yeares understood [...] that the denomination of these must be Jesus."

Figure 6 Mary Ward's First Word, *Painted Life*, painting 1. (Photograph: Studio Tanner, Nesselwang; © Center Maria Ward, MEP Munich.)

If the name of Jesus is the first word in Mary Ward's life it is also the last. Her tombstone is now the center of a shrine in her honor in the Anglican church of Osbaldwick, outside York, where at her death she was buried by an Anglican priest whom her sisters found "honest enough to be bribed" to give a resting place to a Catholic.[61] The huge stone, roughly carved during the siege of York in the English Civil War reads, "To love the poore, persever in the same, live, dy and rise with them was all the ayme of Mary Ward."[62] It is not fanciful to find in this an encrypted reference to her "taking the same of the Society [of Jesus]." From first to last, Mary's companions,

60 Peters, *World in Contemplation*, 252–253, 577.

61 Kenworthy-Browne, *A Briefe Relation*, 74.

62 "Mary Ward," The Parish of Osbaldwick with Murton, www.osbaldwickandmurtonchurches.org.uk.

whether in writing or in painting and carving, found ways to immortalize the claims implicit in her vision which dared not be spoken aloud for centuries.[63]

In her book *Keeping God's Silence*, Rachel Muers speaks of the "dumb silencing" of women, in which they are ignored and excluded from public discourse dominated by men. Women become absent or trivial and irrelevant in contexts where their experience is not thought to count.[64] In *A Room of One's Own*, Virginia Woolf suggests that women are also silenced by being talked about.[65] One of the most comprehensive ways of silencing Mary Ward were the reports on her which flowed into the papal and Jesuit curias and into the English government of the time. What arouses particular anger and resentment is Mary and her followers' claim to speak for themselves and to teach others to speak. Mary's enemies accuse her and her followers of scandalizing Catholics and rendering themselves ridiculous to heretics by aspiring to preach and teach, and also teaching their pupils to act in plays so that later on they might preach from the pulpit. Mary herself is reported as being a "*Vergine d'animo virile*," disporting herself around England and Flanders in a coach and four, claiming to be a duchess *incognita*, preaching from a chair placed in front of the altar and giving instructions on the Our Father.[66] Her insistence on the importance of teaching Latin, the *lingua franca* of theologically and scientifically educated men, to the sisters and girls in her schools is testimony to her dedication to giving the women of the future access to leadership through theological training and intellectual rigor. In a letter of 1627 she writes to Mother Winifred Bedingfield from Vienna:

> Cheifly to congratulate the unexpected progress of your lattin Schools. You cannot easily beleeve the content I tooke in the theams [written exercises] of thos tow towardly [highly promising] girels. You will worke much to your owne happines by advanceinge them a pace in that learninge [...] All such as are capable, invite them to yt. And for such as desirs to be of ours, noe tallant ys so much to be regardded as the lattin tounge,

She is a seasoned educator, however, warning, "I fear thos subtill wenshes have some help at home to make ther Theams." Elsewhere she connects such learning with spiritual growth and virtue,

> I would have Cicilia and Catherina to begin out of hand to learn the rudiments of lattin, fear not ther loss of virtue by that means, for this must and wilbe so common to all as ther wilbe noe caus of complicence etc. [...] what time can be otherwyse fownd besyds ther prayr let yt be bestowed on ther lattin.[67]

In a speech to her own sisters, however, she balances the women's lack of access to the education common among Jesuits with another type of knowing:

63 See Kenworthy-Browne, *A Briefe Relation*, xiv.

64 Rachel Muers, *Keeping God's Silence: Towards a Theological Ethics of Communication* (Oxford: Blackwell, 2004), 32–33.

65 Virginia Woolf, *A Room of One's Own* (London: Penguin, 1945), 27–28.

66 Dirmeier, *Mary Ward und ihre Gründung*, 2, 324–327.

67 Orchard, *Till God Will*, 95–96.

> I beseech you all to understand and note well, wherefore you are to seeke this knowledge, not for the content and satisfaction it bringeth, though it be exceeding great [...] but for the end it bringeth you unto which is god.[68]

Women's participation in speech denotes both equal recognition for themselves as speaking subjects and the articulation of a different voice from the distinctive realm of "women's experience."[69] Mary defends this differentiated equality against another unfortunate Jesuit, who ill-judgedly remarked that while the Jesuitesses' fervor was impressive, "when all is done they are but wemen." To her sisters she counters,

> I would know what you all thinke he meant by this speech of his: But wemen: and what ferver is: ferver is a will to doe well [...which] wemen may have as well as men [...] Ther is no such difference between men and weomen that weomen may not doe great matters.

Her cultural and theological mental landscape did not allow her to think of women's ordination, but she had certainly travelled far from her childhood assumption that women could do good to none but themselves:

> I confes wifes are to be subject to ther husbants, men are head of the church, weomen are not to administer sacraments, nor to preach in publike churches, but in all other things wherin are we soe inferiour to other creatures, that they should terme us but weomen [...] as if we were in all things inferiour to soum other creature which I suppose to be man, which I dare be bould to say is a lye, and with respect to the good father may say it is an errour.[70]

Mary Ward's most insidious and effective silencing came, however, at the hands of her own followers. Pope Benedict XIV's Bull *Quamvis Justo* of 1749 recognized the sisters' right to exist as a religious foundation and the office of General Superior but insisted that this Institute was quite separate from the one condemned in 1631, upholding Urban VIII's Bull of Suppression. It issued a ban, lasting until her official vindication in 1909, on naming Mary Ward as the founder of this 'second' Institute. This provoked a silencing which all but obliterated her memory as founder. In Germany hymns and prayers in honor of Mary Ward were forbidden, though sisters hid away quantities of biographies, even those on the Index of Forbidden Books. Precious letters and documents were burned by a novice who knew that the order to do so was a terrible mistake, but felt bound to observe obedience. While the written word was destroyed, portraits and the *Painted Life* were saved, though remaining hidden. News of Pope Benedict's ban did not reach England until the early nineteenth century, but it unleashed an orgy of zealous obedience in which sisters in York tracked down

68 Dirmeier, *Mary Ward und ihre Gründung*,1, 363–364.

69 Muers, *Keeping God's Silence*, 36–37.

70 Dirmeier, *Mary Ward und ihre Gründung*, 2, 357–359. On the history of women's ordination, see Gary Macy's essay in the present volume, "The Treatment of Ordination in Recent Scholarship on Religious Women in the Early Middle Ages" (chapter 16).

and destroyed pictures, letters, papers and anything relating to Mary Ward. In the library her very name was cut out from the pages of books. Visits to her grave were discontinued for fifty years.

The *Painted Life* remains a cryptic source of the dangerous memory of Mary Ward. It is full of scenes where she breaks the boundaries of enclosure to follow the mysterious will of God. The theme of mobility features equally in the *Painted Life* and in the critical reports sent to Rome about the self-motivated and public activities of the "Jesuitesses." Mary is frequently portrayed as on the move: on horseback, in coaches and boats.[71] Spies' reports complain of the sisters as gadabouts, "galloping girls," and "wandering gossips," acting in contravention of the role prescribed for women in the scriptures and the restrictions placed on the mobility of female religious by the Council of Trent.[72] Painting 26 shows Mary quelling a mutiny on board a ship, her calm demeanor mirroring that of another highly mobile apostle, St. Paul, during the shipwreck in Acts 27. The parallels to Saints Peter and Paul are perhaps a silent way of emphasizing the leadership and holiness inherent in this forbidden apostolic way for women.

While the textual evidence for a direct relationship between Mary Ward and the other women leaders and intellectuals in this collection remains circumstantial, she stands as a link between the relative prominence and freedom of women in the medieval church and the position gained in church and society by women from the twentieth century onwards. She died in 1645, her dream of a female branch of the Jesuits apparently destroyed forever.[73] The "poisonous growths in the church of God" had been torn up by the roots, as the Bull demanded, but their extinction "lest they spread themselves further" was not achieved. It would take another 300 years from the year of foundation for her official recognition as foundress of a congregation of women living self-governing religious lives under vows without enclosure.[74] In 1951 Pope Pius XII would pay tribute to Mary Ward, calling her "that incomparable woman, given to the church by Catholic England in her darkest and bloodiest hour."[75]

As a woman both writing and written about, whose words were suppressed but whose dangerous memory was recorded in cryptic images, she holds, as a leader and intellectual in the medieval tradition, a vision for women of the future, seeking to find their own voice and mobility in a church which often still appears to prefer them to stay quietly at home: "Ther is no such difference between men and weomen that weomen may not doe great matters [..] and I hope in god it will be seene that weomen in tyme to come will doe much."[76]

71 *Painted Life*, paintings 8, 26 and 37.

72 Orchard, *Till God Will*, 49–50 and Dirmeier, *Mary Ward und ihre Gründung*,1, 521–528, 660–661, 762–765. See also 1, 778–779, part of the remarkable testimony of "Sister Dorothy," an otherwise anonymous "Jesuitess" living clandestinely in England.

73 Orchard, *Till God Will*, 115–119.

74 The Congregation of Jesus and the Institute of the Blessed Virgin Mary (Loreto sisters). See Mary Wright, *Mary Ward's Institute: The Struggle for Identity* (Sydney: Crossing Press, 1997).

75 John Saward, John Morrill and Michael Tomko, eds., *Firmly I Believe and Truly: The Spiritual Tradition of Catholic England 1483–1999* (Oxford: Oxford University Press, 2011), 187.

76 Dirmeier, *Mary Ward und ihre Gründung*, 1, 358.

# PART III

# RECOVERING LOST WOMEN'S AUTHORSHIP

## Preface to Part III

# RECOVERING LOST WOMEN'S AUTHORSHIP: NEW SOLUTIONS TO OLD PROBLEMS

KATHRYN KERBY-FULTON

As anyone knows who regularly reads manuscripts, and especially miscellanies, vast numbers of texts and authors go unidentified in medieval transmission. As E. P. Goldschmidt wrote long ago: "Whoever enters upon any investigation in the field ... cannot fail to be bewildered by the extraordinary uncertainty and elusive fluidity of the authors' names. Almost every other book seems to be known habitually under a name which cannot possibly be that of its true author."[1] Anonymous, then, is our most prolific medieval author, but somehow "Anonymous" nearly always gets voted male. There are, of course, many reasonable excuses for this, and the obstacles to recovering medieval women's authorship remain enormous. But the chapters in Part III demonstrate, often magisterially, solutions to the many conundrums scholars face in recovering women's authorship. Together they function almost as a masterclass in the art, pedagogically so helpful that I've tried to enumerate their techniques in the hope that other scholars will see parallel possibilities elsewhere and apply them to future cases.

In "A Woman Author? The Middle-Dutch Dialogue between a 'Good-willed Layperson' and a 'Master Eckhart'" (Chapter 8), John Van Engen brings us an anonymous *Dialogue* ostensibly between an unnamed layperson and "Eckhart," a whopping great text some 60,000 words in length. The text contains tantalizing parallels to Marguerite Porete's theology and, I would note, was written during the single most dangerous medieval period for dissenters (the first quarter of the fourteenth century).[2] One could add that during this time, Porete and her book were tragically burnt, the papal decrees known as the Clementines were published, and persecutions of beguines, Franciscan Spirituals, Joachite thinkers, and countless university academics (at Oxford, Paris, Cologne, and elsewhere) arose – persecutions that only increased as the vicious papacy of John XXII got fully underway by 1317. It is not an accident then, I think, that both the *Dialogue* Van Engen discusses, and the Bridget of Autrey text Nicholas Watson discusses here too, were produced at exactly this time, both bearing a history of censorship in some way.

The Middle Dutch *Dialogue* evokes this period vividly, with its author declaring that the persecutions of the poor sisters and beghards awoke such empathy in her that

1 See E. P. Goldschmidt, *Medieval Texts and their First Appearance in Print* (London: Oxford University Press, 1943), 87.

2 For a Chronology Chart listing the key condemnations of this period, see Kerby-Fulton, *Books Under Suspicion: Censorship and Tolerance of Revelatory Writing in Late Medieval English* (Notre Dame: University of Notre Dame Press, 2006), xxv–xxx.

she turned, in prose, to Meister Eckhart, a hero known to her only by reputation and, in 1323, not yet himself under inquisition. Caught between, in her words, the "Habits" [clergy in religious orders] and the "Priestly Types" [secular clergy], and uttering complaints, as Van Engen shows, far more common to the period's many *laywomen's* groups than its few laymen's, the author wrote a vernacular text nearly devoid of academic or monastic citation. Together these point strongly to female authorship. A later book by a self-identified English laywoman, *The Book of Margery Kempe*, presents striking parallels: Kempe, too, endured public condemnation delivered by a friar from the pulpit, and she suffered clerical contempt for the idea that a layperson could experience contemplation – to be a layperson was to be second-class citizen intellectually. Both also apparently had wide access to vernacular devotional texts. Excitingly, the Dutch author is perhaps, on Van Engen's surmise, even nameable: the elusive Bloemardinne, a woman, other sources say, confident and wealthy enough to teach and write sitting in "a silver seat" (*in sede argentea*). Her teachings so distressed her famous contemporary, Jan van Ruysbroeck, that he was prompted to write in the vernacular to counter them.[3] As a codicologist, I would just add to Van Engen's argument the observation that this author was likely a layperson of some real social means, someone with the financial resources to produce and launch a 60,000-word text – yet another corroboration.

Methodologically, Van Engen contextualizes his evidence by reminding us of the early strength and high quality of women's vernacular writing in the Low Countries. His methods are instructive for anyone faced with anonymous sources. To situate this author as female, he takes into account:

1. The indicators in the historical context – for example, that many more women's groups than men's were currently subject to the persecutions described;
2. The redaction of the text into a dialogue, its transmission history in anonymity, and eventually as excerpts in manuscripts often but not always via women's houses;
3. The absence of academic sources or biblical quotation, and the absence of Latin, but the presence of learning in the vernacular;
4. The author's sympathies – for example, for Eckhart as hero and for the many "poor sisters."

Van Engen notes that women writers of vernacular romance from the early twelfth century broke a path for later women writers of religious prose to follow, and Jocelyn Wogan-Browne's essay discusses one such important writer. In "Recovery and Loss: Women's Writing around Marie de France" (Chapter 9), we are in the secular realm of Marie – or more likely, as Wogan-Browne argues Marie*s* – de France. Wogan-Browne's essay is a *tour de force*, building upon new linguistic and metrical evidence from Ian Short and showing persuasively that there were a legion of "Maries de France." She

3 See Kerby-Fulton, "Eciam Lollardi," in *Voices in Dialogue: Reading Women in the Middle Ages*, ed. Linda Olson and K. Kerby-Fulton (Notre Dame: University of Notre Dame Press, 2005), 276, note 44 for the full Latin text, from *Analecta Bollandianna* (Paris–Brussels, 1882), 4: 286.

suggests that we have an original Marie and several admiring imitators who caught a ride into the literary future on her coattails (as also happened in the case of Marie's contemporary, Hildegard of Bingen, who had documentable literary coteries and imitators).[4] Wogan-Browne's extraordinarily exciting work, based in part on Short's discovery of discrepancies in rhyme phonology in various Marie-attributed texts, has therefore revealed multiple new women authors we never suspected we had. In fact, one could take Wogan-Browne's argument still further by wondering whether at least a few of the conscious imitators of Marie could even have been *men*? If so, that would be an *even* greater accolade still to Marie, since medieval pseudonym appropriators were both pragmatic and opportunistic, and "being" Marie de France must have been a great temptation.[5] Logically, however, it seems mostly likely that most or all of the writers who would adopt a female pseudonym were women, and Wogan-Browne has uncovered these new authors with a ground-breaking set of methods comparable to Van Engen's, but this time employing literary, socio-literary, bibliographic, and philological approaches. She proceeds by examining:

1. The philology, especially the phonology of the rhymes, and the dialect;
2. Scribal vs. authorial issues (for example, can a poet's language modify over time?);
3. The complexities of the medieval narratorial voice, with its tendency to slippage, and its use of performance identities (with analysis that adds new complexity, by the way, to modern theories of the narrator);[6]
4. Transmission issues in the cases of other contemporary women writers, such as the nuns of Campsey and loss or suppression of women's signatures;
5. Theoretical implications (for example, she applies Sarah Kay's theory that Chrestien de Troyes's name may be a soubriquet to the elusiveness and ubiquity of Marie's name).

These, like Van Engen's, are also highly sophisticated methods of proceeding, drawing on a range of disciplines, inventively and broadly applicable, I'd suggest, to other unsolved mysteries of authorial attribution. These tools, too, can be added to our kit for "how to recover women authors."

4 See, for instance, "Pseudo-Hildegardian Prophecy and Antimendicant Propaganda in Late Medieval England: An Edition of the Most Popular Insular Text of 'Insurgent gentes,'" co-written and co-edited by K. Kerby-Fulton, Magda Hayton, and Kenna Olsen, for *Prophecy, Apocalypse and the Day of Doom*, Harlaxton Medieval Studies, vol. XII, ed. Nigel Morgan (Oxford: Blackwell, 2004), 160–193; "Prophecy and Suspicion: Closet Radicalism, Reformist Politics and the Vogue for Hildegardiana in Ricardian England," *Speculum* 75 (2000) 318–341.

5 See Goldschmidt, *Medieval Texts*, 98.

6 See A. C. Spearing, *Medieval Autographies: the 'I' of the Text* (Notre Dame: University of Notre Dame Press, 2012).

We move now from these two cases demanding *deductive* methods (where few indicators survive) to Nicholas Watson's case study of a rare and differently challenging type, one in which a male author describes how a real collaboration with an historical woman actually worked. Such cases are scarce as hen's teeth. As Van Engen notes, modern studies of collaboration abound, but these are of necessity often conjectural as to how or how much the woman contributed. But Watson shows in "The Visions, Experiments, and Operations of Bridget of Autruy (fl. 1303–15)" (Chapter 10) how John of Morigny actually tells us *what* his sister contributed. Bridget, clearly a remarkable teenager, constantly exceeds his expectations, and he is honest enough to say so: she is so naturally adept at learning that he eventually regrets his assumption that she'd need magical help to learn – for modern readers a welcome overturning of endless medieval tropes of miraculous female literacy, usually based on the conviction that women could read only through divine intervention.[7] John in fact soon even becomes dependent on Bridget, which he also candidly records. I would add, further to Watson's observations, that modern studies of language acquisition suggest that there is likely no need to downplay or doubt Bridget's ability to acquire Latin as a teenager. This bright 15-year-old apparently graduated to collaborative status, as John of Morigny's fascinating use of the plural in spots (such as "*We* wrote this down…") indicates a kind of parity in literacy.[8]

Other features of John of Morigny's text readers will find fascinating, but which would take us too far off topic here, are its burnable and retractable books, its controversial *figurae* (reminiscent, though in a different genre, of the Joachite *Liber figurarum* tradition, which also at times drew suspicions),[9] and its dangerous historical context. Watson also discusses many nuggets of interest to codicologists and book historians: e.g., the challenges of a medieval author trying to "cancel" an earlier version (a hopeless enterprise in a manuscript culture) – John of Morigny's text would deserve to be better known for this alone. Other intriguing parallels one might cite, again without space to develop them here, are those to the magician figure in Chaucer's "Franklin's Tale," also a student at Orléans, a university Chaucer portrays as home to magic scholars.[10] More to the point for our discussion of women's authorship is the evidence Watson reveals of Bridget as part of *an inner circle of named academics*. This record of acceptance is so striking, much more so than in other cases of high profile brother–sister relationships, for example, with Douceline de Digne, whose brother was the great Franciscan Joachite theologian, Hugh of Digne; or with Eckbert of Schönau and his famous visionary sister, Elizabeth (Eckbert's witness, indeed much more

7 For multiple cases, see *Medieval Holy Women in the Christian Tradition, c. 1100–1500*, ed. Alastair Minnis and Rosalynn Voaden (Turnhout: Brepols, 2010).

8 For a recent study of the acquisition of Latin and extant grammars, see Christopher Cannon, "Vernacular Latin," *Speculum* 90/ 3 (2015), 641–653; and Jocelyn Wogan-Browne, "'Invisible Archives'? Later Medieval French in England," ibid., 653–673, on acquisition of written and spoken French later in life.

9 See Marjorie Reeves and Beatrice Hirsch-Reich, *The Figurae of Joachim of Fiore* (Oxford: Clarendon Press, 1972); and Kerby-Fulton, *Books Under Suspicion*, chapters 2, 3, 9, and 10 on various cases of book burning and book retraction.

10 See *The Riverside Chaucer*, ed. Larry Benson, 3rd ed. (Boston: Houghton Mifflin, 1987), Explanatory Notes to the "Franklin's Tale," V.1118, on Orléans, known for the study of astrology.

controversial).[11] In both cases we have actual independent writings surviving from the sister but fewer clues as to how or to what extent the brother drew his sister into a circle of male intellectuals as did John of Morigny.

Watson's key findings are also extremely applicable to the recovery of women's voices elsewhere, both methodologically and by extrapolation to less well-documented cases. Watson has given us:

1. A rare set of evidence for male–female *intellectual* collaboration;
2. John of Morigny's record of and respect, virtually scientific, for Bridget's "experimentum" (which he is unable to replicate himself but happily does not suppress);
3. Bridget's membership in a *male* circle of named clerics and academics;
4. A strong suggestion in Bridget's collaboration that she was able to *compose* as well as read.

This volume has several other articles exhibiting new methods for recovering women's texts, small and large. But what our authors here have helped us see is specific: first, that where we get hints of collaboration with a woman, it could indeed have been *very* concrete (like that of Watson's John of Morigny). Second, as Wogan-Browne shows, that *multiple women writers* might hide behind a pseudonym or a convenient soubriquet in medieval book culture – a culture in which a real name was less important than a *successful* name and in which publication was more about patrons than authors. And, as Goldschmidt showed many decades ago, this was *not just a woman's issue*. Medieval writers, both male and female, were likely to suffer authorial misattribution.[12] Third, that large anonymous texts sometimes are by women and that forensic textual and historical work can sometimes uncover an author's gender and caste, as Van Engen shows, if not her name. Finally, to this impressive list of methodologies and findings in all three of the writers in Part III, I would add that the shadow of later history can too often fall over our women writers during the reception process. As some of my own work in tracing once well-known but later submerged medieval women authors has shown, women's texts, sadly, were too often *redacted into anonymity* over time and repurposed to highlight male figures.[13] But with skill and patience, as our three contributors show here, we can sometimes reverse the obliteration.

11 On Douceline de Digne, see Kerby-Fulton, "When Women Preached," in *Voices in Dialogue*, 42–48; on Eckbert, see Anne L. Clark, *Elizabeth of Schonau: A Twelfth-Century Visionary* (Philadelphia: University of Pennsylvania Press, 1992), chap. 4; Clark credits Eckbert with saving and recording Elizabeth's visions, though he was perhaps an unreliable editor.

12 See Goldschmidt, *Medieval Texts*.

13 Kerby-Fulton, "Skepticism, Agnosticism and Belief: The Spectrum of Attitudes Toward Vision in Late Medieval England" in *Women and the Divine in Literature before 1700: Essays in Memory of Margot Louis*, ed. K. Kerby-Fulton (Victoria: English Literary Studies Series, 2009), 1– 18, on the suppression and redaction of works by St. Perpetua and Christina of Markyate.

8

# A WOMAN AUTHOR? THE MIDDLE DUTCH DIALOGUE BETWEEN A "GOOD-WILLED LAYPERSON" AND A "MASTER ECKHART"

JOHN VAN ENGEN

Eighty years ago, Herbert Grundmann proposed that religious writing moved from Latin into the vernacular initially to meet the needs of women, especially those active in what he called a "women's movement." That writing, he further held, was not inherently suspicious simply by virtue of being in the vernacular – as post-Reformation interpreters had often instinctively held, and some scholars do still. Either men or women, likewise, might have authored or compiled such works, even if, he tacitly presupposed, it was mostly men and especially friars writing for women.[1] Religious prose writings in the vernacular first emerged on any scale during the thirteenth century, grew exponentially during the fourteenth and especially the fifteenth centuries, and are today still abundantly represented in surviving manuscript materials.[2] At issue, perhaps now more than ever, is how we are to situate all this work: Is it friars writing for their charges, as with many sermons delivered by Meister Eckhart and Johannes Tauler? Women writing for women, or for women and men, or in not a few cases women and men writing collaboratively? Were these vernacular books actually meant particularly for lay sisters or brothers inside religious orders? Or generated especially by and for

1 Grundmann first mooted this in "Die geschichtlichen Grundlagen der Deutschen Mystik," *Deutsche Vierteljahrsschrift für Literaturwissenschaft und Geistesgeschichte* 12 (1934): 400–29. See also Grundmann, *Religious Movements in the Middle Ages*, trans. Steven Rowan (Notre Dame, IN: University of Notre Dame Press, 1995), 187–201. For critiques of "women's movement" as a helpful rubric, see for instance Martina Wehrli-Johns, "Voraussetzungen und Perspektiven mittelalterlicher Laienfrömmigkeit seit Innozenz III: Eine Auseinandersetzung mit Herbert Grundmanns 'Religiösen Bewegungen,'" *Mitteilungen des Instituts für Österreichische Geschichtsforschung* 104 (1996): 286–309, and idem, "Das mittelalterliche Beginentum: Religiöse Frauenbewegung oder Sozialidee der Scholastik?," in *Fromme Frauen oder Ketzerinnen? Leben und Verfolgung der Beginen im Mittelalter*, ed. Martina Wehrli-Johns and Claudia Opitz (Freiburg: Herder Verlag, 1998), 25–52.

2 For the Low Countries and Middle Dutch, see Thom Mertens, *Boeken voor de eeuwigheid: Middelnederlands geestelijk proza*, Nederlandse literatuur en cultuur in de middeleeuwen 8 (Amsterdam: Prometheus, 1993), as well as Karl Stooker and Theo Verbeij, *Collecties op orde: Middelnederlandse handschriften uit kloosters en semi-religieuze gemeenschappen in de Nederlanden*, Miscellanea Neerlandica 15–16, 2 vols (Louvain: Peeters, 1997). For engaging introductions and overviews, see Frits van Oostrom, *Stemmen op schrift: Geschiedenis van de Nederlandse literatuur vanaf het begin tot 1300* (Amsterdam: Bert Bakker, 2006) and *Wereld in Woorden: Geschiedenis van de Nederlandse literatuur 1300–1400* (Amsterdam: Bert Bakker, 2013).

"quasi-religious" groups? Or aimed rather at educated and aspiring laypersons? Or indeed written by and for circles of dissenters? All these are variously true, none exclusively so. No one approach will account for the range and multiplicity of surviving vernacular religious writing. We must expect and perceive multiple authorial situations and vernacular readers. This essay takes up, too briefly, one dimension of the issue, that of female authorship, and with respect to one little-studied work in Middle Dutch.

Vernacular writing on religious life undertaken by women, apart from earlier hagiography reconfigured as epic poetry, appeared in Latin Christendom first during the early thirteenth century.[3] Earlier women authors on matters religious, thus Dhuoda or Heloise or Hildegard, wrote in Latin. Courtly epic, Romance, and lyric would move into written vernaculars during the twelfth and early thirteenth centuries, and some of these composers were women, thus "Marie de France" along with trobairitz and trouvères.[4] A generation or so later women also began writing religious lyric in the vernacular, often now appropriating romance tropes and forms for religious ends. These same women went on to write in the vernacular on religion in prose as well, thus visions, letters, and teachings ("leer" in Middle Dutch). In the surviving works of, for instance, Beatrice of Nazareth (1200–68) and Hadewijch (c. 1250?), the debt to prior "worldly" forms is patent – links still obscured at times by artificial divides among scholars between secular and religious writing.[5] Also easily overlooked is that this religious writing by women flourished initially in the Low Countries, whether it was written in Middle Dutch or Picard French, even as it moved across the north German plain in Low and Central German and up the Rhine to Strasburg and Basel and Bavaria in High German.[6] Already at mid-century (c. 1250), a male writer in Bavarian Regensburg registered this broader phenomenon and its prominence in the Low Countries with a witty if not sardonic edge: "This art has arisen in our day in Brabant and Bavaria among women. Lord God, what sort of art is it that an old woman grasps better than a clever man?"[7] The "art" (or "craft": kunst) was that of communicating religious experience and teaching

3 This turn is central to the third volume of Bernard McGinn's history of mystical teaching and writing: *The Flowering of Mysticism: Men and Women in the New Mysticism (1200–1350)* (New York: Crossroad, 1998), 1–69.

4 See further Jocelyn Wogan-Browne's contribution to this volume (Chapter 9, "Recovery and Loss: Women's Writing around Marie de France").

5 A fine starting point now, in part with a reversed thematic as its title suggests, is Barbara Newman, *Medieval Crossover: Reading the Secular against the Sacred* (Notre Dame, IN: University of Notre Dame Press, 2013).

6 See now Elizabeth Andersen, Henrike Lähnemann and Anne Simon, *A Companion to Mysticism and Devotion in Northern Germany in the Late Middle Ages* (Leiden–Boston: Brill, 2014), which begins with Hadewijch and Mechthild of Magdeburg.

7 Lamprecht von Regensburg, *Tochter Syon*, lines 2838–43. Published in Karl Weinhold, ed., *Lamprecht von Regensburg: "Sanct Franciskus Leben" und "Tochter Syon"* (Paderborn, 1880), 431. Geert Warnar has interpreted this altogether ironically and argued that Hadewijch and other women writers had little reception among more famous male authors. See his "*Ex levitate mulierum*: Masculine Mysticism and Jan van Ruusbroec's Perception of Religious Women," in *The Voice of Silence: Women's Literacy in a Men's Church*, ed. Thérèse de Hemptinne and Mariá Eugenia Góngora (Turnhout: Brepols, 2004), 193–96. Lamprecht's verse seems to me born of mocking wonder, while Ruusbroec arguably wrote in the vernacular precisely in counterpoint to women religious and authors.

in vernacular verse and prose. A German prologue to select translated works of Hadewijch identified her retrospectively as that "great holy person" whose "productive teaching" (nucze lere) spawned (lebende von) and enlightened (erlúhtet) all those "friends of God in Brabant"[8] – referring hereby to the women modern scholarship identifies especially with Liège and regions around Brussels as "beguines."[9]

It is also easy to overlook, given a plethora now of ready anthologies and translations as well as all the recent scholarly attention, that the transmission of these writings was tenuous. Beatrice of Nazareth in Lier wrote a religious commonplace book in Dutch prose, the earliest of its kind known and perhaps the earliest first-person document in Middle Dutch, now lost – though claimed as a source for a more conventional *vita* written in Latin by a chaplain after her death.[10] Her Middle Dutch *Seven Modes of Love* is the earliest significant extant piece of Middle Dutch prose, and it exists in three manuscripts. Within a generation (1290/1300) of her death it had been anthologized, ultimately twice, in the so-called *Limburg Sermons*, the earliest extant broad collection of religious prose in Middle Dutch, assembled seemingly in the later thirteenth century in that same region of eastern Brabant or Liège. Another copy of her work survives in an anthology featuring Jan van Ruusbroec (1293–1381), the most famous of the later male religious writers in Dutch.[11] Hadewijch in turn, far more prolific and equally or more influential, survives now by way of three copies of her "collected works" written a good century after her death by copyists in Brabant among reforming circles of Carthusians and canons regular. Earlier to be sure, single works of these women, or clusters assembled by them, had circulated, probably initially in loose quires or small bundles and within particular religious circles. Visions and some letters by Hadwijch demonstrably circulated independently early on (her *Letter* 10 entering the *Limburg Sermons*); moreover, some or all of her work was soon translated into Latin (that also now lost).[12] But such works seemingly had little chance

8 Quoted here from Veerle Fraeters, "Hadewijch of Brabant and the Beguine Movement," in *A Companion to Mysticism and Devotion in Northern Germany in the Late Middle Ages*, ed. Elizabeth Andersen, Henrike Lähnemann, and Anne Simon (Leiden–Boston: Brill, 2014), 62.

9 For the complexities and pitfalls in labeling these women, see now, for instance, *Labels and Libels: Naming Beguines in Northern Medieval Europe*, ed. Letha Böhringer, Jennifer Kolpacoff Deane, and Hildo van Engen (Turnhout: Brepols, 2014).

10 Roger De Ganck, *The Life of Beatrice of Nazareth*, Cistercian Fathers (Kalamazoo, MI: Cistercian Publications, 1991), and Amy Hollywood, "Inside-Out: Beatrice of Nazareth and her Hagiographer," in *Gendered Voices: Medieval Saints and their Interpreters*, ed. Catherine M. Mooney (Philadelphia: University of Pennsylvania Press, 1999), 78–98. The conversation over this work, whether it existed, and its possible visibility in the chaplain's Latin *vita*, continues. I do not doubt the existence of such a work, nor the ineptitude of the chaplain, whose "wit" and spiritual courage was far inferior to Beatrice's, as he in effect admitted. See the engaging remarks of Van Oostrom, *Stemmen*, 403ff.

11 See Wybren Scheepsma, *The Limburg Sermons: Preaching in the Medieval Low Countries at the Turn of the Fourteenth Century*, trans. David F. Johnson (Leiden–Boston: Brill, 2008).

12 For orientation to the complex issues surrounding Hadewijch's transmission, see Saskia Murk-Jansen, *The Measure of Mystic Thought: A Study of Hadewijch's Mengeldichten* (Göppingen: Kümmerle Verlag, 1991), 9–13, 21–24; idem, "Hadewijch," in *Medieval Holy Women in the Christian Tradition c. 1100–c.1500*, ed. Alastair Minnis and Rosalynn Voaden (Turnhout: Brepols, 2010), 663–85; and Fraeters, "Hadewijch of Brabant," 49–71. See too Scheepsma, *Limburg Sermons*.

of survival unless they were anthologized, and those anthologies then housed in a cloister. Even more complex and troubled, at this same time, was the transmission of Mechthild of Magdeburg/Helfta's *Flowing Light of the Godhead*, extant in whole or in fragments in various Germanic dialects, if little of it in her own native speech. This work too was translated early into Latin (surviving), and various vernacular fragments attest to excerpted reading across the north German plain.[13] Of another Netherlandish author, Marguerite Porete of Valenciennes in the 1290s, we have only a tenth of her work still in her native Picard French (more in any case than of Mechthild's Low or Central German), but again the whole *Mirror of Simple Souls Reduced to Nothing* translated into Latin, English, and later medieval Parisian French.[14] These translations attest to interest and audiences, the few surviving manuscripts to their tenuous transmission. The same holds in the fifteenth century for Julian or Margery's English writings, and Alijt Bake's Middle Dutch works. Especially in the thirteenth and into the fourteenth century, if writings were deemed worthy of wider reading, they got translated soon into Latin, still the era's *lingua franca*. This was true for Beatrice, Hadewijch, Mechthild, and Marguerite (and Jan van Ruusbroec on the male side). But in truth we would have little still of many women's religious writings in the vernacular were it not for the real interest of late fourteenth- and fifteenth-century Carthusians, Modern-Day Devout, Observants, and other reforming groups.

What went missing, what we do not have – that remains largely an imponderable.[15] But we do have many vernacular religious texts circulating anonymously or with dubious authorial attributions. And we would do well to approach these with an open mind, rather than reflexive assumptions that they too likely originated with some male cleric. The work taken up here, called by scholars "Eckhart and the Layman," is some 60,000 words in length, 170 pages of dense Middle Dutch prose, and has come down to us without title or author. First noted and partially edited at the beginning of the twentieth century by a young C. G. N. de Vooys, it was edited in full only fifteen years ago,[16] and has as yet received minimal scholarly attention, brought to notice outside

13 See now Sara Poor, "Transmission and Impact: Mechthild of Magdeburg's *Das fließende Licht der Gottheit*," in *Companion to Mysticism and Devotion*, 73–101.

14 See Michael G. Sargent, "Marguerite Porete," in *Medieval Holy Women*, 291–309. For the fragment of her original Picard French, see now Geneviève Hasenohr, "Retour sur les caractères linguistiques du manuscript de Chantilly et de ses ancètres," in *Marguerite Porete et le "Miroir des simples âmes": Perspectives historiques, philosophiques et littéraires*, ed. Sean L. Field, Robert E. Lerner, and Sylvain Piron (Paris: Vrin, 2013), 103–26. For locating Marguerite in the Low Countries, see Van Engen, "Marguerite (Porete) of Hainaut and the Medieval Low Countries," in *Marguerite Porete et le "Miroir des simples âmes"*, 25–68.

15 There is a good general orientation to women vernacular religious writers in the Low Countries in Walter Simons, "'Staining the Speech of Things Divine': The Uses of Literacy in Medieval Beguine Communities," and Thérèse de Hemptinne, "Reading, Writing, and Devotional Practices: Lay and Religious Women and the Written Word in the Low Countries (1350–1550)," both in *The Voice of Silence*, 85–110, 111–26.

16 Franz Josef Schweitzer, *Meister Eckhart und der Laie: Ein antihierarchischer Dialog des 14. Jahrhunderts aus den Niederlanden* (Berlin: Walter de Gruyter, 1997). See the penetrating review by Robrecht Lievens, "Eggaert en de (nog steeds) onbekende leek: Enkele overwegingen," *Leuvense bijdragen: tijdschrift voor germaanse filologie* 88 (1999): 15–49.

Middle Dutch circles owing mainly to the alert eye of a young Robert Lerner.[17] This work presents itself as an extended dialogue between a "Master Eckhart" and a "layperson," the layperson no ordinary soul but a "blessed soul" (*salige siele*), a layperson of good will (*de goetwillige leek*). That term, used constantly, pointed toward those dedicated types whom we broadly label, if not always accurately or carefully, as "beguine" or "third-order" or "zealots" or "dissenters." A work in German partly similar to this one in Middle Dutch, and better-known, is the dialogue called *Schwester Katrei*, likely composed near Strasburg (or at least the upper Rhine) at roughly the same time (c. 1320), it too sometimes associated with "Meister Eckhart," though not as explicitly as our work.[18]

Our Middle Dutch dialogue survives in "complete" form in only one manuscript copy (Brussels, Royal Library 888–90). That copy is very late, and was undertaken by lay brothers at the Windesheim house of Bethlehem outside Louvain in 1543/1547. They added the work to a copy they had made of the "collected works" of the lay cook at Groenendael, Jan van Leeuwen (d. 1378), a close companion of Jan Ruusbroec. The "Good Cook," one of the more famous or infamous lay religious male authors of this era, wrote twenty-two known works in his native Dutch (many still unedited). Like those of his father-confessor Jan Ruusbroec, these were accounted worthy early on of varied "collected" editions produced at their home house of Groenendael outside Brussels, even as both were graced as well a generation later with a Latin *vita*.[19] Our dialogue is preserved, thus, in the same Modern-Day Devout network which was also copying or preserving Beatrice and Hadewijch, and alongside a lay vernacular author. In the manuscript this work is headed with a simple marker: *Dit es een ander boexken* ("This is another little book") – "little book" being a common term in the language of the day for such religious works. Whatever it was copied from, that earlier exemplar was likely borrowed from another house in their network, possibly relatively nearby Groenendael. Presumably that exemplar too bore neither author nor title, whether lost, suppressed, or never present. In this case, as with the women noted above, excerpts attest to earlier circulation of this dialogue in whole or part by the later fourteenth century, with bits found in six miscellanies, three from women's houses, another two

17 C. G. N. de Vooys, "Twee Christen-Demokraten uit de veertiende eeuw," *De XXe Eeuw* (1903): 280–310; C. C. de Bruin, *Middeleeuws "Verlicht" Christendom: Kerkhistorische achergronden van een anoniem vraaggesprek met meester Eggaert* (Leiden: Brill, 1956); Robert E. Lerner, *The Heresy of the Free Spirit in the Later Middle Ages* (Berkeley: University of California Press, 1972), 213–15.

18 For an edition, dating, and the manuscripts, see Franz-Josef Schweitzer, *Der Freiheitsbegriff der deutschen Mystik: Seine Beziehung zur Ketzerei der "Brüder und Schwestern vom Freien Geist," mit besonderer Rücksicht auf den pseudoeckartischen Traktat "Schwester Katrei"* (Frankfurt: Peter Lang 1981).

19 For an orientation to Jan van Leeuwen, with manuscripts, see D. Geirnaert and J. Reynaert, "Geestelijke spijs met zalige vermaning: Verspreiding, overlevering en receptie van Jan van Leeuwen," in *Boeken voor de eeuwigheid*, 190–209, 426–34; and now especially Eva Vandemeulebroucke and Youri Desplenter, "How Jan Van Leeuwen († 1378) was Made an Author: *Opera Omnia and* Authority," in *Shaping Authority*, ed. Brigitte Mijns (Turnhout: Brepols, 2016): 363–87. See too Bernard McGinn, *The Varieties of Vernacular Mysticism (1350–1550)* (New York: Crossroad, 2012), 71–76, 512–13.

with women scribes or addressees.[20] Further, an abbreviated version was copied into another famous collection of Middle Dutch religious prose and poetry made around 1400, likewise in regions around Brussels. In it we have no reference to "Eckhart" or a "layperson," the dialogue sustained rather simply by an "I ask" and "I say," with only thirty-eight questions. Its rubric labels this work "questions of a good simple person to which the most superior king of his/her soul answers"[21] – that is, these materials staged, or understood here, as an internal dialogue between faculties of the soul. In five of the six fragments with short excerpts, however, "Master Eckhart" does appear. It was thus the form in which this work most commonly reached readers. That also makes it seemingly the earliest and largest of those items Eckhart scholars have labeled "Eckhart-Legende," that is, appropriations by others of Eckhart's name or reputation beginning already in his lifetime.[22]

In its one known "complete" manuscript version this work contains repetitions, and its thematic development is more episodic than sustained. Some have imagined a dossier built up over time, others a body of writing structured as a complete work. Both seem more or less true. The work, to be sure, offers an intentional opening and closing meant to frame and position the whole. Yet within its considerable length we find various distinct blocks of material and threads of dialogue, teachings built up perhaps over years, some themes coming up for repeated treatment – perhaps not so unlike Beatrice's lost book a century earlier. Schweitzer's edition has divided its text into 141 exchanges. Both he and our one extant manuscript, however, lost their way at times when trying to distinguish the two voices (easily done). A young Dutch scholar has separated out twenty-five more exchanges, and I would add another dozen, bringing the total to nearly 180. In addition, a distinguished Middle Dutch scholar edited a plausible fragment not found in the "complete" manuscript.[23] Further, in the dialogue, some exchanges between "Master Eckhart" and the "layperson" are brief and curt, some paragraph-long questions with page-long answers. In sum, this work represents a significant body of teaching, but with its authorial origin deliberately masked by the dialogue's conceit: a "layperson" who presents leading, probing, or aggrieved questions and a "Master Eckhart" who provides most of the answers and teaching.

To examine authorship, we would do well to begin by locating the work in time and space. As to its likely point of origin, scholars lean to Brabant (De Bruin) owing especially to language, or southern Holland (Schweitzer). Its lay *persona* traveled seemingly across the region (allusions to Aardenburg in Zeeland and also to Aachen), listened to quite a few preachers and questioned quite a few priests, also visited con-

20 Schweitzer, *Meister Eckhart*, lxxxi–lxxxvii.

21 For an edition, see *Het Wiesbadense handschrift: Hs. Wiesbaden, Hessisches Hauptstaatarchiv, 3004 B 10*, ed. Hans Kienhorst and Kees Scepers, with Amand Bertelot and Paul Wackers (Hilversum: Verloren, 2009), 520–33. Its hand, and to some extent its orthography, is distinct from the other eight, but the editors still place it in the same core region of this manuscript: Aalst–Oudenaarde–Brussels.

22 See still Ingeborg Degenhardt, *Studien zum Wandel des Eckhartbildes* (Leiden: Brill, 1967).

23 Yves van Damme, "De rolverdeling in de *Dialoog van meester Eckhart en de leek*: Een herbeschouwing," *Ons geestelijk erf* 84 (2013): 202–43. Robrecht Lievens, "Eggaert en de (nog steeds) onbekende leek: Enkele overwegingen," *Leuvense bijdragen: tijdschrift voor germaanse filologie* 88 (1999): 35, 44–45.

vents (including Rijnsburg west of Leiden). The lay *persona* refers too to a presumed place of origin (*hier voertijts doen ic ionc was*: "Here earlier when I was young"), while projecting Rijnsburg and the bishopric of Utrecht as elsewhere (117:105, 108). Other dioceses with goodly numbers of Dutch speakers would include Tournai and Liège. But Cambrai fits best, and would encompass Brussels as well as Beatrice's Nazareth, Hadewijch's "Brabant," and Marguerite's Romance-speaking Valenciennes. Schweitzer noted echoes of Hadewijch throughout, possibly Beatrice too, and Lerner pointed toward passages possibly echoing "Free Spirit" discourse.

As for a time-span, the dialogue itself refers forcefully at its beginning and end, also generally throughout, to troubled times at present. The "sixth" question has the layperson ask: "Master, from what sins then do these great tribulations (*plagen*) come which have happened during the past twelve years, out of which so much distress [*vernooij*] has come?"[24] Another question recurs more often in varied forms: "Master, why then are the Priestly Types [secular clergy and parish priests] and the Habits [professed religious in their distinctive garb] so very harassing and scornful of the Good-willed Laity, who have scorned themselves and cast themselves under others' feet?" (73:62: *Meester, waer om soe es die paepscap ende die abijt soe seer vervolghende ende versmadende dit goet willeghe leeken, die hem selven hebben versmaet ende gheworpen onder ander menschen voeten?*).[25] Past scholars have suggested time frames between 1306 and the 1340s, some pointing particularly to 1325/26 (Warnar), 1336/37, or 1340/41 (Schweitzer).[26] Any claim to an exact dating turns on an ambiguous passage close to the end (136:169). Here "Eckhart" fits the current outbreak of troubles into a scheme whereby in biblical history tribulations strike every thirteen hundred years. The passage reveals, I have argued, a time early in the year 1325.[27] While we cannot know in what order the work's varied parts were first penned, or over how many months or years, we can conclude that this work arose in the immediate aftermath of attempts by pope and council from 1311/1314 onwards to ban or rein in "Free Spirits" and "beguines" by way of the decrees *Ad nostrum* and *Cum de quibusdam mulieribus*. This brought unprecedented pressure on "Good-willed Laypeople" to prove themselves the "right sort" or be closed down.[28] In 1319 Count Robert of Flanders intervened amidst this

24 Schweitzer, *Meister Eckhart*, 20. Hereafter, as a matter of economy, references will be given in the text in brackets, the number Schweitzer assigned a question his edition, then the page in his edition, thus here (6:20).

25 This, softened, appears in the "Questions of a good simple person" (Q. 28) as: "I ask why the Learned scorn the lowly simple people who have humbled and disparaged themselves." *Wiesbadense handschrift*, 529.

26 Schweitzer, *Meister Eckhart*, lii–liv, lxi, lxv–lxix for the older literature and Schweitzer's position; for Warnar, see the following note.

27 In agreement with this, if not on some other interpretive matters, is Geert Warnar, "Meester Eckhart, Walter van Holland en Jan van Ruusbroec: Historische en literaire betrekkingen in de Middelnederlandse mystiek," *Ons geestelijk erf* 69 (1995): 3–25.

28 For a summary as it applies to the Low Countries, see Van Engen, *Sisters and Brothers of the Common Life: The Devotio Moderna and the World of the Later Middle Ages* (Philadelphia: University of Pennsylvania Press, 2008), 37–44. For a similar nuancing of the originating "beguine persecution" in Strasburg, see Jörg Voight, "Beginen, Bischöfe und Bettelorder in Straßburg: Zu den sogenannten Straßburger Beginenverfolgungen im 14. Jahrhundert, in *Mystik, Recht*

on behalf of all "beguines" in his lands, now, he says, driven out of religious households and into the streets, away from their "upright" way of life.[29] In a document dated 23 May 1319 the large beguine community in Brussels appealed to the pope, and the earliest copies of Pope John XXII's response, which began reactively to license the "right sort" of "religious women," then went out to the dioceses of Cambrai (Brussels) and Tournai (Flanders). We have here, in sum, a vernacular "dialogue" written wholly or in part during or immediately after papal attempts to regulate or suppress "Good-willed Laypeople," groups comprised overwhelmingly of women.

But was this teaching dialogue written by a woman? All have seen him ("him" always presumed) as a free and critical spirit, deeply empathetic with these "Good-willed Lay," whether himself just within orthodoxy or daringly outside. Since 1903 he has been labeled a "Christian Democrat" (then a new and radical type), an "enlightened Christian" (also a radical combination), likewise a "Beghard" or a "Free Spirit." Dutch-speaking scholars have labeled the work itself, and a few others, "anti-hierarchical" owing to its critique of clergymen. Its lay *persona* indeed complains critically about ill-treatment from the clergy, but then anti-clericalism was, so to speak, also normal in the later middle ages. And this person is forever visiting churches, listening to sermons, and querying or consulting priests and friars, if also asking them hard questions. The work's teachings are projected mostly on "Eckhart," a revered figure here, not yet charged with heresy. Scholars have imagined this author too as a secular priest offering the women sympathetic care and cover amidst new pressures. Warnar, rightly, points insistently to rhetorical features at work in the "dialogue" genre, and has suggested that the work may echo prosecutions at Cologne by Dominican inquisitors of a Dutch "Beghard" figure named Walter in 1325/26 – thus from or for a "beghard" milieu, again male.[30]

If we turn to the two *personae* projected in the dialogue, what seems clear is this. The author's "Good-willed Layperson," as Schweitzer noted, is overwhelmingly female, while the "Eckhart" figure is creatively built upon images of the friar and master spreading already in his lifetime as a perceptive spiritual teacher uncommonly open to teaching and counseling women.[31] Now, we must be clear: None of the dialogue's teachings echo or paraphrase Eckhart as such. Translations of his work into Middle Dutch would begin only a generation later. As for Cologne, where Friar Eckhart ministered after 1323 (also earlier), the lay *persona* in the dialogue professes admiration for beghards and poor sisters there without ever having met them or been there. "Their persecution so hurt me," she says, "that my soul opened for you, Master Eckhart," and further "what someone does to my fellow Christian, that the person does to me"

*und Freiheit: Religiöse Erfahrung und kirchliche Institutionen im Spätmittelalter*, ed. Dietmar Mieth and Britta Müller-Schauenburg (Stuttgart: Kohlhammer, 2012), 51–68.

29 See Walter Simons, "In Praise of Faithful Women: Count Robert of Flanders's Defense of Beguines against the Clementine Decree *Cum de quibusdam mulieribus* (ca. 1318–1320)," in *Christianity and Culture in the Middle Ages: Essays to Honor John Van Engen*, ed. David C. Mengel and Lisa Wolverton (Notre Dame, IN: University of Notre Dame Press, 2015), 331–57.

30 Schweitzer, *Meister Eckhart*, lxii–lxv, with a summary of earlier positions; Warnar, "Meester Eckhart," 10ff.

31 Schweitzer, *Meister Eckhart*, li.

(118:121: *Als ic dat hoer, soe quetset my om dat mijn siele es vry voer u. Al daer ome so heb Ic gheclaecht gode ende u. Want dat men minen evenkersten doet, dat doet men my!*) – hints of a possible inciting moment for the fictive frame. Elsewhere the dialogue also projects Cologne as a "time-zone away" (138:174). With such severe pressures on beguines or beguine-like figures at home, these rumors of an empathetic "Eckhart" in a distant city, never seen in person, may have suggested an avenue forward for presenting this author's teachings and opinions (doubtless worked up over years), and in a frame that could appear mischievously safe. In most of the dialogue, questions or objections from the "layperson" are addressed simply to a "master," presumably "Eckhart," though this too could betray stages in the dialogue's conception and composition. At any rate, early or late, our author lent this dialogue its distinctive rhetorical frame by presenting its teachings, the author's own, as born of an extended dialogue with Meister Eckhart, soul to soul, as we will see. Whether undertaken as a deliberate move to mask identity under such a renowned name, or as a cover adopted in dangerous times, or a presumptuous bid to speak here as a religious equal, this text would enter into circulation thus – though some locally no doubt knew the authorial source.

For the gender and identity of this author there is finally no absolute evidence. We must work with interpretive probabilities. In my view those strongly favor a lay or semi-lay woman. First consider the negative evidence. For the author of this dialogue being a cleric or a priest there is, as I see it, no evidence whatsoever of the kind we would expect. In its thousands of words, we find not the slightest hint of Latin or Latin tags, whether from the Psalms or Latin school texts or the Bible more generally, or of materials echoing preachers' or confessors' manuals, or of anything homiletic or distinctively liturgical. The work evidences intelligence and reading – but all in the vernacular, with virtually no direct citation. When the Bible gets invoked, then it is mostly in the form of stories, characters and their deeds or moral teachings, such as one might find in say Jacob van Maerlant's *Rhymed Bible* from a generation or two earlier. Only very occasionally does the author invoke biblical verses as such, then short tags any attentive person would know from church or vernacular liturgy or common sayings. We find here evidence of a probing mind and spiritual intensity but nothing "clerical" in tone or language. That could of course also fit a lay Beghard, though interestingly we have virtually no such lay male writers.

Pronouns are no help, though in Middle Dutch they color the dialogue's effect. Much talk turns on the "blessed soul" (*salige siele*) and "soul" in Middle Dutch is feminine, hence "she" throughout rather than an English "it." Much talk turns likewise on humans generally (*mensch*: "man"), and as in traditional English that becomes "he." So when the "layperson" (*leek*) recounts conversations or encounters with religiously aspiring "young persons," the grammar is male though the person may well be female – and in Dutch the article "*de*" serves masculine and feminine alike. This author on occasion reverses the trope of masculine "spirit" and feminine "body," thus "Eckhart" saying that the soul is lady of the body, and body the male servant or slave (*knecht*) of the soul (76:65). So too a shameful loving of God merely for reward becomes a maidservant honoring her lady for gifts (51:49, 68:59, 69:60). The term for chastity means female in usage (*maagdelijk*, as in "maiden," where *rein* or "pure" is more common). The image of true humility (foundational) invokes a mother nursing and so embracing all virtue (101:77). Eve is described as Adam's "heart's love" (whence he accepted her offer of the apple), as Jesus was Mary Magdalene's. And all rational beings know that "one will love an extraordinarily handsome good man" (28:31). All these are but relative indicators, though noteworthy alongside the text's lack of clerical language or tone.

The material this author presents is serious, instructive, sometimes provocative, but also shrewdly careful. In an early duo of questions (14–15:23–25), a block found too in some of the fragments, the layperson is made to ask whether she can or indeed must speak about the fathomless Godhead such as the blessed soul feels and grasps at that point when the self, in God, has become entirely nothing in perfect love – an echo seemingly of Marguerite's central theme, whether with knowledge of Marguerite or simply as part of a broader religious conversation. The Master replies yes indeed, at least for those to whom this is permitted and who understand. The layperson then retorts that you and people like you (friars, university men) have the understanding and permission, and presses him to speak, thus placing the answer in "Eckhart's" mouth. Ten questions later the layperson asks: If a person has set her life on love of God alone and neither desires nor wills anything of evil, wherein does she still sin if she is also free in conscience? "Eckhart" answers that no person is without sin, and no person can be free in conscience *unless* (in Middle Dutch: *'t en sij*) she lives by the uppermost reason of her soul and exercises herself in all virtue and religious life. Then he tempers that, noting one should always retain the fear of God. An intense exchange follows, culminating in the layperson objecting that proud Priestly Types and Habits harass such people when they speak of these high things. "Eckhart" then explains that these clerics do not comprehend the graces given to Good-willed Laypeople. He "counsels" them to separate themselves from others and to exercise themselves with God in solitude and silence and so restfully enjoy God in their souls. The layperson responds: Yes, she has a sense indeed of what happens when she has spoken of God or spiritual matters before the uncomprehending (*onbekende*). But "Eckhart" explains that if and when the Good-willed Lay by contrast encounter "good humble spiritual people" they "may freely – or they could" (!)[32] – hold religious conference (*vrilike collacien*) over heavenly matters (25:27–29). This theme and praxis stand central for the author: freedom to converse and teach about "God and heavenly matters" without harassment.

The work achieves this end in effect on its own, covertly, staging a dialogue with teachings provided by a revered male friar. Yet, the conversing and teaching that go on within the dialogue also suggest an open and varied world, a large horizon, not a cloistered one. The "layperson" alludes to conversations or sermons at various convents, shrines, and churches with snippets, real or quasi-real, of interchanges with local priests and friars as well as both Good-willed and common laity. The lay *persona*, and the author too, seem neither a nun nor a beguine, and she straightway dismisses the spiritual profit of visions, pilgrimages, and shrines as limited at best in this spiritual quest. The matter of obedience arises, but its form is promptly turned against the cloistered: the highest obedience is to order the will in love of God and obedience to the Ten Commandments (in effect, the lay "rule"), nobler to live thus

32 Did this startling correction, placed in Eckhart's mouth, echo directly the recent new laws?

than under the coercion of a "superior," better also to live untainted by sin among the worldly than be "good" among the "good" (118:117). The orientation here is strongly lay, with a focus then mostly on the "Good-willed Lay," described on several occasions as people of whom no evil is ever heard, whom God has preserved from grave sin since childhood, and who keep themselves apart from the world and in a virginal state (136:166). This lay *persona* also has no automatic reverence for nuns or friars. At a nuns' house outside Leiden she once heard a Dominican preach against Beghards as heretics, and quips that the friar should have spent his time instead teaching these nuns to train their desires on the noble love of God and tasting spiritual joy in their souls (117:105) – what this dialogue is about. The lay *persona* regularly moves about listening to sermons, also visiting convents – that a particular much more likely true of a woman. One passage, locatable perhaps in Brabant or even Brussels (again, *hier*), tells of a Dominican friar preaching there publicly in a "convent." In his sermon he crudely shamed a particular Good-willed Layperson for having expressed (*een woert ghesproken hadde*) a view with which he disagreed. When several Good-willed women (of this convent?) then objected, he retorted that it was as impossible for a layperson to be at rest in God as to jump over that church (117:109). There follows then, in the voice of "Eckhart," a lengthy account of contemplative rest and knowing God's being even in his divinity (presumably the contested issue), and that as coming only through separation from all that is not God and by loving God alone and only for himself. Very likely we have an oblique reference here to the author as having spoken a word on "high matters" before other "Good-willed Laity," then getting castigated for it by a visiting Dominican friar in a public sermon. This met objections from other women (*vrouwen*), whereupon she (and all laity) were dismissed by him in a disparaging retort.[33] In the dialogue these teachings were then placed here ironically in the mouth of another Dominican, "Master Eckhart."

With this incident as background, and allusions in the dialogue to varied encounters with Priestly Types, consider now how the author framed the entire work. This "prologue" deftly opened the way to a work precisely on "God and heavenly matters." The "layperson" greets "Master Eckhart" (not "Father" or "Friar") as an "extraordinary light of divine wisdom," and presents herself as a "silly fool, a foot-wipe of priests," yet as someone who "in the spirit has loved his soul" (Prologue: 17):

> You have found fault with me before your religious brothers because I do not want to speak before you. The highest reason of my soul has forbidden me to speak about God and about heavenly matters because I know very well the notions of the priestly types, who for their own peace choose not to allow that laypeople say things about God or about heavenly matters.
>
> Master, my soul is free to speak before you about God and about heavenly matters. You know me in the spirit, and my soul knows you in God.

33 For another such confrontation, less fully set out, see 112:193.

Amidst new pressures on self-styled religious, doubtless real for the author too, this opening sets up the "layperson" and "Master Eckhart" as being one in spirit, he the only priestly soul before whom her soul will or can speak. Fictively this stages a confidential spiritual conversation, becoming then in practice a massive dialogue all written out in the vernacular. At its halfway point this opening greeting reappears, but interestingly with "Eckhart" now protesting that the "layperson" is asking things too high for what befits her – a critique the author had doubtless encountered in real life. But the lay *persona* responds: "Master, you have given me permission to ask all that I want concerning heaven and earth, and my soul is free before you above all people to speak of God and heavenly matters" (116:100).

Then once again in the epilogue, which was not distinguished as such by Schweitzer in his edition, this motif returns in lengthier form and with a new twist (140:180–83):

> ["Eckhart"]: You have asked much, and spoken as an ignorant idiot [*sod*] above what befits you. But a silly fool and an idiot can ask more than the wise can well provide for.
>
> [Layperson]: I know it well, that I have asked much and spoken above what befits me. It comes from my fault, that I cannot overcome myself but must from time to time speak of God and heavenly matters. Your religious brothers, they have stirred and brought me to this, that I have asked so much above what befits me.[34] Because my soul is free before you above all others, I have spoken freely therefore of the divine being, and because you reproached me before your religious brothers because I did not want to speak before you [...] I have often prayed God for a bridle for my tongue, and never indeed could constrain it [...].
>
> ["Eckhart"]: Even so I counsel you that you keep silent. It is now come to this: To the degree that you and those like you speak of God and heavenly matters, so far will you be persecuted and turned into a scandal by the proud who are now too many on earth. If you want peace and to have rest, flee and keep silent and bridle your tongue [...].
>
> [Layperson]: I will happily follow your counsel unto death. I recognize my guilt, that I have asked too much and spoken above what befits me, because I am a silly fool and an idiot and a foot-wipe of the clergy and of all the Habits.

34 Again, because they would not or could not deal with her queries and views, or she dared not bring this all to them, or dared not answer when interrogated.

With this exchange, brash and ironic and yet strikingly true to the existential situation, this dialogue ends. While its language and tone might fit a lay man as well, the tenor and frame are those of a friar in spiritual converse with a "good-willed" lay woman. In the face of contempt from the Habits, this unbridled tongue speaks nonetheless, at length and soulfully to a Habit she knows "in the spirit," a "speaking" that is in fact a vernacular written script, with the teaching mostly projected as that of "Master Eckhart," including ironically counsel to keep silent – though this may also be heard as real and prudent advice for lay and women readers now under threat. But that makes it however no less ironic and amusing, no less double-tongued – all the more so if we grasp its author as not only "lay" but a woman writing out a dialogue in thousands of words.

Can we imagine such an author and such a woman? We might think of quasi-religious women such as Hadewijch two or three generations earlier, or Catherine of Siena forty years later, both major vernacular writers, both with circles of followers around them, both in varied respects teachers.[35] The author of this dialogue, as mirrored in the lay *persona* as well as its "Master Eckhart," is independent, lay, religiously driven, with social and material means to travel, prone to visit churches and convents, to query priest and friars, also literate so as to acquire and read books in the vernacular, intelligent enough too to turn over in her own mind serious religious and theological questions, sufficiently engaged to develop a big heart for the quasi-religious, leisured enough to write at length, and self-confident enough to act as a teacher, even to present her views by way of dialoguing with "Master Eckhart." Independent lay writers did exist, witness Jacob van Maerlant (1230/40–1288/1300). The most famous or infamous one lived in Brussels at exactly this time, Heilwig Bloemaert (1265?–1335). Daughter of a distinguished burger family with connections to the duchess of Brabant, she was said to teach from a chair, enjoy the protection of local lay authorities, and write a book that annoyed a young local priest named Jan Ruusbroec living just blocks away. And by later reports that book of hers was present at Groenendael (whence it could have reached Bethlehem outside Louvain).[36] My point is not to argue that "Bloemardinne" – about whom there exist too many specious musings – authored this dialogue, though her dates fit, and we certainly should not exclude the possibility. The point is that this dialogue best fits a woman author writing amidst the anti-beguine legislation, a person who enjoyed the social, intellectual, and religious position of a Heilwig Bloemaert.

Accepting such a woman author renders more intelligible not only this text, I would argue, but larger contexts. We have here then an independent lay woman thinker and vernacular author at work in an urban religious setting alive with friars and other quasi-religious women. We also have a distinctive and expansive body of teaching coming more or less directly out of milieus then under attack – for which we have now nothing at all comparable. We would have too a lay woman writer who set out to be a teacher only a decade or so after a woman in that same diocese was shut down

35 For inserting Catherine more accurately in her social and religious milieu, see F. Thomas Luongo, *The Saintly Politics of Catherine of Siena* (Ithaca, NY: Cornell University Press, 2006), as well as his contribution to this volume.

36 Van Engen, *Sisters and Brothers of the Common Life*, 33–36.

and finally burned for her book.[37] Her presence and writings such as these, as scholars have noted of Heilwig Bloemaert, render more intelligible the resolve of a local diocesan priest of no university education to write large works in the vernacular conceived partly as religious correctives, often for women, though also and certainly for "converts" like himself as well. Ruusbroec wrote not in dialogue but in a compelling Middle Dutch expository prose. However, we have here in this dialogue a work brimming with passionate words and beliefs, born of a sometimes embittered spirit and anguished heart but no less a brave and searching spirit, a person of firm resolve to speak and in difficult circumstances to speak freely, finally to teach other "Good-willed Laity" and "Blessed Souls." We also have, not least, a person brazen and crafty enough to cast those complaints and teachings, thousands of words, as a soulful encounter between herself and Master Eckhart – who was, ironically, himself about to be charged with heresy.

37 See Van Engen, "Marguerite of Hainaut and the Medieval Low Countries."

9

# RECOVERY AND LOSS: WOMEN'S WRITING AROUND MARIE DE FRANCE

JOCELYN WOGAN-BROWNE
WITH AN APPENDIX BY IAN SHORT

In medieval English literary culture of the twelfth and thirteenth centuries, the number of really well-known women, certainly if we define 'well-known' as 'taught on undergraduate courses', is, perhaps, two: Christina of Markyate, a religious leader, and Marie de France, acclaimed as the first woman writer in French vernacular literature. This essay looks at the recovery, or better, the creation of Marie de France, and some of its implications. There are several aspects to this examination: although presented in its full detail at the end of the essay, the most original and important is the phonological evidence of Professor Ian Short concerning the texts currently ascribed to Marie de France.[1] My own contribution is less original: I want to reprise some arguments for thinking that looking for authorship and authorial canons is not the only way of seeing medieval women's literary and intellectual engagement, and to argue that the canonical impulse obscures the literary culture in which the works now ascribed to Marie de France were created. Such arguments have quite a long genealogy in work on Marie de France, but still seem to need restating in each generation. Given that it is still possible for scholars to celebrate Marie de France as a *lusus naturae*, bravely inserting herself into "an exclusively male literary system,"[2] it seems pertinent to invoke these arguments in the context of a volume dealing with medieval women's intellectual contributions.

As is well known, the name "Marie de France" is noticed in the sixteenth century in the collection of Aesopic *Fables* ascribed to her, but the canon attributed to Marie

1 In a February 1998 lecture to the Collège de France, Ian Short discussed *Le Problème des trois Maries:* L'Espurgatoire *de Marie dite de France*, noting that Warnke's evidence for the linguistic similarity of the three works currently attached to Marie de France holds good, but is not definitive proof that the three are by a single person, let alone that that person was Marie "de France". He has since analysed the phonology of all works attributed to Marie de France, and, though there is still more work to be done on their morphology, has graciously permitted the use of his evidence here. On Christina of Markyate, see Ian Short, ed., *The Oxford Psalter (Bodleian MS Douce 320)*, Anglo-Norman Text Society 72 (Oxford: ANTS, 2015) where it is shown that this earliest francophone psalter (*olim* the Montebourg Psalter) was made, probably c. 1145, by a St Albans scribe–translator for the Markyate priory.

2 *A Companion to Marie de France*, ed. Logan E. Whalen, Brill's Companions to the Christian Tradition 27 (Leiden: Brill, 2011), 5.

"de France" is an eighteenth-century creation.[3] The first scholar to assign both *Lais* and *Fables* to her is Thomas Tyrwhitt in his 1775 edition of Chaucer, as part of a wider conversation about Armorican lays and the primacy – or not – of Arthurian materials in Geoffrey of Monmouth versus stories from Brittany.[4] (It is significant that the manuscript known to both Tyrwhitt and his predecessor, Warton, is London, British Library MS Harley 978, the only extant medieval manuscript, as discussed below, to contain both *Lais* and *Fables* with each of them having text-internal ascriptions to "Marie"). The *Espurgatoire* was added to "Marie's" oeuvre by the Abbé de La Rue in 1800.[5] This canon was accepted and adopted in the first nineteenth-century scholarly editions from Roquefort's *Recueil de lais, fables et autres productions de cette femme célèbre* (1819–20) onwards.[6] More recently, canon-building has resumed with June Hall McCash's 2002 *Speculum* article arguing for the inclusion of the early thirteenth-century verse *Vie de sainte Audrée* (Æthelthryth of Ely), and with her co-authored English translation of *Audrée*, published as "a work by Marie de France" in 2007.[7] The initial evidence for this latest attribution, as for others in the canon, consists of "signatures" embedded in the texts (though other factors such as stylistic, verbal and thematic commonalities or the lack of them of course also enter the discussion). *Audrée* has a signature in its final couplet:

> Ici escris mon non Marie
> Pur ce ke soie remembree (v. 4624) ;

and this seems at first glance readily alignable with three others associated with Marie "de France". From the *Lais*:

3 See Karen Jambeck, "Warton, Tyrwhitt, and de La Rue: Marie de France in the Eighteenth Century", in *The Reception and Transmission of the Works of Marie de France, 1774–1974*, ed. Chantal Maréchal (Lewiston, Queenstown, Lampeter: Edwin Mellen, 2003), 31–89 (Fauchet's mention of Marie de France in his *Recueil de la langue et poesie françoise* of 1581 at 37). Fauchet owned a copy of the *Fables* (BnF f. fr. 1593): his hand picks out as authorial the name "Marie … de France" on f. 99vb.

4 As Jambeck shows, Tyrwhitt builds on Thomas Warton ("Warton, Tyrwhitt, and de La Rue", 50–1). For the Armorican discussion see Warton's *History of English Poetry from the Close of the Eleventh to the Commencement of the Eighteenth Century* (London: J Dodsley, 1774), vol. 1, Dissertation 1: "Of the Origin of Romantic Fiction in Europe", esp. sig.a (Harley 978 citations on a2 recto, subsequently identified with Marie de France in the revised edition (London: Thomas Tegg, 1824), a2 (= iii).

5 Abbé de La Rue "Dissertation on the Life and Writings of Mary, an Anglo-Norman Poetess of the Thirteenth Century", *Archaeologia* 13 (1800): 35–67. Legrand D'Aussy had already noticed the name Marie in his 1781 summary of the *Espurgatoire*: see Jambeck, "Warton, Tyrwhitt, and De La Rue", 60, 62–3.

6 B. de Roquefort, ed., *Poésies de Marie de France, poète anglo-normand du XIIIe siècle, ou recueil de lais, fables et autres productions de cette femme célèbre* (Paris: Chasseriau et Hécart, 1819).

7 June Hall McCash, "*La Vie seinte Audree*: A Fourth Text by Marie de France?" *Speculum* 77.3 (2002): 744–77; McCash and Judith Clark Barban, eds., *The Life of Saint Audrey: A Text by Marie de France* (Jefferson and London: McFarland Press, 2006). The principal modern edition is *La vie seinte Audree, poème anglo-normand du XIIIe siècle*, ed. Östen Södergård (Uppsala: Lundequistska bokhandeln, 1955). The text is also available from its unique extant copy in BL Add. 70513 on D. W. Russell's Campsey manuscript site at http://margot.uwaterloo.ca/campsey/cmpoverview_e.html.

> Oëz, seignurs, ke dit Marie
> Ki en sun tens pas ne s'oblie.[8]

From the *Espurgatoire*:

> Jo, Marie ai mise en memoire
> Le livre de l'Espurgatoire.[9]

And from the *Fables*:

> Me numerai pur remembrance:
> Marie ai nun, si sui de France.[10]

Close to, and especially with regard to the manuscript witnesses, the evidence becomes less clear-cut.[11] The self-attribution of the *Lais* to "what Marie says" (*ke dit Marie*) does not occur in the celebrated (but anonymous) general prologue to them (extant only in the fullest manuscript collection of the *lais* now ascribed to Marie de France, Harley 978, which is perhaps datable c. 1261–65). The attribution is, rather, just in one *lai*, *Guigemar*, the first of the *lais* copied in Harley 978.[12] *Guigemar* itself is found in only three of the extant five medieval manuscripts containing *lais* now ascribed to Marie de France. Of these, BN fr. 2168 reads "*Marit*" (fol. 48ra, "*Gugemer*", v. 5), and in BN f. fr. 1104, the relevant passage is omitted (fol. 1ra). Arguments that "Marie" is a retrospectively imposed name have not been lacking, and, as Keith Busby has pointed out, text-type plays a role here: the *lais* are perceived as an anonymous genre and any authorial identity is quickly lost in the manuscript tradition after Harley 978.[13] The manuscripts thus present the *lais* now ascribed to Marie de France as a

8 Alfred Ewert, ed., *Marie de France: Lais*, introduction and bibliography by Glyn S. Burgess (Oxford: Blackwell, 1995), *Guigemar*, 3, vv. 3–4.

9 Yolande de Pontfarcy, ed. and trans., *Marie de France, L'Espurgatoire Seint Patriz. Édition du ms Paris B.N. fonds fr. 25407, accompagnée du De Purgatorio Sancti Patricii (éd. de Warnke), et d'une traduction*, Ktêmata 13 (Louvain, Peeters and Paris: Vrin, 1995), Epilogue, vv. 2297–300.

10 Charles Brucker, *Les Fables de Marie de France: Édition critique accompagnée d'une introduction, d'une traduction, de notes et d'un glossaire*, Ktêmata 12, 2nd ed. (Louvain: Peeters and Paris: Vrin, 1998), 364, Epilogue, vv. 3–4.

11 For a helpful account, see Sharon Kinoshita and Peggy McCracken, eds., *Marie de France: A Critical Companion* (Cambridge: D. S. Brewer, 2012), 201–18.

12 London, British Library, MS Harley 978, fol. 118rb, online at http://www.bl.uk/catalogues/illuminatedmanuscripts/ILLUMIN.ASP?Size=mid&IllID=14694.

13 Attributions to Marie de France are questioned by Richard Baum, *Recherches sur les œuvres attribuées à Marie de France*, Annales Universitatis Saraviensis, Philosophische Facultät, 9 (Heidelberg: C. Winter, 1968), 197–216; see also the valuable and informed scepticism of Bernadette A. Masters, "Anglo-Norman and *dreit engleis*: The English Character of the *lais* of Harley MS 978 in the British Library", *Parergon* 10.2 (1992): 81–115. Keith Busby discusses the manuscript tradition of the *lais* in his *Codex and Context: Reading Old French Narrative Verse in Manuscript*, Faux Titre 221–2, 2 vols (Amsterdam: Rodopi, 2002), vol. 1, 466–73, and now in his "The Manuscripts of Marie de France" in *Companion to Marie de France*, ed. Whalen, 303–18. Sylvia Huot's study "The Afterlife of a Twelfth-Century Author: Marie de France in the Later Middle Ages" confirms that though the *lais* themselves were widely influential in later medieval literature, "Marie" is never mentioned in connection with them ("*Li premerains vers*": *Essays for Keith Busby*, ed. Catherine M. Jones and Logan E. Whalen (Amsterdam: Rodopi, 2011), 191–204).

formally introduced body of work only once, in Harley 978. The *lais* are not a stable collection, rarely "complete" (two manuscripts contain only one *lai* each, for instance), and some manuscripts mingle *lais* now considered anonymous and *lais* now ascribed to Marie de France.[14]

As with the attributions in the *Lais* and in *Audrée*, the signature in the unique extant manuscript of the *Espurgatoire saint Patrice* (*Jo, Marie ai mise en mémoire* ... v. 2297) is unspecific. Only in the Epilogue to the *Fables* is a Marie attribution particularized to Marie de France (*Marie ai nun, si sui de France*, v. 4). Being found as a higher proportion of a more extensive textual tradition (fifteen out of twenty-five manuscripts), this signature is better witnessed than in the case of the *lais*.[15] Nevertheless, although fables are a genre where the transmission of authority from Aesop to medieval commissioners and translators is a strong convention, the *Fables* are not a stable collection either, and many of their manuscripts also combine texts ascribed to Marie de France with those now deemed anonymous.[16] The later thirteenth-century Harley 978 remains the chief witness to the creation of Marie de France as author figure in more than one genre, though a number of *Fables* manuscripts contain author portraits.[17]

As is also well recognized, we have little to go on in identifying a specific historical woman as the author, "Marie". Invocations to patrons within the texts, one of the better indications of textual production circles, are inconclusive. The king addressed in several of them may be Henry II (1154–89) or possibly his son, the young king Henry (crowned 1170–d.1183), but the other patron or *destinateur* could

14 See Prudence Mary O'Hara Tobin, ed., *Les Lais anonymes des XIIe et XIIIe siècles* (Genève: Droz,1976), 11–12 (for *lais* in MSS BnF fr. 2168 and BnF nouv. acq. 1104); *Eleven Old French Narrative Lays*, ed. and trans. Amanda Hopkins, Glyn S. Burgess and Leslie Brook, French Arthurian Literature IV (Cambridge: D. S. Brewer, 2007); Glyn S. Burgess, "Marie de France and the Anonymous Lays", in *Companion to Marie de France*, ed. Whalen, 117–56.

15 See the table of twenty-four manuscripts (twenty-five if the small fragment in Nottingham University Library Mi. Lm.6 is counted) in Logan E. Whalen, *Marie de France and the Poetics of Memory* (Washington, D.C.: Catholic University of America Press, 2008), 184–5.

16 Five of the twenty-five manuscripts contain 100 or more fables: others have smaller selections. The boundaries between fables by different authors and even between individual fables are not always stable in the manuscripts. (My sense of this textual tradition is indebted to the work of my former student Breeman Ainsworth, whose University of York 2009 unpublished MA thesis on "Knowledge and the *Fables* of Marie de France" tabulates disruptions to Warnke's "standardized" order and includes systematic attention to the effects of particular arrangements and compilations of fables, especially in the earliest extant manuscript, York Minster MS XVI K 12 (early s. xiii), where "anonymous" translations from Romulus Nilanti and Avianus mingle with those thought to be by Marie de France.)

17 For detailed discussion of Harley 978 see Andrew Taylor, *Textual Situations: Three Medieval Manuscripts and their Readers* (Philadelphia: University of Pennsylvania Press, 2002) and Rupert T. Pickens, "Reading Harley 978: Marie de France in Context," in *Courtly Arts and the Arts of Courtliness*, ed. Keith Busby and Christopher Kleinhenz (Cambridge: D. S. Brewer, 2006), 527–42. Keith Busby discusses the creation of authors and translators as authority figures in the manuscript transmission of the *Fables* in his *Codex and Context*, vol. 1, 473–80; vol. 2, 498–9; on the manuscripts' presentation of the fables as learned material, see Logan E. Whalen, "*Ex libris Mariae*: Courtly Book Iconography in the Illuminated Manuscripts of Marie de France", in *Courtly Arts*, ed. Busby and Kleinhenz, 745–53.

be any one of a number of Count Williams.[18] Some confirmation seems to come from the celebrated allusion made by Magister Dionysus, in all probability at one time the cellarer of Bury St Edmunds, in his Life of Bury's patron saint, Edmund of East Anglia, composed 1190–1193.[19] "Dame Marie," says the prologue to this text, is "much praised" (*mult loee*) and her verse "loved everywhere" (*partut amee*) for her *lais*.[20] It should be recalled that this vernacular Life of St Edmund credits itself not to the Magister Dionysus who probably wrote it, but to a repentant narratorial presence named Denis Piramus (*Jeo ay noun Denis Piramus*, v. 16). As in the prologue claims of several other Anglo-Norman clerical writers, this figure has spent its youth writing short-form courtly entertainments, but is now writing veraciously and seriously (but still entertainingly, he says) about St Edmund.[21] Piramus is, of course, a suspect name, more likely to do with Ovid and perhaps the contemporary anonymous *lai* of Piramus and Thisbe than anything else, and perhaps an acknowledged soubriquet for a poet who claims to repent writing verse lines that "might bring [lovers] together" (v. 10).[22] Relations between such performance identities and historical figures are complicated, and no basis for literary biographies reporting either Piramus or Marie de France as becoming more sober and thoughtful as they get older and so turning away from *lais* and *serventais* and other courtly short forms, and eventually each producing a saint's life.

If the attribution of single authorship to the *Lais*, *Fables*, and *Espurgatoire* is more complex and doubtful than the modern author-figure "Marie de France" has made it seem, the recent ascription of *La Vie seinte Audrée* to Marie de France makes an especially shaky fourth element in this canon. The case in my view has always suffered from its dependence on resemblances in lexis, topoi, and preoccupations that can be paralleled outside works ascribed to Marie de France,[23] as well as from its failure

18 See further the discussion in Kinoshita and McCracken, *Marie de France*, 43–4 and n. 46.

19 For the dating see D. W. Russell, ed., with an art historical excursus by Kathryn A. Smith, *La Vie seint Edmund le Rei*, Anglo-Norman Text Society 71 (Oxford: ANTS, 2014), 8.

20 This prologue, often cited, as it is here, primarily for its allusion to "Dame Marie", is an important literary discussion, fully analysed by Ian Short (in his "Denis Piramus and the Truth of Marie's *Lais*", *Cultura Neolatina* 67 (2007): 319–40), who also makes the case for the later dating of Piramus' life, confirmed by Russell in the edition cited in n. 19 above.

21 See Short, "Denis Piramus and the Truth", 321–2: Short shows that Piramus' diagnosis that Dame Marie's *lais* are not verifiable (*ne sunt pas de tut verais*: Russell, ed., *Vie seint Edmund*, v. 37–8) is another topos: see e.g. Rauf de Linham in his *Kalender* of 1256: … *mut i ad cuntes e fables / Ke ne sunt pas veritables* (v. 12). Both these prologues are edited, translated and introduced in Jocelyn Wogan-Browne, Thelma Fenster and Delbert W. Russell, eds., *Vernacular Literary Theory from the French of Medieval England: Texts and Translations c. 1120–c. 1450* (Cambridge: D. S. Brewer, 2016, pbk 2018), no. 27, 270–6; no. 40, 363–7.

22 The passage plays on the notion of joining couplets and couples together: *Mult me penay de tels vers fere, / Ke assemble les puise treire, / E k'ensemble fussent justez, / Pur acomplir lur voluntez* (I worked hard to write those lines that might bring them together, so that they could be side by side to do as they wished), ed. Russell, *Vie seint Edmund*, vv. 9–12.

23 I do not have the space here to discuss these aspects in detail: my argument is in any case principally concerned with the value of attending to the wider literary culture around Marie "de France". Delbert W. Russell shows the value of wider reading in his discussion of the use of "mettre en memoire" and "faire la memoire" in *Audrée* (argued as meaning "to create memories",

to confront the obvious stylistic and thematic differences between *Audrée* and, particularly, the *lais* and the *fables*. Most surprisingly, there is the slightness of the linguistic evidence adduced. This is concerned to distinguish scribal and authorial language in the extant manuscript of *Audrée* in order to argue that the text is earlier than the manuscript and originally continental, though such a case is not precisely the same as an argument for similarities between the authorial language of *La Vie sainte Audrée* and that of Marie "de France". When the *Audrée* attribution was first made, one might have expected more evidence from the phonology of the rhymes: that is, rhymes not in the sense of which words a writer is in the habit of pairing in verse, but what sounds the writer thinks can make a rhyme. In the always tricky business of making an argument for authorial identity out of the linguistic phenomenology of Old French verse texts, rhyme is among the better forms of evidence available. The greater space available in the *Audrée* translation has not however been used for a full linguistic analysis: the evidence remains as a small sample of general distinctions between scribe as insular, and author as continental, none of them sufficiently determinative.[24] My own knowledge being enough to make me distrust the attribution, but not expert, I appealed some time ago to Ian Short for his opinion, and he has both graciously sent his preliminary conclusions and allowed them to be cited in this essay and included in their detail (Appendix II).

Short's conclusions are firstly that "The proposition that Marie's *Vie seinte Audrée* was written by the Marie of the *Lais* is ... without linguistic foundation." His analysis shows that the Marie of the *Lais* has some general Western French features in her rhymes, but that they are much less pronounced than the fully Anglo-Norman features of *Audrée*, which, Short reaffirms, is by an insular writer (Appendix II, p. 189 below). Secondly, the linguistic evidence for the three texts traditionally ascribed to Marie de France is itself not secure: "Unless ... it could be argued, and shown," says Short, "that a poet's language can modify significantly over time, and that a poet's choice of rhymes can likewise radically differ in the course of their career, it looks very much, from the selection of evidence presented here, as if we are in fact dealing with four separate individuals" (p. 189 below). There will be room for some debate and discussion here, but the opinion of Anglo-Norman's most distinguished philologist and literary scholar

as opposed to hagiography's "more typical" usage of these terms to mean "commemorative, celebratory ritual", and hence typical of *Audrée*, and of secular romance, but not of hagiography: McCash, "*La Vie seinte Audree*", 2002, 751–3). Russell's check of the Campsey manuscript in which *Audrée* is extant along with other saints' lives provides fifty-one examples of "memoire", with "faire la memoire" or "mettre en memoire" used in *St Edmund of Canterbury* (three times) and *St. Modwenna* (eight times), versus five examples in total in *Audrée* (paper delivered in "The MARGOT Project: Making Public Knowledge / Making Knowledge Public", Canadian Society of Medievalists, University of Saskatchewan, Congress of the Humanities and Social Sciences, Saskatoon, 29 May 2007). Yet other saints' lives exemplify similar usage in the AND entry on *memoire*. Keith Busby also shows the value of contextual study of Anglo-Norman writings in his "'Ceo fu la summe de l'escrit' (*Chevrefoil*, line 61) again", *Philological Quarterly* 74 (1995): 1–15, where he illuminates the resonance of a line (used to celebratedly ambiguous effect in the *lai* of *Chevrefoil*) by examining its uses in other insular francophone writing. Busby argues for a shared literary environment rather than common authorship (tempting though the latter may seem when two women writers, Marie and the Nun of Barking, share the line).

24 See Appendix I.

has an evidential weight of itself. While there is more to be done, this is occasion enough to take us back to the drawing board and prompt us to reconsider why we should even *want* just one writer, Marie?

To this question there are obvious common-sense answers and ones that make medievalists' fierce wish to populate the medieval past with unmistakably visible women well justified. The latent allegory of women as ideas to think with that bedevilled scholarship on women writers in the 1980s and 1990s, and which never entirely goes away, means that women writers are readily used to embody critical desires of various kinds, and their historicity is absorbed into other agendas.[25] Jennifer Summit has written forcefully against the assumption, formed in early modernity, that the woman writer is not only always already lost, but embodies the "lostness" of vernacular and early literature to the formation of later literary tradition.[26] Against tendencies to allegorize or lose women, enlarging the canon of particular women writers seems an obvious defense: the bigger their *oeuvre*, the harder to mislay these writers or render them invisible. For Marie "de France" studies, a permanent and sometimes productive tension exists between, to borrow Miranda Griffin's terms from a valuable 1999 article, "escaping the fetishized outline of a fantasy author, and rescuing a lost canon of texts from its shadow, in order to hear the authors of these *lais* as a 'voice'" on the one hand, and, on the other, hearing this voice (as Jane Burns has said) neither as "an embodied essence that communicates the personalized and individual identity of a historical female nor as the depersonalized voice of literature or poetic craft," but as a dialogue between the two.[27]

Sarah Kay's work on courtly culture has long provided one such mediation over what an authorial signature might mean, one, moreover, where inaccessibility to the historical writer does not dissolve their presence. In her classic article of 1997, "Who was Chrétien de Troyes?" Kay took to pieces the evidence for "Chrétien de Troyes", arguing that "Crestien" is a *soubriquet*, that is, not a name, but a description, deployed as a "signal of friendship and participation in poetic exchange."[28] Kay used her disman-

25 For a fascinating analysis of influential medievalists on such points, see Arlyn Diamond, "Engendering Criticism", *Thought* (Special Issue on Gender and the Moral Order in Medieval Society) 64.3 (1989): 298–309, and on essentialist allegorizing of women see the comments in Thelma Fenster, gen. ed., *Forum for Medieval Feminist Scholarship* (*Medieval Feminist Newsletter*) 6.1 (1988): 1–17, and the response by Howard Bloch, "Commentary", *Forum for Medieval Feminist Scholarship* (Medieval Feminist Newsletter*)* 7.1 (1989): 7–12 (http://ir.uiowa.edu/mff/vol6/iss1/ and http://ir.uiowa.edu/mff/vol7/iss1/ respectively).

26 Jennifer Summit, *Lost Property: The Woman Writer and English Literary History 1380–1589* (Chicago: Chicago University Press, 2000).

27 Miranda Griffin, "Gender and Authority in the Medieval French *Lai*", *Forum for Modern Language Studies* 35.1 (1999): 42–56 (at 54, with citation from Jane Burns in E. Jane Burns, Sarah Kay, Roberta L. Krueger, and Helen Solterer, "Feminism and the Discipline of Old French Studies: *Une Bele Disjointure*", in *Medievalism and the Modernist Temper*, ed. R. Howard Bloch and Stephen G. Nichols [Baltimore: Johns Hopkins University Press, 1996], 225–66, at 243).

28 Sarah Kay, "Who was Chrétien de Troyes?" *Arthurian Literature* 15 (1997): 1–35 (see further her *Courtly Contradictions: The Emergence of the Literary Object in the Twelfth Century* (Stanford: Stanford University Press, 2001) on the textual instability of Adgar's *Miracles* and the *Lais*, 205–15), and for a full exploration of the article's implications, Zrinka Stahuljak, Virginie Greene, Sarah Kay, Sharon Kinoshita, and Peggy McCracken, *Thinking through Chrétien de Troyes* (Cambridge: D. S. Brewer, 2011).

tling of the Chrétien canon to offer new readings of the romances regarded as his across secular and sacred divides, and also to look at other works with the soubriquet *Chrestien*. Thus, she discusses the verse Gospel of Nicodemus and the romance of *Guillaume d'Angleterre* without their modern relegation to secondary status, a relegation to being, in effect, anonymous works that aspired to the Chrétien canon, but failed to make it. In Kay's argument, *Chrestien*, the medieval signature of these texts, is an unsurpassable version of Christian brotherhood – a *nec plus ultra* of reciprocal *soubriquets* (an idea that would only be strengthened were it ever possible to show, as some have thought possible, that Chrétien was a Jewish *conversus*).[29] Arguing for anonymity as a component of the medieval author-function, Kay suggests that *Chrestien* is an "anonym", part of medieval authorial self-presentation in narrative (though not therefore an unknown identity for historically contemporary audiences), and that *Marie* may be the female version of such an identity.[30] Kay memorably concludes the article by saying that "where there was light, [I hope to have] shed a little darkness."

This darkness is something from which the study of Marie "de France" can benefit. Spurred by Short and Kay, we might want to consider what Marie as a soubriquet rather than an essentialized authorial identity might do. For after all, *what would be lost if we say that only the* Fables *are by a Marie "de France"*? What we are talking about here is 102 fables extant in 25, mostly later thirteenth-century manuscripts in England and Europe, 15 of them preserving the epilogue naming Marie de France. This is not a mean survival by manuscript culture standards, not so easy to make disappear as an *oeuvre*, and something that might be envied by many male medieval writers of French. Moreover, not only is a canon superfluous to appreciating the brilliant and, in medieval culture, highly respected *Fables*, but disassembling the canon for Marie de France can give us more medieval women writers. And what *is* that name Marie "de France"? In Chrétien de Troyes' modern oeuvre, only *Erec et Enide* ascribes itself to Chrétien "de Troies" in a possibly meaningful opposition between classical (*de Troies*) and Christian (*Crestien*) writing: among the "Marie" texts, only the *Fables* name Marie "*de France*" and this in a context where an English king (*Li reis Alvrez*) is invoked as a prestigious translator ([Alfred] *Le translata puis en engleis / Et jeo l'ai rimee en franceis / Si cum jeo poi*...).[31] The argument that the name "Marie" used in different works is not a sign of common authorship but of allusion or citation (a recognised "anonym" in Kay's terms), would leave room for different Maries. Some of these may even have been cashing in on the soubriquet value of "Marie" and perhaps on the cultural stir around *lais* and the question of their authorship. Piramus seems a witness to that much at least: a certain amount of talk in court and cloister about the new form of *lais* and about a Dame

29 First suggested by U. T. Holmes in *A New Interpretation of Chrétien's Conte del Graal* (Chapel Hill: University of North Carolina Press, 1948): for a review of the discussion since, see Hanna Liss, *Creating Fictional Worlds: Peshat-Exegesis and Narrativity in Rashbam's Commentary on the Torah* (Leiden: Brill, 2011), 29–31: see now Naomi Howell, "Reflecting (on) the Other: Jewish-Christian Relations in *Cligès* and MS Michale 569 (*)" Speculum 91.2 (2016), 374–421. For the Rabbinic school at Troyes, see Stahuljak et al., *Thinking through Chrétien*, 5–7.

30 Kay, "Who Was Chrétien de Troyes?", 32.

31 *Fables*, ed. Brucker, Epilogue, 366, vv. 16–19.

Marie as a composer of them.[32] "Marie" is of course also the name of a supreme figure of patronage, authority and inspiration, as when an anonymous Nun of Barking models her own production of a new life on the Virgin's:

> Si requierez le Fiz Marie
> Pur cele sainte cumpaignie,
> Od ki mainte *cele Deu ancele*
> *Ki fist ceste vie nuvele* (italics mine).

> (Pray to the Son of Mary on behalf of the holy religious order where lives *the handmaiden of God, who has produced this new Life* [of Saint Edward]).[33]

Barking Abbey is the very institution to which Carla Rossi, author of the latest scholarly biography for Marie de France and an *Audrée* believer, attaches the figure of Marie de France, identifying her as Marie Becket, appointed abbess by Henry II in partial satisfaction for the murder of her Archbishop brother (a position she held for two years before her death in 1175).[34] Thus, at a single stroke, up to four writing Maries and one leadership Marie are amalgamated into one woman, and the late twelfth and early thirteenth centuries are deprived of potentially four female figures of interest. Rossi's is a plausible case, more likely than some previous Marie de France biographies, but also a circumstantial case with no definitive proof. Its value perhaps lies less in identifying Marie de France, than in reminding us, especially in its further detailing of the ties between Barking and Canterbury, of the interactions between learned women and men in the networks of cloister and court (matrices of a literary culture by no means exclusively male).[35] At the same time Rossi's case may serve to point up how much attention to "Marie de France" distracts from the women writers and patrons around her.

32 For the uncertainties around the modern category of the Breton *lai* and the question of whether the term can properly be applied to narrative verse as opposed to song, see Horst Bader, *Die Lais: Zur Geschichte einer Gattung der altfranzösischen Kurzererzählungen* (Frankfurt am Main: Klostermann, 1966), esp. 37–73. On talk and its role in medieval literary cultures see Felicity Riddy, "'Women talking of the things of God': A Medieval Literary Sub-Culture?", in *Women and Literature in Britain, 1050–1500*, ed. Carol M. Meale, 2nd ed. (Cambridge: Cambridge University Press, 1996), 104–27 (online edition 2009, http://dx.doi.org/10.1017/CBO9780511582073.008), and Elizabeth Tyler, *England in Europe: English Royal Women and Literary Patronage, c. 1000–c. 1150* (Toronto: University of Toronto Press, 2017) and its important methodological introduction. See also the important collection, *Fama: The Politics of Talk and Reputation in Medieval Europe*, ed. Thelma Fenster and Daniel L. Smail (Ithaca: Cornell University Press, 2003).

33 Östen Södergåard, ed., *La Vie de saint Edouard le confesseur* (Uppsala: Almqvist & Wiksells, 1948), vv. 5326–7 (ed. and trans. Wogan-Browne, Fenster and Russell, *Vernacular Literary Theory*, 19–25).

34 Carla Rossi, *Marie de France et les érudits de Cantorbèry* (Paris: Garnier, 2009), 186–92.

35 Matthew Paris and Gervase of Canterbury state that the Barking abbacy was given to Becket's sister at the instance of Odo, prior of Christ Church, Canterbury (E. A. Loftus and H. F. Chettle, *A History of Barking Abbey* (Barking, UK: Wilson and Whitworth, 1954), 30, citing RS 44 *Historia Anglorum*, i, 376 and RS 73, *Chronicles*, i, 242); Guernes de Pont Ste Maxence's epilogue to his life of Becket mentions the Abbess of Barking and Odo, Prior of Christ Church, Canterbury as supporters of his work (ed. and trans. in Wogan-Browne, Fenster and Russell, *Vernacular Literary Theory*, no. 11b, 108–13: see further Thomas O'Donnell, "'The ladies have made me quite fat': Authors and Patrons at Barking Abbey", in *Barking Abbey and Medieval Literary Culture*, ed. Jennifer N. Brown and Donna Arfana Bussell (York: York Medieval Press, 2012), 94–114).

Barking itself is the abbey of one and perhaps two women writers, authors of a *Romanz de saint Edward, rei e cunfessur* and a *Vie de sainte Catherine*, who may have written earlier than the Marie of the *Lais* and perhaps have a better claim to priority as women writers.[36] At Barking we have, as we do not for so many medieval writers, a historical context, a particular institution and quite a lot of information about its learning, opportunities for women, its networks and its political significance.[37] Nevertheless, efforts to create a single authorial canon out of the two saintly biographies with signatures identifying their authors as women at Barking have been notably less frenzied than those around Marie "de France" and the vacuum of unidentified institutions and networks in which she exists for us. Indeed, the very richness of context that one might have thought would help us to separate the two writers at Barking contributes to the difficulty of doing so, since the influence of shared environment and one writer on another in the same community is hard to quantify. We could, following the thinking on Chrétien de Troyes inspired by Kay's article, consider them as texts "produced by a milieu rather than an author."[38] Most scholars have seen Clemence of Barking's late twelfth-cen-

36 Södergaard, ed., *La Vie d'Édouard le confesseur*; Jane Bliss, trans., *La Vie d'Edouard le Confesseur, by a Nun of Barking Abbey* (Liverpool: Liverpool University Press, 2014); William MacBain, *The Life of St. Catherine,* Anglo-Norman Text Society 18 (Oxford: ANTS, 1964); Jocelyn Wogan-Browne and Glyn S. Burgess, trans., *Virgin Lives and Holy Deaths: Two Anglo-Norman Biographies for Women* (London: Dent, 1996). The Edward life must be after its principal source text, Aelred's *vita* of 1163, and *Catherine* after Thomas's *Tristan* (of which it makes use) had begun to circulate, while the earliest extant manuscripts of the Barking biographies are early s. xiii (*Édouard*) and c. 1200 (*Catherine*). This gives a window of some thirty or forty years before the end of the twelfth century for these texts, while the new dating of Piramus' *Edmund* to the 1190s by Short and Russell suggests that a later date for the *Lais* than the 1160s–70s to which they are traditionally ascribed is possible.

37 Important studies include Catherine Batt, "Clemence of Barking's Transformations of *Courtoisie* in *La Vie de sainte Catherine d'Alexandrie*", *New Comparison* 12 (1991): 102–23; Duncan Robertson, "Writing in the Textual Community: Clemence of Barking's Life of St Catherine", *French Forum* 21 (1996): 5–28; *Barking Abbey and Literary Culture*, ed. Brown and Bussell. On Barking's intimacy to court politics, it is worth noting, *inter alia*, that Marie Becket was swiftly replaced at her death by Henry II's illegitimate daughter Matilda, and that her initial appointment had been balanced by that of Henry's half-sister Marie as Abbess of Shaftesbury. Emily J. Mitchell has argued that the Barking Edward life was written for Abbess Matilda to counter Barking's recent patronage of Becket biography with a royal life affirming the continuities between the Confessor and Henry II: she parallels St Catherine's position as heir to her father's realm with that of Matilda the Empress, Henry II's mother ("Patrons and Politics at Twelfth-Century Barking Abbey", *Revue Bénédictine* 113.2 (2003): 347–64, at 360–1), and suggests that both abbesses are defending their families in their commissions (364). Women's roles in the transmission of Barking's literary works have also been noted: see e.g. Duncan Robertson's argument for a Picard female scribe in Paris, MS BnF fr 23112 who, after copying Clemence of Barking's *Vie de sainte Catherine* and a Mary of Egypt life adds a prayer on the three "Maries" on ff. 344a–344d (*The Medieval Saints' Lives: Spiritual Renewal and Old French Literature* [Lexington, KY: French Forum, 1995], 262–8). On the St Pol noblewomen and the Edward life on the continent, see Delbert W. Russell, "The Cultural Context of the French prose remaniement of the Life of Edward the Confessor by a Nun of Barking Abbey", in *Language and Culture in Medieval Britain: The French of England c.1100–c.1500*, ed. J. Wogan-Browne et al. (York: York Medieval Press, 2009, pb 2013), 290–302.

38 Stahuljak et al., *Thinking through Chrétien*, 13; O'Donnell, "'The ladies have made me quite fat'".

tury *Vie de sainte Catherine* and the anonymous late twelfth-century Barking *Life of Edward the Confessor* as having a finally imponderable mixture of similarities of lexis and phraseology, and similarities and differences of tone and theme.[39] It seems impossible to settle definitively for common authorship as against the influences of a shared community, of contemporaneity and genre. And whether Clemence, an uncommon name in Anglo-Norman England, is Clemence or a soubriquet *Clementia*, is unknown, while her *consoeur* insists on the anonym of "ancele Deu" for herself.[40] Thus, although authorial names are not necessarily fictional, we often cannot do as much as we might like with them. On the other hand, considering the *soubriquet* value of names, as Kay suggests, reminds us of the social conditions in which high medieval texts live. We need to be reserved about making authorial names the founding category of literary production if we are to make sense of a culture where a patron's name can confer more authority on a vernacular text than a writer's, and where authorship is differently conceptualised than it has been since the eighteenth century.

None of this however means that women lack authority in the regional and supra-regional cultures of high medieval England. This is in fact a literary culture humming with women's participation and leadership but distributed according to different models from those we have most readily recognised. Do we really need a biography crediting as many works as possible to a single Marie in order to have a poster-girl for female authority and leadership? There is a substantial scholarly literature on the significance of Anglo-Norman women patrons,[41] but their importance can be perhaps most quickly

39 See D. W. Russell, "'Sun num n'i vult dire a ore': Identity Matters at Barking Abbey", in *Barking Abbey and Medieval Literary Culture*, ed. Brown and Bussell, 17–34; Jane Bliss, "Who Wrote the Nun's Life of Edward?" *Reading Medieval Studies* 38 (2012): 77–98.

40 Scholars have sometimes assumed that *Edouard* is an apprentice work by an author who named herself (as Clemence) only in her second work (*Catherine*), but there is no clear evidence as to the order of composition. Clemence, unlike Matilda/Maud, Alice, Aline/Eleanor, Cecily, seems to be a comparatively rare name in insular culture. Marie is also interestingly less common as an elite personal name in the twelfth century than it later became, to judge by Henry II's list of widows and heiresses (one Marie for twenty-four Matildas): see John Walmsley, ed., *Widows, Heirs, and Heiresses in the Late Twelfth Century: The Rotuli de dominabus et pueris et puellis* (Tempe, AZ: Arizona Center for Medieval and Renaissance Studies, 2006).

41 This is not to suggest that patrons' names themselves can be simply accepted as historical: for a brief account of what patronage may and may not mean, and its status in relation to authorship, see Wogan-Browne, Fenster and Russell, *Vernacular Literary Theory*, 89–95. The foundational study for Anglo-Norman patronage is Ian Short, "Patrons and Polyglots: French Literature in Twelfth-Century England", *Anglo-Norman Studies* 14 (1992): 229–49. On women's patronage, see June Hall McCash's pioneering collection, *The Cultural Patronage of Medieval Women* (Athens, GA: University of Georgia Press, 1996): on Anglo-Norman women's patronage, see e.g. Loveday L. Gee, *Women, Art and Patronage from Henry III to Edward III: 1216 to 1377* (Woodbridge: Boydell Press, 2002); Susan Johns, *Noblewomen, Aristocracy and Power in the Twelfth-Century Anglo-Norman Realm* (Manchester: Manchester University Press, 2003), esp. the overview on 30–49; Emma Bérat, "The Patron and her Clerk: Multilingualism and Cultural Transition", *New Medieval Literatures* 12 (2010): 23–45 (with extensive bibliography in n. 1); Jocelyn Wogan-Browne, *Saints' Lives and Women's Literary Culture: Virginity and its Authorizations, c. 1150–1300* (Oxford, 2001), 151–76; on their institutional patronage, O'Donnell, "'The ladies have made me quite fat'".

and vividly illustrated here by two portraits, one visual, one verbal. In Figure 7, from Baroness Joan de Tateshul's manuscript of the *Manuel des pechez*, Grosseteste's *Chasteau d'amour* and other works of doctrine, the patron is almost twice the height of the scribe preparing her copy of the *Manuel*.[42] (In a further image at the head of the manuscript's text of the *Chasteau*, she is represented as of comparable stature with Grosseteste himself: only his bishop's mitre gives Grosseteste a small advantage in height over the secular female patron; see Figure 8 in Chapter 12 below).[43] The authority represented here, furthermore, may be not only that of Joan de Tateshul's commissioning the manuscript but of her using its contents for teaching within the baronial household, whether in reading with her women, or in teaching children.[44]

Figure 7 Image of Joan de Tateshul. (Taylor Medieval MS 1, fol. 1r; courtesy of Princeton University Library.)

For a verbal portrait of a patroness we might look beyond the well-known Lady Constance Fitzgilbert, patron of Gaimar's *Estoire des engleis*, to Lady Alice de Condet in the 12,000-line verse commentary on Proverbs made for her by Sansun de Nanteuil. Sansun says that

42 For Joan de Tateshul, and her manuscript, see Adelaide Bennett, "A Book Designed for a Noblewoman: An Illustrated *Manuel des pechés* of the Thirteenth Century," in *Medieval Book Production: Assessing the Evidence*, ed. Linda L. Brownrigg (Los Altos, CA: Anderson Lovelace, 1990), 163–81. The manuscript is digitized at http://pudl.princeton.edu/objects/tq57ns412 under the title *Manuel des pechiez*.

43 See discussion and Figure 8 in Chapter 12 by Anna Siebach-Larsen in this volume.

44 On teaching by women, see Michael Clanchy, "Did Mothers Teach their Children to Read?" in *Motherhood, Religion and Society in Medieval Europe, 400–1400: Essays Presented to Henrietta Leyser*, ed. Conrad Leyser and Lesley Smith (Farnham: Ashgate, 2011), 129–53; Jocelyn Wogan-Browne, "Invisible Archives? Later Medieval French in England", *Speculum* 90.3 (2015): 653–73; Thomas Hinton, "French and Anglo-French in the Thirteenth Century: A Reappraisal of Walter de Bibbesworth's 'Tretiz'", *Modern Language Review* 112 (2017): 848–74.

sovient
De sa dame qu'il aime e creient,
Ki mainte feiz l'en out preiéd
Que li desclairast cel traitéd.
Le nun de ceste damme escrist
Cil ki [la] translatïon fist:
Aëliz de Cundé l'apele,
Noble damme enseigné e bele.
Ne quident pas li losengier
Qu'ot eus se voille acompaigner,
Kar trestut cil de sa contree
Unt ben oï sa renumee,
E cil ki mentir l'en orreient,
Tot sun traitét en blasmereient.
Pur ço l'en fist translatïun
Qu'il conut sa devotïon,
Kar des escriz ad grant delit,
Molt volenters les ot e lit.
Nel pot laisser ne li traitast,
Coment que l'enui li grevast (vv. 195–214).

(he remembers his lady whom he loves and fears, who asked him many a time to elucidate this treatise for her. He who has made this translation writes the name of this lady: she is called Alice de Condet, a noble and beautiful, educated lady. May lying sycophants not think he would want to be one of them, for everyone where she lives knows her reputation, and those who heard it lied about would blame the author's treatise entirely. He did this translation because he knows her devotion, for she takes great delight in writings of the faith and she hears and reads them with great pleasure. He could not avoid writing for her though he is weighed down by weariness).[45]

As in Chrétien's *Lancelot ou Le Chevalier avec la charrette*, Sansun suggests an element of *force majeure* ("she made me do it"), and his prologue expresses both courtly fealty (his love for his lady, effectively his female lord, v. 196) and fear or respect. His prologue of 218 lines copiously addresses his patron's educated status and her interest in learning. He provides an account of Solomon as the wise king and Hebrew originator of Proverbs, of Jerome's assembly and translation of the Hebrew scriptures, and of the etymologies of the Hebrew titles for the three books of Proverbs. Sansun presents Jerome to Alice as a jeweller polishing up Hebrew gems for Latin consumption and as a household retainer, serving up tasty spiritual dishes – St Jerome "our steward" (*nostre despenser*, v. 113). Much goes on in this prologue toward Sansun's own

45 The commentary is edited by Claire Isoz, *Les Proverbes de Salemon by Sanson de Nantuil*, 3 vols., Anglo-Norman Text Society 44, 45, 50 (London: ANTS, 1988–94). The text and translation here is taken from Wogan-Browne, Fenster and Russell, *Vernacular Literary Theory*, no. 39, 361, vv. 195–214.

valorisation as translator, but it is in relation to his patron's power, authority and learning (and perhaps again to the patron's desire for a teaching textbook).

Authority in this literary culture is distributed across office, networks, socio-economic status and cultural patronage, rather than necessarily in canons. Although there are some male vernacular Anglo-Norman writers (such as Wace and Guillaume le Clerc) from whom we have multiple works, many are anonymous or known for a single text, often produced as an adjunct to their professional work.[46] Moreover, women's writing seems no different from men's when it comes to that standard medieval expression of respect – unattributed reproduction and adaptation. Clemence of Barking's narrative verse, for instance, is borrowed as Mary Magdalene's authoritative preaching voice in a West Midlands trilingual collection of the third quarter of the thirteenth century. Here we find an extract of narrative commentary from the *Vie de sainte Catherine* appearing as *Proverbia Mariae Magdalenae*.[47] Even more notably, Clemence provides the voice of Roland, the *chanson de geste* hero, in the Christian apologetics with which Roland tries to convert the giant Ferragu in the Anglo-Norman prose *Pseudo-Turpin Chronicle* of c.1210–20 (a work commissioned by Alice de Courcy and her husband Warin Fitzgerold).[48] The rash of vernacular verse Catherine-lives at the turn of the early thirteenth century has yet to be fully investigated, but it seems at the least interesting that Gui d'Amiens' prologue to his version celebrates St Catherine's life with topoi close to those of the Barking Life.[49]

46 Exceptionally, two thirteenth-century bishops, Robert Grosseteste and St Edmund of Abingdon, archbishop of Canterbury are awarded contemporary *auctor* status (by attributions of pseudonymous works and by the treatment of their texts in some manuscripts) across the Latin and French writings associated with them. Authors from whom a single work is known include Benedeit (author of the *Voyage de saint Brendan*), Denis Piramus, Gaimar, Guernes de Pont Ste Maxence, Robert of Greatham, Simon of Walsingham, Ralph of Linham, Thomas of Kent, Sansun de Nantuil etc.

47 Karl Reichl, *Religiöse Dichtung im Englischen Hochmittelalter: Untersuchung und Edition der Handschrift B. 14.39 des Trinity College in Cambridge* (München: Wilhelm Fink, 1973), 463, fol. 80v. Twelve lines of octosyllabic verse under the rubric *Hic incipiunt proverbia Maria Magdalene* are virtually identical, apart from minor orthographic variation, with a discussion of inner and outer demeanor in Clemence of Barking's *Catherine* (ed. MacBain, vv. 599–610).

48 The borrowing is demonstrated in Jocelyn Wogan-Browne, "Women's Formal and Informal Traditions of Biblical Knowledge in Anglo-Norman England", in *Saints, Scholars and Politicians: Gender as a Tool in Medieval Studies*, ed. Mathilde van Dijk and Renée A. Nip (Turnhout: Brepols, 2005), 85–109 (at 106–7). Clemence's verses from vv. 722–1006 are the source of lines in Roland and Ferragu's debate, for which see Ian Short, ed., *The Anglo-Norman Pseudo-Turpin Chronicle of William de Briane*, Anglo-Norman Text Society 25 (Oxford: ANTS, 1973), 53, ll. 792–810: for Alice de Courcy, 4–6 (Alice de Courcy is also attributed with the ownership of a large oneiromancy encyclopaedia possibly made, and certainly copied for her: see Michelle C. Glover, "*Critical Edition of the Middle French Version of Achmet Ibn Sirin's Oneiromancy Found in Ms. francais 1317, folios 51r – 106v, Paris, Bibliotheque Nationale, Entitled (Cy commence la table des) Exposicions et significacions des songes par Daniel et autres exposez*", unpublished PhD thesis, University of London, 1992, 282–9).

49 See Gui d'Amiens, *Vie de sainte Catherine*, early thirteenth century: Henry A. Todd, ed., "*La vie de sainte Catherine d'Alexandrie* as contained in the Paris manuscript *La Clayette*", *PML* 15.1 (1900): 17–73, vv. 11–22 for discussion of Christ as the source of *toutes bontez* in whom *toz biens abonde*, and for whose love the author wishes "*la vie et la sant'estre / D'une seu amie retraire / Et de latin en romanz treire*" (points which echo Clemence of Barking's prologue, vv. 7–10),

This literary culture is stamped with female authority and initiatives and the participation of women in teaching, learning, the production and dissemination and, on occasion, the composition of texts. But not, apparently, with special clinging to female authors. One place where female signatures to texts do not usually appear is the Augustinian nunnery of Campsey in Suffolk. Its large collection of Anglo-Norman verse saints' lives, possibly made within the nunnery, which may have been given to the house by a noblewoman named within the collection, includes all the three saints' lives we know of explicitly ascribed to women: Clemence of Barking's Life of Catherine, the Barking Life of King Edward the Confessor and the *Audrée* life by a Marie. Campsey is about ninety modern road miles up the East coast north from Barking. But the female Benedictine signatures from Barking are omitted from these texts when owned by this Augustinian house. Only that floating signifier, the anonym "Marie" is retained, at the very end of the Campsey manuscript's life of *Sainte Audrée*.[50]

Culting Marie "de France" sucks up a great deal of scholarly energy and generates strange excesses: Richard Baum's 1968 questioning of the canon, for instance, was compared to "*une bombe au souffle dévastateur*" and treated by some scholars as heretical.[51] More is written about Marie and the works ascribed to her as author figure than any other aspect of high medieval women's writing in Britain (1,622 items in Glyn Burgess's third supplementary Marie de France bibliography of 2007 alone).[52] Even though the prologues and epilogues to the Barking saints' lives are contemporaneous with the *Lais* or slightly earlier, and even though they are complex and thoughtful about interpretation, time and *translatio*, and share some common topoi and themes with the *Lais*, the prologue attached to Marie de France is usually discussed in isolation from them.[53]

---

thereby replacing an earlier translation which *por ce que normant estoit /... ne pleisoit mie au[s] François* (this has analogies with Clemence's own displacement of a vernacular predecessor, Prologue vv. 35–46, and may possibly even be a reference to Clemence's own work and a justification for Gui's new version in the Île-de-France).

50 Delbert Russell ("The Campsey Collection of Old French Saints' Lives: a Re-examination of its Structure and Provenance", *Scriptorium* 58 [2003]: 51–83) first pointed this out (he also notes that the scribe of the main late thirteenth-century sections of the manuscripts has done little to smooth out the features of the texts copied, *pace* McCash's insular scribe imposing on a continental writer in Campsey's *Audrée*). See also Sara Gorman, "Anglo-Norman Hagiography as Institutional Historiography: Saints' Lives in Late Medieval Campsey Ash Priory", *Journal of Medieval Religious Cultures* 37.2 (2011): 110–28.

51 Philippe Ménard, *Les Lais de Marie de France* (Paris: Presses universitaires de France, 1979), 24.

52 Glyn S. Burgess, *Marie de France: An Analytic Bibliography, Supplement no. 3* (Woodbridge and Rochester: Tamesis, 2007).

53 An exception is Diane Watt, *Medieval Women's Writing* (Cambridge: Polity, 2007), who compares the prologues' opening topoi (72–3) and the two writers as commentators on earlier vernacular tradition (it is not, however, the case, as Watt seems to suggest, that Clemence of Barking *translates* from the vernacular: her Catherine life is intertextual with many vernacular works and traditions but her main source is the Latin *Vulgata* version of the *Passio sanctae Katerine*). That such commentary is both a topos and an indication of the status of vernacular writing is further suggested by Gui d'Amiens' use of it (n. 49 above), and Guernes de Pont Ste Maxence alludes to other lives, whether by "*clerc u lai, muïne u* dame" in his Becket *Life*.

Within this literary culture, as Elizabeth Salter long ago pointed out, the literary and cultural influence of individual highly placed women is very great and extends at least as far as the many courts and principalities in which elite women were brides, mothers and sometimes rulers.[54] Literary culture, if defined as the production of texts and manuscripts, is the activity of a tiny elite minority and almost always requires patronage whether secular or ecclesiastical/monastic. Writing "literature" is not a professional identity in the post-medieval sense. Excepting some but not all monastic/ecclesiastical professed religious (male or female), composition is often occasional, a by-product of, or dispensation from, other duties in a clerical or administrative career, whether in religious or secular houses. In this culture, we do not necessarily find large authorial canons, but rather, multiple and varied acts of commissioning, composition, circulation and performance. We could thus usefully choose to work with the possibility of multiple Maries and with the many other women in their literary culture. And in that way, we could free up desire and energy for work on the elucidation, not of a fetishized eighteenth-century author figure, but of a medieval literary landscape populated with the cultural authority and activity of women.[55]

54 Elizabeth Salter, *English and International: Studies in the Literature, Art and Patronage of Medieval England*, ed. Derek Pearsall and Nicolette Zeeman (Cambridge: Cambridge University Press, 1988, repr. 2010), 12–17.

55 I am grateful to the conference organisers and proceedings editors of *Women Intellectuals and Leaders in the Middle Ages*; to Ian Short for the privilege of bringing his linguistic analysis to the conference and this volume, to Thelma Fenster and Delbert Russell for much helpful discussion, especially over prosody and phonology, to the Columbia Medievalists group, especially Christopher Baswell who read as well as heard a draft, and to Ellis Light, PhD candidate at Fordham University, for valuable assistance with copy-editing.

## Appendix I: The Linguistic Case for La Vie sainte Audrée

In their 2007 translation, McCash and Barban note scribal orthography for the manuscript and also adduce five points of evidence for *Audrée* as a work by Marie "de France".[56] These latter are dedicated to showing that the language of the text, as opposed to the scribe, is continental. Among them is the question of Anglo-Norman reduction of vowels in hiatus versus continental retention of hiatus: the argument is that when this occurs in the rhyme word, the underlying language of the author requires diaeresis to maintain hiatus, and that the insular scribe has not realised that lines with such rhymes are short by a syllable of the regular eight.[57] No specific examples are given, but among the couplets that might have been adduced there are a number where eight syllables can be produced with or without hiatus, depending on how the syllables are counted: e.g. *Del conseil k'ele avoit eu / Et ke de Deu out recue*, vv. 1063–4. Here -e in v. 1063 could be maintained in *ele* before *avoit*, *or* before *oe/u* in *eu* at the end; in v. 1064, *Deü* or *Deu*, and *receü* or *receu* are both possible. At vv. 1087–8, *Ceste dame dont nos parlum / Ama sainte religiun*, diaeresis is maintained in "religiun", but the line is plausible with or without, in the same text, whether continental or insular. At vv. 985–6, *Ceste chose fu espandue / Par Engleterre et bien sue*, *sue* is presumably eye-rhyme for *seue*, but eight syllables could be counted in v. 986, even if sue has no diaeresis, and was indeed understood by the scribe as monosyllabic: for instance, by maintenance of the final -e in *Engleterre* (where it should otherwise drop before the following vowel). In other words, the argument for this point has not been made: it would require examination of all cases and even then would be imponderable. Moreover, earlier editorial practices regarding diaeresis are no longer automatically accepted, the flexibility and variation of Anglo-Norman prosody and its changes over time and place being currently more fully recognised. Verse that had been originally syllabically counted in early Anglo-Norman writing, but which continued to be composed in an accentual environment developed, so to speak, regular flexibilities and variations, so that, for instance, heptasyllabic lines quite commonly occur within octosyllabic matrices.[58]

Four further points are adduced for continental language underlying the Campsey scribe in *Audrée* and *hence* being Marie de France's language:

1. (i) *en* and *an* are not rhymed (but this seems wrong as stated: it is in *Anglo-Norman* and in some Western areas that this distinction before nasals is maintained).[59]

56 McCash and Judith Clark Barban, eds., *The Life of Saint Audrey: A Text by Marie de France* (Jefferson and London: McFarland Press, 2006), 9–10.

57 McCash and Barban, *The Life of Saint Audrey*, 9–10.

58 For a more detailed exposition, see "Does the French of England Count?" in *Vernacular Literary Theory*, ed. Wogan-Browne, Fenster and Russell, 414–24.

59 Ian Short, *Manual of Anglo-Norman*, 2nd ed., Anglo-Norman Text Society OPS 8 (Oxford: ANTS, 2013), §1.4.

2. (ii) Elision of *ke* or *que* is optional: but this is true both in insular and continental varieties of French and not a determinative linguistic marker.
3. (iii) Instability of final -e. This again is not a determinative criterion, the more so as final -e is unstable in continental as well as insular French.
4. (iv) e used for i in pretonic positions as in *devin* for *divin* (cited from *Eliduc*, v. 1180). But this can hardly be a determinative feature because it is possible in both insular and continental French, and examples are far from unique to *Audrée* and the *Lais*.

## Appendix II: The Three (or Four?) Maries: some philological notes, by Ian Short[60]

Specialists in Anglo-Norman are justly proud of the number of women authors and patrons who made such an important contribution to the precocious flowering of literature in French which is one of the least-sung glories of twelfth-century Britain. Admittance to the Anglo-Norman canon has traditionally been made on strictly philological grounds, with the result that writers such as Wace, for example, Benoît de Sainte-Maure, Guernes de Pont-Sainte-Maxence and the Marie who composed the *Lais* have been excluded – or accorded the status of honorary or adoptive Anglo-Normans by virtue of the contributions which they made to Insular culture as immigrants or visitors. The French that they used, as preserved in their rhymes or syllable-count, as opposed to the linguistic veneer with which successive scribes may have adorned their texts as they copied and recopied them, lacks those phonological features widely recognised as being characteristic of Insular French. Philology – predominantly the phonological analyses of Karl Warnke dating back to the 1880s – has also been the yardstick for the identification of the Marie who wrote the *Fables* with her namesake who wrote the *Espurgatoire seint Patriz*, and of both of these with the more celebrated author of the *Lais*, universally if inaccurately (ever since Fauchet in 1581) referred to as "Marie de France".

There are, however, not just three Maries, but four: to be added to Marie$^1$, author of the celebrated *lais* writing at some indeterminate point in the 1160s; to Marie$^2$, author of the *Fables* (*Isopets*) dating from some time in the 1180s; to Marie$^3$, author of the *Purgatoire seint Patriz* from soon after 1190, is Marie$^4$, author of the Anglo-Norman *Vie seinte Audree*, traditionally dated to the first half of the thirteenth century. This verse life of St Audrey of Ely, also known as Etheldreda (more accurately Æthelthryth) is a 4620-verse rendering of the twelfth-century *Vita sanctae Ethelredae* by one Thomas of Ely.[61] A twice-married virgin of royal East Anglian descent, Æthelthryth died in 679 at the abbey of Ely which she had founded. To judge by the churches dedicated to her and by her calendar mentions, she must have been among the most revered of all Anglo-Saxon women saints.[62] Dominica Legge suggested that Marie$^4$ might be identified with Marie de St Clare, a thirteenth-century abbess of St

60 Titles of manuals used in abbreviation here are Pierre Fouché, *Phonétique historique du français*, 2nd ed. (Paris: Klincksieck, 1969); Yorio Otaka, *Lexique de Marie de France* (Tokyo: Kazama, 1994) and Marie de France, *Œuvres completes*, ed. Yorio Otaka (Tokyo: Kazama, 1987); Mildred K. Pope, *From Latin to Modern French with Especial Consideration of Anglo-Norman* (Manchester: Manchester University Press, 1934, rev. reprs. 1952, 1954); Ian Short, *Manual of Anglo-Norman*. Editions cited by abbreviation are Ewert, *Lais*; Jean Rychner, *Les Lais de Marie de France* (Paris: Champion, 1981). For Karl Warnke's phonological analyses see his editions: *Die Fabeln der Marie de France* (Halle: Niemeyer, 1898) and *Die Lais der Marie de France* (Halle: Niemeyer, 1895).

61 On the source text for the life see Rupert T. Pickens, "Marie de France *Translatrix* II: *La Vie seinte Audree*", in *Companion to Marie de France*, ed. Whalen, 267–302.

62 Virginia Blanton, *Signs of Devotion: The Cult of St. Æthelthryth in Medieval England, 695–1615* (University Park, PA: Pennsylvania State University Press, 2007); cf. Susan Ridyard, *The Royal Saints of Anglo-Saxon England: A Study of West Saxon and East Anglian Cults* (Cambridge: Cambridge University Press, 1988).

Mary's at Chatteris in Cambridgeshire, a conjecture better described as a guess. Equally speculative but more plausible is Virginia Blanton's suggestion of a link between *La Vie seinte Audree* and the saint's translation by the bishop of Ely in 1252.[63] Be that as it may, the French of Marie[4] has always been deemed sufficiently Insular for her to merit a place in the pantheon of Anglo-Norman authors.

Most characteristic of all (though the phenomenon happens to be restricted to only a handful of examples in the extant text) is the Anglo-Norman rhyming of /ü/ with /u/. In *plus: deus* 641, the /ou/ diphthong in the reflex of DŬOS must have levelled to /u/, as in Gaimar's *dous: vus* 4325 (cf. *Roland* 2905). The appearance of *pertus* (= *pertuis* < *PERTŪSIU) in rhyme with *en sous* (= *ensus*) 2580 and with *desus* 2432 points to /üi/ levelling to /ü/, but whether this then velarised to /u/ is unclear. In *uus* (< *USTIU < OSTIU): *sus* (< *SUSU < SŪRSU) 4084 we might have a similar reduction of the /üi/ diphthong, though Pope considers *uus* (for SMF *uis*) to be an undiphthongised Western form (cf. MAN § 15.4), and indeed Marie[1] can be found rhyming *us* with *desus* in Lanval 637 and with *sus* in Guigemar 673 and in Yonec 55. This, and the reduction of /üi/ to /i/ after initial velars (*quisse: guarisse* Guigemar 113, and *guise* in rhyme with *assise* Guigemar 447, *chemise* Guigemar 729 and *mise* Bisclavret 279) are characteristic of Western texts in general and are not specifically Anglo-Norman [Pope 1952: §§ 514–17, Fouché 1969: 286–8, cf. MAN § 15.3]. The same usage is found in Marie[2] (53.15, 62.15, 72.87).

When Marie[1] uses /ü/ elsewhere at the rhyme, she never identifies it with /u/. Neither of the two apparent exceptions proves to be valid: parallels to *ebenus: plus* Guigemar 157 are found in Chrétien's *Perceval* where *ebenus* rhymes with *nus* (= *nuls*) at 3272, and with *desus* at 7683 (cf. *T–L* 3, 10). In *hure: desure* Guigemar 539, *desure* is a graphy for *desore*, a recognised variant of *desor* (Chrétien's *Erec* 6798 [6736] rhymes *dessore* with *more* (< MŌRA); see *T–L* 2, 1665–8, and cf. *AND2* 762b). Marie[2], on the other hand, uses the Anglo-Norman rhyme *dur: poür* 18.14. [The rhymes *eür* (< *AGŪRIU)*: mur* 73.57, and *fu: cuccu* (< CUCŪLU) 46.9 do not belong in this category, *pace* Otaka 1987: 12.] There is nothing comparable in Marie[3], whose French has no example of this particular dialectal feature. [Cf. Otaka 1994: 744a §§ 186–9.]

Equally characteristic of Anglo-Norman, and somewhat better illustrated in Marie[4], is the rhyming together of /e/ and /ie/ in contradiction of "Bartsch's Law": *garderes: peres* 517, *loër: conseillier* 1437, *iré: repeiré* 1371 (though there is a dual form *irié / iré*; see Suchier 1906: 86.) The mixed Anglo-Norman rhyme *pere: matere* 527, 561 probably shows /é/ < Latin A opening to /e/ and then to /ɛ/ and falling together with the reduced diphthong /ie/ > /e/ > /ɛ/. [Södergård's additional illustrations of /e/: /ie/ from 2342 [guerdon et grié/Trinité], 2990 [geté/esté], 3580 [porter/ herbergier], 3538 [refree/ tuee], 4572 [hostés/getez] do not withstand scrutiny.] Whereas Marie[2] also avails herself of a rhyme such as *veritez: jugez* 88.17, no such mixed forms are encountered in Marie[3] [cf. Otaka 1994: 739b §§ 82–6, 741b §§ 117–28.] A handful of possible examples in Marie[1] prove, on closer investigation, to be cases where

63 Blanton 2007; cf. Jocelyn Wogan-Browne, *Saints' Lives and Women's Literary Culture c. 1150–1300* (Oxford: Oxford University Press, 2001), 172 and n. 204.

well-attested alternative forms co-exist. *Mercïer*, for instance, can rhyme either in /e/ (Eliduc 1268) or in /ie/ (Chaitivel 27), and *ancïens: tens* Milun 63 is found next to *bien: auncïen* Milun 531. In *pesé: cungié* Chievrefoil 99, *cungié* is for *cungeé*, the infinitive form *cungeer* being attested in Lanval 460 (similarly for *cunreer* Guigemar 870, Lanval 174, Chaitivel 166), while *avillier* Lanval 306 and 365 rhymes in /ie/. In *bachelers: pers* Laustic 17, we have the reflex of *BACCALARE which coexisted with *bachelier* deriving from a form with an -ARIU agent suffix [Fouché 1969: II 264, 484; cf. also 411–15]. Editorial emendation at Lanval 139–40, Laustic 107–8, Chaitivel 137–8 and Eliduc 1131–2 removes the few remaining anomalies, and it can be confidently concluded that, unlike Marie$^{4}$, Marie$^{1}$ does not interchange /ie/ and /e/ at the rhyme.

The general levelling of diphthongs is another Anglo-Norman characteristic, and here again the usage in Marie$^{4}$ is distinctive. The rhymes *feus* (< FIDĒLES): *eus* (< ĬLLOS) 21, 2028 show the reduction of the /ei/ diphthong to /e/ and, in all likelihood, the levelling of the subsequent /eu/ to /œ/, a thirteenth-century development in Anglo-Norman. [*MAN* § 12.2; Warnke and Rychner (but not Ewert) reject the rhyme *eus: leaus* found in MS H only after Milun 112. Elsewhere in Marie$^{1}$ *leal* invariably rhymes in /al/.]

Marie$^{4}$ observes the Anglo-Norman distinction between /ã/ and /ẽ/, and between /ãi/ and /ẽi/, while allowing interchange in feminine rhymes such as *fonteine: meine* 4102 (also 167, 343, 971). In Marie$^{1}$, on the other hand, the interchange is attested in addition in masculine rhymes such as *pleint* (= *plaint*): *destreint* Guigemar 429, *destreint*: *remeint* (= *remaint*) Eliduc 447, *ceins: meins* (= *mains*) Guigemar 819. Such mixtures are also a feature of the language of Marie$^{2}$ (*meint: ateint* 42.29, *feint: pleint* 29.91, *preinz* < *PRÆGNIS: *einz* 43.9), and of Marie$^{3}$ (*plein: main* 287, 1211, *esteint: remeint* 905, *certeins: meins* < MINUS 111).

There are, however, morphological features which could point to differences between the languages of our four Maries. [Otaka 1987: 10 § 2.4 is in need of clarification: its statistics refer only to the order of frequency of rhymes, and not to the overall occurrence of rhymes, which Otaka presents and tabulates in Otaka 1994: 690–747 §§ 5–5.3.2. Marie's *–ier* and *-iere* rhymes are listed in Otaka 1994: 705–6 §§ 246–72, her *-ai* rhymes at 691 §§ 7–15, and her *-eir* rhymes at 696 §§ 114–17.]

Unless, therefore, it could be argued, and shown, that a poet's language can modify significantly over time, and that a poet's choice of rhymes can likewise differ radically in the course of their career, it looks very much, from the selection of evidence presented here, as if we are in fact dealing with four separate individuals.

The proposition that Marie's *Vie seinte Audree* was written by the Marie of the *Lais* is, in other words, without linguistic foundation. Such an attribution is extremely doubtful, not to say implausible, from a philological point of view. It should not be transformed into a statement of "fact" on the title-page of an academic book. The rightful place which the Medieval French life of St Æthelthryth of Ely has traditionally occupied within Insular literature can safely be reaffirmed.

10

# THE VISIONS, EXPERIMENTS, AND OPERATIONS OF BRIDGET OF AUTRUY (FL. 1303–15)

NICHOLAS WATSON

"Bridget of Autruy" is the moniker used here for a recently rediscovered medieval visionary, the sister and intimate associate of John of Morigny, author of the *Liber florum celestis doctrine*: a work of visions, prayers, rituals, and experiments written in stages between 1301 and early 1316. This work, which at present remains our only source for Bridget's life and thought, was burned as heretical in Paris in 1323 but was widely copied, read, and used as an orthodox expression of Marian devotion for the next two centuries in Germany, Austria, Poland, Italy, Spain, and England, as well as France, especially, it seems, in Benedictine and Augustinian houses. After almost half a millennium of obscurity it has recently been published in full for the first time.[1]

A decade younger than her brother, Bridget was born into a seigneurial family of no great wealth in the late 1280s, probably in Autruy, a village in the Loiret on the river Juine, midway between Orléans to the south and Étampes and nearby Morigny to the north, in the archdiocese of Sens.[2] Here her devout mother owned a house on two floors adjoining a walled field, while the parish church, dedicated to St. Peter, contained a painted wooden statue of the Virgin of a kind widely dispersed across the region.[3] After offering her virginity to God in her teens, partly as a result of a series of visions involving the devil, God, the Virgin, and the angels, Bridget may have lived as a beguine or other semi-religious before becoming a nun in her mid-twenties. It is not unlikely that we should be referring to her as Bridget of Rozay, the Benedictine house near Sens she may well have joined. There are signs that around this time she also became, at least briefly, a public figure. However, nothing is known about her later life or in what year she died.

1 John of Morigny, *Liber florum celestis doctrine*, ed. Claire Fanger and Nicholas Watson, Studies and Texts 199 (Toronto: Pontifical Institute of Mediaeval Studies, 2015). All citations in this essay are to this book unless stated otherwise. For an overview of the referencing system, see Table 1 (xvii–xxi). On manuscript copies and versions, see Claire Fanger, "Introduction B: The Manuscripts and Their Uses," 90–137. Many copies refer to John's sister not as "Burgeta" (Bridget) but as "Gurgeta" (Georgette).

2 See Nicholas Watson, "Introduction A: John of Morigny and His Book," 1–89, at 7 n.9.

3 According to two of John's visions, at I.i.4 and I.ii.5. The Autruy Virgin, which plays an important part in the writing of *Liber florum* for John and (probably) Bridget, does not survive.

Although she could read and write Latin, and although one passage may derive from her pen, there is no evidence that Bridget recorded or publicized her own visions. Nor does her status as a medieval woman intellectual rest only on the eight or so of these visions detailed in the *Liber florum*. Important though these are, they take up fewer than a thousand words of a text well over fifty times this length and share the same emphasis on achieving practical goals that typify many of her brother's considerably more numerous visions. Bridget's significance to this volume derives, rather, from the nature of her engagement in her brother's book and the extraordinary standing it affords her. Not only does she figure in a wide variety of situations in many key passages, as her brother's first and closest reader and user, she appears to have influenced the book in fundamental, albeit not readily determinable, ways.

The attempt to reconstruct Bridget's career in general and her contributions to the *Liber florum* in particular involves us in complex textual details whose historical implications require a mixture of lateral thinking and careful guesswork to tease out. This is partly due to the character of the work itself, which is highly responsive to the charged and fluid situation in which it was written but less informative about a number of details than we need it to be. But it is also a product of the range of Bridget's appearances in the work: now as an exemplary figure whose spiritual experiences are adduced in support of its arguments; now as a named participant in the work and its rituals; now as a character in one of her brother's visions; now, more problematically, as an actant behind the scenes, whose direct or indirect influence can be more or less confidently inferred.

Speculative as any results must remain, however, the attempt is well worth it, and not only for the local insights it offers. Scholars of medieval women visionaries have devoted careful attention to the relationship these remarkable figures had to the confessors and other clerics who acted as their consultants, scribes, apologists, publicists, and collaborators.[4] While the *Liber florum* recounts Bridget's visions as well as those of her brother and while it initially represents John in the role of his sister's guardian and educator, the work reverses the expected polarities of these relationships. Here, a young woman plays a major part over the course of many years in the creation of a long work by an older visionary man, despite both this work's apparent address to a primary audience of university-educated scholars and monastics and its grounding in texts, practices, and disciplines usually understood as clerical preserves. Although her education was at once belated and idiosyncratic, Bridget emerges from the *Liber florum* as her brother's full colleague, well able to take her place as a distinctive member of the community of learned visionaries it aspires to produce. Indeed, her presence in the work and active engagement in its production do much to shape its vision of this community, enabling John to realize the spiritual potential of his project in a manner he could not have accomplished on his own.

4 See especially the essays gathered in the collection *Gendered Voices: Medieval Saints and their Interpreters*, ed. Catherine Mooney (Philadelphia: University of Pennsylvania Press, 1999).

### *Liber florum*

The *Liber florum* is a linked anthology of works initially borne of John's desire to petition the Virgin Mary to communicate with him through lucid dreams composed as an outgrowth of his practice of a private ritual known as the *Ars notoria*: one of several such works said to derive from King Solomon himself in broad circulation across late medieval and early modern Europe.[5] The prayer rituals of the *Ars notoria* provide the means for users to petition God and the angels to instill knowledge in their minds and hearts: specifically knowledge of the "arts and sciences," that is, the chief disciplines of the university curriculum, which the work identifies with the wisdom to discern just judgment that God promised to Solomon when he appeared to him in a dream at Gabaon (I Kings 3). Likely written in Bologna in the late twelfth century and widely used as an adjunct to formal study in monasteries and universities, the work was celebrated enough to be the subject of early attacks by theologians, including Alexander of Hales and Thomas Aquinas.[6] These attacks inflected but did not destroy its reputation. When John found a richly decorated copy of the *Ars notoria* at the University of Orléans around 1301 – near the outset of an eight-year residence there as a law student, which began roughly four years after he took his vows at Morigny – it struck him at first as "of all books the most beautiful and most useful and even the most holy."[7]

Although the main goal of the *Ars notoria* is to acquire formal knowledge, visions play an important role in the work, whose users not only anticipate but actually require repeated interactions with angels and other divine beings in order to be sure they have license to perform or "operate" the work. It thus includes several rituals that petition for these visions, which are typically granted to the sleeping operator in the form of meaningful dreams. John's first prayers, which he collected in a *libellus* called the Grace of Christ in 1304, seem to have arisen in part from frustration at the failure of these rituals to lead to dream visions whose source he could be confident was divine rather than wholly or partially diabolical.[8] But they were also the product of his growing sense that his first impression of the *Ars notoria* had been wrong and that its opponents were, after all, correct to argue that the work was not holy (as it fervently claims) but perverted – with the result that the dream visions he received as he used it were sent by the devil as well as God.[9] As he became confident of this, and as he found that his

5 The following reconstruction of the *Liber florum* and the process of its composition are based on Watson, "Introduction A." For the *Ars notoria*, see *L'Ars notoria au Moyen Âge: Introduction et édition critique*, ed. Julien Véronèse (Florence: Sismel, Edizioni de Galluzo, 2007), cited here as *Ars notoria*. For a general introduction to the *Liber florum*, see Claire Fanger, *Rewriting Magic: An Exegesis of the Visionary Autobiography of a Fourteenth-Century French Monk* (University Park: Pennsylvania State University Press, 2015).

6 See Watson, "Introduction A," 14–15 and the further references given there.

7 I.i.3: "omnium librorum pulcherrimus et vtilissimus et eciam sanctissimus." Translations of the *Liber florum* in this essay are from John of Morigny, *The Flowers of Heavenly Teaching*, trans. Claire Fanger and Nicholas Watson (forthcoming).

8 Watson, "Introduction A," 20–27.

9 This is the story told in the first two parts of the Book of Visions. For John's use of *Ars notoria* vision rituals, see Source Notes to I.i.4, 5, 8, 10.

prayers to the Virgin led to visions that lacked the demonic entanglements of his earlier ones, he gained her permission to produce a new work that would stand in for the *Ars notoria* but (for those who petition successfully for her leave to use it) would be as holy as its predecessor only claimed to be. In the Book of Prayers that became the core of *Liber florum,* the Grace of Christ prayers thus become a prologue to a set of "only thirty simple prayers," finished in 1307.[10]

Following the *Ars notoria* but also drawing on a scholarly tradition of philosophical didascalica descended from Hugh of St Victor, these prayers petition Christ, the Virgin, and the angels for intellectual and spiritual illumination; for the purification and renovation of the senses and soul; and, finally, for infused knowledge of each of the branches of the seven liberal arts, philosophy, theology, and other sciences useful to the pursuit of wisdom and instruction. In the prayer for philosophy (Prayer 28, "O altitudo"), for example, the operator petitions the cherubim to know and understand natural philosophy, metaphysics, and the branches of moral philosophy (political, economic, and monastic); to remember what is learned of these disciplines; and to be given the fluency and skill to deploy and discuss or dispute them. Those who say the Thirty Prayers do not only acquire knowledge and an enhanced mental capacity to retain and articulate it. By receiving it direct from its heavenly source, as *wisdom*, and by learning to situate it within the divine work of creation and restoration to which it is intimately related, they are placed in right relation to knowledge, as intimate members of the household of the Virgin – queen of heaven but also of the arts and sciences – that is the court of God himself.[11]

For all their beauty, the Thirty Prayers were perhaps less clearly efficacious than the Grace of Christ prayers, whose success in petitioning for visions was proved experimentally, and John at some stage realized that it would be necessary to supplement them. The *Ars notoria* derived much of its felt power from the language of its prayers, which invoke many thousands of otherwise unknown angels by name in what is said to be a sacred mix of Latin, Greek, Chaldean, and Hebrew.[12] It was by now clear to him that the reason the work was unusable was that these names had come to include those of *fallen* angels, who had smuggled their presence into the holy prayers so successfully they could not be extricated.[13] But the *Ars notoria* was also famous for its figures: inscribed and purposefully obscure diagrams the operator inspects repeatedly at the climax of each of the work's prolonged rituals that play a crucial (if inchoate) role in how knowledge is actually communicated.[14] Despite the commitment to clarity symbolized by John's use of Latin in place of the sacred language of the *Ars notoria,* his obvious next move was thus to produce figures of his own. Now the operator, having completed the nine-week program for reciting the Thirty Prayers on their own called the First Procedure, could say them again with the help of the figures in an

10 I.ii.5.a: "vnum librum tantummodo de triginta oracionibus simplicibus."

11 Watson, "Introduction A," 27–41, especially Tables 7 and 8 (31–32 and 38).

12 See, e.g., *Ars notoria* B §§6–6b glose.

13 I.i.9.

14 See Michael Camille, "Visual Art in Two Manuscripts of the *Ars Notoria*," in *Conjuring Spirits: Texts and Traditions of Medieval Ritual Magic*, ed. Claire Fanger (University Park, PA: Pennsylvania State University Press, 1994), 110–39.

advanced Second Procedure, petitioning for knowledge in much more specific detail: "May I know and understand the books *Elenchi*, *Topics*, *Posterior*, and *Prior Analytics*, *Perihermenias*, *Predicamenta*," goes one petition, linked to the figure of dialectic.[15] Thus did a book that began as an idiosyncratic contribution to religious pedagogy take on a new identity as something like an academic exercise or even a discipline: no longer merely a means to acquire the arts and sciences, but an art, indeed an "ars arcium," in its own right.[16]

John's attempt to produce the figures and the rituals associated with them seems to have thrown his project into temporary crisis, caused partly by his continuing ambivalence over the significant complexities of the new rituals he was devising, partly by his increasing doubts over the astrological character of the figures, which were difficult to reconcile with orthodox Christian theologies of intercession.[17] Now back at Morigny and the abbey's provost and third most senior official,[18] it took him several years to produce a Book of Figures that addressed these difficulties, beginning to send the book out in instalments to his fellow-operators (as was his usual practice) only after a series of frustrating visions seemed to threaten the project with breakdown. One of these visions features Bridget herself in the role of interpreter and comforter. A many-layered work, organized around no fewer than ninety-one figures and completed after several drafts in 1311, the Book of Figures depicts a vastly more difficult as well as a more ambitious ritual than is envisaged by the Book of Prayers.[19]

For all their anxieties, however, these were also the years when John emerged as a public figure. Realizing he had received the spirit of prophecy, he expressed his new understanding of his work by prefacing it with a Book of Visions that tells how his work came about and argues its eschatological significance.[20] The new book describes the radically contrasting dream visions that followed from the use of the *Ars notoria* and of the Grace of Christ prayers respectively, breaching the *Ars notoria*'s prohibition against publicizing dream visions that earlier parts of the work had largely respected.[21] Adducing not only his experience but those of two "witnesses," one of whom is Bridget, the Book of Visions sets out a formal case against the *Ars notoria* and stakes a claim for what is for the first time called the *Liber florum celestis doctrine*, representing it as an intervention by the Virgin in his own spiritual life and that of his times.[22]

15 OC III.18.c.i: "Vellem scire et intelligere librum *Elencorum*, *Topicorum*, *Posteriorum*, *Priorum*, *Periarmenias*, *Predicamentorum*; arguere, disputare, soluere, et opponere, sophisticare, et verum a falso discernere."

16 OC I.iv.4, 12.

17 Watson, "Introduction A," 58–59. See also OC I.iv.10.g.

18 I.i.1.b, "prepositus nostre camere factus," and Source Note. As John notes, as *praepositus* he had an "officium mobile," being obliged to leave the monastery regularly in order to oversee the community's scattered holdings.

19 For a summary of the installments in which the work may have been sent to readers, see Table 14 (134–37). For a summary of the rituals associated with the figures, see the appendix, "Overview of Ritual Operations in *Liber florum*," 602–16, *passim*, under the heading of "Old Compilation." For the figures themselves, see Table 17 (616).

20 OC III.21–25, 28. For this phase of the work, see Watson, "Introduction A," 61–71.

21 Watson, "Introduction A," 67.

22 I.iii.1; I.Prol, opening rubric.

The first version of *Liber florum* was fully published by late 1311 and reissued in 1313, presumably in response to growing demand.[23] While John had done a good deal to resolve their problems at a theological level, however, the work's figures were as controversial in aspect as he admits they were hard to use in practice. In 1315, they came under fierce attack from certain people who likened the uses of crosses and circles in the figures to those in works of necromancy and scorned its reliance on visionary dreams. Although the work calls these critics only "barking dogs" ("canes latrantes"), they evidently had sufficient official status to require drastic action. In early August – mindful, perhaps, of the lethal recent heresy trials of the Knights Templar and of Marguerite Porete, both conducted under the aegis of Philip of Marigny, archbishop of Sens – he thus declared the old version of the Book of Figures null, arguing that the scandal arising over its use had rendered its rituals inoperable.[24] He then wrote a new Book of Figures in three books which reduces the ninety-one figures to seven and greatly simplifies the rituals that involve them. The new work also includes descriptions of the dream visions that accompanied its composition and a series of formal scholarly defenses of visionary dreaming as a spiritual practice.

The urgency John felt in undertaking this revision can be gauged by the fact that he began the new figures against the Virgin's express wishes, as communicated to him by no less than the archangel Michael: an error he felt obliged to correct by admitting it penitentially in the work itself, before setting out painstakingly to petition for her visionary approval of every detail of their form and lettering. The revision was mostly written between early August 13 and October 28. Subsequent adjustments and additions were likely completed by early the following year.[25]

Despite the occasion that caused it, however, this New Compilation (as it is called) is more than an embattled response to criticism. Reflecting developments that may have been set down in a work, presently lost, called the Book of Particular Experiments (likely finished in 1314), which contained new prayers, rituals, and perhaps figures, the New Compilation evinces remarkable ritual flexibility and a new emphasis on the pastoral.[26] Featuring Bridget in so many different contexts that it seems clear she figured largely in its composition, it provides rituals to assist those of limited education who wish to participate in the work and enroll themselves in the family of the Virgin. Secular priests, the laity, the sick, the old, even John and Bridget's unlettered mother, are all invited to participate in the rituals of the *Liber florum* in any way they can.[27] The new ritual also takes on an important additional element: the operator may now petition for visionary leave to make a special ring, engraved with the Virgin's image, to be worn in the daytime while saying the prayers and at night while experiencing visionary dreams.[28] Such evidence as we have suggests that

23 Watson, "Introduction A," 72–74.

24 NC III.i.1.b. On Philip of Marigny's role in these trials, see Sean L. Field, *The Beguine, the Angel, and the Inquisitor: The Trials of Marguerite Porete and Guiard de Cressonessart* (Notre Dame, IN: University of Notre Dame Press, 2012), 148–53.

25 NC III.i.4.a–b; NC III.iii.1–8, *passim*. Watson, "Introduction A," 75–81; Table 11 (77–78).

26 Watson, "Introduction A," 74–75; Source Notes to NC III.ii, *passim*.

27 NC III.i.12.d–g and Source Notes.

28 NC III.iii.27–29.

the New Compilation largely displaced what John now calls the Old Compilation. We do not know whether or not the critique of the *Liber florum* by the barking dogs was connected to the burning of the work eight years later, publicly on the grounds that it revived, rather than displaced, the *Ars notoria*, unofficially (it may be) because the work had become worryingly popular among Paris's students and clerics.[29]

## Visions

The *Liber florum* has a powerful impulse towards literary and ritual coherence. However, as a visionary work it is also properly concerned to convey both the tumultuous story of its own development and the disturbance felt by those swept up into that story, as they find their daily lives and aspirations ineluctably transformed into eschatological signs. Visionary works pass on only such personal details as are taken to be relevant. But despite the gaps in the record this leaves, their sense of what counts as relevant, while often unexpected, can occasionally be blessedly expansive, not least because the meaning of the events that underlie them is still only partly clear to those most closely involved in them. Thus it is that we can infer a good deal of information about Bridget's life, including information that at first blush might appear to be merely incidental to the central project of the *Liber florum*, from the moment she is unexpectedly drawn into the work's ambit.

Bridget enters the Book of Visions as the first and more important of John's witnesses against the evils of the *Ars notoria* (the other is the Cistercian monk, John of Fontainejean, perhaps a contemporary of John's at Orléans). Fifteen and marriageable ("uiripotens"), she asks her brother, deep in his studies, to teach her letters ("litteras"), despite his view that "considering her advanced age ... she would not now become very good."[30] After delaying in order to try her resolve (following I Jn 4:1, "test the spirits to see if they be of God," a verse the Benedictine Rule applies to postulants),[31] he assists her with a ritual from *Ars notoria* whose uses include teaching boys to write, versify, sing, and play musical instruments ("dictando, versificando vel cantando vel organizando"), as well as helping less educated boys to learn Latin.[32] The pupil is "shown the letters" in the same way as was often done using a Prayer Book, then reads the prayers word by word after a master seven times a day for a week.[33] The ritual involves the repetition (in front of a figure) of four two-part prayers, the first parts ("Ezethomos," "Domine sancte pater," "Lemogethon," and "Omaza") consisting of angelic and divine names, the second of Latin petitions for illumination: "Everlasting God, way, life, truth, grant that your light may flower in my thought and in my mind through the power of the Holy Spirit" begins one.[34]

29 On the burning, see Watson, "Introduction A," 88; Fanger, "Introduction B," 121–22.

30 I.iii.1: "Cuius etatem considerans ita magnam dixi ei se in eis de cetero non posse proficere."

31 I.iii.1 and Source Note: "Probate spiritus si ex Deo sint."

32 *Ars notoria* B §97, usefully explicated by the rewritten version of this ritual in the *Liber florum*, II.iii.cap 3.14–15.

33 I.iii.3: "literas ei ostendi."

34 *Ars notoria* B §§90–96; "Deus semper, via, vita, veritas, da lucem tuam florere per uirtutem Spiritus Sancti in conscientiam meam et mentem meam" (§93).

Her success is remarkable. As John proudly notes, "she learned so much – she who had never seen letters – that within the reckoning of half a year she was reading and writing everywhere; and what's more, in the church before all the people sang an alleluia perfectly all by herself, without help, as graciously as an angel," taking a role in parish worship usually reserved for boy choristers.[35] Indeed, she begins formal operation of the *Ars notoria*, undertaking its use "in the customary manner," presumably in the hope of studying the liberal arts.[36] In the process, she becomes the only medieval woman we know to have engaged in this type of ritual practice, demonstrating the usefulness of knowledge rituals such as the *Ars notoria* to women and other non-clerics in a manner that directly anticipates her subsequent roles in the *Liber florum*.

As she proceeds, however, learning to "test the spirits" on her own, she begins to share John's own suspicions about the ritual as haunted by demonic as well as angelic powers. She is repeatedly crushed by a "malign spirit" when she is asleep, who "pressed so hard upon the girl's sides and back that she could neither speak nor cry out," all the while "threatening that he would kill her and torment her and not leave her in peace," and terrifying her in this way on so many occasions that it becomes impossible for her to go to bed on her own any longer.[37] This happens most severely one night when Bridget and another girl are sleeping in a room with John, perhaps on one of his visits to the family home in Autruy. Despite her plea, "My brother, the spirit is here, I feel him, for God's sake chase him away if you can!" and his advice to "commend yourself to God, cross yourself and say an Our Father and the Creed and Hail Mary, and he will do you no harm," the spirit only comes closer. "Oh my brother, look, he's got me now," she cries. The spirit retreats only after she has heeded his guilt-stricken advice to "renounce the *Ars notoria* and its pomps and works," and to "promise God and the blessed Mary before her image in church that you won't operate through this art any more."[38] Thus is she forced to cut herself off from the only route to Latinate learning that had appeared to be open to her.

These events, although set down only near the end of 1310, seem to belong to 1303/1304, when John was himself moving uncertainly away from the *Ars notoria*, completing work on the Grace of Christ, and beginning to meditate the Thirty Prayers. But the Book of Visions does not stop at Bridget's experience of the *Ars notoria*. Paralleling its account of John's early visionary life, it moves on to describe the "good visions" that shape her career as an aspiring religious, as she uses her new skills as a literate visionary to step firmly away from whatever dynastic plans had been made for her. Rapt in ecstasy

35 I.iii.1: "et in tantum didicit ipsa que numquam vidit literas infra computacionem dimidij anni quod legebat et ubique scribebat; et quod plus est, in ecclesia coram omni populo sine defectu vnum Alleluia sola sine adiutorio graciosissime tamquam angelus decantabat."

36 I.iii.2.a: "Postquam predicta soror mea Burgeta Artis notorie vt mos est ingressa fuit."

37 I.iii.2.a: "Videbat, eciam senciebat, dormiendo in extasi venire quemdam spiritum malignum et iuxta latus suum in lecto suo stabat, et tunc ille malignus spiritus illam puellam ita per latera et dorsum stringebat fortiter ita quod nec loqui nec clamare poterat," etc.

38 I.iii.2.b: "'Frater mi, adest spiritus ille, sencio illum, pro Deo fugetis eum si potestis!' Cui respondi 'Soror mea, quid habes tu? Commendes te Deo, et signes te, et dicas Pater noster, Credo in Deum, Aue Maria, et nullum malum tibi faciet'"; "'Ha, frater mi, ecce iam tenet me'"; "'Soror cara, renunccia Arti notorie et pompis eius et operibus, et cras promitte Deo et beate Marie coram ymagine in ecclesia quod de cetero per ipsam Artem non operaberis,'" etc.

in sleep, and now apparently using John's Grace of Christ prayers instead of any *Ars notoria* ritual, she finds herself kneeling, naked, before a "great table in a certain church," at which sits "the Creator of all in three persons." Weeping, she offers her virginity to him and is accepted, once she can confirm that she has "the power to do this," able to decide for herself and not yet promised in earthly marriage.[39] Despite the *Ars notoria's* admonitions on this score, she at once tells John what has happened, declaring her vision openly to her brother without inhibition, as seems to have been her normal practice from the start.

In a vision that takes place "on another day" and is reiterated several times, the Virgin then instructs her that she will serve her son "in our church at Rozay-le-Jeune."[40] Although "Le-Jeune" ("minori" in the manuscripts) remains a puzzle, this is most likely a prestigious Benedictine convent near Sens, founded by Elizabeth de Crépy (St. Elizabeth Rose, d. 1130) at roughly the same time as Morigny.[41] Soon after, and again several times, the Virgin tells Bridget to cut off her "very beautiful hair" and to do penance by renouncing fine linen clothing, in return for being able to speak with her "at will" – perhaps a reference to the fact that Bridget later gains the capacity to communicate with the Virgin even when awake. Having performed these difficult sacrifices, and in implied repudiation of the *Ars notoria*'s claim to offer direct access to the angelic powers, she sees "the nave of a certain church which was filled with choirs of angels in the air."[42]

Finally, the Virgin announces to Bridget that "in order to get your place in the said Abbey of Rozay, someone other than I must speak," with the result that John travels there at her behest to negotiate with the abbess on her behalf, demonstrating the resourcefulness that the Virgin expects of all her servants.[43] "I know and believe without doubt that when you ask a place for me, it will be granted and given us," she says to her reluctant brother when he tries to refuse. To his great surprise, he is successful in reserving her a vacancy, although he has never visited the house before and "neither I nor you nor anyone in our entire family knows anybody there."[44] To his

39 I.iii.3.a, a chapter entitled "De visionibus bonis sororis mee postquam dimisit Artem notoriam": "Vidit in vna nocte in extasi posita Creatorem omnium in tribus personis ad mensam magnam in quadam ecclesia sedentem, et ipsa erat tota nuda ante eum. Que lacrimabiliter flexis genibus dixit ei, 'Miserere mei quia dono me ipsam tibi integram.' Cui respondens ait, 'Habes tu potestatem dandi te?' Respondit, 'Domine mi, habeo.' Et ait illi 'Et Ego te recipio, filia mea.'"

40 I.iii.3.b: "'Et in ecclesia nostra de Roseto Minori et ibi nobis seruies.'"

41 Source Note to I.iii.3.b. "Minori" might reflect the fact that Rozay (often spelled "Rozoy") is sometimes referred to as Rozoy-le-Jeune, were it not that this title is often understood to have been conferred on it after its move to a new location (at Villechassons) during the fifteenth century. The word evidently does not here refer to Minorites.

42 I.iii.3.n: "Item, vidit pluries in sompnis quod beata Maria dixit ei, 'Filia, remoue capillos tuos' (quia habebat pulcherrimos capillos), quod sic fecit. Item, dictum fuit sibi quod si uellet loqui ad voluntatem suam cum gloriosa virgine Maria quod ageret penitenciam, que sic fecit, quia post hoc non vsa fuit pannis lineis. Item, uidit nauim ecclesie cuiusdam in sompnis quod in aere plena angelorum choris."

43 I.iii.i3.c: "'Filia, ad impetrandum locum tuum in abbacia Roseto predicta oportet quod alter quam ego loquatur.'" See also NC III.iii.20.c, where this scene is recalled and moralized.

44 I.iii.3.c: "'et scio et credo sine dubio quod dum ipsum locum meum impetrabitis, et nobis concedetur et dabitur'"; "'Et quomodo esse potest, cum nec ego nec tu nec aliquis de parentela nostra tota aliquam noticiam ibi habemus?'"

further astonishment, the Virgin has even informed Bridget of this happy event before she greets him, weeping with joy, upon his return.[45] As mindful of Bridget's economic situation as the Trinity was of her marital one, the Virgin also promises John that she will find a dowry for her when the time comes, overriding his anxious question, "how is it possible that she can become a nun when she needs so many worldly goods to give to the said abbey before she can enter, and when as to worldly goods, she seems to have few or none?" Bridget has not only lost nothing from transferring her hopes of learning from the *Ars notoria* to her brother's successor to this work, but she has gained the most powerful of heavenly patrons. Obstacles that might derail the careers of many women of meagre means in quest of a religious life appear to melt before the Virgin's calm "I will provide the necessaries for her."[46]

## Experiments

We can date most of Bridget's visions to between 1304, when she was perhaps sixteen (a standard age to enter a convent), and 1308, when she was about twenty. This was the period when her brother, still in Orléans, was writing the Book of Prayers and slowly thinking towards the Book of Figures. After this, the record is patchy for several years, picking up again only with the New Compilation Book of Figures, by which time her relationship with her brother's project, like the project itself, had become less straightforward. Up to 1308, when the Book of Prayers was finished, the *Liber florum* was well-suited to the needs of users such as her and was clearly developed partly with these needs in mind. The work does not associate her directly with its own writing. But in style and form it honors the fact that the book John had petitioned the Virgin to license – in an Autruy vision probably featuring the same image before which Bridget had renounced the *Ars notoria* – was to contain "only thirty *simple* prayers."[47] It also directs itself not only towards monks and priests who say the full canonical hours but towards those who use the Little Office of the Virgin, as Bridget probably did at this early stage of her career.[48]

Now, however, almost despite itself, the work became inexorably more exclusive. Even if John later exaggerates when he states that, once it was finished in this form, it "could scarcely be managed by anyone," few of the completed rituals involving the Old Compilation figures would have been easy to use independently by an operator inexperienced in the full liturgical round.[49] Indeed, the consequence of this development for Bridget is the implied subject of one of a set of Morigny visions from this period in which she makes a sudden appearance, solidifying next to John as he stands before the Virgin, "painted on a sort of pillar and suddenly transmuted into

45 I.iii.3.c according to the earlier version of this passage: see "Variants," 403.

46 I.iii.3.d: "Item, postea apparuit michi virgo Maria et dixit michi petenti eam de hoc – quomodo posset esse quod ipsa monialis esset, cum tanta temporalia sibi oportet habere et abbacie predicte dare antequam posset eam intrare, cum de predictis temporalibus pauca vel nulla uidebatur habere? – que respondit, 'Sibi de necessarijs prouidebo.'"

47 I.ii.5.a: ""vnum librum tantummodo de triginta oracionibus simplicibus.'"

48 II.iii.prol.

49 NC III.iii.1.c: "quia vix posset ab aliquo adimpleri."

the likeness and form of a beautiful woman," in order to advise him how to interpret the Virgin's refusal to license the Book of Figures, despite her willingness to "look at it." "What the virgin Mary said should be enough for you," the dream Bridget urges, "go ahead and make your book, and when it is made she will look to see if it is well done or not, and she will respond to you accordingly."[50] Although suggestive both of her engagement in John's project and of his sense of her importance to it, Bridget's words here imply that the book has moved so far from its first design that he needs her reassurance, as well as the Virgin's, in order to go on.

It bears noting that the years in which John was busy making his book more academic were the same years in which Bridget allowed herself to be written into the Book of Visions, thus both endorsing the *Liber florum* publicly by associating herself irrevocably with the project and standing in as a symbol for the breadth of its intended reach. It also bears noting that, during these years, John not only worked hard to maintain this breadth by creating a new version of the same *Ars notoria* literacy ritual Bridget had used earlier, but began to encourage her and others to build their own rituals focused around petitions for visions, inaugurating the developments that eventually led to the Book of Particular Experiments (now lost).[51] Moreover, as we shall see, there is good evidence that she did make use of the figures, albeit not in a standard way. Nonetheless, by creating a route to knowledge of the arts and sciences that could only be followed by a few, the Old Compilation Book of Figures threatened a rupture within the textual community that had formed around the *Liber florum*, limiting Bridget's access to it in ways that the New Compilation later found itself scrambling – with what was evidently her considerable help – to undo.

If Bridget's relationship to the *Liber florum* changed after 1308, as the work grew into what was meant to be its final form, the same may have been true with the visionary relationship with the Virgin it had initially seemed to make easy, but which now entered a period of deferral. Because she had obtained the third vacancy at Rozay, not the first, her entry into the house was long delayed. Punctiliously updating the record of the Virgin's interventions to the day (as was increasingly John's habit), the final references to Bridget in the two recensions of the Book of Visions note that, as of December 2, 1310 (in one case), and June 1, 1313 (in the other), she is still waiting patiently for her "promise" and her "place."[52] During these years, her vow to God made visible to all in her cropped hair, rough clothing, and unmarried state, she may have lived as a semi-religious. This would have been an obvious move for a woman in her situation, given the existence of beguinages in Orléans and

50 OC III.5: "Apparuit michi virgo Maria in quodam pilario depicta et subito in specie et forma pulcherime mulieris transmutata ... Et videbatur michi quod soror mea Burgeta erat iuxta me quando virgo Maria dixit michi verba predicta. Et dixit michi soror mea, 'Sufficiant vobis que dixit virgo Maria; faciatis librum vestrum, et quando erit factus ipsa videbit si bene erit factus vel non, et secundum hoc vobis respondebit.'"

51 OC III.15, 24.

52 I.iii.d: "Quam promissionem et locum deuote a tempore illo exspectauit predicta soror mea; et ad hoc exspectabat tempore illo quo paginam isti scripsi (scilicet anno incarnacionis Dominic mo. ccco. 3o decimo, kalendis Iunij)"; see Variants for the version of this passage containing the earlier date.

(intriguingly) also Étampes, where seventeenth-century evidence suggests the existence of a semi-religious community near the church of St. Gilles, only a mile from Morigny.[53] The second part of the New Compilation Book of Figures – a shortened revision of the earlier Book of Particular Experiments, which gives ground-rules for operators hoping to develop their own rituals – introduces an experiment of Bridget's devising as the work of "a religious woman" ("mulierem religiosam"), a phrase often used to designate those living an semi-religious life. It also adds the clarifying "in corde et animo" perhaps to imply by omission that, at the time to which it refers (before 1314), she was not yet religious by profession.[54]

In a careful adaptation of a passage from the *Ars notoria* that may well have been made by Bridget herself, the work then details her use of the Grace of Christ visionary petition prayer, the brief "O reuelatrix" – "O revealer of all secrets, O teacher of all the ignorant, reveal to me and teach me (*Here make your petition*) through your supernal power and grace" – at the bedside:[55]

> See then my sister's experiments. If someone wants to have a definite diagnosis about any sickness, whether it will lead to life or death, if the patient is lying down, stand before him and say secretly, "O reuelatrix," etc. And conclude the petition where it is supposed to be concluded. Afterwards question him as it occurs to you. If he answers you, "I am getting better," or something like that, know without doubt that the sick person is to live. But if he answers, "poorly" or "badly" or something similar, know without doubt that the sick one is to die. And if he does not answer at all, know that he is to die. And if he answers, "I don't know," he is likewise dead, or his sickness will change for the worse.[56]

53 For the royal beguinage at Orléans, see Tanya Stabler Miller, *The Beguines of Medieval Paris: Gender, Patronage, and Spiritual Authority* (Philadelphia: University of Pennsylvania Press, 2014), 250. The evidence for Étampes is sparse, but see Dom Basille Fleureau, *Les Antiquitez de la Ville et du Duché d'Estampes* (Paris, Coignard, 1683), Deuxième Partie, Chapitre XXIV, which references "un lieu d'assemblée de ces femmes devotes que l'on appelloit anciennement Beguines, dont la place est encore aujourd'huy appellée le Carrefour des Beguines. Il est situé au bout de la ruë de la Foulerie, vers saint Gilles, & il en est fait mention dans les vieils papiers terriers de l'Abbaye de Morigny," a claim further supported by a sixteenth-century street-name. See the online edition of this text at http://www.corpusetampois.com/che-17-fleureau-c24.html. Few Morigny records from the period now survive.

54 NC III.ii.4.a: "quandam sororem, mulierem religiosam corde et animo, ego habebam et habeo"; the unusual "habebam et habeo" presumably reflecting the fact that this passage is being recopied from the earlier book.

55 Prayer *5.4: "O reuelatrix omnium secretorum, O doctrix omnium ignorancium, reuela michi et doce me (hic exprime peticionem); per tuam supremam potenciam et graciam. Amen." Repeated in amplified form at NC III.i.3.c.

56 NC III.ii.4.b: "Ecce itaque experimenta sororis mee. Si enim aliquis voluerit habere congnicionem certam de aliqua egritudine, vtrum sit ad vitam vel ad mortem, si iacuerit langwens, assiste coram eo dic secrete, 'O reuelatrix,' et cetera. Et conclude peticionem vbi concludenda est. Postea interrogabis eum sicut tibi videtur. Quod si respondit tibi, 'bene conualescenciam,' vel aliquid talem, scias proculdubio quod ad vitam est infirmus. Si autem respondit, 'grauiter,' vel 'male,' vel aliquid simile, scias proculdubio quod ad mortem est infirmus. Si autem tibi non responderit, scias quod ad mortem est. Si autem responderit 'nescio,' similiter mors est, vel infirmitas mutabitur in grauius."

The prayer can also be used in situations when the patient is a child unable to speak or an older person is unwilling or unable to reply; when the sick person is far away; when feeling any sick person's pulse; in determining whether a girl is pregnant and whether she will then bear a girl, a boy, or twins; and so on. Many semi-religious were involved in visiting the sick, tending both to bodies and to souls. Knowledge of sickbed outcomes would have been invaluable, affecting whatever action had to be taken. Although the wording of the passage stays close to its source, Bridget must have had a specific need to develop this group of experiments, which required a personal license from the Virgin to operate. Indeed, John includes the ritual in part to give an example of an operation he has not himself won heavenly permission to use, in part, perhaps, because it involves communication with the Virgin in a waking state.[57] Bridget's interest in diagnosis, and her decision to develop an original experiment out of one of the most frequently used prayers of the *Liber florum,* presumably grew out of the exigencies of her life at the time.

Only at the outset of the third part of the New Compilation Book of Figures do we find a hint that, at some moment since June 1313, the Virgin had at last kept her promise of a place at Rozay to Bridget. Introducing the first vision of his new book in late September of 1315, and still stinging from the recent attacks of the barking dogs, John writes:

> And so, with the most fervent zeal for lofty contemplation coming to flower, with the grace of holy *Ruh* or *Pneuma* or Spirit proceeding from the Father and the Son marvelously indicating and administering it, and with the ardor of heavenly desire for salvation straightaway prevailing, the plough lately (in a sense) laid aside by me and my sister for a legitimate reason was again taken up by us. And afterwards just as before, by the selfsame promised counsel of the glorious Virgin, we were equally bound together by the bond of holy charity and set under the rein of holy obedience and the constraint of humility; and these things restrained us, and guided our way.[58]

Whatever is going on in detail in this complicated passage, it presents brother and sister as now "bound together" in a single way of life, yoked under one "plough," constrained by "charity," "obedience," and "humility," and lifted up by a "zeal for lofty contemplation" that circumstances had conspired for a time to thwart. By alluding to a principle laid down in Luke 9:62, "No man putting his hand to the plough, and looking back, is fit for the kingdom of God," a verse often used to attack those who desert the cloister, and by using the legal "ex causa legitima" to justify Bridget and

57 NC III.ii.4.

58 NC III.iii.1.a: "Florenti namque summe contemplacionis feruentissimo studio; Ruhi vel Pneumatis aut Spiritus Sancti a Patre et Filio procedentis gracia sugerente et mirabiliter ministrante; celestisque desiderij ardore continuo preualente salutis; aratro quodammodo a me et mea sorore ex causa legitima iam dimisso; et postea ipsa monicione promissa Virginis gloriose iterum a nobis similiter ut prius – eque sancte caritatis vinculo insimul colligatis et freno sancte obediencie et humilitatis coartacione iam positis et stringentibus iterque nostrum dirigentibus – reassumpto:"

John's apparent breach of this principle, the passage assumes a direct institutional parallel between the two.[59] This makes no sense if Bridget was still living as a semi-religious, a way of life that was canonically defined around the absence of the formal obligations to which John alludes here. It therefore seems probable that, like him, she had now become a Benedictine.

If so, however, the passage is as far as possible from being redolent of prayerful ease. On the contrary, as John goes on to imply in introducing the vision that grew out of this situation, it describes a scene of exhausted relief in which brother and sister are both worn out by the "extreme labors and struggles" that have been necessary in order to defend *Liber florum* "against those who were declaring this science to be fantasmic" – the barking dogs mentioned in the first part of this book.[60] In other words, almost as soon as Bridget entered the cloister it seems she had to leave it again, suspending her vow of stability (and the obligation to strict enclosure laid down in Boniface VIII's "Periculoso" of 1298).[61] I will go on to suggest that this may have been on account of the charges brought against the figures and dreams of *Liber florum*. Having risked one kind of danger in beginning her journey to the cloister by working with the spiritually perilous *Ars notoria*, she now risked the new dangers arising from her temporarily anomalous status as an uncloistered nun on the one hand and her association with the scandal consuming her brother's book on the other.

Although it surely implies more than John's need to have his sister at his side in a crisis, in the absence of any external evidence, we can only guess what had taken place to precipitate this passage. It seems possible, however, that Bridget and her brother had been obliged to attend an enquiry into the *Liber florum* in order to rebut the charges laid against its figures and dreams, and had (for the time) been successful. Such a formal or informal enquiry, possibly but not necessarily related to the work's later burning, could have been called by Morigny's archbishop or bishop in response to a complaint laid by the critics John calls "canes latrantes." These might have been Dominicans, "domini canes" as they were sometimes nicknamed.[62] Two likely venues would have been the archdiocesan court at Sens and the diocesan one at Paris.[63]

The passage marks the end of a hiatus of some weeks in the New Compilation, from mid-August when most of the first part of the work was written. During this hiatus, John presumably drafted the *questiones* he later copied into the book as defenses "against the gnawing of dogs and against poisoned tongues."[64] Two of these

59 "Ait ad illum Iesus nemo mittens manum suam in aratrum et aspiciens retro aptus est regno Dei."

60 NC III.iii.1.b, the opening of a description of a vision that takes place "post maximos labores et certamina et maxime post certamen obtentum contra illos qui dicebant scienciam istam esse fantasticam."

61 See Elizabeth Makowski, *Canon Law and Cloistered Women: Periculoso and Its Commentators, 1298–1545* (Washington, D.C.: Catholic University of America Press, 1999).

62 For this pun, see, David Burr, *Spiritual Franciscans: From Protest to Persecution in the Century After Saint Francis* (University Park, PA: Pennsylvania State University Press, 2001), 55–56 (thanks to Robert Lerner for this reference). Although Dominicans would indeed make the likeliest critics of the *Liber florum,* Burr offers few specific examples.

63 For the available processes used in investigating works suspected or doctrinal error, see Field, *The Beguine, the Angel, and the Inquisitor*, especially Chapters 3–4.

64 NC III.i.i.5.a: "Contra morsus latrancium et adversas lingwas toxicatas."

"invoke and adduce" the experience of "my sister, Bridget" as witness: one as proof that "this holy and marvelous science" is "stable, holy and true," not least because of its antagonism to the "nefarious arts" in general and the *Ars notoria* in particular; the other as proof that it is permitted by God, since it "augments faith, ... nurtures charity, confirms hope, instructs devotion, and constrains sin."[65] In the midst of the hiatus, on September 8, he also had a vision in which the Virgin spoke scornfully to him, "indignantly moving her entire head, nostrils and eyes" before exclaiming, "you are the fantasm of all the others,'" apparently acknowledging that "this science [of visionary dreams] is fantastical."[66] Clearly he was still under the same pressure he had been some weeks earlier, when (perhaps preparing for what lay ahead) he moved to replace the offending figures of the Old Compilation against the Virgin's wishes. It seems that Bridget, too, was under pressure. Having been imagined as a prosecuting witness in a fictive enquiry into the *Ars notoria* in the Book of Visions, she may have had to become a real witness at a public enquiry, this time for the defense.

## Operations

The many references to Bridget in the New Compilation Book of Figures allow us to go some way towards reconstructing the progress both of her professional career and of her role as an advocate for the "holy and marvelous science" communicated by the Virgin. In general terms, the references continue a literary strategy developed in the Book of Visions, in which Bridget's testimony is enfolded into the permanent record the book hands down to "successors" in order to exemplify the workings of its "science" and secure its claims to authenticity.[67] More locally, here relying on the ease with which medieval visionary women could be identified with sincere devotion – and potentially with their great heavenly exemplar, the Virgin – they invite us to associate her with the New Compilation's stated desire to prune away the elaborations of the Old Compilation and return the *Liber florum* to the primal simplicity it had temporarily lost.

But these references – a total of two to "sister," eight to "my sister," two to "my sister Bridget," and originally (we shall see) seven simply to "Bridget" – also return us to the question of the larger place she played in shaping the work, not as an inscribed character but as an early user, consultant, and colleague. Certain of them in particular ascribe to her a key role in two ritual innovations, one related to the sickbed "particular experiments" described in part two of the New Compilation Book of Figures, the

65 NC III.i.5: "ista sancta sciencia et mirabilis ... sit stabilis, sancta, et vera"; "invoco et adduco"; NC III.iii.3.g, "omne enim quod fidem auget, quod karitatem nutrit, spem firmat, devocionem instrvit, et quod peccatum constringit hoc dicitur esse permissiuum"; "artibus nepharijs." Compare NC III.iii.33.i.

66 NC III.iii.5.d: "Item, ex dictis Virginis gloriose, que dixit michi in quadam visione viijo ydus Septembris, petenti ab ipsa quid sibi videbatur de me. Que respondens ait, 'Tu es Spiritus Sancti receptaculum.' Et statim, sine interuallo, cum indignacione mouens capud omne, naribus et oculis subsannando subiunxit, 'Et tu es fantasma omnium aliorum' ... Ergo, ista sciencia fantastica est." See NC III.iii.5.h for John's positive interpretation of this difficult vision.

67 For "successores," see, e.g., NC III.iii.7.a.

other to the seven figures of the Virgin that become the book's substitute for the more specialized figures of its predecessor. Like the rest of the New Compilation Book of Figures, both innovations emphasize the availability of its "science" to a range of users. Yet neither of them features Bridget simply as a pastoral target. Rather, her part is to act as bridge between the non-clerical world and a ritual system that principally targets learned operators, but in which she herself has deep experience. As such, they exemplify relatively clearly what may in fact have been Bridget's most important contribution to the *Liber florum*: to keep the work true to its universalizing vision of learning in which the acquisition of knowledge of the world and God is taken to be so fundamental to human identity that it needs to be made available to all. It is Bridget who ensures that this vision – laid out in principle in didascalica from Hugh of St. Victor onwards but more often assumed to be attainable only through formal, clerical education – is honored in practice, not merely in theory.

Despite their emphasis on operating in the waking world, Bridget's sickbed experiments, which offer the most sustained example of personalized rituals provided by the New Compilation Book of Figures, are an outgrowth of several initiatives intended to tailor the work to different kinds of operators. Some of these operators are assumed to have worked through the entirety of the First and Second Procedures before deciding to specialize, garnering advanced knowledge of one or more single disciplines, petitioning for answers to specific questions, and so on.[68] Others, "who do not want to work through the whole body of this science, or cannot do so, but only [to use it] for having a vision," will have omitted this step, using a shorter version of the *Liber florum*, which is organized primarily around vision rituals and thus omits the prayers for the arts and sciences along with much else.[69] Although John's copy of the New Compilation was consecrated in such a way that it could also be used by Bridget, the personal copy that she would have needed once she was enclosed as a nun could, in principle, have provided the model for books of this shorter type, which are referred to in both versions of the Book of Figures.[70] Whether or not this is so, the versatility of the prayer "O reuelatrix" she demonstrates is key to the particular experiments for clerical and non-clerical operators alike. "For so great is the power of the prayer uttered in the aforesaid experiments and others like them," the work states on the basis of her achievement, "that it can be uttered effectively, as set forth above, without figure or ring."[71]

Yet while Bridget seems to have helped spearhead the shift towards the "particular experiment" that is a marked feature of the *Liber florum* in its later stages, the New Compilation Book of Figures is clear that she was not thereby to be excluded from the knowledge rituals of the First and Second Procedures. A distinctive feature of the Old Compilation figures was their inclusion of the names of their operator,

68 NC III.ii.2.a and 5.a.

69 NC III.iii.5, rubric: "qui nolunt operari per totum corpus huius sciencie, vel non possunt, set solummodo ad habendam visionem."

70 OC III. 24; NC III.i.11.b; NC III.iii.29.b; NC III.iii.5.a.

71 NC III.ii.5.f: "Tanta enim est virtus oracionis prefate in experimentis predictis et similibus – licencia prius operandi obtenta a Virgine gloriosa – quod sine figura et annulo proferri possit, ut premittitur, cum effectu."

"mixed with the name of the blessed Mary, and with the letters of the names of the property of the figures, and situated in the figures in the form of a cross," in such a way that customized versions with the proper lettering had to be produced for each new copy of the book.[72] John retained the basics of this structure, and thus of the principle that operators each require their own, ritually confirmed copy of the work, in devising his new figures. But in his first, failed effort to produce changes against the wishes of the Virgin he also attempted to introduce a system in which operators might add the names of "male or female colleagues, one or more" into the figures, alongside their own names, at will.[73]

Even after the Virgin unexpectedly forbade him to implement this system, responding "there is no way that this can be done" to his request "that all men and women whose names are written in the circumference can operate through [the figures], just as I do," he continued to petition for it in different form, asking her to "concede" to him "by special grace" to "set my sister's name there together with mine."[74] Indeed, he began the ritual process of drawing the new figures into his book immediately after he was sure he had won this concession, which happened only at his second attempt. The first vision which seemed to grant this concession he judged to have been infused with the presence of "a malign and fantasmal spirit," revealed to him in the contradictory nature of the Virgin's words and in the temptation to "a sin of the flesh" with which it ended – a clear, if "doubtful," sign of the urgency of the concession he was seeking.[75] Together with the defense of the *Liber florum* and the making of the "ring of the glorious Virgin," the effort to establish Bridget's name with John's "in the lower part of the figure to the right and the left of the feet of the image" in his exemplary copy of the figures is a key topic of the third part of the book.[76]

The system adopted for the New Compilation figures throws valuable incidental light on Bridget's relationship with the figures of the Old Compilation, suggesting that she had been making use of her brother's copy, rather than one of her own, but also indicating that she did perform rituals involving the figures with some regularity, either on her own or with John. Some such arrangement would have been a practical

72 OC I.iv.6: "Litere uero figurarum litere sunt nominis operantis mixte cum literis nominis beate Marie et cum literis nominum proprietatis figurarum et situate in figuris ad modum crucis."

73 NC III.i.2.d: "Et nomen opificis et sociorum suorum vel suarum, vnum vel plura, secundum quod sibi placuerit, scribat vel faciat scribi in circuitu figure."

74 NC III.iii.4.c: "Et postea pecij, 'Domina, confirmetis, supplico vobis, istas figuras tali modo quod omnes illi et ille quorum nomina in circuitu sunt scripta possunt per easdem operari, sicut et ego.' Que respondens, 'Hoc nequaquam fieri potest'"; "quod ex speciali gracia vellet michi concedere quod nomen sororis mee ibidem vna cum meo apponerem."

75 NC III.iii.11.a: "Postquam locuta fuit mecum beata Virgo, ita subtiliter inmiscuit se maligus spiritus et fantasticus verbis et dictis ipsius Virginis … quia finis responsionis ipsius visionis principio contrariebatur. Et illusione fantastica et in recessu carnis peccato temptauit me, et ideo de ipsa tota dubitaui."

76 NC III.iii.23.a: "Nomen vero opificis et illorum quos de gracia speciali poteris inpetrare in inferiori parte figure a146 dextris et a sinistris pedum ymaginis collocuntur." For examples of New Compilation figures with single names inscribed in them see *Liber florum*, Plates 7 and 9 (after 394). No figures with paired names are presently known.

response to the difficulties, not to say financial cost, of the Old Compilation, and might have allowed Bridget to participate in the development of certain of its rituals. More locally, the system also raises questions about how she used the new figures in practice, seeing that she and John seem by this point to have been separated by a two-day journey as well as by their respective cloister walls. Such evidence as we have gives ambiguous support for what would otherwise be one obvious possible answer, that the presence of a second name in the figures implicitly allowed for the production of a second copy.

However, the effects of John's success in petitioning the Virgin for special leave to "set my sister's name there together with mine, and that she might be able to operate as I do" are clear.[77] Not only does Bridget acquire the right to operate all the New Compilation rituals open to John – and in his absence as well as in his presence, if we are to take "operate as I do" seriously. It opens the door for subsequent operators in her situation to follow their joint lead, potentially makes each copy of the work into the center of a tiny textual community. Even though John states that "the name of my sister ... set in the figures of this book" is not intended to be "drawn" into later copies of the *Liber florum*, "since it is not part of the substance of the figures," its trace remains in surviving copies made for those who have achieved their own "special grace" from the Virgin and thus contain the names of two or three operators, not one.[78]

At a rhetorical level, moreover, the pairing of Bridget's name with John's in the visionary quest for the new figures that allows the book to conclude gives further color to the remarkable passage with which its final part opens, as brother and sister, having faced down the threat from the barking dogs, return with "fervent zeal" to their lives of "lofty contemplation." Physically separated as they are, they are now joined imaginatively in the "ardor of heavenly desire for salvation" every time either of them uses the figures of the Virgin containing their paired names. An analogous effect is available for those who come after, for whom the part that Bridget's name plays in her brother's figures serves as a reminder that the "science" of infused wisdom tends towards a collective good, not an individual one, and is ultimately a work of charity, who "gives away her own property," as John explicitly gives the book to the world.[79] John is conscious that he alone is the human author of the *Liber florum*, noting the day and time he finishes the book in the Lady Chapel at Morigny and adding both an affirmation of Catholic faith and a clause aimed at protecting associates such as Bridget: "whatever we ourselves have said is not to be imputed to

77 NC III.iii.4.c: "quod nomen sororis mee ibidem vna cum meo apponerem et quod posset operari sicut et ego."

78 NC III.iii.32.a: "Notandum vero est quod nomen sororis mee quod appositum est in figuris huius libri non est de substancia figurarum, vna cum meo, cum illud de gracia speciali inpetrauimus. Et ideo non est trahendum ad consequencia." For confirmation prayers that include two or three names, see Variants at NC III.iii.29.

79 NC III.iii.36.c: "Caritas ... propria largitur eius." as does John in ending his book: "Eciam virtutem nostram, propria largituri sumus, et largimus, et bonum nobis visum fuit, et videtur, elargiri."

others."[80] But as their paired names remind us, she is the first link in the chain of its users. It is only on the basis of her witness that these "successors" know that the book "came from the blessed Mary."[81]

## Conclusion

In setting out to follow the contemplative trail her brother had blazed, Bridget met the obstacles endemic to being younger and a girl: the assumption that she would marry, a consequent lack of education, small choice of religious houses, and initially insufficient family funds to finance a second monastic career. These obstacles took a decade to overcome. Bridget may never have acquired flawless Latin and spent years tending the sick at a time of life when her brother was at university improving his education. She survives to us as a historical actant, fragments of whose career can be speculatively reconstructed, only because he wrote about her. Despite the many and varied traces she leaves across the *Liber florum,* we are likely never to know the extent of her role in the composition and dissemination of the work, nor just how, over time, she used it.

Nonetheless, these traces are too strong for it to be credible that the *Liber florum* could have taken anything like the forms it did without her. John often wrote with her in mind; drew on her experience as a user of his and others' rituals; made prominent use of her experiments; asked her to testify to the holiness of his work and of his intentions in producing it; and clearly consulted with her on numerous occasions. Especially as the work draws to a close, signs multiply of her presence behind the scenes and of her brother's unabashed dependence on her.

It remains possible, moreover, that Bridget opened a way into the *Liber florum* for other women anxious to share the opportunity to benefit from the access to earthly and heavenly knowledge it promised. Although the search is far from complete, the more than twenty copies of the work found so far are linked to male users and religious houses. But in one form or another the work seems likely to have played a part in convents such as Rozay. The small body of evidence uncovered so far that some of its prayers circulated independently already suggests it moved beyond the monastery and the clerical world.[82] It is possible that an account of how this happened and with what consequences may one day make a further chapter in Bridget's story.

80 NC III.iii.36..c: "Quidquid enim diximus ipsi non alijs inputetur."

81 NC III.iii.7.a: "quod ipsa erat ex parte Virginis."

82 See Fanger, "Introduction B," Table 13 (133), items 20–24.

# PART IV

# MULTIDISCIPLINARY APPROACHES TO GENDER, PATRONAGE, AND POWER

Preface to Part IV

# METHODOLOGICAL INNOVATIONS FOR THE STUDY OF WOMEN'S AUTHORSHIP AND AGENCY

NICHOLAS WATSON

Until not many decades ago, despite the pioneering early efforts of Eileen Power and a few others, it seemed to most scholars that there was too little evidence to say anything much about the role of women in medieval intellectual and institutional culture.[1] David Knowles, great student of English monasticism, considered the materials surviving from convents too sparse and confusing to be worth detailed study, devoting a distinguished career to the study of monks and their foundations in incongruous isolation from their female counterparts.[2] As happens all too often in medieval studies, absence of evidence was confused with evidence of absence. Unaware of the great trove of surviving Latin, French, and English books associated with late-medieval nuns and too ready to equate learning with Latin learning, even Power imagined that, after the Anglo-Saxon period, England's convents had become intellectually stultified, ripe for the teasing treatment Chaucer metes out to the Prioress with her bad French, genteel preciosity, and passionate anti-intellectualism in *The Canterbury Tales*.

Although feminist scholarship has been justly critical of certain of the assumptions earlier generations brought to the study of medieval women, this was not necessarily anyone's fault. After all, if prejudice and even misogyny were sometimes part of the problem, even now new evidence for medieval women's roles and activities remains far from easy to come by. This seems to be partly because, in a patriarchal society, women were at a nearly consistent disadvantage when it came to building the kinds of institutions that kept and preserved records and partly because these records, which seldom set out to answer the specific questions we ask of them, are so often silent about issues of gender at just the moments when we most want them not to be. In many medieval contexts, gender offered a less pertinent basis for categorization than social estate, ecclesiastical estate, citizenship, or affiliation with parish, guild, manor, or household. Women escape notice for the reason that the records for the most part

1 Eileen Power, *Medieval English Nunneries, c. 1275–1535* (Cambridge: Cambridge University Press, 1922).

2 David Knowles, *The Monastic Order in England: A History of Its Development from the Times of St Dunstan to the Fourth Lateran Council, 943–1216* (Cambridge: Cambridge University Press, 1940); *The Religious Orders in England*, 3 vols. (Cambridge: Cambridge University Press, 1948–59). For a critique, see Marilyn Oliva, *The Convent and the Community in Late Medieval England: Female Monasteries in the Diocese of Norwich, 1350–1540* (Woodbridge: Boydell Press, 1996), 3–4.

treat them, simply, as people. To search for traces of the intellectual activities of all but the most prominent medieval women – or even to seek to discover how such activities were regarded in practice, rather than institutional theory or literary fiction – we must thus not only work from the particular to the general, reconstructing women's intellectual culture from the study of individual books, texts, records, and details. We must also cultivate a supple and imaginative attitude to what constitutes evidence and how it is best to be read. Even more than in other areas of medieval studies, most of the real advances made in the field over the past thirty years are the product of a mixture of patient research and methodological innovation.

The chapters gathered in this section offer excellent examples of this mixture at work. Diverse in subject-matter, spanning multiple centuries of English history, and equally diverse in approach, drawing on different kinds of record and advancing different kinds of argument, they share a common concern with unearthing new information and a common awareness that to do so requires thinking resourcefully on one's methodological feet. They recognize that scholarship in this field is accretive and slow. Through the fiercely focused energies the authors bring to their several topics, they nonetheless remind us that all advances in this particular field are of consuming interest.

The first chapter in Part IV, Leanne MacDonald's "Written with her Own Hand: Perpetua's Representation of Non-Binary Gender in Old English Hagiography" (Chapter 11), works outwards from an Old English account of "virile women": the brief narrative of Perpetua and Felicity that constitutes the entry for March 7 in the early ninth-century legendary known as the *Old English Martyrology*. Others have written about the complex gender play in this work, but MacDonald asks us to attend to two details that seem to reflect individualized responses to that play among the communities that made and copied it. In reporting Perpetua's premonitory dream of martyrdom in which she becomes a man to fight the enemy, the *Martyrology* uniquely bestows on her a sword and describes her, not as undergoing bodily transformation, but as *looking like* a man, representing the shift less as metamorphosis than as a performance. As MacDonald explains:

> Perpetua of Carthage was an extremely rare example of a woman intellectual whose words appear in the Old English vernacular. As a person who experienced gender identity as non-binary, albeit briefly, Perpetua sets an example for later Anglo-Saxon writers on saints who live with both masculine and feminine gender identities, like Ælfric in *Lives of Saints* and the compiler of the *Old English Martyrology*. Thus, although she lived several centuries before the Anglo-Saxon period, Perpetua stands as an influential woman intellectual in Anglo-Saxon England.[3]

As MacDonald has shown elsewhere, copyists of Ælfric's account of Eugenia's life as abbot of a male religious community similarly negotiate the awkward business of how to refer to a saintly woman in her male guise, representing the author's decisions

3 Private correspondence, Dec. 15, 2018.

differently, "divided" on "whether or not they recognize [the saint's] masculinity." Source study is an established way for scholars to explore medieval gender trouble, but the analysis of textual variants to this end is more or less new. MacDonald not only puts this approach on the map; she shows us scribes worrying over the same issues as authors and translators, participants in what emerges as a continuing cultural conversation about the carefully constructed conundrum represented by the saintly figures whose memories they are laboring to preserve.

If the *Martyrology* is silent about the fact that Perpetua wrote part of her own *passio*, Ælfric draws a clear link between Eugenia's education and her conversion and election as abbot, presenting her explicitly as a Christian woman intellectual, learned in Greek philosophy and Latin eloquence ("Greciscre uðwytengunge and Lædenre getingnysse").[4] But as the two other chapters in Part IV show, intellectualism comes in different guises. For Anna Siebach-Larsen, an aristocratic patroness may also require us to consider her in this light. The illuminated *Q* that begins Robert Grosseteste's great theological romance, the *Chasteau d'amour*, in a sumptuous late thirteenth-century insular French compilation represents Joan Tateshal, who commissioned the book, in intimate colloquy with the learned bishop. Clearly Tateshal, whose likeness appears elsewhere in the book, expects us to see her as a model beneficiary of its teaching. We might also see the image as representing her claim, as an aristocratic laywoman who is properly addressed in French verse, to be accepted as the co-creator of the works contained in the book, hailing them, as it were, into being. Yet these images do not only depict the book's spiritual and material economy, they are part of that economy, as co-producers of its meaning. Musing on the methodological opportunities and pitfalls the text/image relationship sets up for discussions of women's intellective experience, Siebach-Larsen argues that the Tateshal images ask to be understood through the metaphysics of light expounded in the *Chasteau*, especially around the figure of the Virgin Mary, earthly vehicle of divinity itself. Illuminated by the gold that surrounds her image, the wealthy patroness gives herself to the reader-viewer as an object of contemplation in her own right, a light-filled medium of the transcendent. The "cognitive life" sustained by thirteenth-century books like this one is embodied as well as abstract, conceptually as well as sensually grounded in its own material form. As we found in MacDonald's study of a different kind of neglected evidence, textual variants, to recognize this fact is to engage more closely with the intellectual world of the book than we can hope to do through study of its texts alone.

The well-born wife of a powerful baron, Joan Tateshal had the wealth and social capital to leave behind compelling evidence not only of her reading and thinking, but also of how she hoped to be remembered: as a lively and generative presence in the religious culture of her era. In thirteenth-century England, lucid self-memorialization like this was difficult for women even a few rungs down the social ladder, such as the London sisters whose wills are the focus of Amanda Bohne's chapter, Isabella Bukerel and Johanna Vyel. Our access to their intellectual and emotional lives is restricted to what we can deduce from the legally savvy ways in which they disposed their goods

4 Ælfric, "Natale Sancte Eugenie Virginis," in *Ælfric's Lives of Saints*, ed. and trans. W.W. Skeat, Early English Text Society o.s. 76 (London: N. Trübner, 1881), 26, line 21.

and chattels and the spiritual, familial, and perhaps romantic concerns implied by the specific decisions they made. Bukerel was wealthy by most standards, a property-holder with sufficient capital to keep a chaplain and endow a chantry chapel without neglecting the economic future of her kin. Vyel, who was single, may have been less so but had sufficient resources both to carry out her sister's dying wishes and to imitate her sister by making a special gift to this chaplain, William de St. Alban, later vicar of Kenardington in Kent. Bohne intriguingly suggests that Bukerel and her cleric were sexually attached in the informal fashion preferred both by many late-medieval minor clergy hoping for career advancement and, no doubt, by many well-off widows and that Vyel's further bequest to him acknowledged the abiding importance of this relationship to the family. It is perhaps not out of the question that it was Vyel, presumably the younger of the sisters, to whom de St. Alban was, for a time, "unmarried." At any event, the two wills and the fragments of further evidence that relate to the sisters and their properties offer precious testimony to the complex lives lived by later medieval urban women of conventional piety and their capable efforts to balance competing demands and desires. Chaucer's parodic portrait of a wealthy urban laywoman, the Wife of Bath, childless and without family responsibilities as she is, massively and doubtless purposefully misses the point.

11

# WRITTEN WITH HER OWN HAND: PERPETUA'S REPRESENTATION OF NON-BINARY GENDER IN OLD ENGLISH HAGIOGRAPHY

LEANNE MACDONALD

The intellectual influence of women of letters in Old English can be difficult to detect. The evidence for women's participation in Latin literary culture is more readily available: the correspondence of Boniface, for example, reveals a network of learned women religious involved in the exchange and production of religious books.[1] The English nun Leoba even sends Boniface a sample of original poetry, explaining that she has been taught to compose verse by her abbess Eadburga.[2] There is also evidence of women as historians and hagiographers in early medieval England, as Diane Watt has recently argued – the compiler of the ninth-century *Old English Martyrology* and Bede were likely indebted to the work of nuns' local historiography and hagiography as sources for the lives of the holy women of their communities.[3] Although the traces of women-authored texts may be detectable in the *Old English Martyrology*, one of the earlier extant texts in Old English, there are no known women writers in that language before 1150.[4] According to Lees and Overing, however, the apparent lack of women writers in Old English represents not a dead end in the historiography of British women's writing, but an opportunity to expand our notion of what it means to participate in the production of writing in early medieval England: "these problems become opportunities to revise the scholarly paradigms of how we think about and identify women's agency as writers, readers, and participants in the production of literature and of culture."[5] One way of revising these scholarly paradigms is to pay due attention to the models of authorship and literary agency that are particular to

1 Clare A. Lees and Gillian R. Overing, "Women and the Origins of English Literature," *The History of Women's Writing*, 700–1500, ed. Liz Herbert McAvoy and Diane Watt (London: Palgrave MacMillan, 2010), 35.

2 *The Letters of Saint Boniface*, trans. Ephraim Emerton (New York: Columbia University Press, 1940), 37–38.

3 Diane Watt, "The Earliest Women's Writing? Anglo-Saxon Literary Cultures and Communities," *Women's Writing* 20.4 (2013): 537–54 and Christine Rauer, *Old English Martyrology: Edition, Translation, and Commentary* (Cambridge: D. S. Brewer, 2013). For more on Bede's relationships with intellectual women colleagues, see Sarah Foot's "Bede's Abbesses," Chapter 14 in this volume.

4 Lees and Overing, "Women and the Origins of English Literature," 31.

5 Ibid., 32.

the manuscript culture, in which a text is created throughout the transmission process of translation, copying, and compilation. Another is to reconsider early medieval notions of auctoritas, which gave more currency to ancient writers like Augustine and Orosius than any contemporary English writer, expanding our notion of early medieval English literary culture temporally to consider a potential auctrix: Perpetua of Carthage.[6]

Perpetua is unusual among women saints venerated in the Middle Ages in that she tells her own story in the form of prison diaries that were incorporated into the third-century *Passio Sanctarum Perpetuae et Felicitatis*. The autohagiographical account of Perpetua's martyrdom, "conscriptum manu sua et suo sensu reliquit" [written with her own hand and according to her experiences], is remarkable in its early date and partial authorship by the saint herself in an era with very few women writers.[7] Furthermore, the *Passio* stands out as an early example of a text featuring the first-person experience of gender identity that falls outside a socially and biologically determined gender binary, in the form of a divine vision in which Perpetua relates "facta sum masculus" [I became a male].[8] While there were other accounts of Perpetua's passion available in the early Middle Ages, such as a narrative from the *Acta Sanctorum* that does not incorporate Perpetua's writings, Margaret Cotter-Lynch has demonstrated that the *Old English Martyrology* follows the pattern of other early English accounts of Perpetua by eschewing the *Acta*, the more popular version on the continent. Cotter-Lynch writes that "whereas the *Acta*, Augustine's sermons, and the works of Ado of Vienne and Notker all downplay or eradicate the gender ambiguity suggested by the *Passio*, English texts often emphasize the gladiatorial aspects of Perpetua's story, depicting her sanctity in ways that, like the *Passio*, challenge conventional gender categories."[9] Thus, though the intervening centuries have resulted in many mediations of the *Passio*, English authors perennially return to Perpetua's words.

Not only does the *Old English Martyrology* turn to Perpetua's written words as a primary source on the subject of martyrdom, but the text highlights and augments the unconventional aspects of her gender identity. The format of the collection only allows for a brief description of each saint, and the compiler has chosen to focus almost entirely on this vision: "þære Perpetuan mætte þa heo wæs on mædenhade þæt heo wære on wæres hiwe ond ðæt heo hæfde sweord on handa, ond ðæt heo stranglice fuhte mid þy" [Perpetua dreamt when she was a maiden that she had the appearance of a man and that she had a sword in hand and that she fought strongly with it].[10] Though the Old English version describes this transformation as gaining "wæres hiwe" rather than literally becoming a man, it also goes as far as to claim that her dream is actually fulfilled: "þæt wæs eall eft on hire martyrdome gefylled, ða heo

6 Alistair Minnis, *Medieval Theory of Authorship: Scholastic Literary Attitudes in the Later Middle Ages* (Philadelphia: University of Pennsylvania Press, 1984), 12.

7 Thomas Heffernan, *The Passion of Perpetua and Felicity (New York, Oxford University Press, 2012)*, 5.

8 Ibid., 112. All translations are mine, unless otherwise noted.

9 Cotter-Lynch, *Saint Perpetua across the Middle Ages: Mother, Gladiator, Saint (New York: Palgrave Macmillan, 2016)*, 113.

10 Rauer, *Old English Martyrology*, 62.

mid werlice geðohte deofol oferswiððe ond þa hæþnan ehteras" [That was all fulfilled afterwards in her martyrdom, when she overcame the devil and heathen persecutors with manly determination].[11] Masculinity is asserted as being a crucial part of Perpetua's identity when it is "gefylled" [fulfilled] in waking life rather than simply relegated to a dream state. The original suggestion that Perpetua experiences more than one gender identity in the course of her martyrdom comes from the saint herself, and the compiler of the *Old English Martyrology* has the power to legitimize Perpetua's simultaneous masculine and feminine identities by selecting and shaping the details of the martyrology entry.[12]

A reconsideration of Perpetua's place in the culture of early medieval England gives a fuller picture of the influence of women intellectuals in general during the period as well as highlighting greater gender diversity among writers on gender that were read in early medieval England. One of the effects of the apparent dearth of women writers in this period, according to Helene Scheck, is that representations of women are shaped by the goals and biases of male writers:

> Masculinist constructions of the female subject dominate, therefore, especially in the later Anglo-Saxon period, often representing women stereotypically and artificially in a few carefully delineated domestic, rather than public, roles. Devoid of any connection to active female subjectivity, such representations of women become a mirror, the perfect reflection of the patriarchal order.[13]

She argues that those writers who had a vested interest in the Church as the central power in England, including Ælfric, employed this "linguistic monopoly" to retain tight control over any potential subversion in circulating religious texts.[14] The potential for subversion of the patriarchal order is particularly salient in a set of texts that appears to undermine the very concept of binary and hierarchal gender that constitutes the patriarchal order in the first place. The *vitae* and *passiones* of saints designated as female (or occasionally male) early in life who live part of their lives under the name, clothing, and identity of another gender, often called "transvestite" or "cross-dressing" saints, appear in many hagiographic collections throughout the Middle Ages from Northern Europe to North Africa and Western Asia. This subgenre is represented in Old English by Eugenia and Euphrosyne in Ælfric's *Lives of Saints* as well as Pelagia, Eugenia, and Thecla in the *Old English Martyrology*. We may also add Perpetua in the *Old English Martyrology* to this number; although she does not take on the clothing or identity of a man in any sustained way during her life, she describes herself as taking on aspects of both masculine and feminine identities in the time leading up to her martyrdom. Perpetua's words and their use in the *Old English Martyrology* stand out as a rare example

11 Ibid.

12 For commentary on Perpetua's gender in the Latin *passio*, see Craig Williams, "Perpetua's Gender," *Perpetua's Passions: Multidisciplinary Approaches to the Passio Perpetuae et Felicitatis*, ed. Jan N. Bremmer and Marco Formisano (Oxford: Oxford University Press, 2012).

13 Helene Scheck, *Reform and Resistance: Formations of Female Subjectivity in Early Medieval Ecclesiastical Culture* (Albany: State University of New York Press, 2009), 24.

14 Ibid., 84.

of the intellectual influence of a named woman writer appearing in Old English. Moreover, Perpetua's participation in the early medieval English representation of gender provides an opportunity to listen to more voices on the topic of gender diversity.

### Auctoritas, Augustine, and Reception of the *Passio*

The identification of Perpetua as both a "woman" and a "writer" is rather complicated and has been the subject of some debate. Perpetua is identified as a female saint and uses feminine language to refer to herself in general but also experiences complexity in her gender identity when she receives a vision in which she becomes male. The competing and multilayered representations of Perpetua's gender begin with the *Passio Sanctarum Perpetuae et Felicitatis* itself, in which Perpetua's declaration that she becomes a man in her divine vision appears in a complex narrative voice. This voice is created when Perpetua relates the aforementioned gladiatorial dream vision in her *Passio*. The most explicit complication of Perpetua's gender identity comes the day before the saint is sent to her death in the Carthage amphitheatre, when she finds herself in the arena with an Egyptian wrestler who is so large that he exceeds the size of the amphitheatre.[15] As the would-be wrestler prepares for the ensuing match, the narrative voice reports: "Et expoliata sum, et facta sum masculus" [And I was stripped naked, and I became a male].[16] Perpetua, as a male wrestler, is then rubbed with oil by assistants before successfully causing the massive Egyptian to fall to the ground. Perpetua's nakedness and the practice of rubbing a wrestler with oil before a match place emphasis on concrete physicality and mean that the saint does not metaphorically, mentally, or emotionally become a man in the vision – Perpetua's male body is seen by everyone and touched by several other men. Within the same text, Perpetua's physical body is highlighted in her account of herself as a lactating mother, which shows her physical body performing an act with deep connections to social constructions of womanhood and a female reproductive role.[17] This highlights her fulfillment of both masculine and feminine roles as she describes her final days. Within the short space of Perpetua's imprisonment and martyrdom, the saint's maleness and femaleness, as well as her masculinity and femininity, are crucial elements in her journey towards God.

Some modern scholars, like Craig Williams, have argued that Perpetua's vision is to be read as a dream and a metaphor for her active struggle and endurance of violence on behalf of her faith, rather than any definitive declaration of gender transformation.[18] Perpetua's status as a writer and a person who challenged normative gender binaries was reinforced by an undisputed *auctor* in early medieval England: Augustine of Hippo. Aaron J. Kleist points out that nearly a tenth of surviving manuscripts from the period contain material attributed to Augustine, and King Alfred declared Augustine's *Soliloquies* to be one of the essential texts "ða ðe niedbeðearfosta sien eallum monnum to wiotonne" [that are the most necessary for all people to

15 Heffernan, *The Passion of Perpetua and Felicity*, 112.

16 Ibid.

17 Stamiata Dova, "Lactation Cessation and the Realities of Martyrdom in *The Passion of Saint Perpetua*," *Illinois Classical Studies* 42. 1 (2017).

18 Williams, "Perpetua's Gender," 54–77.

know].[19] Augustine comments on Perpetua in *De natura et origine anima*, which can be found in three extant manuscripts, and Rauer has suggested that his *Sermones* 280–82 influenced the Perpetua and Felicity entry in the *Old English Martyrology*.[20] While, as Vincent Hunink points out, "even Augustine cannot be blindly trusted" when it comes to the facts surrounding Perpetua and her authorship of the *Passio*, the Church Father's authoritative opinions on Perpetua provide a window into how at least some of her early Christian readers interpreted the *Passio*. Moreover, Augustine's *auctoritas* in early medieval England indicates that his opinions on the saint were likely within the mainstream.

Others have voiced skepticism over whether we can be certain that Perpetua was the true author of the first-person section of the *Passio*. Heffernan and Hunink posit that many of these objections, however, are based on entrenched assumptions about the nature and abilities of women in late antiquity, rather than on concrete textual or historical evidence that might cast doubt on the narrative attribution of authorship.[21] In the Middle Ages, the textual attribution of authorship to Perpetua herself was reinforced by Augustine's commentary on the text, as Augustine straightforwardly presents the work as that of the future martyr, describing it as a text that "beata Perpetua… narravit" [the blessed Perpetua told was revealed to her about herself]. Clearly, Augustine and his readers from late antiquity onward did not necessarily find this claim to authorship suspect or problematic.[22] Even if other models of authorship are proposed, such as Ronsse's suggestion that Perpetua may have delivered her testimony orally, Augustine's commentary establishes a tradition of Perpetua as a woman writer in the eyes of her medieval readers and translators.[23]

Just as Augustine lends veracity to Perpetua's role as an early woman writer, he also establishes that although Perpetua's transformation into a man takes place in a dream vision, it held more significance to its early Christian audience than a mere fantasy or a metaphor. In his treatise *De natura et origine animae*, Saint Augustine cites Perpetua's nocturnal masculinity as evidence of the soul's ability to take on a likeness that differs from the body:

19 Aaron J. Kleist, *Striving With Grace: Views of Free Will in Anglo-Saxon England* (Toronto: University of Toronto Press, 2008), 3 and Daniel Anlezark, "Which Books are 'Most Necessary' to Know? The Old English Pastoral Care Preface and King Alfred's Educational Reform," *English Studies* 98.8 (2017): 760.

20 Helmust Gneuss and Michael Lapidge, *Anglo-Saxon Manuscripts: A Bibliographical Handlist of Manuscripts and Manuscript Fragments Written or Owned in England up to 1100* (Toronto: University of Toronto Press, 2014), 894 and Rauer, *The Old English Martyrology*, 243.

21 Heffernan, *The Passion of Perpetua and Felicity*, 3–6 and Vincent Hunink, "Did Perpetua Write Her Prison Account?" *Folia Philologica* 133.1 (2010): 147–55.

22 Augustine, "Sermones, Part 1," *Saint Augustine: Opera Omnia – Corpus Augustinianum Gissense. Electronic Edition*, ed. Cornelius Mayer (Charlottesville, VA: Intelex Corp., 2000), 1281–86. For skeptics, see Ross S. Kraemer and Shira L. Lander, "Perpetua and Felicitas," *The Early Christian World*, ed. Philip F. Esler (London and New York: Routledge, 2000), 1048–68 and Heidi Vierow, "Feminine and Masculine Voices in the 'Passion of Saints Perpetua and Felicitas,'" *Latomus* 58.3 (1999): 600.

23 Erin Ronsse, "Rhetoric of Martyrs: Listening to Saints Perpetua and Felicitas," in *Journal of Early Christian Studies* 14.3 (2006): 300.

> quis autem dubitet in illa similitudine corporis animam eius fuisse, non corpus, quod utique in suo femineo sexu manens sopitis sensibus iacebat in stratis, quando anima eius in illa uirilis corporis similitudine luctabatur?
>
> [But who can doubt that it was her soul in the likeness of a body, not a body, which surely remained in its female sex, and lay in bed with its senses having been lulled to sleep, while her soul struggled in the likeness of a man's body?][24]

Augustine maintains that Perpetua's soul is in the "similitudine" or *likeness* of a body, since he denies that souls have a corporeal form and rejects the notion that Perpetua has undergone any literal physical transformation. Although her soul lacks a physical form, however, it is nevertheless actively engaged in a struggle rather than passively receiving a vision or slumbering along with the rest of Perpetua as she visualizes an imagined conflict. The soul in the likeness of a man's body is real because it is actually "struggling" [luctabatur], rather than experiencing the sensation of a struggle. Augustine aims to clear up any confusion about Perpetua's transformation but retains a sense that both the female body that sleeps and the soul (which is not given a natural gender) in the likeness of a male body that struggles are simultaneously participating in Perpetua's narrative. Despite any ambiguities raised by Augustine over whether Perpetua really was transformed into a man in body as she slept, he is clear that Perpetua has a dual identity in this moment.

Augustine's shaping of opinion on Perpetua in early medieval England is apparent in the influence of *Sermones* 280 through 282 on the *Old English Martyrology*. As J. E. Cross points out, "the phrase 'mid werlice geðohte' echoes *virilis animus* in Augustine… and the idea that Perpetua was manly in behaviour although feminine in form is one emphasized in the sermons."[25] Indeed, *Sermo* 280 begins with a reference to Perpetua's experience of multiple gender identities and how we, as the audience, should understand them.[26] Augustine alludes to Galatians 3:28 and the idea that there is no male or female in Christ and attributes this lack of gender to the "interior man": "secundum interiorem hominem, nec masculus, nec femina inueniuntur" [According to the interior man, neither male nor female is found]. [27] He goes on to argue that we ought not pay attention to Perpetua's outward sex if it does not match her deeds: "ut etiam in his quae sunt feminae corpore, virtus mentis sexum carnis abscondat, et in membris pigeat cogitare, quod in factis non potuit apparere" [So that even in those who are women in body, the strength of the mind conceals the sex of the flesh, and it grieves one to think about that in the members which

24 Augustine, "De anima et eius origine," in *Saint Augustine: Opera Omnia – Corpus Augustinianum Gissense. Electronic Edition*, ed. Cornelius Mayer (Charlottesville, VA: Intelex Corp., 2000), 405.

25 J. E. Cross, "The Latinity of the Ninth-Century Old English Martyrologist," *Studies in Earlier Old English Prose*, ed. Paul E. Szarmach (Albany: State University of New York Press, 1984), 298.

26 Augustine, "Sermones, Part 1," *Saint Augustine: Opera Omnia – Corpus Augustinianum Gissense. Electronic Edition*, ed. Cornelius Mayer (Charlottesville, VA: Intelex Corp., 2000), 1281–86.

27 Ibid., 1281.

could not appear in deeds].[28] Here Augustine depicts a "sexum carnis" [sex of the flesh] that may or may not be reflected "in factis" [in deeds]. To focus solely on the sex of the flesh is not only reductive, but something to be avoided, as Augustine emphasizes with the word "pigeo" [to feel annoyance or reluctance at]. Perpetua's experience of non-binary gender comes from her own text, but Augustine's authority helps to reinforce and further disseminate Perpetua's narrative characterization of gender.

## Perpetua in the *Old English Martyrology*

The compiler of the *Old English Martyrology* places attention on Perpetua's own narrative voice, though the short entry is told in the third-person narrative, by recognizing Perpetua's masculinity and its ultimate fulfillment by singling it out as an important aspect of her martyrdom alongside her femininity. In her study of the medieval reception and transmission of Perpetua and Felicitas, Erin Ronsse notes the rhetorical agency of the *Old English Martyrology* compiler by arguing that "the *Old English Martyrology* innovatively highlights the personal force of Perpetua and Felicitas in achieving visionary and prophetic knowledge that enabled their public triumphs."[29] Ronsse also notes that Early English Text Society editor George Herzfeld sees the differences between the *Old English Martyrology* text and Latin sources as erroneous and especially focuses on the detail of the sword in Perpetua's hand, writing: "it is therefore wrong to say that P. had a sword in her hand."[30] Herzfeld argues that this and other so-called mistakes make for a "confused and unsatisfactory presentment of the legends," which he attributes to Latin incompetence on the part of the compiler.[31] Cross and Ronsse both defend the interpretive agency of the compiler, with Cross asserting the martyrologist's "right of choice to include or omit what he wished"[32] and Ronsse affirming that "where Herzfeld sees confusion, I suggest that we may see interpretive sensitivity and skill, complexity and commemorative sophistication."[33] In embracing Perpetua's multivalent gender identity as she presents it with her own hand, the narrative affirms Perpetua's vision and prioritizes her actions as the source of her holiness.

The compiler's rhetorical skill in placing emphasis on Perpetua's agency as well as her dual gender identity is evident in the text's description of the saint's sword-wielding masculinity and the ultimate fulfillment of her dream in the *Old English Martyrology*.[34] In choosing not to narrate any portion of Perpetua's life except this dream, omitting any details of Perpetua's imprisonment or the contents of her other extraordinary dreams, the martyrologist keeps the Anglo-Saxon audience

28 Ibid.

29 Ronsse, "Rhetoric of Martyrs: Transmission and Reception History of the "Passion of Saints Perpetua and Felicitas," PhD dissertation, University of Victoria, 2007, 106.

30 *An Old English Martyrology*, ed. George Herzfeld (London: EETS, 1900), 226.

31 Ibid.

32 Cross, "The Latinity of the Ninth-Century Old English Martyrologist," 284.

33 Ronsse, "Rhetoric of Martyrs: Transmission and Reception," 116.

34 Rauer, *Old English Martyrology*, 62.

focused on gladiation. The martyrologist complicates the simplicity of "facta sum masculus" by reminding the reader that Perpetua was "on mædenhade" [in her maidenhood], either using the term to connote any young woman or glossing over the saint's recent motherhood. After seemingly tempering Perpetua's masculinity by bringing together her "mædenhade" and "wæres hiwe," as well as maintaining feminine pronouns throughout, the *Old English Martyrology* takes Perpetua's complex gender identity a step further than does the *Passio*. The text affirms that it has been "gefylled" in waking life and repeats that Perpetua is as "werlice" in her battle with her earthly persecutors as she is in her battle with a dream giant. In doing so, this brief passage collapses Perpetua's multiple textual *personae*, as well as her unconscious and waking lives, into a complex whole that allows masculinity and femininity to exist at the same time.

The translator and compiler of the *Old English Martyrology*'s choice to make Perpetua's self-described masculinity a central feature of the text was not a foregone conclusion. The dream in which Perpetua is transformed so that she has the appearance of a man is a striking episode in the *Passio*, to be sure, but it is not necessarily the inevitable point of focus in such an abbreviation. Bede's *Martyrologies*, for example, which were used as one of the sources for the *Old English Martyrology*, recount that "Perpetuae inter alia concessum est ut eius mens quodammodo avertaretur a corpore, in quo vaccae impetum pertulit: ...gestum esse nesciret" [Among other things it was granted to Perpetua that her mind would somehow be turned away from her body, in which she endured the attack of a cow: ... she did not know what was then happening].[35] Instead of praising Perpetua's masculinity in fighting against adversaries, Bede's account emphasizes Perpetua's miraculous ability to mentally suppress pain by separating body and mind over her military prowess. This quality associates the early martyr with other female virgin martyrs who are known for their passive endurance of pain and torment and recalls a passage from the *Passio* that explicitly frames Perpetua as a woman: "Puellis autem ferocissimam vaccam, ideoque praeter consuetudinem conparatam, diabolus praeparavit, sexui earum etiam de bestia aemulatus" [For the young women, however, the devil prepared a ferocious cow, contrary to custom, matching their sex with that of the beast].[36] Furthermore, the actual events of Perpetua's martyrdom that Bede narrates come from the latter portion of the *Passio*, after Perpetua has left off writing and the story has been taken up by an anonymous narrator. While the compiler of the *Old English Martyrology* had access to Bede's *Martyrologies*, and thus precedent for emphasizing Perpetua's straightforward femininity as constructed by the later editor of her *Passio*, he or she nevertheless sticks to the portion of the text written by the saint herself. At least seven centuries after her death, Perpetua's work shines through into early medieval England and gives her the rare distinction of being a named women writer whose words appear in Old English.

35 Bede, *Edition pratique des martyrologes de Bède, de l'anonyme lyonnais et de Florus*, ed. Jacques DuBois and Geneviève Renaud (Paris: Editions du Centre national de la recherche scientifique, 1976), 46. See also Henri Quentin, *Les martyrologes historiques du moyen âge* (Paris: Librairie Victor Lecoffre, 1908), 88.

36 Heffernan, *The Passion of Perpetua and Felicity*, 121.

### The Afterlives of the *Passio Sanctarum Perpetuae et Felicitatis* in Early Medieval England

The existence of contrasting representations of Perpetua in the *Old English Martyrology* and Bede's *Martyrologies* shows that while Perpetua's words in the *Passio* continued to have influence over English knowledge of Perpetua, there was still ample room for multiple narratives to coexist. Neither the Perpetua who "became a man" nor the one who is straightforwardly presented as a Roman lady has complete dominance or edges out other versions. As well as exerting influence on the *Old English Martyrology*, the *Passio Sanctarum Perpetuae et Felicitatis* appears in full in the Cotton-Corpus legendary. This collection, named for the earliest version now split between two manuscripts in the British Library (MSS Cotton Nero E.i, pt. 1–2) and one in Corpus Christi College, Cambridge (CCCC 9), dates from the late ninth or early tenth century and contains some 165 saints' lives.[37] It was also used as a source by Ælfric for his *Lives of Saints*, including his Life of Saint Eugenia, and likely known to the majority of the reading public at the time.[38] Ælfric does not include a translation of the *Passio Sanctarum Perpetuae et Felicitatis* among the saints in his *Lives of Saints*, but he does include another saint's life that features a saint originally identified as a woman but who lives as a man for a time in the lead-up to martyrdom, the *Life of Saint Eugenia*.[39] As Ælfric worked with a source that contained Perpetua's own perspective on gender complexity and sainthood, it would have been difficult to ignore her words as he adapted his own narrative of a gender non-binary saint.

The presence of Perpetua's *Passio* within the Cotton-Corpus legendary prevents a monolithic interpretation of gender among saints' lives in general, as those readers familiar with the genre had access to multiple narratives. In a forthcoming book project, I will trace the ways in which Ælfric's choices as a translator of the *Passio Eugeniae* in the Cotton-Corpus legendary and his scribes' different uses of gender

37 Peter Jackson and Michael Lapidge, "The Contents of the Cotton-Corpus Legendary," *Holy Men and Holy Women: Old English Prose Saints Lives and Their Contexts*, ed. Paul E. Szarmach (Albany: State University of New York Press, 1996). While some scholars have begun to doubt the extent to which Ælfric used the Cotton-Corpus legendary as an exclusive source, it is likely that he knew some version of the text, and it is certainly very close to Ælfric's source for Eugenia. See Rhonda McDaniel, *The Third Gender and Aelfric's Lives of Saints* (Kalamazoo: Medieval Institute Publications, 2018), 130, n.1.

38 Ibid., 134.

39 *Ælfric, "Natale Sancte Eugenie Virginis," Ælfric's Lives of Saints*, ed. and trans. W. W. Skeat, Early English Text Society o.s. 76 (London: N. Trübner, 1881), 24–51. Recent scholars to discuss the *Life of Saint Eugenia* include McDaniel, *Third Gender and Aelfric's Lives of Saints*, Robert Mills, *Seeing Sodomy in the Middle Ages* (Chicago: University of Chicago Press, 2015), David Clark, *Between Medieval Men: Male Friendship and Desire in Early Medieval English Literature* (Oxford: Oxford University Press, 2009), Helene Scheck, *Reform and Resistance: Formations of Female Subjectivity in Early Medieval Ecclesiastical Culture* (Albany: State University of Nnew York Press, 2008), and Anke Bernau, "The Translation of Purity in the Old English Lives of St. Eugenia and St. Euphrosyne," *Studies in Anglo-Saxon England (Special Issue of the Bulletin of the John Rylands University Library of Manchester 86)*, ed. Kathryn Powell and Donald Scragg (Manchester: University of Manchester Press, 2006).

pronouns preserve diverse multiple narratives in the continuing conversation about the representation of gender. Just as Bede and the *Old English Martyrology* compiler made different assertions about the significance of gender in the story of Perpetua's martyrdom, different readers of the *Life of Saint Eugenia* had varying perspectives on what aspect of Eugenia's life ought to be emphasized: her role as a Christian brother and abbot or an enduring feminine identity. The continuing intellectual consideration of pronouns and gender for early medieval English scribes shows that even within a literary culture that made very little space for voices other than those that belonged to outwardly gender-normative clerical men, gender representation could not be flattened into homogenous clerical control. The written words of women can be difficult to uncover in early medieval England, especially in the vernacular, but the persistence of Perpetua's striking visions indicates that women and gender non-conforming people cannot be erased from the written record.[40]

40 I would like to thank the organizers and participants of "Women Leaders and Intellectuals of the Medieval World" and "Holy Water and Saintly Ink: Papers on Medieval Women and Religious Writing," at which I presented versions of this paper, for their attention and suggestions. In particular, I would like to thank Katie Bugyis, Kathryn Kerby-Fulton, Nicholas Watson, Gopa Roy, Marjorie Harrington, Angel Matos, and Eric Lewis for their helpful suggestions.

12

# THE MATERIALIZATION OF KNOWLEDGE IN THIRTEENTH-CENTURY ENGLAND: JOAN TATESHAL, ROBERT GROSSETESTE, AND THE TATESHAL MISCELLANY

ANNA SIEBACH-LARSEN

This chapter will consider the case of Joan Tateshal, a thirteenth-century noblewoman in England who was closely tied to the diocese of Lincoln after the death of Bishop Robert Grosseteste, and one of her manuscripts, Princeton University Library, Taylor Medieval MS 1 (hereafter referred to as the Tateshal Miscellany).[1] Through a combination of visual depiction and an understanding of Grosseteste's cognitive theories and their place within the theological system he creates in his *Chasteau d'amour*, Joan positions herself as co-creator of her transformed self, alongside her spiritual advisors and models, particularly Grosseteste himself.[2] The manuscript page is a key locus for this positioning. It functions as a material ground of thought and experience, a ground on which visible things – whether words, pictorial images, or otherwise – participate in a network of signification. Considered expansively, that network of signification incorporates *what* is apprehended and *how* it is apprehended through the process of cognition. It is in the cognitive process that the intellect and the body are brought together and, in its exercise, that aristocratic lay women, such as Joan Tateshal, were

1 The manuscript has been digitized and is viewable online: "Le manuel des péchés," http://arks.princeton.edu/ark:/88435/tq57ns412, accessed August 20, 2016.

2 In her article, "A Book Designed for a Noblewoman: An Illustrated 'Manuel des Péchés' of the Thirteenth Century," in *Medieval Book Production: Assessing the Evidence*, ed. Linda Brownrigg (Oxford: Anderson-Lovelace, 1990), 173, Adelaide Bennett remarks that Joan Tateshal's visual presentation is imperious and commanding, representing a "dialogue, as it were, between the laywoman and the ecclesiastic." In this essay, I take Bennett's observation a step further, situating Joan's self-presentation within Grosseteste's cognitive system and visual theories in order to uncover how she functioned as a co-creator of her spiritual education and transformation. Bennett's remains the most substantive exploration of this manuscript; see also Don C. Skemer, *Medieval & Renaissance Manuscripts in the Princeton University Library* (Princeton: Department of Art and Archaeology and the Princeton University Library in association with Princeton University Press, 2013), I.399–404. See also Gustav Haenel, *Catalogi Librorum Manuscriptorum qui in Bibliothecis Galliae, Helvetiae, Belgii, Britanniae M., Hispaniae, Lusitaniae asservantur* (Leipzig: I. C. Hinrichs, 1830), 879, no. 2223; Nigel Morgan, *Early Gothic Manuscripts II: 1250–1285*, A Survey of Manuscripts Illuminated in the British Isles 4 (London: Harvey Miller, 1988), 194; Jean Preston, "More Taylor Medieval Manuscripts," *PULC* 47.2 (1986), 262. See also my essay "Structures of Thought in the *Chasteau d'amour* and the Tateshal Miscellany" in the forthcoming volume *Literary Echoes of the Fourth Lateran Council in England and France (1215–1405)*, ed. Maureen Boulton (Toronto: PIMS, 2019), 170-196.

able to transcend the mind/body, text/image binaries, becoming agents and instruments in their own theological investigations and self-transformations.

Joan Tateshal (d.1310) was the daughter of Ralph FitzRanulf of Middleham, Yorkshire. She married Robert Tateshal of Tattershall Castle, Lincolnshire and Buckenham Castle and Manor, Norfolk in 1268. She commissioned the Tateshal Miscellany, which was created in upper East Anglia or in the East Midlands, in the late thirteenth century.[3] Joan is depicted twice in the manuscript: on fol. 1r in the historiated initial opening the *Manuel des pechiez*, she wears the heraldic garments of her father and is depicted in discussion with a tonsured cleric (see Figure 7, in Chapter 9 above).[4] In the opening initial of the *Chasteau d'amour*, fol. 173, she wears a dress with the heraldic garments of Robert Tateshal and is pictured alongside Robert Grosseteste, who is wearing his bishop's mitre (see Figure 8).[5] The lavish manuscript contains five texts of religious instruction, including a heavily illustrated *Manuel des pechiez* and ending with the *Chasteau d'amour*.[6]

The exchange depicted in the *Chasteau*'s miniature is a historical impossibility. Grosseteste died in 1253, fifteen years before Joan FitzRanulf married Robert Tateshal the 5th. However, it does embody the centrality of Grosseteste's work to the texts in the Tateshal Miscellany, the manuscript's entire pastoral project, and his role in the public and private religious life of the Tateshal family. Robert Tateshal owned extensive properties in Lincolnshire and Norfolk, holdings that included Wymondham Abbey, Buckenham Castle and Manor, and Tattershall Castle. He was one of at least seventeen lay Lincolnshire inhabitants who sought Grosseteste's canonization in 1286/87.[7]

3 For dating and provenance, see Bennett, "Book," 172–3 and Skemer. Bennett connects the Tateshal Miscellany with the Salvin Hours (1270–80) and the Huth Psalter (c. 1280) on stylistic grounds. Both were associated with the Lincoln diocese.

4 A chief indented azure. For Ralph FitzRanulf's arms: Glover's Roll [B], c. 1255, no. 140. T. D. Tremlett and H. S. London, *Rolls of Arms: Henry III*, Aspilogia II (London: Society of Antiquaries, 1967), 142; Robert W. Mitchell, *English Mediaeval Rolls of Arms, I: 1244–1334* (Peebles: The Heraldry Society of Scotland, 1983), 29; Anthony R. Wagner, *Historic Heraldry of Britain* (London, 1939), 37–8.

5 Chequy or and gules, a chief ermine. For Robert Tateshal's heraldry: St. George's Roll [E], c. 1285, no. 71 (Mitchell, 125); Charles's Roll [F], c. 1285, n. 38 (Mitchell, 154); Collins' Roll [Q], c. 1296, Copy I, Erdeswicke's Version, no. 52 (Mitchell, 178); Copy II, Dethick's Version, no. 52 (Mitchell, 202); Gullim's Roll [J], c. 1295–1305, no. 58 (Mitchell, 221); Falkirk Roll [H], 1298, no. 9 (Mitchell, 227). For an overview of the FitzRanulf and Tateshal families, see Bennett, "Book," Appendix 2, 176–8.

6 The other contents are: a prefatory series of circular and arboreal theological and moral diagrams, a Latin verse prayer to the Virgin, the *Roman des romans*, the *Plainte de la Vièrge*, an incomplete version of Maurice de Sully's Homily on the *Pater Noster* and an Anglo-Norman translation. The manuscript is fairly small but also rectangular and narrow, measuring 245 x 125–138mm. For other narrow, holster-style books, see G. S. Ivy, "The Bibliography of the Manuscript-Book," in F. Wormald and C. E. Wright, eds., *The English Library before 1700* (London, 1958), 55, n. 71. A similar codex is New York, Pierpont Morgan Library, MS M. 761, an early fourteenth-century copy of the *Lumière as lais*. The Tateshal Miscellany is written continuously throughout by a single hand; the instructions to the illuminator are visible particularly in the illustrations of the exempla in the *Manuel des pechiez*. On these instructions, see Bennett, "Book," 167–72.

7 Grosseteste was never canonized, but he was, on occasion, referred to as "sanctus" or "beatus," as in the Salvin Hours and in the Tateshal Miscellany's version of the *Chasteau*. The rubric at

Figure 8 Historiated initial depicting Joan Tateshal and Robert Grosseteste opening the *Chasteau d'amour*. (Taylor Medieval MS 1, fol. 173r; courtesy of Princeton University Library.)

By depicting herself along Grosseteste, Joan claims a degree of participation in his authorial and ecclesiastical authority and also ties herself to Lincolnshire and those who continued to venerate Grosseteste after his death.

In this initial, Joan Tateshal and Robert Grosseteste stand closely together in a carefully framed niche. They face each other, each mirroring the other's glances and raised hands, the red of the woman's checked dress reflecting the red and pink of the man's robe. They are connected and separated by the scroll which they each clutch in one hand, its unfurling shape mirroring the verticality of its holders. It is a moment of intimacy and of reciprocity: though the man is clearly an ecclesiastical figure, with his robe, crozier, and mitre, the woman's height and her firm grasp of the scroll subvert any assumed power balance, replacing submission with equality and promoting a visual dialogue between collaborators. The two figures are closely framed by curved pink walls, set within a larger square frame. A diffuse golden light highlights the scene and removes them from time and a discernible location: they are both transitory and eternal, always beginning but never completing the conversation and the actions upon which they are forever embarking. They are always already here. We as viewers are always already intruding upon their exchange – their feet are partially obscured by the niche in which they stand, and they are closely surrounded by the curves of the mauve oval, pressing them together and underscoring the spontaneity and the intimacy of the scene as well as its occurrence at a remove from its viewers. And yet, we are invited to see and to read them, to engage in their dialogue as we read the letters descending upon the scroll which joins and divides them: "ci cumence ici."

This scroll works as a clever visual/verbal play: it visualizes the text and codex in which it appears, and it directs the reader – both the woman in the miniature and the assumed reader holding the codex – to begin her study at the miniature and the first word of the text, Robert Grosseteste's *Chasteau d'amour*. While we may assume that a painting of a woman and an ecclesiastical authority would fall into the standard generic conventions of female suppliant, or perhaps that of a donor portrait, this miniature resists such a reading. It participates in the same networks of signification as a suppliant image: the inculcation of lineal duty, a reflexive mode of address, the play between the inward and the outward gaze, the act of looking as devotional and efficacious. However, Joan's self-presentation image in our miniature is not that of the female suppliant in a mid-twelfth-century miscellany of Anselmian prayers,[8] the prostrate suppliant at the foot of the cross in an early fourteenth-century French Book of

the outset of this text refers to "Seint Robert first eveske de Nichole" (fol. 172v). The same rubric is in the London, British Library, Royal MS 20.B.xiv (fol. 87v) and Oxford, Bodleian MS Laud Misc. 471B (fol. 94). See Bennett, "Book," 167. On the attempted canonization of Grosseteste, see Eric W. Kemp, "The Attempted Canonization of Robert Grosseteste," in *Robert Grosseteste: Scholar and Bishop: Essays in Commemoration of the Seventh Centenary of His Death*, ed. D. A. Callus (Oxford: Oxford University Press, 1955), 244, n. 7; F. S. Stevenson, *Robert Grosseteste, Bishop of Lincoln* (London, 1899), 327–9; R. E. G. Cole, "Proceedings Relative to the Canonization of Robert Grosseteste, Bishop of Lincoln," *Associated Architectural Societies' Reports and Papers* 33 (1915–16): 1–34; D. A. Stocker, "The Tomb and Shrine of Bishop Grosseteste in Lincoln Cathedral," in *England in the Thirteenth Century: Proceedings of the 1984 Harlaxton Symposium*, ed. W. M. Ormrod (Nottingham: Nottingham University Press, 1985), 143–8.

8 Oxford, Bodleian Library, MS Auct. D.26, fol. 158v.

Hours,[9] or, starkly, the male suppliant in the lower margin of fol. 44 of the Tateshal Miscellany.[10] It is also not that of a privileged mystic or authority figure with a more direct relationship with the divine, in the model of Christina of Markyate in the St. Alban's Psalter, Hildegard von Bingen, or the nuns of Hohenburg Abbey and the convent of St. Walburg.[11] Rather, Joan seems to be creating a space for a reader, speaker, and director, an object of intellectual and devotional vision and cognition, depicted in the act of seeing and cogitating – under direction, as appropriate for a laywoman, but also as an autonomous, creating subject, working within the overarching institutional Church yet outside of the physical and organizational institution of a monastery or even anchorhold.[12]

The *Chasteau d'amour*, the text which opens with the miniature on fol. 173r, is a theological treatise, characterized by Grosseteste in his prologue as having been written "pur ceus ki ne sevent mie / Ne lettreüre ne clergie" [for those who have no acquaintance with letters of Latin].[13] This introduction can be misleading if interpreted as marking the text for the unlearned: the *Chasteau d'amour* is neither simple nor solely for the intellectual elite. For Grosseteste, theological discourse was, at its core, pastoral, contributing to the Church's administration of salvation by engendering good works and preaching, and the *Chasteau* was "the nearest [Grosseteste] came to a *Summa theologiae*."[14]

9 Cambrai, Bibliothèque municipal, MS 87, fol. 178 (Cambrai Hours). This image is very similar to the marginal supplicating friar on fol. 44 in the Tateshal Miscellany.

10 On this point, see Adelaide Bennett, "A Book Designed for a Noblewoman: An Illustrated 'Manuel des Péchés' of the Thirteenth Century," in *Medieval Book Production: Assessing the Evidence*, ed. Linda Brownrigg (Oxford: Anderson-Lovelace, 1990), 173.

11 On Christina of Markyate and the St. Albans Psalter, see Kristen Collins, *The St. Albans Psalter: Painting and Prayer in Medieval England* (Los Angeles: Getty Publications, 2013); Jane Geddes, *The St. Albans Psalter: A Book for Christina of Markyate* (London: British Library Publications, 2005); the essays in Jochen Bepler, Peter Kidd, and Jane Geddes, eds., *The St Albans Psalter (Albani Psalter)* (Simbach am Inn: Müller & Schindler, 2008). On the nuns of St. Walburg and their devotional drawings, see Jeffrey Hamburger, *Nuns as Artists: The Visual Culture of a Medieval Convent* (Berkeley, Los Angeles, London: University of California Press, 1997). On Herrad and the nuns of Hohenburg, see Danielle Joyner, *Painting the Hortus deliciarum: Medieval Women, Wisdom, and Time* (University Park, PA: Penn State University Press, 2016), especially 17–21 for discussion of Herrad, Hildegard, and Christina of Markyate and the St. Albans Psalter. On author portraits generally, see Randall Rosenfeld, "The Prophets and Apostles Write: Images and the Medieval Understanding of Writing," in "Writing and the Growth of Culture in the Mediterranean," ed. Domenico Pietropaulo, *Scripta Mediterranea* 12–13 (1991–92): 53–95; Ursula Peters, *Das Ich im Bild: Die Figure des Autors in volkssprachigen Bilderhandschriften des 13. bis 16. Jahrhunderts* (Cologne: Böhlau Verlag, 2008); Johann Konrad Eberlein, *Miniatur und Arbeit* (Frankfurt am Main: Suhrkamp, 1995).

12 In this sense, Joan's self-presentation is closer to that of Blanche of Castile as depicted in the Bible of St. Louis (New York, Morgan Library & Museum, MS M.240, f. 8).

13 ll. 27–28, 16–19. All quotations are taken from Murray, unless the reading from the Tateshal Miscellany differs from Murray's edition. All translations are taken from Maureen Boulton, *Piety and Persecution in the French Texts of England*, FRETS 6 (Tempe, AZ: Arizona Center for Medieval and Renaissance Studies, 2013), with silent emendations.

14 James R. Ginther, *Master of the Sacred Page: A Study of the Theology of Grosseteste, ca. 1229/30–1235* (Burlington, VT: Ashgate, 2004), 243; Richard Southern, *Robert Grossteste: The Growth of an English Mind in Medieval Europe*, 2nd ed. (Oxford: Clarendon Press, 1982), 224–5.

Written prior to 1235, and wildly popular amongst a wide range of readers,[15] the *Chasteau* is a complex treatise structured around the allegory of a multi-colored, glorious castle,[16] which represents Mary,[17] the heavenly Jerusalem, and possibly even Lincoln Cathedral itself.[18] Its ultimate goal is that the reader come to know the whole Christ (*Christus integer*) through the work – and the physical process – of thought.[19] Thus Grosseteste opens his text with *how* the reader must know what she is to know: "Sanz penser ne poet suffire / De nul bien fet commencer" [Without thinking rightly one cannot be prepared to begin any good work].[20]

15 On the *Chasteau* and its dating and audience, see Evelyn Mackie, "Scribal Intervention and the Question of Audience: editing Le Château d'amour," in *Robert Grosseteste: Papers Given at the Thirty-Sixth Annual Conference on Editorial Problems. University of Toronto, 3–4 November 2000*, ed. Evelyn A Mackie and Joseph Goering (Toronto: University of Toronto Press, 2003), 61–77. See also C. W. Marx, *The Devil's Rights and the Redemption in the Literature of Medieval England* (Cambridge: D. S. Brewer, 1995), 65–79. Marx describes all the Anglo-Norman and English manuscripts: see 160–70. For the Middle English versions, see Kari Sajavaara, *The Middle English Translations of Robert Grosseteste's Château d'amour* (Helsinki: Société Néophilologique, 1967), 54–101. For an edition of the text, see Jessie Murray, *Le Chateau d'amour de Robert Grosseteste évèque de Lincoln* (Paris: Champion, 1918). There are two modern English translations: Evelyn Mackie, "Le Château d'Amour: An English Prose Translation," in *Robert Grosseteste and the Beginnings of a British Theological Tradition*, ed. Maura O'Carroll (Roma: Instituto Storico dei Cappuccini, 2003), 151–79; Boulton, *Piety and Persecution*, 3–14, 61–89.

16 On the relationship of the *Chasteau*'s castle allegory to more widespread uses of martial and castle imagery, see Christiania Whitehead, *Castles of the Mind: A Study of Medieval Architectural Allegory* (Cardiff: University of Wales Press, 2003). See also Whitehead, "A Fortress and a Shield: The Representation of the Virgin in the *Château d'amour* of Robert Grosseteste," in *Writing Religious Women: Female Spiritual and Textual Practices in Late Medieval England*, ed. D. Renevey and C. Whitehead (Cardiff: University of Wales Press, 2000). R. D. Cornelius, *The Figurative Castle: A Study in the Mediaeval Allegory of the Edifice with Especial Reference to Religious Writings* (Bryn Mawr, 1930); Paul Binski, *Becket's Crown: Art and Imagination in Gothic England, 1170–1300* (New Haven: Yale University Press, 2004), 182–88; Abigail Wheatley, *The Idea of the Castle in Medieval England* (York: York Medieval Press, 2004).

17 On the exegetical connection between the Virgin Mary and the figure of the castle, which dates to the ninth century, see Wheatley, 81; Cornelius, 37–50; and B. E. Kurtz, "'The Small Castle of the Soul': Mysticism and Metaphor in the European Middle Ages," *Studia Mystica* 15.4 (1992): 19–39; Jill Mann, "Allegorical Buildings in Mediaeval Literature," *Medium Aevum* 63 (1994), 198. Grosseteste's basis for the allegory is John 10:38 and may be drawing on Aelred's Sermon XVII. See Wheatley, 78–88 and Aelred of Rievaulx, "Sermo XVII: In Assumptione beatae Marie," *Patrologiae Latinae*, ed. J. P. Migne (Paris, 1844–64), 195, cols. 303–4.

18 On the relationship between Grosseteste's cosmology and Lincoln Cathedral, see John Shannon Hendrix, *Architecture as Cosmology: Lincoln Cathedral and English Gothic Architecture* (New York: Peter Lang, 2001). See also the essays in Nicholas Temple, John Shannon Hendrix, and Christian Frost, eds., *Bishop Robert Grosseteste and Lincoln Cathedral: Tracing Relationships between Medieval Concepts of Order and Built Form* (Farnham, Surrey: Ashgate Publishing Ltd., 2014), particularly Cecilia Panti, "Robert Grosseteste's Cosmology of Light and Light-Metaphors," 59–80.

19 On Grosseteste's argument that the whole Christ is the subject matter of theology – including the Trinity, the Incarnation, the Church, and all creation – see Robert Grosseteste, *Hexaëmeron*, ed. Richard C. Dales and Servus Gieben, *Auctores Britannici Medii Aevi* 6 (London: British Academy, 1982), 1.1.1–1.2.3 (pp. 49–52). See also Ginther, 33–47.

20 ll. 2–3.

For Grosseteste, the object of thought and the mechanics of thought are inseparable: his goal is to structure the workings of the intellect and thus the soul. The object of thought is God, who is light, and it is through light that we are able to see the material and immaterial objects through which our apprehension of God is facilitated. He connects this divine illumination with the material world in his commentary on Ecclesiasticus 43:1–5, in a passage in which the world is a legible book that leads its reader upward to invisible truths:

> since the species and forms and figures of things are like a kind of writing, and the sensible causes, up to the reasons in the divine mind, are like certain spoken words, the course of the sun is hastened at [God's] words because in the forms, figures and species impressed by the sun, or drawn out through its efficacy, a course to the visible causes is prepared for human intelligence and inquiry, as if in its word, by ascending in sequence to the invisible things of God that are clearly seen, being understood through those visible things that were made.[21]

The created world is doubly illuminated by physical and spiritual light: we see things (*res*) with our physical eyes thanks to the sun and understand them inwardly thanks to divine illumination.[22] Our understanding of the world is grounded in material substance and immaterial light – as well as the Light that imbues and makes visible all creation and truth and gives material objects their meaning. The language that Grosseteste uses in his discussions of cognition in his scientific and theological works is both that of light and of vision: he discusses the mind in terms of *aspectus mentis*, or the gaze of the mind's eye, and *affectus mentis*, or desire or will. For Grosseteste, the mind's gaze – its rational powers – must be awakened because it is not separated from the mind's desires, which are oriented toward physical needs and thus away from the light. The more the mind's desire can be diverted from the corporeal and corruptible to the eternal, the more the gaze will "come to the light it needs to see."[23]

The physical process of studying the text and accompanying images is inseparable from inward rumination and is also fundamental to Joan's eventual glorification, a task that is a cooperative effort between herself and God. Our physical eyes can only see when there is light present. And as the thinking goes, all objects emanate light, and as these rays emanate and impress images of objects upon our mind – whether

21 "Item cum species et formae et figurae rerum quasi quaedam litterae sint et quaedam verba loquentia sensibiles causas usque ad rationes in mente divina, in sermonibus solis est iter festinatum, quia in formis et figuris et speciebus a sole impressis, sive per eius efficaciam eductis, quasi in eius verbo paratur iter humanae intelligentiae et investigationi ad causas visibiles, ascendendo seriatim usque ad invisibilia Dei, quae conspiciuntur intellecta per ea quae facta sunt visibilia." Grosseteste, *De operationibus solis,* ed. James McEvoy, "The Sun as *res* and *signum*: Grosseteste's commentary on *Ecclesiasticus* ch. 43, vv. 1–5," *Recherches de théologie ancienne et médiévale* 41 (1974): 90–91. Translation, with slight emendations, by Aden Kumler, in Aden Kumler and Christopher Lakey, "*Res et significatio*: The Material Sense of Things," *Gesta* 51.1 (2012): 5.

22 See Kumler and Lakey, 5.

23 Ginther, 248. See Grosseteste, *Commentarius in posteriorum analyticorum libros*, ed. P. Rossi (Florence: Olschki, 1981), 1.14 (215–16).

images of physical castles or images of words describing allegorical ones – our comprehension of their truth through the vision of the mind (*aspectus*) is based upon the mind's disposition (*affectus*).[24] Our intellective, or spiritual, eyes can only comprehend sensorial information, and then interpret its spiritual significance, through inward illumination by God. This inward illumination is achieved through the appropriate ordering of desire: true seeing and cogitating are truly transformative acts, as the viewer is physically transformed by the impression of viewed images upon her brain and spiritually transformed through her alignment of her will and the focus of her desires on God. This inward remaking is reflected in the reader's outward appearance, as she is eventually transformed into light, as enacted and facilitated in the *Chasteau*.

Grosseteste's epistemological formulation is essentially Neoplatonic and Pseudo-Dionysian: God is both the true light and the source of light, and the means of coming to understand that Light is analogous to corporeal vision as a process.[25] Grosseteste expands upon Augustine's formulation of cognition as analogous to vision in his *Commentary on the Posterior Analytics*, articulating that divine illumination is "a spiritual light which is shed upon intelligible things and the eye of [the] mind and which has the same relation to the interior eye and to intelligible things as the corporeal sun has to the bodily eye and to visible things."[26]

Grosseteste connects this epistemology of light to a cosmogony of light, in which corporeity finds its origins in a primordial point of light created by God, which then extended to create the universe in all its components.[27] We can understand how the

24 On the *aspectus* and *affectus mentis*, see Ginther, 248. Much of Grosseteste's cognitive and optical theory is contained in his treatises on light and color. For the latter, see the essays, edition, and translation of *De Colore* in Greti Dinkova-Bruun et al., *The Dimensons of Color: Robert Grosseteste's De Colore. Edition, Translation, and Interdisciplinary Analysis* (Toronto: PIMS, 2013); on light, see Robert Grosseteste, "Robert Grosseteste's *De Luce*: A Critical Edition," ed. Cecilia Panti, in *Robert Grosseteste and His Intellectual Milieu*, ed. J. Flood, J. R. Ginther, and J. W. Goering (Toronto: PIMS, 2013), 193–238; Robert Grosseteste, "Robert Grosseteste's *On Light*. An English Translation," trans. Neil Lewis, in *Robert Grosseteste and his Intellectual Milieu*, 239–47. See also Cecilia Panti, "Robert Grosseteste's Cosmology of Light and Light-Metaphors," in *Bishop Robert Grosseteste and Lincoln Cathedral*, ed. Nicholas Temple and John Shannon Hendrix (Farnham: Ashgate, 2014), 59–80. For an overview of ancient and medieval theories of vision, see David C. Lindberg, *Theories of Vision from Al-Kindi to Kepler* (Chicago: University of Chicago Press, 1976); for Grosseteste particularly, see 96–99. See also Suzanne Conklin Akbari, *Seeing through the Veil: Optical Theory and Medieval Allegory* (Toronto: University of Toronto Press, 2004), especially 3–44. For a discussion of medieval theories of cognition, see Michael Camille, "Before the Gaze: The Internal Senses and Late Medieval Practices of Seeing," in *Visuality Before and Beyond the Renaissance: Seeing as Others Saw*, ed. Robert S. Nelson (Cambridge: Cambridge University Press, 2000), 197–223; Karl Whittington, *Body-Worlds: Opicinus de Canistris and the Medieval Cartographic Imagination* (Toronto: PIMS, 2014); Michelle Karnes, *Imagination, Meditation, and Cognition in the Middle Ages* (Chicago: University of Chicago Press, 2011).

25 Thus, Augustine: "But we ought … to believe that the intellectual mind is so formed in its nature as to see those things, which by the disposition of the Creator are subjoined to things intelligible in a natural order, by a sort of incorporeal light of a unique kind; as the eye of the flesh sees things adjacent to itself in this bodily light, of which light it is made to be receptive, and adapted to it." Quoted in Lindberg, 96.

26 Quoted in Lindberg, 96.

27 See Lindberg, 96–7.

universe was created by studying physical light; optical theory reveals how nature itself works. Grosseteste developed his theory of the multiplication of the species in order to account for the Neoplatonic and Aristotelean explanations of the physics of light and optical theory, following Avicebron and al-Kindi's arguments of emanation in his own development of the theory by which every natural agent emanates its own power from itself to other bodies. These emanating self-representations Grosseteste calls *species in medio*, and they fill the distance between the object and the perceiver, according to the rules of geometrical optics, the study of which could reveal the very nature of "material reality, of cognition, and indeed of God himself."[28] As he sought to make compatible Aristotelian ideas of optical geometry with Neoplatonic notions of divine light, Grosseteste developed an optical theory that posited that truly seeing – comprehending – a thing physically would transform an individual, as light as she is suffused by light, which impresses true and beautiful images upon her mind according to her desire for God.

This complex relationship between light, the material, and the immaterial undergirds the project of the *Chasteau* and is the defining feature of the castle itself. Mary as the castle becomes full of light through her goodness: the multi-colored castle is crowned by crimson, which is the fiery light of the Virgin's "seinte charité, / Dunt ele est enluminee / E esprise del feu d'amur / De servir Deu sun creatur" [holy charity, [with which she is] set aflame by the fire of love to serve her creator].[29] This light renders Mary an appropriate *locus* for the residence of Christ, who is light: "Mes Deus ne voleit herberger / Fors en beau lu e en cler" ['God could not take shelter except in a beautiful and clear place'].[30]

Mary is not the only participant in this allegory who is full of light: as the reader works through the significations of the various objects that fill the text, made visible through the light of God that suffuses the reader and illuminates her understanding and her being, the reader will become "cler cum li solaus" ['bright as the sun'] as she is transformed and purified to the point that she too can join the ranks of the saved who are depicted at the end of the *Chasteau*. This glorification is achieved through a careful study of the content of the text as it elucidates the creation of the world, the virtues and vices, and the claims of the devil and the role of mercy in our salvation. As the reader studies and comprehends these fundamental tenets of religious belief, she invariably aligns herself more closely with God's will.

Keeping Grosseteste's cognitive framework in mind, we return to the miniature that begins the *Chasteau* in the Tateshal Miscellany. Joan is almost equal in stature with Grosseteste; not only is she raising her hand in reciprocity to him, she firmly

28 Lindberg, 99.

29 ll. 697–700. The description of the castle draws on the celestial city of the *Apocalypse* and references to other biblical references, including Ezekiel's temple. On the integration of biblical texts into the allegory of the castle, see Wheatley, 95–7 and Sajavaara, 100.

30 ll. 567–8. On Mary's beauty as colorful light, see Grosseteste's c. 1230 sermon *Tota pulchra es et macula non est in te*. The text is published in Servus Gieben, "Robert Grosseteste and the Immaculate Conception, With the Text of the Sermon *Tota Pulchra Es*," *Collectanea Franciscana* 28 (1958): 211–27. See also E. Longpré, *Robert Grossetête et l'Immaculée Conception*, *Arch. Franc. Hist* 26 (1933): 551; S. H. Thomson, *The Writings of Robert Grosseteste, 1235–1253* (Cambridge: Cambridge University Press, 1940), 172.

grasps along with the bishop the scroll containing the directive to "ci cumence ici," asserting her role as reader but also as something more: as co-creator, through the commissioning and possibly the design of the manuscript. While the initial depicts Joan as a powerful agential commissioner of the physical manuscript, helping bring the text into being, it also depicts a woman who has worked through or is in the process of working through a text in which created beings, such as herself, are the means by which God is apprehended in this world. This functions as a depiction of exchange but also an enactment of the process of cognition: the words on the scroll and the figures are made visible and comprehensible by means of the light – represented and created by the gold leaf – that suffuses the space. This ground of light, signifying the light by means of which our physical eyes see and the light by which our mind apprehends, is the ground for Joan herself. It is upon and through this light that Joan is transformed into an object of contemplation as she participates more fully in the divine light and is made more bright and more visible herself through repeated contemplation of the truths made comprehensible in the *Chasteau*.

The *Chasteau* is a translation and materialization by Grosseteste of the intersection of his theology and psychology. It is informed by his understanding of the material and immaterial nature of light and the role of light in the bodying forth of meaning and the cognitive process. That comprehension also lays the groundwork for the multiple levels of work that the manuscript object and the pictorial image undertake, and Grosseteste's own pastoral project justifies and enables Joan Tateshal's visual claims as collaborator in the pursuit of theological instruction and in her own spiritual and thus physical transformation.

Thus, the Tateshal Miscellany is an excellent example of one way in which women could participate in their own religious formation through the commissioning of books: Joan Tateshal's depiction in her manuscript highlights her active role in the discussion and formulation of the codex as she directs the writing of her cleric on fol. 1 and shares possession of the written word with Grosseteste on fol. 173. However, by thinking more expansively both about the possible ways in which lay women may have interacted with images, as well as the intellectual and theological discourses in which they may have participated, we can discern how her manuscript was a site for Joan Tateshal to participate in her formation in a more material way. Placing the images of Joan within the framework of Grosseteste's theories of cognition and the fundamental role of the material world in the understanding of spiritual truths illuminates the manner in which Joan's image also participates in the economy of signification: Joan's painted body becomes a material means by which Joan the reader can contemplate the theological precepts and the process of transformation articulated in the *Chasteau d'amour*. The double reading of image and text is mirrored in the double transformation of body and mind articulated in Grosseteste's description of the ascent of the blessed, modeled on the perfect virtue and beauty of the Virgin Mary – a double transformation entered into by Joan Tateshal through engagement with her manuscript. In the exercise of her cognitive faculties, then, Joan becomes a co-creator of her own spiritual progression, alongside Robert Grosseteste as author and as spiritual mentor and God as the object of desire and the source of physical and spiritual illumination. Joan thus participates as co-creator of her self and her manuscript on material and immaterial levels, encompassing the transformation and engagement of her body, mind, and soul. For, after all, "without thinking rightly one cannot be prepared to begin any good work."[31]

31 For a greater exploration of the relationship between Joan Tateshal and the *Chasteau d'amour* and the directives of Lateran IV, see my forthcoming essay in *Literary Responses to the Fourth Lateran Council*, ed. Maureen Boulton (Toronto: PIMS, 2019), 170-196.

13

# NETWORKS OF INFLUENCE: WIDOWS, SOLE ADMINISTRATION, AND UNCONVENTIONAL RELATIONSHIPS IN THIRTEENTH-CENTURY LONDON

AMANDA BOHNE

Isabella Bukerel and Johanna Vyel lived and moved in a society in which women of their class and station understood the law, especially as it pertained to their estates and inheritance, and knew how to use it. The methods by which women acquired this acumen are not explicitly recorded, but it seems to have been almost the rule, and certainly not the exception. Barbara Hanawalt finds that in London dower cases between 1301 and 1306, forty-five percent of widows in recorded cases represented themselves.[1] Sue Sheridan Walker writes, "The control of property – as heiresses, landholders by their own acquisition, joint tenants, and doweresses – gave medieval women power, status, and a need to be familiar with land law. ... Litigation about real property and appurtenant rights required that women, especially widows, be an active part of that pervasive legal culture."[2] Extant wills demonstrate that as they prepared for their deaths, late thirteenth-century London women capably prioritized not only their own material and spiritual interests, but also those of their family members and other loved ones, including other women. Walker writes, "The frequency with which women used the law courts and bureaucratic tribunals of the King, the church, and the town is one of the most striking features of medieval England."[3]

This chapter uses historical documents to examine the end-of-life decisions of the widow Isabella Bukerel, one of the wealthiest women in late thirteenth-century London, through her will and other documents relating to her family. Extant wills demonstrate that as they prepared for their deaths, thirteenth-century London women capably prioritized not only their own legal, material, and spiritual interests, but also those of their family members and other loved ones, including other women. These women used their status as wealthy, influential movers in the City's mercantile culture to arrange their own postmortem affairs and those of their families and to advocate for those concerns in the courts when it was necessary. Bukerel is an early example of

1 Hanawalt, "The Widow's Mite," in *The Widdow's Mite:Provisions for Medieval London Widows*, ed. Louise Mirrer (Ann Arbor: University of Michigan Press, 1992), 28–29.

2 Sue Sheridan Walker, "Litigation as a Personal Quest: Suing for Dower in the Royal Courts," in *Wife and Widow in Medieval England*, ed. Sue Sheridan Walker (Ann Arbor: University of Michigan Press, 1993), 82.

3 Walker, *Wife and Widow in Medieval England*, 1.

the kind of widow Rowena Archer and B. E. Ferme use Christine de Pisan to invoke, "[taking] up the challenge of sole and indefinite administration of estates."[4] Bukerel's will and her sister Johanna Vyel's place them at the center of a network of women from different branches of one family, coordinating as they judiciously attend to their own legal and religious concerns and to the obligations they owe their families. The Vyel and Bukerel families were, Gwyn Williams writes, "enmeshed in a web of marriage-relationships.... Towards the end of the century, as social mobility accelerated, the marriageable daughters of aldermanic families were acting as a stabilizing influence, preserving old standards of conduct and belief in a time of disconcerting changes."[5] In this particular network of related families in the late thirteenth century, men have left few extant wills, and property was bequeathed through women. Although testators were typically male – eighty-eight percent of the Husting Court wills were made by men, in fact – most of the wills considered in this essay are those of women.[6]

Bukerel and Vyel each see to the other's worldly or spiritual interests and to those of other family members and loved ones.[7] Vyel also makes bequests suggesting a romantic relationship between Bukerel and her clerk, as we will see below. Lastly, two nieces of Vyel and Bukerel who challenged Vyel's will provide another example of independent, proactive female participation in late thirteenth-century London courts. Knowledge of the concerns of this small network can refine our understanding of the ways in which women relied upon each other's abilities and understanding, even after death, and of their proficient use of the legal system to ensure not only the postmortem care of their own souls and the souls of their family members, but also the material well-being of their families and friends. Vyel and Bukerel participated not just actively, but adeptly in the creation of documents that would ensure the correct passage of property through the courts following their own deaths and the deaths of others.

The Bukerel and Vyel families were those of well-off merchants, prominent and powerful in thirteenth-century London.[8] There has been no dedicated scholarship

4 Rowena E. Archer and B. E. Ferme, "Testamentary Procedure with Special Reference to the Executrix," *Medieval Women in Southern England*, ed. Keith Bate, *Reading Medieval Studies* 15 (1989): 3.

5 Williams, *Medieval London: From Commune to Capital* (London: Athlone Press, 1970), 75.

6 Kate Kelsey Staples, *Daughters of London: Inheriting Opportunity in the Late Middle Ages* (Leiden: Brill, 2011), 21.

7 All of the wills discussed in this essay are preserved in the London Husting Rolls of Deeds and Wills. In addition to the rolls themselves, now held by the London Metropolitan Archive, the images of the rolls are available on microfilm: G. H. Martin, *Husting Rolls of Deeds and Wills 1252–1485* (Cambridge: Chadwyck-Healey, 1988). Additionally, there is a calendar of abstracts, Reginald Sharpe, *Calendar of Wills Proved and Enrolled in the Court of Husting, London A.D. 1258–1688*, 2 vols. (London: John C. Francis, 1889). For Isabella Bukerel, see Corporation of London Records Office, Husting Roll (cited hereafter as CLRO, HR) 11 (68) or Sharpe, *Calendar of Wills*, 1:49–50. For Johanna Vyel, see CLRO, HR 24 (13) or Sharpe, *Calendar of Wills*, 1:115–16. Sharpe's entries are abstracts of the wills entered on the court rolls and so often omit certain details, particularly about bequests made outside the family, and also when one beneficiary is the recipient of multiple bequests. Spelling of "Bukerel" varies throughout documents. Outside of quotations or references to specific documents, I have used "Bukerel," the spelling most other scholars use.

8 For the Vyel family, in particular, see Williams, *Medieval London*.

of any significant length on the families, but members frequently appear in historical records and merit passing mention in relevant studies. A bibliography of such references to the family comprises a significant overview of scholarship on thirteenth-century London. Most usefully, Gwyn A. Williams provides a family tree demonstrating relationships between the sisters and other family members who appear in their wills and other documents.[9] This table, titled "The Viels and Their Kin," shows Isabella Bukerel and her sister Johanna Vyel as the daughters of Isabella and John Viel, Senior, along with five other siblings. Williams and many other scholars focus on Margery and John Vyel, seemingly Isabella and Johanna's grandparents, and Margery's efforts to appeal to the king when she was unhappy with the decision of the city authorities regarding the settlement of her husband's estate.[10] Further work on all of these families could yield a fruitful longer study, but Margery is the earliest example we have in this family of a widow or single woman strongly advocating for her own rights to her family's estates in the courts. Both families had established themselves in London around the time of the Conquest. According to Williams, the Bukerels were descended from an Italian pepper merchant and had been in London since the Conquest, while the Viels had been aldermen since the eleventh century.[11] There is no independent mention of Johanna in scholarship on thirteenth-century London, but Isabella, who married into the wealthy Bukerel family, figures in several studies because of her significant wealth, her own efforts to secure her rights to her rebellious husband's property after his death, and because of the chantries her family founded and maintained in St. Paul's Cathedral and the Church of St. Mary Aldermanbury.[12]

For the purposes of this chapter, four wills, all concerned with the property of Isabella Bukerel and Johanna Vyel and extant in the Husting Rolls of Deeds and Wills, occupy our primary attention. The Husting Court Rolls of Deeds and Wills contain transcripts of testaments submitted to the court in medieval London by the executors of the deceased. As Kate Kelsey Staples notes in her thorough study of the inheritances of daughters recorded in these wills from 1300 to 1500, the Husting Court only enrolled the wills of testators who were citizens of London and whose

9 Williams, *Medieval London*, Appendix, Table B.

10 Williams, *Medieval London*, 206–07. This case figures in several other studies as well, including Jonathan Andrews et al., *The History of Bethlem* (New York: Routledge, 1997), 27–35; Caroline Barron, "The 'Golden Age' of Women in Medieval London," *Reading Medieval Studies* 15 (1989): 35–58, see 53n31; this article reprinted in Martha Carlin and Joel T. Rosenthal, eds., *Medieval London: Collected Papers of Caroline M. Barron* (Kalamazoo, MI: Medieval Institute Press, 2017), 361–83; Nicholas Vincent, "Goffredo de Prefetti and the Church of Bethlehem in England," *Journal of Ecclesiastical History* 49 (1998): 213–35, see 225.

11 Williams, *Medieval London*, 50, 74.

12 Many of these works are cited throughout, but the most substantial and readily available mentions of these cases are Sharpe, *Calendar of Wills*, x, particularly n3; Marie-Helene Rousseau, *Saving the Souls of Medieval London: Perpetual Chantries at St Paul's Cathedral, c. 1200–1548* (Farnham, Surrey: Ashgate, 2011), 178 (as Bokrel), 16n26, 97, 178; Walter Besant, *The Survey of London, vol. 8: The City* (London: Adam and Charles Black, 1910), 71; Williams, *Medieval London: From Commune to Capital*, 54, 236, 243, 245; Caroline Barron, *The Medieval Guildhall of London* (London: The Corporation of London, 1974), 17, 45n21.

estates came to the value of £10 or more.[13] The earliest extant roll begins in 1252, but this first roll does not contain any testamentary records, only a mention of one in a charter and a marginal note for an entry that was perhaps planned but not completed.[14] Wills are consistently recorded from the second roll on. Moving chronologically, the first will is that of Isabella Bukerel.

Bukerel was perhaps the most prominent woman in the Vyel and Bukerel families and one of the wealthiest women in late thirteenth-century London. Williams writes that she "owned most of the Drapery, Ropery, Saddlery, and Peltry in Cheap and Walbrook."[15] She exercised effectiveness in dealing with legal matters in a number of ways. In her lifetime, she strenuously advocated for the return of her confiscated property as well as administering her own estate and acting as her son's executor after his death. In her will, she made bequests to establish and maintain chantries for the family at two churches and bequeathed property and income to address the material and spiritual needs of other family members and loved ones. Her will was enrolled in 1280.[16] Her husband, Stephen Bukerel, who died in 1268, supported Simon de Montfort in his rebellion against Henry III.[17] The king confiscated his house on Aldermanbury Street in retribution and awarded it to Roger de Mortimer in October 1265.[18] Isabella successfully advocated to have the house returned to her. There is a brief mention in the Latin and Anglo-Norman Liber de Antiquis Legibus of her suit to recover the house, remarking that the mayor "himself was impleaded as to a certain tenement which Isabella Bukerel demanded of him by plea between them moved."[19] In his Calendar of Wills, Sharpe expands on this account of Isabella's efforts to advocate for the return of her property, which "according to the law and custom of

13 Staples, *Daughters of London*, 21. In addition to Staples, whose study focuses on recipients of bequests, several other scholars have utilized the Husting Court wills to complete their studies: Kristen Burkholder, "Material Culture and Self-Representation in Late Medieval England," (Ph.D. Dissertation, University of Minnesota, 2001); John M. Jennings, "The Distribution of Landed Wealth in the Wills of London Merchants 1400–1450," *Mediaeval Studies* 39 (1977): 261–80; Harry A. Miskimin, "The Legacies of London 1259–1330," in *The Medieval City*, ed. Harry A. Miskimin, David Herlihy, and A. L. Udovitch (New Haven: Yale University Press, 1977), 261–80.

14 G. H. Martin, *The Husting Rolls of Deeds and Wills, 1252–1485: Guide to the Microfilm Edition* (Cambridge: Chadwyck-Healey, 1990), 9.

15 Williams, *Medieval London*, 54.

16 CLRO, HR 11 (68); Martin, Reel 2; Sharpe, *Calendar of Wills*, 1:49–50. Having examined the roll entry in person, I will cite only the roll in future notes.

17 Williams, *Medieval London*, 248.

18 David Bowsher et al., *The London Guildhall: An Archaeological History of a Neighborhood from Early Medieval to Modern Times*, vol. 1 (London: Museum of London Archaeology Service, 2007), 123, 134. Caroline Barron, *London in the Later Middle Ages: Government and People* (Oxford: Oxford University Press, 2004), 16–17. Williams, *Medieval London*, 220, 225–26, 236, 237–38.

19 Arnold Fitz-Thedmar, *Chronicles of the Mayors and Sheriffs of London, A.D. 1188 to A.D. 1274, Translated from the Original Latin and Anglo-Norman of the* "Liber de Antiquis Legibus" *in the Possession of the Corporation of the City of London: Attributed to Arnald Fitz-Thedmar, Alderman of London in the Reign of Henry III*, ed. and trans. Henry Thomas Riley (London: Trübner and Company, 1863), 164. This is Riley's translation. A new edition of Arnold Fitz-Thedmar's work is forthcoming by Ian Stone. See also Ian Stone, "Arnold Fitz Thedmar: Identity, Politics and the City of London in the Thirteenth Century," *The London Journal* 40 (2015): 106–22.

the City," were rightfully hers.[20] The first roll of the Husting Rolls of Pleas of Land records that after proceedings were begun to return the house to Isabella in the fifty-third year of Henry III's reign (1268–69), she finally regained the house in the second year of Edward I's reign (1273–74).[21] It is unclear if Bukerel administered her husband's estate after his death, but she certainly took it up after the death of their son, whose executor she was. Bukerel's son, William, named her and his wife, Dyonisia, as co-executrices, and they can be seen in the Husting Court Letter Books, attending to the business of his estate.[22] Staples notes that testators often named their wives executors, along with other family members or business associates.[23] William's decision to appoint his mother to execute his will alongside his wife, rather than a business associate, indicates his confidence in her superior abilities.

Bukerel's bequests further make her wealth and foresight evident. At the time of her death in 1280, a chantry dedicated to her husband and sons had already been established at St. Paul's, and her will particularly mentions that it should be maintained for the benefit of their souls.[24] The family may have been buried in St. Paul's or at St. Mary Aldermanbury, where another chantry was later established, but Bukerel's will only makes a general reference to burial at one of the churches where the two chantries are located. Rousseau tentatively suggests that she may have been buried at St. Paul's, at the altar of St. Margaret.[25] Bukerel's son, William, a draper, gave his mother the power to bequeath her dower where she liked to provide for prayers for herself and the family.[26] Bukerel's dower, one-third of her husband's estate, would have been hers only for life and certainly reverted to William's family after her death.[27] William had died in 1278, and his mother and his wife, Dionisia, had acted as his co-executors.[28]

20 Sharpe, *Calendar of Wills*, x, note 3.

21 Ibid.

22 Reginald R. Sharpe, *Calendar of Letter-Books Preserved Among the Archives of the City of London at the Guildhall: Letter-book A* (London: J. E. Francis, 1908), 23. As Dionisia might often have done for him when he was alive and as Isabella had probably done for Stephen. As Carruthers notes, wives were often left to manage the business affairs of their husbands in their absence. Mary Carruthers, "The Wife of Bath and the Painting of Lions," in *Feminist Readings in Middle English Literature*, ed. Ruth Evans (London: Routledge, 1994), 28.

23 Staples, *Daughters of London*, 18–19.

24 CLRO, HR 11(68) or Sharpe, *Calendar of Wills*, 1:59–50; Rousseau, *Saving the Souls of Medieval London*, 178 (as Bokrel). Rousseau records that in the late fourteenth and early fifteenth centuries, John Tyckhill, the chaplain of a St. Paul's chantry, dedicated to the family of Isabella Bukerel, made serious efforts to save it, writing petitions to the king and the bishop of London when the chantry ran out of funds.

25 Rousseau, *Saving the Souls*, 178.

26 Sharpe, *Calendar of Wills*, 1:36; Corporation of London Records Office, Husting Roll 9 (81). The entry for William's will spells their surname "Bukerell," but the references that his mother makes back to his will confirm that this is Isabella Bukerel's son.

27 Marie-Françoise Alamichel, *Widows in Anglo-Saxon and Medieval Britain* (Oxford: Peter Lang, 2008), 228. Barbara Hanawalt, "The Widow's Mite," 25.

28 CLRO, HR 9 (81). The entry also appears in Sharpe, *Calendar of Wills*, 1:36, but Sharpe does not include executors in his abstracts. See also Reginald R. Sharpe, *Calendar of Letter-Books Preserved Among the Archives of the City of London at the Guildhall: Letter-book A* (London: J. E. Francis, 1908), 23, where the two are named as executors while carrying out business related to the estate.

Bukerel left bequests to William's daughter – her granddaughter, another Isabella – and charged her with the responsibility for using the tenements that comprised her grandmother's dower to establish a chantry in the parish church of St. Mary Aldermanbury for her benefit. Bukerel's decision to charge her namesake with this responsibility fits a pattern in the family of women tending to the family's postmortem legal and religious business. By the time this younger Isabella had lost the grandmother who shared her name, her father had been dead for approximately three years, and it was her turn to see to the same matters her mother and grandmother had overseen. Other documentary evidence shows that this younger Isabella undertook the task her grandmother assigned her. The will of the draper John Tours, enrolled in 1386, bequeathed two shops in Westchepe to support a chantry in St. Mary Aldermanbury, "founded by Isabella, daughter of William Bokerell."[29] The property that the older Isabella Bukerel bequeathed might have been non-dower property that she inherited from her husband, or it may have come from other interests. In any case, the property was hers outright, to bequeath as she wished; it was not intended to devolve to anyone else after her death. As a London widow, in addition to her dower, she was entitled to occupy the marital home until she remarried or died. It was the responsibility of London widows to maintain their husbands' households and businesses and continue training their apprentices. Elsewhere in England, she would have been obligated to vacate after forty days in favor of her husband's heir.[30]

Bukerel's sister, Johanna Vyel, whose will was enrolled in 1294, acknowledged social ties established by her deceased sister and made arrangements for the care of her own soul and her father's after her own decease.[31] She was likely a single woman, never married. The Husting Court record identifies her not as the widow of any man, but as the daughter of John Vyel, Sr. This mention of her role as a daughter indicates that she was never married because, if she were a widow, the will would mention her husband, rather than her father. If her father were still alive, she would not have made her own will. As an unmarried daughter, Vyel was likely to have been one of the least wealthy members of the family.[32] She still, however, had ample resources to bequeath the property she inherited from her sister as well as other assets. The source of the rest of her property is not clear, especially since the will (or parts of it) was contested, but she seems to have been quite comfortable at the time of her death. She had rental income in the Ropery, in the neighborhood of St. Mary Woolchurch, in Old Fish Street, in the Saddlery, and in Bredestrete.

Both Bukerel and Vyel demonstrated themselves to be forward-thinking testators who were aware of the laws and statutes or who took advice from people who were. Vyel's nomination of William de St. Alban as her executor indicates that she trusted

29 Sharpe, *Calendar of Wills*, 2:259.

30 Barron and Sutton, *Medieval London Widows, 1300–1500* (London: Hambledon Press, 1994), xvii.

31 CLRO, HR 24 (13); Martin Reel 3; Sharpe, *Calendar of Wills*, 1:115–16. I have not examined this entry in person, as the microfilm image is very good. Subsequent citations will refer to the roll entry, as it is the most specific way of locating the entry on the microfilm. Thanks to my colleague Marjorie Harrington for providing my first copy of this image at the beginning of my research.

32 Alamichel, *Widows in Anglo-Saxon and Medieval Britain*, 259.

him to oversee her legal affairs. Bukerel and Vyel each allowed for contingencies if the king voided a legacy in her will. Bukerel's will stipulated that if her bequest to the various clergy members at St. Paul's was void because of the king's statute, the rents should be sold and the proceeds substituted in their place.[33] Vyel likewise ordered that if her bequests to the prioress and convent of Stratford for her father's soul and hers were opposed by the king or for any legal statute, the rents should be realized and the prioress and convent should receive the proceeds instead.[34] Sharpe remarks in a note that this likely demonstrates concern about statutes prohibiting religious houses and individuals from buying, selling, or receiving lands or tenements as gifts.[35]

The particular bequests made by the sisters strongly demonstrate their mutual interests and concerns. Rather than movables, the bequests largely consisted of real estate and rental property.[36] The older Isabella Bukerel left her sister, Johanna Vyel, quitrents in the Ropery, in the parish of St. Mary Woolchurch, in Old Fish Street, and in the Saddlery, thus addressing any of her possible material needs.[37] This might have been out of concern for Vyel's unmarried status or with the intention that she would continue to devolve Bukerel's property in specific ways at her own death. Additionally, Bukerel left her clerk, William de St. Alban, a house in the parish of St. Mary Aldermanbury and rents from a tenement on Thames Street. She left bequests to St. Paul's, to the church of St. Mary Aldermanbury, and to the community of priests in London for various prayers and services for the good of her soul and the souls of her family members.[38] Vyel left the same William de St. Alban, one of her executors, income from various rental properties. Of those, the most interesting are those she inherited from Bukerel – near the church of St. Mary Magdalene at the Old Fish Market and in the Saddlery of Westchepe. She carefully specifies that she received these properties from her sister before bequeathing them to de St. Alban. She charged him with the responsibility of having a priest celebrate Mass for her soul a year after her death. She also left rental income from property in Bredestrete to the prioress of the convent at Stratford to provide for prayers and donations to the poor on the anniversaries of her father's death and hers.

Vyel's will also implies an unusually close connection between the family and Bukerel's clerk, William de St. Alban, and relevant church records cast light further light on the possible nature of that relationship. Both Bukerel and Vyel made significant provision for de St. Alban in their wills. Bukerel's will names him as a beneficiary and identifies him as "clerico suo."[39] Vyel maintained the reciprocity of this network by giving him responsibilities as her executor and making her very first bequest to him.

33 Sharpe, *Calendar of Wills*, 1:49; CLRO, HR 11 (68).

34 Sharpe, *Calendar of Wills*, 1:115; CLRO, HR 24 (13).

35 Sharpe, *Calendar of Wills*, 1:116, n. 1.

36 For a discussion of the bequest of real estate as opposed to movables, see Staples, *Daughters of London*, 33, 55–71, and 111–51.

37 A quitrent, *quietus redditus* in Latin, is a rental payment that either excuses the payer from feudal service or reserves the use of the land solely to the tenant without interruption from the owner or others who might have rights of use.

38 CLRO, HR 11 (68); Sharpe, *Calendar of Wills*, 1:49–50.

39 CLRO, HR 11 (68).

The entry for her will in the Husting Court Roll says, "qui quondam fuit cum Isabella sorore mea" [who was formerly with Isabella my sister].[40] After acknowledging that her ties to the clerk stemmed from his association with Bukerel, Vyel left him property she had received from Bukerel. The remark and bequest raise questions about the precise nature of the relationship between Bukerel and de St. Alban. Was he a previous employee of Bukerel's who continued to do other work for the family? If this were the case, why, after fourteen years, would Vyel still refer back to her sister in making a bequest to William de St. Alban? It seems highly possible that there was a romantic partnership between them, an "unmarriage," as Ruth Mazo Karras would define it.[41] They may have maintained a romantic union or partnership that had not been officially affirmed by the church:

> The idea that some churchmen keep their vow of celibacy in the technical sense of being unmarried, but not in the more common sense of abstaining from sexual activity surprises no one, whether we are talking about the Middle Ages or today. ...Some women may have been driven into such unions by economic necessity, but some women may have had other reasons to choose them, ranging from personal affection, to social advantage, to involvement in the church.[42]

Karras' research focuses on priests who were ordained in higher orders and prohibited from marrying. Using the court records of the archdeaconry of Paris as an example, Karras writes that the only traces of the relationships are most often records of a fine paid by the priest.[43] Another complicating factor is the fact that the "fuit cum" might not be a Latin translation of Vyel's words, but the assessment of those who enrolled her will or the wording of the clerk. It is consistent, however, with other cases that record relationships between clergy members and laywomen. Kathryn Kerby-Fulton's work on the fifteenth-century Acta Capitularia, the records of the York chapterhouse, notes fornication cases that use similar language. She writes that on fol. 12v of the Acta, a Johannes Ellys is brought to the court after being caught "cum Agnetis ffauconberg" as well as "cum Emmeta Sargant."[44] "With" also seems an odd preposition for a professional relationship, but if that were the case, Bukerel's 1280 bequests of a house and further rents might be a plausible, if extravagant, gesture to a former employee. For Vyel to name him her executor fourteen years later and make further bequests to him, but still identify him most closely with her sister in her own will, however, strongly implies a particularly significant relationship between Bukerel and de St. Alban, romantic or otherwise. As de St. Alban seems to have been without a benefice at the time, a relationship between him and Bukerel may have been more difficult to detect. Whatever the particular nature of that relationship, the sisters used their legal skills to acknowledge and strengthen this important connection on their own terms.

40 CLRO, HR 24 (13); Sharpe's translation, *Calendar of Wills*, 1: 115–16. Sharpe's translation.

41 Ruth Mazo Karras, *Unmarriages: Women, Men, and Sexual Unions in the Middle Ages* (Philadelphia: University of Pennsylvania Press, 2012).

42 Karras, *Unmarriages*, 115.

43 Karras, *Unmarriages*, 153.

44 Kathryn Kerby-Fulton, *The Clerical Proletariat* (forthcoming).

The combined bequests to de St. Alban by Bukerel and Vyel demonstrate de St. Alban's close relationship with the family through Bukerel. In her own will, Bukerel left de St. Alban a house in the parish of St. Mary Aldermanbury and rents from a tenement in Thames Street.[45] Although the will does not provide any direct indication that their relationship was particularly special, it is noteworthy that the house in the parish of St. Mary Aldermanbury would have been quite near her marital home, the same house she had gone to some lengths to recover after Henry III confiscated it from her husband. The marital home itself passed to her son William, who left it to his wife Dionisia for her life, and to their daughter, Isabella, after Dionisia's death.[46] De St. Alban himself actually used this younger Isabella's property as a landmark for his in his 1313 will.[47] For Vyel to name de St. Alban her executor fourteen years later and make further bequests to him, but still identify him most closely with her sister in her own will, however, strongly implies a lasting and meaningful relationship not only between de St. Alban and the family, but in particular between Bukerel and de St. Alban. Marie-Françoise Alamichel observes that in sermons and didactic treatises, "widows are constantly advised to be the embodiment of discretion, reserve, moderation."[48] Bukerel may have found a way to embody these ideals while also using her powerful position to keep a unique relationship private.

Bukerel's economic power enhanced her agency and protected her social standing. Many or most women who entered into lasting or brief partnerships with members of the clergy occupied relatively unstable positions. If a woman was nominally living with a priest as his employee, rather than as a wife, she had no legal recourse if he died or threw her over. Karras notes that it was unusual for the woman in such a situation to have more stability than her male partner, but Bukerel was a wealthy widow and de St. Alban appears to have been unbeneficed at the time of her death and her sister's. His lack of position may have made their relationship less conspicuous, as extant records show most investigations into clerical misconduct stemming from episcopal visitations and complaints made by parishioners. If the association was romantic, or even if it was a less concrete matter of de St. Alban's "frequenting" Bukerel (an expression Karras compares to the modern "hanging out"), Bukerel still ran a social risk. Her position as a widow, however, left her with more freedom to choose with whom she spent her time, and her personal wealth made it possible for her to make bequests as she liked.

De St. Alban's will affirms his connection with the family, particularly the elder Isabella Bukerel, from whom so much of his property derived. In addition to using

45 Sharpe, *Calendar of Wills*, 1:49–50, and CLRO, HR 11 (68).

46 Sharpe, *Calendar of Wills*, 1:36 and CLRO, HR 9 (81).

47 CLRO, HR 41 (67). Sharpe's *Calendar* does not include this remark. As de St. Alban's will also refers to his own property as a "tenement," it is difficult to ascertain how the properties may or may not have been joined, but he likely meant that his house was connected to properties owned by Isabella or on the same plot of land. The archaeology of that part of the Guildhall neighborhood is not as clear as other excavations in the area, but "tenement" was also a broader term for more than one building or for a lot that contained multiple buildings. Bowsher, *The London Guildhall: An Archaeological History*, 134–36, 166–67.

48 Alamichel, *Widows in Anglo-Saxon and Medieval Britain*, 181.

the younger Isabella's property as a landmark for the property he wishes to be sold, he also identifies it as a legacy he received from her grandmother, the Isabella who mainly occupies this discussion. He orders the sale of all the tenements in the parish of St. Mary Aldermanbury "ex legato domine Isabelle Bokerel pro ut situm est inter tenementum Isabelle filie & hered[is?] William Bukerel" [from the legacy of Isabelle Bukerel just as it is situated between (among) the tenement of Isabelle, daughter and heir of William Bukerel].[49] He again refers to a legacy from Isabella Bukerel as he gives instructions for the sale of rents in the parish of St. Mary Magdalene, in the Old Fish Market, and in the Saddlery of Westchepe, despite the fact that these were technically properties that Bukerel had left to her sister, Johanna Vyel, and which Vyel had later bequeathed to him. It is not impossible, of course, that thirty-three years after Bukerel's death and nineteen years after Vyel's, de St. Alban might simply forget which properties had derived from which sister. As one aspect of many suggestive pieces of evidence, however, the associations de St. Alban incorporated into his will further point to a particularly close relationship with Bukerel.

The agency, foresight, and coordination of Bukerel and Vyel provided de St. Alban with more economic stability than many unbeneficed clergy at the time. He may be a lucky example of those among the "clerical proletariat" about whom Kathryn Kerby-Fulton has recently published, putting together a living working in private homes or other smaller positions while waiting for a benefice.[50] It is possible that Bukerel or Vyel, aware of the precarious state of many under-employed clerics, found it in their power to do more for de St. Alban than one might have expected. Vyel's careful bequest of the same property that Bukerel left her, however, does seem to point to something more significant than professional regard. If de St. Alban was waiting, it seems to have paid off, as his 1313 will, in which he left directions for the bequests he received from Isabella Bukerel and Johanna Vyel to be sold, identifies him as the rector of St. Mary de Kenardyntone in the diocese of Canterbury.[51] Ultimately, therefore, he took full orders, but his closeness with the sisters, particularly his identification in Bukerel's will as "clerico suo" [her clerk] is consistent with someone in the position of an unbeneficed member of the clergy.[52] John Moorman's analysis of ordination lists and the number of parishes in the late thirteenth century shows that there were many more clerics than parish positions to employ them.[53] Kerby-Fulton writes that these clerics were "dependent

49 CLRO, HR 41 (67). Sharpe's abstract of this will, 1:239, is very brief, only listing the properties to be sold without further identifying narration. As I mention above, the properties were quite close. David Bowsher et al. locate both properties in the area they label Tenement 4, west of the Guildhall, along Aldermanbury Street. The property the younger Isabella inherited from her father and grandmother was the main house, although *The London Guildhall: An Archaeological History* mistakenly identifies it as having remained in the possession of Roger de Mortimer (or perhaps this refers to yet another dwelling on the lot). The house William de St. Alban inherited from the older Isabella Bukerel was located to the north of that property. Bowsher et al., 166–67.

50 Kathryn Kerby-Fulton, "The Clerical Proletariat: The Underemployed Scribe and Vocational Crisis," *Journal of the Early Book Society* 17 (2014): 1–34.

51 Sharpe, *Calendar of Wills*, 1:239; Corporation of London Records Office, Husting Roll 41 (67).

52 CLRO, HR 11 (68) or Sharpe, *Calendar of Wills*, 1:49–50.

53 John Richard Humpidge Moorman, *Church Life in the Thirteenth Century* (Cambridge: Cambridge University Press, 1945), 53.

on the laity for their livelihood."[54] This kind of dependence could foster a strong and confident relationship if the sisters found de St. Alban to be a trustworthy and reliable advisor. The care that Vyel took to bequeath more of Bukerel's property to de St. Alban and to deliberately associate him with Bukerel in her will after such a long time is the most impressive indicator that his primary association with the family was through Bukerel. If this were simply a longstanding business relationship concerning the family, there would have been no reason to associate him particularly with Bukerel. Vyel clearly trusted de St. Alban with her own affairs as well, or she would not have made him an executor of her will. It may be that, as either sister dictated her will or as it was entered into the court roll, remarks were changed or omitted. The connection between de St. Alban and these two families underscores how little we know about the relationships between clerics and individual families and how they and the people in their lives were impacted as they waited for benefices.

Bukerel and Vyel were not the only women in their family to exercise legal acumen through their use of estate documents. Their nieces, Isabella de Basinges and her sister Johanna, appeared in court on their own behalf to contest Vyel's will on the grounds that she only held the tenements in question for life.[55] Isabella de Basinges and her sister assessed, perhaps correctly, that their rights to some of Vyel's property had been overlooked and took appropriate steps to assert their rights and those of their heirs. Caroline Barron writes, "The rights of the widow might be ignored by heirs and other interested parties. Often ignorance arose from obscurity of kin and complicated relationships which were the result of high mortality and a high rate of remarriage."[56] Unfortunately, the record does not indicate what the outcome of the challenge was or specify which tenements the sisters called into question. This second set of identically named sisters is yet another example of women with an understanding of the law and the ability to take action to protect their rights and ensure the correct passage of property from hand to hand. According to the entry for her will in the Husting Court Roll, this new Isabella, the widow of Nicholas de Basinges, died in 1297.[57] Isabella de Basinges and this younger Johanna argued that Johanna Vyel only had a life interest in some tenements; but the court roll does not specify which tenements, nor does it record the outcome of the challenge as it sometimes does in other cases. It does seem, however, that there was a ruling to change at least one of the bequests or that it came to the de Basinges family in another way. In 1297, this Isabella – de Basinges – bequeathed to her own daughter the rents that Vyel had originally intended for the other executor of her will, Sir John de Chyvele.[58] The bequests to William de St. Alban were apparently upheld, as he left instructions for them to be sold in his own will of 1313.[59] The brief note in the margin of the Husting Court Roll entry offers no clue

54 Kerby-Fulton, "The Clerical Proletariat," 2.

55 Sharpe, *Calendar of Wills*, 1:115–16; CLRO, HR 24 (13).

56 Barron and Sutton, *Medieval London Widows*, xxi.

57 Isabella de Basinges' will is CLRO, HR 27 (1); Sharpe, *Calendar of Wills*, 1:130. Nicholas de Basinges' will has not been identified.

58 For Isabella de Basinges, Sharpe, *Calendar of Wills*, 1:130. For Johanna Vyel, Sharpe, *Calendar of Wills*, 1:115–116, or CLRO, HR 24 (13).

59 Sharpe, *Calendar of Wills*, 1:239, CLRO, HR 41 (67).

as to why Isabella de Basinges and her sister had an interest in Vyel's properties or even if they argued that the property was meant to devolve to one of them or to another party, although it seems likely they were concerned about their own interests. William's family tree shows that Isabella Bukerel and Johanna Vyel's brother John Vyel, Jr. was the father of Isabella de Basinges and Joanna, strongly suggesting that the property might have been the legacy of another common ancestor.[60] Isabella de Basinges' will included a bequest to maintain a chantry in St. Michael Queenhithe, specifying that prayers be said for the souls of John and Margery Vyel, among others. As this couple were Isabella de Basinges' paternal grandparents, they seem likely candidates.[61]

Isabella Bukerel and her sister Johanna Vyel used their wills to make sure the emotional and material needs of their female family members and other loved ones were met. Bukerel's husband predeceased her, and in 1280, she left a considerable number of rents to Vyel, perhaps ensuring her material comfort and certainly enabling her to leave further bequests to the clerk, William de St. Alban, to whom Bukerel had also left a house and other property. Whether she was following up on something her sister had asked her to do or simply acting out of a desire to acknowledge the relationship between de St. Alban and Bukerel more fully than Bukerel had been able to do, Vyel acted out of concern for her deceased sister's social and emotional ties when she gave her final instructions in 1294. When Vyel's will was enrolled, Isabella de Basinges and her sister appeared in order to challenge it and protect their rights and the rights of their heirs. All of these women used their economic power and social positions in late thirteenth-century London to adeptly govern their own affairs and advocate for themselves in the Husting Court.[62]

60 Williams, *Medieval London*, Appendix, Table B.

61 CLRO, HR 27 (1). Sharpe's entry, *Calendar of Wills*, 1:239, does not mention this bequest and the image on the microfilm, Martin, Reel 3, is very unclear, so it is necessary to consult the will directly.

62 Acknowledgements: I would like to thank Marjorie Harrington for providing me with an image of the entry for Johanna Vyel's will in the Husting Court Roll ahead of the October 1–3, 2015 conference; Nicole Eddy for invaluable consultation on the contents of the wills; and Melissa McCoul and Leanne MacDonald for their helpful reading of this paper.

# PART V

# RELIGIOUS WOMEN IN LEADERSHIP, MINISTRY, AND LATIN ECCLESIASTICAL CULTURE

## Preface to Part V

# RELIGIOUS WOMEN IN LEADERSHIP, MINISTRY, AND LATIN ECCLESIASTICAL CULTURE

JOHN VAN ENGEN

Distinguishing religious women from lay came naturally in a world that looked upon those consecrated to the church or to God as set apart from this world's society spiritually and physically. That observation is only partially true, however, and will take us only a little way toward understanding all the human and social realities. In truth, interactions abounded, and complementarities were self-evident. Queens came to be consecrated for office, as abbesses were into theirs, each a figure of public female authority with their respective duties and powers blessed by these rites. The women in both also came, with few exceptions, from the upper reaches of society, social distinctions arguably being as important, or more so. In this case, the authority of an abbess was in principle more autonomous and absolute than that of a queen – except when a king was away, or she came to serve in a regent capacity as queen-mother. In social and political practice, abbesses worked with lay benefactors or advocates reporting ultimately to her on abbatial lands. Future queens in turn may well have been reared partly in convents, where they learned there a little Latin, or a lot, and they might also return as widows to retire, while abbesses might well find themselves on occasion in court circles. Below these highest levels of leadership, sisters in convents also mostly retained contact to varying degrees with their families (a regular complaint of reformers), and lay women might well visit monastic complexes, male or female, on special feast days or to pray at particular shrines.

But what then of obedience: the profession sworn by a sister to her mother superior and those marriage vows pledging a woman to her husband? This was a culture inclined to hierarchies, usually male hierarchies, but in practice nonetheless much came down to persons and communities. For medievalists, despite some revealing accounts scattered through the centuries of relationships both hopeful and cruel, all this is not so easy to get at in practice, also despite satirical writings full of naughty nuns, unfaithful queens, and shrewish wives. Wives may well have found somewhat more space to look after themselves, or even on occasion to take the lead, than did sisters subject to a rule and bound to the community disciplines of cloister and choir. Exceptions there were and especially in the grandest convents housing the truly elite. And elsewhere too, in the German lands for instance, there were those called "secular canonesses," who in considerable measure could govern their own lives, even leave to marry – if then too sometimes the objects of reformers' complaint. Moreover, even in the case of recluses and anchoresses, those committing themselves to a status somewhere between religious and lay, enclosed alone for a life of prayer, complaints suggest nonetheless that such persons might well emerge by way of their talk windows as in effect local centers of counsel and communication ("gossip" to reformers).

To be sure, medieval women in leadership would certainly face differing expectations, circumstances, opportunities, and limitations if they found themselves in lay or in religious life – but not always all that different. We do well to bring nuance, not binaries, and to pay close attention to practices articulated or presumed rather than to construct rigid strawmen in effect replicating normative utterances. Nor should we limit instances of female leadership or authoritative utterance to the standout cases of a visionary or the austerely ascetical, important a role as those forms certainly played in medieval culture and religion. Finally, practices on the ground, those normative utterances too, varied century by century and region by region, even case by case.

Sarah Foot takes up a famous case, that of abbesses in early Anglo-Saxon England who instantiated many characteristics of leadership; one, Hild of Whitby, hosting a signal event in its religious history, a council that resolved the clashing tensions between Roman and Irish observances. These women were to varying degrees Latinate. Some may have been authors or copyists. But the interpretive challenge here is of another sort, one Foot takes up directly. Much of our evidence in this case comes by way of one male historian, Bede, supplemented by a few hagiographic texts. The accounts do not always synchronize, also on matters pertinent to teasing out underlying attitudes toward women, especially these women manifesting leadership. And of course, we ourselves come to these texts with expectations of women as potentially notable actors and authors or as inevitably suppressed and disparaged. Foot handles this deftly and even-handedly by going back to the sources themselves, where basic interpretive issues immediately arise: first, with respect to Bede's intent in writing (which may well have had little to do with our questions about women's roles and status); second, what he presumed with respect to these women acting as leaders of their religious communities and players in the high ranks of their society; and third, what these women routinely did as Latin-literate chanters of the divine office and keepers of religious libraries. A further matter of interpretation turns on finding the right tone or timbre with respect to characteristics ascribed to women active in their society, whether socially or religiously. Foot notes two terms which may rightly be translated as "bold" or "brash," in effect the women's presence as "outsize," and readily understood as put-downs or gendered smears. They almost certainly spring from gender rivalries or stereotypes, but they may also inadvertently disclose these women as truly actors in society and religion, even routinely so, and self-confident ones, whether or not the men knew how to handle assertive female self-confidence. Here, as Foot notes, a comparison to Bede's ways of handling queens could be revealing. Thus too, as alluded to by Foot, we must consider the patterns at conferences where male laity and clergy routinely interacted, and the king was a player: at these early medieval synods, did men and women also interact, thus these abbesses and bishops and lords? And with no need particularly to note that in his account, what the attitudes were when some women made their views known?

With Megan J. Hall's study of the Ancrene Wisse, or more accurately the Latin glosses on one of its early and most important manuscripts, she moves this macaronic text into a world of Latin and vernacular, of male cleric and quasi-lay or quasi-religious women, of external instruction and personal appropriation. And, at least in the first instance, for this text which will have a long and varied history, we are in the world still of aristocratic women pursuing religion, whose position and options in the world were not always strictly bounded by religious status or by language. Some measure of Latin could often be expected among such women. As Hall rightly notes, Aelred, whose Old English was beyond doubt (his father and grandfather were married priests in northern English parishes), wrote out his instructions for anchorites, here his very own sister, in his glowing Latin – or maybe Aelred wrote out too some version in English now long gone? The author of Ancrene Wisse, almost certainly also a cleric, chose to write in English, indeed at a time when the vernacular for many of the elites might have been French. Hall however chooses to focus on its considerable number of Latin glosses and its familiarity with the format of Latin manuscripts, the directional signals. One may, if one wishes to retain the binaries, ascribe these to a male reader, and some probably were, but in fact, the manuscript is material evidence for a world in which its female readers knew and could work with such signals and with some measure of Latin, particularly perhaps bits close to liturgy and the psalms. Hall analyses comparatively the extent or difficulty of Latin abbreviations in the early manuscripts, the amount of Latin left untranslated in the text, and advice given to the women in the text itself on how to read. Anchoresses were expected to have pens, parchment, and ink and to use these materials to conduct correspondence and offer counsel in their communities. Even the female servants of these women might be expected to have some of these skills. Hall offers further evidence elsewhere that at least some of the extant manuscripts were likely used in an anchorhold, and their marginalia could well be by women readers. Moreover, intriguingly, drawing on her own observations of the restricted physical circumstances of anchorholds (Hall has traveled to many of the extant anchorholds in England), she concludes that there was neither time, space, nor necessity for most early anchoresses to be dependent on male clergy for all their understanding of untranslated Latin text – this reinforced by how much Latin remains untranslated and the level of difficulty involved in the Latin abbreviations in this text.

The worlds of medieval religion and culture, as of writing and reading, were multiple, and we do ourselves little good trying to cram them into unilineal straightjackets. Glossing was active reading, its notes and signals sometimes an active parsing of the text. Women of a social lineage to have access to tutors or schools, also with the religious drive to seek access to holy and instructive texts, might well leave precisely these kinds of evidences behind of their own religious and intellectual life. And, importantly, the scholarly ability to "read" a manuscript for all it might have to tell us, as Hall demonstrates here superbly, can be as important as the ability to read the letters that form its text and to read that text for what it may have to offer.

Gary Macy provides us in effect with an "interlude" reviewing scholarship and calling sharply to our attention ways in which the understanding of Europe's past remains painfully at work still five centuries on. We are all aware of a more general fascination with the Middle Ages, on-again, off-again, also the scholarly study of those subsequent and sometimes very influential visions of its violence and its romance which we call "medievalism." All this informs our entertainment still, at times politics and social outlooks, even as we teachers meet people and students who want to know from us "what was real." Now the same holds for religious groups, be they churches, or Jewish and Muslim communities, anxious to uphold their heritages, and in this case, the consequences reach beyond entertainment and video games. Macy, a student of historical theology, did his early work on the emergence of "transubstantiation" as a technical term approved in the thirteenth century by medieval professors and churchmen as a way to define what happened in the Christian sacrament of sharing bread and wine. For these past years, he has worked in depth on medieval meanings of "ordination" and, particularly, with the notion's implications subsequently for women and laypeople. His essay offers an overview of studies and positions, in part from the perspective of an able medievalist, often too in the defiant stance of a frustrated and aggrieved member of his own religious community. There is an irony here, which also partly informed Foot's essay. Both traditionalists on the status and roles of women and varied progressive feminists may end up, for contrary reasons, consciously or unconsciously, insisting on seeing the past in terms of quite rigid positions, here regarding medieval ordination, where the realities, as Macy has tried to point out, could be more muddled and flexible, thus queens consecrated as well as kings, and both rites accounted by some as "sacraments" – and as Bugyis too will highlight in her essay on liturgical practices.

For those not as conversant with liturgy or sacramental theology as Macy, it may help to position the point he wishes to make by setting out as background four important historical shifts, here described broadly. In the late antique period, as Christianity became the authorized religion, with an exception clause for Judaism, churchmen, many from the finest Roman families and education, appropriated Roman concepts and practices in setting up Christian institutions and laws, including those pertaining to the "ordaining" of people into certain "offices" or tasks– which in some cases plainly included women. This is not to declare Roman and Christian practices synonymous, but they were patently inter-related; and "ordaining" applied to a host of acts. Second, until after the mid-twelfth century, there was no common agreement – beyond baptism, the eucharist, and confirmation – on those rites specially set apart as "sacraments," with varied lists that ranged from three to a dozen or so. The longer ones regularly included the consecration of both nuns and monks as well as abbesses and abbots, sometimes that of both queens and kings, often that of bishops (beyond, or distinct from, priests), while arguments were fierce over whether marriage (involving sexual union) was in or out (a "blessing" – yes; a "sacrament" – how or why?). In the later twelfth century, a narrowing and stabilizing took place, now in the heat and aftermath of the Gregorian Reform and Investiture Controversy. The ordinations of worldly bishops and the status of priests with female companions thus became important considerations in adjudicating a theological issue that turned more largely on which exclusively mediated true saving grace. Furthermore, third, during what we call broadly the movement from the early to the high Middle Ages, a mostly silent shift was taking place with respect to how one thought theologically and ecclesiastically about the sacraments, which now came into fruition. While baptism had been the paradigmatic sacrament for centuries and was still in many of the contentious pamphlets of the Gregorian Reform, the eucharist now emerged for theological purposes as the paradigmatic sacrament. Women (especially midwives) and laypeople could perform a christening, albeit chiefly in emergencies or the absence of a priest, but only priests could confect the eucharist. Finally, and fourth, this same narrowing, after another long battle involving both theologians and canon lawyers, also ruled out the episcopacy (and thus also the papacy) as being a distinct sacramental order (in that respect, both were and are priests). For theology, it all culminated in, or came to be understood in terms of, the priesthood's power to confect the Body and Blood of Christ, whereas for canon law at issue were differing levels of jurisdiction culminating in bishops and popes or, for women, effectively in abbesses. Also now at issue, in an age that newly valued preaching, was its status, how limited to the sacramental priesthood, how much instead a juridically conferred mandate which could thus potentially extend to, say, prioresses or abbesses or recognized visionaries – as it did still in the mid-twelfth century to Hildegard, outside her cloister as well as to her nuns, and as it did in practice within a number of late medieval communities. Forms of personal confession, interwoven with spiritual guidance (its origin), went on in practice too inside convents, as did forms of preaching.

In a world disposed to gendering authority as male, the result of shifts in sacramental theology across the twelfth century became clear enough, even if plenty of exceptions persisted – and women were if anything even more prominent in religious life in the later Middle Ages. Macy's complaint in this "roar of silence," which could easily be replicated in other religious communities, is against an institution, in his case a church that went through a major "updating" (aggiornamento) in the mid-1960s, that refuses to acknowledge its more diverse and changing history in its fullness (also in its theology) but in some cases even insists upon rewriting past history, which is the stuff of authoritarian political regimes.

If it has become a commonplace to see women as taking an ever larger part in religious movements during the later Middle Ages, their presence has meantime also become deeply linked to an astonishing expansion in the writing, copying, and reading of vernacular religious literature during this same era. Herbert Grundmann first posited this connection some eighty years ago – a fruitful suggestion. Scholars now however have begun making more nuanced assessments as to whether the vernacular was intended only or primarily for women, whether Latin then somehow disappeared from the divine office in women's houses (it did not for the professed), what a "movement" is or how we should talk about it historically, and what roles men played too in founding new and experimental communities. At the same time, it often remains commonplace as well to hold, contrariwise and paradoxically, that religious life was variously in steep decline in the later Middle Ages, which then made explosive dismissals of all that was foregoing, if not inevitable, at least intelligible in the Reformation or the Renaissance. This view, though still everywhere to be found, has come in for even more severe critique during the last few years, such that most historians now look to upheaval and startling new energies as present all at once, even if group interests subsequently sliced out one piece of the story for their purposes.

This is precisely what Renate Blumenfeld-Kosinksi does in the case of Colette de Corbie (1381–1447), a figure wholly underappreciated until very recently. Here we have, first of all, a reversal in social class from what we came largely to expect with regard to women leaders or writers prior to the thirteenth century. A girl of the artisan class who lost both parents early on, she emerges, not unlike Joan of Arc, as a leader, in this case a bold and determined religious leader, who is eventually interacting with, also exchanging letters with, great figures both secular and religious. We also find in her story that of a leader and organizer who somehow emerged not only from lower social origins, but also from a first religious life as a recluse to become arguably the most significant representative of the "Franciscan" way in her era, at least as she understood and meant to live it – so determined about adhering to the strictest forms of that life and in her intense admiration of St. Francis (and by extension Clare) that she refused to submit her own followers and their houses not only to the "Conventual" (the traditional or "slack") Franciscans, but even to their Observant branch, to which her own radically austere way of life is however most akin. We find a woman leader who pens a version of the Testament of Francis that insists upon strict obedience and enclosure, as well as poverty, while herself traveling and interacting with donors to build up her own "Franciscan" community. And despite her humble origins, she could apparently write in a French vernacular, unless we are to understand her signature to three dozen or more surviving letters as what she added to something dictated to others – a point still open.

Blumenfeld-Kosinski is a master of religious women writers in French during this era and here builds her account primarily upon two lives written soon after Colette's death, both in French, one by a longtime confessor and advisor, the other by a longtime companion and fellow sister. Blumenfeld-Kosinski notes similarities, also differences, in their accounts. Unlike Bede's account of those early English abbesses, here we have contemporary accounts, indeed by a man and a woman, and are still left with many interpretive issues. Their intentions were certainly to celebrate their friend and companion and leader. But in their writing, do they draw upon hagiographical commonplaces while still attempting to capture the fullness of their friend and leader, or do they rather make their companion into a hagiographical type? What should we make of supposed authorizing visionary experiences in a figure who plainly in actual practice was forceful and shrewd and, in the end, created and led a Franciscan order of her own? How do we, reading or interpreting these accounts, both grasp as scholars and leave room for wonder that a woman of lowly origins assumed such leadership and re-appropriated the Franciscan model for her own modern world? There is an important turn over the last generation of focused scholarship to urban Carthusians, Observant religious, Modern-Day Devout, and many other such groups and types, but we have hardly as yet created a conceptual landscape fit to account for the energy set loose in all these movements, the roles of women in them direct and indirect, and a female leader and reformer of Colette's spirit and power.

Our last essay in Part V, Chapter 18, presents in some sense a reversed interpretive dynamic. If in those Lives written by two of Colette's companions who knew her well, Blumenfeld-Kosinski presents us with an opportunity to observe medieval authors trying to contain a life that burst the boundaries more or less of conventional hagiography, in the Ordinal which Katie Bugyis mines for this chapter, we are privileged to watch her turn a very conventional medieval source into a document revelatory of women's lives and ministerial aspirations. Ordinals were common but important books that literally ordered the liturgical life of a community, setting out their performance of prayer and praise, written in Latin, also for women's houses. Barking, from which this particular ordinal survives (many do not survive, and perhaps even more go unstudied), was not just any house, but another of those great women's houses from the Anglo-Saxon era, comparable to the ones Foot studied in the north, but in this case just east of London. It enjoyed elite patronage and also housed elite women, with those women coming increasingly in the mid-twelfth century from a new Anglo-Norman elite, such that they were now more likely conversant in French, though possibly bilingual, and the staff, the servants and cooks and such, who almost never get mentioned, likely speaking English. The nuns' prayers and praise would have been spoken and sung in Latin. The book on which Bugyis has worked dates from the early fifteenth century (1404).

Now, medieval liturgical books often give medievalists pause on two counts: they require a specialized learning much like any who would research medieval account books or canon law or theology, and they are prescriptive without our knowing exactly how closely any person or community followed them in practice – perhaps reasonably closely, but in the end, we cannot be utterly sure. Bugyis has acquired the liturgical expertise, also the manuscript skills, and brings to the interpretation of this ordinal a historian's imagination. Her interest is in what she calls here, and elsewhere in her work, "ministries," that is, religious acts and services which in medieval (and some modern) contexts may be constricted to certain ordained offices – thus, not unlike the issues Macy is raising. But what do we find here in this medieval convent and resting on what kind of evidence? What Bugyis finds are women, here on the highest feast days of the Christian year, assuming garments and roles normally borne by priests. To be sure, this takes place in what are understood as enactments or performances, but all the same, the roles are assumed, here especially in liturgical drama. Now, she notes contextually that medieval culture incorporated, willy-nilly or shrewdly, moments such as especially the "Feast of Fools" celebrated on Holy Innocents' day, in effect inviting, or at least allowing, sportive inversions of this hierarchical society. But this is something else, built into the liturgical year, an annual performance wherein women in part assumed roles usually reserved for priests and enactments that touch on the very center of Christian belief and worship: the death, burial, and resurrection of Jesus.

This preface began by drawing attention to complementarities and exchanges between the lay and religious worlds in medieval culture and society. The same holds to varying degrees, as these chapters in their different ways show, for female and male, Latin and the vernacular, high and low social class. These chapters draw, often ingeniously, upon five genres of sources: chronicles, glosses, lives, liturgies, and ordination rites. They encourage and sometimes demand fresh looks at the possibilities for female religious leadership in a world gendered male. The powers of abbesses were real, whatever the ritual status of their ordinations, and in effect preaching, confession, spiritual guidance, and more often went on whatever the formal rules. Latin and the vernacular could often prove complementary rather than adversarial and were not gendered strictly male and female. Circumstances and cases always count, for women as for men. Leadership could burst expected boundaries, as could reading and writing. As scholars, we must not, by reverting to a rigid reading of normative texts, or by not making every effort to enter into female life as lived in all its complexity, if too within its limits and cruelties, thus make ourselves as interpreters a caricature of the stance of that same medieval clerical caste we so often critique.

14

# BEDE'S ABBESSES

SARAH FOOT

Historians have traditionally depicted the Age of Bede as a golden age for women in the medieval English church. They have seen this as an era in which women faced a range of opportunities by which to explore their religious vocations and to enjoy significant economic, social and political power, as well as to exercise spiritual authority in ways not open to their sisters in later centuries. Female actors assumed important roles in early narratives of the conversion of the English kingdoms, and the names of many of these feminae gloriosae are well known, thanks in large measure to Bede's vivid and memorable accounts of their activities.[1] Bede's apparent willingness to accord equal attention to female as to male religious has done much to bring the female *vita religiosa* in early Anglo-Saxon England to our attention; so prominent are his detailed descriptions of the holiness and virtue of several abbesses that the fourth book of his Historia ecclesiastica has even been termed 'the book of the abbesses'.[2]

The names of Bede's most celebrated abbesses – Hild of Whitby, Æthelburh of Barking and Æthelthryth of Ely – come so readily to mind that one might imagine them as representative of a much larger group of lesser-known religious women leaders active in his day. It thus proved rather sobering to discover that a systematic search of all of Bede's historical and hagiographical writings reveals the names of only twelve other women who served as abbesses between the mid-seventh and early eighth centuries. Three of those identified by Bede exercised authority over monasteries in northern Gaul in the era before the creation of the first monasteries for women in Anglo-Saxon England: "the most noble abbess called Fara", abbess of Brie, near Meaux in northern France;[3] Æthelburh, daughter of Anna, king of East Anglia; and Sæthryth, Anna's stepdaughter, who both also became abbesses of Brie, "by merit of their virtues".[4] Of the remainder, eight ruled over six different houses in Bede's

1 Joan Nicholson, "*Feminae gloriosae*: Women in the Age of Bede", in *Medieval Women: Dedicated and Presented to Professor Rosalind M. T. Hill on the Occasion of her Seventieth Birthday*, ed. Derek Baker, Studies in Church History, Subsidia, 1 (Oxford: Blackwell, 1978), 15–29.

2 Virginia Blanton, *Signs of Devotion: The Cult of St Æthelthryth in Medieval England, 695–1615* (University Park, PA: Pennsylvania State University Press, 2007), 23.

3 Bede, *Historia ecclesiastica* [hereafter *HE*] III.8: *Bede's Ecclesiastical History of the English People*, ed. B. Colgrave and R. A. B. Mynors (Oxford: Clarendon Press, 1969), 236–7.

4 Bede, *HE* III. 8, 238–9. For the foundation of the first religious houses for women in England see Sarah Foot, *Veiled Women I: The Disappearance of Nuns from Anglo-Saxon England* (Aldershot: Ashgate Publishing, 2000), 35–60; Barbara Yorke, *Nunneries and the Anglo-Saxon Royal Houses* (London: Continuum, 2003), 17–46.

native Northumbria (Coldingham, Hartlepool, Partney, Watton, a house on the River Wear, and Whitby),[5] while the other four governed just two double houses in southern England: Barking in the kingdom of the East Saxons and Ely in East Anglia.[6] Other sources provide the names of some of the abbesses who governed further communities that we know to have housed women in the second half of the seventh and first half of the eighth centuries;[7] whether Bede's silence about the activities of those women arose from deliberate choice or his ignorance of their activities remains imponderable.

Despite the fact that he identified only a small number of different abbesses active during the first Christian centuries in England, Bede still represents an important and informative source for the role of senior women in the church; he seems to have showed himself favourably disposed towards the life and witness of these women. Yet, in recent years, scholars have begun to argue that Bede portrayed women in negative terms, maintaining that he went out of his way to stress their alterity from men and therefore their unsuitability to participate in the divine mysteries.[8] Further, some have deemed his accounts of Anglo-Saxon monasticism to display marked gender asymmetry, arguing that he tended to play down accounts of women in authority, giving a patriarchal structure to his narratives, and often minimized, or overwrote the authority of women.[9] One scholar has even suggested that Bede "felt uncomfortable with, and therefore tried to contain textually, the degree of autonomy and power wielded by the early abbesses – autonomy and power which was subsequently circumscribed by monastic reform".[10] In keeping with this volume's focus on women in leadership, this essay seeks to question the view that Bede showed some antipathy towards women in power by reinvestigating his attitudes towards the women who held the sole position of authority open to them in the early English church: that of abbess.[11]

5 Æbbe at Coldingham: Bede, *Vita S Cuthberti* [hereafter *VSC*], ch. 10, ed. Bertram Colgrave, *Two Lives of Saint Cuthbert* (Cambridge: Cambridge University Press, 1940, repr. 1985), 188–9; Heiu and Hild over Hartlepool: Bede, *HE* IV. 23, 406–9; Æthelhild at an unnamed house near Partney: *HE* III. 11, 246–51; Verca perhaps at South Shields: *VSC*, ch. 37, 272–3; Hereburh at Watton: *HE* V. 3, 460–1; Hild over a monastery on the north bank of the Wear: *HE* IV. 23, 404–7; and Hild, Eanflæd and Ælfflæd at Whitby: *HE* IV. 23, 408–15; *HE* IV. 26, 428–31.

6 Æthelburh and Hildelith at Barking: Bede, *HE* IV.6–10, 354–65; Æthelthryth and Seaxburh at Ely: Bede, *HE* IV. 19, 392–3.

7 Yorke, *Nunneries*, 17–46.

8 Stephanie Hollis, *Anglo-Saxon Women and the Church* (Woodbridge: Boydell Press, 1992), 179–207.

9 Clare A. Lees and Gillian R. Overing, "Birthing Bishops and Fathering Poets: Bede, Hild, and the Relations of Cultural Production", *Exemplaria* 6 (1994), 35–65, 56–8; Diane Watt, "The Earliest Women's Writing? Anglo-Saxon Literary Cultures and Communities", *Women's Writing* 20 (2013), 537–54, at 540.

10 Watt, "Earliest Women's Writing", 538.

11 There would, manifestly, have been a larger paper to write that additionally took account of Bede's attitudes towards secular women leaders, especially queens, but space does not permit their inclusion in this essay, which has a narrower, ecclesiastical focus.

## Bede's Words for Abbesses

If we begin by exploring the language that Bede used to describe abbesses, it appears unexceptional at first glance, at least in the circumstances in which Bede sought to indicate that these women had chosen to adopt lives in religion. He identified Heiu, *religiosa Christi famula* ("a devout handmaid of Christ") as the first Northumbrian women to take the vows and habit of a nun.[12] Verca, abbess of a monastery on the Tyne, perhaps at South Shields, Bede described as a *nobilissima famula Christi* ("a most noble handmaiden of Christ") and "a woman beloved of God" (*dilecta Deo femina*);[13] Æbbe of Coldingham he called *sanctimonialis femina* [14] whereas Hild he termed *religiosissima Christi famula* ("most devout servant of Christ").[15] Bede paid particular attention to women whose devotion to religion found expression in a vocation to virginity. He thus described Ælfflæd (King Oswiu's daughter) as a royal virgin (*regia uirgo*) and observed that Æthelburh, daughter of Anna of the East Angles, "preserved the glory of perpetual virginity, which was pleasing to God". When Æthelburh's tomb was opened some time after her death, her body appeared "as untouched by decay as it had been immune from the corruption of fleshly desires".[16] Most strikingly, Æthelthryth apparently contrived to "preserve the glory of perfect virginity" through two marriages (to a Northumbrian nobleman, Tondberht, and then to King Ecgfrith of Northumbria) before she finally obtained her desire to adopt the religious life, first entering her aunt's community at Coldingham and then founding a monastery at Ely.[17] Bede called her *sancta et perpetua uirgo christi* ("holy and perpetual virgin of Christ"),[18] and used the evidence of the finding of her body incorrupt six years after her death as evidence of her pure state.[19] Whether Bede's contemporaries considered virginity a pre-requisite for those women who aspired to exercise the most senior roles within the church we cannot tell, but clearly it constituted a useful attribute. To most of the women already mentioned who assumed the leadership of their congregations, Bede also gave the title *abbatissa* (the female equivalent of *abbas*, derived from the Hebrew word for father, *abba*). Thus, Bede described Fara, abbess of Brie, as *abbatissa nobilissima* and he called Æthelhild *abbatissa quaedam uenerabilis*.[20]

Bede's choice of language appears more interesting when we focus on the other nouns that he attributed specifically to abbesses, marking them out from other religious

12 Bede, *HE* IV. 23, 406–7.

13 Bede, *VSC*, ch. 35, 264–5; *VSC*, ch. 37, 272–3.

14 Bede, *VSC*, ch. 10, 188–9.

15 Bede, *HE* IV. 23, 408–15.

16 Bede, *HE* IV. 26, 428–9; III. 8, 240–1.

17 Bede, *HE* IV. 19, 390–3.

18 Bede, *De temporum ratione*, ch. 66, *s.a.* 4639, ed. Charles Williams Jones, Corpus Christianorum Series Latina [hereafter CCSL], 123B (Turnhout: Brepols, 1977), 463–534, at 528; trans. Faith Wallis, *Bede: The Reckoning of Time*, Translated Texts for Historians, 29 (Liverpool: Liverpool University Press, 1999), 157–237, at 232.

19 Bede, *HE* IV. 19, 394–5.

20 Bede, *HE* III.8, 236–7; *HE* III. 11, 246–7.

women. Æbbe of Coldingham was "a monastic woman and mother of handmaidens" (*sanctimonialis femina et mater ancillarum*);[21] Æthelthryth of Ely he described as "virgin mother of many virgins dedicated to God" (*uirginum Deo deuotarum perplurium mater uirgo*),[22] while Hild, abbess of Whitby, enjoyed the role of mother of them all (*mater illarum ominium*).[23] We may readily understand why the image of maternity should have seemed appropriate. Early medieval religious life modelled itself closely on that of earthly families; those women and men who aspired to devote themselves to the service of God renounced their connections with their blood kin in order to attach themselves to like-minded sisters and brothers, living under the overall authority of a mother (or father) in religion.[24] Yet, Bede applied the imagery of motherhood to abbesses more than he chose to talk about the role of abbots to act as fathers to the monks in their care (with the notable exception of the abbots of his own monastery, Wearmouth Jarrow).[25] He might have sought in this fashion to draw attention to the cherishing and nurturing role of abbesses; note how he described Æthelburh, sister of Eorcenwald, bishop of London and first abbess of Barking, as *mater ac nutrix* ("mother and nurse") of a community of women dedicated to God.[26] We should not, however, assume that he chose such language as a subtle way of diminishing these prominent women, downplaying their status to reduce their leadership and power, by reducing them to roles we might deem conventionally passive and subordinate. It seems more relevant that Bede himself was probably an orphan; by his own account, "relatives" (not parents) put him into the monastery at Wearmouth at the age of seven, and he was remarkably close emotionally to Abbot Ceolfrith at Jarrow.[27] Had he never known his own mother, nor enjoyed a meaningful relationship with any other adult female relative, he might well have found himself drawn to praise the example of these women who "nurtured spiritual children brought into one family of holy profession although in terms of the flesh they were born of different parents".[28]

21 Bede, *VSC*, ch. 10, 188–9.

22 Bede, *HE* IV. 19, 392–3.

23 Bede, *HE* IV. 23, 412–13.

24 Sarah Foot, "Anglo-Saxon Ecclesiastical Households", in Benjamin T. Hudson, ed., *Familia and Household in the Medieval Atlantic Province* (Tempe, AZ: Arizona Center for Medieval and Renaissance Studies, 2011), 51–71, at 55–7.

25 Compare Bede's homily for the feast of the first abbot of Wearmouth, Benedict Biscop, Bede, *Homiliarum euangelii*, I. 13, ed. David Hurst, CCSL, 122 (Turnhout: Brepols, 1955), 91–3; trans. Lawrence T. Martin and David Hurst, *Bede the Venerable: Homilies on the Gospels I, Advent to Lent*, Cistercian Studies, 110 (Kalamazoo, MI: Cistercian Publications, 1991), 128–31 [hereafter *Hom*]. Also his description of Abbot Ceolfrith as "noster parens": *Historia abbatum*, ch. 23, ed. and trans. Christopher Grocock and I. N. Wood, *Abbots of Wearmouth and Jarrow* (Oxford: Clarendon Press, 2013), 74–5 [hereafter *HA*].

26 Bede, *HE* IV.6, 356–7.

27 Bede, *HE* V. 24, 566; for full discussion of this issue see my "Bede's Kings", in *Writing Kingship and Power in Anglo-Saxon England*, ed. Rory Naismith and David Woodman (Cambridge: Cambridge University Press, 2017) , 25-51, at 49-51.

28 Bede, *Hom*. I. 13, 93. See also David Pelteret, "Bede's Women", in *Women, Marriage, and Family in Medieval Christendom: Essays in Memory of Michael M. Sheehan, C.S.B.*, ed. Constance M. Rousseau and Joel T. Rosenthal (Kalamazoo, MI: Medieval Institute Publications, 1998), 19–46, at 25.

Yet, while our minds turn naturally to earthly families when we think about mothering, Bede found the ultimate model for family life in heavenly family, where Mary, the blessed virgin, was both virgin and mother. In his homilies for Advent and Christmas (and the feast of the purification) and his commentary on the gospel of Luke, Bede stressed Mary's divine maternity (using on one occasion the Greek noun *Θεοτόκος*, which he translated as *dei genitrix*).[29] He drew attention to her role in showing humanity the path of humility by the example of her religious devotion and venerable chastity, repeatedly emphasising her purity and her perpetual virginity, as well as her freedom from subjection to the law.[30] Interestingly, he attributed to two of our abbesses, both as it happens abbesses of Whitby, the noun *ancilla* ("handmaid"), the word that the evangelist Luke put into the mouth of the Virgin in his account of the annunciation.[31] Linking motherhood and virginity in his description of Ælfflæd of Whitby in his *Life of Cuthbert*, Bede depicted her as sharing Mary's attributes: "the venerable handmaiden (*ancilla*) of Christ, who to the joys of virginity added a maternal and pious care of no small company of the servants of Christ.[32] Of Hild, Whitby's first abbess, Bede said that all who knew Hild, "the handmaiden of Christ and abbess (*Christi ancella et abbatissa*) used to call her mother because of her outstanding devotion and grace"; her example provided opportunities for salvation not only to those who lived in her monastery, but to others far away who heard of her industry and virtue.[33]

## The Role of the Abbess

Having looked at the terms in which Bede described our women leaders in the church, let us consider further what the role of abbess involved, over what sort of institutions these women exercised headship, and what Bede says of how they functioned as leaders. While the earliest English religious houses for men date from the conversion period, communities for women emerged rather later. The first attempts to create such congregations date from the 640s and 650s, but the majority were established during the last three decades of the seventh century; in the earlier period pious women had to go to Gaul to satisfy their spiritual ambitions.[34] Even so, the idea of female monasticism had become well established by the time that Bede wrote and a number of houses for women – or rather, double houses, of men and women living together under the overall authority of an abbess – existed across England by c. 700.[35] The advantages of mixed communities are obvious: ordained clerics could provide sacraments for the

29 Bede, *In Lucae euangelium expositio*, I. 1, ed. David Hurst, CCSL 120 (Turnhout: Brepols, 1960), 34 [hereafter *In Luc.*].

30 Bede, *Hom.* I. 4, 21; I. 5, 35, I.18, 129.

31 Luke 1: 38: "Dixit autem Maria: Ecce ancilla Domini"; cf. *In Luc.* I. 1, 35.

32 Bede, *VSC*, ch. 23, 230–2. Compare Pelteret, "Bede's Women", 35–6. We might also, of course, note the echo of Pope Gregory's description of himself as "seruus seruuorum dei", as for example in letters of his quoted by Bede, *HE* I. 23, I. 24, I. 29, I. 30, 70–1, 106–7, 108–9.

33 Bede, *HE* IV. 23, 410–11.

34 Bede, *HE* III. 8, 236–9; Yorke, *Nunneries*, 23–8.

35 Foot, *Veiled Women*, 35–49.

nuns and say masses on behalf of the souls of the abbey's dead, including their founders; men could perform any necessary heavy labour, both in fields and in building and repairing the fabric of monastic dwellings; they also offered potential protection for the nuns from the physical or sexual attack from outside, to which the women might otherwise have been thought especially vulnerable. As an institution, the double house arose only in Frankia, Spain and England (although the notion subsequently spread from England to Germany thanks to the work of Anglo-Saxon missionaries in the eighth century); it differs both from the earlier mixed houses of the Eastern Church and from later medieval double houses such as those founded by Gilbert of Sempringham which men always governed.[36] The fact that these institutions had female headship gave religious women among the Anglo-Saxons opportunities to exercise social, economic, cultural and political power. Although we know of occasions on which men performed different roles on behalf of their abbesses, none of them exercised ultimate authority over a mixed-gender community and its affairs, either internally or in the wider world: that power lay firmly in female hands. We need not be surprised, therefore, to discover how many of the women who held such positions came from royal or aristocratic families.

Discussion of what Bede had to say about how women fulfilled those positions of responsibility raises an immediate methodological problem. For the supplying of information about the leadership roles occupied by women in the church lay far from Bede's wider purposes in writing history. He constructed his narrative to continue that of the Acts of Apostles, in order to show the fulfilling of Christ's injunctions to his apostles to take the gospel "to Jerusalem, to Judea and Samaria and to the ends of the earth".[37] Bede saw Britain as lying at the ends of the earth, and its conversion – and the bringing of almost all its peoples, save the recalcitrant British, to the Roman faith – as the completion of the divine charge. Within the wider frame of the story of Christian development in these shores, Bede displayed a natural interest in the part played by women in that process. But he proved most interested in women who manifested particular holiness: those who showed the working of the grace of God through their lives, especially those who experienced visions and angelic visitations, and those through whom miracles were worked or prayers answered. He thus devoted most space in his *History* to accounts of women for whom he had obtained written hagiographical materials: the nuns of the community at Barking in Essex; Hild, abbess of Whitby (and her successor Ælfflæd); and Æthelthryth, abbess of Ely. The latter he so admired that he had previously written a poem in her praise, comparing her with virginal martyrs of the early church.[38] This should prepare us for what we will find; we should remember that his questions are not ours, and be cautious of applying inappropriate standards when he fails to tell us what we had hoped to hear.

Bede demonstrated the ability of women to act as powerful political agents most obviously in describing the part they played in the foundation and endowment

36 S. E. Rigold, "The 'Double Minsters' of Kent and their Analogies", *Journal of the British Archaeological Association*, 3rd ser. 31 (1961), 27–37; Foot, *Veiled Women*, 49–56.

37 Acts 1: 9; Sarah Foot, *Bede's Church*, Jarrow Lecture 2012 (Jarrow: St Paul's Church, 2013), 10–12.

38 Bede, *HE* IV. 20, 396–401.

of monastic communities. Thus, the former Northumbrian queen, Æthelthryth, having achieved her ambition to take control of her life by leaving her marriage, built a monastery at Ely in her homeland of East Anglia. Bede shows her exercising patronage as well as instigating the formation of the community that gathered around her.[39] Æthelburh, Æthelthryth's sister, was among those women who went to Frankia to adopt the religious life before the foundation of English houses, but Bede described her also acting as a patron and initiating the building of a new church, dedicated to the apostles at Brie where, although a foreigner, she had become abbess.[40] Other examples could also be cited of women who, either alone or with male relatives, acted to create monastic houses, but our interest in this volume lies in women who not only provided materially for the creation or support of institutions housing women, but also took on the leadership of those communities. The difficulty of exploring just how women performed such roles lies in the paucity of concrete evidence that Bede provided beyond that already mentioned. In the case of Æthelthryth indeed, Bede took less interest in her leadership of her community than in manifestations of her spirituality and devotion. As Pelteret has argued, "the literary virtuosity of Bede's composition serves only to distract us from Æthelthryth's physical presence and her accomplishments by shifting our focus away from her to the abstraction celebrated by the poem on virginity".[41] Similarly, in his portrait of another Æthelburh, sister of Eorcenwold, bishop of London, the first abbess of Barking, Bede dwelt more on her illness and death than on her actions in managing and controlling the everyday affairs of her monastery.[42] On the one occasion on which she might have made an executive decision and ordered those under her to take action (in the matter of deciding where to create a cemetery for the female members of the congregation), "divine providence" made the choice on her behalf, shining a light on the most suitable portion of the enclosure.[43]

Bede made only occasional direct reference to individuals employed to work on an abbess's behalf. In recounting the story of the herdsman-poet Cædmon, Bede left the abbess of Whitby unnamed (although the events clearly occurred in Hild's day), presumably to focus attention on the main protagonist himself. His tale required mention of the reeve at Whitby, who served as the abbess's deputy in charge of the agricultural labourers on the estate and thus became the first to hear of Cædmon's marvellous talents in versifying.[44] Her deputy having made his report, the abbess herself decided to receive Cædmon into the community of brothers and have him instructed in the course of sacred history.[45] A nun called Frigyth also assumed a role on the abbess's behalf: she presided over the monastery at Hackness (a daughter house of

39 Bede, *HE* IV. 19, 392–3.

40 Bede, *HE* III. 8, 238–41

41 Pelteret, "Bede's Women", 37.

42 Bede, *HE* IV. 6–9, 354–63; Peleteret, "Bede's Women", 36.

43 Bede, *HE* IV. 7, 356–9.

44 Bede, *HE* IV. 24, 416–17. It does not seem necessary to assume, with Diane Watt, that Bede deliberately wrote out Hild's crucial role as Cædmon's patron: "Earliest Women's Writing", 543.

45 Bede, *HE* IV. 24, 416–19.

Whitby) "in place of the abbess".[46] Æthelthryth's successor at Ely, Seaxburh, instructed some of the brothers to go out from the monastery to look for blocks of stone from which to make a new coffin for their former abbess; they had to travel some way from the Isle of Ely before they found a deserted fortress.[47] Otherwise Bede did not consider it relevant to his wider purpose to include accounts of the actions of abbesses in, for example, arranging for the clearance of trees from a site suitable for the erection of new buildings, the diversion of water supplies, the acquisition of stone for construction, or the collection of the harvest. Equally, he did not describe abbesses engaged in the organisation of their material resources in the same way that the hagiographer Stephen described how Wilfrid supervised the building of stone churches at Ripon and Hexham; placed charters recording his landed endowments onto the altar of the church at Ripon on the day of its dedication; or divided his money on his deathbed.[48] This silence probably arises from the nature of the sources at Bede's disposal rather than any intention on his part to diminish women's pragmatic or leadership roles. Only in the case of the abbots of his own community at Wearmouth and Jarrow could Bede provide a first-hand account of their involvement in practical day-to-day affairs.[49]

Responsibility for offering hospitality on a community's behalf fell frequently to abbesses. For example, Abbess Verca received Cuthbert when he came to her monastery on the Tyne (perhaps at South Shields) and arranged for him to be suitably refreshed (supplying water which he then turned into wine).[50] Yet here, and on the occasion on which Ælfflæd organised a feast in Cuthbert's honour on one of Whitby's estates the evening before he was to dedicate a new church,[51] we can struggle to disentangle the conventional Anglo-Saxon female role in hospitality from either the specifically monastic responsibility to offer succour to guests, or the particular role of an abbess to fulfil that obligation.[52] Female leadership may perhaps be better demonstrated by the fact that the bishop sometimes visited specific double houses at the direct invitation of abbess: thus Æbbe (the sister of kings Oswald and Oswiu) "asked Cuthbert to come and visit her and her monastery at Coldingham for the sake of exhorting them".[53] In her role as abbess of Whitby, Ælfflæd clearly felt herself empowered to demand Cuthbert's presence, asking him to meet her at Coquet Isle so that she might converse with him, or to come and dedicate a church for her.[54] Whether this behaviour genuinely illustrates female leadership, or rather reflects the capacity of royally born women to summon men to attend them when they wished remains

46 Bede, *HE* IV. 23, 412–13.

47 Bede, *HE* IV. 19, 394–5.

48 *The Life of Bishop Wilfrid by Eddius Stephanus*, chs. 17, 22–3, 63, ed. and trans. Bertram Colgrave (Cambridge: Cambridge University Press, 1927; reprinted 1985), 36–7, 44–7, 136–7.

49 Consider, for example, the remarkably detailed account of the agricultural activities supposedly performed by Hwætberht, even after his assumption of the abbacy: Bede, *HA*, ch. 8, 42–3.

50 Bede, *VSC*, ch. 35, 264–7.

51 Bede, *VSC*, ch. 34, 262–3.

52 Christine Fell, *Women in Anglo-Saxon England and the Impact of 1066* (Oxford: Blackwell, 1984), 49–50.

53 Bede, *VSC*, ch. 10, 188–9.

54 Bede, *VSC*, chs. 24 and 34, 234–9, 262–3.

uncertain. In large measure, the two sorts of status will have merged to the point of becoming indistinguishable, yet Bede may deliberately have sought to draw attention to the *religious* status of these women to counter any implication that these male ecclesiastics had responded to royal whim.

In the case of Hild, abbess of Whitby, Bede did, however, provide unequivocal evidence of the exercise of significant leadership by a woman, showing her engaged both practically in the administration of the mixed-gender institution of which she had charge, and also more widely assuming authority over churchmen in her region. Hild also came of royal stock; her father, Hereric was a nephew of King Edwin, and as a teenager, she had been baptised into the Christian faith at the same time as that king, in the year 627.[55] Tellingly, Bede never described her as a virgin and indeed, since she spent thirty-three years living in the world before adopting the religious life, it seems most likely that she had been married, possibly even to someone who remained a pagan.[56] Far from evidence of gendered antipathy, we might interpret Bede's silence about Hild's former marital status as an attempt on his part to enhance her reputation for sanctity. Hild's first experience of monasticism came when Bishop Aidan established her, with a small group of companions, on the north side of the River Wear. After a year, she assumed the leadership of the house at Hartlepool on the retirement of its founder and first abbess, Heiu. Having ruled there for some years (attracting the admiration of Bishop Aidan and other devout men who used to visit her and loved her for her innate wisdom), Hild then "undertook either to found or to set in order a monastery at a place called *Streonæshalch*, a task imposed upon her which she carried out with great industry".[57] Whether or not this was a pre-existing religious community, Bede shows clearly how firmly Hild took charge of the ordering of the community, imposing the same rule of life on the new congregation that she had followed at Hartlepool; her rule promoted various Christian virtues and was modelled on the way of life followed by the earliest Christian community in Jerusalem as described in the Acts of the Apostles. After her move to Whitby, Hild's influence and authority as a leader were not restricted to her own community. Bede reported that her prudence (*prudentia*) led not only ordinary people but also kings and princes to seek her counsel when in difficulty.[58] Her role as counsellor not just within, but beyond the church marked her out as exercising a specific kind of leadership.

Hild also famously played some part in the great synod to discuss the date of Easter that was held in her monastery in 664. Some have argued that Bede wrote Hild out of this narrative, but such a reading fails to recognise the place the Synod of Whitby occupied in overall structure of his *Historia*. In Bede's schema by which he modelled his work on the Acts of the Apostles, the council of Whitby lay at the centre point and climax of the volume, serving the same function as had the Council of

55 Bede, *HE* IV. 23, 406–7.

56 Christine Fell, "Hild, abbess of Streonæshalch", in *Hagiography and Medieval Literature: A Symposium*, ed. Hans Bekker-Nielsen *et al.* (Odense: Odense University Press, 1981), 76–99, at 78–9.

57 Bede, *HE* IV. 23, 408–9; Fell, "Hild", 81–2.

58 Bede, *HE* IV. 23, 408–9, quoting Acts 2: 44–5 and Acts 4: 32–4.

Jerusalem in Acts;[59] the place for narrating Hild's story would come later, in the following book. That Hild acted in some sense as the host of Whitby seems correct. Bede tells us that the synod took place in the abbey over which she exercised authority and Stephen, author of *The Life of Bishop Wilfrid*, also said the synod was held "in the presence of the holy mother and most pious Hild".[60] Yet Bede cannot deliberately have concealed Hild's role in these events, for no woman would have overseen the formal sessions of the synod itself. Kings presided at royal councils (just as archbishops and bishops did over ecclesiastical ones); Oswiu took the chair, opening the proceedings with his relatio, the statement of the issue that the meeting had to resolve.[61] Rather than imagining that Bede deliberately wrote Hild out of the proceedings, we may wonder that this one woman found mention at all among the catalogue of men who dominated Bede's (and Stephen's) accounts of the discussion. No evidence supports Diane Watt's assertion that the relative invisibility of Hild on this occasion meant that "Bede may have been unsettled by Hild's public and political life";[62] nor do we have to wonder with David Pelteret if Bede "baulked at the idea that a woman could help shape ecclesiastical doctrine".[63] Bede did indeed fail to put words into Hild's mouth when recounting the deliberations of the council, even though he reported a number of lengthy speeches made by various different men, notably King Oswiu, Colman, bishop of Lindisfarne, and Wilfrid. Wilfrid, not Hild, lies at the centre of his narrative; by Bede's account, the successful outcome of the synod arose in large measure from that bishop's rhetorical skills. Misogyny did not drive Bede either to diminish Hild's role or depoliticise her sanctity;[64] he did, indeed, leave her silent, but he also silenced all the Irish participants apart from Bishop Colman, and further on the Roman side, put no words into the mouths of the priest Agatho, James the deacon, or the cleric called Romanus.[65] Hild's role required no further description beyond the fact that, as Bede noted, it was within the monastery over which she presided that the synod took place.

Education represents an important sphere in which Bede portrayed abbesses as leaders, not merely through their roles in training the members of their communities to high levels of Latin learning but also, arguably, by the encouragement they offered for new writing. Although there survive almost no manuscripts or texts from this period that can with certainty be attributed to female production, significant evidence

59 Roger Ray, "What Do We Know about Bede's Commentaries?", *Recherches de théologie ancienne et médievale* 49 (1982), 5–20, at 19–20.

60 *The Life of Bishop Wilfrid*, ch. 10, 20.

61 Bede, *HE* III. 25, 298–9: "First King Oswiu began by declaring that it was fitting that those who served one God should observe one rule of life and not different in the celebration of the heavenly sacraments." For discussion of the procedure followed at Anglo-Saxon synods, specifically who chaired the sessions, see Catherine Cubitt, *Anglo-Saxon Church Councils c. 650–c. 850* (London and New York: Leicester University Press, 1995), 87–92.

62 Watt, "Earliest Women's Writing", 543.

63 Pelteret, "Bede's Women", 27.

64 Watt, "Earliest English Lives", 544.

65 For a more positive reading, arguing that Bede put Hild "on par with other men", see Jean A. Truax, "From Bede to Orderic Vitalis: Changing Perspectives on the Role of Women in the Anglo-Saxon and Anglo-Norman Churches", *Haskins Society Journal* 3 (1991), 35–51, at 43.

points both to the engagement of female communities in intellectual activity, and to the leadership offered by abbesses in that endeavour. Barking constitutes an obvious example: Aldhelm dedicated his tract *De virginitate* to Hildelith and the nuns of Barking, apparently expecting the women to cope with its demanding prose.[66] The nuns may themselves have written the small book (*libellus*) that provided Bede with his information about the visions seen in the East Saxon abbey; perhaps Hildelith herself commissioned it.[67] Archaeological evidence of the survival of styli (for writing on wax tablets) and book-clasps from Whitby supports Bede's assertions about the promotion of learning by the community's abbesses.[68] He reported that Hild compelled all those under her direction to devote as much time to the study of the holy Scriptures as to the performance of good works, stressing the fact that her energies ensured the provision in her abbey of men trained for holy orders, that is for the services of the altar.[69] Among these were five men who ultimately became bishops, one of whom (Oftfor) had studied with Hild at Hartlepool, before moving with her to the new monastery at Whitby.[70] Again the narrative makes Hild's implicit role stand out; far from keeping these men at bay, Hild enabled them to achieve their full potential by nurturing them as future church leaders.

Much discussion has surrounded the gender of the author of the earliest example of hagiographical writing to survive from England: the anonymous Life of Pope Gregory the Great, composed at Whitby. Internal evidence from the text suggests that it was written between 704 and 714, during the lifetime of Ælfflæd, and quite possibly under her abbacy.[71] Diane Watt recently made a convincing case for seeing a vibrant literary culture among the women at Whitby, producing not only the now-lost life of Hild to which we know that Bede had access (traces of which are also apparent in the *Old English Martyrology*),[72] but also the Life of Gregory, apostle to the English. In his *Historia*, Bede drew attention to Ælfflæd's learning. Reporting her move to *Streonæshalch* with Hild, he said that the king's daughter had been first a pupil and then a teacher (*magistra*) of life under the rule.[73] At a later point, he described

66 Sarah Foot, "*Flores ecclesiae*: Women in Early Anglo-Saxon Monasticism"; *Female vita religiosa between Late Antiquity and the High Middle Ages: Structures, Developments and Spatial Contexts*, ed. Gert Melville and Anne Müller, *Vita Regularis: Ordnungen und Deutungen religiosen Lebens im Mittelalter* 47 (Berlin: Lit, 2011), 173–85, at 173–5.

67 Diane Watt, "Lost Books: Abbess Hildelith and the Literary Culture of Barking Abbey", *Philological Quarterly* 91 (2012), 1–21, at 2.

68 Rosemary Cramp, "Monastic Sites", in *The Archaeology of Anglo-Saxon England*, ed. David Wilson (Cambridge: Cambridge University Press, 1976), 201–52, at 228; cf. Patrick Sims-Williams, *Religion and Literature in Western England, 600–800* (Cambridge: Cambridge University Press, 1990), 185–6.

69 Bede, *HE* IV. 23, 408.

70 Bosa, became bishop of York; Ætla was bishop of Dorchester; John (of Beverley) became bishop of Hexham; and Wilfrid (not the famous Wilfrid), bishop of York. For Oftfor see Sims-Williams, *Religion*, 186–7.

71 Colgrave, *The Earliest Life*, 45–9.

72 *The Old English Martyrology*, 17 November: Hild, ed. Christine Rauer (Cambridge: D. S. Brewer, 2013), 217, and see n. 226, at 306.

73 Bede, *HE* III. 24, 292: "primo discipula uitae regularis, deinde etiam magistra".

Ælfflæd as a devout *doctrix* ("teacher"), using, in its feminine form, his favourite word for a teacher: *doctor*. For Bede *doctores* were those whose knowledge and understanding enabled them to get behind the veil of the literal meaning of scripture to the deep meanings underneath. As he explained on various occasions, one who sought to become a *doctor* needed to combine active pursuit of learning with contemplative prayer and exemplary living, in order to inspire in others not just basic understanding but right doctrine and true ideals.[74] That group did not, however, consist exclusively of men.

For Bede, the church's *doctores* were those charged with transmitting the church's heritage, faithful interpreters of scripture who acted as a defence against heresy.[75] As well as ordained clergy, they included others from the wider ecclesial community, including significant monastic leaders, and even the devout heads of secular households.[76] Bede may even have envisaged that women might preach.[77] He dedicated just one of his biblical commentaries to a female reader: the commentary on Canticle of Habakkuk, written in response to the request of an unnamed nun whom he addressed as his "dearly beloved sister in Christ".[78] While he devoted much of that text to advising his female reader to listen to the teaching of male preachers, he also seemed to argue that his dedicatee should not just listen, but should act on the teaching she had heard. Perhaps we could read this text as commending the activity of oral preaching to a female audience.[79] While Bede may, of course, have written the commentary for an abbess whose name we will never know, Ælfflæd of Whitby (who did not die until c. 714) seems a likely recipient, bearing in mind the favourable terms in which he described her, terms which pointed towards her learning.

### Women who Transgressed

As we have already seen, some recent historians have argued that Bede was unfavourably disposed towards women in positions of leadership, arguing that he disliked the notion that women might assume prominent status in his own society.[80] That he could articulate discontent is most sharply apparent in the letter that he wrote to his local diocesan Ecgberht, bishop of York, in 734 to complain – in distinctly frank and un-

74 Alan Thacker, "Bede and the Ordering of Understanding", in *Innovation and Tradition in the Writings of the Venerable Bede*, ed. Scott DeGregorio (Morgantown, VA: West Virginia University Press, 2006), 27–63, at 43.

75 Alan Thacker, "Bede's Ideal of Reform", in *Ideal and Reality in Frankish and Anglo-Saxon Society*, ed. Patrick Wormald *et al.* (Oxford: Basil Blackwell, 1985), 130–53, at 130–1.

76 Bede, *Hom.*, I. 7, 49.

77 Thacker, "Bede's Ideal", 131; Sarah Foot, "Women, Prayer and Preaching in the Early English Church", in *Prayer and Thought in Monastic Tradition: Essays in Honour of Sr Benedicta Ward*, ed. Santha Bhattacharji *et al.* (London: Bloomsbury, 2014), 59–76, at 73–5.

78 Benedicta Ward, "'To my dearest sister': Bede and the Educated Woman", in *Women, the Book and the Godly*, ed. Lesley Smith and Jane H. M. Taylor (Cambridge: D. S. Brewer, 1995), 105–11, at 107.

79 Foot, "Women", 61–3.

80 In addition to the works cited above see Clare A. Lees and Gillian R. Overing, *Double Agents: Women and Clerical Culture in Anglo-Saxon England* (Philadelphia, PA: University of Pennsylvania Press, 2001), 15–39.

modulated tones – about a variety of abuses he perceived in the church of his own day. Among these, he identified the lay foundation of monasteries, and commented on the outrage of laymen "who even go so far as to ask for places to build monasteries, as they themselves put it, for their wives, who in equal foolishness, although they are laywomen (*laicae*), allow themselves to be rulers/governesses/mistresses (*rectrices*) of the maidservants of Christ (*famularum Christi*)".[81] He had no hesitation in voicing his disapproval of the manner in which aristocratic social norms had come to dominate establishments that should have devoted themselves exclusively to consideration of the things above. In that light, his choice of the noun *rectrix* to refer to those who lead or guide such congregations, instead of the term *abbatissa*, which more usually denoted the rulers of female communities, tells its own story.[82] Whether some other passages in his writings should also be read as expressing varying degrees of antipathy to more orthodox female leadership seems to me to be far less obvious. When in his *History*, Bede praised Ælfflæd as *doctrix*, he also pointed out that Trumwine, former bishop of Abercorn, retired to Whitby, where Ælfflæd and her mother Eanflæd were ruling; he asserted that Ælfflæd "found the bishop a great help in the government of the monastery as well as a comfort in her own life".[83] Stephanie Hollis has read this to mean that Trumwine assumed the governance of Whitby, acting as Ælfflæd's superior, as if Bede wished to signal Ælfflæd's inability to manage the governance of her community without input from a retired bishop.[84] With Christine Fell, I am more inclined to imagine that Ælfflæd would neither have needed, nor welcomed such help.[85] Two passages in Bede's *Life of Cuthbert* do, however, appear at first sight to portray this abbess more negatively.

Once Ælfflæd – "most reverend virgin and mother of the virgins of Christ" (*reuerentissima uirgo et mater uirginum Christi*) – asked Bishop Cuthbert to meet and talk with her; they both travelled to an island by the mouth of the River Coquet, famous for its companies of monks. After conversing for a while, Ælfflæd fell at the bishop's feet and begged him to use his gifts of prophecy to reveal how much longer her brother would live and rule over the Northumbrian kingdom. In the earlier, anonymous version of this story written by a monk of Lindisfarne, although the bishop had begun by speaking "in an indirect way about the brevity of man's life", he went on to tell the abbess that her brother had only a year to live.[86] But Bede handled the whole episode completely differently, making Cuthbert rebuke her: "It is wonderful that you, a wise woman and learned in the Holy Scriptures (*sapiens femina et in sanctis erudite scripturis*), should be willing to speak of the term of our human life as if it were

81 Bede, *Epistola ad Ecgbertum episcopum*, §12, ed. and trans. Grocock and Wood, *Abbots*, 148–9, where *rectrices* is translated as "abbesses".

82 The feminine noun *rectrix* (equivalent to the masculine *rector*) derives from the Latin *regere*, to rule, with the suffix *-trix*. We might read Bede's use of it here as ironical; their lay status and lack of any training or education in the religious life of course made the wives of these laymen utterly unfit to rule any sisters of Christ.

83 Bede, *HE* IV. 26, 430–1.

84 Hollis, *Anglo-Saxon Women*, 129.

85 Fell, "Hild", 86.

86 Anon., *VSC*, III. 6, ed. Colgrave, *Two Lives*, 102–5.

long, when the Psalmist says that "our years pass away like those of a spider" (*anni nostri sicut aranea meditabuntur*), and when Solomon warns us that "if a man live many years and rejoice in them all, yet let him remember the days of darkness, for they shall be many; when they come the past is reckoned as vanity."[87] Similarly, when Ælfflæd persisted, despite this rebuke, to try and push the saint on the identity of Ecgfrith's successor, Bede described her enquiry as made "with womanly daring" (*audacia feminea*).[88] This comment on Ælfflæd's brashness seems secondary to the real issue at stake in this episode; Bede's disapproval related to the exploitation of the saint's prophetic insights for worldly ends, which he thought represented an inappropriate melding of the religious and the secular.

Another episode in the same text involving the same abbess, Ælfflæd, seemingly presents a similarly ambivalent (even overtly misogynistic) view of her authority.[89] Cuthbert had come to an estate belonging to the monastery of Whitby both to converse with the abbess and to dedicate a church. During a feast on the evening before the dedication ceremony, Cuthbert went pale and dropped his knife, having seen something that shocked and appalled him.[90] In the anonymous version of his Life, Cuthbert seemed to have experienced an involuntary premonition; what should have been a time of joy and conviviality at the feast was transformed into one of grief. Ælfflæd apparently noticed Cuthbert's altered demeanour immediately, and in response to her enquiries about what had happened, the bishop gave her an admittedly partial and cryptic answer, but an answer of sorts.[91] In Bede's version of this event, however, Ælfflæd was so busy acting as hostess to her table that she failed even to notice what had happened; the bishop's chaplain had to prompt her to enquire.[92] It transpired that Cuthbert had seen a vision of the soul of a holy man from one of the abbess's own estates being carried to heaven by angels, but in both versions he refused to identify the dead man, despite some pressure to do so. When the next day Ælfflæd found out that it was one of her own shepherds who had fallen from a tree and died, in the Anonymous Life she contrived to arrive to share this news with the bishop just when, in the mass he was celebrating to mark the dedication of the church, he had reached the point where it says "Remember Lord your servants". Ælfflæd could thus declare the name Hadwald aloud without disrupting the solemnities.[93] In Bede's version, on the other hand, Ælfflæd behaved in a completely inappropriate manner: she approached the bishop while he was in the very act of dedicating the church and "with woman like astonishment [*stupore femineo*], as if she were announcing something new and doubtful", blurted out the name of her shepherd who had died.[94] Stephanie Hollis has argued that Bede deployed a polemical tool in this text as part of "a wider conflict

87 Bede, *VSC*, ch. 24, 234–7; quoting Ps 89[90]: 9 and Ecclesiasticus 11: 8.

88 Bede, *VSC*, ch. 24, 236–7; see Pelteret, "Bede's Women", 26. Hollis, *Anglo-Saxon Women*, 194–5, 207; Lees and Overing, *Double Agents*, 51–2.

89 Pelteret, "Bede's Women", 26.

90 Bede, *VSC*, ch. 34, 262–3.

91 Anon., *VSC*, IV. 10; ed. Colgrave, *Two Lives*, 126–7; Hollis, *Anglo-Saxon Women*, 203.

92 Bede, *VSC*, ch. 34, 262–3.

93 Anon., *VSC*, IV. 10, 126–7.

94 Bede, *VSC*, ch. 34, 264–5.

between churchmen and royal women, whether queens or abbesses, whose employment testified not to royal women's absence of status but to their power and prestige in contemporary society and especially within the Church".[95] It seems relevant that these negative portrayals of a powerful abbess occur only in Bede's *Life of Cuthbert*, a work designed primarily for a monastic audience, not for a wider, lay readership. Yet, Cuthbert's criticism of Ælfflæd for her failure to apply her (not inconsiderable) learning does not appear out of line with the terms in which Bede expressed negative opinions about the behaviour of others, even those within the church. Perhaps her gender caused him to voice that criticism in slightly different language from that which he might have used to censure a male cleric, but Bede had no hesitation in articulating his disapproval of ecclesiastics of both sexes. Leaders could reasonably, to his mind, expect to be judged by higher standards than those demanded of the monks and nuns in their care.

## Conclusion

In this brief investigation we have seen that Bede presented the lives and activities of abbesses in the early English church in a more complicated fashion than we might have anticipated. On the one hand, his abbesses were women of action; most of them royally born, all of them noble. Bede showed effectively how they used their family ties and associated wealth and influence to invest in the new communal institutions that became the defining feature of the early Anglo-Saxon church. Founded with family money, often on dynastic lands, these monasteries provided women (and their male and female relatives) with novel ways of expressing their commitment to the new faith. But more than that, they offered to those who would act as leaders of their communities the opportunity to exercise significant economic, cultural, and arguably political, influence in their immediate locality and farther afield. Abbess Hild stands out among all those considered here, partly because Bede had the most to say about her (clearly having benefited from access to hagiographical materials collected by women from her own congregation). It remains to ask whether Hild was genuinely remarkable, witnessing uniquely to a particular kind of spiritual authority in addition to her pragmatic, administrative skills. Or was she merely the best known of a larger group of women, who also provided leadership in similar ways, but for whom less information survives. As this essay makes clear, I have little sympathy with readings that have depicted Bede as misogynistic and do not believe that he ever deliberately downplayed the role of women.

Overall, I would argue that Bede presents us at various points in his historical and hagiographical writings with images of active and powerful women, women who while capitalising on their family background and influence, proved capable of using their own minds to determine their futures. Bede's abbesses appear frequently as forceful political agents; rigorous, and even transgressive thinkers; innovative authors; and courageous champions of the monastic way of life among the early English.

95 Hollis, *Anglo-Saxon Women*, 206.

15

# WOMEN'S LATINITY IN THE EARLY ENGLISH ANCHORHOLD

MEGAN J. HALL

The anchoritic life was first attested among women in England in the early twelfth century and became an increasingly popular choice that continued up to the Reformation.[1] In the thirteenth century, the time period under consideration here, the anchoritic life was flourishing, particularly for aristocratic women.[2] The *Ancrene Wisse*, or *Ancrene Riwle* as it is alternatively known, was written in the West Midlands of England in the early thirteenth century as a handbook for such solitary women who sought physical enclosure, away from the world, in order to pursue a higher spiritual calling.[3] The *AW* author's autograph text does not survive, but the unrevised version does, at one or two removes from the original, in the Nero manuscript (London, British Library, Cotton MS Nero A.xiv, henceforth "Nero"), dedicated to three aristocratic sisters who took up the anchoritic life and for whom the text was composed.[4] The text was revised, possibly by the author himself, for a wider group of anchoresses, and this revised version is preserved in the Corpus, Cleopatra, Titus, Vitellius, and

1 Surviving Latin letters of Anselm of Canterbury to female recluses date from c. 1102. The textual tradition runs up to *The Myrour of Recluses*, extant c. 1450. Goscelin of St. Bertin wrote his *Liber confortatorius* for Eve of Wilton c. 1080, though she went to the church of Saint-Laurent du Tertre in Angers to became an anchoress (for discussion, see particularly the first chapter of Mari Hughes-Edwards, *Reading Medieval Anchoritism: Ideology and Spriritual Practices*, Religion and Culture in the Middle Ages (Cardiff: University of Wales Press, 2012).

2 Ann K. Warren notes of anchoritism in this century that there were about four anchoresses to every one anchorite (in the previous century the ratio had been five to three), and increasing numbers of cells were built to house this growing population. Most parishes supported anchoresses (*Anchorites and their Patrons in Medieval England* [Berkeley: University of California Press, 1985], 18–20).

3 For the most up-to-date survey of the *Ancrene Wisse* [hereafter *AW*] and all concomitant areas of inquiry, see the General Introduction in Bella Millett, ed., *Ancrene Wisse: A Corrected Edition of the Text in Cambridge, Corpus Christi College, MS 402, with Variants from Other Manuscripts*, 2 vols, EETS o.s. 325–26 (Oxford: Oxford University Press, 2005–06), II.ix–lvii, henceforth referred to as Millett, EETS. *AW* quotations are drawn from this edition unless otherwise noted. To avoid confusion, I cite page and line references from this edition as, e.g., EETS I.65.5–6, and part and section number of the *AW* text as, e.g., 3.31.

4 See Millett, EETS I.73 n.4. Millett discusses the audience of the *AW* in *Ancrene Wisse, the Katherine Group, and the Wooing Group*, Annotated Bibliographies of Old and Middle English Literature 2 (Cambridge: D. S. Brewer, 1996), 15–17 (henceforth referred to as Millett, *AnnBib*), and EETS II.xix–xxiv.

Vernon manuscripts.[5] These, with the exception of Vitellius, make up the early manuscripts of the *AW*.

Particularly in the past thirty years, though studies of the readership of the *AW* have grown, few have probed more than superficially the relationship between the text and its thirteenth-century women readers. Even these studies typically consider English and French devotional literacy; questions of Latin literacy among this readership are often dealt with briefly and then set aside on the grounds that Latin literacy among thirteenth-century laywomen readers was exceptional, and the Latin that appears in the *AW* was not in the main directed at the women readers but at their supervisors. The predominant language of literacy was shifting;[6] this shift is highlighted by the composition of the *AW* in English rather than in the Latin of Aelred of Rievaulx's anchoritic guidebook *De institutione inclusarum* only sixty or so years earlier. Also, the remarkable texts of the contemporary Katherine Group (KG) and the Wooing Group

5 London, British Library, Cotton MS Nero A.xiv – Mabel Day, ed., *The English Text of the Ancrene Riwle, Edited from Cotton MS. Nero A.*XIV, on the basis of a transcript by J. A. Herbert, EETS o.s. 225 (London: Oxford University Press, 1952, for 1946); Cambridge, Corpus Christi College, MS 402 – J. R. R. Tolkien, ed., *The English Text of the Ancrene Riwle, Ancrene Wisse, Edited from MS. Corpus Christi College Cambridge 402*, EETS o.s. 249 (London: Oxford University Press, 1962, for 1960); London, British Library, Cotton MS Cleopatra C.vi – E. J. Dobson, ed., *The English Text of the Ancrene Riwle, Edited from B.M. Cotton MS. Cleopatra C.vi.*, EETS o.s. 267 (London: Oxford University Press, 1972); London, British Library, Cotton MS Titus D.xviii – Frances M. Mack, ed., *The English Text of the Ancrene Riwle, Edited from Cotton MS. Titus D. XVIII; together with the Lanhydrock Fragment, Bodleian MS. Engl. th. c. 70, ed. Arne Zettersten*, EETS o.s. 252 (London: Oxford University Press, 1963, for 1962); London, British Library, Cotton MS Vitellius F.vii – J. A. Herbert, ed., *The French Text of the Ancrene Riwle, Edited from British Museum MS Cotton Vitellius F vii*, EETS o.s. 219 (London: Oxford University Press, 1944); Oxford, Bodleian Library, MS Eng. poet. a.1 – Zettersten and Bernhard Diensberg, eds., *The English Text of the Ancrene Riwle: The 'Vernon' Text, Edited from Oxford, Bodleian Library, MS Eng. poet. a.1.*, EETS o.s. 310 (London: Oxford University Press, 2000); see also the digital facsimile by Wendy Scase, ed., *A Facsimile Edition of the Vernon Manuscript: A Literary Hoard from Medieval England*, Bodleian Digital Texts 3 (Oxford: Bodleian Library, 2011), DVD–ROM. In the fourteenth, fifteenth, and sixteenth centuries the text was adapted further for an even wider readership; the *AW* survives in this adapted form in an additional eleven manuscripts. The dedication to the three sisters, contained in the Nero text, has been generally accepted by scholars as accurate, rather than a rhetorical device. On this, see Millett, EETS I.xii–xlv and *AnnBib* 49–59 and 31–34. On the early transmission of the *AW*, see particularly Dobson, "The Affiliations of the Manuscripts of *Ancrene Wisse*," in *English and Medieval Studies Presented to J. R. R. Tolkien on the Occasion of His Seventieth Birthday*, ed. Norman Davis and C. L. Wrenn (London: George Allen & Unwin, 1962), 128–63; and ibid., *The Origins of Ancrene Wisse* (Oxford: Clarendon Press, 1976); as well as Roger Dahood, "The Use of Coloured Initials and Other Division Markers in Early Versions of the Ancrene Riwle," in *Medieval English Studies Presented to George Kane*, ed. Edward Donald Kennedy et al. (Woodbridge: D. S. Brewer, 1988), 79–97.

6 See, for instance, the discussions in Michael Clanchy, *From Memory to Written Record: England 1066–1307*, 3rd ed. (Oxford: Wiley-Blackwell, 2013), 226–54; Brian Stock, *The Implications of Literacy: Written Language and Models of Interpretation in the Eleventh and Twelfth Centuries* (Princeton, NJ: Princeton University Press, 1983); and Alexandra Barratt, "Small Latin? The Post-Conquest Learning of English Religious Women," in *Anglo-Latin and Its Heritage: Essays in Honour of A. G. Rigg on His 64th Birthday*, ed. Siân Echard and Gernot R. Wieland, Publications of the Journal of Medieval Latin 4 (Turnhout: Brepols, 2001), 51–65.

(WG) have often been taken as evidence that vernacular literacy among their women readers was supreme.[7] For such reasons, as well as the usual gendered assumptions about Latin as a male default and the vernacular as a female, critical consensus generally dismisses more advanced Latinity among women as exceptional, beyond the ability of such readers to perhaps pronounce Latin, or follow it in the liturgy.[8] In this essay, I reexamine this assumption, offering evidence from the earliest text and manuscripts of the *AW*, that the thirteenth-century readers of the text enjoyed a greater degree of Latin literacy than has been credited to them. This evidence includes not just the use of Latin text within the manuscripts by author and scribe but the use of scribal abbreviation by, ostensibly, the anchoresses themselves (see, for example, Figure 9). Specifically, I argue for their ability to read and comprehend Latin – not just *legere*, or the pronunciation of Latin, but *intellegere*, the comprehension of Latin. Much of this evidence has not been discussed before in the scholarship and arises from my close examination of the manuscripts.[9]

Though the *AW* is a macaronic text, it is composed primarily in English.[10] That Latin makes up a much smaller percentage of the text than English has been interpreted by many scholars as a sure indicator that the readers of this text were Latin-illiterate. Certainly it is possible that not all Latin composition would have been comprehensible to the earliest lay readers of the *AW*; but while more formal registers of Latin, such as those in academic treatises, Biblical commentaries, and Chancery

7 The KG texts are the alliterative Middle English prose lives of Saints Katherine of Alexandria, Margaret of Antioch, and Juliana of Nicomedia together with the Middle English homilies *Hali Meiðhad* and *Sawles Warde*. WG texts are *Þe wohunge of ure Lauerd*, *Ureisun of God Almihti*, "Lofsong of ure Lefdi," and "Lofsong of ure Louerde" (for an overview of these texts, see Millett, ed. and trans., *Ancrene Wisse: Guide for Anchoresses: A Translation Based on Cambridge, Corpus Christi College, MS 402*, Exeter Medieval Texts and Studies (Exeter: University of Exeter Press, 2009), ix–xx; Millett, EETS II.lvii; and Anne Savage and Nicholas Watson, trans. and intro., *Anchoritic Spirituality: Ancrene Wisse and Associated Works* (New York: Paulist Press, 1991), 7–15.

8 See particularly Millett, "Women in No Man's Land: English Recluses and the Development of Vernacular Literature in the Twelfth and Thirteenth Centuries," in *Women and Literature in Britain, 1150–1500*, 2nd ed., ed. Carol Meale, Cambridge Studies in Medieval Literature 17 (Cambridge: Cambridge University Press, 1997), 86–103; and Susan Uselmann, "Women Reading and Reading Women: Early Scribal Notions of Literacy in the Ancrene Wisse," *Exemplaria: A Journal of Theory in Medieval and Renaissance Studies* 16.2 (2004): 369–404.

9 In my dissertation, "Learning and Literacy Outside the Convent: Early Middle English Women Readers and the *Ancrene Wisse*" (University of Notre Dame, 2016), I lay out and analyze the evidence in detail; here, for the sake of space, I wish to present an overview of the main points.

10 Though the "English" text is not strictly English but is heavily influenced by a multitude of languages, including, naturally, Anglo-Norman. For discussion, see D. A. Trotter, "The Anglo-French Lexis of *Ancrene Wisse*: A Re-Evaluation," in *A Companion to Ancrene Wisse*, ed. Yoko Wada (Cambridge: D. S. Brewer, 2003), 83–101; Zettersten, *Studies in the Dialect and Vocabulary of the Ancrene Riwle*, Lund Studies in English 34 (Lund: Gleerup, 1965); ibid., "French Loan-Words in the *Ancren Riwle* and Their Frequency," in *Mélanges de philologie offerts à Alf Lombard à l'occasion de son soixante-cinquième anniversaire par ses collègues et ses amis*, Études Romanes de Lund 18 (Lund: Gleerup, 1969), 227–50; and Richard Dance, "The AB Language: the Recluse, the Gossip and the Language Historian," in *A Companion to Ancrene Wisse*, ed. Yoko Wada (Cambridge: D. S. Brewer, 2003), 57–82, esp. 74–76. The *AW* was translated into both French and Latin, though most of the surviving manuscripts contain English versions.

records, might have been out of reach, less formal Latin texts, for example letters, estate management records, primers, and the Latin found in surviving multilingual miscellanies, could have been accessible.[11] There are indeed places in the *AW* where the author translates passages from Latin to English, such as in Part 4, when he quotes a lengthy excerpt from Chronicles and follows it with a translation introduced by "Þis is þet Englisch" (This is the English).[12] In many more passages, however, and particularly in the Preface, the author cites the Latin but does not follow it with a translation.[13] Latin appears primarily for incipits, antiphons, versicles, and prayers, likely familiar to readers, as well as citation of *auctoritates*. When Latin passages appear at length, they function primarily to authorize the English exegesis and expansions that often follow. Siegfried Wenzel comments on this macaronic structure and notes that it is characteristic not only of Middle English devotional material but of Middle English sermons.[14] Despite Wenzel's characterization of the Latin in the *AW* as fairly ordinary for religious writing, he fails to emphasize that there are passages that remain untranslated which are crucial to understanding the structure so explicitly emphasized throughout the text. Indeed, many of the quotations serve other than strictly authoritative functions, such as the moments when the author directs his (female) readers to refer to Biblical passages they have read, or religious materials they have written out, or in the rhetorically sophisticated use of untranslated Latin in the opening portion of the Preface to establish the importance of a rule to the three sisters.

It is commonly suggested that supervisors might have read the text aloud to the anchoresses, explaining the Latin and any difficult passages. There are certainly references in the text to support the anchoresses' being counseled and taught orally.[15] The author cautions, though, that the anchoresses must be careful that unless they have a male or female witness who can hear the conversation, they should not speak for very long.[16] Clearly, limitations existed for how much an anchoress could or should be instructed, supporting the idea that the author certainly intended the *AW* primarily for private study, which would require a fairly advanced degree of personal reading comprehension.

11 On the kinds of Latin consumed by aristocratic households, see Christopher Cannon, "Vernacular Latin," *Speculum* 90.3 (2015): 641–53, particularly at 647; and Malcolm B. Parkes, "The Literacy of the Laity," *Scribes, Scripts, and Readers: Studies in the Communication, Presentation, and Dissemination of Medieval Texts* (1976; London: Hambledon Press, 1991), 275–97, particularly at 284–85.

12 Millett, EETS I.101. Similar passages appear in 4.81 and 5.11.

13 For example, in Millett, EETS P.1–2, P.4, and P.5.

14 *Macaronic Sermons: Bilingualism and Preaching in Late-Medieval England* (Ann Arbor: University of Michigan Press, 1994), 5.

15 In 3.19, for example, the author briefly cites the Old Testament figures Isaac, Rebecca, Jacob, Moses, and Elijah, and adds that someone will tell the anchoresses these stories, because they are too long to write out in the text, and in 4.39 he advises the women to listen to instructive stories their male visitors will tell them. Part 2 gives some idea of who these visitors were: gossips, the curious, self-important clerics, malingerers, and honest friars and priests; the anchoress might ask the latter to hear her confession and give spiritual instruction.

16 See, for instance, Millett, EETS 2.14 and 2.16.

The appearance of the Latin in the early manuscripts also suggests a degree of Latin literacy among the earliest anchoresses.[17] Nero and Titus present themselves fairly homogeneously, the text body written in lettering all of one size and uniform color on plain parchment punctuated by enlarged, colored initials, some with pen-decoration (more in Titus than Nero). Both the Latin and the vernacular are abbreviated, though the Latin generally receives heavier abbreviation than the vernacular, as is standard. Otherwise no visual markers, such as rubrication, underlining, hierarchy of script or differing sizes of letters, distinguish the Latin from the vernacular. Neither are alternate letter forms employed.[18] By contrast, in Vitellius various visual elements, including elaborately decorated initials, distinguish hierarchies of text.[19] Latin passages are typically underlined in red, and are sometimes written in red letters. Generally, though, red lettering is used as a reading or finding aid; for enlarged initials; for directions to the reader; for distinction of sections, both between and within parts; and to introduce and describe quoted or paraphrased material.[20] As with Nero and Titus, the Latin in Vitellius is generally more heavily abbreviated than the vernacular; the Vitellius text on the whole, however, is less abbreviated. Also worth noting is the reduced presence of Latin in Vitellius: the Latin excerpts have in the main been edited down.[21]

These differences in manuscript layout and visual elements between the earliest manuscripts and a later one may be accounted for by changing style, under the influence of the university and other pressures.[22] Perhaps the changing style also suggests something about the readership of the manuscripts. The marking of Latin passages, stronger emphasis of visual hierarchies, and increase in finding aids might have assisted later readers less able to approach the Latin material privately, while the relative simplicity of Nero and Titus might have been appropriate for readers accomplished in Latin.

17 Nero and Titus are the earlier manuscripts; Vitellius the later. Further, Titus was adapted at certain points for male recluses, providing additional contrast to Nero and Vitellius.

18 Except for the *ð* used occasionally, instead of a crossed *d*, to abbreviate names that use the letter *d* (e.g., *ðo* for *Domino*, *ðs* for *Deus*, or *dð* for David).

19 Vitellius sustained serious damage in the Ashburnham House fire, and while a good deal of the interior text is in the main visible, the edges of all leaves have been burned beyond readability. The red ink shows quite starkly against the darkened leaves.

20 Red initials are generally decorated with purple penwork and alternate with blue initials decorated with red penwork. An example of direction in red to the reader comes at fol. 5a, "Coment vous deuez dire voz pater nostres en lonourance de la trinitee" (How you must say your *Pater Nosters* in reverence of the Trinity; Herbert, *The French Text* 18.7–10). One instance of a distinction between parts is on fol. 22b, "Ici commence la tierce distinction de ceste liure qe fet comparison des recluses a vne maniere doisels" ("Here begins the third part of this book which compares recluses to a kind of bird"; Herbert 96.24–28). An Old Testament example is pointed out with "Essample del vieil testament" in red on fol. 29a (Herbert 127.11–12).

21 Nero generally preserves longer Latin quotations.

22 On this see the discussion in Malcolm B. Parkes, "The Influence of the Concepts of *Ordinatio* and *Compilatio* on the Development of the Book," in *Medieval Learning and Literature: Essays Presented to Richard William Hunt*, ed. J. J. G. Alexander, M. T. Gibson, and R. W. Southern (Oxford: Clarendon Press, 1976), 115–41 and plates.

The degree of abbreviation in the manuscripts deserves brief consideration as well. Whether or not scholars can formally determine what amount of scribal training laywomen would have received, textual evidence in the manuscripts suggests that their early female readers would have been familiar with the accepted principles of scribal abbreviation, for the principles are used to abbreviate the vernacular text as well as the Latin, with a few differences.[23] In abbreviating the vernacular text of Nero, Titus, and Vitellius, the scribes employed the usual methods: suspension, contraction, and superscripting of a letter to indicate elision. A few vernacular *notae* appear, usually sigla for "þat" or "þuruh" or the Tironian "*et*." Unlike the scribes of Nero and Titus, the Vitellius scribe used much more frequent abbreviation for personal pronouns, possibly because they are quite close to the Latin.

As noted earlier, the Latin is more heavily abbreviated than the vernacular in all three manuscripts. Scholars have frequently assumed that more heavily abbreviated Latin in the presence of less heavily abbreviated vernacular signified a more educated reader. In the *AW* manuscripts, at least, a complementary and perhaps alternate explanation may be identified. Rather than abbreviating Latin more heavily than vernacular on principle, the scribes appear in general to abbreviate *familiar* passages or words most heavily. The heaviest Latin abbreviation tends to be found in Nero and Titus, in strings of individual letters to indicate familiar Biblical passages and other *auctoritates*; in expected ritual formulae; for *nomina sacra*; and in standard *notae* and abbreviations.[24] Such abbreviations result in tight, compact sections of text looking almost alchemical in their jumble of symbols. In Vitellius, by contrast, most abbreviations are accomplished rather simply through suspension marks or superscripting of a letter or letters to indicate an elision, and an isolated few through individual sigla or special characters.

The text of the *AW*, being new and unfamiliar, and written in the vernacular, might have been less suitable for heavy abbreviation. As Malcolm Parkes points out, the system of scribal abbreviation was "much more fully developed for writing the Latin language than for the vernaculars," partly because "the methods of indicating abbreviations in Latin had been evolved in the course of a long established tradition," but also because "these methods depended on the consistency with which the morphological structure of paradigmatic forms in Latin was manifested in the written medium – unaffected by major dialect differences which might arise in the spoken equivalent."[25] Parkes writes here of the scribal abbreviation system in the context of

23 Certainly the abbreviation of Latin requires greater grammatical knowledge; yet the point I wish to make is that in order to understand an abbreviated vernacular, the readers would have needed to understand the principles of scribal abbreviation.

24 Some examples of ritual formulae are abbreviations for *kyrieleison*, *christeleison*, *pater noster*, *in nomine patris et filii et spiritus sancti amen*; standard abbreviations include "÷" for "*est*," "z" for "*et*," or "·i·" for "*id est.*"

25 Malcolm B. Parkes, "Tachygraphy in the Middle Ages: Writing Techniques Employed for *Reportationes* of Lectures and Sermons," in *Scribes, Scripts, and Readers: Studies in the Communication, Presentation, and Dissemination of Medieval Texts* (1976; London: Hambledon Press, 1991), 19–33, at 27. See also Ann Blair, "Student Manuscripts and the Textbook," in *Scholarly Knowledge: Textbooks in Early Modern Europe*, ed. Emidio Campi (Geneva: Librairie Droz, 2008), 39–74; and Giorgio Cencetti, *Lineamenta di storia della scrittura latina* (Bologna: Pàtron, 1956), 353–475, on the development of abbreviations.

shorthand and *reportationes*, the development of abbreviated stenography systems for fast writing, used by scribes who were taking down and copying out lectures and sermons as they were delivered, but the principles are well applied to other writing in Latin.[26] He describes a system in which, by the end of the twelfth century, scribes had developed a range of abbreviations more numerous than those in the Tironian *notae*, an "almost limitless number of simplified forms," using some of those *notae* and the principles of abbreviating syllables (e.g., through suspension), and using multiple abbreviations in the same word; further, "quotations from familiar auctoritates, and especially the Bible text, were usually indicated only by the first letter of each word." The skill of tight abbreviation reached a peak in the thirteenth century.[27]

It should also be noted that in Nero the Latin is heavily abbreviated in the beginning, though the amount of abbreviation lessens as the manuscript goes on.[28] The English is likewise less abbreviated the farther through the manuscript one proceeds. It also appears at times that the scribe abbreviated the English more heavily if it preceded an abbreviated Latin passage, whereas in lengthier English-only passages abbreviation is more minimal later in the manuscript.[29]

A third type of Latin presence in the early manuscripts, particularly Nero, further testifies to the Latinity of the earliest readers of the *AW*: marginal additions. I focus primarily on Nero because it is the only surviving *AW* manuscript to represent the text before it was revised for a broader audience of more mixed literacy, and on its face it is directed at women readers and appears to preserve annotations made by women readers. It is also one of the earliest manuscripts, dating to the second quarter of the thirteenth century. In Nero, in addition to the lengthier Latin additions Mabel Day notes in her 1952 EETS edition, I have catalogued a number of hitherto unnoted words, symbols, navigational and indexing aids, and additional marginalia from the thirteenth, and possibly early fourteenth, centuries. Altogether I have identified in Nero at least three thirteenth-century hands in both ink and drypoint, together with a body of markings not attributable to a specific hand. The marginal annotations include devotional or meditative glosses, references to other works, navigational aids, and systems for marking items of interest.[30] The marginal additions appear next to

26 Friars would have been well familiar with this system.

27 Parkes, "Tachygraphy," 24–25.

28 There is no obvious explanation for this phenomenon. It might signify simply that, as the scribe went on, he had more or less room than expected. There are a number of places in which a fair amount of text – from a few lines to entire paragraphs – is scraped out and rewritten, seemingly after correction with an exemplar (perhaps more than one, given how much text is at times reworked). Tighter abbreviation might appear in places where additional text had to be squeezed in after correction, though I have not yet been able to study this in detail.

29 Some exceptions prove generally true, though: throughout the text, "eu̓" is used regularly to abbreviate "ever," and a suspension mark regularly indicates the abbreviation of an "m" or "n" (e.g., "hā" for "h").

30 In selecting this terminology, I have consulted taxonomic systems proposed for late Middle English texts: Stephen Partridge, for example, has proposed categories for Chaucer glosses in "Glosses in the Manuscripts of Chaucer's *Canterbury Tales*: An Edition and Commentary" (Dissertation, Harvard University, 1992). See also A. I. Doyle and Malcolm B. Parkes, "The Production of Copies of the *Canterbury Tales* and the *Confessio Amantis* in the Early Fifteenth

Latin as well as vernacular passages, indicating an anchoritic reader or readers capable of responding not just to the English but also to the Latin passages. The text is not formally or scholastically glossed, underscoring that this book was for a time in the hands of a non-university-trained reader. This new evidence, alongside what Day notes, strongly suggests that at least two early anchoresses might have used and annotated the Nero manuscript in their cells.

Nero contains no absolute evidence that women readers added these annotations. It does not have a colophon specifying a female scribe, nor does it contain thirteenth-century women's ownership marks.[31] Different scholars might imagine different kinds of scribes at work here in the margins: correctors, pastoral caregivers, later (male) owner–annotators, friars who supervised anchoresses, parish priests, and the like. This is the default position: that women were not capable of the kind of literacy it would have taken to reflect upon the text and annotate it. I base my conclusion that women added these annotations on the totality of the evidence. Most thirteenth-century anchoresses would have possessed sufficient literacy: typically aristocratic, they could have benefited from an advanced education, whether obtained at home or in a nunnery, and had the time, space, and direction from trained clerics to increase that education.[32] Friars were busy and likely lacked the time to spend annotating the manuscripts of the women they counseled. Many of the annotations highlight passages critical to maintaining sanity in the confines of the anchorhold: the topics of self-control, encouragement, lust, deprivation, secular and spiritual attack, and limiting ascetic excess are marked repeatedly. None of the annotations, beyond one or two odd instances, is repeated in the other early manuscripts[33]; they are all highly

Century," in *Scribes, Scripts, and Readers: Studies in the Communication, Presentation, and Dissemination of Medieval Texts* (1976; London: Hambledon Press, 1991), 201–48. For Langland, David C. Benson and Lynne Sandra Blanchfield have suggested a system in *The Manuscripts of Piers Plowman: The B-version* (Cambridge: D. S. Brewer, 1997), particularly 9–27 and 116–17. Kathryn Kerby-Fulton has proposed another in *Iconography and the Professional Reader* (with Denise Despres, *Iconography and the Professional Reader: The Politics of Book Production in the Douce Piers Plowman* (Minneapolis: University of Minnesota Press, 1999)). Likewise Carl Grindley has laid out a detailed taxonomy in "Reading *Piers Plowman* C-Text Annotations: Notes toward the Classification of Printed and Written Marginalia in Texts from the British Isles 1300–1641," in *The Medieval Professional Reader at Work: Evidence from Manuscripts of Chaucer, Langland, Kempe, and Gower*, ed. Kathryn Kerby-Fulton and Maidie Hilmo, English Literary Studies Monograph Series 85 (Victoria, BC: ELS Editions, 2001), 73–142. Such systems have yet to be devised for early Middle English texts.

31 The lack of a colophon is not surprising, though. Only one surviving manuscript from this period contains one: the early twelfth-century Oxford, Bodleian Library, MS Bodley 451, produced at Nunnaminster. On this, see P. R. Robinson, "A Twelfth-Century Scriptrix from Nunnaminster," in *Of the Making of Books: Medieval Manuscripts, Their Scribes and Readers. Essays Presented to M. B. Parkes*, ed. P. R. Robinson and Rivkah Zim (Aldershot: Scolar, 1997), 73–93.

32 I review this in detail in "*Ancrene Wisse* and the Education of Laywomen in Thirteenth-Century England," *Early Middle English* 2.1 (forthcoming, 2020). On the typical social class of anchoresses, see Warren, *Anchorites and their Patrons*, 25–26. On the formal schooling of girls, see Daniel Klein, "Female Childhoods" in *The Cambridge Companion to Medieval Women's Writings*, ed. Carolyn Dinshaw and David Wallace, *Cambridge Companions Online* (Cambridge, 2003), 13–20.

33 The name "Ana," for example, is recorded in the margins of both Nero and Cleopatra; certain of the deadly sins are indexed in several of the manuscripts.

individualized and are not accumulated glosses as in university texts of the same period or as in later vernacular English manuscripts such as those of Chaucer.[34] Moreover, the strange placement of the bulk of the annotations and the non-professional hands in which they are written confirm, in my view, that these particular additions were inserted by anchoritic women readers.

It is important that I clarify the types of annotations that I present here. The manuscripts, once written, were corrected, generally by their main scribes.[35] At times (particularly in Cleopatra), the correctors added marginal text meant for insertion into the main text. I do not include these kinds of corrections in my analysis of annotations, as I assume – based in part on the identification of the main scribe with the corrector in several cases, the trained professionalism of those hands, and the expected placement of text for correction or insertion – that such corrections were added by (likely) male scribes, and my intention is to isolate those additions most likely made by women.[36] For this purpose I use the term "annotation" to signify mainly items added by hands other than those of the main scribes or correctors.

Nero exhibits two ruling patterns; though both are unusual, they serve the normal utilitarian function of delimiting those areas of the page meant for text and those meant for margins. In both patterns, the ruler has added several vertical lines to create dedicated blank columns on either side of the text block; the two patterns are differentiated by the number of columns created, and on some leaves trimming or sewing has reduced the available column area. A number of annotators availed themselves frequently of these blank columns, writing in both Latin and English, though none of the annotations appear scholarly.[37] The informal hand and the content of these marks suggest that the annotators were anchoresses themselves, and the accretion of their responses over time suggests the circulation of this manuscript among several devout readers, particularly in its early years.[38]

Space does not allow for a detailed review of all of the evidence, so I present here a few of the most remarkable examples.[39] One early person, acting as both meditative

34 On the matter, see Graham D. Caie, "The Manuscript Experience: What Medieval Vernacular Manuscripts Tell Us about Authors and Text," in *Medieval Texts in Context*, ed. Graham D. Caie and Denis Renevey (New York: Routledge, 2008); Grindley, "Reading *Piers Plowman* C-Text Annotations"; Kerby-Fulton and Despres, *Iconography and the Professional Reader*; A. J. Minnis, *Chaucer's* Boece *and the Medieval Tradition of Boethius*, Chaucer Studies 18 (Cambridge: D. S. Brewer, 1993), esp. 5–6; Parkes, "*Ordinatio* and *Compilatio*."

35 Cleopatra is exceptional, as the early text was written by one hand (Dobson's Scribe A), corrected contemporaneously by another (Scribe B), and later by yet a third (Scribe D); see Dobson's discussion in *The English Text*, xlvi–clxxii and "The Affiliations of the Manuscripts."

36 Indeed, with the exception of two, none of the marks is positioned as a scholastic gloss; nor, given the genre of the text, would we expect to see such glosses. For further discussion of friars' hands, see John Scahill, "Friars' Miscellanies," in *Medieval England: An Encyclopedia*, ed. Paul Szarmach et al. (New York: Garland, 1998), 306–07.

37 Examples survive, for instance, at fols. 61b–62a and 76b–77a.

38 For a fuller discussion of this, see Megan J. Hall, "At Work in the Anchorhold and Beyond: A Codicological Study of London, British Library, Cotton MS Nero A.xiv," in *Journal of the Early Book Society* 20 (2017): 18–28, at 8–9.

39 A more complete discussion may be found in "Learning and Literacy Outside the Convent", in which I also catalog the markings in Titus, little-discussed in scholarship.

reader and corrector, added Latin marginalia, as well as a handful of interlinear corrections, at various points throughout the manuscript in a later thirteenth-century hand. One of the lengthier additions comes at fol. 78b (see Figure 9). Into the left margin, this annotator has copied Scriptural excerpts from the body of the *AW* text, meditations from the Psalter against lechery.[40] The text in its usual macaronic and exegetical style contains both Scriptural excerpts and vernacular commentary on them; the annotator copies only the Latin incipits – and at that does not copy blindly but changes about a third of the scribal abbreviations, indicating that she understood the principles of abbreviation and could manipulate them for herself.[41]

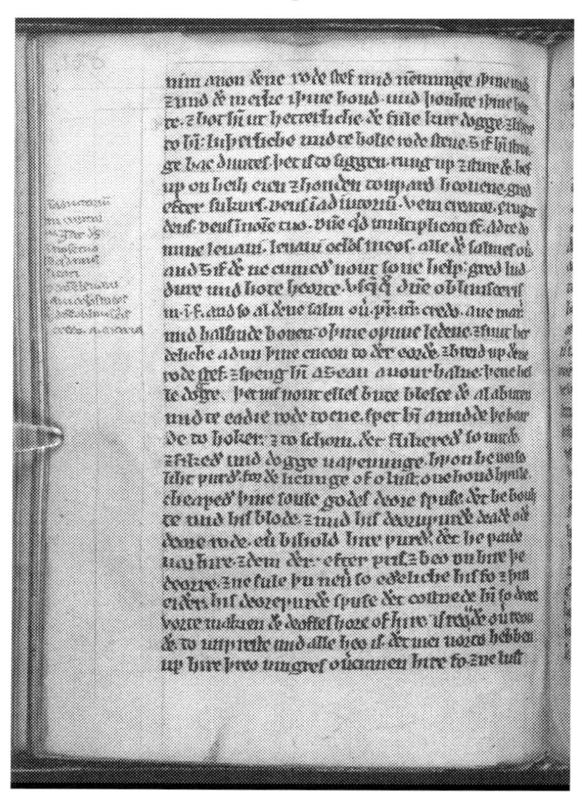

Figure 9 Marginal annotation added in the outer margin by the first annotator. Marginal symbols faintly visible in outer margin at lines 3, 21–2, and 28–9. (British Library, Cotton MS Nero A.xiv, fol. 78b; © The British Library Board, London.)

40 The passage appears in Nero at fol. 78b.5–12.

41 "Deus," in line 8, becomes "ðs," "domine" in lines 8–9 becomes "dn̄e," "obliuisceris" in lines 11 becomes "obliuiscis," and "aue mar." in line 12 becomes "a. maria." While "ðs" and "dn̄e" are common abbreviations for names of God, particularly in this manuscript, the annotator's use of "obliuiscis" particularly demonstrates that she understood the principles of scribal abbreviation, as she has used a suspension mark to elide the "er" that appears in the main text. Annotations in the same hand appear farther down the page, at line 16, and again at 75a.8–9 and 77a.3.

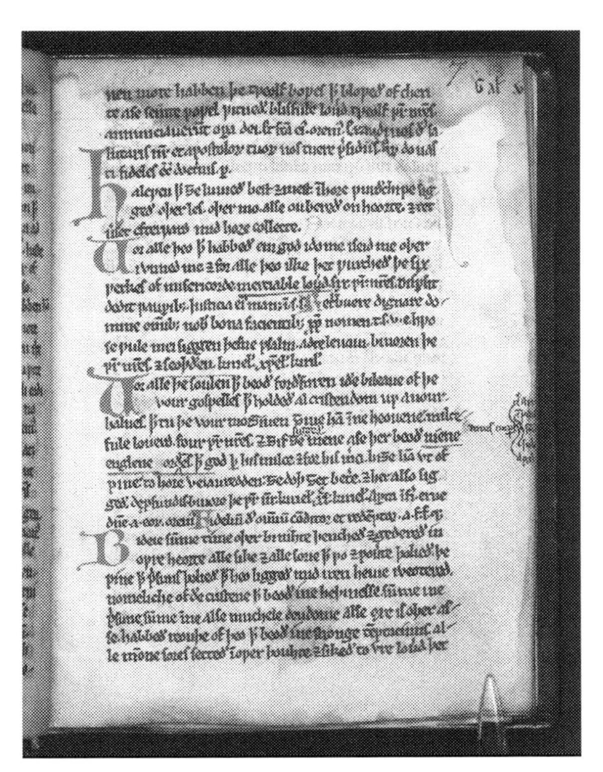

Figure 10 The marginal addition of Grosseteste appears in the outer margin at lines 17–20. The main hand corrects line 19. (British Library, Cotton MS Nero A.xiv, fol. 7a; © The British Library Board, London.)

A different thirteenth-century annotator, functioning as a glossator, has added other Latin material.[42] The professionalism of the hand might mean that a trained scribe added these items, though the passages and themes they highlight suggest that an anchoritic reader may have been responsible. First, on fol. 7a appears a likely cross-reference to Grosseteste's *De dotibus* (see Figure 10). In the outer margin the annotator writes, "dotes corp*oris* { clari[tas] / i*m*pass[ibilitas] / sui / sub[tilitas] / agil[i-tas]"[43]; the text has been trimmed. The annotator has, notably, used abbreviation, visible in "corp*oris*" and "i*m*pass[ibilitas]." This commentary on the *dotibus corporis* (wedding gifts given from groom to bride the morning after the wedding, in this context given to the resurrected body as bride of Christ) appears next to a passage on the "vour

42 Day dates the hand in *The English Text*, 13 n.8 and 15 n.19ff.

43 This is one of the marginal additions Day notes; she characterizes the hand as thirteenth century and links it to Grosseteste (Day, *The English Text*, 13 n.8). On the *De dotibus*, see Joseph Goering, "The *De Dotibus* of Robert Grosseteste," *Mediaeval Studies* 44 (1982): 83–109, who establishes the popularity of this theological subject in the early to mid-thirteenth century. Millett comments on this passage in EETS II.31, n. I.190–1; she briefly mentions the annotation in Nero, and links the passage to Thomas of Chobham.

morȝiuen" ("four morning-gifts") given to the "soulen *þat* beoð forðfaren" ("departed souls"), in Part 1.14.[44] The annotator might have had access to *De dotibus*, or have had a text like the *Summa de arte praedicandi*, material from which appears elsewhere in the *AW*.[45] She might also have been taught this text or these principles orally.

Similarly, the same hand has also indexed each of the Five Joys of Mary discussed on fols. 8b and 9a by adding Latin headings in the outer margin (see Figure 10). The *AW* text directs anchoresses to recite five *Aves* after each of the Joys. Making special note of the Joys is a not-unexpected move on the annotator's part, as Marian devotion was an integral part of the anchoritic life, and this section falls in Part 1, given over to the daily devotions of the anchoress, who might have wanted quick access to this section. Interestingly as well, as Sitwell points out, the *AW* "seems to give the earliest known example of devotion to the Five Joys of Mary set out in an elaborate form," and the annotation underscores the importance of this particular devotion in the thirteenth century.[46]

Another early reader, judging by the faded quality of the ink, the general aspects of the formation of characters, and the few letters that appear to be by the same hand, has annotated the manuscript using a series of symbols reminiscent of Robert Grosseteste's.[47] The non-professional hand suggests a parish priest, friar, or – given the context – a personal user. An anchoress could certainly have received instruction from her fraternal supervisor in how to do this. A good number of these symbols seem to indicate an indexing, or perhaps mnemonic, effort, marking passages of meditative interest to the reader. While many of them mark vernacular passages, some also point

44 The *AW* author does not specify those *dotes* in this passage – the annotator has added this cross-reference – though he picks up the subject again in 2.33 and names "swiftnesse. ant leome of a briht sihðe" ("swiftness and the light of clear sight") as two of the morning-gifts.

45 As Malcolm B. Parkes points out in "Book Provision and Libraries at the Medieval University of Oxford," friars were part of a network circulating a "constant traffic in books," and may easily have lent anchoresses edifying works that they recommended for reading (in *Scribes, Scripts, and Readers: Studies in the Communication, Presentation, and Dissemination of Medieval Texts* (1976; London: Hambledon Press, 1991), 299–310, at 301).

46 Sitwell, quoted in M. B. Salu, ed. and trans., *The Ancrene Riwle (The Corpus MS: Ancrene Wisse)* (Notre Dame: University of Notre Dame Press, 1956), 196; see also Millett, EETS II.38, n. I.275.

47 The symbols are very faint and do not photograph well. I discuss them in detail in "Learning and Literacy Outside the Convent". Whether the annotator read *De dotibus* and was also influenced by Grosseteste's symbols system, or whether this connection is coincidence, is unknown. The symbols that appear in Nero are not those of Grosseteste, though there are some similarities, such as in the use of arabic numerals. It is possible, if the annotation on fol. 7a is an indication, that the annotating reader was familiar with Grosseteste's system and may have been influenced by it. Grosseteste used a system of symbols to form a topical concordance. His system has been identified in several extant manuscripts, including Oxford, Bodleian Library, MS Bodley 198 (ca. 1225), Lyons MS 414, fols. 17a–32a (c.1235x1250), and London, British Library, Royal MS 5 D.x, fol. 49a (late thirteenth century). See Richard W. Hunt, "Manuscripts Containing the Indexing Symbols of Robert Grosseteste," *Bodleian Library Record* 4 (1953): 241–55. Mary Carruthers discusses the use of such systems, including Grosseteste's, in *The Book of Memory*, remarking that graphic *notae* used as mnemonic signs, in systems devised by individual readers, are commonly found in manuscripts starting in the twelfth century (*The Book of Memory*, 2nd ed., Cambridge Studies in Medieval Literature (Cambridge: Cambridge University Press, 2008), 135–52, at 136).

up Latin material.[48] Other marks that appear include *manicula*, faces, *nota bene* signs, exemplum marks, marginal comments, and navigational aids. All of these marks reveal the early audience carried out close reading of Nero, and the marks they have left indicate that their reading was likewise devotional and meditative; some of the marks appear as well to be spontaneous glosses, having meaning primarily to the annotator but not to us. The text is not formally or scholastically glossed, suggesting perhaps that this book was for a long time in the hands of a reader not trained at a university, rather than with academics.

Though for the sake of space the review of the evidence has been brief, I hope I have conveyed sufficiently that the early text and manuscripts argue strongly for greater Latinity and literacy among the earliest anchoresses for whom the *AW* was written than previous scholars have acknowledged. We perhaps will never know precisely who its earliest audience was or how they were educated; nor does the evidence reveal who, exactly, annotated Nero. It does seem most likely, though, given the context and other evidence I have drawn out and presented here, that these annotations were made by a female user of the text, quite possibly an anchoress in her cell. Understood in this way, the idea of an accomplished thirteenth-century female reader of Latin, one who need not read her text through a clerical intermediary, is not farfetched. A clear picture of an educated, private, lay female reader emerges.

48 Some vernacular examples are found at 105b.14, 64a.12–13, and 52a.8; Latin at 16a.2–4, 65a.25–26, and 42a.11–12.

16

# THE TREATMENT OF ORDINATION IN RECENT SCHOLARSHIP ON RELIGIOUS WOMEN IN THE EARLY MIDDLE AGES

GARY MACY

The purpose of this essay is to review recent literature on the role of medieval religious women in the period before the reform movement often attributed to Gregory VII that took place between the eleventh and early thirteenth centuries.[1] The reason for choosing this particular period in Christian history will become clear, one hopes, in the course of the essay. It is divided into three sections. The first will offer a brief summary of historical studies of women religious in the early Middle Ages (roughly 500–1200 CE). The second will offer a summary of scholarly theological discussion of the ordination of women in Christian history. The third will summarize studies of the meaning of ordination, and more importantly, the change in the meaning of ordination in Christian history. Finally, a brief conclusion will offer suggestions for a more integrated study of these three areas in order to more precisely understand the role religious women played in the early medieval Church.

More precisely, this essay attempts 1) to demonstrate that the majority of scholarship on early religious women in Western Christianity has failed to address the extensive scholarship demonstrating that women were designated as ordained in this period, and 2) that this is in part because they are assuming an anachronistic definition of ordination in their studies.

## Discussions of the Ordination of Women in Historical Studies of Women Religious

Suzanne Wemple in her 1981 study, *Women in Frankish Society*, offers one of the few and most complete discussions of women deacons and the roles that they may have played in early medieval ecclesiastical circles.[2] She notes that the attempts to exclude women from the diaconate in the sixth and seventh century failed, and the "Gallican church had ordained deaconesses who regarded themselves as equals to the male clergy."[3] By the end of the sixth century, however, the office of deaconess had been abolished, and women were removed from ministry. Monastic women continued to defy ecclesiastical legislation by participating in liturgical rites, a practice forbidden

1 This essay represents the *status quaestionis* at the time the original paper was delivered in 2015. It does not discuss or intend to discuss studies published in the intervening years.

2 Suzanne Fonay Wemple, *Women in Frankish Society: Marriage and the Cloister, 500 to 900* (Philadelphia: University of Pennsylvania Press, 1981), 136–48, 160, 173.

3 Ibid., 138.

by new legislation during the Carolingian period. Women continued to assume the title of deacon at least into the tenth century, although by that time, the title was applied to abbesses. Wemple relies on an impressive array of primary sources, but also several important studies by theologians, including Karl H. Schäfer,[4] Adolf Kalsbach,[5] Josephine Mayer,[6] Haye van der Meer,[7] and Roger Gryson.[8]

The most extensive investigation of women's liturgical roles in the Middle Ages is surely Gisela Muschiol's 1994 study, *Famula Dei: Zur Liturgie in merowingischen Frauenklöstern*.[9] She cites instances of women hearing confessions,[10] serving at the altar,[11] reading the Gospel,[12] and preaching.[13] Despite this invaluable work, Muschiol does not discuss how or why the ecclesiastical structure of the time might have allowed the women to perform functions later reserved to ordained men.

Sarah Foot reviews the position of widows in her 2000 study, *Veiled Women*. Based on the work of Gryson, she states: "That widows remained laywomen and were never to be ranked with the clergy is clear from these early Church councils, yet the liturgical evidence demonstrates quite clearly that entry into the *ordo viduarum* was formally marked by a ceremony involving prayers, and a formal re-clothing."[14] Foot goes on to study these ceremonies in depth,[15] noting that they bear a resemblance to the rite of ordaining of a woman deacon, a title which she believes, "seems not to have denoted a true function in the West."[16]

A thorough discussion of the ordination of women deacons occurs in Dyan Elliott's 2012 monograph, *The Bride of Christ Goes to Hell*. In her analysis of the correspondence between Abelard and Heloise, Elliott concludes: "Abelard was intent on claiming the

4 Karl H. Schäfer, *Die Kanonissenstifter im deutschen Mittelalter. Ihre Entwicklung und innere Einrichtung im Zusammenhang mit dem altchristlichen Sanktimonialentum* (Stuttgart: W. Kohlhammer, 1907; repr. Amsterdam: P. Schippus, 1965).

5 Adolf Kalsbach, *Die altkirchliche Einrichtung der Kiakonissen bis zum ihrem Erlöschen* (Frieburg im Breisgau: Herder, 1926).

6 Josephine Mayer, *Monumenta de viduis diaconissis virginibusque tractantia. Florilegium patristicum tam veteris quam medii aevi auctores complectens*, 42 (Bonn: Peter Hanstein, 1938).

7 Haye van der Meer, *Priestertum der Frau? Eine theologiegeschichtliche Untersuchung, Quaestiones disputatae*, 42 (Freiburg: Herder, 1969). For the English translation, see *Women Priests in the Catholic Church: A Theological–Historical Investigation* (Philadelphia: Temple University Press, 1973).

8 Roger Gryson, *Le ministère des femmes dans l'Église ancienne : Recherches et syntheses, section d'histoire*, 4 (Gembloux : Éditions J. Duculot, 1972). For the English translation, see *The Ministry of Women in the Early Church* (Collegeville: Liturgical Press, 1976).

9 Gisela Muschiol, *Famula Dei: Zur Liturgie in merowingischen Frauenklöstern*, Beiträge zur Geschichte des alten Mönchtums und des Benediktinertum, 41 (Munster: Aschendorff, 1994).

10 Ibid., 222–63

11 Ibid., 219–20.

12 Ibid., 10–11, 94–100.

13 Ibid., 98–99.

14 Sarah Foot, *Veiled Women I: The Disappearance of Nuns from Anglo-Saxon England* (Aldershot: Ashgate, 2000), 118.

15 Ibid., 127–34.

16 Ibid., 117.

title of deacon for Heloise."[17] This leads Elliott to investigate the role and status of women deacons in the early Middle Ages. She reports that the title "deaconess" was applied to widows, virgins, the wives of deacons, and, most importantly for Abelard, abbesses who had previously been married. Elliott does not doubt that women deacons were ordained, and continued to be so into the twelfth century, as least as abbesses.[18] Elliot's study relies on historical, theological and liturgical sources to place the elusive woman deacon and in doing so updates and corrects Wemple's earlier study. It is an unusually detailed account of the role of women deacons in the Middle Ages by an historian of women religious.

By far the most complete study of women deacons in an historical work occurs in Mary Schneider's monograph, *Women in Pastoral Office* (2012).[19] Schneider not only provides a complete discussion of all the liturgical rites that exist for the commissioning of women, but also includes an extensive analysis of the roles of women deacons. She concludes that women were indeed ordained deacons and performed that function even in Rome itself. The author, however, unlike the others mentioned here, was also a theologian and professor of theology and so also belongs to another tradition of scholarship on this subject that will be discussed below

Several other studies allude to women's ordination but provide no discussion of the issue. I am including a sample of such studies, but the examples could be greatly amplified. Stephanie Hollis's 1992 study, *Anglo-Saxon Women*, which relies on Wemple's examination, but is at best ambiguous about women's ordination, concludes: "The office of deaconess was outlawed by the 5th and 6th c. bishops in the West, and it is unclear whether the title, continuing in use, signified ordination or merely marriage to an ordained man."[20] Pauline Stafford's 1999 article "Queens, Nunneries and Reforming Churchmen: Gender, Religious Status and Reform in Tenth and Eleventh-Century England" hints that women may have participated in the Eucharist when she cites Ælfric as desiring "holy *þenas* and *þinena* (male and female servants) who will offer with cleanness of mind and body the holy Eucharist. It is chastity which equips men and women equally for such offering, just as it transforms them equally into vessels through which God may speak."[21] She offers no further speculation about the eccesiastical status of these female servants.

Jocelyn Wogan-Browne's 2001 monograph, *Saints' Lives and Women's Literary Culture, c. 1150–1300*, simply notes that abbesses were "forbidden in canon law to preach or read the gospel in public, to veil consecrated virgins, hear confession, or give liturgical blessing."[22] Helene Scheck's 2008 study, *Reform and Resistance: Formations*

17 Dyan Elliott, *The Bride of Christ Goes to Hell: Metaphor and Embodiment in the Lives of Pious Women, 200–1500* (Philadelphia: University of Pennsylvania Press, 2012), 140.

18 Ibid., 140–47.

19 Mary M. Schneider, *Women in Pastoral Care: The Story of Santa Presede, Rome* (New York: Oxford University Press, 2012).

20 Stephanie Hollis, *Anglo-Saxon Women and the Church: Sharing a Common Fate* (Woodbridge: Boydell Press, 1992), 77, n. 3.

21 Pauline Stafford, "Queens, Nunneries and Reforming Churchmen: Gender, Religious Status and Reform in Tenth and Eleventh-Century England," *Past and Present* 163 (1999): 10.

22 Jocelyn Wogan-Browne, *Saints' Lives and Women's Literary Culture c. 1150–1300: Virginity and its Authorizations* (Oxford: Oxford University Press, 2001), 191, n. 6. This is a summary of Innocent

*of Female Subjectivity in Early Medieval Ecclesiastical Culture*, raises obliquely the issue of women serving at the altar when she conjectures that Alcuin's gift of ampulla and paten to Æthelburga, abbess of Fladbury, "is not urging her to perform the Eucharistic function of a priest, but to perform the offertory, the offering of bread and wine to the priest for blessing. He is stressing her active participation in the rite, in other words, rather than somehow restricting the practice for women as in the later Carolingian church." She offers no particular evidence for this analysis besides a note to an unidentified page of *The Concise Oxford Dictionary of the Christian Church*.[23] Her discussion of the ordination of English queens also offers no opinion on what such ordination might have meant in such a case.[24] Lisa Bitel describes the ordination of Brigit of Kildare as a bishop in one amazing hagiographic account, but does not further analyze the meaning such a claim might have for its author.[25] Barbara Newman accepts that the ordination of women was still a debated issue in the twelfth century in her 2010 essay, "Coming Out of the (Sacristy) Closet" but offers no further description or analysis of that debate.[26] This brief summary at least gives a feel for the way in which historians of women religious in the early Middle Ages tend to address the question of the ordination of those religious.

So much has been written so well on the role of women in this era that is very likely that my cursory survey has missed some significant discussion of the issue among historians. Even given this caveat, it is safe to estimate that fewer than a dozen historians of women in the early Middle Ages entertain the possibility that women were ordained during that period. Even within the discussions that do exist, reluctance to admit that women were ever ordained dominates. The exceptions are the discussions by Suzanne Wemple, Sarah Foot, and Dyan Elliott. The work of Mary Schaeffer, as one might expect, shows an intimate knowledge of the scholarly theological discussions of the role of women in the early Middle Ages and it is to that tradition that we now turn.

## Theological Discussions of the History of the Ordination of Women

In contrast to the thin historical literature in this subject, nearly 1,000 articles on the ordination of women have appeared in scholarly theological articles. Between 1960 and 2001 alone nearly 800 books and articles were written on the subject. Though I have not kept up with recent bibliographies on the subject, I am quite aware that the

III's influential letter of 1210 to the Bishop of Burgos and the Abbot of Morimundo directed at the Abbess of Las Huelgas in Burgos (Corpus Iuris Canonici, Decretales l. 5, t. 38, c. 10, ed. E. Friedberg (Graz, 1959), 2:886–87). The standard work on the complicated and continuing episcopal and liturgical privileges of the Abbess of Las Huelgas is José María Escrivá de Balaguer, *La abadesa de las Huelgas: studio teologico juridico*, 3rd ed. (Madrid: Edicione Rialp, 1988).

23 Helene Scheck, *Reform and Resistance: Formations of Female Subjectivity in Early Medieval Ecclesiastical Culture* (Albany: State University of New York Press, 2008), 63 and n. 33

24 Ibid., 81. For a summary discussion of the ordination rites of queens, see Julie Ann Smith, "The Earliest Queen-Making Rites," *Church History* 66 (1997): 18–35. This article includes useful references to earlier studies.

25 Lisa Bitel, *Landscape with Two Saints: How Geneovesa of Paris and Brigit of Kildare Built Christianity in Barbarian Europe* (Oxford: Oxford University Press, 2009), 180.

26 Barbara Newman, "Coming Out of the (Sacristy) Closet," *Religion & Literature* 42 (2010): 286.

subject is still under lively debate. While historians seem loath to take a stand on whether or not women were ordained in the past, theologians have no such reluctance. A brief review of the most important literature is useful in understanding how thoroughly the historical sources have been analyzed by these many authors.

Jean Morin, writing in the seventeenth century, was the first, to my knowledge, to argue that women were ordained validly as women deacons since the same rites were used for male deacons and female deacons in the most ancient Greek rituals. Morin was also the first, again to my knowledge, to set forth criteria for deciding whether the ordinations of women referenced in historical documents were "true" ordinations. Morin specified (1) that the ritual be called a valid ordination, (2) that the ritual be celebrated at the altar by the bishop, (3) that hands be laid upon the one to be ordained, (4) that the stole be placed on the one to be ordained, (5) that the ordained receive communion under the forms of both bread and wine, and most importantly (6) that the ordination be to one of the "major orders," that is, priest, deacon, or subdeacon. In short, the ancient ceremonies had to meet the requirements for ordination as they would have been understood in the seventeenth century.[27]

The Jesuit Jean Pien in the eighteenth century and Arcadius Pankowski in the nineteenth century dismissed Morin's conclusions. Women in the past had only received a ceremonial, not a sacramental, ordination, since their ordination did not allow them to preach or administer the other sacraments, particularly the sacrament of the altar. In short, these ordinations did not meet Morin's sixth criterion since the ordinations of women did not result in the priesthood. Josephine Mayer, Adolf Karlsbach, and Santiago Giner Sempere writing in the early twentieth century gave more nuanced responses. Ordination was a loosely used term in the early church, and so did not, and indeed could not, refer to full sacramental ordination.[28] This position would be advocated particularly by Marie-Josèphe Aubert in 1987 when he quoted Yves Congar's astute evaluation of the question:

> [Whether or not women were ordained in the past] is a bad question. I think that there is a certain *quiproquo* [sic] about the notion. Order in the ancient church, "*ordo*," "*ordinare*" meant to establish a certain "order" in the Church. The question does not present itself as knowing whether this is the sacrament of Orders. Without doubt one might ask that today if one thinks of things in this way. But the ancients did not work like that. The question solely to be established about an "*ordo*" was whether it is authentic, the "order" of the female diaconate.[29]

According to Congar, then, the question of the validity of orders in the past might be interesting, or even necessary to determine if women should be ordained now, but it was a question the early church would not have asked and was, thus, anachronistic.

27 Jean Morin, *Commentarius de sacris ordinationibus secundum antiques et recentiores latinos, graecos, syros et babylonios in tres partes distinctus* (Amsterdam, 1695; repr. Farnsborough, 1969), iii. 143–51.

28 Macy, *The Hidden History of Women's Ordination: Female Clergy in the Medieval West* (Oxford: Oxford University Press, 2007), 8–10.

29 Marie-Josèphe Aubert, *Des Femmes Diacres: Un nouveau chemin pour l'église* (Paris, 1987), 127–28.

Jean Daniélou was one of the first in a long line of recent scholars to review the historical data and conclude that the rituals for male deacons and female deacons certainly seemed to be the same, but since women deacons could not become priests, they were not truly ordained. That is, Morin's criteria 1 through 5 were met, but not, once again, criterion 6.

The most famous debate over the validity of the ordination of women in the past occurred between the French scholars Roger Gryson and Aimé George Martimort.[30] Both provided lengthy examinations of the documents relating to women's ordination but with different conclusions. Gryson concluded that women deacons were really ordained because they received a laying on of hands during their ordination (Morin's criterion 3). Martimort rejected this ordination as valid, as had Daniélou, because women deacons did not serve at the altar nor continued on to be priests (Morin's criterion 6).

In 1997, Hans Jorissen and Peter Hünermann summarized the arguments for and against the ordination of women deacons in contrasting articles. Both scholars agreed that the basic argument against the ordination of women deacons in the past was based on the definition of ordination as sacerdotal service at the altar. Since women deacons had never served at the altar, then any ceremony that they may have undergone could not be a true ordination (again Morin's criterion 6).[31]

This brief survey of the theological debate makes several important points. First, the historical documents that refer to women as ordained have long been readily available to scholars. Most of the important documents were collected in single volume by Josephina Mayer in 1937. Since then, all of the important documents have been translated into English and German.[32] Second, historians of women religious, on the whole, appear to be unaware of this extensive literature. The question of why this is so is beyond the scope of this essay and is perhaps best explained by the growing specialization of academic fields. It is difficult enough to master one field let alone two. Finally, studies on the ordination of women (or indeed men) inevitably raised the issue of the meaning of ordination. Clearly the requirements for a valid ordination seem to have changed over the centuries. It is now the scholarship available on the history of ordination to which we turn.

### Ordination in the Period before the Reforms Initiated in the Eleventh Century

Theologians have a particular interest and concern to determine whether the ordinations of women in the past were "real." This is an important theological question because of its immediate relevance to the ordination of women today. It is quite proper

30 Macy, *Hidden History*, 10.

31 Ibid., 11–13.

32 For English translations, see Kevin Madigan and Carolyn Osieck, *Ordained Women in the Early Church: A Documentary History* (Baltimore and London: Johns Hopkins University Press, 2005); *A History of Women and Ordination*, ed. Bernard Cooke and Gary Macy, vol. 1: John Hilary Martin, *The Ordination of Women in a Medieval Context*, and vol. 2: Ida Raming, *The Exclusion of Women from the Priesthood* (Lanham and London: Scarecrow Press, 2002). For German translations, see Heike Grieser, Rosemarie Nurnberg and Gisela Muschiol, "Texte aus der kirchlichen Tradition und lehramtliche Dokumente," in *Diakonat: Ein Amt für Frauen in der Kirche—Ein frauengerechtes Amt?* ed. Peter Hünermann, Albert Biesinger, Marianne Heimbach-Steins and Anne Jenson, 367–411 (Ostfildern: Schwabenverlag, 1997).

for theologians to raise the issue and to try to answer it. On the basis of the review that I have offered, it is abundantly clear that the criteria used to determine the validity of ordination were all developed long after the ordinations of medieval women. Yves Congar is the clearest on this point. The ancients would never have asked the question, much less used the criteria listed by Morin and assumed by writers ever since. The inevitable question must be: what did ordination mean at the time when women could still be considered to be ordained?

Fortunately, we have fairly extensive studies of this question, once again, however, by theologians. Beginning with the seminal studies on sacramental character by Franz Gillman in the early decades of the twentieth century,[33] theologians have substantially changed our understanding of how Christians of the first millennium described and practiced ordination. Based on these studies, scholars now can discern how early definitions of ordination underwent a significant revision and redefinition during the great eleventh century reform movement, reaching their culmination in the decrees of the Fourth Lateran Council in 1215. The differences between the earlier and later understandings of ordination are extremely significant and are essential in understanding references to ordained women in the first millennium of Christianity.

Originally, Christians understood ordination to denote the appointment to a particular role in the community. This should not be the least bit surprising for, as Pierre van Beneden demonstrated in his study of the concept of *ordo* in the first three centuries of Christianity, Christians simply adopted the concept of *ordo* from everyday usage. According to Beneden, *ordinatio* for the early Christians indicated the appointment and consecration of a person to a particular charge or function.[34] Ordination, thus, was linked not to an irrevocable power, but to a particular role in a particular community.

This understanding of ordination remained unchanged until the second half of the twelfth century. *Ordinatio* denoted not only the election and consecration to a particular liturgical function, but also to any function considered of service to the Christian community. An *ordo* would be a role within the community that included not only roles that are now considered spiritual, but also political and civil roles. According to Pierre- Marie Gy, "at least in the patristic era, *ordinare* is greater than *consecrare* or *benedicere* and designates not only the prayer of ordination but all the ecclesial processes of which this was a part. As we have already seen, the term *ordinatio* had, after all, been applied in the high Middle Ages to kings, abbots, abbesses, and by imperial Christian law, to civil functionaries."[35]

33 Franz Gillmann, "Der 'sakramentale Character' bei dem Glossatoren Rufinus, Johannes Faventinus, Sicard von Cremona, Huguccio und in der Glossa ordinaria des Decrets," *Zeitschrift für katholische Wissenschaft und kirchliches Leben* 90 (1910): 300–13; idem, "Der 'sakramentale Character' bei Petrus von Poitiers und by Stephan Langton," *Zeitschrift für katholische Wissenschaft und kirchliches Leben* 93 (1913): 74–76; and idem, *Zur Lehre der Scholasik vom Spender der Firmung und des Weihesakraments* (Paderborn, 1920).

34 Pierre Van Beneden, *Aux origines d'une terminologie sacramentelle:* Ordo, ordinare, ordinatio *dans la littérature chrétienne avant 313*, Spicilegium sacrum Lovaniense, Études et documents 38 (Louvain : Spicilegium Sacrum Lovaniense, 1974).

35 Pierre-Marie Gy, "Les anciennes prères d'ordination," *La Maison-Dieu* 138 (1979): 108–9.

Ordination in the first millennium included the entire process whereby a person was selected and appointed by the community to a particular service to the community. Yves Congar pointed out, for instance, that ordination is the term used for the appointment to an ecclesiastical post by a secular ruler. He also noted the many instances in which contemporaries referred to secular rulers as ordained. Charlemagne, Otto II, and Otto III were all so designated; and, according to Congar, "'To be ordained' was the official formula for their coronation."[36] Of course, contemporaries of those emperors, as well as the emperors themselves, would have understood their role as spiritual as well as secular *ordines*.

So, it would seem, did the important religious authorities. Pope Urban II in a letter dated 1089 to Rainold, archbishop of Rheims, affirmed the archbishop's power to ordain the kings and queens of France.[37] The Western rite for the coronation of the emperor is called in the tenth-century Romano-Germanic Pontifical "*benedictio ad ordinandum imperatorem secundum occidentalis* [blessing for the ordaining of emperor according to the Western [rite]."[38] The coronation rite contained in a Florentine sacramentary from the second half of the tenth century describes the blessing of the empress as an ordination.[39] This usage fits perfectly with the ordination rites for English queens discussed by Wogan-Browne. The Rule of Benedict, of course, used *ordinatio* frequently to refer to the installation of an abbot. The chapter in the Rule concerning the choosing of an abbot is simply entitled "*De ordinando abbate*."[40] Abbots, monks, and others entering the religious life were referred to as ordained throughout the early Middle Ages.

In summary, ordination in the early centuries referred essentially to a function, a role within the community, not to the conferral of an irreversible power, detached from any particular community. This definition of ordination encompassed many different roles within the community and certainly was not limited to those who served at the altar, as the later definition would. Yves Congar put it succinctly:

> ordination encompassed at the same time election as its starting-point and consecration as its term. But instead of signifying, as happened from the beginning of the twelfth century, the ceremony in which an individual received a power henceforth possessed in such a way that it could never be lost, the words *ordinare*, *ordinari*, *ordinatio* signified the fact of being designated and consecrated to take up a certain place, or better a certain function, *ordo*, in the community and at its service.[41]

36 Yves Congar, "Note sur une valeur des termes 'ordinare, ordinatio,'" *Revue des sciences religieuses* 58 (1984): 7–8.

37 *Epistola* 27, *PL* 151:310 B–C.

38 Cyrille Vogel, *Medieval Liturgy: An Introduction to the Sources*, trans. William Storey and Niels Rasmussen (Washington, D.C., 1986), 182.

39 Reinhard Elze, ed., *Die Ordines für die Weihe und Krönung des Kaisers und der Kaiserin*, MGH Fontes juris Germanici antiqui 9 (Hanover, 1995), no. 4b, 12.

40 A thorough discussion of the ordination of abbots in the Rule can be found in Robert Somerville, "Ordinatio abbatis in the Rule of St. Benedict," *Revue Benedictine* 77 (1967): 246–63.

41 Yves Congar, "My Path-Findings in the Theology of Laity and Ministries," *The Jurist* 32 (1972): 180.

Several important implications follow from this definition. First, an ordained person was expected to be from the community that chose her or him and to remain bound to that community. "Absolute ordination," that is ordination not tied to a particular community was explicitly forbidden, although sometimes practiced, until the twelfth century.[42] It was only in 1198 that Pope Innocent III lifted the longstanding ban on absolute ordination, requiring only that the ordained be supplied with a reliable income.[43] The connection between a particular community and the person ordained from and to it was legally severed.

A second important implication of the earlier definition of ordination was that the priesthood was not understood as the pinnacle of the ordained state. Each ordo was equally ordained, if not of equal importance. In fact according to John St. H. Gibault in his study of the *cursus honorum*, "the presbyterate was a dispensable grade in the *cursus* towards the episcopate."[44] In the see of Rome, for instance, up until the mid-eighth century, it was quite customary for deacons to ascend to the episcopate, including such luminaries as Leo the Great (440–461) and Gregory the Great (590–604). This practice continued in Rome into the tenth century. The first deacon elected pope who insisted on presbyteral ordination before consecration as pope was Gregory VII himself in 1073.[45] This was also the practice in other sees. Ambrose famously became bishop of Milan without ever holding any other clerical post.[46]

Further, not only a priest or deacon could celebrate the rituals of the Eucharist, give penance, read the Gospel, or preach. Theologians in the twelfth century, for example, would still debate whether an ordained minister was necessary to consecrate the bread and wine in the Eucharist. Teaching in the middle of the twelfth century, Bernard and Thierry of Chartres were described by Peter Abelard as teaching that the words of consecration confect the sacrament no matter who pronounced the words, even if that should be a woman (*etiam mulier*). A similar position was taken at the same time by the Parisian theologian John Beleth (fl. 1135–1182) who held that the words of institution effected the change, even if pronounced by accident and by the laity. Only with the Fourth Lateran Council in 1215 would the Church officially teach that only a properly ordained priest could consecrate the Eucharist.[47] To summarize:

42 Vincenz Fuchs, *Der Ordinationstitel von seiner Entstehung bis auf Innocenz III* (Amsterdam : Schippers Verlag, 1963).

43 "Licet autem praedecessores nostri ordinationes eorum, qui sine certo titulo promoventur, in iniuriam ordinantium irritas esse voluerint et inanes, nos tamen, benignus agere cupientes tam diu per ordinatores et successores eorum provideri volumus ordinatas, donec per eos ecclesiastica beneficia consequantur." Quoted and discussed by Fuchs, *Der Ordinationstitel*, 274–75.

44 John St. H. Gibaut, *The "Cursus Honorum": A Study of the Origins and Evolution of Sequential Ordination*, Patristics Studies, 3 (New York, 2000), 239.

45 Ibid., 136–37, 233–34, 296.

46 Ibid., 138–42.

47 See Gary Macy, "Theologies of the Eucharist in the High Middle Ages," in *A Companion to the Eucharist in the Middle Ages*, ed. Ian Levy, Gary Macy and Kristen Van Ausdall, 366–70 (Brill: Leiden, 2011).

> the definition of ordination that dominated the late Middle Ages and that is still the definition of orders accepted by most Christians was [by the early thirteenth century] now complete. Ordination was no longer a ceremony that marked the entry of a member of the church into some new service or ministry. Ordination was a ceremony empowering a member of the church for only one purpose, the consecration of the bread and wine during the liturgy in order to make the risen Christ present at that liturgy. All other *ordines* (now the minor orders) either led to the priesthood or, as in the case of the episcopacy, made the priesthood possible. Any *ordo* that did not relate directly to the priesthood was not an *ordo* at all.[48]

This change in the definition of ordination has not gone unnoticed in other areas of medieval history. An important new study, *A Companion to Priesthood and Holy Orders in the Middle Ages*,[49] concurs with these findings. Robert Swanson in an introductory essay puts it clearly and succinctly:

> The tectonic shift of the long 12th century brought fundamental changes in the way that episcopacy and priesthood were defined and described within the Western church, to clarify the status and role of bishops and priest both for themselves and for the laity to whom they offered the hope of salvation. Collective amnesia soon obscured the extent of the transformation as the new (but soon engrained and traditional) understanding of priestly ordination and episcopal authority congealed into a system and theology of "order," which had supposedly existed since apostolic times and became a spinal feature of late medieval catholicism. In particular, the sacramental priesthood, imbued with the character infused by ordination, became foundational for the whole sacramental system and for the whole hierarchical order.[50]

In summary, then, ordination was understood quite differently in the first millennium of Christianity. This has important implications for understanding what it meant for women to be ordained during that period. It meant (as indeed it did for men) that they were chosen by their communities to perform a certain function or role in that community. Ordination was not tied to, nor limited to, the celebration of the Eucharist, as it would become by the early thirteenth century. Determining, then, whether women (or indeed men) were priests was not at all the same question as whether women (or men) were ordained. However, as those ordained to the leadership of a community would be the ones most likely to lead those communities in their rituals, it should not be surprising if women performed rites within their communities which would later be attributed to male priests. Abbesses, for example, would be the

48 Macy, *Hidden History*, 108.

49 *A Companion to Priesthood and Holy Orders in the Middle Ages*, ed. Greg Peters and C. Colt Anderson, Brill's Companions to the Christian Tradition, 62 (Leiden: Brill, 2016).

50 Robert Swanson, "Apostolic Successors: Priests and Priesthood, Bishops, and Episcopacy in Medieval Western Europe," in *ibid.*, 41.

most likely people to hear the confessions of those under their care, and indeed this seems to have been the case. Scholars still have much to learn about the roles that ordained women played in such a society. Scholars, such as Dr. Katie Bugyis, are carefully uncovering these roles.[51] Understanding what ordination meant, and more importantly what it did not mean, for such women and the men with which they worked creates the possibility of reimagining the society in which they operated.

## Conclusions

A fuller and more robust understanding of the role women played in the church of the early Middle Ages can be gained by considering the possibility that they were understood as ordained by the society in which they lived. This assumes, of course, an understanding of ordination quite different from what would prevail after the great reforms of the eleventh through the thirteenth centuries. One cannot assume, for example, that women were not ordained because they were not priests, or because they did not lead the liturgy. Such assumptions would be at best anachronistic.

Granted, the tendency to read the later understanding of ordination back into the earlier Middle Ages is very strong among both historians and theologians. The advocates of the Gregorian Reform, and their followers down through the centuries, have accomplished one of the most successful rewritings of history in Western civilization, and we are still held in the spell of their propaganda. As Marianne Delaporte rightly points out, "historians and theologians have long fogged up the question of women's ordination by using a modern definition to the term even while discussing ordination in the church prior to this time. The reason that the practice of women's ordination has been hidden is largely due to a matter of semantics, as the term ordination has been limited to the modern understanding which confines ordination to priests and deacons."[52] We need to escape from the enchantment of the Reformers. They wanted to convince their readers that the changes they were introducing were eternal truths from which the Church practice had strayed. The problem is further complicated by the sources with which we have to work. Many of them are precisely the ones the Reformers preserved in their vast collections of church law and, as they were intended, the sources they preserved support their reform agenda.

An integration of the insights gained by both historians and theologians can go a long way in helping to construct a different history of women religious, one more faithful to their true role in society. One of the main goals of this essay is to foster such an integration in the hopes of recovering a more accurate picture of the amazing women who inhabited the Church of the past.

51 See, for example, Katie Ann-Marie Bugyis, "The Practice of Penance in Communities of Benedictine Women Religious in Central Medieval England," *Speculum* 92 (2017): 36–84; eadem, *The Care of Nuns: The Ministries of Benedictine Women in England during the Central Middle Ages* (New York: Oxford University Press, 2019).

52 Marianne Delaporte, Review of Gary Macy, *The Hidden History of Women's Ordination* in *Anglican and Episcopal History* 78 (2009): 217.

17

# SAINT COLETTE DE CORBIE (1381–1447): REFORMIST LEADERSHIP AND BELATED SAINTHOOD

RENATE BLUMENFELD-KOSINSKI

Colette de Corbie was one of the most important reformers of the Franciscan order in the late Middle Ages. Looking back at her long career, one has to conclude that she was a natural-born leader, inspiring some of the most powerful men and women of her time, both secular and ecclesiastical, to lend support to her foundations and reforms. This support was monetary as well as spiritual and crossed the "party lines" drawn in the last stages of the Hundred Years War. Together with other saintly personages, like Saint Vincent Ferrer (1350–1419), she worked to end the Great Schism of the Western Church (1378–1417).[1] She lived to see the end of that Schism at the Council of Constance, but not the end of the next conflict that pitted Pope Eugene IV (d.1447) against Amadeus of Savoy (1383–1451), elected as antipope Felix V in 1439 during the long drawn-out Council of Basel (1431–1449). In the midst of seemingly endless war and multiple ecclesiastical conflicts Colette managed to steer a course focused on founding new Franciscan houses and reforming existing ones. It is Colette's identity as a reformist leader and the strategies she used to implement her reforms that are at the center of this essay.[2]

1 See Renate Blumenfeld-Kosinski, *Poets, Saints, and Visionaries of the Great Schism (1378–1417)* (University Park, PA: Pennsylvania State University Press, 2006), chaps. 2 and 3.

2 It would be instructive to compare Colette's career as a founder and reformer with those of Saints Clare (1193/94–1253) and Birgitta of Sweden (1303–1373). How did they realize their leadership roles? What was the importance of their social class, that is, the upper-class and noble origins of Clare and Birgitta versus Colette's lower-class background? How crucial was male–female cooperation in the development of their orders? What was the role of the papacy? The function of visions? How much pressure were these two women able to exert to achieve their goals? We could think of Saint Clare's skillful strategies to obtain the "Privilege of Poverty" from pope Gregory IX in 1228 or look at the many decades it took Saint Birgitta to transform her 1340s vision of Christ giving her the Rule for her future order into the Birgittine Order (which she did not live to see, however.) Unfortunately, this kind of comparison lies beyond the scope of the present article. The literature on Saints Clare and Birgitta is vast. For concise information on some of these issues see Joan Mueller, "Female Mendicancy: A Failed Experiment? The Case of Saint Clare of Assisi," in *The Origin, Development, and Refinement of Medieval Religious Mendicancies*, Brill's Companions to the Christian Tradition 24, ed. Donald S. Prudlo (Leiden: Brill, 2011), 59–81 and Bridget Morris, "The Rule of the Savior," in *The Revelations of St. Birgitta of Sweden*, translated by Denis Searby with introductions and notes by Bridget Morris (Oxford: Oxford University Press, 2006), vol. 4, 109–47.

Colette's identity has a variety of facets, some of them contradictory; there appears to be a tug-of-war between acknowledgment of her leadership qualities and efforts to "contain" her in a straitjacket of saintly models, depending on the witnesses we consult. Thus, the image that her biographers Pierre De Vaux and Perrine de la Roche created of her in two biographies,[3] dating from shortly after Colette's death in 1447 and around 1477 respectively,[4] do not always correspond to the testimonies of other people who knew her or to those of the chroniclers who wrote about her. Nor do they square with the Colette we find in her long-delayed bull of canonization in 1807.[5] Her quest for authority – and its success – is depicted differently in all these sources, yet a number of coherent strategies emerge. In the framework of this chapter I can touch only briefly on some of the elements that come together to create our view of Colette as a charismatic and forceful leader.

Given her leadership qualities, it took Colette a remarkably long time to find her true vocation. Colette was born in 1381 in Corbie in Picardy as the daughter of an elderly carpenter, Robert Boulet, who worked for the local Benedictine abbey, and his equally elderly, extremely pious wife Margaret Moyon, for whom this was a second marriage.[6] Colette was a puella senex who despised childish games and, like Saint John the Baptist, at age four had "knowledge of God." Also, like Saint John she would have liked to live in the desert, a desire she could not fulfill, as Pierre de Vaux states "because she was a girl." Instead, she chose to live secretement et solitairement (apart

3 Pierre de Vaux was Colette's confessor and Perrine de la Roche or de la Baume was the niece of Colette's confessor Henry de Baume (d. 1439), a Colettine sister and Colette's companion of many decades. She was born in 1408, during or just after Colette visited her father's castle in Burgundy. See Elisabeth Lopez, *Colette of Corbie (1381–1447): Learning and Holiness*, trans. Joanna Waller (St. Bonaventure, NY: The Franciscan Institute, 2011 [originally published in French in 1994]), 4.

4 Pierre de Reims dit de Vaux et Soeur Perrine de la Roche et de Baume, *Les Vies de Ste Colette Boylet de Corbie, Réformatrice des Frères Mineurs et des Clarisses (1381–1447)*, Archives Franciscaines 4, ed. Ubald d'Alençon (Paris: Picard, 1911). Both biographies were written in French. All translations are my own. I am currently preparing an English translation of these Lives. References to the two texts will be made parenthetically as Vaux and Perrine.

5 A comprehensive and strangely neglected study of Saint Colette and her reform is Joan Marie Richards, "Franciscan Women: The Colettine Reform of the Order of Saint Clare," PhD dissertation, University of California at Berkeley, 1989. The *Companion to Colette of Corbie*, Brill's Companions to the Christian Tradition 66, ed. Joan Mueller and Nancy Bradley Warren (Leiden: Brill, 2016), contains a number of insightful essays. I thank Nancy Warren for sharing this volume with me in the proof stage. On the different images of Colette, including in some modern scholarship, see also the important article by Bert Roest, "A Textual Community in the Making: Colettine Authorship in the Fifteenth Century," in *Seeing and Knowing: Women and Learning in Medieval Europe 1200–1550*, ed. Anneke Mulder-Bakker (Turnhout: Brepols, 2004), 163–80.

6 This fact is the subject of a rather heartless remark Colette makes to her mother: "I wish you had not remarried," she tells her, and when the mother observes that in that case Colette would not have been born, the young girl replies: "then I would have been born by one of your neighbors," thus rejecting her mother's logical and loving argument (Vaux, 62). The fact that her biographer Pierre de Vaux reports this exchange in the context of Colette's later reluctance to accept non-virgins into her Order, does not much mitigate the harsh tone of the girl's reproach to her mother. This episode is an early illustration of Colette's toughness.

and in solitude; Vaux, 7–8). Colette attended the school for children run by the local abbey and also seems to have received some religious instruction from an older woman whom, according to Perrine, she called her maistresse (Perrine, 203). Colette could certainly read and most likely also write. In later life her letters were probably dictated, as was common in the Middle Ages, but they bear her signature.[7] But Colette was also rebellious, as we learn from a passage that only Sister Perrine reports: at night she would often climb out of the window when her parents were asleep to meet her friend Adam Mangnier in order to attend night services (Perrine, 203)! At age nine Colette received a revelation of the spirit of the Franciscan Order and the need for its reform.[8] Sharing her religious fervor proved difficult, however, because of her small stature, which caused detractors to speak to her parents and urge them to rein in her pious overtures to "poor and dissolute women" in Corbie. After a pilgrimage and a prayer to Christ, the fourteen-year-old girl experienced a miraculous growth spurt and could henceforth spread her pious messages unimpeded (Vaux, 12–13).

When Colette was eighteen her parents died within months of each other and, having refused marriage plans proposed to her by the abbot of the monastery where her father had worked, Colette decided to become a beguine after getting rid of everything she owned. This was the beginning of a search for her true vocation: disliking the beguine life, she became a *conversa* with the Benedictines in Corbie, then moved to the royal abbey of Moncel near Pont Saint-Maxence as a "servant."[9] However, the lack of true poverty of this abbey of Urbanist Poor Clares, which followed the rule of Isabelle of Longchamp,[10] left her dissatisfied and she returned to Corbie, where her mentors became impatient with her lack of direction. One of these mentors, the reformist Franciscan Jean Pinet, guardian of the Hesdin friary, advised Colette to become a recluse since none of the available convents was strict enough for her. From 1402 to 1406 she lived in an anchorhold constructed for her adjacent to the church of Saint Etienne.[11] But again she had to move: Saint Francis appeared to Colette in a vision urging her to reform his three orders. Having obtained permission to leave her an-

7 See Lopez, *Learning and Holiness*, 165–66. For a list and analysis of Colette's letters, most of them written after 1439, see Lopez, *Learning and Holiness*, 175–212. Whether Colette knew Latin, German, and other languages, as Pierre de Vaux claims (Vaux, 151), cannot be confirmed. Vaux evokes the apostles here who "spoke all languages" and we therefore most likely deal with a hagiographic topos. On this topos see Christine Cooper Rompato, *The Gift of Tongues: Women's Xenoglossia in the Later Middle Ages* (University Park, PA: Pennsylvania State University Press, 2010).

8 Simone Roisin, "Colette de Corbie (Sainte) (1381–1447), réformatrice du premier et du second ordre franciscains," *Dictionnaire d'histoire et de géographie ecclésiastique*, vol. 13 (Paris: Letouzey, 1956), cols. 238–46; at col. 239.

9 Pont-Saint-Maxence is in southern Picardy. See Roisin, "Colette de Corbie," col. 239.

10 Isabelle (1224–1270) was the daughter of Louis VIII and Blanche of Castille and the sister of King Louis IX, Saint Louis. She founded the Poor Clares of Longchamp in 1256 and was canonized in 1696. See Sean L. Field, *Isabelle of France: Capetian Sanctity and Franciscan Identity in the Thirteenth Century* (Notre Dame: University of Notre Dame Press, 2006). "Urbanist" refers to Pope Urban IV (pope from 1261 to1264) who had relaxed the strict rules on poverty for most communities of Poor Clares.

11 Bert Roest, "The Poor Clares during the Era of Observant Reform: Attempts at a Typology," *Franciscan Studies* 69 (2011): 343–86; at 348.

chorhold, Colette met with the Avignon Pope Benedict XIII (1394–1423[12]) in Nice in 1406 and – with and sometimes against the great reformers Saint Bernardino of Siena (1380–1444) and Saint John Capistrano (1386–1456) – became one of the greatest reformers of the Franciscans Orders. She died on March 6, 1447 in her convent in Ghent with her confessor and future biographer Pierre de Vaux by her side.

How did this woman, who took a while to find her path, become what John Moorman calls "a leader – a woman of great force of character, determined, competent, autocratic, and self-confident" and normally getting what she wanted, a woman "who held the love and loyalty of those over whom she ruled"?[13] A look at a few authorizing moments and strategies can help explain her rise to leadership.

The impetus for Colette's reforming mission came from a series of dramatic visions that propelled her out of her anchorhold and into the world of the Franciscans. These visions are described almost identically by her two biographers, Pierre de Vaux and Sister Perrine, Colette's loyal companion through decades of convent life and frequent travel. An important difference is that Perrine often appeals to male authorities who "told" her about Colette's visions, while Pierre's voice makes no appeal to such intermediaries. This series of visions is so crucial that it needs to be cited at length:

> A marvelous and frightening vision was shown to her by God. In this vision she saw and recognized all the different estates of the Church and of secular society, from the highest to the lowest, and the system of government of each of these estates. Then were shown to her the faults and offenses that each of these estates, from the highest to the lowest, had committed against their governments and against God, to His great displeasure. She also saw the horrible pains and grievous torments with which every one of them was punished according to his just deserts. She was so terribly frightened by these horrible pains and grievous torments that for eight days it seemed to her that she herself had to fall into these horrible torments. And when this vision was finished she suddenly found an iron bar in the middle of her window that was strong enough to support her,[14] and she grabbed it and held

12 Although deposed at the Council of Constance, Benedict, supported by some loyal followers, believed himself to be pope until his death in 1423 at the age of ninety-five.

13 J. R. H. Moorman, *A History of the Franciscan Order* (Oxford: Oxford University Press, 1968), 554.

14 This window bar expands into an iron cage attached to the outside of a chapel, protecting Colette from the fires and demons of hell, in the image accompanying this passage in Manuscript 8 of the Monasterium "Bethlehem" of the Zusters Clarissen-Coletienes in Ghent. See *Vita Sanctae Coletae (1381–1447)*, ed. Auspicius van Constantje et al. (Leiden: Brill, 1982), fig. 6, fol. 19r. This volume offers color reproductions of all the miniatures in Manuscript 8. On this manuscript and its illustrations see Andrea Pearson, "Imaging and Imagining Colette of Corbie: An Illuminated Version of Pierre de Vaux's *Vie de Colette*," in *A Companion* (above n. 5), 130–72. Pearson shows that the illustrations had no particular iconographic models and were inspired by Pierre de Vaux's *Vie de Sainte Colette*. See also Erica O'Brien, "The Politics of Perception: A Duchess' Devotional Skill in *La Vie de Sainte Colette* (MS. 8)," in *The Image and Perception of Monarchy in Medieval and Early Modern Europe*, ed. Sean McGlynn and Elena Woodacre (Newcastle: Cambridge Scholars Publishing, 2014), 110–27.

on to it with her hand so that she would not fall into these torments, and she later had great trouble letting go of it. And this vision of the estates and their faults and punishments was so firmly imprinted in her heart for the rest of her life that she always remembered them. And because of these offenses and faults that she knew had been committed against the divine sovereign majesty, she carried in her heart great sadness and enormous pain for a long time. Several times each day and night she prayed humbly and fervently to God for the correction of the poor sinners, which devout prayers God by His sovereign grace and merciful compassion listened to and granted.

And it was shown to her that this correction would be done through the reformed orders that Saint Francis had instituted.[15] In order to correct and reform these orders we can take the example of the glorious Virgin Mary and our savior Jesus Christ, her dear child, who wanted to throw three lances in order to confound and destroy the world, especially for the sins of pride, avarice, and voluptuousness. But the Virgin Mary presented to Him Saint Francis and Saint Dominic as two champions who could virtuously fight and preach against these vices for the correction of these sinners. Similarly, our lord Saint Francis, in the presence of the glorious Virgin Mary and the blessed angels of paradise, presented his handmaid to our glorious savior Jesus Christ and humbly asked Him that He should let her undertake the above-mentioned reform of his orders. Thus she would correct the sinners of all the estates that she had seen in her vision, and he asked that she should be the first and principal person to undertake this reform; and this presentation was pleasant and agreeable to our Lord. And He graciously granted the request and petition of lord Saint Francis that he had presented to Him. This permission regarding the reform and correction that should be undertaken filled the above-mentioned handmaid of Our Lord with great joy, but she also felt great sadness because her glorious beloved mother and lord Saint Francis wanted that she should be the first and principal person to undertake this reform, and she believed herself to be incapable and unworthy. She could not wholeheartedly consent, even though it was made clear to her in her prayers that it had to be done this way and that it was God's will. At one point

15 Orders, in the plural, presumably refers to the first Order of Saint Francis and the Poor Clares though Saint Dominic is mentioned below. It is interesting that here the foundation of both the first and second order is attributed to Saint Francis (1181–1226) alone. The foundation of the Poor Clares has a problematic history; its founding is "shrouded in myth," as Alison More puts it. See More, *Fictive Orders and Feminine Religious Identities, 1200–1600* (Oxford: Oxford University Press, 2018), 33. More shows that many communities of pious women were retrofitted as "orders" in later documents and chronicles. The Poor Clares were in fact founded, that is, institutionalized by Pope Urban IV in 1263, ten years after Clare's death in 1253. See More, *Fictive Orders*, 32–35. See also Lezlie Knox, *Creating Clare of Assisi: Female Franciscan Identities in Later Medieval Italy*, The Medieval Franciscans vol. 5 (Leiden: Brill, 2008), chaps. 1–2.

> she excused herself by saying that she was a simple young woman who knew nothing, at another point by mentioning the vow she had made never to leave her anchorhold. And several times she feared that the devil from hell tried to deceive her.
>
> Because of these difficulties she humbly approached all devout people she knew and whose acquaintance she could make, and from the learned and knowledgeable people, who loved and feared God, she sought counsel and advice. All of them, uniformly and by God's grace, judged that she should do it and told her so. And so that she could be sure and have no doubt that it was God's will that she should undertake this reform and correction she asked that God by His grace show her some visible signs as evidence. The first sign was that she became mute like Zacharias, the father of Saint John the Baptist, and for three days she did not say anything; then she was blind for three days and did not see anything. And when she consented [to undertake the reform] she spoke and saw again. (Vaux, 28–30)

Thus, in these dramatic visions Saint Francis appears accompanied by the Virgin Mary to present Colette to Christ as the future reformer of his orders so that the world can be saved from the horrors Colette had seen in her vision.[16] The iron bar that protects Colette from these infernal horrors seems to represent the strength that Christ gives her for the coming reform. Thus, Christ authorizes Colette to embark on this new path, but Pierre de Vaux makes certain to report that Colette's professed humility and "ignorance" led her to seek the advice of learned people. This important move into the real world of human counsel is followed by three divine signs, that is, the blindness and muteness described in the passage just cited plus another vision: a big tree begins to grow in her anchorhold, accompanied by lots of little trees.[17] Fearing diabolical deception, Colette throws them out, but they keep on coming back. Finally, God interprets the trees for her: the fact that they move, their *transportacion*, signified "that she would have to go and build and do good in several different regions" (Vaux, 31); and indeed, in her future life Colette seems to be constantly on the move. Somewhat later, when Colette has begun her reforming activities, Pierre de Vaux adds an extremely important interpretation to the vision of Saint Francis saying "that the said

16 Clare of Assisi is notably absent from this vision in de Vaux's version, but she does make an appearance in the version reported by sister Elisabeth of Bavaria whose source apparently was Henry de Baume. She asks for a reform of her order as well. This variant is in the Mémoire de Hesdin, Archives d'Amiens, no. 11, liasse 23 (Lopez, *Learning and Holiness*, 42 n. 6). Elisabeth also speaks of Saints Mary Magdalene and John the Baptist as present in this vision. All of them are united with Christ and Mary on the frontispiece of *La Règle de Sainte Claire avec les statuts de la Réforme de Sainte Colette* (Bruges: Desclé de Brouwer, 1892).

17 See illustration in Elisabeth Lopez, *Petite Vie de Sainte Colette* (Paris: Desclée de Brouwer, 1998), 27 (from Bibliothèque Municipale of Arras, manuscript 461–74, fol. 2v) and in Manuscript 8 of the Monasterium "Bethlehem" of the Zusters Clarissen-Coletienes in Ghent, fol. 30r, which shows indistinct figures planting trees. Reproduced as fig. 9 in van Constantje, ed., *Vita Sanctae Coletae*.

reform and correction that were to be accomplished by her were to be effected not just in one order but in all three orders that lord Saint Francis instituted, as it appears through the convents that were built or reformed by her, as much for men as for women, for friars and sisters" (Vaux, 43). In a further vision a white cord descends from heaven into Colette's arms, signifying the purity of Colette and the pleasure God takes in her reforms (Vaux, 45).[18] However, as we will see in a moment, Pierre de Vaux's interpretation amounting to an endorsement of Colette's triple reformist mission does not have an equivalent in real life.[19] Pierre de Vaux, writing in 1447 after Colette's death, extrapolates here from the saint's future successes by situating the divine authorization for the reform of all three orders even before her meeting with Pope Benedict XIII.

Looking at Pierre de Vaux's version of Colette's mission in its early stages as a whole, we see that he assembles all the elements necessary for a woman to gain a leadership role as a reformer: authorizing divinely sent visions featuring the founder of the Franciscan order as well as the Virgin Mary and Christ, who Himself commands reforms from Colette.[20] And on the worldly level she seeks advice from trusted counselors, advice that is then confirmed by further divine signs.

However, visions and divine signs were not sufficient to authorize the kind of enterprise Colette was embarking on in 1406. She also needed the endorsement of the pope, in her case that of Benedict XIII, the powerful and tenacious former cardinal Pedro de Luna, who was ensconced at Nice during a critical period of the Great Schism. Interestingly, Pierre de Vaux gives us a kind of preview of this meeting, outside of the chronological order of Colette's biography: in chapter 2 entitled "About Her Profound Humility" we learn (and this passage occurs before the text's description of the vision of Saint Francis) that although Saint Francis had commanded that Colette function as "the mother and the principal" of his three orders, she felt not up to this task and "unworthy." Then, in a rather breathtaking move, Pierre de Vaux tells us "she would never consent to doing this [the reform] and proposed that she would even go so far as to seek the pope's presence to beg him humbly to order the reform of these orders, and that she would implore the Holy Father to let her become a servant of the reformed order of Saint Clare, which is the second order of Saint Francis." And so Colette, "the small, humble and unworthy servant of Our Lord, a poor and useless sister of the order of Saint Clare, who never allowed anyone to say or write anything honoring or praising her," managed to be made "lady, mother, and abbess" (*dame, mere et abbesse*) of this entire reform (*de toute la dicte reforme*), without her actually knowing about it (*sans ce qu'elle en eust cognoissance*) (Vaux, 15–16). The last phrase is puzzling but may refer to the historical detail that the

18 Illustrated in Manuscript 8 of the Monasterium "Bethlehem" of the Zusters Clarissen-Coletienes in Ghent, fol. 30r, left compartment.

19 As Elisabeth Lopez puts it "the power of the legend has covered up history" (*Petite Vie*, 35).

20 Once launched, Colette's mission was endorsed by more visions of which one of the most touching is reported only by Perrine: one day, when Colette was gravely ill and thought she was dying, Saints Mary Magdalene and Clare appear to her, asking the Lord to make her die so that she could join them in heaven. But Saint Francis does not agree: he insists that he still needs her for the reform of his orders. The Lord sides with Francis, and Colette, though "unhappy" about this decision (she states, "*je suys bien mal contente*") must continue her work (Perrine, 257).

bull Benedict XIII issued in April 1406 did not in fact authorize Colette's activities as a reformer, but merely gave her permission "to found a monastery with the privilege of observing the strictest poverty."[21] In other words, there was no mention of *toute la dicte reforme*. Indeed, Duncan Nimmo puts his finger on the central paradox of Colette's early career when he observes, "it must be granted that in strict canonical terms the notion of a nun empowered to reform an Order of men makes no sense. Nevertheless, the evidence of the biographical sources is hard to deny."[22] In 1447 it was clear what kind of a leadership role Colette had played for the Franciscan orders; consequently, Pierre de Vaux's strategy of coupling Colette's utter humility with her proposal to go and see the pope may strike the modern reader as ironic, but it fits into Pierre de Vaux's efforts to reconcile hagiographic conventions with the reality of a forceful and determined leader.[23] This leader comes to the fore when Pierre de Vaux once again recounts her meeting with Pope Benedict XIII, this time at the correct chronological point in Colette's life and not in a chapter devoted to the virtue of humility.

In that section (chapter 5) we see how Colette, still in her anchorhold and now convinced of the divine truth of her visions, developed a plan of action that looks surprisingly modern: she put together a team and wrote a memo. This *memoriael* was a small scroll (*petit rolet*), containing the details that God had revealed to her for "the things necessary for her business" (*les choses qui luy estoeint neccessaires pour ses affaires*; Vaux, 32).[24] This is the crucial moment in Colette's career: we can assume that the scroll may have contained a reference to the vision she had received, providing divine authorization for this next phase of her life. The support team that agreed to accompany her to Pope Benedict XIII consisted of one of her confessors, the Franciscan Henry de Baume (d. 1439), and Isabeau de Rochechouard, baronesse de Brisay from Besançon. They provided the social support network for a young woman from a humble milieu, for Henry was well connected in the noble circles of his region as was of course the baronesse. On their way to Nice, "flying" (Vaux, 34) over stones and difficult terrain they stop to engage a "respected and discreet woman" (*une notable et discrete femme*) who is to announce their arrival to the pope. However, this woman promptly goes crazy, starts spouting "disordered and dishonest" things (Vaux, 37), and strips naked in public, an act that jeopardizes their admittance to the pope. In the illustrated manuscript of

21 Lopez, *Petite Vie*, 34–35 and for the quote Lopez, *Learning and Holiness*, 54. Benedict issued three bulls, the first in April 1406 and the other two in October 1406. The second authorized the foundation at Hesdin, and the third allowed that two friars could assist Colette.

22 Duncan Nimmo, *Reform and Division in the Medieval Franciscan Order: From Saint Francis to the Foundation of the Capuchins* (Rome: Capuchin Historical Institute, 1987), 448.

23 I cannot agree here with Jane Marie Pinzino who states that "Pierre's text ironically bears responsibility for a future that downplayed rather than embraced the tangible leadership in male spheres that Colette in fact exercised" and that "Pierre chose to depict Colette's holiness in the *vita* as that of a visionary and ecstatic contemplative." See "But Where to Draw the Line: Colette of Corbie, Joan of Arc, and the Expanding Boundaries of Female Leadership in the Fifteenth Century," in *A Companion to Colette of Corbie*, 66 (as in n. 5). I believe he skillfully combines the many aspects of Colette's holiness, including her reformist leadership.

24 Perrine says nothing about God giving her the words, she just mentions the *rolet* that Colette carries in a *petite boursette* hanging from her belt and that contained all that Colette wanted to request from the pope (Perrine, 215).

de Vaux's *Vie de Sainte Colette* in Ghent we see an image of this scene in which demons are tearing open her dress.[25]

Eventually the woman recovers (a miracle showing that the devil has been thwarted) and Colette is admitted to the chambers of the pope who promptly stumbles. This incident may be related to Benedict XIII's role in the Great Schism, which he was accused of prolonging through his refusal to abdicate.[26] After this brief contretemps Benedict receives Colette graciously and, according to Pierre de Vaux, grants her the two things she wants: To enter the order of Saint Clare and to be allowed to reform the orders (plural) that Saint Francis instituted (Vaux, 38). However, as we saw earlier, the second request was not part of the formal papal bull. Once again Pierre de Vaux inserts a fictitious authorization for Colette's reformist leadership. In a continuation of the scene at Nice we find the cardinals, who think that at twenty-five Colette is too young to accomplish all these tasks, quickly dying of the plague.[27] These details are missing from Perrine's account of Colette's visit to the pope. In Pierre de Vaux's version Benedict grants Colette even more than she asked for: he immediately makes her an abbess in addition to authorizing her reforming activities.

The accumulation of "signs" in this scene is remarkable,[28] none more so than the crazed naked woman. I suggest that she may represent an out-of-control sexualized bodily female danger that threatens to invade the papal court. The association of demons with sexuality was a given at the beginning of the fifteenth century.[29] Thus the first phase of Colette's visit to the pope took place under the double threat of the demonic and the sexual, the two forces that Colette's holiness and asceticism could defeat. Only after this woman is "tamed," dressed again and back to normal – the threats resolved – can Colette appear, a marked contrast with her sober and pious presence, a woman with a plan showing a truly intellectual approach to her mission.[30] What is this mission and how can she accomplish it in the face of many obstacles?

The support of highly placed nobles was crucial for the creation of Colette's authority.[31] Dukes, duchesses, even kings all lent support to Colette's foundations and

25 Manuscript 8 of the Monasterium "Bethlehem" of the Zusters Clarissen-Coletienes in Ghent, fol. 23r, reproduced as fig. 7 in van Constantje, ed., *Vita Sanctae Coletae.*

26 The complex question of Colette and Benedict's tenuous position after the French Withdrawal of Obedience (1398–1403) and its restitution cannot be treated here. See Lopez, *Petite Vie*, 34; and Blumenfeld-Kosinski, *Poets, Saints, and Visionaries,* 94.

27 Doubters, persecutors, and detractors have similar fates later in the *Vie*: certain "clerks" slander Colette and accuse her of being a heretic, a Hussite, and a follower of Jerome of Prague, even of being a usurer. They are quickly punished by illness and death (Vaux, 160).

28 Lopez, *Learning and Holiness*, 49.

29 See Renate Blumenfeld-Kosinski, *The Strange Case of Ermine de Reims: A Medieval Woman between Demons and Saints* (Philadelphia: University of Pennsylvania Press, 2015), esp. chap. 4.

30 While the text offers these scenes as sequential, the image shows them as simultaneous and thus highlights the contrast between the sexually aggressive demons and the figure of Colette, soberly dressed in black. See van Constantje, ed., *Vita Sanctae Coletae*, fig. 7, fol. 23r.

31 See Nancy Bradley Warren, "The Life and Afterlives of St. Colette of Corbie: Religion, Politics, and Networks of Power" and Monique Sommé, "The Duchesses of Burgundy as Benefactors of Colette de Corbie and Colettine Poor Clares," in *A Companion to Colette of Corbie*, 6–31 and 32–55 respectively.

reforms. But her hometown of Corbie violently rejected her first planned foundation, indeed Colette was accused of being a "witch, a magician, an invoker of demons" and "other horrible things" and was therefore forced "to go into foreign lands" (*estrainge pays*; Vaux, 41).[32] Colette found refuge at the castle of Blanche of Geneva (the sister of Robert of Geneva [d. 1394] who as Pope Clement VII was the first pope of the Great Schism on the Avignon side) and used half of Blanche's castle for the first foundation. From there she went on to Besançon and beyond, for a total of seventeen foundations and reformations of existing houses, both male and female.[33] This decades-long activity, entailing extensive and dangerous travel in regions still in the throes of the Hundred Years War, cannot be detailed here. Rather I will now look at just a few moments that presented challenges to Colette's leadership while often confirming it.

Colette's reforms were part of the larger Franciscan reform movement of the late fourteenth and fifteenth centuries, marked by the conflict between the Conventuals and the Observants.[34] The Conventuals were accused by the reformers of having abandoned the true Franciscan spirit by becoming lax in their conduct and allowing themselves to own property. But, although Colette's goals were more or less identical to those of the Observants, she did not want to merge with them. Her insistence on absolute poverty, strict enclosure, chastity, asceticism, and obedience, the cornerstones of the *Constitutions* (inspired by the Rule of Saint Clare) she composed around 1430,[35] certainly conformed to the Observants' ideals, but a merger with them would have meant, among other things, that the new Colettine foundations would have been absorbed into the larger Observant movement and, most important, that the friars would have taken over as directors of the convents and as Visitors would have had the power to dismiss the abbesses elected by the nuns.[36] Colette would not allow her authority to be diminished. William of Casale, the Minister General of the Franciscan Order, acknowledged this authority in a rather bemused (or frustrated?) tone when in a letter from around 1437 he admitted that Colette's "daughters" would not "dare to obey my orders or suggestions without a special order from you" (*sine vestro speciali mandato*).[37]

32 Her hometown rejected her again decades later in 1445 and even threatened her with a lawsuit. See Monique Sommé, "Sainte Colette de Corbie et la réforme franciscaine en Picardie et Flandres au XVe siècle," in *Horizons marins, itinéraires spirituels (Ve – XVIIIe siècles)*, vol. 1: *Mentalités et Sociétés*, ed. Henri Dubois, Jean-Claude Hocquet, and André Vauchez (Paris: Publications de la Sorbonne, 1987), 255–64; at 258.

33 On all of Colette's foundations and reforms see in addition to Warren and Sommé (as in note 31) the Introduction of d'Alençon's edition of the two *Vies de Sainte Colette*.

34 In addition to Roest, "The Poor Clares" and Nimmo, *Reform and Division*, see Marie Richards, "The Conflict between Observant and Conventual Reformed Franciscans in Fifteenth-Century France and Flanders," *Franciscan Studies* 50 (1990): 263–81.

35 See *La Règle de Sainte Claire avec les statuts de la Réforme de Sainte Colette* (Bruges: Desclée de Brouwer, 1892). For an analysis of this Rule and its relation to the Rule of Saint Clare see Joan Mueller, "Colette of Corbie and the 'Privilege of Poverty,'" in *A Companion to Colette of Corbie*, 101–29. Richards indicates that William of Casale wrote them in Latin for her at her request and under her direction ("Franciscan Women," 19, as in n. 5). Sommé, on the other hand, writes that Colette herself redacted (*rédigea*) the *Constitutions* ("Sainte Colette de Corbie," 256; as in n. 32).

36 Lopez, *Petite Vie*, 76.

37 See Ubald d'Alençon, "Lettres inédites de Guillaume de Casal à Sainte Colette et notes pour la biographie de cette sainte," *Etudes franciscaines* 19 (1908): 460–81 and 668–91; at 476.

One of the most powerful men Colette had to contend with was Saint John of Capistrano, who in 1437 had been appointed as "reformer of all the convents of Saint Clare,"[38] and in 1442 had arrived as papal legate at the court of Philip the Good of Burgundy to persuade him to support Pope Eugene IV against the antipope Felix V. Colette enjoyed strong support from the house of Burgundy, as Nancy Bradley Warren and Monique Sommé have shown clearly.[39] But Colette vehemently opposed the merger desired by Capistrano, for merging with the Observants would mean that her hard-won Rule and the authority it gave her would disappear. The conflict between Colette and Capistrano was not of a spiritual or even ideological nature but centered, as indicated above, on the question of the authority of the abbess which Capistrano sought to undermine. In the chronicle of the Colettine house in Vevey, Colette's position is described dramatically: "And our saintly mother exhorted her sisters with urgency that they should never join the above-mentioned 'family' [the Observants], for it would result in their destruction and great desolation." Colette exhorted her nuns that they "should rather die than submit" to the Observants.[40] Capistrano finally had to accept her refusal and even allowed her to appoint her own Visitors. A letter to Colette in 1442 affirmed his consent.[41]

Interestingly, Pierre de Vaux omits this entire conflict from his *Vie*. But Colette's nineteenth-century biographer, the abbé Florimond Auguste Douillet gives us a dramatic version of Colette's struggle in face of Capistrano's demands. Together with her nuns Colette prayed for guidance, asking herself whether her own sins may have brought "the divine work that was entrusted to her so close to ruin." Colette drags herself on her knees through the cloister, one "can follow the trace that her injured knees leave with their virginal blood on the stones." Finally, Capistrano, "filled with admiration and afraid all at once" relents, and henceforth "the union of these two great souls was perfect" and they worked together even more ardently "for the triumph and the pacification of the Church."[42] In this version Colette's extraordinary piety and willingness to suffer physically are highlighted as the means with which she gains what she wants in the power struggle with Capistrano. We can juxtapose this incident

38 See d'Alençon's Introduction to the *Vies*, xi.

39 See Warren, "The Life and Afterlives," and Sommé, "The Duchesses of Burgundy as Benefactors," in *A Companion to Colette of Corbie*, 6–31 and 32–55 respectively.

40 Document from the Clarisses at Poligny (Amiens 23.21) quoted by Richards, "The Conflict," 275. Richards adds that this exhortation is preceded by an unflattering description of John Capistrano.

41 This letter was translated by the Poor Clare community Ty Mam Duw in Hawarden, Wales, on their website (poorclarestmd.org/colette/letters/letters/john.html). More than twenty letters to and from Colette are also available in translation on this site.

42 Florimond Auguste Douillet, *Ste Colette, sa vie, ses oeuvres, son culte, son influence* (Paris: Bary et Retaux, 1869), 277. Douillet was "curé et doyen" in Corbie, Colette's hometown. As was the custom in many of these nineteenth-century biographies, no sources are provided, but Douillet was probably inspired by the report of an anonymous sixteenth-century Franciscan who mentions in the so-called chronicle of Vevey that one could still see the blood on the stones. See Richards, "Franciscan Women," 50 and n. 66. Douillet's rosy vision of Colette and John's "union of souls" did not exactly correspond to the reality of their relationship which showed "no spiritual bond" between the two reformers (Richards, "Franciscan Women," 49).

with a brief scene in Pierre de Vaux's *Vie*, which deals with Colette's desire, early on in her reforms, to have the office sung rather than read. She consults with her confessor Henry de Baume and almost instantly an angelic voice fills the church, confirming Colette's desire for a sung office.[43] And henceforth it was "instituted and ordered" that the office should be sung like this (Vaux, 66). Thus, as in the conflict with Capistrano, Colette's visionary gifts confirm a policy choice. It would thus be a mistake to separate Colette's ascetic and visionary qualities from her political and diplomatic talents.[44]

Colette's refusal to merge with the Observants was a true test for her leadership and led to accusations that Colette had introduced a schism into the Franciscan order. In particular, this accusation is attributed to Bernardino of Siena by the copyist of a letter of William of Casale, who as Minister General of the Franciscans from 1430 to 1442 was one of Colette's strongest supporters. In this letter Casale confirms Colette's *Constitutions*.[45] The copyist, who was active in the second half of the fifteenth century, added a double sheet in which he identifies himself as a *translateur* and a *bien povre frere mineur*. Referring to the ever-greater division in the Franciscan Order, this friar cites Saint Bernardino of Siena who is said to have accused Colette of causing a schism in the Franciscan Order (*scisme en l'ordre de saint francois*). That this accusation dogged Colette during her lifetime becomes clear in a letter that Pierre de Vaux sent to the citizens of Amiens in 1443, trying to persuade them to accept a Colettine house. He stresses Colette's peaceful influence by saying that no "sedition, quarrel or division" (*sedicion, debat, ou division*) ever occurred in places where Colette's Poor Clares settled; on the contrary, Colette "pacified many cities."[46] This remark reminds us that Colette's many foundations and reforms required extensive travel. Although the Hundred Years War was winding down after the 1435 Treaty of Arras between the French king Charles VII and the duke of Burgundy, roads were still dangerous. Colette and her nuns were attacked repeatedly and escaped only through Colette's miraculous talent of pacifying would-be robbers. Colette also intervened in a number of conflicts and managed to prevent bloodshed, notably in one instance when her

43 The Rule of Saint Clare had specified that the office should be recited, not sung (*La Règle de l'Ordre de Sainte Claire*, 69). Colette thus revises – even contravenes – Clare's Rule by angelic command. One can think here of Saint Birgitta's "dictating angel" and the question of the sung and read liturgy. See Katherine Zieman, "Playing *Doctor*: St. Birgitta, Ritual Reading, and Ecclesiastical Authority," in *Voices in Dialogue: Reading Women in the Middle Ages*, ed.Linda Olson and Kathryn Kerby-Fulton (Notre Dame: University of Notre Dame Press, 2005), 307–34; at 315.

44 I therefore cannot quite agree with Ludovic Viallet who states that "Colette did not use her visions to further her action as a reformer." See "Colette de Corbie and the Franciscan Reform: The *Observantia* in the First Half of the Fifteenth Century," in *A Companion to Colette of Corbie* (as in n. 5), 76–100; at 96. However, he is right concerning the initial visions in which Saint Francis authorized her reforms of the First and Second Orders. These visions are not referred to explicitly in her later reform work.

45 Ubald d'Alençon, "Lettres inédites," 468–69. Quotations of this letter come from these two pages. For an analysis of other letters by important Churchmen and officials of the Franciscan order affirming Colette's leadership and her role as "spiritual mother" see Roest, "A Textual Community in the Making" (as in note 5), 168–69.

46 Ubald d'Alençon, "La Lettre de P. Pierre de Vaux aux Habitants d'Amiens (1443)," *Etudes franciscaines* 23 (1910): 651–59; at 654.

entreating letters kept warring factions from engaging in a battle, or when through her prayers she managed to protect a village from rapidly approaching and threatening marauders. Indeed, in a letter from 1438 or 1439 that Colette sent to the citizens of Ghent who had sponsored a new convent and awaited her arrival, she explained that merchants told her that the roads were too dangerous "especially for women and nuns" and that therefore she would not be able to come, nor could she send anyone else for fear of their safety.[47]

In the letter to Amiens, Pierre de Vaux also spoke of her reforms of many Poor Clare convents and male Franciscan houses as well as of the strong support she enjoyed from notable people, many of whom even travelled long distances to join her. According to its editor Ubald d'Alençon, this letter is an important document for the history of the Colettine reform movement because it was written during Colette's lifetime and thus precedes the biography, which was so much shaped by hagiographical conventions. In this letter Pierre de Vaux wages a campaign on Colette's behalf by painting her as an effective and unifying leader of the reform.

But unity of the Franciscan Order was not imminent in 1443. The conflict between the Observants and Conventuals was not completely resolved until 1517 when Pope Leo X promulgated the bulls *Ita vos* and *Omnipotens Deus* which designated the Observants

> as the true heirs of St. Francis, the Order of Friars Minor; the Conventuals were defined as a smaller and separate order. *Ita vos* also required that all the fragmented groups within the Franciscan reform (including the Coletans, drawn from the Conventuals) join the main Order, that is, the Observants. This should have meant the end of the Coletan–Observant dispute, but the bitterness lingered.[48]

Throughout the sixteenth century some Colettine convents petitioned to be exempted from Observant jurisdiction and often succeeded.[49]

Colette the reformer had thus in many ways been successful, and chroniclers both criticized her and paid tribute to her, some depicting her reforms as divisive, others as major achievements. Nicholas Glassberger (d. 1508), an Observant Franciscan chronicler working in Nuremberg, recognized her reforms but, in his epitaph for Colette, characterized her withdrawal from "the governance of the Observant Fathers" as "female fickleness" that introduced pernicious divisions into the Franciscan Order.[50]

47 The letter to the citizens of Ghent is translated in Lopez, *Petite Vie*, 89–92. For the other incidents see Vaux, 27, 51, and 69–73 (accounts of several attacks, one of them thwarted by Colette "speaking in tongues" to the highway robbers), 124 (preventing a battle), 143 (a miracle thwarting an attack). Perrine traveled with Colette and gives an eye-witness account of the incident of the would-be robbers pacified by Colette's addressing them in their language (226).

48 Richards, "The Conflict," 278. On the spirituality of the Coletans, the friars attached to Colette's convents who followed the Statutes written by Henry de Baume, see Nimmo, *Reform and Division*, 467–77. For an excellent concise analysis of the Coletans' history see Richards, "Franciscan Women," 58–60.

49 Richards cites among other documents a 1536 letter from the Emperor Charles V to that effect ("The Conflict," 278).

50 Cited by Richards, "The Conflict," 279.

By contrast, Johannes Nider, also working in Nuremberg but a Dominican, spoke of Colette as a *virgo sancta et prudens* in his *Formicarius* (1436–1438), contrasting her with other visionaries he considered dangerous and deceitful. Ludovic Viallet is right in interpreting the term *prudens* as "referring to the way in which Colette conducted herself and behaved in the world."[51] Prudence was seen as a political virtue in this period, indeed one that Christine de Pizan, for example, prized above all others.[52] Olivier de la Marche (1425–1502), working for Duke Charles the Bold of Burgundy, not surprisingly praised Colette, describing somewhat too enthusiastically how Colette, a "devout and holy woman, [...] traveled throughout Christendom" and built 380 monasteries "of the religion of Saint Francis and Saint Clare." He also tells in detail of the encounter between King Jacques II of Bourbon (1370–1438) and Colette, where she persuaded the king to become a penitent member of the Third Order of Saint Francis by citing the reversals of fortune and the "brevity of this life."[53] Jacques' two daughters became Colettine nuns, and Colette's influence over him was assumed by Cardinal Cesarini, legate of Pope Eugene IV and president of the Council of Basel, who appealed to her in a letter of 1436 to intervene with King Jacques in a case involving the bishop of Albi.[54] Jacques II of Bourbon was just one of the many powerful people Colette encountered and influenced.

Long after Colette's death another powerful personage, the English king Henry VIII, praised her virtues in a letter to Pope Leo X in September 1513, acting in concert with Margaret of Austria and the emperor Maximilian. For Henry, Colette was a Burgundian saint and could thus be used "as a sign of unity of the anti-French powers."[55] He lauded her as "a diligent bee" who brought "exquisite honey to the celestial gardener" in the form of the Franciscan houses she founded. "Why has she not been canonized?" he asks the pope.[56] This is indeed a good question, and one that has now been answered in great detail by Anna Campbell.[57] In 1807, 360 years of repeated efforts to surmount countless obstacles finally came to fruition when Pope Pius VII canonized Saint Colette. In the canonization bull there is little mention of her reform of the First Order of Saint Francis (though the accusations against her as "sorceress and invoker of demons" are cited!), and there is only a brief

51 See Viallet, "Colette of Corbie and the Franciscan Reforms," 97–98. Viallet cites the relevant passage from the *Formicarius*, book 4, chap. 9, at length in note 57.

52 See for example Michael Richarz, "Prudence and Wisdom in Christine de Pizan's *Livre des fais et bonnes meurs du sage roy Charles V*," in *Healing the Body Politic: The Political Thought of Christine de Pizan*, ed. Karen Green and Constant J. Mews (Turnhout: Brepols, 2005), 99–116.

53 Olivier de la Marche, *Mémoires*, ed. Henri Beaune and J. D'Arbaumont (Paris: Renouard, 1883), 1:192–93. On the importance of this king for Colette see Lopez, *Learning and Holiness*, 303–7.

54 Translated by the Poor Clares of Hawarden (as in n. 41). In 1438 Cesarini wrote a very emotional letter to Colette addressing her as "beloved Mother" and sending her twelve "Rhenish florins" for her garments.

55 For the complicated political situation surrounding this petition to the pope see Anna Campbell, "Colette of Corbie: Cult and Canonization," in *Companion to Colette of Corbie*, 185–86.

56 Cited by Louis Sellier, *Vie de Sainte Colette* (Paris: Caron, 1855), 144–46. He comments on Henry VIII: "Heureux prince, s'il avait persévéré dans des sentiments si catholiques..." (144), but the split from the Roman Catholic Church was to come about twenty years later.

57 Campbell, "Colette of Corbie: Cult and Canonization," 173–206.

reference to her founding a new order of female religious and of the reforms of the Second Order.[58] Colette's great visions of the estates of this world in hell and of Saint Francis authorizing her reforms are reduced to a celestial voice that told her what to do. What is stressed in the bull are her asceticism and her humility. Thus the forceful and skillful leader, a woman who drew authority from her visions and commanded the respect of powerful contemporaries, vanishes in this canonization bull at the expense of a more generalized classic paradigm of female holiness.

58 The bull is transcribed in French and Latin by Sellier. Quote on *veneficam, sortilegam, et demonorum invocatricem* on 230.

18

# WOMEN PRIESTS AT BARKING ABBEY IN THE LATE MIDDLE AGES

KATIE ANN-MARIE BUGYIS

In around 1404, Sibyl de Felton, the abbess of Barking Abbey in Essex from 1394 to 1419, granted, "with divine permission," an ordinal "for the use of the abbesses in the said house into perpetuity."[1] This book, now Oxford, University College, MS 169, includes many of the features proper to medieval ordinals: it details the Masses and hours of the Divine Office that were to be celebrated throughout the entire year, negotiating the coincidence of multiple feasts on a given day; providing incipits to chants, prayers, and readings; assigning roles to specific monastic officers, other community members, and attendant clergy; and supplying performative cues for the intonation of chants and for the staging of processions, liturgical dramas, and other rituals. This book – with its clear articulation of the procedures for the yearly distribution of books at Chapter on the first Monday of Lent,[2] the profession of new members,[3] and the election, consecration, and installation of a new abbess[4] – was also to double as a customary for the abbey. Details culled from the ordinal's rubrics reveal that the purpose behind the book's production was, in part, to organize and preserve Barking's liturgical practices, many of which were first initiated in the more distant reaches of the abbey's past, some even date to the period soon after the Norman Conquest.[5] And the list of abbesses found near the book's end suggests that the ordinal remained in use until at least the death of Abbess Elizabeth Lexham in 1479, if not until the abbey's formal surrender to King Henry VIII's commissioner on 14 November 1539.[6] Barking's ordinal is

1 Sibyl de Felton's *memorandum* is found on fol. 6r of Oxford, University College, MS 169. See J. B. L. Tolhurst, ed., *The Ordinale and Customary of the Benedictine Nuns of Barking Abbey*, Henry Bradshaw Society 115–116 (London, 1927), 1:13. All translations are my own unless noted otherwise. Barking's surviving books are catalogued and discussed in David N. Bell's *What Nuns Read: Books and Libraries in Medieval English Nunneries* (Kalamazoo, MI: Cistercian Publications, 1995), 107–120.

2 *Ordinale*, 1:69.

3 Ibid., 2:350–351.

4 Ibid., 2:349–350, 351–353.

5 Anne Bagnall Yardley, *Performing Piety: Musical Culture in Medieval English Nunneries* (New York: Palgrave Macmillan, 2006), 194; Katie Ann-Marie Bugyis, *The Care of Nuns: The Ministries of Benedictine Women in England during the Central Middle Ages* (New York: Oxford University Press, 2019), chap. 3.

6 This list records the names of the abbesses who founded and supported the hospital at Ilford, beginning with Adeliza (d. 1173); *Ordinale*, 2:361.

the only comprehensive liturgical plan to survive from a women's monastic house located in medieval England and, thus, offers a unique record of how at least one late medieval community of Benedictine nuns not only participated in but also scripted, orchestrated, and starred in its various liturgical performances.

Among the ordinal's most remarkable directives for performance are the physical and spiritual transfigurations envisioned for the Barking nuns, which often were to exceed the limits of liturgical precedent, gender, and ecclesiastical status. So transfigured, the nuns were to fulfill ministerial roles that had been routinely carried out by their consorors in the early Middle Ages, but had increasingly become the preserve of male clerics over the course of the central and late Middle Ages.[7] Liturgical dramas especially created the necessary liminal spaces in which the nuns could reclaim past ministries and still deny charges of illicit or improper activity from ecclesiastical authorities. They could always claim that they were only acting *as if*.

For example, at Barking, on the Feast of the Holy Innocents (or Fools) on 28 December, young novices (*scolares*) could become the abbess or other senior officers.[8] Through the celebration of the *Decensus/Elevatio* during Easter Matins, the entire convent, vested in copes, joined by certain priests and clerics, were to become the patriarchs and prophets that Christ liberated from hell, as well as the disciples who followed Christ to Galilee after his resurrection.[9] The performance of the *Decensus* is rarely attested in extant liturgical books from medieval England, and does not appear in any of the twenty-three Easter dramas performed in communities of religious women either in England or on the continent.[10] In light of the surviving evidence, the Barking women appear to be unique in their roles as male biblical figures, and "complicate the common metaphor of nuns as 'brides of Christ,'" as Anne Yardley has observed.[11] Similarly, on the Feast of Pentecost, on two separate occasions, first at the hour of Terce, during the hymn "Veni Creator Spiritus," and then at the main Mass of the day, during the sequence "Sancti Spiritus assit nobis gracia," the choir was transformed into the apostles locked in the upper room, awaiting the Holy Spirit's advent. The Spirit's gifts were bestowed on the nuns first in the form of a dove surrounded by seven candles, and then as scattered flowers of diverse kinds. On both occasions, the Spirit's descent was confined to the choir; thus, not the attendant priests or clerics, but only the nuns were to appear as the apostles, for they alone were to

7 See Bugyis, *Care of Nuns*, for evidence of Benedictine nuns serving as preachers, liturgical readers of the gospels, and confessors during the central Middle Ages. For religious women's gradual exclusion from "ordained" ministries in Western Europe during the central Middle Ages, see Gary Macy, *The Hidden History of Women's Ordination: Female Clergy and the Medieval West* (New York: Oxford University Press, 2007) and his essay in this volume (chapter 16).

8 *Ordinale*, 1:33–34. See Anne Bagnall Yardley, "The Musical Education of Young Girls in Medieval English Nunneries," in *Young Choristers, 650–1700*, ed. Susan Boynton and Eric Rice 49–67 (Woodbridge: Boydell Press, 2008), 54.

9 Anne Bagnall Yardley and Jesse D. Mann, ed. and trans., "The Liturgical Dramas for Holy Week at Barking Abbey," *Medieval Feminist Forum* 3 (2014): 1–39, at 18–22.

10 Dunbar Ogden, "Women Play Women in the Liturgical Drama of the Middle Ages," in *Shakespearean Illuminations: Essays in Honor of Marvin Rosenberg*, ed. Jay L. Halio and Hugh Richmond, 336–360 (Cranbury, NJ: Associated University Press, 1998), 346.

11 Yardley, "Liturgical Dramas," 7.

receive material signs of the Spirit's gifts.[12] More remarkably still, the dramatic action of the nuns playing the three Marys in the *Visitatio Sepulchri* at Easter Matins seems to have been viewed as "sacerdotal" by the community, for in the closing rubrics to this drama, the women were identified as "priests":

> And meanwhile the aforementioned [women] priests, putting back on their own clothes in the chapel, passing through the choir with candelabras, should go to the sepulcher to give thanks, and there they should offer a brief prayer. Then they should return to their station until the abbess commands them to go to rest.
>
> (Et interim predicte sacerdotes in capellam propriis vestibus reinduentes cum candelabris per chorum transeuntes orandi gratia sepulcrum adeant et ibi brevem orationem faciant. Tunc redeant in stacionem suam usque abbatissa eas iubeat exire ad quiescendum.)[13]

Until Anne Yardley's recent edition and translation of Barking's Holy Week dramas, the Marys' identification as "priests" had been "overlooked, ignored, or misread."[14] Nearly all of the previous editions, translations, and commentaries interpreted the feminine past participle "predicte" and/or pronoun "eas" as scribal errors and, thus, exchanged them for masculine grammatical forms to refer to the "sacerdotes et clerici" representing the disciples.[15] More likely "sacerdotes" is a holdover from the exemplar consulted by the ordinal's scribe, or that exemplar's exemplar, but someone along the way decided to retain "sacerdotes" while adjusting the adjective and pronoun referring to it for the Barking nuns' use. Arguably, "sacerdotes" should be emended to "sorores," but even this editorial intervention fails to capture the preceding dramatic action scripted for the Marys. Building on Yardley's suggestion that these women "were in some sense seen as clerics or priests," I argue in this essay that, through chants sung, postures and positions assumed, vestments worn, and objects handled and mediated, the sisters playing the Marys, not the priests and clerics figuring the disciples, were to assume sacerdotal roles.[16]

Walther Lipphardt's prodigious nine-volume edition of medieval Easter dramas includes over 830 plays that were performed in cathedrals, monasteries, and parishes

12 *Ordinale*, 1:135–136.

13 "Liturgical Dramas," 30.

14 Ibid., 10.

15 In their editions of Barking's *Visitatio*, Karl Young and Walther Lipphardt both replaced "predicte" with "predicti." Young, *The Drama of the Medieval Church*, 2 vols. (Oxford: Clarendon Press, 1933), 1:384; Lipphardt, *Lateinische Osterfeiern und Osterspiele*, 9 vols. (New York: De Gruyter, 1975–1990), L770. Dunbar Ogden and Kay Slocum have independently read "sacerdotes" as a reference to the clergy playing the disciples. Ogden, *The Staging of Drama in the Medieval Church* (Newark: University of Delaware Press, 2002), 149; Slocum, "Ritual and Ceremony at Barking Abbey," *Magistra* 16, no. 2 (2010): 94–110, at 107. Only J. B. L. Tolhurst and Pamela Sheingorn retained both "predicte" and "eas." *Ordinale*, 1:109–110; Sheingorn, *The Easter Sepulchre in England* (Kalamazoo: Medieval Institute Publications, 1987), 137. For related attempts made by modern editors to "normalize" queer readings in medieval texts, see Leanne MacDonald's essay in this volume (chapter 11).

16 Yardley, "Liturgical Dramas," 10.

throughout Western Europe, dating from the tenth through the sixteenth centuries, yet his edition, as Margaret Pappano has noted, is "scarcely complete"; many liturgical books across Europe still remain unedited.[17] Twenty-three of those that have been edited can be linked to women's communities, and twenty-one of those feature women playing the three Marys.[18] Many of the *Visitationes* from these communities contain unique elements not found at other sites; their geneses are likely owed to the creative directions of abbesses, prioresses, cantors, sacristans, and other officers charged with liturgical responsibilities.[19]

According to Barking's ordinal, Katherine de Sutton, abbess from 1358 to 1376, should receive some credit for the form of the Easter dramas preserved in the book. Though she was unlikely to have been the sole genius behind their initial orchestration, she was certainly the motive force behind changing the time when the *Decensus/Elevatio* and *Visitatio* were to be performed.[20] Contrary to "ancient ecclesiastical custom," she moved their performance from before Matins to after the third responsory "to root out torpor completely and to stir more devotion in the faithful for so great a celebration."[21] The ordinal highlights Katherine's solicitude for the people

17 Pappano, "Sister Acts: Conventual Performance and the *Visitatio Sepulchri* in England and France," in *Medieval Constructions in Gender and Identity: Essays in Honor of Joan M. Ferrante*, ed. Teodolinda Barolini, 43–67 (Tempe: Arizona Center for Medieval and Renaissance Studies, 2005), 44, n. 4. Notably, the *Visitatio* from Wilton Abbey in Wiltshire does not appear in Lipphardt's edition. The late thirteenth- or early fourteenth-century processional containing Wilton's *Visitatio* was long considered to be lost and only to survive in a later copy made at Solesmes Abbey in 1860, until Alison Altstatt's recent discovery of thirty-four single leaves of the original manuscript; "Re-membering the Wilton Processional," *Notes: The Quarterly Journal of the Music Library Association* 72, no. 4 (2016): 690–732.

18 The frequency with which nuns played the roles of the Marys in performances of the *Visitatio Sepulchri* in women's communities is often unacknowledged in the scholarship on this Easter drama. Fiona Griffiths has provided a short history of "the resurrection as a drama featuring female players" in *Nuns' Priests' Tales: Men and Salvation in Medieval Women's Monastic Life* (Philadelphia: University of Pennsylvania Press, 2018), 61–66.

19 Dunbar Ogden only credited the creative geniuses of abbesses for these liturgical innovations; "Women Play Women," 337–339. But, as I have demonstrated elsewhere, the contributions of cantors and sacristans in communities of Benedictine nuns should not be discounted. See Bugyis, "Female Monastic Cantors and Sacristans in Central Medieval England: Four Sketches," in *Medieval Cantors and Their Craft: Music, Liturgy, and the Shaping of History, 800–1500*, ed. Katie Bugyis, A. B. Kraebel, and Margot Fassler, 151–169 (York: York Medieval Press, 2017).

20 Nancy Cotton attributed the versions of the *Decensus/Elevatio* and *Visitatio* found in the ordinal to Katherine de Sutton alone; "Katherine of Sutton: The First English Woman Playwright," *Educational Theatre Journal* 30 (1978): 475–481. For more measured accounts of Katherine's involvement in the drama's initial orchestration, see Santha Bhattacharji, "Sutton, Katherine (d. 1376)," *Oxford Dictionary of National Biography* (Oxford: Oxford University Press, 2004); Anne Bagnall Yardley, "Liturgy as the Site of Creative Engagement: Contributions of the Nuns of Barking," in *Barking Abbey and Medieval Literary Culture: Authorship and Authority in a Female Community*, ed. Jennifer N. Brown and Donna Alfano Bussell, 267–282 (York: York Medieval Press, 2012), 274; Yardley, "Liturgical Dramas," 4.

21 Ibid., 18: "Nota quod secundum antiquam consuetudinem ecclesiasticam, resurexio dominica celebrata fuit ante matutinas et ante aliquam campane pulsacionem in die pasche. Et quoniam populorum concursus temporibus illis videbatur devocione frigessere et torpor humanus maxime accrescens, venerabilis domina Domina Katerina de Suttone, tunc pastoralis cure gerens vicem,

entrusted to her "pastoral care," not only for her fellow sisters, but also for the laity who belonged to Barking's parish church, St. Margaret's, and attended services at the abbey to celebrate important feasts, especially the abbey church's dedication (13 July) and Easter.[22] The ordinal notes their presence as spectators of the Holy Week dramas, twice directing the actors' words and actions "toward the people [ad populum]."[23] The ordinal also mentions that Katherine consulted the members of her community before making the change to the time of the Easter dramas, and they gave their unanimous consent. Their endorsement raises the possibility that some of these women collaborated in the dramas' orchestration, perhaps composing some of the unique chants or staging the other distinctive dramatic elements.[24] As this essay shows, close study of Barking's *Visitatio* reveals that it was a living script, able both to accommodate chants and cues that were fixtures of the long tradition of the drama's performance at the abbey, and to incorporate modifications from later directors and actors.

In preparation for the *Visitatio*'s performance, during Chapter on the previous day, Barking's abbess was to select three of her consorors to play the roles of the women who visited Jesus' tomb.[25] Out of the twenty other extant *Visitationes* that explicitly

desiderans dictum torporem penitus exstirpare et fidelium devocionem ad tam celebrem celebracionem magis excitare, unanimi consororum consensu instituit ut statim post tercium responsorium matutinarum die pasche fieret dicte resurexionis celebracio."

22 Among the directives for the feast of the abbey church's dedication included in the ordinal is the notice that Katherine de Sutton had ordered, through Simon Sudbury, bishop of London (1361–1376), that all Barking's parishioners gather in the nave of the church and listen to the divine services on this day as well as on Easter under punishment of excommunication; *Ordinale*, 2:257. During Sibyl de Felton's abbacy, relations between the abbey and its parishioners were contentious. In 1395, the bishop of London had to intervene to stop the "strife and debate between her and her parishioners"; H. C. Maxwell Lyte, ed., *Calendar of the Close Rolls Preserved in the Public Record Office: Richard II*, 6 vols. (London, 1914–1927), 5:500. See also Winifrid M. Sturman, "Barking Abbey: A Study in its External and Internal Administration from the Conquest to the Dissolution" (Ph.D. diss., University of London, 1961), 135–137.

23 "Liturgical Dramas," 22, 28. Establishing the precise location of the actors when they directed their performance "toward the people" is made difficult, if not impossible, by the ordinal's ambiguous directives, which only stipulate that the actors stand "before the altar" located near the sepulcher and "turn" to face the people, but neither identifies the name of the altar nor specifies where it or the sepulcher were situated within the sanctuary. Kate Matthews and David Wiles, building on Winifrid Sturman's reconstruction of the locations of the abbey church's various altars, have argued for identifying the altar in question as the Altar of the Resurrection, which was dedicated to John the Evangelist and Mary Magdalene on 18 August 1331; Matthews, "The Bride of Christ: An Exploration of Convent Drama c. 1100–1500" (Ph.D. diss., Royal Holloway, University of London, 2002), chaps. 5 and 6; Wiles, *A Short History of Western Performance Space* (Cambridge: Cambridge University Press, 2003), 45–49. Cf. *Ordinale* 2:282. According to Sturman, this altar was "probably situated just outside of the rood-screen," which would have allowed any action performed at it to be seen clearly by the people gathered in the nave; "Barking Abbey," 158. Yet in the absence of more definitive textual or archaeological evidence, such claims cannot be verified definitively.

24 Many of the distinctive dramatic elements are analyzed in what follows. Unfortunately, the complete texts and music for the seven unique chants are missing.

25 *Ordinale*, 1:103: "provideat abbatissa tres sorores quesituras in sepulcro nocte sequenti crucifixum scilicet mulieres prefigurantes que ad monumentum Domini cum aromatibus venerint. Singulis autem illarum due iuvencule adhibeantur que candelabra iuxta eas circumferant."

script women for these roles, only those from Origny-Sainte-Benoît (c. 1286 and s. xiv), Troyes (s. xiii), and Wilton (1250–1320) feature these roles in several scenes with extended sung dialogues like Barking's. The *Visitationes* from these convents share a number of structural, textual, and musical correspondences, though each integrates distinctive elements, as Susan Rankin, Dunbar Ogden, and Margaret Pappano individually have observed.[26] Yet to be analyzed in any study of these texts are the Barking ordinal's unique directions to the women playing the three Marys on the use of certain liturgical vestments and objects, and how these directions staged them in roles in which they would have appeared both as the women in Matthew's gospel and as priests.

The ordinal's instructions on how the three women were to be prepared for their roles are quite detailed:

> The three sisters previously elected by the abbess are to proceed to the chapel of blessed Mary Magdalene and take off their black habits. They are to be clothed in the whitest of surplices, and snow-white veils are to be placed on their heads by the abbess. When they are thus prepared, and holding silver ampullas in their hands, they are to say the *Confiteor* to the abbess and be absolved by her and stand in the established place with candelabras.
>
> (Procedant tres sorores a domina abbatissa preelecte, et nigris vestibus in capella beate Marie Magdalene exute nitidissimis superpelliciis induantur, niveis velis a domina abbatissa capitibus earum superpositis. Sic igitur preparate et in manibus ampullas tenentes argenteas dicant *Confiteor* ad abbatissam, et ab ea absolute in loco statuto cum candelabris consistant.)[27]

Only the Marys at Barking were to wear clerical vestments.[28] Troyes's were to remain in their own habits.[29] Wilton's also were not to change out of their habits, but only to replace their black veils with white ones "in the likeness of women [in similitudine mulierum]."[30] And Origny's were to be clothed in white tunics, cloaks, and kerchiefs without a veil.[31]

26 Rankin, "A New English Source of the Visitatio Sepulchri," *Journal of the Plainsong and Mediaeval Music Society* 4 (1981): 1–11; Rankin, "The Mary Magdalen Scene in the 'Visitatio Sepulchri' Ceremonies," *Early Music History* 1 (1981): 227–255; Ogden, "Women Play Women in the Liturgical Drama of the Middle Ages," *On-Stage Studies* 19 (1996): 1–33; Ogden, *Staging of Drama*, 143–153; Pappano, "Sister Acts."

27 "Liturgical Dramas," 24.

28 In the ordinal's script for the *Visitatio*, only the Marys were instructed to change their garments in the chapel of Mary Magdalene, which cue led Anne Yardley to conclude that the "sacerdotes," who were directed to return to the chapel to change back into "their own clothes" in the drama's final rubric, referred to the nuns playing the three Marys, not to the male priests playing the disciples (ibid., 11).

29 *Lateinische Osterfeiern und Osterspiele*, L170: "dames en lor habiz et li enfant si sont toutes blanches et crevechie blanc sor lor testes."

30 "Visitatio Sepulchri," 6: "Dum cantatur tertia lectio levent tres cantrices et lavent manus suas, et absconso velamine, candidum velum capitibus suis imponant in similitudine mulierum."

31 *Lateinische Osterfeiern und Osterspiele*, L303: "Et doivent estre appariellies des le derrainne

The surplice first emerged among the articles of clerical dress in the eleventh century as a late modification to the alb; it was similar in material and length, often made of white cotton or linen and reached to the feet, but its sleeves were wider and longer to fit better over a fur-lined cassock – hence its name, *superpellicium*. Over the course of the thirteenth and fourteenth centuries, surplices were increasingly worn by ordained clergy in both major and minor orders during the performance of sacerdotal functions.[32] In the *Visitationes* performed at Augsburg, Dublin, and Gerresheim, which variously date from the fourteenth to the late fifteenth centuries, the clerics or priests playing the Marys were to wear surplices, sometimes under copes.[33] Only on two other occasions does Barking's ordinal stipulate the wearing of surplices: during the censing of the entire monastery at None on the Feast of the Ascension and at Sext on the Feast of the Annunciation.[34] On both occasions, the presiding priests alone were instructed to wear this vestment. The restricted liturgical use of surplices by Barking's priests surely heightened the visual effect of the three women wearing these vestments during the performance of the *Visitatio*, investing their roles with an apparent solemnity and clerical authority.

The silver ampullas (small cruets or flasks) that the women were to carry would have reinforced the surplices' association with priests' sacramental roles. Though thuribles were the insignia of choice to represent the jars of spices prepared to anoint Jesus' body,[35] gold and silver ampullas or vessels (*vasa* or *vasculae*) or alabaster jars (*alabastra*) were specified in several *Visitationes*.[36] When such containers were to be

noturene devant l'autel le Madellainne et doivent estre en lours blans chainges et leurs mantiaus et en blans cueurechies sans voil."

32 Herbert Norris, *Church Vestments: Their Origin and Development* (New York: E. P. Dutton & Co., 1950), 168–169; Janet Mayo, *A History of Ecclesiastical Dress* (New York: Holmes & Meier Publishers, Inc., 1984), 45–46, 49–50, 174–175.

33 See *Lateinische Osterfeiern und Osterspiele*, L213 (Gerresheim, s. xv), L522 (Augsburg, 1487), and L772 (Dublin, s. xiv). At Gerresheim, two or three clerics were to be clothed in surplices; at Augsburg, two priests were to wear copes over surplices; and at Dublin, three "persons [personae]" were to wear surplices and copes. In the *Visitatio* performed at Soissons in the thirteenth century (L167), after the three Marys had announced Christ's resurrection, the chaplain, clothed in a surplice, was to bring out a vessel containing a consecrated host. In *Visitationes* performed at other monastic and ecclesiastical sites, albs, chasubles, copes, dalmatics, stoles, and/or amices often appear among the vestments that were to be worn by the Marys.

34 *Ordinale*, 1:129: "Interea sacerdos ebdomadarius et sacerdos misse matutinalis, superpelliciis induti et capis, ter thurificent altaria, virginumque feretra et tociens conventum, clericis cum candelabris preeuntibus"; and 2:210: "Interea predictus sacerdos et sacerdos beate Marie, superpelliciis indutis et capis semel thurificent altaria et conventum ut predictum esset clericis cum candelabris preeuntibus." The censing of the altars and convent on the Feast of the Annunciation only occurred if the feast fell on a Sunday.

35 Notably, thuribles were assigned to the Marys in one of the source-texts for Barking's *Visitatio*: the *Regularis Concordia*, the customary promulgated by the Council of Winchester in c. 970, which was to be applied to every monastic community in England. Thomas Symons, ed., *Regularis Concordia* (London: Thomas Nelson and Sons Ltd., 1953), 49–50: "Dumque tertium percelebratur responsorium residui tres succedant, omnes quidem cappis induti, turibula cum incensu manibus gestantes."

36 *Lateinische Osterfeiern und Osterspiele*, L97 (Bourges, s. xv): boys or clerics were to carry "vasa aurea vel argentea"; L116 (Narbonne, n.d.): the cleric playing Mary Magdalene was to carry

carried, deacons, clerics, or canons were to play the Marys, except in the case of the *Visitatio* performed at St. Guilia in Brescia in the mid-fifteenth century. There, the Marys were to be played by three nuns of this Benedictine monastery, and each was to carry a silver ampulla and offer it at the main altar after visiting the sepulcher.[37] None of the other *Visitationes* performed in communities of religious women script the Marys' use of liturgical vessels. Wilton's Marys were entrusted with cases enclosing relics (*filateria*);[38] Origny's were handed four candelabras (*candelabres*) and a censer (*l'encensier*);[39] and, more ambiguously, Troyes's were each given a candle (*un cierge*), a cloth (*une touelle*), and a box (*une boite*).[40] Barking's ordinal does not state whether the Marys' ampullas were to be filled with anything, but if they were taken from the church's sacristy – which they likely were, along with the surplices – then they would have contained water or wine or, more fittingly given the vessels' intended use within the dramatic action of the *Visitatio*, holy oil.[41] Vessels filled with oil were to be carried by the Marys in the *Visitationes* performed at Jerusalem in the twelfth century and at Padua Cathedral in the thirteenth.[42] Yet, during Barking's performance of the *Depositio* on Holy Friday, two priests, "in the appearance [in specie]" of Nicodemus and Joseph of Arimathea, were to carry the cross to the high altar where they removed the *imago* from the wood and washed the Crucified's wounds with wine and water.[43] Perhaps the same vessels of wine and water were to be used again by the nuns playing the Marys in the *Visitatio* in order to foster greater visual continuity across the Holy Week dramas, and to highlight more clearly the correspondences between the Marys' dramatic actions and priests' sacramental roles.

The final step in the ordinal's directions for the Marys' preparation required the women to recite the *Confiteor* before their abbess and to receive absolution from her. Origny's Marys were to recite a related form of confession before their abbess at the altar of Mary Magdalene;[44] Troyes's recited the same prayer but before a priest at the

an "ampullam argenti"; L168 (St. Aper, Toulouse, s.xiv): "vascula"; L172 (Troyes, s.xiv): three deacons were to carry "vasa aurea vel argentea"; L404 (Fécamp, s. xiv): three monks were to carry "vasa in modum pissidarum"; L407 (Jerusalem, 1133): three young clerics each were to carry "vasa aureum vel argenteum intus habens aliquod ungenteum"; L773 (Mont Saint-Michel, s. xiv): three youths were to carry "alabastra"; and L776 (Rouen, s. xiv): three canons of the grade of deacon were to carry "vascula."

37 Ibid., L8: "Et tres Marie vadant deorsum tunc ad altare maius ad offerendum tria vasa argentea."

38 "Visitatio Sepulchri," 6: "Et tres Mariae ante hostium chori tria filateria manibus gestante, duabus candelabra, turibula cum incensu ante eas deferentibus."

39 *Lateinische Osterfeiern und Osterspiele*, L303: "Et li tresoriere doit faire aporter les saintuaires par .i. prestre et les .iiii. candelabres et l'encensier par les jovenes demiselles."

40 Ibid., L170: "un cierge et une touelle et une boite."

41 In Latin sources from England dating from the early to the late Middle Ages, the term "ampulla" most frequently refers to a small cruet or flask used to store holy oil or to transport the wine and/or water at the offertory during Mass; *Dictionary of Medieval Latin from British Sources*, fasc. 1: *A–B*, ed. R. E. Latham (Oxford: British Academy, 1975).

42 For Jerusalem's *Visitatio*, see *Lateinische Osterfeiern und Osterspiele*, L407 in n. 36 above. L427 (Padua Cathedral, s. xiii): three *scholares* were to carry "unguenta," along with thuribles.

43 "Liturgical Dramas," 16: "Deferant crucem ad magnum altare ibique in specie Ioseph et Nichodemi de lingo deponentes ymaginem crucifixi vino abluant et aqua."

44 *Lateinische Osterfeiern und Osterspiele*, L303: "Et devant çou qu'elles saroient, elles se doivent

main altar;[45] and Wilton's were to perform a more literal act of cleansing by washing their hands.[46] Notably, none of the extant *Visitationes* that cast men as the Marys prescribed such acts. These acts, however, bear a very close resemblance to the rites of purification undertaken by priests prior to the celebration of Mass, as Dunbar Ogden has observed.[47] The question of why the female Marys had to be ritually cleansed and not the male Marys is perhaps answered by concerns over women's bodily purity in sacred spaces,[48] but for Barking's Marys such an explanation fails to consider their penitential act in view of the other actions that they were to perform in the *Visitatio*.[49]

On three separate occasions, the Marys were commanded to announce the good news of Christ's resurrection to the disciples: first, by the angels waiting at the empty tomb to all three Marys; then, by Christ to Mary Magdalene when he appeared to her alone; and finally, by Christ to all three Marys.[50] Somewhat in keeping with the second command, but utterly original to Barking's *Visitatio*, Mary Magdalene was to proclaim the good news to her companions first, "communicating her joy with a jubilant voice," singing the unique chant "Gratulari et letari" – a moving expression of the enduring bonds of sorority that united the Marys, past and present.[51] Confirmed in the knowledge they had received from both Mary Magdalene's proclamation and their physical encounter with the risen Christ, all three Marys were then to move to the step before the altar, turn "toward the people," and together sing the responsory,

confessier et aler a me dame aus cantiques des Matines, et doivent rendre leur proprietet chascune par li et meitre quanques elles ont de propre volenté et doivent dire *Confiteor*. Et me dame doit dire *Misereatur* et *Indulgentiam*."

45 Ibid., L170: "Et viennent les .iii. Maries devant le grant autel, la on a appareillie ces choses, et viennent et sagenoillent et dient *Confiteor* et li prestes dist *Misereatur*."

46 See n. 30.

47 Ogden, *Staging of Drama*, 145–146.

48 Ogden offered the following explanation: "It is a rite that not a single member of the male clergy underwent before playing in a liturgical drama – a rite that links to numerous religious acts where women must be cleansed in some special way before participating in a sacred observance" (ibid., 146).

49 Perhaps significantly, at Origny, Troyes, and Wilton, the Marys had to confess before receiving their objects to carry. Barking's Marys were to perform this penitential act after changing their clothing and receiving the ampullas, suggesting that their confessions were not to be given in preparation for being arrayed as sacerdotal figures.

50 These commands were to be articulated in the chants sung by the angel, "Non est hic, surrexit," and by Christ, "Noli me tangere" and "Avete. Nolite timere"; "Liturgical Dramas," 26–28.

51 Ibid., 28: "Cum persona disparverit, Maria gaudium suum consociabus communicet voce letabunda hos concinendo versus: *Gratulari et letari* et cetera." Notably, Mary Magdalene was also said to have first reported the good news of Christ's resurrection to the other Marys, before journeying on to Jerusalem to find the disciples, in the pseudo-Bonaventure's *Meditationes vitae Christi* and in Nicholas Love's Middle English translation, *The Mirror of the Blessed Life of Jesus Christ*. See A. C. Peltier, ed., *Meditationes Vitae Christi*, in *S. Bonaventure Opera Omnia*, vol. 12 (Paris, 1868), 618; and Michael G. Sargent, ed., *The Mirror of the Blessed Life of Jesus Christ: A Full Critical Edition based on Cambridge University Library Additional MSS 6578 and 6686 with Introduction, Notes, and Glossary*, Exeter Medieval Texts and Studies (Exeter: University of Exeter Press, 2005), 199.15–20. The possibility that the Barking ordinal's production of the *Visitatio* was influenced by the account of Christ's resurrection found in Nicholas Love's *Mirror* is raised in what follows.

"Alleluia surrexit Dominus de sepulchro."[52] This announcement of Christ's resurrection was to be echoed immediately by the choir, thereby affirming the truth of their fellow sisters' report and becoming messengers of the good news, too.[53] After this call and response, priests and clerics representing the disciples were to approach the woman playing Mary Magdalene, and one was to question her about what she had seen on the way to the tomb, singing "Dic nobis Maria," a verse taken from the popular Easter sequence, "Victimae paschali laudes."[54] She was to answer with the two succeeding verses of this sequence – "Sepulchrum Christi" and "Angelicos testes" – and then point to the place in the tomb where the angel was sitting, show them the *sudarium*, or head shroud, that she had found among Jesus' burial cloths, and hold it up for them to kiss.[55] So scripted, Mary Magdalene was not to preach the good news with words alone; she also was to extend an embodied kerygma – visible and tangible proof that the one whom they mourned had indeed conquered death. This scene, though found in many of the *Visitationes* featuring male Marys, has no scriptural warrant. John's gospel does not recount Mary Magdalene's mission to the disciples, nor their reaction to her good news. Yet, in Barking's *Visitatio*, she was to be hailed by both the disciples and the choir as "truthful Mary [veraci Marie]," one whose witness "is to be believed [credendum est]."[56] So affirmed, Mary Magdalene was then to sing the good news a final time to the assembly, chanting "Christus resurgens," with the clergy and choir accompanying her, after which the *Visitatio* and Matins was to conclude with the "Te Deum."

Beyond their roles as proclaimers of Christ's resurrection, Barking's Marys were also granted privileged access to their beloved's bodily presence. Like the Marys in many other *Visitationes*, Barking's were to respond to the angel's invitation to "come and see" the empty tomb by entering and kissing the spot where the Crucified's *imago* had been placed during the *Depositio*.[57] However, unlike any of the other Marys, Barking's were not restricted to handling a mere contact relic. Upon Christ's appearance to the three women on the right side of the altar, and his assurance to fear not,

52 "Liturgical Dramas," 28: "Finitis hiis versibus tunc Marie stantes super gradus ante altare vertentes se ad populum canant hoc responsorium: *Alleluia. Surrexit Dominus de sepulchro.*"

53 Ibid.: "choro eis respondente."

54 Ibid.: "Finitis hiis, sacerdotes et clerici in figuram discipulorum Christi procedant dicentes: *O gens dira.* Tunc unus illorum accedat et dicat Marie Magdalene: *Dic nobis Maria* et cetera." "O gens dira" is a unique chant in Barking's *Visitatio*. The widespread development of incorporating all or part of the Easter sequence "Victimae paschali laudes" into forms of the *Visitatio*, from the twelfth century on, was first traced by Karl Young, *Drama of the Medieval Church*, 1:273–288, 336–350. Milburn Price speculated that this sequence was incorporated to allow "further expansion of the dramatic action to accompany the text, such as the displaying of the gravecloth and gestures toward the sepulchre"; "The Visitatio Sepulchri of the Medieval Church," *The Choral Journal* 11 (1971): 12–15, at 13.

55 "Liturgical Dramas," 28: "Illa autem respondeat: *Sepulchrum Christi. Angelicos testes.* Digito indicet locum ubi angelus sedebat, et prebeat illis ad deosculandum."

56 Ibid.: "Tunc subiunga[n]tur a discipulis et a choro hii ultimi versus: *Credendum est [magis soli Marie veraci quam Iudeorum turbe fallaci]* et *Scimus Christum [surrexisse a mortuis vere; tu nobis, victor rex, miserere].*"

57 Ibid., 26: "Cumque dixerit *venite et videte*, ingrediantur sepulcrum et deosculentur locum ubi positus erat crucifixus."

they were to "prostrate themselves on the ground, take hold of his feet, and kiss them."[58] The directive to kiss Christ's feet is remarkable because it is not attested in any other *Visitatio*, likely because it is not supported by the account of the Marys' encounter with the risen Christ recorded in Matthew's gospel, which only recalls that they "took hold of his feet and adored him."[59] Only the Marys at Origny came closest to touching Christ's body when they were to prostrate themselves at his feet, but they were still not explicitly directed to have physical contact with him.[60] More often than not in extant *Visitationes*, the only mention made of touching Christ's body is one of prohibition: "Noli me tangere [Don't touch me]," Christ was to chant to Mary Magdalene, while drawing away from her desirous reach, nearly in keeping with the gospel of John's portrayal of this scene.[61] Initially, the touch of Barking's Mary Magdalene was to be rebuked in this very way, but, in the end, her hand was not to be stayed.[62] Together with her two companions, she was permitted to kiss her teacher one last time. The seeming audacity of the Marys' kisses has long puzzled scholars, as it seems to "fly in the face of ... dominant ecclesiastical codes" upheld in other *Visitationes* performed at religious women's communities, as Margaret Pappano

58 Ibid., 28: "Quibus finitis persona in dextera parte altaris tribus simul occurrat mulieribus dicens: *Avete. Nolite timere*. Tunc ille humi prostrate teneant pedes eius et deosculentur."

59 Mt 28:9: "et tenuerunt pedes eius, et adoraverunt eum"; *Biblia sacra: iuxta Vulgatam versionem*, ed. Bonifatius Fischer and Robert Weber (Stuttgart: Deutsche Bibelgesellschaft, 1994), 1574.

60 *Lateinische Osterfeiern und Osterspiele*, L825: "Ces deus Maries gisent as piés nostre Signeur."

61 Jn 20:16: "Dicit ei Jesus: 'Noli me tangere.'" John's gospel does not indicate that Christ drew his body away from Mary Magdalene's touch, but this scene captured the imaginations of later theologians and artists, from biblical exegetes to manuscript illuminators, and was expanded to include Christ's decisive withdrawal from Mary's reach. Christ's refusal of Mary's touch, through both word and gesture, was explicitly directed in *Lateinische Osterfeiern und Osterspiele*, L771 (Coutances, 1400); L773 and 774 (Mont-Saint-Michel, s. xiv); L775 (Rouen, s. xiii); L776 (Rouen, s. xiv); L777 (Rouen, s. xv); L779 (Saint-Lomer, Blois, s. xiii); L798 (St. George, Prague, s. xii); L802 and 803 (St. George, Prague, s. xiv). Differently, in the fifteenth- and sixteenth-century versions of the *Visitatio* from Nottuln, Christ was also to rebuke Mary's touch, but after singing the "Noli me tangere," he was to help lift her up from the ground and then bless her before sending her on her way to proclaim the good news of the resurrection to the disciples; L794 and 795. For studies tracing the historical development of the cult of Mary Magdalene from the early Church to the late Middle Ages, see Victor Saxer, *Le culte de Marie Madeleine en Occident: Des origines à la fin du moyen âge*, 2 vols. (Paris: Clavreuil, 1959); Katherine L. Jansen, *The Making of the Magdalen: Preaching and Popular Devotion in the Later Middle Ages* (Princeton: Princeton University Press, 2000); Aina Trotzig, "L'apparition du Christ ressuscité à Marie Madeleine et le drame liturgique: Étude iconographique," *Revue de Musicologie* 86 (2000): 83–104; Ann Graham Brock, *Mary Magdalene, the First Apostle: The Struggle for Authority*, Harvard Theological Studies 51 (Cambridge, MA: Harvard University Press, 2003); Sherry Reames, "The Legend of Mary Magdalen, Penitent and Apostle: Introduction," in *Middle English Legends of Women Saints*, ed. Reames, 51–57 (Kalamazoo: Medieval Institute Publications, 2003), 51; and the essays in Peter Loewen and Robin Waugh, eds., *Mary Magdalene in Medieval Culture: Conflicted Roles* (New York: Routledge, 2014). For a more focused study on the development of Mary Magdalene's cult in late medieval England, see Theresa Coletti, *Mary Magdalene and the Drama of Saints: Theater, Gender, and Religion in Late Medieval England* (Philadelphia: University of Pennsylvania Press, 2004).

62 "Liturgical Dramas," 26–28: "Tunc illa agnoscens eum pedibus eius prostrenatur dicens: *Raboni*. Persona autem se subtrahens dicat: *Noli me tangere*."

has wondered.[63] Yet to be considered is the possibility that Barking's dramatic deviation from other *Visitationes* was encouraged and authorized by other sources.

In the original Greek of Matthew's account of the Marys' encounter with the risen Christ, the verb used to describe what the women did after they took hold of their beloved's feet – "prosekynesan" – could be translated as "worshipped," "bowed down," "performed obeisance," or, from the second century on, "approached with a kiss."[64] Significantly, the last meaning of the verb is not reflected in the *Vetus Latina* – the catchall title for the sizable and varied collection of Latin translations of biblical texts used by Christian communities from the second century until they were superseded by the translation of the Bible produced by Jerome in the late fourth century – or in the Vulgate – the title eventually given to Jerome's translation. In both the *Vetus Latina* and the Vulgate, the translation of "prosekynesan" as simply "adoraverunt" predominates.[65] However, the meaning of "prosekynesan" as "kissed" is conveyed in the seventh verse of "Aurora lucis rutilat," an anonymous Ambrosian hymn of unknown origins:

> While they, eager, were on their way
> to the apostles this to say,
> seeing that he was alive,
> they kissed the feet of the Lord.
>
> (Illae dum pergunt concitae
> apostolis hoc dicere
> videntes eum vivere
> osculant pedes Domini.)[66]

63 Pappano, "Sister Acts," 49: "Why do the nuns touch at Barking while they stay their hands at Wilton and Origny? Why does one Benedictine nunnery fly in the face of convention while the others appear to uphold it? … Even wealthy and socially prominent nuns (like Wilton) could not always transform dominant ecclesiastical codes."

64 Mt 28:9: "αἱ δὲ προσελθοῦσαι ἐκράτησαν αὐτοῦ τοὺς πόδας καὶ προσεκύνησαν αὐτῷ"; Barbara Aland,, et al., eds., *The Greek New Testament*, 5th ed. (Stuttgart: Deutsche Bibelgesellschaft, 2014). Quite literally, *proskuneō* comes from *pros* ("towards") and *kuneō* ("to kiss"). Henry Liddell, Robert Scott, Henry Jones, and Roderick McKenzie, *A Greek–English Lexicon* (Oxford: Oxford University Press, 1966), 1518; W. E. Vine, *An Expository Dictionary of New Testament Words with their Precise Meanings for English Readers* (Nashville: T. Nelson, 1952), 1247–1248; and Joseph H. Thayer, *A Greek–English Lexicon of the New Testament: Being Grimm's Wilke's Clavis Novi Testamenti* (Grand Rapids: Zondervan, 1977), 548. Matthew Bowen has analyzed the incidence of proskynesis before Jesus in the gospels and set these acts within their wider biblical and historical context in "'They Came and Held Him by the Feet and Worshipped Him': Proskynesis before Jesus in its Biblical and Ancient Near Eastern Context," *Studies in the Bible and Antiquity* 5 (2013): 63–89. I owe a debt of gratitude to Mary Rose D'Angelo for drawing my attention to the ambiguous meaning of *proskuneō* and to Ian Werrett for advising me on the scholarship on this word.

65 *Vetus Latina Database*, s.v. "Matthaeus [Mt] 28.9" (Turnhout: Brepols, 2002). For the Vulgate's translation of Mt 28:9, see n. 59 above.

66 Clemens Blume, ed., *Thesauri hymnologici hymnarium: Die Hymnen des Thesaurus Hymnologicus H. A. Daniels und anderer Humnen-Ausgaben*, Analecta hymnica medii aevi 51 (Leipzig: O. R. Reisland, 1908), no. 84.

This hymn first appears in the sixth century in Italy and southern Gaul in the Old Hymnal for use on Easter Day, but over the course of the Middle Ages, beginning in the ninth century in northern Francia with the New Hymnal, it was increasingly sung not on Easter itself, but throughout Eastertide at Lauds.[67] According to the Barking ordinal, the community was to sing "Aurora lucis rutilat" every day at Lauds beginning on the Monday following Easter up to the Feast of the Ascension.[68] The music and text of this hymn are preserved in an early fifteenth-century liturgical manuscript from the abbey that contains many of the hymns that were to be sung during the temporal and sanctoral cycles.[69] Given the frequency with which this hymn was sung during Eastertide at Barking, its alternative reading of Matthew 28:9 alone may have inspired the inclusion of the Marys' kiss of Christ's feet in the *Visitatio*, yet another source may have offered additional direction.

Sibyl de Felton, the abbess who gave the ordinal to Barking, was the owner of a copy of Nicholas Love's *Mirror of the Blessed Life of Jesus Christ*, a Middle English translation of the pseudo-Bonaventure's *Meditationes vitae Christi*. Her copy belongs to a recension of the text that predates its official examination and approbation in c. 1410 by Thomas Arundel, archbishop of Canterbury (1396–1414), the much-maligned menace to vernacular theological productions in early fifteenth-century England.[70] Elsewhere I have shown that the recension of Love's *Mirror* in Sibyl de Felton's possession conveys the Carthusian translator's deep pastoral concern for lay and religious women, which he expressed through the addition of unique features to the portraits of the Virgin Mary and Mary Magdalene presented in his Latin source and in the gospels.[71] In his translation of the meditation on the encounter between the three Marys and the risen Christ, Love did not simply reiterate Matthew's account of the women's embrace of Christ's feet, as the pseudo-Bonaventure did; instead, he added: "& þei so ioyful of his presence, þat it may not be seide, felle done at hees feete &

67 *The Canterbury Dictionary of Hymnology*, s.v. "Aurora lucis rutilat" (Norwich: Canterbury Press, 2013); A. S. Walpole, ed., *Early Latin Hymns* (Cambridge: Cambridge University Press, 1922), no. 111; W. Bulst, ed., *Hymni Latini Antiquissimi LXX. Psalmi III* (Heidelberg: F. H. Kerle, 1956), 114–115, 195; and Helmut Gneuss, *Hymnar und Hymnen im englischen Mittelalter*, Buchreihe der Anglia 12 (Tübingen: M. Niemeyer, 1968), no. 41. This hymn appears in several manuscript copies of the New Hymnal from late Anglo-Saxon England studied by Inge Milfull, *The Hymns of the Anglo-Saxon Church: A Study and Edition of the 'Durham Hymnal'* (Cambridge: Cambridge University Press, 1996), no. 72.

68 *Ordinale*, 1:112–126. I am grateful for Anne Yardley's guidance on tracing the appearance of "Aurora lucis rutilat" in the Barking ordinal.

69 Cambridge, Trinity College, MS 1226 (O.3.54), fol. 15r–v. For studies of the music contained in this manuscript, see Yardley, *Performing Piety*, 192–198; Yardley, "Was Anonymous a Woman?" in *Women Composers: Music through the Ages, Volume 1: Composers Born before 1599*, ed. Martha Furman Schleifer and Sylvia Glickman, 69–72 (New York: G. K. Hall, 1996), 70.

70 Sibyl de Felton's copy of Love's *Mirror* was once owned by William Foyle and identified as Beeleigh Abbey, Maldon, Essex, Foyle MS, but it is now privately owned.

71 Bugyis, "Through the Looking Glass: Reflections of Christ's 'trewe louers' in Nicholas Love's *The Mirror of the Blessed Life of Jesus Christ*," in *Devotional Culture in Late Medieval England and Europe: Diverse Imaginations of Christ's Life*, ed. Stephen Kelly and Ryan Perry, 461–484 (Turnhout: Brepols, 2015).

clipped [embraced] hem & kissede with ioyful teres & speken also with him."[72] Love's addition of the Marys' kissing Christ's feet appears fitting when read immediately after the preceding chapter, in which he, like the pseudo-Bonaventure, expressed his belief that Christ, despite his initial prohibition, ultimately "suffrede [Mary Magdalene] to touch him, & to kysse boþe handes & fete, or þei departeden."[73] Love, perhaps interested in figuring greater equality among Christ's most devoted female followers, granted all three Marys the opportunity not only to touch, but also to kiss their teacher with tears of joy, and Sibyl de Felton, perhaps inspired by this meditation on Christ's post-resurrection appearance, decided to replicate this scene in Barking's *Visitatio*, creatively exercising her abbatial prerogative in order to heighten the drama's visual effect and spiritual meaning. Only the women playing the Marys, not the clerics and priests representing the disciples, were to be seen intimately handling the body of Christ, in very close proximity to the principal site where the abbey's priests consecrated the eucharistic elements – a visual parallel likely intended by the drama's directors, and evident to its participants and viewers.

This parallel would have been made even more apparent by Mary Magdalene's presentation of the *sudarium* to each of the disciples to kiss.[74] In Wilton's version of this scene, the Marys were to receive the *sudarium* from a subdeacon and kiss it before it was offered to the rest of the people.[75] Margaret Pappano, in her analysis of Wilton's *Visitatio*, has likened the *sudarium* to the *pax* passed around the congregation after the consecration as a substitute for the Eucharist, as both objects were clearly invested with "clerical authority."[76] Yet, in late medieval piety the *sudarium* was much more closely connected, even conflated, with the Eucharist itself than with its substitute, the *pax*, because both objects were believed to communicate in their very substance Christ's bodily presence to those who consumed them physically, whether by sight, touch, or taste.[77] In the late fifteenth-century *Visitationes* from Frankfurt and Mainz, a corporal – the liturgical cloth placed on the altar under the paten and chalice holding the bread and wine for the consecration of the Eucharist – was used to represent the *sudarium*, an appropriate choice given that, at both sites during the *Depositio*, a consecrated host was to be placed in the sepulcher to figure Jesus' burial.[78] Though the

72 This passage occurs in all three of the recensions of Love's *Mirror* identified by Michael Sargent; *Mirror*, 199.25–27. The pseudo-Bonaventure only partially cites Mt 28:9, omitting the Marys' adoration of Christ: "Illae vero ultra quam dici posset exhilaratae, *procidentes tenuerunt pedes eius*"; *Meditationes*, 618.

73 *Mirror*, 198.38–39. Cf. *Meditationes*, 618: "Licet autem sic eidem a principio Dominus responderit, vix credere possum quin eum familiariter tangeret antequam inde discederet, deosculando pedes et manus."

74 "Liturgical Dramas," 28–29.

75 Rankin, "New English Source," 9: "Subdiaconus accipiat textum; ostendat eis quem ipse adorent prius, et osculetur postea omnis et populus."

76 Pappano, "Sister Acts," 60.

77 Jeffrey Hamburger, "Vision and the Veronica," in *The Visual and the Visionary: Art and Female Spirituality in Late Medieval Germany*, 317–358 (New York: Zone Books, 1998), 336.

78 See *Lateinische Osterfeiern und Osterspiele*, L207 (Frankfurt, 1486): "corporali accepto"; L256 (Mainz, 1480): "persone accepto corporali." Blandine-Dominique Berger briefly discussed the use of the *sudarium* in Easter dramas in *Le Drame liturgique de Paques du Xe au XIIIe siècle*,

rubrics to Barking's Holy Week dramas are more ambiguous as to the type of cloth that was to be used for the *sudarium* – the only stipulation is that the burial cloths be made of "the whitest linen"[79] – it is possible that a corporal was supplied because, during the *Elevatio*, the officiating priest was to enter the tomb, remove the host representing the Lord's body from its burial cloths, place it in a monstrance, and process with it to the altar of the Holy Trinity.[80]

Even if a corporal was not used for the *sudarium*, within the reality of the drama, Mary Magdalene was still to handle and present for veneration one of the holiest contact relics: the cloth within which Jesus' *imago* was wrapped for burial. This object, much like the Eucharist, would have served as a potent witness to Christ's continued, real, palpable presence, and Mary alone was to mediate access to this presence – and to ordained men no less. Like Wilton's Marys, the priests and clerics playing the disciples in Barking's *Visitatio* were not granted direct contact with Christ's body; instead, they depended on the ministrations of another whose touch was so authorized. The Barking nun playing Mary Magdalene was invested with such authority by virtue of both the drama's script and her very performance of it; thus, it is not surprising then that she, along with her two companions, had to perform a rite of purification similar to the ones undertaken by priests before the celebration of Mass. Through wearing clerical vestments, carrying liturgical vessels, preaching Christ's resurrection, and handling his body, these women would have assumed a distinctly sacerdotal cast and, thus, were identified as "priests" in the *Visitatio*'s concluding rubric. Their appearance was to exceed a mere *similitudo mulierum*; they were vested, purified, and directed to act *in persona sacerdotum*, too.

The identification of the women playing the Marys as "sacerdotes," though arguably grammatically correct and fitting within the drama's logic, is nevertheless utterly unique, thus raising the pressing question of how the nuns at Barking were able to script and perform such a daring transformation of three of their sisters without provoking ecclesiastical censure. The abbey had long exercised primary control over its liturgical dramas, despite attempts made by ecclesiastical officials to reform them. Most notably, among the injunctions that John Peckham, archbishop of Canterbury (1279–1292), issued against the abbey in 1279, after the visitation of John de Chishull, bishop of London (1274–1280), was a strong disapproval of the reversal of roles between novices and senior officers that took place in the celebration of the Feast of the Holy Innocents. He worried that, in the officers' absence, no one could ensure that "divine praise was not turned into a mockery."[81] Yet, despite Peckham's displeasure,

Théologie Historique 37 (Paris: Éditions Beauchesne, 1976), 264.

79 "Liturgical Dramas," 16: "Cumque in predictum locum tapetum palleo auriculari quoque et lintheis nitidissimis decenter ornatum illam cum reverencia locaverint."

80 Ibid., 22: "Et cum ad sepulcrum pervenerint, sacerdos ebdomadarius sepulcrum thurificet et intret sepulcrum incipiendo versum *Consurgit* … Et interim asportabit corpus dominicum de sepulcro incipiendo antiphonam *Christus resurgens* coram altari versu vultu ad populum tenendo corpus dominicum in manibus suis inclusum cristallo."

81 C. T. Martin, ed., *Registrum Epistolarum Fratris Johannis Peckham, Archiepiscopi Cantuariensis*, Rolls Series 77, 3 vols. (London, 1882–1886), 1:82–83: "Festi etiam Innocentum celebritas, quam agi a parvulis non approbamus, sed cum displicentia sustinemus, nullatenus ab eisdem parvulis inchoetur, nec aliqualiter se immisceant, usque post Beati Johannis Evangelistae vesperas

Barking's ordinal attests to the community's continued performance of this drama into the early fifteenth century.[82] Clearly they were not deterred from performing their feasts according to their own traditions. Such evidence of the Barking nuns' agency in the production and performance of their liturgies is perhaps not surprising given the abbey's considerable wealth, prestige, and venerability. It was the only community of religious women that could claim an early medieval foundation; it attracted the daughters of royalty and nobility as members; the abbess had carried the title of baron since the Norman Conquest; and, at its dissolution in 1539, it was the third wealthiest nunnery in England.[83] In my book, *The Care of Nuns: The Ministries of Benedictine Women in England during the Central Middle Ages*, I have uncovered evidence of the Barking nuns assuming roles long considered to be the exclusive province of male priests: serving as confessors and "evangelists" in both senses of the word, scribes and proclaimers of the gospels.[84] The abbey's storied history of casting women in sacerdotal roles surely set the necessary preconditions for identifying the *sorores* playing the Marys in the *Visitatio* as "sacerdotes." They were simply following their foremothers' lead.

consummatas. Consequenter autem moniales ipsi officio se non subtrahant, sed exclusis a choro tunc temporis omnibus masculis et mulieribus, etiam quae ad crementi terminum pervenerunt, ipsae defectus suppleant parvularum, ne, quod nefas est, vertatur in ludibrium laus divina."

82 See n. 8 above.

83 For comprehensive studies of Barking's history, see William Page and J. Horace Round, eds., "Houses of Benedictine Nuns: Abbey of Barking," in *The Victoria History of the County of Essex: Volume* 2 (London, 1907), 115–122; E. A. Loftus and H. F. Chettle, *A History of Barking Abbey* (Barking, 1954); Sturman, "Barking Abbey"; Sarah Foot, *Veiled Women: The Disappearance of Nuns from Anglo-Saxon England*, 2 vols. (Aldershot: Ashgate, 2000), 2:27–33; Yardley, *Performing Piety*, esp. chap. 7; and the contributions to *Barking Abbey and Medieval Literary Culture*.

84 Bugyis, *Care of Nuns*.

PART VI

# OUT OF THE SHADOWS: LAYWOMEN IN COMMUNAL LEADERSHIP

## Preface to Part VI

# LAYWOMEN AS LEADERS

DYAN ELLIOTT

In a patriarchal culture where female influence often seems thin on the ground, the essays in Part VI offer a refreshing perspective on the contributions of the elusive laywoman. Maureen Miller (in Chapter 19) focuses on the eleventh century, examining elite women's roles as patrons of monastic foundations in Italy. Rachel Koopmans' study (Chapter 20) provides an interesting contrast through its orientation around the prominent role that non-elite women played in English miracles stories from the mid-twelfth to mid-thirteenth century. And Barbara Newman's essay (Chapter 21) examines the impact of the spirituality of the laywoman – the Beguine, Mechthild of Magdeburg – on the cloistered nuns of Helfta. If the introduction of the category of gender into academic discourse has sometimes led to consternation and self-doubting among historians, these three chapters reassure us that the traditional category of "women" is still an effective tool for historical analysis.[1] They also provide new opportunities for assessing how the analysis of women engages many familiar historical tropes, while at the same time revealing some telling changes over time.

Maureen Miller's study "follows the money," pointing to the number of elite women who responded to clerical requests for financial support of reformed monastic communities. Appeals to elite women have always been a reliable index for discerning contemporary concerns. For the Venerable Bede, it was the conversion of the husband that was at stake; for the eleventh-century clergy, it was reform. And yet, despite this venerable coalition between elite women and the clergy, I am nevertheless struck by the altered terms of engagement. For example, Bede recounts that when Pope Boniface attempted to hasten Queen Ethelberga's progress in the conversion of the husband, he offered a silver mirror and an ivory comb inlaid with gold.[2] In Miller's analysis, however, the gifts seem to be moving in a different direction. It is the English queen, Matilda, being solicited to provide priestly garments for Bishop Ivo of Chartres who, as inducement, promises to remember Matilda as he says Mass. Miller interprets this as a tacit invitation "to be present at the altar with him" – a promise of spiritual intimacy that a pious woman would doubtless

1 The possibilities for the separation of gender from biological sex were set out clearly in Joan Scott's ground-breaking, "Gender: A Useful Category of Historical Analysis," *American Historical Review* 91 (1986): 1053–75. They were even more potently realized in theoretical works like Judith Butler's *Gender Trouble: Feminism and the Submersion of Identity* (New York: Routledge, 1990).

2 Bede, *A History of the English Church and People* 2.2, rev. ed., trans. Leo Sherley-Price (Harmondsworth: Penguin, 1968), 120–22.

value much more highly than paltry babbles of silver and gold. And yet Ivo, the reformer, should perhaps be distinguished from Ivo, the solicitor of royal favor. In his *Decretum,* Ivo cites a canon that bars women from touching any fabric or vessels at the altar in two separate instances – an interdict that would be repeated in Gratian.[3] One wonders how Matilda would have responded, had she known, or if the bishop himself could appreciate this irony.

Miller distinguishes no marked preference among female patrons for communities associated with a reformist agenda over those that were not. Yet, she demonstrates convincingly that elite women were still well worth courting: the benevolence of one great lady was all it took to ensure the future of a given foundation. Indeed, one could well argue that the entire papal reform was dependent on Matilda of Tuscany, a celebrated benefactress who was prepared to make epic sacrifices for the cause. Miller notes how Matilda of Tuscany left her vast inheritance to the papacy. But her contributions to the papacy went far beyond the terms of a will. During her lifetime, Matilda bankrolled the reform movement, led troops into battle, and, despite her predilection for chastity, married at forty-three "not so much from incontinence as out of obedience to the Roman pontiff."[4]

The laywomen represented in Rachel Koopmans' analysis of miracles are less prominent socially and, hence, more obscure historically than our Italian patronesses. And yet we can still discern in them a number of familiar patterns that are omnipresent in women's temporal and spiritual roles. The efficacious use of martyrs' blood in effecting cures both alludes to women's traditional role as healers even as it anticipates future depredations attributed to women witches. A female figure in a stained-glass window is featured in the *orans* posture in which women were frequently depicted in the earliest examples of early Christian art, hearkening back to their more visible role in the church. This impression is confirmed by the instance in which the child dies in the bath, and the widow asks "Do we not have five widows here?" – recalling another time when women as widows and/or deaconesses occupied a prominent place in public worship.[5] Indeed, women's very role in initiating miracles through relics is reminiscent of the ancient narrative of St. Helena and her invention of the True Cross. The quasi-legal function fulfilled by these women as witnesses to the efficacy of a given saint's power, and hence the cult, is also notable for its singularity in this period – a reminder of the drastically curtailed

3 Ivo of Chartres, *Decretum* 2.72, 3.265, *PL* 161: 176, 259. This canon, attributed to Pope Soter (d. c. 174), is, in fact, one of the False Decretals. It made its way into Gratian's *Decretum* Dist. 23 c. 25, in A. Friedberg, *Corpus Iuris Canonici*, 2nd ed. (Leipzig: B. Tauchnitz, 1879), 1:86.

4 *Bernoldi Chronicon* a. *1089*, ed. G. H. Pertz, MGH, Scrip. 5 (Hanover: Hahn, 1844), 449. On Matilda's financial and military support of the reform movement, see Demetrius B. Zema, "The Houses of Tuscany and Pierlone in the Crisis of Rome in the Eleventh Century," *Traditio* 4 (1944): 155–75, esp. 157–69. Jo Ann McNamara notes the reformers' insensitivity to the preference for chastity expressed by both Matilda and her mother Beatrice – "Chaste Marriage and Clerical Celibacy," in *Sexual Practices and the Medieval Church,* ed. Vern L. Bullough and James A. Brundage (Buffalo: Prometheus, 1982), 32.

5 See Gary Macy, *The Hidden History of Female Ordination: Female Clergy in the Medieval West* (Oxford: Oxford University Press, 2008).

ability of women to bear witness in ecclesiastical and civil courts alike in the high Middle Ages.[6]

Finally, Barbara Newman's chapter attests to the difference in mentality between a spiritual entrepreneur like the Beguine, Mechthild of Magdeburg, when compared with her younger cloistered namesake, the nun Mechthild of Hackeborn. The older woman was a self-deprecating individualist – a *minnesinger* whose love of God sometimes teetered on the edge of heresy. After being buffeted around in secular society, she finally found respite at the community of Helfta, where she died. The writings, and doubtless the personalities, of the two Mechthilds were sufficiently different that the impact of the elder Mechthild's vernacular works on her Latinate namesake has hitherto gone unnoticed. Yet Newman's analysis also points to a number of things that seem to have gotten lost in translation. Even as the Beguine's spectacular vernacular was Latinized, so too was her imagery sanitized, and her individualism communalized. The younger Mechtilds's Latin homage remains, however, a stirring insight into how the elder Mechthild was revered, and probably feared, by the community of Helfta. One can only imagine the nuns' anticipation/ anxiety when it was her turn to say grace.

Taken together, these essays both affirm the analytic category of "women" while at the same time inviting us to explore its limitations. In the case of a religious community, it is clear that such a classification makes sense. Mechthild of Hackeborn even presents salvation as a group endeavor, projecting the virginal brides of her community into heaven, where they rally around their celestial groom. But one wonders if the same kind of potential for collective analysis holds true for women in secular society. There is little doubt that women partook of the same set of liabilities imposed on them by virtue of their sex, but do such restrictions alone provide sufficient motive to approach them as a meaningful collective? As Denise Riley has demonstrated, one of the reasons that modern men saw fit to deny women the vote was the fear that they would vote in a block.[7] There are aspects of the medieval misogynist tradition that parallel this fear. The women of the fabliaux are often depicted as a dark sorority, competing with one another to see who can make the biggest fool of their husbands. The women of the *Wife of Bath's Tale* are portrayed as united in their desire for sovereignty over men. In the later Middle Ages, the clerical elite became convinced that female witches congregated at diabolical orgies.[8]

Does history vindicate this propensity for collective agency projected upon women by their detractors? Did women inside the cloister identify with women on the

6 On female subordination in Common Law, see F. Pollock and F. W. Maitland, *The History of English Law*, 2nd ed. (Cambridge: Cambridge University Press, 1952), 2:406–407; in canon law, see Elliott, *Spiritual Marriage*, 155–58. One of the few reasons that women can appear as independent witnesses in court is to testify to male impotence. See Jacqueline Murray, "On the Origins and Role of 'Wise Women' in Causes for Annulment on the Grounds of Male Impotence," *Journal of Medieval History* 16 (1990): 235–49.

7 Denise Riley, "Am I That Name?" *Feminism and the Category of "Women" in History* (Minneapolis: University of Minnesota, 1988), esp. 67–95.

8 The belief in the witches' Sabbath begins to take shape in the first half of the fifteenth century. For the five formative texts, see *L'Imaginaire du sabbat: Edition critique des textes les plus anciens (1430 c.–1440 c.)*, ed. Martine Ostorero et al. (Lausanne: Cahiers lausannois d'histoire médiéval, 1999).

outside? Did laywomen, who did not experience the commonality implicit in an enclosed community, nevertheless feel a sense of common cause? Did they have the capacity to act collectively? If there was a sense of commonality, did it transcend social divisions? For instance, did the elite women who animated the papal reform ever think about the sad fate of clerical wives, who were denigrated and persecuted by the reformers?[9] What if these elite women knew that the number of female saints (never prolix), declined dramatically during the reform, as did the number of female religious communities, while those in existence became progressively impoverished? Would this knowledge have changed their patterns of donation?[10] Or is it likely that gender was not an important category for elite women, who may have experienced greater empathy and shared common purpose with members of the clergy? Even if this were the case, the bonds between elite women and their clerical companions were fraught with incommensurate measures of dependence that had the potential to foster division. For while a cleric might sometimes be dependent on an elite woman for patronage, this would not efface his superiority in terms of gender or sacerdotal privilege. Nor can we ignore the fact that most women, elite and non-elite alike, relied upon the clergy for representation in script.[11]

Here too the deeply learned nuns of Helfta stand apart from laywomen, and even from most nuns. But if these women are not dependent on men for writing in Latin, it is nevertheless the clergy who provide the measure for what may be written: what is deemed orthodox and what is deemed heretical. Indeed, we can sometimes sense the sisters looking over their shoulders as if to discern this invisible metric. Newman recounts one telling scene from the revelations of Gertrude the Great, protégée of Mechthild of Hackeborn, in which Gertrude asks Christ to glorify the late Mechthild of Magdeburg with miracles in order to validate her visions. He refuses, his stated reason being that it is the inner experience of God that counts – not outer signs. As spiritually edifying as Christ's comment might be, Newman interprets this to mean that there would be no saint's cult around the elder Mechthild. This serves as a reminder that times had changed since the martyrdom of Becket, when the translation of a saint's relics was still a local affair. By the time Gertrude was writing, canonization had been centralized through the papacy for over a century, and more and more communities, religious and secular, would run afoul of papal authorities through supporting unauthorized cults.[12] So the nuns of Helfta played it safe: there was no cult for the elder Beguine, and hence no vita – the first step toward initiating a process of canonization. It was different for men. If clerics, such as Jacques de Vitry, Thomas of Cantimpré, or Goswin of Bossut had been constrained by parallel considerations, there would be virtually no vita for any Beguine.

9 See Dyan Elliott, *Fallen Bodies: Pollution, Sexuality, and Demonology in the Middle Ages* (Philadelphia: University of Pennsylvania, 1999), 81–106.

10 Jane Tibbets Schulenburg, "Sexism in the Celestial Gynaeceum, from 500 to 1200," *Journal of Medieval History* 4 (1978): 117–33; eadem, *Forgetful of their Sex: Female Sanctity and Society, ca. 500–1100* (Chicago: University of Chicago Press, 1998), 108.

11 See, however, Megan J. Hall's essay in this volume (Chapter 15).

12 See Janine Larmon Peterson's "Holy Heretics in Later Medieval Italy," *Past and Present* 204 (2009): 3–31.

It is inspiring to discover instances of collective action among women who did not live in a female community and could, in all probability, not write: the non-elite women of Koopmans' miracle stories. These women are presented as a self-referential female collective; a veritable sisterhood of healing. Are they the invention of a clerical scribe, or do they in some way represent the self-understanding of real women? Of course, one wishes for the latter to be true. Yet either way, they provide a stirring reminder that the papal reformers could not have it all their own way. They may have barred women from altars, expelled clerical wives, and devalued female religious communities, but these miracle-women still remained. Nevertheless, the shifting patterns of veneration suggest that the English landscape has not escaped the occlusion of reform. The cults of women like Margaret, Frideswide, or Aebbe of Coldingham are represented as a distinct minority among active cults. They were destined to be over-shadowed by contemporary superstars like William of Norwich, Thomas of Becket, Gilbert of Sempringham, Hugh of Lincoln, and Richard of Chichester. Did the miracle-women inadvertently foster these trends?

Whatever the answer may be to this question it is important for historians of women to cultivate something of a parallax view: a shifting perspective that can identify constraining gender roles, but still appreciate the ways in which laywomen overcame such constraints and found meaning in their lives. When seen from this angle, the women in these three chapters not only demonstrate leadership, but true heroism.

19

# WOMEN DONORS AND ECCLESIASTICAL REFORM: EVIDENCE FROM CAMALDOLI AND VALLOMBROSA, c. 1000–1150

MAUREEN C. MILLER

Advocates for ecclesiastical reform in the eleventh and early twelfth centuries notably used letters to spread their ideas as well as to recruit and encourage supporters. In a study of Pope Gregory VII's register, Ian Robinson dubbed these communities of correspondents "friendship circles" and underscored their importance in advancing ecclesiastical change.[1] Subsequent scholarship has used network theory to deepen this emphasis on discrete human connections across considerable distances and upon letters as key tools of reform.[2] In my own research on clerical clothing, I was struck by the number of letters sent to elite women by episcopal advocates of reform. Bishops such as Ivo of Chartres wrote to queens and countesses, generally asking support for their churches but often specifically requesting liturgical vestments. While such requests tapped into women's control of textile workshops, and traditional associations of feminine virtue with needlework, they also proffered a spiritual relationship to women. Ivo, for example, promised Queen Matilda of England that if she sent him "an alb or some other priestly garment," he would wear it as he celebrated Mass, implicitly inviting Matilda through her handiwork to be present at the altar with him.[3] We know, moreover, that at least some women seem to have cherished such spiritual intimacy: according to Eadmer of Canterbury, Countess Adela of Blois had chosen Bishop Anselm as "the instructor and tutor of her life," and the intensity of

1 I. S. Robinson, "The Friendship Network of Gregory VII," *History* 63, no. 207 (1978): 1–22; idem, "The Friendship Circle of Bernold of Constance and the Dissemination of Gregorian Ideas in Late Eleventh-Century Germany," in *Friendship in Medieval Europe*, ed. Julian P. Haseldine (Thrupp-Stroud: Sutton, 1999), 185–98.

2 Julian P. Haseldine, "Friends, Friendship and Networks in the Letters of Bernard of Clairvaux," *Cîteaux: Commentarii Cistercienses* 57, no. 3–4 (2006): 243–79; Uta-Renate Blumenthal, "Poitevin Manuscripts, the Abbey of Saint-Ruf and Ecclesiastical Reform in the Eleventh Century," in *Readers, Texts and Compilers in the Earlier Middle Ages: Studies in Medieval Canon Law in Honour of Linda Fowler-Magerl*, ed. Martin Brett and Kathleen G. Cushing (Farnham: Ashgate, 2009), 87–100; Barbara H. Rosenwein, "Circles of Affection in Cluniac Charters," in *Ecritures de l'espace social: Mélanges d'histoire médiévale offerts à Monique Bourin*, ed. Didier Boisseuil, Pierre Chastang, Laurent Feller, and Joseph Morsel (Paris: Publications de la Sorbonne, 2010), 397–415; Guido Cariboni, "'Archiabbatum numquam invenimus annotatum' : Una svolta del monachesimo sotto I pontificati di Urbano II e Pasquale II," *Bullettino dell'Istituto storico italiano per il Medio Evo* 115 (2013): 171–207.

3 "A Letter from Ivo, Bishop of Chartres (1100s)," in *Epistolae: Medieval Women's Latin Letters*, ed. and trans. Joan Ferrante, http://epistolae.ccnmtl.columbia.edu.

Matilda of Canossa's relationship with Pope Gregory VII aroused rumors of scandalous impropriety.[4]

Might women, then, have been key supporters of reform? Might their traditional roles as religious educators of their children and stewards of the pious commemoration of deceased members of their families have made them particularly interested in the quality of prayer offered in ecclesiastical institutions? Opponents of some of the ecclesiastical changes advocated in the late eleventh century voiced anxiety about the power of elite women: the imperial bishops who renounced Gregory VII's leadership at Worms in 1076 accused the pope of running the church with "a new senate of women."[5] Invective this certainly was. But were there important ties of support between women and advocates for ecclesiastical change in the eleventh and early twelfth centuries?

I sought some preliminary answers to this question through an evaluation of donations to two prominent reformed monastic communities in Tuscany: the hermitages of Camaldoli, founded by Saint Romuald of Ravenna between 1023 and 1027,[6] and Vallombrosa, established by Saint John Gualbert c. 1038.[7] Both went on to reform other religious communities, building congregations of linked institutions across northern and central Italy.[8] The results presented here are based on the charters

4 Maureen C. Miller, *Clothing the Clergy: Virtue and Power in Medieval Europe, c. 800–1200* (Ithaca: Cornell University Press, 2014), 183–87, 239–40.

5 *Die Briefe Heinrichs IV*, ed. Carl Erdmann (Leipzig: K. W. Hiersemann, 1937), *MGH Deutsches Mittelalter* 1:68: "In qua re verecundia nostra magis quam causa laborat, quamvis haec generalis querela ubique personuerit: omnia iudicia, omnia decreta per feminas in apostolica sede actari, denique per hunc feminarum nouum senatum totum orbem ecclesiae administrari."

6 Giovanni Tabacco "La data di fondazione di Camaldoli," *Rivista di Storia della Chiesa in Italia* 16 (1962): 451–55; Wilhelm Kurze, "Campus Maldoli: Die frühgeschichte Camaldolis," *Quellen und Forschungen aus Italienischen Archiven und Bibliotheken* 44 (1964): 1–34; Giuseppe Vedovato, *Camaldoli e la sua congregazione dalle origini al 1184: Storia e documentazione* (Cesena: Badia di S. Maria del Monte, 1994), 7, 15–23; Cécile Caby, *De l'érémitisme rural au monachisme urbain: Les Camaldules en Italie à la fin du moyen âge* (Rome: École française de Rome, 1999), 70–71.

7 Brunetto Quilici, "Giovanni Gualberto e la sua riforma monastica," *Archivio Storico Italiano* 99, no. 1 (1941): 113–32; 99, no. 2 (1941): 27–62; 100 (1942): 45–99. Robert Davidsohn, *Geschichte von Florenz* (Berlin: E. S. Mittler und sohn, 1908–27); trans. Giovanni Battista Klein and Roberto Palmarocchi, ed. Ugo Procacci as *Storia di Firenze*, 8 vols. (Florence: Sansoni, 1969), 1: 242–52; Denis Meade, "From Turmoil to Solidarity: The Emergence of the Vallumbrosan Monastic Congregation," *American Benedictine Review* 19 (1968): 328.

8 Nicola Vasaturo, "L'espansione della congregazione vallombrosana fino alla metà del sec. XII," *Rivisto di Storia della Chiesa in Italia* 16 (1962): 456–85; Vedovato, *Camaldoli*; Giovanni Spinelli, "Note sull'espansione Vallombrosana in alta Italia," in *I Vallombrosani nella società italiana dei secoli XI e XII, Vallombrosa, 3–4 settembre 1993*, ed. Giordano Monzio Campagnoni, Archivio Vallombrosano 2 (Vallombrosa: Edizioni Vallombrosa, 1995), 179–201; Jean Pierre Delumeau, *Arezzo Espace et sociétés, 715–1230. Recherches sur Arezzo et son* contado *du VIIIe au début du XIIIe siècle*, Collection de l'École française de Rome 219, 2 vols. (Rome: École française de Rome, 1996), 1:580–94, 1:712–41; Wilhelm Kurze, "La diffusione dei vallombrosani : Problematica e linee di tendenza," in *L'Ordo vallisumbrosae tra XII e XIII secolo. Gli sviluppi istituzionali e culturali e l'espansione geografica (1101–1293)*, ed. Giordano Monzio Compagnoni, Archivio Vallombrosano 3 (Vallombrosa: Edizione Vallombrosa, 1999), 595–617. This collection also offers regional studies of Vallombrosan expansion in Sicily (365–73), Piedmont (619–725), Romagna (809–39), Umbria (841–83), and Sardegna (885–902), in addition to more focused

of the two "mother" houses of these eremitic congregations, San Salvatore at Camaldoli and Santa Maria d'Acquabella at Vallombrosa, compared with those of the traditional Benedictine monastery of Santa Maria della Badia in the city of Florence. The charters of all these institutions are available online in the "archivi digitalizzati" of the Florentine state archive, facilitating detailed analysis of individual donations as well as simple quantitative analyses of donations in the context of each community's surviving parchments.[9] A comparison of donors supporting new reformed institutions to those patronizing a traditional Benedictine monastery reveals no simple, direct correlation between gender and support for reform. It does, however, make obvious why advocates of change were importuning *elite* women, even as new religious initiatives were attracting donations from people of modest means. And it suggests that, at least in Tuscany, the approbation of the ecclesiastical hierarchy was more important to women donors than to their male counterparts. Finally, a focus on women donors reveals some reasons why contestation over ecclesiastical change was so protracted over the eleventh and twelfth centuries. After some background on all three institutions, the statistics on women's donations these collections yielded will be presented, and then a more fine-grained analysis of women's relations with new reforming movements in Tuscany.

## The Institutions

It is worth noting at the outset that the documentation for Florence is extremely sparse before the tenth century, so the most venerable Benedictine monastery geographically proximate to Camaldoli and Vallombrosa with some documentation for analysis is Santa Maria della Badia within the city of Florence (usually referred to as the Badia Fiorentina). The work of Wilhelm Kurze has established that this was not a noble

analyses of the Vallombrosan houses around Bologna (727–63) and in the mountainous zone between Pistoia and Bologna (765–808).

9 I thank Mahel Hamroun, a doctoral candidate at the University of California Berkeley, who collected the data and created the initial databases from the *fondi* Archivio di Stato Firenze, Diplomata [hereafter ASF Dip.], Firenze, Santa Maria della Badia detta Badia fiorentina; Camaldoli, San Salvatore (eremo); Vallombrosa, Santa Maria d'Acquabella (badia vallombrosana). On the histories of these collections see Luigi Schiaparelli, Anna Maria Enriques, eds. *Le carte del monastero di S. Maria in Firenze (Badia)*, 2 vols., Regesta Chartarum Italiae 41–42 (Rome: Istituto storico italiano per il medioevo, 1990), 1: XI–XIII; Luigi Schiaparelli, Francesco Baldasseroni, and Ernesto Lasinio, eds., *Regesto di Camaldoli*, 4 vols., *Regesta chartarum Italiae* 2, 5, 13–14 (Rome: E. Loescher, 1907–1928), 1: VII–X; Lucia Roselli, *L'Archivio del Monastero di Santa Maria di Vallombrosa: Inventario* (Lucca: Istituto Storico Lucchese, 2006), 29–39; Francesco Salvestrini, "La vita di un istituto attraverso i suoi documenti," in idem, *Disciplina caritatis: Il monachesimo vallombrosano tra medioevo e prima età moderna* (Roma: Viella, 2008), 109–27, especially 125–27. All documents before 1150 were surveyed for each institution. While the *fondo* for Vallombrosa did not include more than sporadic documents regarding affiliated institutions, the Camaldoli *fondo* had incorporated a large number of eleventh- and early twelfth-century parchments regarding its daughter-house Santa Maria in Prataglia (not affiliated with San Salvatore until 1157). This required a patient pruning of the original database to remove these documents, a process aided by the *Regesto di Camaldoli*.

*Eigenkloster*, as some contended, but an imperial monastery.[10] Founded on May 31, 978 by Countess Willa – daughter of Boniface, the Margrave of Tuscany, and widow of Uberto, Margrave of Spoleto and Camerino – and subsequently also patronized by her son, Ugo Margrave of Tuscany, other Frankish elites, Emperor Otto III, and his successors, the Badia was richly endowed with public lands and fiscal rights: it served, basically, to organize and administer the imperial patrimony in the Tuscan march. Throughout the Middle Ages, it was the city's richest monastery.[11]

Both the hermitages of Camaldoli and Vallombrosa had much humbler beginnings, although both were eventually enriched through donations. The origins of Camaldoli have proven a vexed question, primarily because Peter Damian's life of its founder, Saint Romuald, never mentions the hermitage.[12] Contemporary documentary sources, however, indicate that sometime between 1023 and 1027 Romuald had established a hermitage in the Tuscan Apennines at the northernmost edge of the county and diocese of Arezzo. The bishops of Arezzo were early patrons of the hermitage and at Rome in January of 1047, Emperor Henry III confirmed the see's gifts to the community. From 1059 monasteries began to be donated to Camaldoli so that its hermits could renew the religious life of these other institutions. Papal confirmations quickly followed and by Pope Honorius II's bull of March 7, 1125, forty-four monasteries and churches, in central Italy as well as in Sardinia, were part of the Camaldolese congregation.[13]

Vallombrosa's origins also feature hermits, but violent public strife over ecclesiastical practices gave this institution a much higher profile. Its founder, John Gaulbert, had been born into a knightly family with lands in the Val di Pesa, southeast of Florence. According to Atto of Pistoia's *Vita*, an encounter with the murderer of a member of his family led to John's conversion to religious life: he was moved to compassion when the killer fell to his knees and in surrender extended his arms in the form of a cross.[14] John entered the monastery of San Miniato al Monte, probably in

10 Wilhelm Kurze, "Monasteri e nobiltà nella Tuscia altomedievale," in idem, *Monasteri e nobiltà nel senese e nella Toscana medieval: Studi diplomatici, archeologici, genealogici, giuridici e sociali* (Siena: Accademia senese degli intronati / Ente provinciale per il turismo, 1989), 295–316.

11 Davidsohn, *Storia di Firenze*, 1: 173–75, 181–93, 203; Anne Leader, *The Badia of Florence: Art and Observance in a Renaissance Monastery* (Bloomington: Indiana University Press, 2012), 11–19.

12 See above note 6, and Umberto Longo, *Come angeli in terra: Pier Domiani, la santità e la riforma del secolo XI* (Rome: Viella, 2012), 249–51.

13 ASF Dip. 000074024, August 1027 (privilege of Bishop Teodald of Arezzo); 00000745, January 3, 1047 (confirmation and privilege of Emperor Henry III); 00003893, March 7, 1125 (bull Honorius II); transcriptions of all the early privileges of bishops, popes, and emperors may be found in Vedovato, *Camaldoli* (above, n. 6), for those cited here, see 126–28, 188–89, 240–41. Briefer registrations of the full corpus of documents are in Schiaparelli et al., *Regesto di Camaldoli*, 1: 35–36 (no. 86), 98–99 (no. 239), 150 (no. 373). The best studies of the origins and early development of Camaldoli are Vedovato, *Camaldoli*, and Wilhelm Kurze, "Sulla storia di Camaldoli all'epoca delle riforme," in idem, *Monasteri e nobiltà*, 275–94; Caby, *De l'érémitisme*, 9–56, provides a critical review of the historiography and of the medieval sources for the congregation.

14 Atto of Pistoia, *S. Ioanis Gualberti Vita*, cap. 2, *PL* 146: 672; this life was probably written between 1127 and 1133 when Atto was abbot of Vallombrosa. For brief biographies see Antonella Degl'Innocenti, "Giovanni Gualberto," *Dizionario Biografico degli Italiani* (Rome: Isti-

1033. Hagiographical accounts relate that c. 1038 he accused the newly elected abbot of his house, Uberto, of having bought his office from Bishop Atto of Florence; shortly thereafter he left San Miniato. After taking counsel with a hermit named Teuzo and with the abbot of the monastery of Settimo, John was said to have gone to the old marketplace in Florence, publicly denounced both Uberto and the bishop as simoniacs, and provoked a riot.[15] His strident rigorist position having been rejected by the populace, John fled the city and at a place called Acquabella in the hills east of Florence joined two other hermits in a life of fasting and prayer.[16] By the end of 1038 a church had been consecrated at the site and from 1048 other institutions began calling upon Gualbert and his brothers to reform their communities.[17] Vallombrosa's development of a network of institutions occurred, therefore, earlier than Camaldoli's, but it also differed from Camaldoli in another respect: it fairly quickly abandoned its eremitic origins and embraced cenobitic life.[18] Gualbert and his monks continued their

---

tuto della Enciclopedia italiana, 1960–) (hereafter *DBI*), 56: 341–47; Meade, "From Turmoil to Solidarity," 323–57. The earliest life, written by Andrea da Strumi c. 1092, surviving in one incomplete copy, and an anonymous twelfth-century life, were both edited by F. Baethgen, *MGH*, *SS* 30/2, 1076–1110. A valuable collection is *Vallombrosa: Memorie agiografiche e culto dell reliquie*, ed. Antonella Degl'Innocenti (Rome: Viella, 2012), which republished Sofia Boesch Gajano's first systematic study of Vallombrosan hagiography along with additional recent work, including Degl'Innocenti's extremely useful "Da Andrea di Strumi a Sante da Perugia: l'agiografia su Giovanni Gualberto fino al XV secolo" (117–40) – the most current overview of the various lives. The volume also includes Degl'Innocenti's edition (273–97) of an early fourteenth-century anonymous life from the Biblioteca Laurenziana (ms. Plut. 35 sin. 9) first published by W. Goez and C. Hafner, eds. "Die vierte Vita des Abtes Johannes Gualberti von Vallombrosa," *Deutsches Archiv* 41/2 (1985): 418–37.

15 The best, brief, critical account of these events is Nicolangelo D'Acunto, "Lotte religiose a Firenze nel secolo XI: Aspetti della rivolta contro il vescovo Pietro Mezzabarba," *Aevum* 67, no. 2 (1993): 280–84; but now see William D. McCready, *Odiosa sanctitas: St Peter Damian, Simony, and Reform* (Toronto: Pontifical Institute of Mediaeval Studies, 2011), 130–33. Still essential is Giovanni Miccoli, *Pietro Igneo: Studi sull'età gregoriana*, Istituto Storico Italiano per il Medio Evo Studi Storici 40–41 (Rome: Istituto Storico Italiano per il Medio Evo, 1960), especially 1–45.

16 Several springs on the site explain its name. The location was in the diocese of Fiesole: Davidsohn, *Storia di Firenze*, 1: 250; Meade, "From Turmoil to Solidarity," 327–28.

17 Meade, "From Turmoil to Solidarity," 333, 337–55; Vasaturo, "L'espansione," 463ff.; a useful list of the early affiliates of Vallombrosa is both in Vasaturo and *Alle origini di Vallombrosa: Giovanni Gaulberto nella società dell'XI secolo*, ed. Giovanni Spinelli and Giustino Rossi (Novara: Europìa, 1984), 159–63 (map on 147). On the religious ideals and practices constituting and informing ties between Vallombrosa and its associated communities, see Francesco Salvestrini, "La strutturazione dell'Ordine dalle origini al *Capitulum generale* del 1216," in idem, *Disciplina caritatis*, 181–244, but especially 181–205, on the period from the life of the founder to the constitutions of 1095–1101.

18 In 1039, it was called an *eremus* and simply a *locus* and in 1043 John Gualbert was addressed as *praepositus*; the foundation charter of 1048 for its first subject house at S. Salvi, however, established a *monasterium secundum ordinem Sancti Benedicti*, and subsequent charters to Vallombrosa are to the *ecclesia et monasterio* there. ASF Dip. 00074035 (July 3, 1039); 00000687 (August 27, 1043); 00000872 (June 1, 1054); 00001209 (May 1068); Meade, "From Turmoil to Solidarity," 328–30; Francesco Salvestrini, "Eremitismo-cenobitismo. La realtà di Santa Maria di Vallombrosa in età medievale," in *Architettura eremitica. Sistemi progettuali e paesaggi culturali: Atti del Secondo Convegno Internazionale di Studi Vallombrosa 24–25 Settembre 2011*, ed. Stefano Bertocci and Sandro Parrinello (Firenze: Edifir-Edizioni, 2011), 33–39.

advocacy against simony, most notably in their campaign against Bishop Peter Mezzabarba of Florence (1061–1068).[19] The Vallombrosan congregation continued to expand after Gualbert's death in 1073.[20]

## Rates of Donation by Women

Women acting alone making donations or testamentary bequests were very few across all three institutions. They account for eleven percent of the donations to the Badia, ten percent of those to Camaldoli, and eight and a half percent of those to Vallombrosa.[21] If we combine the number of women acting alone with the number of women donating with husbands or other male relatives, all three institutions received roughly similar percentages of their support from benefactions involving women: thirty-three percent of the Badia's donations and testamentary bequests, thirty-seven percent of Camaldoli's, and thirty percent of Vallombrosa's.[22] In these Tuscan cases, therefore, women appear to have been no more likely to support a reformed institution than a traditional Benedictine monastery. So, if Vallombrosan or Camaldolese reformers were actively soliciting support from women, their efforts made little difference to the overall rate of donations or bequests by women.

The data makes evident, however, why reforming popes and bishops were writing to queens and countesses: one Willa – the Frankish countess who founded the Badia – was enough to secure the future of a new religious foundation. She endowed the new monastery with its site within the city of Florence and with twenty-one houses and four massive estates (*curtes*), three with castles and churches, in the counties of Florence and Fiesole.[23] Through her relations with other wealthy elites and royalty,

19 On Mezzabarba see Nicolangelo D'Acunto, "Mezzabarba, Pietro," *DBI* 74: 65–66; idem, "Tensioni e convergenze fra monachesimo vallombrosano, papato e vescovi nel secolo XI," in Campagnoni, ed., *I Vallombrosani nella società italiana*, 57–81; McCready, *Odiosa sanctitas*, 7–34, 196–251.

20 Essential overviews of historical work on Vallombrosa are Francesco Salvestrini, "La storiografia sul movimento e sull'ordine monastico di Vallombrosa osb. Uno status quaestionis," *Reti Medievali Rivista* 2, no. 2 (2001): art. 3, www.rmojs.uninia.it; Francesco Salvestrini, "Bibliografia storica ragionata dell'Ordine vallombrosano," *Reti Medievali Rivista* 2, no. 2 (2001): art. 9, www.rmojs.uninia.it; and Giancarlo Andenna, "La storiografia vallombrosana nel Dopoguerra," in *L'Ordo vallisumbrosae tra XII e XIII secolo*, 7–30.

21 The total number of documents surveyed for each institution was 168 for the Badia, 748 for Camaldoli, and 334 for Vallombrosa. Donations and testamentary bequests constituted only eleven percent (18) of the Badia's total documentation, but these few tended to be large gifts of multiple estates. The proportions of donations and testamentary bequests within the documentation as a whole were higher for the hermitages: thirty-nine percent (294) of Camaldoli's and thirty-two percent (107) of Vallombrosa's. There were two donations by individual women to the Badia, twenty-five donations and five testamentary bequests to Camaldoli, and eight donations and one bequest to Vallombrosa.

22 Four women with male relatives donated to the Badia, bringing to six the total number of donations involving women. Camaldoli's total for donations and bequests involving women was 109 (30 individuals plus 79 with male relatives) and Vallombrosa's 32 (9 individuals plus 23 with male relatives).

23 ASF Dip. 00074004; Schiaparelli and Enriques, *Le carte... (Badia)* 1:10–17.

Willa arranged the gifts and privileges that made the Badia the most well-endowed ecclesiastical institution in Florence. As today, radical income inequality gave disproportionate charitable power to the women of the "one percent": the begging letters of popes and bishops might have been long shots, but the ramifications of any success would have been huge.

While generally Camaldoli's and Vallombrosa's elite patrons came from the next level down in the social hierarchy, from Lombard comital families whose patrimonies were substantial but more geographically restricted, there was at the very beginning of these institutions a less obvious, but very important, connection to this highest, margravial, stratum of nobility in northern Italy. This crucial connection to the "one percent" occurred because both Romuald and John Gualbert chose the right wilderness.

## Choosing the Right Wilderness

There may have been men seeking to follow in the footsteps of the desert fathers who wandered randomly into the forest closest at hand. But founders of successful hermit congregations, it seems, had a sort of eremitic GPS: they gravitated toward wilderness owned by prosperous ecclesiastical institutions with very good connections. The proprietors of these wilderness lands were the most essential early donors to each hermitage.

It was Bishop Teodald of Arezzo (1023–1036) who granted Romuald and his early followers at Camaldoli the site where they had erected their hermit cells. Recalling how Saint Romuald had asked him to consecrate to the Saviour "that church in the middle of the mountains which belongs to the see of Saint Donatus," Bishop Teodald proceeded to donate the church and the site to the hermits and additionally to bestow upon them "our forest of Asque" (specifically declared to be part of his lordship), and other properties.[24] The Bishop specified that the lands he gave for the use of the hermits were the property of his see (*iuris episcopii Sancti Donati*) and he also donated the tithes of several churches for their support. So Romuald had chosen a wilderness on lands of the Aretine see, and it may even have been the case that Bishop Teodald had invited him to come.[25] Certainly, Romuald knew that Arezzo's bishop at that time was not a nobody: Teodald, or Tedald, was the son of Tedald, Marquis of Canossa (d. 1012), and the brother of the ruling Marquis of Canossa, Boniface (husband of Beatrix and father of Matilda of Canossa). Peter Damian's life of Romuald depicts him not only in colloquy with emperors but also actively contacting the counts of Camerino about coming to their lands.[26] Surely he did not happen by chance onto lands under the control of Teodald of Canossa. At this early date

24 ASF Dip. 00074024, August 1027; Vedovato, *Camaldoli*, 126–28; Schiaparelli et al., *Regesto di Camaldoli*, 1: 35–36 (no. 85).

25 Caby, *L'érémitisme*, 71; Vedovato, *Camaldoli*, 19.

26 Peter Damian, *Vita beati Romualdi*, ed. Giovanni Tabacco, Fonti per la Storia d'Italia 94 (Rome: Istituto Storico Italiano, 1957), 47–48, 65 (Otto III); 64, 106–8 (Henry II); 74 (sending messengers to the counts of Camerino "seeking where he might find land suitable for bringing forth a harvest of souls").

(1027), there is no evidence of any established ties of the family with reform,[27] but such an association is evident for the see of Arezzo and for Teodald himself. In the late tenth century, Bishop Elimpert of Arezzo (986–1010) reformed the cathedral chapter, instituting the common life in a canonry built adjacent to the new cathedral he began, establishing a school there as well.[28] Teodald was in the chapter from 1009, brought Elimpert's cathedral to completion and, as bishop, consecrated it. In his charter for Camaldoli too, Teobald referred to Saint Romuald as *spiritualis pater noster*.[29]

In the case of Vallombrosa, this earliest key donor and protector was a woman: Itta, abbess of the convent of Sant'Ilario in Alfiano. Although she has not been securely identified, Itta was definitely from a very powerful elite family of either margravial or comital status. The density of landholdings of the comital Guidi family in this zone have led many to identify Itta as a member of this powerful lineage, whose lands extended well beyond the Casentino across Tuscany and the Romagna.[30] An equally compelling hypothesis, however, is that she was daughter of Ugo, marquis of Tuscany (d. 1001), who was a patron of the Badia.[31] Gualbert supposedly sought the advice of the hermit Teuzo, whose urban cell was next to the Badia, and of the abbot of Settimo, two of whose monks were already pursuing the eremitic life at the site that became Vallombrosa. This hagiographical tradition suggests that John knew where he was going when he went off into the "wilderness": he was going to a place already hosting hermits on the lands of a monastery with powerful connections either to the margraves of Tuscany or to the Guidi counts. It was also in the diocese of Fiesole, certainly safer than some place in the Florentine diocese since Gualbert had denounced its bishop.

27 Maria Luisa Ceccarelli Lemut has shown that the family had relations with various Tuscan monasteries and that ties to reform houses only became prominent in the late eleventh century under Matilda: "I Canossa e i monasteri toscani," in *I poteri dei Canossa da Reggio Emilia all'Europa. Atti del convegno internazionale di studi (Reggio Emilia – Carpineti, 29–31 ottobre 1992)*, ed. Paolo Golinelli (Bologna: Pàtron, 1994), 143–61; Peter Damian's letter no. 2, written c. 1042–1043 to Marquis Boniface, asking him to protect the monastery of S. Vincenzo and others in his territory, is the earliest evidence that I know of some connection between reformers and the house of Canossa: *Die Briefe des Petrus Damiani*, ed. Kurt Reindel, 4 vols. (Munich: Monumenta Germaniae historica, 1983), 1: 103–5; Peter Damian, *Letters*, trans. Owen J. Blum, 7 vols. (Washington DC: Catholic University of America Press, 1989–2005), 1:84–86.

28 *Arezzo nel medioevo*, ed. Giovanni Cherubini, Franco Franceschi, Andrea Barlucchi, Giulio Firpo (Rome: Giorgio Bretschneider Editore, 2012), 68–69, 90–91.

29 Maria Grandi, "Elimperto," *DBI* 42 (1993): 477–79; Delumeau, *Arezzo*, 1:498–504, 508–14; Vedovato, *Camaldoli*, 126–30.

30 Anna Benvenuti, "Sant'Ilario, Vallombrosa e Firenze," in Compagnoni, ed., *L'Ordo vallisumbrosae tra XII e XIII secolo*, 393–417, particularly 397–98; Francesco Salvestrini, "I rapporti con la grande aristocrazia rurale: I conti Guidi e i vallombrosani" in *Disciplina caritatis*, 303–26, especially 307–14; for earlier bibliography, see Natale Rauty, *Documenti per la storia dei conti Guidi in Toscana. Le origini e i primi secoli 887–1164*, Deputazione di storia patria per la Toscana, Documenti di storia italiana ser. 2, vol. 10 (Florence: Leo S. Olschki Editore, 2003), 315.

31 Rauty, *Documenti... Guidi*, 315. In a document of December 1058, *Iulitta filia Hugonis marchionis* is identified as abbess of S. Ilario; see Maria Elena Cortese, *Signori, castelli, città. L'aristocrazia del territorio fiorentino tra X e XII secolo* (Florence: Leo S. Olschki Editore, 2007), 90.

We do not know precisely when John arrived (c. 1038?) or when the abbess became aware of his presence. We do know that Itta likely orchestrated at least a modicum of royal approbation for the hermits and then she both sanctioned the community and provided lands to support it. She related in the elaborate preamble to her charter of July 3, 1039 that since, of course, it is laudable to support those who leave the world, throwing themselves upon the mercy of Christ and taking up arms against the devil in unceasing prayer, she "had received, as you know, those men of the monastery of San Miniato, whom we believe to be well known to you, in the hermitage which is called Vallombrosa in the place called Acquabella" (which, she hastened to add, was the property of her monastery, Sant'Ilario in Alfiano).[32] God, seeing their righteous desire to flee the multitude and build a sacred life in a solitary place, caused word of their works to spread, until it reached the ears of Emperor Conrad, his wife the Empress Ghisla, and their son King Henry, when they happen to have come to Florence. The sovereigns diligently inquired about the hermits. When they learned that the oratory there had not been consecrated, due to a vacancy in the see of Fiesole after the death of Bishop Jacopo, they sent a member of their entourage, Rodulf (Rotho), a Cluniac monk and bishop of Paderborn, to consecrate the church. This was likely a reconnaissance mission as well as a diplomatic effort to calm local ecclesial tensions. Regardless of the fact that Gualbert had publicly denounced Emperor Conrad's appointed bishop of Florence, it seems some rapprochement was reached and approbation was given.[33] Bishop Rodulf consecrated the altar of the hermit's oratory and then Abbess Itta conceded to the hermits use of the land where they were staying and the church they had built. She did so with the requirement that they pray for her soul and those of her relatives, and that they annually on the feast of Saint Hilary bring to the altar of the convent's church in Alfiano a pound of wax and another of oil. She underscored that the hermitage was "under the power and defense of the aforesaid monastery of Sant'Ilario, on whose property that church was located, and under my power, and that of my successors, to rule, defend, and order."[34] The revocable character of the concession – this was not an alienation of

32 ASF Dip. 00074035: "quosdam uiros de sancti Miniatis monasterio quos vobis bene notos esse credimus in eremo que Vallisumbrosa vocatur sicut vos scitis suscepimus in loco qui dicitur Aquabella in proprietatem silicet nostri monasterii quidem in onore sancti Illari sito Alfiano." Salvestrini has pointed out that this identification of the hermits as men from the episcopal foundation of San Miniato glosses over Gualbert's flight from, and strident critique of, this monastery: Salvestrini, "I rapporti," 309.

33 Andrea of Strumi's *Vita* (cap. 32) credits the intervention of the emperor's son, Henry, soon to ascend to the throne: *MGH, SS* 30, 2: 1086; see also Nicola Vasaturo, *Vallombrosa: L'abbazia e la congregazione, note storiche*, ed. Giordano Monzio Compagnoni, Archivio Vallombrosano 1 (Vallombrosa: Edizioni Vallombrosa, 1994), 6–8.

34 ASF Dip. 00074035; this section of the charter is given in the partial transcription in Rauty, *Documenti... Guidi*, 315–16: "In ipsa ecclesia et oratorio Sancte Marie pro anime mee remedium et parentum meorum, tam vivorum quam defuntorum, concedo et confirmo in tali tinore ut prenominata ecclesia cum omnibus rebus, quas modo ibi concedo et confirmo, e quas Deo annuente deinceps ibidem pertinere debebunt, semper sit sub potestatem et defensionem prenominati monasterii S. Illari, in cuius proprietatem ipsa ecclesia sita est, et sub mea potestate et mearum subcessorum ad regendum et defensandum, sive ordinandum et ita volo ut prepositus, sive abbas, qui pro tempore ibi e santorum auctoritate et nostra donatione ordinatus fuerit,

property but a grant of *beneficium* – reveals a prudent caution in light of Gualbert's actions, but Itta's support was crucial at this critical moment in the fledgling community's history.

In sum, members of the highest strata of the nobility in northern Italy – of the marquises of Tuscany and of Canossa, or the Guidi counts – were also the key early donors for these two innovative reforming hermitages, only they were acting as leaders of established ecclesiastical institutions. It is worth noting here the importance of these "non-heirs" – that is, those members of great lineages designated for religious life or ecclesiastical careers – as well as the uncanny ability of hermits to find wildernesses under their control.

### Donors of More Modest Means

Although all three institutions received support from the highest strata of elites, not all received gifts from those further down the social pyramid. The Badia received very substantial donations while both Camaldoli and Vallombrosa attracted small gifts, usually of a single piece of land, from small and medium landholders. Some of the earliest donations to Camaldoli – including the earliest donations by women – were such tiny offerings. They cluster in the village of Monte, which was below Camaldoli on the east slope of the Archiano Valley, about two hours from the hermitage by foot. John and his wife Boniza in 1038, for example, gave one piece of land with vines, while Bezza, widow of Pepo, in 1047 gave a single plot of land.[35] Vallombrosa also attracted this tier of small donors. On June 7, 1079, for example, Ghisla, daughter of the deceased Gerardo and wife of Giovanni di Pietro, acting with his consent and that of their two sons, donated a piece of land in a place called Ulmitulo. A married couple, Rodulfo son of Stefano and his wife Liuza, in March of 1088 gave to Vallombrosa one piece of land in Tremoleto (in the Arno Valley south of Pisa).[36]

Although the pattern is less clear with Vallombrosa, Camaldoli's modest donors definitely were neighbors of the hermitage. This accords with the pattern I found at

pro predicta eclesia Sancte Marie et pro omnibus pertenentiis eius, omni anno in festivitate Sancti Illari, in ipsa ecclesia et monasterio sito Alfiano, ante altare eius, sive per se, sive per missum suum, pro singnum pensionis ponat de ceram libram unam et de oleo libram alteram, ad luminaria faciendum." Anna Benvenuti recounts the long sad story of how in the thirteenth century the Vallombrosans turned the tables on S. Ilario, gained control of its monastery, and forced out the women religious there. Benvenuti, "Sant'Ilario," 393–417.

35 ASF Dip. 00000570 March 1038, 00000755 October 1047 and Schiaparelli et al., *Regesto di Camaldoli*, 1: 73, 100 (nos. 173, 242); other small donations from this village were made by Donnello and his wife Gania and by two couples – Vivenzio and Masaria, Crisenzio and Burga – acting together, ASF Dip. 00000530 April 1036, 00000656 March 1042 and Schiaparelli et al., *Regesto di Camaldoli*, 1: 65, 85 (nos. 155, 206). For a discussion of these particular donations in relation to others in the Casentino see Chris Wickham, *The Mountains and the City: The Tuscan Apennines in the Middle Ages* (Oxford: Clarendon Press, 1988), 238, 247–48, 251–52, 259–67.

36 ASF Dip. 00001725 7 June 1079 and 00002277 March 1088; Francesco Salvestrini, "Il patrimonio. Secoli XII–XIII," in idem, *Disciplina caritatis*, 23–62, to this point, 27–30; idem, *Santa Maria di Vallombrosa: Patrimonio e vita economica di un grande monastero medievale*, Biblioteca storica Toscana 33 (Florence: Leo S. Olschki, 1998), 49–50.

Verona in an analysis of all donations in the diocese from the early Middle Ages to 1150: the least affluent donors gave to local institutions.[37] In Camaldoli's case, the institution was associated with reform, but these modest donors were likely motivated more by proximity than by any decided preference for religious innovation. Both Camaldoli and Vallombrosa, however, like innovative ecclesiastical institutions in the Veronese diocese, had a broad social basis of support: they attracted donations from the very wealthiest elites, from more local notables, and from medium and small landholders.

### Conditions Fostering Female Patronage

When we look beyond the key initial donors – those members of the margravial or comital elite who could well be considered founders or at least co-founders of Camaldoli and Vallombrosa – there are slightly different patterns in the chronology of donations involving women to each institution. Individual women and women acting with their male kin started donating to Camaldoli very soon after it was established, whereas individual women and those donating with their male relatives did not start patronizing Vallombrosa until 1068 – that is, three decades after its establishment.

The consistent and strong support of the bishops of Arezzo for Camaldoli likely made a difference in this regard. Donations began within a decade of Bishop Teodald's initial 1027 privilege, remained steady at low levels until the 1070s and 1090s when they peak. The earliest donation involving a woman was in 1036 – Donnello and his wife Maria, called Gania – followed two years later by a gift from John and his wife Bonizia, and in 1042 by a joint donation from two couples – Vivenzio and Massaia acting with Crisenzio and Burga – and in October of 1047, by the widow Bezza.[38] All these were neighbors of the hermitage. The widow Bezza's donation came just after the first imperial confirmation to Camaldoli in 1046, but for the others donating earlier the approbation of their local bishop was enough. And all these came before the first papal grant of protection in 1072.

The delay in women's donations to Vallombrosa was part of a more general pattern of donor reticence that was most likely occasioned by the community's high-profile battles with ecclesiastical authorities.[39] While historians have been fascinated by the dramatic and at points violent conflicts of Vallombrosa's monks

37 Maureen C. Miller, "Donors, their Gifts, and Religious Innovation in Medieval Verona," *Speculum* 66, no. 1 (1991): 27–42, particularly 33–34.

38 ASF Dip. 00000530 (April 1036); 00000570 (March 1038); 00000656 (March 1042); 00000755 (October 1047); Schiaparelli et al., *Regesto di Camaldoli* 1: 65, 73, 85–86, 100 (nos. 155, 173, 206, 242).

39 While beyond the scope of the present inquiry, early support (or the lack thereof) for Vallombrosa merits further investigation. As will be obvious in the discussion that follows, the evidence for significant support before 1068 comes primarily from later hagiographical sources, which might well be more critically evaluated, and not from the extant documentary record. Salvestrini's excellent research on the patrimony of Vallombrosa has focused more on the later period of the fourteenth and fifteenth centuries; he treats the eleventh and twelfth centuries as an undifferentiated "early period." See Salvestrini, *Santa Maria di Vallombrosa*, 41–56, and "Il patrimonio," 26–43.

with the bishop of Florence that culminated in an ordeal by fire at Settimo in 1068, donors reacted with reserve. In the archival collection for Santa Maria d'Acquabella, there are only seven documents in the period from Abbess Itta's concession of July 3, 1039 until the ordeal at Settimo on February 13, 1068. Only one of these is a donation: on August 27, 1043 Grimaldo, son of the deceased Baldo, donated lands with a church in Perticaia (near Rignano sull'Arno, about twenty kilometers west of Vallombrosa).[40] Historians have asserted, however, other significant gifts to Vallombrosa in this period in the form of monasteries given over to be reformed (San Salvatore di Settimo, Santa Reparata di Marradi, San Michele in Passignano) or of lands where monasteries were built (San Salvi, San Pietro di Moscheto, San Paolo di Razzuolo, San Cassiano di Montescalari).[41] The chief, and sometimes only, source for these donations is the c. 1092 life of John Gualbert by Andrea da Strumi. In chapter 25, Andrea recounts,

> At that time noble and faithful men from different places began to flock to such a father. Some offered him lands, begging him to build new monasteries on them; others offered him ancient and dissolute monasteries, urging him with incessant pleas to take them under his governance and try to reform them according to his principles. Thus, he newly built the renowned monastery of San Salvi and in Moscheto another in honor of Saint Peter prince of the apostles and in Razzuolo one in honor of Saint Paul. Then he received the ancient house of Passignano under his governance and another in Romagna named in honor of Saint Reparata. He then built another monastery at Montescalari.[42]

Gifts by three men made in charters dated March 26 and April 16, 1048 provided the land on which San Salvi was built, while Count Anselm of Pietramala and Ottaviano of the Ubaldini donated the properties for San Pietro di Moscheto and San Paolo di Razzuolo respectively.[43] The donor behind San Cassiano di Montescalari remains nameless. For the monasteries given over to Gualbert to be reformed, only the problematic case of Settimo supplies the names of the donors. An anony-

40 ASF Dip. 00000687 (August 27, 1043).

41 Miccoli, *Pietro Igneo*, 135–38.

42 *MGH*, SS 30.2:1086: "Per idem tempus ceperunt at tantum patrem concurrere de diversis partibus viri nobiles et fideles. Alii ei offerebant loca cum suplicatione nimia ad edificanda noviter cenobia; alii vetusta et dissoluta offerebant monasteria et instabant precibus nimiis et importunis, ut ea ipse in suo sumeret regimine et suam normam studeret corrigere. Tunc sancti Salvii famosum cenobium noviter edificavit. Tunc in Musceta alterum in honore sancti Petri apostolorum principis. Tunc in Razolum in honore sancti Pauli. Tunc in suo regimine vetustum suscepit Passinianum et alterum in Romania sub nomine et honore sanctae Reparatae. Tunc aedificavit alium in Scalario monte."

43 ASF Dip. 00000758 (March 26, 1048) in which two brothers, Peter and Gerard, resident in Florence give the church of San Salvi in a place called Carrari as well as lands next to and near the church with the stipulation that a monastery following the rule of Saint Benedict be established there; ASF Dip. 00000763 (April 16, 1048) in which Roland, called the Moor, also donates the church of San Salvi, described as in the *plebs* of Santa Reparata in the city of Florence in the place called Paratinule, along with other lands, with a similar stipulation that a Benedictine monastery be built; Salvestrini, "I rapporti," 306.

mous twelfth-century life of John Gualbert recounts that Count William, called Bulgarello, of the Cadolingi dynasty invited the holy man to the monastery to subject it to his governance. In the 1060s there clearly was some Vallombrosan presence, but San Salvatore at Settimo was not among the houses confirmed to Santa Maria d'Acquabella in Urban II's bull of 1090.[44] In sum, from Vallombrosa's establishment to 1068 there are very few donations and all, save Abbess Itta's, appear to have been made by men.

This period, of course, was most notable for the campaign against simony by John Gualbert, his monks, and their supporters. From 1064 they denounced Bishop Peter Mezzabarba of Florence and so riled up the populace against him that Pope Alexander II (early in 1064?) wrote a letter addressed to the clergy and people of Florence ordering the monks to cease their preaching and return to their cloisters.[45] This too John Gualbert ignored, continuing to agitate, and finally challenging the bishop to undergo the judgment of God in an ordeal by fire. Those angered by the fanaticism of the Vallombrosan supporters – including Goffredo, duke of Lotharingia and Margrave of Canossa, and the imperial chancellor Gregory, bishop of Vercelli – rallied in support of Mezzabarba and it was probably the forces of Goffredo who attacked the Vallombrosan monastery of San Salvi in Florence in the hopes of capturing Gualbert. A delegation of Vallombrosan abbots put their case before the pope at the spring synod of 1067, but the fathers gathered there took their fellow bishop's side and even Peter Damian denounced the monks. Pope Alexander tried to mediate and sent Damian to preach peace in Florence, but his attempts at conciliation failed completely. Even a visit to the city in the summer of 1067 by the pope himself did not calm the strife.[46] Further violence culminated in the trial by fire on February 13, 1068 at Settimo. Bishop Peter, of course, refused to attend, but the chosen monk,

44 *MGH* SS 30.2: 1106; Miccoli, *Pietro Igneo*, 137–38; Salvestrini, "I rapporti," 306.

45 Philip Jaffe, S. Löwenfeld, F. Kaltenbrunner, and P. Ewald, eds., *Regesta pontificum romanorum ab condita ecclesia ad annum post Christum natum MCXCVIII*, 2 vols. (Leipzig: Veit, 1885–88), 1:574 (no. 4552); Davidsohn, *Storia di Firenze*, 1:335–36; Miccoli, *Pietro Igneo*, 13–14; D'Acunto, "Lotte," 285–88; McCready, *Odiosa sanctitas*, 12–13, underscoring that this letter of Alexander is a fragment and undated (Löwenfeld assigned it to early 1064, but it could be from after the Roman synod of 1067); holding to the 1064 date is Kathleen G. Cushing, "Of *Locustae* and Dangerous Men: Damian, the Vallombrosans, and Eleventh-century Reform," *Church History* 74 (2005): 740–57, especially 744. The Italian historiography on the causes and consequences of the Vallombrosan staging of the ordeal is essential. Readers should eschew the naïve interpretation of Colin Morris, "*Judicium Dei*: The Social and Political Significance of the Ordeal in the Eleventh Century," *Studies in Church History* 12 (1975): 95–11, especially 105–7, in favor of the works analyzed by Francesco Salvestrini, "La tradizione storiografica," in *Disciplina caritatis*, 151–79, especially 160–65: in addition to Miccoli (cited above), Yoram Milo, "Dissonance between Papal and Local Reform Interests in pre-Gregorian Tuscany," *Studi Medievali*, ser. 3, 20 (1979): 69–86; Nicolangelo D'Acunto, "Il latte nell'immaginario religioso," in *La civiltà del latte. Fonti, simpoli e prodotti dal Tardoantico al Novecento* (Brescia: Fondazione civiltà bresciana, 2011), 295–308; Anna Benvenuti, "San Giovanni Gaulberto e Firenze," in *I Vallombrosani nella società italiana dei secoli XI e XII, Vallombrosa, 3–4 settembre 1993. I Colloquio Vallombrosano*, ed. Giordano Monzio Compagnoni (Vollombrosa: Edizioni Vallombrosa, 1995), 83–112.

46 Davidsohn, *Storia di Firenze*, 1:339–50; Miccoli, *Pietro Igneo*, 21–24; D'Acunto, "Lotte," 296–303; McCready, *Odiosa sanctitas*, 29–34.

also named Peter (and ever after *Igneo* or Fiery Peter), supposedly walked through fire miraculously unhurt. Radicals, led by the archdeacon Hildebrand, gained the upper hand in Rome, and the Lenten synod that year deposed Mezzabarba.[47]

The long drought in donations ended nearly immediately after these dramatic events. In May, Guido IV, Count of Modigliana, and his wife the Countess Ermellina, ceded a holding (*sors*) in Tavorra. Over the next decade two other couples made donations, and in February 1077 Burga daughter of Berardo, with her father consenting, offered several pieces of land.[48] Although the number of donations overall in these early years for both institutions is meager, the delay in women's donations to Vallombrosa, in comparison to support for Camaldoli, suggests that the approbation of ecclesiastical authorities for a new reforming institution may have been more important to women donors than to their male counterparts.

The Guidi donation to Vallombrosa in May 1068, just weeks after the ordeal at Settimo and the Lenten synod's deposition of Bishop Peter Mezzabarba, opens several other important differences between this reforming institution and Camaldoli. First, although many within Florence and within the curia were opposed to Vallombrosa's public campaign to depose Mezzabarba, it worked – and, importantly, it worked with elite donors. The Guidi's initial donation was modest, but members of this family went on to make much more substantial gifts to the congregation, including that of their family monastery, San Fedele di Strumi. And this comital family's power soared through an alliance with the house of Canossa: Count Guido V was a strong supporter of the Countess Matilda and in 1099 she designated him her adopted son. The great countess and papal ally joined Guido in a donation to Vallombrosa on November 19, 1103 ceding half the castle of Magnale and lands of the estate there.[49] Shortly thereafter, Matilda reconsidered her relationship with Guido, negated her adoption of him and on her death in 1115 left her vast patrimony to the Apostolic See.

Camaldoli's quieter pursuit of reform took a lot longer to attract donations from the wealthiest local lay lineages. Its most important benefactors remained the bishops of Arezzo for some time. It was only in the early twelfth century that donations from lay comital families begin. On February 1, 1109, Count Ugo, son of the deceased Count Uguccione, donated to the hermitage of San Salvatore the church and monastery of Santa Maria at Morrona with all its lands. Part of the powerful lineage of the Cadolingi, who held lands throughout Tuscany, this Count Ugo also added substantially to this donation two months later.[50] The Guidi counts exchanged one piece of land in Soci with Camaldoli and sold the hermitage some lands there too, but it

47 Davidsohn, *Storia di Firenze*, 1:350–59; Miccoli, *Pietro Igneo*, 24–45, 139–57; D'Acunto, "Lotte," 303–9; McCready, *Odiosa sanctitas*, 196–206, 252–76.

48 ASF Dip. 00001209 (May 1068), 00001755 (May 2, 1071?), 00001490 (February 1075), 00001593 (February 1077); also Rauty, *Documenti... Guidi*, 92–94 (no. 49) for the 1068 donation.

49 Rauty, *Documenti... Guidi*, 189–92 (no. 134), and on the ascent of the family, 14–16; Salvestrini, "I rapporti," 323–24.

50 ASF Dip. 00003243 (February 1, 1109), 00003256 (April 6, 1109) and Schiaparelli et al., *Regesto di Camaldoli* 2:29–30, 32–33 (nos. 695, 701). The second document is a sale of half an estate and castle, but at the symbolic price of *unam par pellium*. On the Marchiones, see Delumeau, *Arezzo*, 1:307–37, 2:1417.

was not until the 1130s that the lineage donated to San Salvatore. On April 28, 1134, Countess Imilia and her young son Count Guido VI asked the prior of Camaldoli to institute a female monastery at the church of Santa Maria di Poppiena, promising to provide all that was needed to establish the new institution. And in 1137, Imilia, acting on her own, donated to Camaldoli all her rights in the church of San Giusto near Gricciano and lands attached to it, previously conceded to her daughter the abbess Sofia, in order that a women's monastery be established there under the authority of San Salvatore.[51]

To return to the questions raised at the beginning of this essay, medieval Tuscan women showed no marked preference for reformed institutions, but in the case of Vallombrosa an elite woman, the abbess Itta, was a key early supporter (and perhaps should be considered a co-founder of the institution). The essential roles played by the wealthiest noble families in northern Italy in establishing all three of these institutions, traditional and reformed, make obvious why popes and bishops actively cultivated relations with elite women: the support of the medieval "one percent" assured the success and longevity of ecclesiastical institutions. Anyone trying to foster enduring religious change needed elite support to be successful. It does appear that the agonistic reform strategies of Vallombrosa kept women donors at a distance until seeming divine approbation led to papal and episcopal approval. The success of Vallombrosa's high-stakes gamble on the ordeal at Settimo did pay off with donors and likely influenced similar risky strategies attempted by their supporter Hildebrand when he became Pope Gregory VII. But Vallombrosa was no more successful than Camaldoli: the eleventh-century church embraced both the dramatic, confrontational monks of Santa Maria d'Acquabella and the quiet, retiring hermits of San Salvatore. Not only did two very different interpretations of reform in the religious life both thrive in this Tuscan sample, but so too did earlier traditional Benedictine foundations like the Badia. To a certain degree, lay patronage, including the patronage of laywomen, was relatively evenly apportioned among different visions of the "best" religious life.[52] Little wonder, then, that contestation over reform endured for such a protracted period over the eleventh and twelfth centuries.

51 Rauty, *Documenti Guidi*, 246–47, 250–52 (nos. 179, 184).

52 Although some scholars have posited a strategy among Florentine elites of backing Vallombrosa in order to limit the power in the countryside of the bishops of Florence and their powerful Canossa allies, elites generally tended to hedge their bets and support a range of religious institutions: Salvestrini, "I rapporti," 305, 312–15; D'Acunto, "Lotte," 287–90; Milo, "Dissonance," 78–82; Miccoli, *Pietro Igneo*, 5; Ceccarelli Lemut, "I Canossa," 145–46, 154; Wickham, *Mountains and the City*, 196.

20

# LAYWOMEN'S LEADERSHIP IN MEDIEVAL MIRACLE CULTS: EVIDENCE FROM BRITAIN, c. 1150–1250

RACHEL KOOPMANS

This chapter seeks to highlight an arena in which medieval women exercised religious leadership that has been largely overlooked: the miracle cult. Miracle cults, the phenomenon of people claiming miraculous experiences through the merits and action of deceased saints, were common in the medieval centuries and sprang up in numerous places throughout Europe.[1] Other aspects of saints' cults, such as the composition of hagiographic texts, the performance of liturgies and processions, and the patronage of major works of cultic art and architecture, were largely (though certainly not entirely) governed by religious men with wealth, literacy, and elite status.[2] Miracle cults, in contrast, provided a much more open and freeform arena for religious leadership of people of all social classes, including lay, lower-status, and illiterate women. Thus, analysis of miracle cults is important not only for expanding our sense of how medieval women exercised religious leadership, but also which types of women had the opportunity to lead.[3]

1 For an excellent general survey of the medieval cult of the saints, with good attention to miracle cults, see Robert Bartlett, *Why Can the Dead Do Such Great Things: Saints and Worshippers from the Martyrs to the Reformation* (Princeton: Princeton University Press, 2013), esp. 333–409.

2 Since male religious communities possessed most of the principal relics of the saints, this governance is not surprising. For a handful of medieval female religious communities that produced miracle collections, see Jane Tibbetts Schulenburg, "Women's Monasteries and Sacred Space: The Promotion of Saints' Cults and Miracles," in *Gender and Christianity in Medieval Europe: New Perspectives*, ed. Lisa M. Bitel and Felice Lifshitz (Philadelphia: University of Pennsylvania Press, 2008), 68–86, and for women's writing of saints' *vitae*, see, among much other literature, the studies of Jocelyn Wogan-Browne and Sean Field in this volume. Women's participation in the cults of Anne, Catherine of Alexandria, the Virgin, and such "universal" female saints has been treated by a number of recent scholars (see, for example, Katherine J. Lewis, *The Cult of St Katherine of Alexandria in Late Medieval England* [Woodbridge: Boydell Press, 2000]), but these cults are of less interest here as they were generally not miracle cults.

3 Women of lesser status who found the means to dedicate themselves to informal religious lifestyles have been the subject of increasing attention: see, for example, Anneke B. Mulder-Bakker, "Devoted Holiness in the Lay World," in *The Oxford Handbook of Women and Gender in Medieval Europe*, ed. Judith M. Bennett and Ruth Mazo Karras (Oxford: Oxford University Press, 2013), 464–479. For studies relating to the religious experience of the majority of the female population – that is, laywomen with few financial resources who did not commit themselves to a religious lifestyle – see Peter Biller, "The Common Woman in the Western Church in the Thirteenth and Early Fourteenth Centuries," *Women in the Church*, ed. W. J. Sheils and Diana Wood, Studies in Church History vol. 27 (Oxford: Basil Blackwell, 1990), 127–157;

Evidence for laywomen's leadership roles in miracle cults is largely found within written collections of miracle stories and canonization dossiers, but there are visual sources as well. This essay begins with an analysis of two particularly striking images depicting laywomen from the early thirteenth-century stained glass of Canterbury Cathedral. These two panels, which picture a miracle of Thomas Becket, will serve as springboards into a study of two important aspects of laywomen's cultic leadership: first, the collective leadership of groups of laywomen at saints' tombs and in their local neighborhoods, and second, the creation and distribution of contact relics (dust from saints' tombs, pieces of clothing worn by saints, and the like) by individual laywomen. On both of these topics, I will focus on laywomen's cultic leadership in non-domestic contexts. There is no question that women took on cultic leadership roles within their own families. The vast majority of the nursing of the ill or injured was done by female family members, and these female caretakers were normally the ones who made decisions about whether and how to seek miraculous aid.[4] These decisions focused family resources on particular saints and cultic sites and often had long-term consequences for the entire household, husbands included. Women who decided to appeal to saints on their own behalf, moreover, made up a significant proportion of those claiming miraculous experiences. When they told miracle stories about themselves, these women furthered the cult and made themselves into public figures, sometimes quite remarkably so, such as a woman who, a miracle collector tells us, travelled to Rome to tell her story to the pope himself.[5]

The stories that have received the least attention from scholars, though, are those that show laywomen making cultic decisions and taking leading action on behalf of *non-relatives* – neighbors, friends, acquaintances, and strangers.[6] Because modern

Katherine L. French, "Maiden's Lights and Wives' Stories: Women's Parish Guilds in Late Medieval England," *Sixteenth Century Journal* 29:2 (1998): 399–425; Carole Hill, *Women and Religion in Late Medieval Norwich* (Woodbridge: Boydell Press, 2010); Nicola A. Lowe, "Women's Devotional Bequests of Textiles in the Late Medieval English Parish Church, c.1350–1550," *Gender and History* 22:2 (2010): 407–429; and the studies of female pilgrims cited below.

4 For discussion of women's invocations and pilgrimages, see especially Sari Katajala-Peltomaa, *Gender, Miracles, and Daily Life: The Evidence of Fourteenth-century Canonization Processes* (Turnhout: Brepols, 2009), 115–126 and Leigh Ann Craig, *Wandering Women and Holy Matrons: Women as Pilgrims in the Later Middle Ages* (Leiden: Brill, 2009), 79–130. Craig analyzes stories from seven lengthy fourteenth- and fifteenth-century miracle collections, finding that "in both raw numbers and in proportion to their overall presence, women outstripped men as intercessors. Taking all collections together, more than two-fifths of women, either alone or in groups, sought help for someone else, but only about a quarter of men did the same" (92). Both Craig and Katajala-Peltomaa focus on women's invocations for family members.

5 Thomas of Monmouth, *The Life and Passion of William of Norwich*, trans. Miri Rubin (London: Penguin, 2014), book 6, ch. 14, 163–165.

6 Susan Signe Morrison voices a general assumption in *Women Pilgrims in Late Medieval England: Private Piety as Public Performance* (London: Routledge, 2000), 146, when she writes: "The woman pilgrim rarely exists in literature and history except in terms of family, whether as wife, mother or sister." There is some discussion of the care of children by neighbors in Barbara Hanawalt, "Narratives of a Nurturing Culture: Parents and Neighbors in Medieval England," in *Of Good and Ill Repute: Gender and Social Control in Medieval England* (New York: Oxford University Press, 1998), 158–177, though her focus is on parents. In her study of the late thirteenth-century inquest into the miracles of St Louis, Sharon Farmer has ex-

observers do not expect to see medieval laywomen acting outside of domestic contexts, some of this evidence, such as the panels of Canterbury stained glass, has been strikingly misinterpreted. The majority of the material I will discuss derives from English sources dated c.1150–1250, though to demonstrate the breath of laywomen's cultic leadership and the potential for further study, I will utilize some source material from other places and periods. When our viewfinders are set to see these women, they quickly come into focus. In fact, it is hard to see how medieval miracle cults could have functioned without the ideas, initiative, and collective action of laywomen, both within and without domestic circles.[7]

### The Miracle of Goditha of Canterbury in Canterbury Cathedral's Stained Glass

Near the top of one of the ambulatory windows surrounding Thomas Becket's shrine in Canterbury Cathedral is a panel that pictures six women together (Figure 11, Trinity Chapel nIV 49).[8] Two women stand in a doorway on the left, looking at a middle grouping of three women. The woman at the centre is hunched over, with a bowed head and hands held helplessly before her. She is clearly ill and immobilized: two other women hold her up and move her along a path or street. On the far right, a sixth woman stands at a doorway, her hands open in reception. The narrative is continued in a second panel (Figure 12, Trinity Chapel nIV 50).[9] The ill woman, clothed as she was in the previous panel, is now sitting in a chair at the far left. A woman kneels before her and bathes her leg. Taking up the majority of the panel is a scene set above Becket's tomb, the low structure with two openings on the bottom center right. Three figures stand above the tomb. The central figure, her position accentuated and framed by the candles standing on the tomb, is a woman. She holds a spoon

plored the ways in which these stories show how poor, unattached, and ill women were cared for in Paris, often by other women: see Sharon Farmer, *Surviving Poverty in Medieval Paris: Gender, Ideology, and the Daily Lives of the Poor* (Ithaca: Cornell University Press, 2002), 119–121, 136–138, 160–163.

7 For a compelling article regarding women's "active roles in the creation of various saints' cults" (though in this case not miracle cults, but rather the promotion of female religious companions as saints), see Maiju Lehmijoki-Gardner, "The Women Behind their Saints: Dominican Women's Institutional Uses of the Cults of their Religious Companions," in *Images of Sanctity: Essays in Honour of Gary Dickson*, ed. Debra Higgs Strickland (Leiden: Brill, 2007), 5–24. See also Donald S. Prudlo, "Mothers and the Martyr: The Unlikely Patronage of a Medieval Dominican Preacher," in *Journal of the History of Sexuality* 21:2 (2012): 313–324. Prudlo argues that the presence of an atypically large percentage of childbirth miracles in Peter of Verona's miracle collections represents a "lay appropriation of the cult," (p. 317) though it seems more appropriate to term this a *female* appropriation of the cult.

8 The indispensable guide to the Trinity Chapel ambulatory windows is the work of Madeline Caviness, *The Windows of Christ Church Cathedral, Canterbury*, Corpus Vitrearum Medii Aevi: Great Britain, Volume II (London, 1981), at 177–214; see also her earlier treatment in Caviness, *The Early Stained Glass of Canterbury Cathedral* (Princeton, NJ: Princeton University Press, 1977), esp. 146–150.

9 For description and restoration diagrams of nIV 49 and 50, see Caviness, *Windows of Christ Church*, 182, and for further discussion, Rachel Koopmans, "Kentish Pilgrims in Canterbury Cathedral's Miracle Windows," *Journal of the Warburg and Courtauld Institutes* LXXX (2017): 1–27, esp. 16–18.

Figure 11 Local laywomen help Goditha to Becket's tomb. (Canterbury Cathedral, Trinity Chapel nIV 49; panel dated c. 1213–20. Photograph: The Cathedral Studios, reproduced courtesy of the Chapter, Canterbury Cathedral.)

Figure 12 A woman bathes Goditha's leg while another woman at Becket's tomb holds a bowl and mixes up the relic water. (Canterbury Cathedral, Trinity Chapel nIV 50; panel dated c. 1213–20. Photograph: The Cathedral Studios, reproduced courtesy of the Chapter, Canterbury Cathedral.)

in one hand and a bowl in another. On her right, a layman pours liquid into her bowl from a flask, while on her left, a monk holds a smaller vessel and ladles or spoons something towards the women's bowl. The Latin inscriptions on these two panels are in a sadly scrambled state, but otherwise the panels are in quite good condition, without a great deal of damage or restoration.[10]

There are no known medieval or early modern descriptions of the contents of the Trinity Chapel windows. Deciding whose stories are pictured in this glass means reading through two very lengthy miracle collections composed in the 1170s by Benedict of Peterborough and William of Canterbury, the source texts for the glaziers, and searching for possible matches. The first person who thought he knew what these panels pictured was Dr. Arthur Mason, a canon of Canterbury, who wrote a guidebook to Canterbury's glass in 1925. He suggested, "perhaps the cure of [the nun] Petron[e]lla of Polesworth is depicted. On the left she is being brought to her abbess in a fit of epilepsy… on the right, a bowl is filled with water at the tomb, and the lady is seen seated close by, being bathed with the water."[11] The subjects of the miracle windows were re-evaluated by Bernard Rackham in 1949 and by Madeline Caviness in 1981, and these two panels have been discussed by other more recent commentators as well.[12] Through it all, Mason's supposition has stuck: these panels have been read as picturing the recovery of an epileptic nun.

However, a careful look at Petronella's story, found near the beginning of William of Canterbury's miracle collection, raises serious questions about this identification.[13] In William's description of Petronella's illness and cure, there is no mention of her ever being presented to her abbess. There is no instance in which the nuns (or anyone else) support Petronella as she is in an epileptic fit, nor, most troublingly, is there any mention of the use of the Becket relic water so prominently featured on the second panel. William's story of Petronella's recovery revolves around her rejection of human

10 A copy of nIV 49 made by George Austin, Sr. in 1838 and installed in Thorney Abbey has the inscription CONVALET EGROTAM. When Mason described the panel in 1925, he saw the inscription as something quite different: *"[no]n valet stare."* In 1949, Rackham recorded the inscription as CONVALET EGRO[*EFVNCT*], which is what it reads today. Inscriptions were often swapped between panels by restorers, so even if CONVALET EGROTAM were an original inscription, there is no guarantee that it was originally attached to this panel, and the woman certainly does not seem to be the act of recovering. A copy of nIV 50 made by Austin has the inscription IMPH_NGMNACVMCELOTA; Rackham recorded S:DE*M*IMPHA*T*-*V*NONGINCHOTA, from which Caviness picked out two words, IMPHA [*[l]ympha*] and INCHOTA [*inchota*] – "healing water" and "unfinished."

11 A. J. Mason, *A Guide to the Ancient Glass in Canterbury Cathedral* (Canterbury, 1925), 30.

12 See Bernard Rackham, *The Ancient Glass of Canterbury Cathedral* (London, 1949), 88 and Caviness, *Windows of Christ Church*, 182; for further references, see, for example, Morrison, *Women Pilgrims*, 96; Anne Harris, "Pilgrimage, Performance and Stained Glass at Canterbury Cathedral," in *Art and Architecture of Late Medieval Pilgrimage*, ed. Sarah Blick and Rita Tekippe (Leiden: Brill, 2004), 243–281, at 273; M. A. Michael, *Stained Glass of Canterbury Cathedral* (London, 2004), 106–108; and Marie-Pierre Gelin, *"Lumen ad revelationem gentium": Iconographie et Liturgie à Christ Church, Canterbury, 1175–1220* (Turnhout: Brepols, 2006), 80 and 208.

13 William of Canterbury, *Miracula S. Thomae*, ed. J. C. Robertson in *Materials for the History of Thomas Becket*, vol. 1 (London, 1875), 162–164.

doctors and medical aid. In an extended analogy comparing Petronella to a sick sheep, William describes how Petronella "hastens from the sheepfold and presents herself to her shepherd, the overseer Thomas of Canterbury, just like a shepherd of sheep. The daughter begs the father for her health with prayers, and having been heard, she leaves, not knowing whether she obtained what she had sought."[14] By this, William probably meant that Petronella went on a pilgrimage to Canterbury, though it is possible that William meant simply that she presented herself to Becket in prayer. In any case, William attributes Petronella's recovery to this appeal to her "shepherd," and makes no mention of the relic water at all.

There is a much better match for these panels in Benedict of Peterborough's miracle collection. The glaziers drew most of their stories from his collection, not William's, and they were often highly attentive to specific details in Benedict's accounts. A story found at the close of Benedict's collection's first book begins, "Goditha, the wife of Matthew, a citizen of Canterbury, also presented herself [to the martyr], though supported on the feet of others, not her own: two women supported the third."[15] This seems to be exactly what we see in the first panel of the sequence (Figure 11). Two women supporting a third are moving along a path or street between buildings. Benedict continues, "A terrible swelling was seen from her knees on down. The medicine of the blood and water was put on it, and the swollen members were brought back to their original size." This scene is pictured on the second panel (Figure 12): the blood and water relic, known as the "Water of St Thomas," is being mixed up in the woman's bowl on the right, while on the left, a kneeling woman applies the water to Goditha's swollen legs.

Panels nIV 49 and nIV 50 do not picture nuns. They depict *local laywomen* leading a laywoman to Becket's tomb, procuring and mixing up the Becket water for her, and washing her diseased limbs. Women appear very much in charge on these panels. It could be that Mason could not imagine a context in which medieval women would take on leading roles or act in concert in such a way except inside a convent, and so searched the collections for the story of the healing of a nun. Ellen Shortell has recently discussed a disquieting case about stained glass panels of similar date from Saint-Quentin. In the course of repairing two donation panels, a nineteenth-century restorer at Saint-Quentin removed two female heads and replaced them with male heads (Figure 13).[16] Despite the fact that these panels, dated c. 1200, have an inscription reading "the money of the widows" (*AES VIDVARVM*) the restorer did not seem

14 William, *Miracula*, 163.

15 See Benedict of Peterborough, *Miracula S. Thomae*, ed. J. C. Robertson in *Materials for the History of Thomas Becket*, vol. 2 (London, 1876), I.24, 56. The close of the previous chapter (I.23, 55–56) spoke of how a boy "presented himself to the martyr."

16 See Ellen M. Shortell, "Erasures and Recoveries of Women's Contributions to Gothic Architecture: The Case of Saint-Quentin, Local Nobility, and Eleanor of Vermandois," in *Reassessing the Roles of Women as "Makers" of Medieval Art and Architecture*, ed. Therese Martin (Boston: Brill, 2012), 129–174, esp. 129–130 and 146–153. See also her earlier article, "The Widows' Money and Artistic Integration in the Axial Chapel at Saint-Quentin," in *The Four Modes of Seeing: Approaches to Medieval Imagery in Honor of Madeline Harrison Caviness*, ed. Evelyn Staudinger Lane, Elizabeth Carson Pastan, and Ellen M. Shortell (Farnham: Ashgate, 2009), 217–238.

to be able to countenance panels in which four women (and women only) were pictured, two of them proffering bags of money. The original panels suggested, in Shortell's words, "a [female] group identity... that seems to be neither a familial relationship nor membership in a monastery," very much like the closely contemporary Goditha panels at Canterbury.[17] The Saint-Quentin restorer transformed this all-female pair of images into panels picturing two women and two men, with the men holding the money.

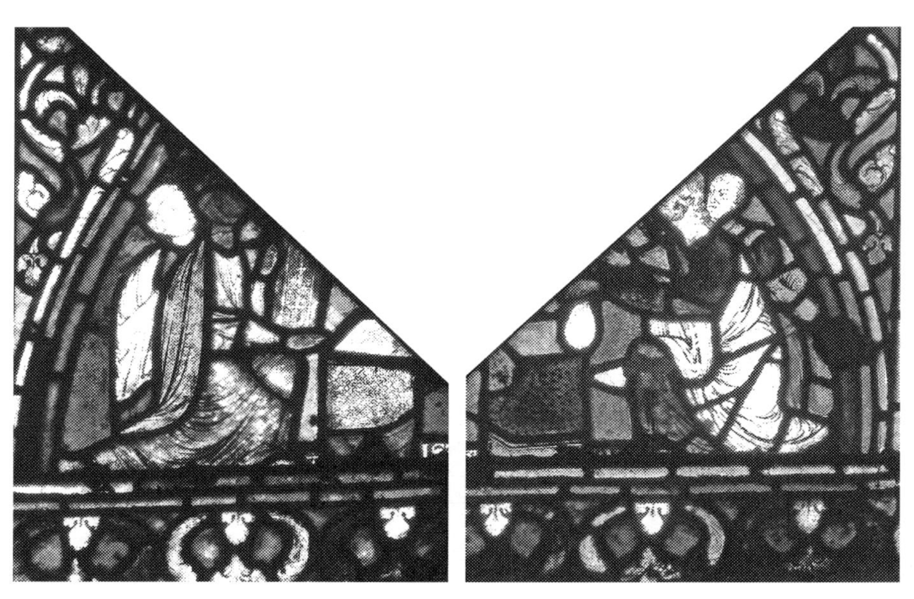

Figure 13 Widows' donation panels from the Glorification of the Virgin window. (Saint-Quentin, former collegiate church; panels dated c. 1200. Photograph: Ellen Shortell.)

The Trinity Chapel glass overlooked and surrounded Becket's shrine, one of the most public forums in the medieval world. There must have been occasions in which the all-female image of nIV 49 was mirrored by actual groups of women arriving together at Becket's shrine, whether from Canterbury or further afield. Only a few chapters after Goditha's story, for instance, Benedict describes how Edilda of Canterbury, who was also lame, was brought to the tomb "by the help of three women," something he repeats again later in the story: "She was brought to the martyr, as already stated, by three women, leaning on a staff."[18] When one looks at more evidence from contemporary miracle cults, particularly the cult of St Hugh in early thirteenth-century Lincoln, it is evident that the scene was not an unusual one: groups of laywomen frequently acted in concert in cultic situations.

17 Shortell, "Erasures and Recoveries," 150.

18 Benedict II.7, 61–62.

## Matrons of the City: Corporate Female Leadership in Miracle Cults

Recent studies have highlighted the number of women who lived independent religious lives as vowesses or as recluses in Britain.[19] Such women were almost always widows or had never married. What is interesting about many of the references to laywomen acting in cultic situations is that they are clearly married women. A rarely referenced early thirteenth-century collection of the miracles of the Carthusian bishop Hugh of Avalon (d. 1200) contains particularly striking references to the actions of "the matrons of the city" (*matrone civitatis*) of Lincoln, married women who took it on themselves to further Hugh's cult. The collection, which contains sixteen miracle stories, was written by Gerald of Wales.[20] He composed this text about a decade and a half after the bishop died and was entombed in Lincoln Cathedral. Gerald was resident in Lincoln for some time, and his accounts appear to be based, at least in part, on his own experience and eyewitness.[21]

"The matrons of the city" are referenced in four of the sixteen stories in Gerald's text. The first of these stories concerns a mute boy who fell asleep at Hugh's tomb, had a vision, and woke cured. "There were a great number of the matrons of the city holding vigil at the tomb with their lamps," writes Gerald: "They knew the mute boy very well, and when they saw this remarkable miracle, they sent messengers to summon their husbands, to whom the boy was also not unknown since they had for a long time supported him by alms." Soon, the entire church "was filled with people of both sexes mingling together, praising and glorifying the Lord and Saint Hugh."[22] In the story that follows, concerning another mute boy, Gerald speaks of matrons again: "Clerics living in Pottergate who knew the mute boy well, as well as matrons of that same neighborhood (*matrone vici eiusdem*) who had fostered him and were then keeping vigil at the tomb, leaped to their feet once they saw the miracle. They went shouting through the neighborhood that the mute boy was now speaking correctly and easily

19 For study of vowesses, see Sarah Foot, *Veiled Women I: The Disappearance of Nuns from Anglo-Saxon England* (Farnham: Ashgate, 2000), esp. 134–144, and Susan Steuer, "Identifying Chaste Widows: Documenting a Religious Vocation," in *The Ties that Bind: Essays in Medieval British History in Honour of Barbara Hanawalt*, ed. Linda E. Mitchell, Katherine L. French, and Douglas L. Biggs (Farnham: Ashgate, 2011), 87–103. For recluses, Tom Licence, *Hermits and Recluses in English Society, 950–1200* (Oxford: Oxford University Press, 2011) provides a good introduction.

20 Gerald of Wales, *The Life of St Hugh of Avalon: Bishop of Lincoln, 1186–1200*, ed. and trans. Richard M. Loomis, Garland Library of Medieval Literature, vol. 31 (New York: Garland Publishing, 1985).

21 For the dating of the collection and a listing of Gerald's other hagiographic works, see Robert Bartlett, *Gerald of Wales, 1146–1223* (New York: Oxford University Press, 1982), 217–218. Despite Gerald of Wales' stature as a major author of the period, this collection has received very little attention aside from a short section in Loomis's introduction to his edition and translation, xlvii–l, and some passages in Loomis's article, "Giraldus de Barri's Homage to Hugh of Avalon," *De Cella in Seculum: Religious and Secular Life and Devotion in Late Medieval England*, ed. Michael G. Sargent (Cambridge: D. S. Brewer, 1989), 29–40.

22 Gerald of Wales, *The Life of St Hugh*, Book II, chap. 10, 59–61.

at the tomb of Saint Hugh."[23] The following story, about the recovery of an insane girl, has yet another reference to Lincoln's matrons: the girl "said and proclaimed in a high voice to those standing there that by the merits of Saint Hugh sanity had been restored to her. Matrons of the city who had fostered her with their alms and who had grieved at the violence of her illness now rejoiced and were glad and did not cease thanking God and Saint Hugh for this miracle."[24]

Though not in the same tier as London, Bristol, or York, Lincoln was a prosperous city in the early thirteenth century.[25] On the Continent at this time period, urban women were energizing early thirteenth-century religious movements.[26] In Lincoln, women take on public, Mary Magdalene-like roles even as they stay firmly within a lay camp: they keep watch by Hugh's tomb; they openly announce and give thanksgiving for the miracles that they see there; and they also provide support and watch over ill people, including, as in all three of these stories, people outside of their family circles. Gerald mentions the matrons of Lincoln again in a story in a section he added sometime after the main body of the text was complete. Here, Gerald speaks of them as having a vision in aid of a seamstress named Matilda who became blind and spent over a year at Lincoln seeking healing: "certain matrons of the city (*urbis matrone*) who used to comfort [Matilda] with their alms as she lay in the precincts of the cathedral told her with conviction that they had seen in a vision that she was sure to receive the happiness of sight through the merits of Saint Hugh. By this hope the woman's spirit was renewed and she bore her deprivation and misery more patiently and begged the help of the holy bishop far more devoutly and confidently."[27] After describing how Matilda regained her sight, Gerald mentions the matrons again at the close of the story: "Since the city was filled at once with the report of the miracle, the matrons I mentioned before, together with a great multitude of people, ran to observe a marvel of such rarity."[28]

Matrons of the city are a distinct and identifiable group in Gerald's text. Perhaps there was some kind of loose women's association connected with the cult of Hugh at Lincoln in the early thirteenth century.[29] Albeit in a much later context, Kather-

23 Gerald of Wales, *The Life of St Hugh*, Book II, chap. 11, 63.

24 Gerald of Wales, *The Life of St Hugh*, Book II, chap. 12, 63–65.

25 Louise Wilkinson, *Women in Thirteenth-century Lincolnshire* (Woodbridge: Boydell Press, 2007), provides a thorough survey of women's social and economic roles in Lincoln and Lincolnshire more generally.

26 For early thirteenth-century religious movements on the Continent, see the summary in Brenda M. Bolton, "*Mulieres Sanctae*," in *Sanctity and Secularity: The Church and the World*, Studies in Church History vol. 10 (Oxford: Basil Blackwell, 1973), 77–95 and John Van Engen, "The Religious Women of Liège at the Turn of the Thirteenth Century," in *Medieval Liège at the Crossroads of Europe: Monastic Society and Culture, 1000–1300*, ed. Steven Vanderputten, Tjamke Snijders, and Jay Diehl (Turnhout: Brepols Publishers, 2017), 339–370.

27 Gerald of Wales, *The Life of St Hugh*, Book III, chap. 3, 71–73.

28 Gerald of Wales, *The Life of St Hugh*, Book III, chap. 3, 73.

29 Gerald highlighted women's input in other miracles, too: he describes how the sisters of the hospital of Lincoln were on vigil at the tomb when a young man for whom they had cared was cured; how the wife of a lord gave advice to a knight about praying to Hugh for healing, advice that worked; and how a mistress, who had brought her servant girl to Hugh's tomb for healing,

ine French has found interesting records relating to all-female parish guilds, including one termed "the wives of the town," in late fifteenth- and early sixteenth-century English sources.[30] Perhaps the early thirteenth-century matrons of Lincoln belonged to the same parish or parishes, and informally organized vigils and fostered ill supplicants in something of the same manner as a parish guild. It could also be that Lincoln's like-minded matrons banded together at Hugh's tomb itself, having been inspired by the saint's recent death and the miracles at Lincoln to devote their energies to the cult. In Adam of Eynsham's *Life of St Hugh*, completed not long after Hugh's death in 1200, women are the first people to experience and announce miracles performed by Hugh in Lincoln Cathedral. One of these stories is about a blind woman who claimed she could see again after touching Hugh's body, while the other centers on a "pious matron" (*matrona deuota*) whose purse was stolen when she was praying near Hugh's body. After this matron retrieved her purse, still with the coins inside of it, she "loudly acclaimed the bounty of the patron whom she had visited with such devotion."[31] One wonders if this woman might have later stood vigil at Hugh's tomb or looked after mute boys and blind seamstresses seeking miracles from the saint. Adam writes that before Hugh's burial, both "men and women" (*uiri et femine*) held vigil around Hugh's body, "holding lighted candles in their hands" – a precursor, it seems, of the matrons on nightly vigil at Hugh's tomb holding lamps described by Gerald.[32]

More traces of laywomen involved in Hugh's cult are found in a canonization dossier compiled in 1219.[33] "Matrons of the city" are never named in the canonization dossier, even though its compiler retold some of the same stories Gerald does. However, the testimony of "two women" or "three women" is frequently invoked by the compiler. In his story regarding the miracle of the first mute boy, for instance, the writer notes that "two women testified that they often saw the [boy] who was cured at the tomb of the said bishop."[34] "Three women" testified to the recovery from madness of

then assembled a group of people to speak to her cure: see *The Life of St Hugh*, Book III, chap. 6, 79; Book III, chap. 5, 75; and Book II, chap. 9, 57–59. Lest it be thought that Gerald simply liked to invoke the presence of matrons in his accounts of miracles, it should be noted that he does not mention matrons either in his account of the miracles of St David or in the miracles of St Remigius. See Michael J. Curley, "The Miracles of St David: A New Text and its Context," *Traditio* 62 (2007): 135–205; Gerald of Wales, *Vita S Remigii et Vita S Hugonis*, ed. James F. Dimock (London, 1877), *Giraldi Cambrensis, Opera* vol. VII, 22–31.

30 See French, "Maiden's Lights and Wives' Stories." Two-thirds of the thirty-three all-female guilds French discusses were dedicated to a named saint, most of them to the Virgin, but one, interestingly, was dedicated to Henry VI.

31 Adam of Eynsham, *Magna vita sancti Hugonis: The Life of Saint Hugh of Lincoln*, ed. D. L. Douie and D. H. Farmer, Oxford Medieval Texts (Oxford: Clarendon Press, 1961–2, reprint with corrections, 1985), vol. 2, 230–231.

32 Adam of Eynsham, *Magna vita sancti Hugonis*, vol. 2, 231.

33 The text is edited in Hugh Farmer, "The Canonization of St. Hugh of Lincoln," *The Lincolnshire Architectural and Archaeological Society: Reports and Papers* 6:2 (1956): 86–117. For analysis of the dossier, see D. H. Farmer, "The Cult and Canonization of St. Hugh," in *St. Hugh of Lincoln: Lectures Delivered at Oxford and Lincoln to Celebrate the Eighth Centenary of St. Hugh's Consecration as Bishop of Lincoln*, ed. Henry Mayr-Harting (Oxford: Clarendon Press, 1987), 75–87.

34 Farmer, "Canonization," no. 22, 103.

a certain Thomas Waneper.[35] In a story about the healing of a crippled woman who was brought to the cathedral in a basket, the "two women who used to bring her to church" (very like the story of Goditha at Canterbury) testified to her healing.[36] In a story about the recovery of a paralyzed girl, her mother "and two other women" are witnesses; in the case of a woman with dropsy, "two women" testify to her cure; "two women" also testify to the paralysis and mute tongue of a woman named Margaret.[37] These multiple references may well indicate the continuing presence of an active group of respected local laywomen within Hugh's cult at Lincoln.

It may be that the prominence of Gilbert of Sempringham (d. 1190) and the Gilbertine Order in Lincolnshire, including the foundation of a Gilbertine house in Lincoln itself (the priory of St Catherine, with some twenty sisters), had an impact on the religious men resident at Lincoln, making them more cognizant of the activity of Lincoln's matrons.[38] Possibly, too, the matrons themselves felt emboldened by knowledge of the new houses for women being established by Gilbert in their region. By providing alms and encouragement to those seeking miracles, holding vigils, and announcing and testifying to Hugh's miracles, married laywomen in Lincoln could take on religious leadership of a kind that provided scope for considerable excitement, visibility, and public speech acts – much more so, in fact, than if they had become cloistered Gilbertine nuns. These women of Lincoln, like the women of Canterbury pictured on the Goditha panels, were leading on the streets and in the churches in public view – and Lincoln's women, too, may be memorialized in stained glass. An intriguing early thirteenth-century panel surviving in Lincoln Cathedral's "Dean's Eye" window (North Transept Rose Window, N31, A4), shows, in Nigel Morgan's words, "four figures, probably women, standing before a doorway" (Figure 14).[39] This panel is contemporary with the miracle glass at Canterbury, and might be part of a series of panels devoted to the Life of St Hugh. A panel with a similar shape and border shows the body of St Hugh being carried into Lincoln.[40]

Matrons taking leading roles in saints' cults are not just found in texts and images relating to Hugh's cult in Lincoln. There are more references to matrons in the late twelfth-century miracle collection termed the "Book of the Foundation of the St Bartholomew's." This text, written by an anonymous author between 1174 and 1189, recounts the story of the foundation, construction, and miracles within the oratory

35 Farmer, "Canonization," no. 27, 104.

36 Farmer, "Canonization," no. 10, 101.

37 Farmer, "Canonization," no. 17, 102; no. 12, 101; no. 13, 101–102.

38 On the Gilbertines, see Brian Golding, *Gilbert of Sempringham and the Gilbertine Order, c. 1130–c.1300* (Oxford: Clarendon Press, 1995), and on townswomen in medieval Lincoln and Lincolnshire, see Wilkinson, *Women in Thirteenth-Century Lincolnshire*, 92–115.

39 N. J. Morgan, *The Medieval Painted Glass of Lincoln Cathedral*, Corpus Vitrearum Medii Aevi, Occasional Paper III, Lincoln Cathedral (London: Oxford University Press, 1983), 14 and 16.

40 See Morgan, *The Medieval Painted Glass of Lincoln*, 16, North Transept Rose Window no. C1. The panel with the four women might also belong to a Life of the Virgin, scraps of which survive in the Dean's Eye as well.

Figure 14 Four women at a doorway, probably from a sequence dedicated to the Life of St Hugh or the Life of the Virgin. (Lincoln Cathedral, North Transept Rose Window ("Dean's Eye"), A4: panel dated early thirteenth century. Photograph: Historic England Archive.)

of St Bartholomew's hospital in Smithfield, London. The author mentions matrons at two key junctures in his text. In his description of the very first healing miracle at the oratory, he describes how matrons came to stand nightly vigil after the miracle, the healing of a crippled man, was made known to the people of the city: "Then noble matrons of the city [*nobiles civitates matrone*] made nightly vigils there, and crowds of clergy and people frequented the place with great devotion of mind and heart."[41] At the very end of the text, the writer mentions women on vigil with lamps again, in a passage in which he assures the reader that "not only men but women, too, are most devout in their regard for his cult and veneration [*cura eius cultum et veneracionem devotissime existunt*]": "so it is that many of them [i.e., the women] are accustomed to visit his holy church annually with their lamps and peace offerings and to recount with joy his many miracles worked among them."[42] The story that follows, the concluding miracle in the collection, is about one of these women, "a worshipful matron by the name of Cecilia," who diverts a fire from her home by invoking Bartholomew.

The wording of these passages implies that the presence of matrons on vigil is not just a result of an active miracle cult, but a visible sign of it, an authentication.[43] References to such women on vigil in cultic contexts in this period can be found in non-English sources as well. In his *Dialogue of Miracles*, compiled in the early thirteenth century, Caesarius of Heisterbach describes "matrons of the city" (*matronae civitatis*) on vigil in Cologne and in Ferrara, a city in Lombardy. In Cologne, the church of St George the Martyr had "a metal cross with an effigy of the Savior, through which many miracles and healings have been worked. Wherefore, the matrons of the city have been accustomed to burn many candles before it."[44] The bellringer of the church used to take the candles for himself until he had a frightening vision and learned more respect. Caesarius states that he himself remembered this miracle and that it was widely known in the city. In another story, this time about Ferrara, Caesarius relates how a simple man named Marcadellus who, greatly devoted to the shrines of saints, was asked by a thief to return a censer he had stolen from a church. Marcadellus agreed, but before he could return it, the censer was discovered in his possession. He was executed as a thief and buried outside the church doors. "On the following night," Caesarius writes, "when certain religious matrons of the city went to the church for matins and came to his tomb, they heard angelic songs there, saw burning candles, and smelled a most sweet smell." When this happened again on the

41 British Library, Cotton Vespasian MS B ix, fol. 11v. The Latin text of "The Book of the Foundation of St. Bartholomew's Church" in Cotton Vespasian B ix is unedited, though an unpublished modern English translation of the Latin text of the *Book* made in the 1920s by Humphrey H. King and William Barnard can be found on the website www.raheresgarden.com. In this translation, the passage referenced above is found in Bk I, chap. 13.

42 BL, Cotton Vespasian B ix, fol. 40r. See the unpublished Book of the Foundation translation referenced in note 35 above, Bk II, chap. 27, 39.

43 For another story revolving around a noble matron at vigil at a tomb, see *Herman the Archdeacon and Goscelin of Saint-Bertin: Miracles of St Edmund*, ed. and trans. Tom Licence with the assistance of Lynda Lockyer (Oxford: Oxford University Press, 2014), 195–197.

44 Caesarius of Heisterbach, *Dialogus Miraculorum*, ed. Josephus Strange (Cologne: H. Lempertz and Co., 1851), vol. 2, book VIII, chap. 25, 101.

second and the third nights, the matrons told the bishop about it. On the fourth night, the bishop too "learned by experience what the women had described," and he ordered a chapel to be built, "where many miracles happen to the present day."[45]

In Lincoln, London, Cologne, and Ferrara, groups of laywomen recognize, mark out, and forward miracle cults. Such cultic leadership by laywomen was possible outside of urban centers as well. The canonization dossier compiled for Gilbert of Sempringham, in c. 1202–1205, contains a remarkable number of stories about women from Anwick, a village about twenty miles from Sempringham. In one passage in the dossier, the compiler begins by stating that a certain Eleanor of Anwick testified that when she was ill, "she found out that two women, neighbours of hers, one deaf and the other partially paralysed, had recovered their health at Master Gilbert's tomb." This caused her to "gain confidence that she too would recover," and she went to Gilbert's tomb. A woman named Lady Hawise of Anwick testified to the truth of Eleanor's cure, and Lady Hawise also described how she herself recovered from a swollen arm through Gilbert's merits. Yet another woman from Anwick, Felice, testified to her cure from lameness, and Lady Hawise testified to her cure.[46] Moreover, the men who had driven the carts that had carried Eleanor and Felice to Gilbert's tomb testified to the women's miracles too. Reading between the lines, it seems very likely that Lady Hawise hired these men with their carts and in effect led a women's delegation from Anwick to testify to Gilbert's miracles. Later on in the dossier there is yet another story of a woman from Anwick being healed, making a total of six women from Anwick who claimed healing from Gilbert.[47] There were surely connections between all of these women.

Groups of unrelated women travelling together, supporting each other and testifying to miracles are also described in the collection of miracles of Æbbe of Coldingham, written c. 1190. In two stories, girls are taken to the oratory at St Æbbe's Head not by their family members, but by neighbors. In the case of one of these girls, the writer notes, "in the morning some of the women who had accompanied her and seen these blessings declared to some of us that she saw, heard and spoke with ready tongue. We believed devoutly but doubted and decided to learn about it more fully from the account of her parents," who only came to the tomb the following day.[48] In the case of the second girl, who had been brought to Dumfermline by her parents but was told she needed to go to St Æbbe's Head as well, "it happened that some women from the same village were travelling to the oratory in order to pray and they brought the girl with them." After her cure, "The priest who had spent the night there along

45 Caesarius of Heisterbach, *Dialogus Miraculorum*, vol. 1, book VI, chap. 33, 384–385. For additional references to matrons of the city in this tremendously rich text, see vol. 1, book VI, chap. 10, 363 and vol. 2, book VII, chap. 49, 69–70.

46 *The Book of St Gilbert*, ed. Raymonde Foreville and Gillian Keir (Oxford: Clarendon Press, 1987), 271–272.

47 *The Book of St Gilbert*, no. 29, 303. A similar set of stories in the dossier revolves around a certain Ysouda of Pickworth, who testified to her brother's miracle, her own miracle, her son's miracle, and the miracle of a non-relative, a woman suffering in childbirth (*Book of St Gilbert* 299–301, nos 26–28).

48 *The Miracles of Saint Æbbe of Coldingham and Saint Margaret of Scotland*, ed. and trans. Robert Bartlett, OMT (Oxford, 2003), no. 1, 33.

with them wished to be more certainly informed about the miracle that had been witnessed and called the women to him. They were prepared to assert on oath that everything occurred just as we have narrated."[49] Female travelling companions play a major role in another miracle of Æbbe, this time concerning an insane woman who was brought to the oratory by two women and her husband. Her husband left, but when "the two little women were also sitting down and vigilantly watching over her," three crows attacked the mad woman: "the women were frightened and stupefied, as women would be, but nevertheless they jumped up with a bold spirit and opposed their hands to the attacks, eventually driving them off more by their faith than by their strength."[50] The insane woman was not healed at this point, but when she was "taken home and brought there by her friends [*a suis*] a second time, while they kept vigils for her recovery and offered devout prayers and tears to God, by the divine gift and because of their faith she immediately recovered her health."[51]

In addition to providing travel support and supplication, laywomen frequently gave creative cultic guidance to their neighbors and acquaintances in emergency situations, as is evidenced in collection after collection. In Benedict of Peterborough's miracles of Thomas Becket, for instance, the women of a village in Kent help a neighbor when her son was found drowned in a tub. When the accident became known, "the women of the neighborhood hastened there; nearly all of the men had gone off to fish or to reap." Eventually, after one person suggested it was time to accept the boy's death, "one of the widows said, 'Do we not have five widows here? Let us invoke the blessed martyr Thomas nine times on our knees, and repeat the Lord's Prayer nine times in his name, and he may give heed.'"[52] In the miracles of John of Beverley, "wise women" tell an ill peasant to select a saint by lot.[53] In the miracles of St Germanus at Selby, a faithful matron (*matrona fidelis*) describes her pilgrimage to Selby and suggests to an ill man that he should appeal to St Germanus;[54] while in the miracles of St Richard of Chichester, a noble girl named Johanna residing at Lewes Castle calls upon St Richard to cure the desperately ill son of the Justiciar of England.[55] In the miracles of William of Norwich, the wife of the monks' cook, Botilda, tells everyone aboard a sinking ship that they must invoke St William. "Everyone was transfixed by [her] voice," writes the collector, "and the hearts of all bowed to the woman's command with an amazing unanimity."[56]

49 *The Miracles of Saint Æbbe*, no. 34, 61–63.

50 *The Miracles of Saint Æbbe* no. 9, 47.

51 *The Miracles of Saint Æbbe* no. 9, 49. For additional stories, see the section on "friends and neighbors" in Anne E. Bailey, "Women Pilgrims and Their Travelling Companions in Twelfth-Century England," *Viator* 46:1 (2015): 115–134.

52 Benedict, IV.63, 228.

53 *Alia Miracula* I, chap. 13, 192–193, ed. in Susan E. Wilson, *The Life and After-Life of St. John of Beverley: The Evolution of the Cult of an Anglo-Saxon Saint* (Aldershot: Ashgate, 2006).

54 *Historia Selebiensis Monasterii*, ed. and trans. Janet Burton with Lynda Lockyer, Oxford Medieval Texts (Oxford: Clarendon Press, 2013), no. 37, 151–153.

55 *Saint Richard of Chichester: The Sources for his Life*, ed. David Jones (Sussex Record Society, 1995), 215–216. See also 224–225, about a "woman among those present" who suggests invoking Richard, and 220–221, for a lord's daughter named Margaret doing the same.

56 Thomas of Monmouth, *The Life and Passion of William of Norwich*, trans. Miri Rubin (London: Penguin, 2014), 117.

This Botilda with the arresting voice was also a creator and distributor of contact relics of St William, one of the most powerful ways in which laywomen took leading roles in miracle cults. The bodies of saints at the heart of miracle cults were typically under the control of male communities, but contact relics – water, dust, oil, clothing, etc. – were acquired and manipulated by lay women and men as well as the religious. Contact relics were personal possessions, and they could be used however the owner desired.

### The Making and Distribution of Contact Relics by Laywomen

In the second panel of the Goditha sequence in Canterbury's Trinity Chapel glass, a woman stands above Becket's tomb holding a bowl into which a layman and a monk ladle Becket's blood and water (Figure 12). She stands taller than both men, her hair is uncovered, and she stirs the mixture with a spoon. Though the paint on this panel has faded, it is still possible to see that the glaziers painted a decorative border on the v-neck of the women's green dress, an unusual feature that seems to be meant as a marker of this woman's importance. Another panel in the miracle windows (nV 7) has this very same composition – a central figure stands above Becket's tomb holding a vessel, into which two smaller flanking figures pour and ladle liquids. In this case, though, the central figure is a priest.[57] On nIV 50, a laywoman takes the priest's place.

The commanding image of this woman has received no comment from scholars, perhaps in part because she may have been thought to be an abbess rather than a laywoman. Benedict's collection contains only a single story about nuns using a Becket contact relic, in this case a glove owned by Becket which a guest of the nunnery happened to have with him.[58] In contrast, Benedict tells numerous stories about laywomen's possession and use of the "water of St Thomas" and other Becket relics. In fact, the very first story Benedict tells in which Becket's blood is used in pursuit of a cure concerns a blind woman in Canterbury who, in the first days after Becket's death, goes to an inn, and there "asked the mother of the household if she had procured something of the martyr, and whether she would lend it to her." This woman "produced a reddened cloth, which was still moist with the martyr's liquid blood."[59] One of the most striking stories Benedict tells about a laywoman's possession of Becket's relics, in this case a piece of Becket's hairshirt, was chosen for presentation in Canterbury's glass. Figure 15, Trinity Chapel panel sVII 8, shows a scene from the story in which the wife of the earl of Hertford, one of the great magnates of the realm, is kneeling

57 See Caviness, *Windows of Christ Church*, 179. Images of this panel and the rest of Canterbury's medieval stained glass are available online through the Corpus Vitrearum Medii Aevi picture archive at http://www.cvma.ac.uk. For further analysis of the priest pictured in nV 7 and the making of the Becket water relic at Canterbury, see Rachel Koopmans, "'Water mixed with the blood of Thomas': Contact Relic Manufacture Pictured in Canterbury Cathedral's Stained Glass," *Journal of Medieval History* 42:5 (2016): 535–558.

58 Benedict III.58, 158.

59 Benedict, *Miracula* I.11, 41. See also I.17, a story about "a certain religious woman" who was the *custos* of an almshouse and acquired a portion of Becket's blood.

Figure 15 The wife of the earl of Hertford kneels before an altar on which her reliquary (containing a piece of Becket's hairshirt) is placed; panel dated c. 1213–20. (Canterbury Cathedral, Trinity Chapel sVII 8. Author's photograph; reproduced courtesy of the Chapter, Canterbury Cathedral.)

in prayer in her local church and being informed by one of her sons that his younger brother has died.[60] The woman's reliquary, containing the piece of Becket's hairshirt that she would use to resurrect the boy, is pictured on the altar before her. This striking panel, with the large figure of the kneeling noblewoman at its center, originally pictured no adult men. The small figure behind the kneeling woman, the boy who announces his brother's death, now sports the head of a bald adult man, placed there by a restorer at the end of the nineteenth or beginning of the twentieth century.[61]

In contrast to references to "matrons of the city" acting in concert in vigils at saints' tombs or aiding individual supplicants, most references to laywomen acting with their relics concern solo individuals. Although women most often utilized their contact relics to the advantage of people within their own domestic circles, neighbors and non-relatives could also feel their benefit. One particularly striking story from the Becket miracles concerns a serving woman in Hampshire who tries to pass on a relic to a neighbor. In the story, a knight and his squire returned from Canterbury with ampullae of Becket water. The knight deposited his ampulla in the local chapel, where the priest doled out its contents. When a serving woman of the knight "heard that the priest was denying the water to many, to one of the women who had been refused she said, 'Why do you thirst? Come to me, and I will give you plenty of the same liquid.'" She then stole the squire's ampulla, intending to give its contents to the woman in need, but before she could do so, she saw her lord approaching. She poured the ampulla's contents into a beaker nearby, and then "filled the ampulla with other water and put it back in its place, bidding the woman to come the next day." But when she came back the next morning to fetch the water, the woman found "thick and congealed blood" in the beaker. She "broke out in great cries as women do," alerting everyone to her theft and to the miracle.[62]

The story interested Benedict because of the transformation of the water into blood, but it is also a striking case of a woman determined to stand in the place of a priest, right a wrong, and provide the water to a non-relative. Stories of enterprising laywomen are found in many other collections of the period, including a striking story about a new-found contact relic in the miracles of Margaret of Scotland. The anonymous compiler of this collection places the story in the period immediately after the translation of Margaret's relics in 1180 in Dunfermline, though the compilation of the collection dates to the later thirteenth century.[63] A woman named Emma was in great pain and had a badly swollen face resulting from a toothache. She had a vision in which she was told to pray at Margaret's tomb and "place your face to the stone

60 On this panel, see Caviness, *Windows of Christ Church*, 214, and for Benedict's description of this story, *Miracula* IV.94, 255–257.

61 Williams, *Notes on the Painted Glass*, 43 and Plate 27. For further discussion of the restoration of window sVII and the panels picturing this miracle, see Rachel Koopmans, "Visions, Reliquaries, and the Image of 'Becket's Shrine' in the Miracle Windows of Canterbury Cathedral," *Gesta* 54:1 (2015): 37–57, at 45–51.

62 Benedict, *Miracula* IV.12, 191–193.

63 On the dating of this collection, see *The Miracles of Saint Æbbe of Coldingham and Saint Margaret of Scotland*, ed. and trans. Robert Bartlett, OMT (Oxford: Oxford University Press, 2003), xxxiv–xxxvii.

and press." She did this, and felt some relief, but later, the pain started to return. At this point "she applied to the tooth the dust which she had taken from the place where the lady had previously rested in the old church and the swelling and pain completely disappeared."[64] The compiler of the collection then tells a story about a monk named Reginald, who had a toothache which he had suffered for a year: "When the previous miracle had been announced in chapter and he had heard what had happened… [he decided] that on the following night he would, after praying, try the same grace of healing which he had heard had taken place in the woman."[65] This strategy worked, and the compiler praises Emma for her resourcefulness, noting that "unless she had gone forth and found grace in the sight of God and the lady, [the monk] might have remained slothful and inactive and prolonged his complaint. He had near to him a hidden medicine by which his pain could be relieved and he did not know it. She did not, but sought it and found it."[66] Later in the collection, another monk, named Lambert, cures a toothache using Emma's method: he "touched with his finger the stone in which her most holy relics rest, then put the finger in his mouth and rubbed both the front and the back of his teeth with it."[67]

Emma, in sum, created a toothache cure in Dunfermline. There was considerable room for creative invention with contact relics. If a woman's invention took hold, it could have a wide impact on people of the neighborhood or surrounding region. In Norwich, Botilda, the wife of the monks' cook mentioned above, unveiled a healing spring. Thomas of Monmouth, who mentions this same Botilda in three different places in his collection, describes how she had a vision of St William of Norwich in which she was told to "approach the tree where once I was thrown by the Jews, where I lay for awhile under the sky, dig around its roots a little and when you find water there, drink it. Having drunk it, you will be freed from the ailment you suffer, and so will your son from his. From then on strive to let all know that a cure will surely come to all those who faithfully drink of that water." Botilda followed these instructions, with the additional precaution of bringing along a priest as a witness, and she indeed discovered a spring. Its water cured her and her son, and "thereafter," Thomas writes, "we also know that many people received the remedy they hoped for by tasting that water."[68] Botilda's relic creativity is evident not only from this story, but from an earlier account in the collection about a fern Botilda found on William's grave. She hung the fern on the wall and "guarded it for future use." Later, when she was in a difficult labor, she saw the fern, asked for it to be immersed in water, drank it, and bore the child.[69] Thomas of Monmouth references this fern miracle again near the end of the collection in a list of three miracles that authenticated the holiness of William's initial burial site.[70]

64 *The Miracles of Saint Margaret of Scotland*, no. 9, 93–95.

65 *The Miracles of Saint Margaret of Scotland*, no. 10, 95–97.

66 *The Miracles of Saint Margaret of Scotland*, no. 10, 97.

67 *The Miracles of Saint Margaret of Scotland*, no. 32, 129. The curing properties of dust from the tomb are also highlighted in a story about a boy with leprosy: see no. 21, 117.

68 Thomas of Monmouth, *The Life and Passion of William of Norwich*, bk 4, chap. 10, 116–18.

69 Thomas of Monmouth, *The Life and Passion of William of Norwich*, bk 2, chap. 6, 51–52.

70 Thomas of Monmouth, *The Life and Passion of William of Norwich*, bk 7, chap. 18, 188.

At the very end of his collection, Thomas of Monmouth copied a letter written by a monk in Worcestershire about another laywoman creating contact relics that were used by non-family members. The monk describes how an ill young woman named Agnes had a vision of St William. To get well, William told her, she was to take holy water, wash a crucifix in the name of the Father, Son, and Holy Spirit, and then "crumble morsels of bread [in it] and consume it in good faith and without delay." There was more: "that will not only be a remedy for your illness, but also relief to all those ill with whatever illness, if they – as we said – use it while invoking God in good faith. And so that you find a good example in it, you will give some of it to the person suffering a fever who is in torment in the new church at Croome, and he will be cured immediately." Agnes followed these instructions, and it worked for her and the man at Croome suffering with fever.[71] Interestingly, the healing material here – crumbs of bread in holy water that had washed a crucifix – have no connection with St William's own bodily remains. Caesarius of Heisterbach tells a somewhat similar story about a young woman named Quida in France who had a vision of the celestial Jerusalem. In the vision, an angel gave her half of a candle, and when she came back to herself, she found she still had it in her hand. "From it," Caesarius writes, "many more candles were fashioned, and their powers exist to this day. For the sick drink water that has been poured over them, and they recover."[72]

We will never know how many people felt benefit from the inventions of Emma, Botilda, Agnes, Quida, and other women like them, but contact relics like these were essential elements of miracle cults, likely responsible for far more claims to healing miracles than pilgrimages to saints' tombs or shrines, something the seriously ill could not attempt. Other laywomen made their relics available for non-relatives to use, such as the women who shared out the water of St Æbbe's fountain to "those in [their] village who were sick";[73] a married woman named Margaret who gave an ampulla miraculously filled with milk by St Frideswide to be held in a chapel "for the necessities of the ill in the future";[74] or Rose, a young woman who, when she heard about the illness of the prioress of St Helen's nunnery in London, brought the prioress a rather gory relic that she possessed, "a rag which had been dipped in St Richard's blood when his entrails were being removed from his body." Rose "unfolded [the cloth] and, entreating the prioress to put her trust in the merits of St Richard… reverently placed the cloth against her cheek and called with all her heart for the help of the saint."[75]

These examples all derive from late twelfth- or early thirteenth-century texts, but stories of female invention and distribution of contact relics can be found in much earlier source material as well. *The Life of Guthlac*, written by Felix of Crowland in the

71 Thomas of Monmouth, *The Life and Passion of William of Norwich*, 188–191.

72 Caesarius of Heisterbach, *Dialogus Miraculorum*, vol. 1, Book VII, chap. 20, 27.

73 *The Miracles of Saint Æbbe of Coldingham*, no. 14, 53. This water had miraculously disappeared and then reappeared in a vessel.

74 Philip of Oxford, *Miracula S. Frideswidae*, ed. B. Bossue, *AASS*, Oct. 8 (1853), 568–589, chap. 104.

75 *Saint Richard of Chichester*, 218–219. See also Katajala-Peltomaa, *Gender, Miracles, And Daily Life*, 126, for water made by a Domina Margarita which cured friends as well as family members.

eighth century within a generation of Guthlac's death in 714, contains notable stories about the actions of Pega, Guthlac's sister. Pega is instrumental in Guthlac's first posthumous miracle. When a blind man comes to Guthlac's body, she takes "a piece of glutinous salt which had previously been consecrated by St Guthlac and, grating it lightly, let the scrapings fall into consecrated water. She made this water drip, drop by drop, under the blind man's eyelids," and cured him.[76] The miracle itself is not pictured in the eighteen roundels drawn on the so-called "Guthlac Roll," a late twelfth- or early thirteenth-century series of line-drawings on a roll of parchment that may have served as preliminary designs for a stained glass series. Pega appears in two of these roundels, though, including one particularly striking image in which Pega holds Guthlac's head and upper body and lowers his corpse into his tomb (Figure 16). Felix had described how Pega was the one who wrapped Guthlac's body in cloths and interred him above ground, so launching his cult.[77] This image is a fitting recognition of Pega's leading role in the creation of the ur-relic of the cult, Guthlac's body itself, as visualized by an artist some four centuries after the event.[78]

## Conclusion

Miracle cults are not usually envisioned as a particularly female zone of operation. The stained-glass panels and the range of textual evidence discussed above, however, suggests that medieval writers and artists saw a different reality. Laywomen were leaders. They sought out miracles for themselves and for members of their households, actions that generated the stories which fill the pages of miracle collections. In public, non-domestic contexts, too, laywomen took the reins. They gave advice to neighbors and acquaintances. They fostered those who were ill and in need of miracles, providing them with alms, praying for them, and not infrequently physically carrying them to a saint's tomb and caring for them there. They held vigils, created and distributed relics, and publicly announced miracles that were not their own. Such actions would have been especially influential in the early stages of a miracle cult, a fluid period in which laywomen's actions and public proclamations could authenticate the existence of a cult and direct its future path, but this was certainly not the only time in which laywomen's leadership mattered. Some miracle cults lasted for years or even across generations, while others fizzled out quickly. The energies and interest of local laywomen may well have been the crucial factor that determined which miracle cults

76 *Felix's Life of Saint Guthlac*, ed. and trans. Bertram Colgrave (Cambridge: Cambridge University Press, 1956), 167.

77 *Felix's Life of Saint Guthlac*, 160–166.

78 On Pega, see Avril Lumley Prior, "Fact and/or Folklore? The Case for St Pega of Peakirk," *Northamptonshire Past and Present* 61 (2008): 7–16. For the very interesting case of a late Anglo-Saxon woman, Seietha, attached to the shrine of St Edmund, see *Herman the Archdeacon and Goscelin of Saint-Bertin Miracles of St Edmund*, 275–289, and the discussion in Elisabeth van Houts, "The Women of Bury St Edmunds," in *Bury St Edmunds and the Norman Conquest*, ed. Tom Licence (Woodbridge: Boydell Press, 2014), 53–73. Lay support for Edmund's cult in the Anglo-Saxon period has been further examined by Sarah Foot, "Households of St Edmund," in *Religion and the Household*, ed. John Doran (†), Charlotte Methuen, and Alexandra Walsham, Studies in Church History, vol. 50 (Woodbridge: Boydell Press, 2014), 47–58.

Figure 16 Pega lowers Guthlac's body into his tomb. Roll dated to the late twelfth or early thirteenth century. (Guthlac Roll, British Library Harley Roll Y 6, roundel 16. Photograph: British Library.)

would continue and which would expire. Some of the women taking on leading cultic roles were of elite status, such as the "noble" matrons on vigil at St Bartholomew's tomb, but there was also plenty of room for the initiative of women of no particular social standing. Botilda, the wife of the monks' cook, called on others to invoke William of Norwich, created a healing spring, and authenticated the holiness of William's initial place of burial. For a woman of Botilda's status, a miracle cult was one of the very few arenas in which she could take on such a public, activist role.

The names and actions of most of the laywomen who forwarded the cults of the saints never found written record, much less visualization in the public forum of stained glass. Still, enough remains to leave little doubt that the ideas, endeavors, and leadership of laywomen were critical forces within the generation and continuance of medieval miracle cults. The scenes pictured on the Goditha panels, in which laywomen lead their neighbor to a saint's resting place, acquire relics for her and enable her pursuit of a miracle, must have been familiar sights in the streets, homes, and churches of medieval Europe.[79]

79 I am grateful for the invitation to speak at the "Women Leaders and Intellectuals of the Medieval World" conference, held at the University of Notre Dame in October 2015, and for the many helpful suggestions I received on this paper, especially those from John Van Engen and Dyan Elliot. I am indebted to the Social Sciences and Humanities Research Council of Canada for financial support and the research assistance of Eun Seon (Ludia) Bae.

21

# MECHTHILD OF MAGDEBURG AT HELFTA: A STUDY IN LITERARY INFLUENCE

BARBARA NEWMAN

Medieval women writers too often confront us as lonely figures, on the margins of the usual networks of literary exchange and influence. It is rare that that we are able to trace one female author's direct influence on another, as we can with Hildegard of Bingen's *Scivias* and Elisabeth of Schönau's *Liber viarum Dei*, or Hadewijch's *Rhymed Letters* (*Mengeldichten*) and those of her disciple, "Hadewijch II." An especially fascinating case is afforded by the beguine Mechthild of Magdeburg and the nuns of Helfta. The mystical beguine is thought to have entered Helfta around 1270 in her old age, though we do not know exactly when she was born or died. What we do know is that, because of encroaching blindness, she had to dictate the seventh and last book of her *Flowing Light of the Godhead* (*Das fließende Licht der Gottheit*) to the nuns.[1] Several of these nuns would soon become authors themselves, recording the revelations of two gifted seers in their midst – Mechthild of Hackeborn and her protégée, St. Gertrude the Great. Between 1291 and 1302 the nuns produced two massive Latin tomes, *The Book of Special Grace* (*Liber specialis gratiae*) about Mechthild of Hackeborn's revelations, and *The Herald of God's Loving-Kindness* (*Legatus divinae pietatis*) about Gertrude's.[2] The last book of *The Flowing Light* includes several remarks about Helfta, while the beguine is referenced in both of the nuns' volumes as "Sister M." Mechthild of Magdeburg looms especially large in the *Book*, where her literary influence is apparent from beginning to end. Although that general fact has long been recognized, there has thus far been no study showing exactly how the fiery German mystic influenced the nuns who cocooned her old age in respect and care.

By the end of her long sojourn in Magdeburg, Mechthild was something of a public figure: she was read, admired, criticized, and feared. Before her departure for

1 Mechthild von Magdeburg, *Das fließende Licht der Gottheit*, ed. and trans. Gisela Vollmann-Profe (Frankfurt: Deutscher Klassiker Verlag, 2003); *The Flowing Light of the Godhead*, trans. Frank Tobin (New York: Paulist, 1998).

2 The sole edition of the *Liber specialis gratiae* is in *Revelationes Gertrudianae ac Mechtildianae*, 2 vols., ed. Louis Paquelin and the monks of Solesmes (Poitiers and Paris: Oudin, 1877), 2:1–421. All translations are from *The Book of Special Grace*, trans. Barbara Newman (New York: Paulist, 2017). For the *Legatus* see Gertrude d'Helfta, *Oeuvres spirituelles*, vols. 2–5, ed. and trans. Pierre Doyère et al. (Paris: Cerf, 1968–1986); *The Herald of God's Loving-Kindness*, trans. Alexandra Barratt, 4 vols. (Kalamazoo: Cistercian Publications, 1991–2020).

Helfta she had become the head of a perhaps unruly beguine community.[3] Books 1–5 of *The Flowing Light* had begun to circulate as a unit, and some individual visions, prophecies, and songs may have travelled independently.[4] In Book 6, for example, Mechthild rails against a blind "Pharisee" who took her to task for a vision in which John the Baptist, a layman, celebrates mass in heaven.[5] Fortunately, her Dominican supporters were able to protect her from more serious harassment. But attacks of this sort, along with increasing debility and blindness, made it clear that her days of self-sufficiency were numbered. The friars perhaps communicated with their confreres at Helfta to find a safer refuge for the "weather-beaten old Sibyl,"[6] with the result that Abbess Gertrude of Hackeborn (reg. 1251–91) invited her to join their monastery.[7] And so she did. In Book 7 of *The Flowing Light*, Mechthild has several dialogues with her new sisters about the convent and her role in it. Once she asks Christ, "Lord, what should I be doing here in this convent?" – to which he replies, "You should illumine and teach them and should remain with them in great honor."[8] She sees the Lord blessing the whole community, promising to make them radiant mirrors in heaven.[9] But these mirrors of wisdom stood in awe of the visionary beguine, seeking her advice about topics of such perennial interest as how to prepare for communion. In response to one query, she answers, "You want to have instruction from me, but I myself am uneducated. What you are searching for you can find a thousand times better in your books."[10]

Yet the beguine's lack of formal learning – especially her ignorance of Latin – was a bulwark of her prophetic authority. No topos of women's writing was more time-honored than that of the "unlearned" but divinely illumined seer.[11] So Mechthild of Magdeburg presented the nuns of Helfta with a challenge. These sisters had immersed themselves in Latin from childhood, ran their own school and scriptorium, pursued advanced studies of Scripture, meditated on the finer points of the liturgy, and rhapsodized about the heavenly rewards of such theologians as Bernard of Clairvaux, Albertus Magnus, and Thomas Aquinas.[12] When they decided to take up visionary

3 "In my community there is a religious person who causes me much distress because of her contrary disposition. This person is not willing to obey me in regard to anything." *The Flowing Light* 6.7, trans. Tobin, 233.

4 Sara S. Poor, "Transmission and Impact: Mechthild of Magdeburg's *Das fließende Licht der Gottheit*," in *A Companion to Mysticism and Devotion in Northern Germany in the Late Middle Ages*, ed. Elizabeth Andersen, Henrike Lähnemann, and Anne Simon (Leiden: Brill, 2014), 73–101.

5 *The Flowing Light* 6.36, trans. Tobin, 262.

6 Hans Urs von Balthasar, "Mechthilds kirchlicher Auftrag," in *Das fließende Licht der Gottheit*, ed. and trans. Margot Schmidt (Einsiedeln: Benziger, 1955), 20.

7 Abbess Gertrude, Mechthild of Hackeborn's older sister, presided over the abbey's golden age of mystical and literary efflorescence.

8 *The Flowing Light* 7.8, trans. Tobin, 283.

9 Ibid. 7.14, 286–87.

10 Ibid. 7.21, 292.

11 Marianne Heimbach, *"Der ungelehrte Mund" als Autorität: Mystische Erfahrung als Quelle kirchlich-prophetischer Rede im Werk Mechthilds von Magdeburg* (Stuttgart-Bad Cannstatt: Frommann-Holzboog, 1989).

12 On the pursuit of education at Helfta see *Liber specialis gratiae* 6.1; on the nuns' admiration for Bernard of Clairvaux, 1.28; on Albertus Magnus and Thomas Aquinas, 5.9.

writing, they needed no male scribes or editors to help them; their books were entirely their own. So, unlike even the formidably learned Hildegard, the nuns of Helfta could never claim to be *indoctae*. As they took Mechthild of Magdeburg's dictation, questioned her eagerly about her experience of God, and perused the earlier books of *The Flowing Light*, they must have wondered if they too could disseminate mystical knowledge. At the urging of a new abbess, Sophia of Mansfeld (reg. 1291–98), they decided they could. Yet they would pursue their project in Latin, renouncing all claims to *docta ignorantia*, but assuring themselves a much wider readership than the beguine could hope to attain in her Low German vernacular.

If Mechthild of Magdeburg arrived at Helfta in 1270, her namesake Mechthild of Hackeborn (the sister of the abbess) would have been twenty-nine years old at the time. She was already serving as *cantrix*, a role she would hold throughout her career because of her fine voice. A chantress was normally in charge of the scriptorium, where liturgical books were copied, and also taught the chant to novices, making her an unofficial director of formation. Since 1261, Mechthild of Hackeborn had been the foster mother and teacher of St. Gertrude, who entered Helfta in that year at the age of five. Gertrude, then, would have been about fourteen when Mechthild of Magdeburg arrived. Either or both could have transcribed dictation from the elderly beguine, though no evidence confirms this. But both fell under her spell, so to speak, and fervently admired her book. In Gertrude's case, we know this from her account of the beguine's last illness in *The Herald*. Mechthild's death was lingering and painful, and toward the end she became delirious. Gertrude, indignantly asking why Christ permitted this, heard him reply, "to make it known that I work more in the depths than on the surface."[13] She then prayed that he would "at least" glorify Sister M. with miracles after death to legitimize her revelations and confound unbelievers. Declining to do so, Christ appears to Gertrude with *The Flowing Light* in his hand. In the past, he asserts, it was necessary to subdue the nations with signs and wonders, but now those who understand the flood of God's grace through their own experience (*per propriam experientiam*) need no external signs to confirm the truth of such visions. Gertrude then sees how pleased the Lord is when the faithful accept the "lavish overflow of divine grace" to chosen souls as a proof of his generosity.[14] This exchange implies that, despite the disappointing lack of miracles ascribed to Mechthild of Magdeburg, her admirers at Helfta were among those whose privileged experience enabled them to trust and (in due time) to imitate her.

It is Mechthild of Hackeborn, however, whose book reveals the more profound literary influence. If this is not at first obvious, it is only because *The Book of Special Grace* does not *sound* anything like *The Flowing Light*. The language difference is just the beginning. Mechthild of Magdeburg, a gifted vernacular poet, echoes the lexicon of minnesang. She oscillates between verse and prose in a book that does not even pretend to generic unity. Items appear in seemingly random order: divine love songs, prayers, moral allegories, otherworld visions, practical advice, accounts of mystical

13 *Legatus divinae pietatis* 5.7.1, in *Oeuvres spirituelles* 5:122.

14 Ibid. 5.7.2, in *Oeuvres spirituelles* 5:124. Mechthild of Magdeburg in the Helfta literature is *Soror M.*, while Mechthild of Hackeborn is identified in the *Legatus* as *domna M. cantrix nostra*.

union, self-defense and self-deprecation, all jostle each other on the page. Theologically, the beguine is audacious, edgy, and sometimes wildly speculative. It is easy to see why she encountered critics. *The Book of Special Grace*, on the other hand, is all of a piece. Despite its collaborative authorship, it is composed in a smooth, uniform style.[15] To borrow two of Mechthild of Hackeborn's favorite words, the *Book* is *mellifluus* and *dulcisonans*. Readers will find nothing to jar or disturb them, though they may be lulled into slumber by a surfeit of sweetness. Visions and allegories cluster around liturgical moments and doctrines dear to the nuns' souls, especially the Sacred Heart and the exchange of merits. The chantress practiced unitive mysticism but had no interest in theological speculation; her emphases are always devotional and practical. It is not surprising, then, that two works so different in language, style, and religious ethos have never been compared in detail.[16] On a deeper reading, however, *The Book of Special Grace* is permeated by the earlier Mechthild's influence. While preparing a new translation of Mechthild of Hackeborn, I found that at least eighteen chapters of *The Flowing Light* are echoed in *The Book of Special Grace* – and that more than two dozen chapters of the latter allude to the former.[17]

The most significant impact of the beguine's work at Helfta may be the least visible. We often take "bridal mysticism" for granted as a normative category in women's writing, derived from such twelfth-century figures as Bernard of Clairvaux and Richard of Saint-Victor. To be sure, the Cistercians and Victorines were important models at Helfta, yet there is a key difference between their bridal mysticism and that of the nuns. Twelfth-century writers keenly analyze the development of the soul's love for God, tracing its progression along trajectories from servile to filial love, from self-seeking cupidity to selfless charity, and so forth. God's love for the soul meanwhile remains constant. He is her bridegroom, yet his love is *agape* rather than *eros*: pure generosity, untainted by the neediness that desire implies. Mechthild of Magdeburg, however, loves an ardent, amorous God who creates a world to fulfill his desire.[18] In one of her speculative dialogues, she imagines the Father telling the Son at the beginning of time, "Son, a powerful desire stirs in my divine breast ... I shall make a bride for myself who shall greet me with her mouth and wound me with her beauty. Only then does

15 Mechthild herself wrote only a single chapter (4.59) of the enormous compilation. The rest was the work of two nun-scribes, one of them almost certainly Gertrude, the other unknown. On the collective authorship see Claudia Kolletzki, "'Über die Wahrheit dieses Buches': Die Entstehung des 'Liber Specialis Gratiae' Mechthilds von Hackeborn zwischen Wirklichkeit und Fiktion," in *"Vor dir steht die leere Schale meiner Sehnsucht": Die Mystik der Frauen von Helfta*, ed. Michael Bangert and Hildegund Keul (Leipzig: St. Benno, 1998), 156–79, and Anna Harrison, "'Oh! What Treasure is in this Book?' Writing, Reading, and Community at the Monastery of Helfta," *Viator* 39.1 (2008): 75–106.

16 For a broader comparison of Mechthild of Magdeburg with the nuns of Helfta, see Caroline Walker Bynum, "Women Mystics in the Thirteenth Century: The Case of the Nuns of Helfta," in *Jesus as Mother: Studies in the Spirituality of the High Middle Ages* (Berkeley: University of California Press, 1982), 170–262.

17 By "chapters" I refer to the numbered editorial divisions of these texts in the editions cited.

18 Barbara Newman, "*La mystique courtoise:* Thirteenth-Century Beguines and the Art of Love," in *From Virile Woman to WomanChrist: Studies in Medieval Religion and Literature* (Philadelphia: University of Pennsylvania Press, 1995), 137–67.

love really begin." The Holy Spirit promises to "deliver the bride to your bed."[19] After the Fall, God is "saddened" because "his darling bride, the noble soul, [is] dead," so he chooses instead the eternal, preexistent Virgin Mary "that he might have something to love."[20] Throughout *The Flowing Light*, especially its first two books, God and the Soul exchange strophes in a wooing song of mutual praise and desire, recalling a genre of minnesang called the *Gesprächslied* or dialogue song. For instance, the Soul effuses: "O you pouring God in your gift! / O you flowing God in your love! / O you burning God in your desire!" He replies, "O you beautiful rose among the thorns! / O you fluttering bee in the honey! / O you unblemished dove in your being!"[21]

The nuns of Helfta do not adopt this vernacular idiom, yet their God is the same desiring, yearning God we meet in *The Flowing Light*, rather than the dispassionately loving God of twelfth-century Latin mystics. In one vision, Mechthild of Hackeborn sees her soul as a small cottage of cedar wood, enclosed in a lofty mansion representing the heart of God. The door of the cottage "had a golden bolt from which a little golden chain was hanging, and that chain reached right into the heart of God. So when the door was opened, the little chain seemed to move his heart. The door, as she understood, designates the soul's desire … But the little chain signifies God's desire that always precedes that of the soul, arousing its desire and will and drawing them toward him."[22] Deliberately or not, this allegory recalls the celebrated Cave of Lovers in Gottfried von Strassburg's *Tristan*. In Gottfried's love idyll, the cave is sealed from within by bolts of ivory and cedar, representing the virtues of Purity, Modesty, Discretion, and Understanding of Love. The golden latch on the door stands for Success, and its hidden lever is a tin spindle denoting "Firm Intent for intimate dealings." There follows a bawdy double entendre: "Any man can guide his Intent to his pleasures, narrow, broaden, shorten, lengthen it, free it, or confine it, here or there, this way or that."[23] While the nuns are less mischievous, their allegory blends chaste modesty with fervent eroticism as surely as *Tristan* does. The golden chain that reaches "right into the heart of God" is his desire, which the soul can arouse by mobilizing her own desire. Yet ultimately, it is his desire that precedes. Surely the underlying thought, if not the language, is closer to Mechthild of Magdeburg than to Bernard of Clairvaux.

The two Mechthilds share an interest in the feminine Divine, which for both takes the form of *Frowe Minne* or Lady Love. In the sacred minnesang of Hadewijch, a Dutch beguine, Minne is an imperious, fluid, ubiquitous presence. Sometimes she is the divine Beloved, sometimes a potent goddess distinct from him, sometimes a personification of the beguine's own love or the power of love in general.[24] Mechthild of Magdeburg introduces Minne unforgettably in the first chapter of *The Flowing Light*, where Lady Love has a bittersweet dialogue with Lady Soul. The Soul con-

19 *The Flowing Light* 3.9, trans. Tobin, 114–15.

20 Ibid. 1.22, 50.

21 Ibid. 1.17–18, 48.

22 *Book of Special Grace* 1.19, trans. Newman, 77.

23 Gottfried von Strassburg, *Tristan*, trans. A. T. Hatto (Harmondsworth: Penguin, 1967), 265.

24 Barbara Newman, *God and the Goddesses: Vision, Poetry, and Belief in the Middle Ages* (Philadelphia: University of Pennsylvania Press, 2003), 169–81; see also "*La mystique courtoise*."

gratulates Minne on "forc[ing] the exalted Trinity to pour itself utterly into the humble virginal womb of Mary."[25] But she goes on to reproach her, for Minne has stolen everything the Soul had – childhood and youth, friends and relations, honors and riches, even her health. Love retorts that the Soul has "made a happy exchange": in return she has received heavenly freedom, sublime knowledge, and the Holy Spirit. Still angry, the Soul charges, "Lady Love, you are a robber; for this as well shall you make reparation." Love replies, "then take me ... [and] in addition you may demand God and all his kingdom!" This riveting exchange sets the tone for all that follows. Minne often returns in the company of other virtues, for as Mechthild explains, they are all her subjects (*Dir sint alle tugende undertan*). "Love passes through the senses and storms the soul with all her might. All the while that Love grows in the soul, she ascends to God longingly and, richly flowing, opens up to receive the wonder that is approaching."[26]

Entranced by the figure of Minne, Mechthild of Hackeborn evokes her even more than Mechthild of Magdeburg does. In Latin, her scribes use the term *amor* rather than *caritas* – a significant choice, for *amor* (like Minne) subsumes both generous, self-sacrificing love and the urgency of erotic desire. Indeed, charity is among the virtues that are subject to her. But *amor* is masculine, so the nuns must convey Minne's gender by describing her as "Love in the form of a beautiful virgin" (*amor in specie virginis pulcherrimae*).[27] In a tender dialogue, Christ reminds Mechthild of Hackeborn that just as she used to call her mother *Minne* – a childish endearment – he is now giving her his own Love to be her mother. "Just as children suck their mother's breasts, you will suck inner consolation from her, unspeakable sweetness; and she will give you food and drink and clothing. In all your needs, she will take care of you as a mother does her only daughter."[28] Love therefore atones for the Soul's negligence; clothes her like a robe of sunlight; takes custody of her good deeds, preserving them in the shrine of God's heart; and compensates her poverty with boundless riches.[29]

Minne also accompanies the incarnate Christ throughout his career. Like the cosmic Minne of Mechthild of Magdeburg, it is Love who "brought Christ from his Father's bosom to his Mother's womb."[30] Speaking as the Virgin Mary's divine double, she proclaims, "It was I who first handled him with virginal hands and wrapped him in swaddling clothes. It was I who nursed him with virginal breasts with his Mother. I warmed him at my bosom and showed him all the service his humanity required, along with his Mother."[31] At his Passion, she dyes his robe with his scarlet blood and pierces his heart with an arrow, producing a salvific flow of blood and water from his side.[32] To compensate, she then "suffuse[s] all [his] limbs with inconceivable joy and

25 *The Flowing Light* 1.1, trans. Tobin, 39–40.

26 *Das fließende Licht* 5.4, ed. Vollmann-Profe, 326; trans. Tobin, 182 (translation altered).

27 *Liber specialis gratiae* 1.28, ed. Paquelin, 98; *Book of Special Grace*, trans. Newman, 103.

28 *Book of Special Grace* 2.16, trans. Newman, 129.

29 Ibid. 2.15–2.16, 128; 2.41, 145; and 3.22, 157.

30 Ibid. 2.31, 137.

31 Ibid. 1.5, 45.

32 Ibid. 4.59, 179, and 1.18, 70.

overflowing sweetness" at the Resurrection.[33] At the Ascension she reemerges as a cosmic force, a double of divine Wisdom.[34] Enthroned as Queen beside Christ the King, Love proclaims that he is the only one in whom she could exercise the full extent of her power, yet she is omnipotent and disposes all that is done on earth (Wisd. 8:1). Again, like Wisdom, she "circle[s] the vault of heaven alone" (Sir. 24:8) because "Love alone had subdued the omnipotence of the divine majesty to herself, made his inscrutable wisdom foolish (so to speak), and poured out all his sweet goodness."[35] As I have argued elsewhere, these medieval avatars of the feminine Divine – Wisdom, the Virgin Mary, and Minne or Caritas – are to some extent interchangeable. They all in their several ways represent God in female form.[36] Lest we should mistake this figure's ultimate divinity, Mechthild of Hackeborn's Christ gazes with love on the "beautiful virgin" Minne and tells her, "You are the same as I am" (*tu es quod ego sum*).[37] Despite this maternal and queenly language characterizing Love, we might miss the chantress's attraction to the feminine Divine (as previous scholarship has done) if we did not read her with one eye on *The Flowing Light*, her hidden vernacular intertext.

Mechthild of Hackeborn's brand of divine eros and her interest in Minne are the most pervasive aspects of the beguine's literary influence. There are many other echoes and allusions to *The Flowing Light* throughout *The Book of Special Grace*. But rather than cataloguing them, in the remainder of this essay I will ask how the nuns of Helfta transform their intertext, both stylistically and theologically. For in the process of latinizing key motifs from Mechthild of Magdeburg, the nuns also domesticated her, softening her sharp edges and removing all trace of heterodoxy. Three examples are especially salient: the celestial masses witnessed by both Mechthilds, the heavenly dance, and the role of the Virgin Mary.

The vision that aroused the ire of the "Pharisee" in Magdeburg is one of the beguine's most striking literary creations.[38] Being sick one day, a "poor girl" (*arme dirne*) mourns that she cannot attend mass, so God grants her something even better. Falling into ecstasy, she finds herself in a heavenly church where courtly youths arrange flowers before the celebrant arrives – a tall, emaciated John the Baptist. John the Evangelist and St. Peter, "a simple man," are also present. Suddenly the church is filled with the whole court of heaven in all their celestial finery. Mortified by her own wretched garb, the poor girl sees herself transformed into a noble maiden "wearing a deep red mantle woven out of love," inscribed in gold with her amorous songs. The Virgin kindly beckons her into the choir, and John the Evangelist hears her confession and reads the Gospel. At the offertory, Mary gives the poor girl a golden penny (symbolizing self-will) to offer Christ. The Baptist then says the Secret of the Mass

33 Ibid. 1.19, 79.

34 Ibid. 1.20, 83–84.

35 Ibid. 2.35, 140. The power exercised over God by a personified female Love is celebrated in Hugh of Saint-Victor's treatise "On the Praise of Charity," trans. Franklin T. Harkins, in *On Love: A Selection of Works of Hugh, Adam, Achard, Richard, and Godfrey of St Victor*, ed. Hugh Feiss (Turnhout: Brepols, 2011), 159–68.

36 Newman, *God and the Goddesses*.

37 *Liber specialis gratiae* 1.23, ed. Paquelin, 82; *Book of Special Grace*, trans. Newman, 92.

38 *Das fließende Licht* 2.4, ed. Vollmann-Profe, 84–90; trans. Tobin, 72–75.

(*die stillen messe*),[39] and at communion, he takes the Lamb of God from the altar and places it in Mechthild's mouth – literally "between her teeth." The Lamb lies down on "its own image in her stable" – her heart – and there begins to suckle.

Mechthild of Hackeborn was clearly taken with this vision, for she borrows its details in several places. On Christmas Eve, the Christ Child suckles from each sister's heart, just as the Lamb does.[40] St. Agnes, like the "poor girl," wears a crimson garment inscribed in gold with her avowals of love.[41] When Mechthild of Hackeborn grieves that she has no worthy offering, the Virgin gives her a golden ring, just as she had given the poor girl a golden penny.[42] Beyond these local borrowings, the chantress adapts the beguine's vision *in toto* at a low point in Helfta's communal life. On the feast of the Assumption, the nuns cannot receive communion because of an interdict.[43] So, to console his heartbroken bride, Christ promises that she will see wonders. Then, like the beguine before her, she witnesses a full-scale celestial mass.[44] But the details differ significantly. In the nun's vision, the celebrant is none other than Christ, while John the Baptist is consigned to the unproblematic role of reading the epistle – something even a subdeacon could do. And in her love for her community, the chantress brings heaven down to Helfta itself. Christ and Mary lead the nuns in a festal procession that winds its way through the close, into their choir, and finally down to the nave. There Christ is fittingly vested in a red chasuble and episcopal mitre. The Virgin offers "a golden brooch like the purest crystal, sumptuously adorned with gems of inestimable value." Every chant is specified, and at the Sanctus, Christ encourages the saints to put some heart into it: "Sing, all of you! Sing and make melody!" At communion, he himself gives his body to each sister. Since nuns could no longer receive the chalice, Mechthild specifies a visionary surrogate, common in the Helfta literature: the Virgin Mary holds a golden bowl to Christ's side to collect the delicious liquid from his heart, which the sisters sip through a golden straw.

In addition to raising the ceremonial level a few notches, Mechthild of Hackeborn omits the self-deprecation that marks the beguine's vision. As Caroline Bynum showed long ago, the storm-tossed Mechthild of Magdeburg had nothing like the serene self-confidence of Gertrude or Mechthild of Hackeborn, raised in the cloister from childhood.[45] Even in the midst of her vision, the beguine calls herself a "poor lazy thing" (*vil armú tregú*), a "foul puddle" (*unselig phül*), a "lowly crow" (*unedele kra*), and a "wretched girl" (*dú snöde*). There is nothing like this in the nun's vision. Rather, the virgins of Helfta confidently approach their own altar and offer golden rings, which Christ at once puts on his fingers. At the end of mass, when he lifts his

39 Both Vollmann-Profe and Tobin misinterpret this phrase – not "low mass" but the Secret of the Mass, the portion of the eucharistic prayer spoken quietly by the priest.

40 *Book of Special Grace* 1.5, trans. Newman, 44.

41 Ibid. 1.11, 57.

42 Ibid. 3.1, 148.

43 This interdict was imposed by the cathedral chapter of Halberstadt in 1296, when the episcopal see was vacant, over a fiscal dispute with the nuns. Gertrude also mentions it in *Legatus divinae pietatis* 3.16, in *Oeuvres spirituelles* 3:66–73.

44 *Book of Special Grace* 1.27, trans. Newman, 101–02.

45 Bynum, "Women Mystics in the Thirteenth Century."

hand in blessing, Mechthild sees that "on every finger he wore a golden ring to signify the betrothal of each virgin who was to marry him. These were set with rubies to show that his blood pertains especially to the adornment of virgins." As always, the nun of Helfta sees, prays, and receives Christ's blessing on behalf of her whole community. In a deep sense, she knows that she and her sisters *belong* with the exalted company of saints, all processing together behind Christ and Mary, whereas the "poor girl" feels herself a solitary outsider, inconceivably lucky to be accepted by the celestial insiders of her vision.

Another case of borrowing and transformation is the heavenly dance. Liturgical dancers and dance historians often cite Mechthild of Magdeburg's play with this image. In *The Flowing Light* 1.44, the Soul goes out to court her "fair youth" and sends messengers to summon him "because she is eager to dance."[46] After the saints have performed a "splendid dance of praise," the young man – not yet identified – invites the Soul to follow their lead. But she replies, "I cannot dance, Lord, unless you lead me. If you want me to leap with abandon, you must intone the song. Then I shall leap into love, from love into knowledge, from knowledge into enjoyment, and from enjoyment beyond all human sensations." The couple then sing a dance-duet, and after their *pas de deux* the youth invites his beloved to his bed, where "you shall have your way with the Son of the Virgin, for you are delightfully weary." But the maiden's senses resist this invitation because they know that in the blaze of the Godhead, they will "go completely blind." So they suggest that the Soul refresh herself instead with the blood of martyrs, the bliss of angels, and so forth, culminating with the Virgin's milk. As if insulted, the Soul replies, "That is child's love, that one suckle and rock a baby. I am a full-grown bride. I want to go to my Lover." When she does so, he bids her take off her clothes – representing her "fear and shame and all external virtues" – to enter the bed of love with nothing but her naked longing.

This chapter has always been a favorite with Mechthild's readers, for it combines the attractive courtly trappings of *hohe Minne* with mystical daring. The Soul cannot be satisfied with the consolations of everyday piety because "the force of love transcends all austerity." Even the infant Christ cannot appease her unabashed desire. In her ascent to mystical union she gladly leaves her body and senses behind, along with all the saints and angels. Interestingly, Mechthild of Hackeborn adopts the image of a mystical dance in several places, yet she never echoes this passage. Perhaps she was shocked by the beguine's rejection of a tryst with the Christ Child. And, despite her own mystical eroticism, she would no more have doffed her soul's apparel of virtues than she would have discarded her veil in choir. *The Book of Special Grace* lavishes so much attention on clothing (mostly vivid, deep-dyed brocades, interwoven with gold and studded with gems) that if Mechthild had not been a nun, she would have had to be a fashion designer. The glorious garb is allegorical, of course, but even so, the difference matters. Where the beguine longs for a naked, apophatic union with God, the nun sighs with St. Paul, "not that we would be unclothed, but that we would be further clothed" (2 Cor. 5:4). At Helfta, "external virtues" cannot hinder mystical union; rather, one can never have enough of them. Moreover, Mechthild of Hackeborn's

46 *The Flowing Light* 1.44, trans. Tobin, 58–62.

loving Soul never performs a solo dance or even a duet with Christ. Instead, all the dancing in *The Book of Special Grace* is communal and courtly. It is a difference of both style and substance.

The *Book* therefore draws not on *Flowing Light* 1.44, but on two less familiar dance scenes. In one of her visions Mechthild of Magdeburg describes the rewards of various saints, especially preachers, martyrs, and virgins. These "three blessed bands go merrily forth into the presence of the Trinity, dancing finely in a circle."[47] Near the end of the book another chapter, composed at Helfta, recapitulates the courtly dance of 1.44 without its bolder elements. At the feast of the Holy Trinity, pure virgins will "follow the noble Youth, Jesus Christ, … who is utterly filled with love, as he was at age eighteen." He will crown them with garlands of virtues as they follow the Lamb wherever he goes, dancing "in untold bliss; from bliss to love, from love to joy, from joy to splendor, from splendor to power, from power to the highest heights."[48]

Touchingly, Mechthild of Hackeborn associates the beguine with her mystical dance so strongly that she envisions dancing saints at her deathbed. When Mechthild of Magdeburg is anointed, the chantress sees "all the saints perform[ing] a dance around her bed; the virgins danced closest to God among them all."[49] In another vision that closely echoes *The Flowing Light*, the saints feast with the Lord, and after the table is removed, the virgins rise for more festivities. "He too rose and led a jolly dance with them as they sang sweet new songs."[50] Among these dancers the *Book* specifically names Sister M., or Mechthild of Magdeburg. When Abbess Gertrude of Hackeborn dies, she too is welcomed into heaven by dancing saints.[51] But Mechthild of Hackeborn's fullest account of the dance graces her vision for All Saints Day. At Matins, the chantress sees Mary standing before Christ with a throng of virgins, linked heart-to-heart in a ring dance: "From [Christ's] overflowing heart, where the plenitude of all bliss lies hidden, a triple golden cord extended through the Virgin Mother's loving heart to the hearts of all the virgins, passing through each one until it circled back from the last virgin into the Lord's heart again, creating a kind of dance as it threaded so marvelously through them. All the other saints of both sexes, those who had not been exalted by this special gift of virginity, danced around the virgins in a separate circle. The choirs of holy angels danced by themselves in the outer ring."[52] This carol expresses the joy and unity of all the saints, as well as their hierarchy; the privileged virgins literally form an inner circle. The dance would also have been very pretty to watch – especially if one imagines the inner and outer rings dancing clockwise, while the middle ring moves counterclockwise. As for the music, it rises directly from the dancers' hearts, for even the smallest virtuous deeds they performed on earth "ring out from their hearts as eternal music to the praise of God and the increase of their joy and glory."

47 Ibid. 3.1, 104.

48 Ibid. 7.37, 308.

49 *Book of Special Grace* 5.6, trans. Newman, 189.

50 Ibid. 4.8, 168.

51 Ibid. 6.6, 210, and 6.9, 214.

52 Ibid. 1.31, 109.

Both Mechthilds use the dance as a figure of heavenly joy, but the nuances differ. For the beguine, dancing signifies passionate young love, as in a courtly romance. The virgins follow Christ "as he was at age eighteen," dancing "with bliss-filled tenderness into the blossoming meadow of their pure conscience." Their dance is also a mystical ascent: the dancers spiral up "to the highest heights" or "beyond all human sensation." Even when there are many, it is as if each virgin dances individually with her Beloved, rising to ineffable heights beyond thought and language. But in *The Book of Special Grace*, the dance signifies the festivity of the heavenly court. Christ and Mary dance in a ring with the other virgins, but Mechthild emphasizes the unity of the saints' loving hearts, manifested in the perfection of their carol. Here as always, beauty in the *Book* makes the glories of an ideal community, the kingdom of heaven, visible and tangible.

According to Sara Poor, the most widely cited chapter in *The Flowing Light* was 1.22 – a remarkable chapter consisting of two parts, a poem on mystical union followed by a speculative dialogue on Mariology.[53] Mechthild of Hackeborn drew on both parts of this chapter, but again we see her taming and correcting the beguine's excesses. In her poem on divine union, Mechthild of Magdeburg stresses its incomprehensible mystery. In the dazzling light of the Godhead the bride becomes blind, but in that blindness she sees most clearly. "The longer she is dead, the more blissfully she lives. ... The richer she becomes, the poorer she is. ... The more she labors, the more contentedly she rests. ... The more quiet her silence, the louder she calls." There is much more in that vein; this classic mystical text is enlivened by the literary devices of paradox and anaphora. Mechthild's poem was incorporated into a fourteenth-century mystical compendium called *The Book of Perfection* (*Das Buch der Vollkommenheit*), which enjoyed wide circulation.[54] As Poor notes, however, not every clause is a paradox. Some are more straightforward, for example, "The more she burns, the more beautifully she glows." In *The Book of Special Grace*, Mechthild of Hackeborn alludes to this poem, even adopting its grammar of correlative comparison. The German parallelism of *ie si ... ie si* (the more she ... the more she) becomes a *quanto ... tanto* construction in Latin. In contrast to the beguine, however, the nun has an aversion to paradox. When God speaks to the Soul, his logic is direct: "The more you distance yourself from all creatures and reject consolation from them, the higher you will be lifted toward the unattainable height of my majesty. The more you extend yourself toward creatures in charity, ... the more tightly and sweetly you will embrace my incomprehensible breadth. The more you humble yourself beneath all creatures, ... the more deeply you will be immersed in me."[55] In fact, the nun has replaced Mechthild of Magdeburg's erotic paradoxes with a gloss on Scripture, for her own account of mystical union relies on Ephesians 3:17–19: "that you, being rooted and grounded in love, may have power to comprehend with all the saints what is the breadth and length and height and depth, and to know the love of Christ

53 *The Flowing Light* 1.22, trans. Tobin, 49–52; Poor, "Transmission and Impact," 87–94.

54 Pseudo-Engelhart von Ebrach, *Das Buch der Vollkommenheit*, ed. Karin Schneider (Berlin: Akademie Verlag, 2006).

55 *Book of Special Grace* 2.34, trans. Newman, 139.

which surpasses knowledge." The dazzling, mind-bending paradoxes that delighted Mechthild of Magdeburg (and Marguerite Porete) simply did not interest the nuns of Helfta.

Finally, the second part of *Flowing Light* 1.22 is an extravagant paean to the Virgin Mary. The beguine embraces a sapiential Mariology that represents her as an eternal being, "the bride of the Holy Trinity," long before the birth of Christ.[56] At Adam's fall, as we have already seen, God chooses Mary as his beloved after the death of his first bride, the Soul. Speaking in the first person, the Virgin tells Mechthild, "When our Father's *jubilus* was saddened by Adam's fall, so that he had to become angry, the Eternal Wisdom of the almighty Godhead intercepted the anger together with me."[57] As *Maria lactans*, Mary is a version of the Great Mother: "my breasts became so full of the pure, spotless milk of true, generous mercy that I suckled the prophets and sages, even before I was born. Afterward, in my childhood, I suckled Jesus; later, in my youth, I suckled God's bride, Holy Christianity." The Virgin's breasts, Mechthild continues, will flow until the Last Day, and the saints will suckle her milk as long as time endures. If this makes her sound very much like a goddess, the beguine does not shy away from that implication, but calls her one outright. "Her Son is God and she Goddess" (*ir sun ist got und si göttinne*); again, she is a "noble Goddess over all pure people" (*edel göttinne ob allen luteren menschen*).[58] God and the Virgin together revive the ailing Soul, who needs to be fed by both parents; she is restored by the blood of Christ and the milk of Mary.

Mechthild of Hackeborn will have none of this. She does allude to the Marian section of *Flowing Light* 1.22, but only to provide a gentle corrective. One of the chantress's most fascinating visions, in fact, can be read as a deliberate revision of Mechthild of Magdeburg. The nun sees divine Love as a beautiful maiden standing in the heart of God, knocking against it with a diamond ring.[59] The diamond, Love explains, "denotes the sin of Adam" because, just as diamonds can be cut only with blood (a belief derived from Pliny's *Natural History*), original sin can be dissolved only in the blood of Christ. Hence Love asserts, "as soon as Adam sinned, I stepped in and intercepted that whole sin. By knocking constantly on the heart of God and moving it to pity, I did not let him rest until, in an instant, I took the Son of God from the Father's heart and laid him in the Virgin Mother's womb." Afterwards Love cared for the Christ Child along with his Mother and followed him in all his works, "until I nailed him to the gibbet of the cross. There I appeased all the Father's wrath and united humanity to God with an indissoluble bond of love." In *The Book of Special Grace*, divine Love thus takes the place assigned to the Virgin Mary in *The Flowing Light*. It is she who "intercepts" the sin of Adam and appeases the Father's wrath, and it is she – not a preexistent Mary – who stands at Christ's side before, during, and after his earthly life. Because Love is a divine, eternal figure, as we have seen, no hint

56 On sapiential Mariology see Newman, *God and the Goddesses*, 194–206, and *Frauenlob's Song of Songs: A Medieval German Poet and His Masterpiece* (University Park: Pennsylvania State University Press, 2006), 97–104.

57 *The Flowing Light* 1.22, trans. Tobin, 50–51.

58 *Das fließende Licht* 3.1 and 3.4, ed. Vollmann-Profe, 150, 166.

59 *Book of Special Grace* 2.17, trans. Newman, 129–30.

of heterodoxy remains. The Virgin Mary is not slighted in the *Book* – far from it. But she suckles no one except the infant Christ, and she is decidedly no goddess.

Mechthild of Magdeburg was an important influence at Helfta: catalyst, inspiration, and direct literary source. But she was also a slightly problematic figure whose visions, though much admired, demanded revisions. In *The Book of Special Grace*, Mechthild of Hackeborn not only latinizes parts of *The Flowing Light*, but bends the beguine's highly individual mysticism toward a more communal and monastic emphasis. Nudging her visions toward orthodoxy, the chantress of Helfta replaces the "layman" John the Baptist with Christ, the eternal High Priest, as celebrant of mass in heaven; rejects the notion that "external virtues" could ever obstruct a union with God; shies away from mystical paradox; and sidelines the beguine's Goddess Mariology, replacing the preexistent Virgin with Minne or divine Love – herself an import from *The Flowing Light*. I hope that this essay, by exploring the ways one mystical Mechthild read another, will help to stimulate new interest in *The Book of Special Grace* and insert more medieval women into the great web of literary exchange, through which we have long read the books of their brothers.

Epilogue

# POSITIONING WOMEN IN MEDIEVAL SOCIETY, CULTURE, AND RELIGION

JOHN VAN ENGEN

Well into the twentieth century, the roles and achievements of women in medieval European society and culture, indeed their very presence, hardly registered in accounts of the ten centuries or so that make up the Middle Ages. Medieval historians, focused primarily on politics, economy, and warfare, mostly left bit-parts at best to women, their roles perhaps as pawns in dynastic arrangements or as queens, very occasionally as a duchess or abbess treated in her own right. Or, alternatively, they were lifted out as wholly extraordinary figures, thus an Eleanor of Aquitaine for instance. In literary and cultural studies, scholars (mostly male) puzzled over the interpretation of texts projecting women primarily as adulterous consorts or distant objects of desire, figures on whose behalf men consumed their strength to prove their virtue. In religious studies, scholars might highlight the role of the Virgin Mary or of female saints, their lives lifted out as exemplary, also their merciful interventions as leavening hardship in a merciless male world. But women as actors or writers in their own right rarely appeared, or then as truly extraordinary figures, even eccentric, a Hildegard of Bingen as prophetic seer or Heloise as early exponent of free love (not as learned abbess). This all may seem overstated on my part, but not by much. The *Booke* of Margery Kempe, rediscovered in the 1930s, 500 years after its initial writing, became no serious part of literary or religious studies until the 1980s. Indeed its reception – scorn first from high literary and religious types for its "gushing" prose, defenses of the *Booke* then as articulating distinctively female attitudes and religious affections, efforts next to credit Kempe with a highly literate authoring of this "Margery" *persona*, arguments too over whether Margery Kempe could oversee the production of her own *Booke* (a female scholar negative on this, a male positive), now new documentary finds seemingly confirming her place in history – it all mirrors, and here only in part, the interpretive world through which approaches to women in the Middle Ages have passed, and debates continue.[1] The writings of a Netherlandish author, a near contemporary of Margery named Alijt Bake (d. 1455), were first rediscovered in the 1930s as well, and her life and works are still not part of our narratives or conversations outside a small Netherlandish circle and the placing of her inside a new religious order.[2] And one could go on.

1 See for instance Nicholas Watson, "The Making of *The Book of Margery Kempe*," in *Voices in Dialogue: Reading Women in the Middle Ages*, ed. Linda Olson and Kathryn Kerby-Fulton (Notre Dame: University of Notre Dame Press, 2005), 395–434; and Felicity Riddy, "Text and Self in *The Book of Margery Kempe*," in ibid., 435–53.

2 I have a full reconstruction and translation of her works nearly finished.

When we then turned to the study of medieval women in earnest, much of the work turned initially on social history, women's roles and powers in local economies and in human and political relationships, particularly evident here in the contributions of Amanda Bohne and Adrienne Williams Boyarin. This early work in social history, pioneering and important, was soon overshadowed somewhat by cultural historical approaches. In literary history, women emerged as writers from the time of Peter Dronke's *Women Writers in the Middle Ages* in 1984 and Alexandra Barratt's *Women's Writing in Middle English* in 1992, among others, here as cultural and religious figures in their own right.[3] Social history, by definition and of necessity, engaged women too as part of a larger world, whether enterprising forces to be reckoned with or consigned to operating mostly in the shadows of men. Literary history by contrast has tended to treat women writers in relative isolation, virtually as their own phenomenon, as more recently (2010) in the fine collective volume of Rosalynn Voaden and Alastair Minnis on *Medieval Holy Women in the Christian Tradition c. 1100–c. 1500*.[4] Singling them out, and as their own story, is wholly intelligible after so many years of neglect, though it has consequences for positioning them more broadly in cultural history, this tendency then reinforced by those who would actively resist "mainstreaming" medieval women and their writings. Religious history turned its attention to women as well – a move anticipated already in 1935 by Herbert Grundmann, if then left dormant for another generation or more, only to become in the last arguably one of the most productive areas of medieval research. From the later 1970s, all these initiatives were energized, even transformed, by approaches and questions promoted from within feminist and cultural studies. For medievalists, that turn often gets associated with the work of Caroline Walker Bynum, and rightly so, though it is important to recognize a broader groundswell around her and to acknowledge in her work inspirations that sprang as well from deep explorations in medieval philosophy and theology and religiosity, thus, into the nature of human beings, body and soul, material and spiritual, this also and particularly with respect to medieval women. Here one may turn for more in this volume to several contributors, including Ruth Mazo Karras and Anna Siebach-Larsen.

There arose simultaneously amidst all this, in very broad terms, interpretive inclinations or predispositions that still inform our scholarship today, consciously or no. One sets out from a position that seems undeniably true in general historical terms: that in medieval society and culture, women were broadly presumed to be of subordinate status and privilege, a presumption expressed and acted out in countless social, cultural, and religious modes, mothers for instance not even allowed to attend the baptism or circumcision of their own children. These outlooks and practices grew out of age-old customs, laws and statutes too, secular or religious, buttressed by rites and rulings which, in a world saturated with religion, placed holy powers disproportionately, often principally, in male hands. A modern scholar is left then with difficult interpretive and narrative choices: whether to invoke these as the actual as well as the normative or rather to seek out and highlight all the exceptions, work-arounds, local customs, and much

3 Peter Dronke, *Women Writers in the Middle Ages (Cambridge: Cambridge University Press, 1984);* Alexandra Barratt, *Women's Writing in Middle English* (London: Longman, 1992).

4 Rosalynn Voaden and Alastair Minnis, *Medieval Holy Women in the Christian Tradition c. 1100–c. 1500 (Turnhout: Brepols, 2010).*

else that could often prevail in local practice – and, further, whether then in one's account to be indignant about the former or to triumph in the latter, or both.

From this arose two inferences that became, in effect, working interpretive assumptions or expectations: that women were consequently found or placed easily or routinely in the position of victims and that women's agency as a result nearly always got expressed indirectly, by alternative means or routes. We might name off a whole series of interpretations-become-narratives that are now common. Thus, more or less excluded from preaching and teaching, women channeled the divine instead as gifted visionaries. With literacy privileged as male and Latinate, women came in time to flourish in the vernacular instead. Tasked with birthing and human care and often enormous physical labor, women represented, or were construed as being of, the flesh rather than the spirit. This was distinct – but not entirely – from notions too of their possessing inordinate erotic powers. Versions of all this could become reified religiously in some devotional and theological notions among Europe's Christian majority, which tended to identify women with Christ's sacrificially crucified body more than his spirit or mind, with his bodily suffering more than his spiritual teaching.

These assumptions, whatever their historical truths, have become in some cases something like functional or narrative binaries, also presuppositions. But they are now coming in for reconsideration and far greater nuance. Nuns read their office in Latin, and women wrote Latin, some spectacularly into the twelfth century, some too beyond – that dimension now under-represented in this volume owing to papers committed elsewhere, but evident still in the work of Megan J. Hall, Sean Field, and Katie Bugyis, among others. Furthermore, later medieval women like Marguerite Porete and Alijt Bake promoted and articulated an all-consuming abstinence grounded now in the spirit rather than the body, and it superior, indeed far superior to fleshly abstinence – teachings Eckhart developed philosophically and Tauler sermonically. These were widespread in the vernacular in the later Middle Ages, especially in women's religious communities, and sometimes too mixed up with charges of "Free Spirit" heresy. Women were copyists and self-conscious authors too, crucial to the essays by Sean Field, Tom Luongo, Sarah J. Pearce, Thelma Fenster, and Nicholas Watson. In religious life, their numbers equaled or exceeded those of men in the high and later Middle Ages. As abbesses or prioresses, or queens or duchesses, they often exercised considerable powers in their own right, evident in the papers of Sarah Foot, Maureen Miller, Renate Blumenfeld-Kosinski, and others. Our vision of women's places and possibilities in the medieval world must become more layered, also within the world of Islam, as indicated by Asma Afsaruddin. This is not to tip the balance unrealistically in the other direction, but to bring layers and nuance and possibility, not to assume that anonymous writings are probably by men or clerics (as in my own contribution). More broadly, in social, cultural, or religious power, if we are to put it in that language, class generally weighed more heavily than gender – and all of this continuously changing, for better and worse, across 1,000 years' time.

The essays in this volume, and the conference that first set it in motion, presume the continuing influence of those earlier paradigms but confidently explore still other ways to approach and understand the roles of women during the 1,000 years that make up what we call the European Middle Ages. The essays come with a variety of scholarly approaches and points of view – that deliberately intended. There is no party line, but there was and is enthusiasm about alternate angles of vision, more ways of approaching and telling the stories of medieval women as actors and thinkers and writers. Amidst still common claims (and some realities) regarding sufficient sources available pertinent to women, this volume draws attention to a variety of lesser or even unknown figures, indeed a far broader and deeper world of women copyists, writers, actors, and more beyond the renowned (Christine de Pizan, Mechthild of Magdeburg), with at least one major figure here, Marie de France, deconstructed into yet more potential authors. This brings us closer to the world as it actually was than do narratives fixated on a handful of major authors or actors; thus Jewish women working in the English court, Muslim women active in the inner circle of male teachers in Afsaruddin's reconstruction. It undoes ready assumptions that anonymous works were probably by males, scribes too usually male, that Latin meant male, and so on – and again, all of this to be approached as differing by time and place.

The change of tone or emphasis lies, one might suggest, in multiple shifts rather than one or two dramatic reversals. It looks for "ordinary" or more routine ways in which women might manifest themselves rather than to approach women actors or writers or thinkers as *ipso facto* extraordinary. Subversion and indirection there may well have been, and often, but we must look as well to local customs and expectations and practices. To turn some version of the normative into a guiding narrative, a temptation in medieval studies when bottom-up sources can be scarce, is as mistaken as to make the role of "victim" in effect the new norm or narrative, which effectively robs human beings, in this case women, of their individuality and possibilities in context. None of this is to deny the reality of gender-based constraints. But the same held for class-based constraints, arguably as great a factor, arguably greater, in shaping the contours and possibilities of medieval persons. Yet it was mostly non-literate peasant women among the Christian majority who taught their children the Lord's Prayer and the Creed and other fundamental rites in acting as christened citizens, subjects set out in articles by Michael Clanchy gathered now in his *Looking Back from the Invention of Printing*.[5] The same holds for the careful and ingenious work which Elisheva Baumgarten has done for women's roles in medieval Ashkenazi communities, thus in her *Mothers and Children: Jewish Family Life in Medieval Europe*.[6] And Rachel Koopmans's study of the glass in Canterbury Cathedral reveals that women assistants were as essential to the functioning of the Becket cult in actual practice as the managing monk-priests. Our witness here is a silent one, if nonetheless also visually stunning.

The term "intellectual" is a troubled one, also a modern one, though Jacques Le Goff in 1955 tried, with some initial success, to transport that term back to high medieval Paris in his *Les intellectuels au Moyen Âge*.[7] But he too was thinking in male terms, whether those thirteenth-century schoolmen or his contemporary post-war pundits and writers. In the Middle Ages, literacy came in multiple forms, as did aspects of what we call learning. In the newer work on cognition as well as affections, the complexity and

5 Michael Clanchy, *Looking Back from the Invention of Printing: Mothers and the Teaching of Reading in the Middle Ages (Turnhout: Brepols, 2018).*

6 Elisheva Baumgarten, *Mothers and Children: Jewish Family Life in Medieval Europe* (Princeton: Princeton University Press, 2004)

7 Jacques Le Goof, *Les intellectuels au Moyen Âoe* (Paris: Éditions du Seuil, 1955).

richness of human engagement with religion and culture and in human relations has only multiplied dimensions and possibilities historically, hence too our ways of entering into and grasping the acts and culture of these medieval persons, including women. Kathryn Kerby-Fulton took this up more fully in the Introduction. To suggest that women did not share in this large cultural world, be it in ways secular or religious, or could not or would not, is exaggerated, and at worst false, their exclusion from the university (until into the nineteenth century) notwithstanding. To set up that one form of mental and cultural life as paradigmatic, also as over against a host of other forms, seems more the binary or ideological preoccupation of some scholars than it does the realities of what we learn from manuscripts, images, and the whole fullness of cognitive practices. Indeed, works of devotion or romance outstripped academic works in notable numbers. So too anti-woman slurs or satire must be weighed in the same scales as the equally common, and sometimes cross-over, anti-clerical satire. If the latter is taken, often, as an indirect witness to clerical power or privilege, what then should we make of anti-women satire? If we fall into the trap of viewing women only through the lens of certain medieval stereotypes, thus of flesh rather than spirit or mind, we perpetuate as history certain attitudes or stances which only partially reflected actualities on the ground. That women found themselves regularly in disadvantaged positions socially, culturally, or religiously is true. But it is not the whole truth, and the essays in this volume open up vistas on whole areas where other perspectives and possibilities are in evidence and ought to become part of our narratives too.

## INDEX OF PERSONS, PLACES AND WORKS

Note: This index covers proper names and geographical locations, as well as major works and themes; however, some selected items, such as geological features, have not been indexed in this list.

Printed in the United States
By Bookmasters